# XANTO

POTTERY-PAINTER, POET,
MAN OF THE ITALIAN RENAISSANCE

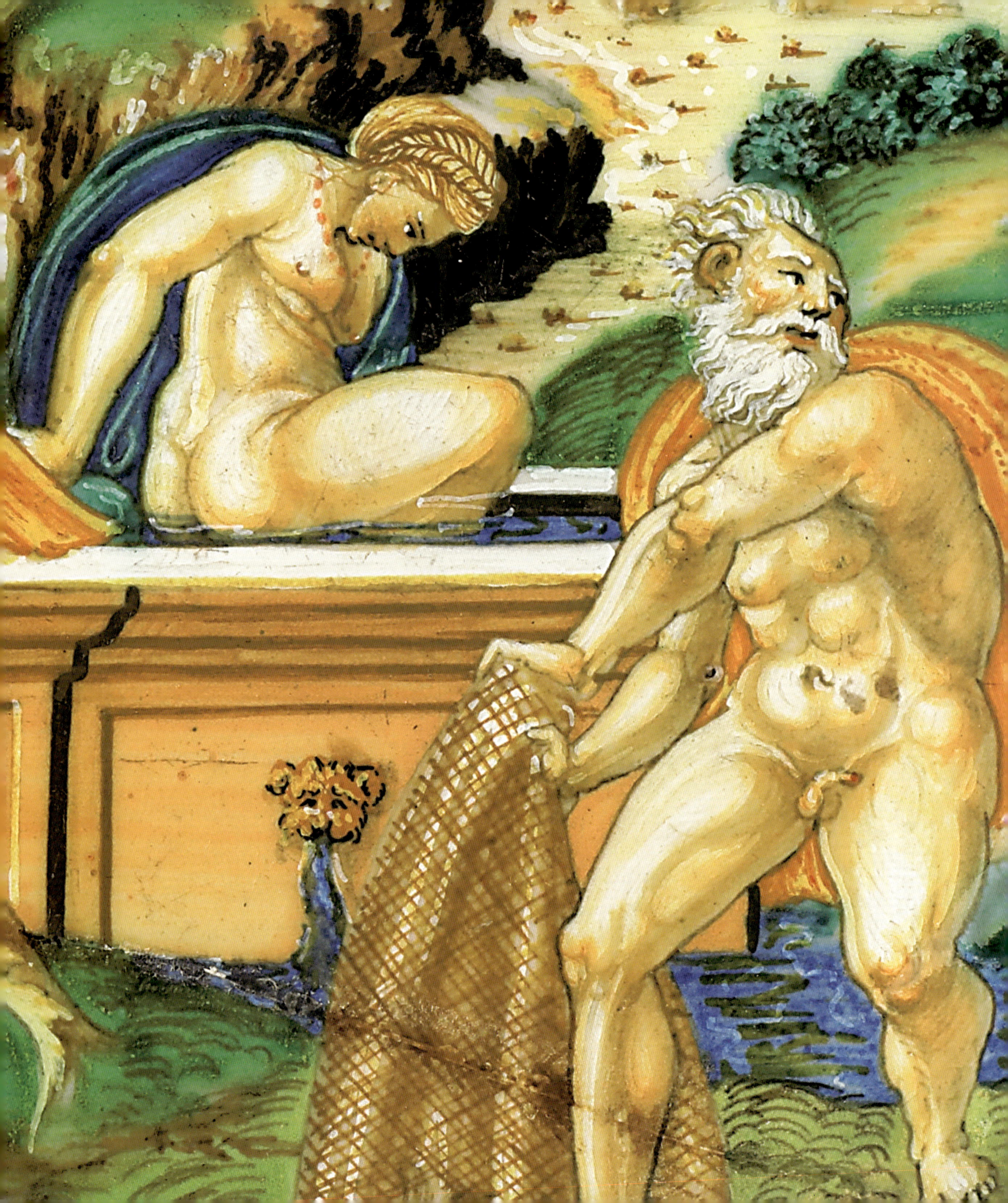

# XANTO

## POTTERY-PAINTER, POET, MAN OF THE ITALIAN RENAISSANCE

J.V.G. Mallet

WITH CONTRIBUTIONS FROM

Giovanna Hendel, Suzanne Higgott
and Elisa Paola Sani

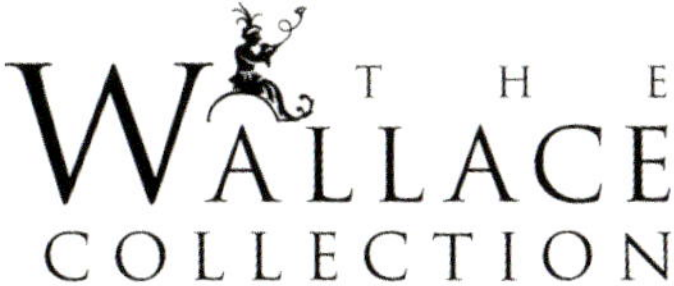

THE WALLACE COLLECTION

Published by the Wallace Collection
to accompany the exhibition,
*Xanto: Pottery-painter, Poet, Man of the Italian Renaissance*,
at the Wallace Collection, London,
25 January–15 April 2007

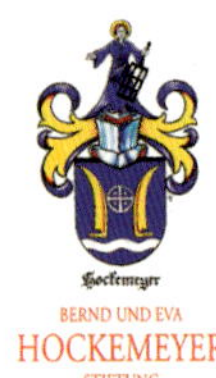

with the support of the
Italian Cultural Institute

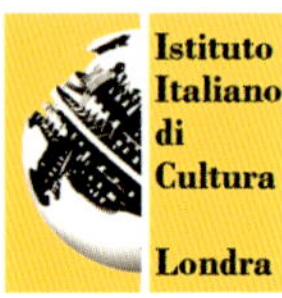





Designed by Philip Lewis
Printed by Graphic Studio, Verona, Italy

Produced and published for
the Wallace Collection by
Paul Holberton publishing
Third Floor
89 Borough High Street
London SE1 1NL
www.paul-holberton.net

FRONT COVER: Incorporates detail from bowl
attributed to Francesco Xanto Avelli, *Hippolytus
escaping from the Wrath of Theseus*, Urbino,
*c.* 1527–28, cat. 24
BACK COVER: Sonnet VIII from Francesco Xanto
Avelli's sonnet sequence, *Il Ritratto*, sixteenth
century, manuscript, Biblioteca Apostolica
Vaticana (Vatican), Urb. lat. 794,
(Appendix A), p. 169.
FRONTISPIECE: Cat. 49 (detail, enlarged)
PAGE 8: Cat. 10 (detail)
PAGES 46–47: Cat. 40 (detail)

# Contents

# Director's Preface

Francesco Xanto Avelli, or Xanto as he is familiarly known, was one of the most fascinating, resourceful and prolific maiolica painters of the Italian Renaissance. Several of his richly coloured and beautifully painted dishes are amongst the highlights of the Wallace Collection's superb holdings of Italian Renaissance maiolica. We are, therefore, immensely proud to be hosting the first exhibition ever to be devoted to this versatile and intriguing artist.

Xanto's working life spanned turbulent times. Italy was a major platform for the playing out of tumultuous shifts in political allegiance, with the resultant battles and sacks that helped to define the wider European stage. The Holy Roman Emperor Charles V and Pope Clement VII were key players and the devastating Sack of Rome in 1527, when the pope was forced to take refuge from Imperial troops in the Castel Sant'Angelo, was a major episode in sixteenth-century Italian history. The Sack is rarely represented by artists but it is the subject of a number of Xanto's allegorical dishes. At the same time, this was a period of phenomenal cultural activity, profoundly influenced by the artistic and literary legacy of Classical Antiquity. Religious subject-matter rubbed shoulders with pagan mythology. All this provided Xanto with a wealth of subjects, depicted in a rich and vibrant palette that does not fade, appearing as fresh to us today as it did to Xanto's patrons, as they turned pieces carefully to reveal the inscriptions often painted on the reverse. Here you can abandon yourself to a host of themes, from the colourful exploits of Hercules or Samson to the serenity of *The Three Graces*.

We are supremely honoured to have the great ceramic scholar John Mallet as the curator of this exhibition. As well as being my own mentor when he was Keeper of Ceramics at the Victoria and Albert Museum, he has also guided and advised us about maiolica in the Wallace Collection for many years. When he asked if we would be interested in holding an exhibition dedicated to Xanto we were delighted: as the acknowledged authority on Xanto's maiolica there could be no one better qualified to mastermind this project. John Mallet's long-standing interest in Xanto's development, collaborators, pupils and followers is admirably reflected in his selection of works included here. We are hugely grateful to him for bringing his lifetime of expertise on this subject to the Wallace Collection.

I would also like to thank the lenders: the Ashmolean Museum, Oxford; the Biblioteca Apostolica Vaticana; the British Museum, London; English Heritage and the Wernher Foundation; the Fitzwilliam Museum, Cambridge; Glasgow City Council Museums; the Museo d'Arte Medievale e Moderna, Arezzo; the National Trust and the Victoria and Albert Museum, London for so generously enabling us to incorporate their documentary works, as well as Manny and Brigitta Davidson and Family, the Bernd und Eva Hockemeyer Stiftung, the Italian Cultural Institute, Professor Elisa Provini Walker, Sotheby's and Rainer Zietz Ltd. for their kind support of the exhibition.

Preparation of this catalogue has revealed the wealth of talent and expertise among the staff at the Wallace Collection under the guidance of Jeremy Warren, Assistant Director: Head of Collections. I am filled with admiration for all those involved. Suzanne Higgott, Curator of Glass, Limoges Painted Enamels and Earthenwares, who has devoted her professional life to studying the Renaissance works of art in the Wallace Collection and is widely recognised for her dedication and scholarship in her field, has been the prime mover behind this exhibition. Giovanna Hendel has transcribed and translated into English for the first time Xanto's sequence of forty-four eulogistic sonnets dedicated to Francesco Maria I Della Rovere, Duke of Urbino, the fiery-tempered soldier duke whose patronage Xanto sought to attract. These provide great insight into Xanto's life and times. And Elisa Sani has compiled the very first extensive list of works by or attributable to Xanto. They have all contributed new insights to our knowledge and understanding of these remarkable works of art.

We hope that this exhibition and the catalogue, which has been generously subsidised by the Ceramica – Stiftung Basel, will finally do the great Xanto justice. Our aim is to create a new generation of students and devotees of Italian maiolica who can marvel at his genius, enjoy his artistry and be inspired by his contribution to Renaissance art.

ROSALIND SAVILL, DIRECTOR
January 2007

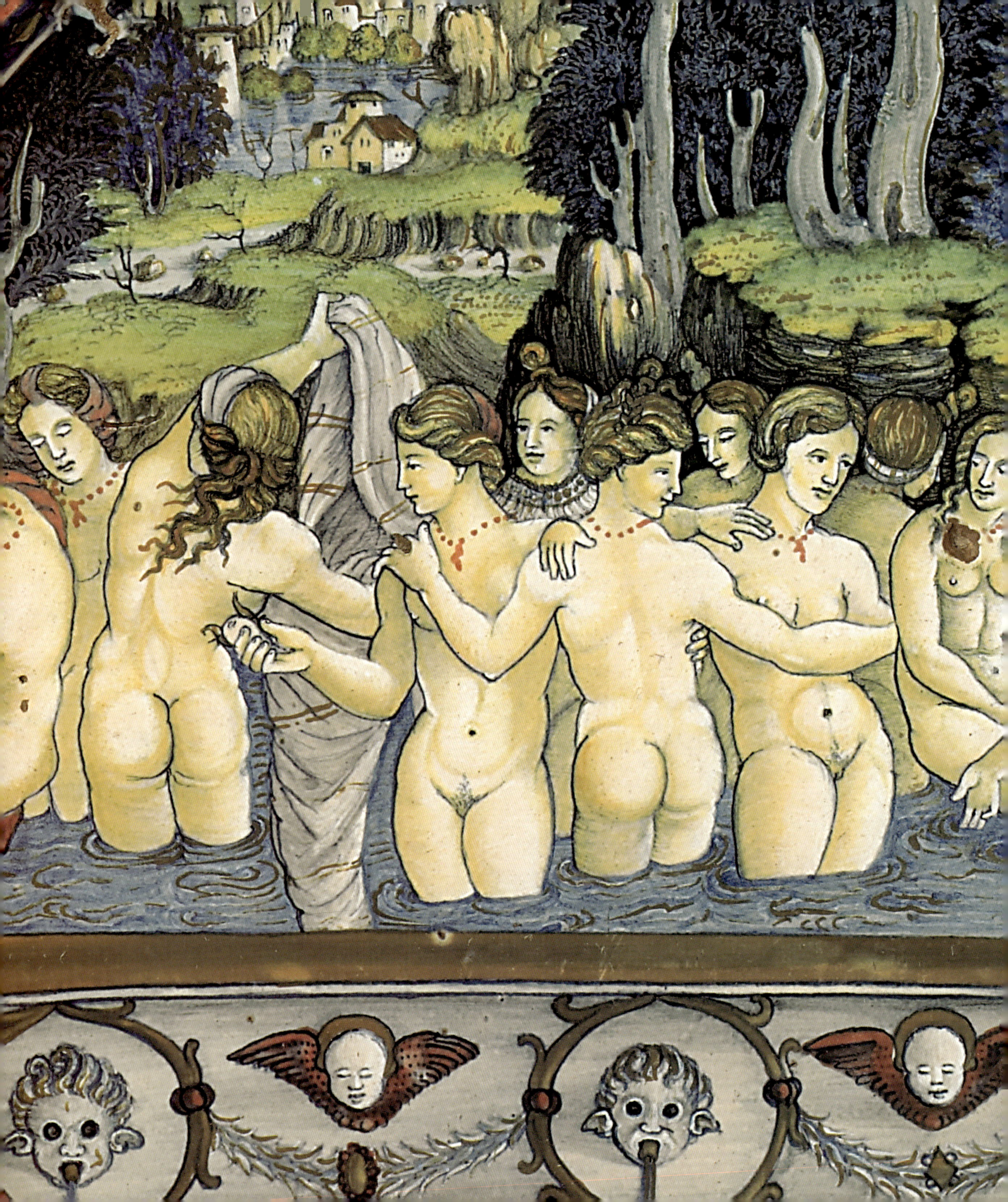

# Acknowledgements

This exhibition and its catalogue would not have come to fruition without the support of the Wallace Collection's Director, Rosalind Savill, who enthusiastically took me up on a remark that Great Britain, and London in particular, has unmatched holdings of key works by the maiolica painter, Francesco Xanto Avelli. Jeremy Warren has exercised wise control over the project, while Suzanne Higgott has shown a very necessary dedication to its detailed realisation, cajoling out of me a quantity of work of which I might otherwise have thought myself incapable. It has been a further pleasure to be flanked by Elisa Sani and Giovanna Hendel. Elisa, besides other aid, has compiled the list of works by or attributable to Xanto that features as *Appendix C*; Giovanna, in *Appendix A*, has rendered into English Xanto's somewhat contorted sonnets, besides performing, in *Appendix B*, the same task for two of the fine sonnets by Petrarch with which Xanto shows himself to have been familiar.

It is impossible to recognise the aid, practical and scholarly, of all those who have helped to make this exhibition and catalogue possible. Amongst those outside the Wallace Collection must be included: Maria Grazia Albertini, Bridget Allen, Cardinale Tarcisio Bertone, Claude Blair, Terry Bloxham, Marijke Booth, Christopher Brown, Chezzy Brownen, Lucia Burgio, Giuliana Cangini, Stephen Cannon-Brookes, Vera Carasso, the staff in Ceramics and Glass Conservation at the Victoria and Albert Museum, Cecil H. Clough, Patricia Collins, Consultants in Design, Simon Cottle, Judith Crouch, Amalia D'Alascio, Alan Darr, Paul Dearn, Jane Donnini, Rembrandt Duits, Jeff Dunn, Sabine Eiche, Caroline Elam, Virginia Ennor, Marianne Eve, Don Raffaele Farina, Carola Fiocco, Mirjam Foot, Alexandra Gaba van Dongen, Brian Gallagher, Gabriella Gherardi, Charlotte Grant, Anthony Griffiths, Javis Gurr, Tjark Hausmann, Sabine Hesse, Gordon Higgott, Paul Holberton, Alessandra Holly, Nikita Hooper, Ulla Houkjaer, Annie Kemkaran-Smith, Ann Katrin Koster, Sebastian Kuhn, Johanna Lessmann, Philip Lewis, Reino Liefkes, Ines Lindam, Denise Ling, the late Giuseppe Liverani, Helen Lloyd, Giangiacomo Martines, Christopher Maxwell, Elizabeth McGrath, Jessie McNab, Katja Miksovsky, Jennifer Montagu, Claudia Montuschi, Tessa Murdoch, Padre Franco Negroni, Sue Newell, the late Vesey Norman, Anthony North, Laura Nuvoloni, Jock Palmer, James Peters, Roxanne Peters, Julia Poole, Carmen Ravanelli Guidotti, Janice Reading, Fernando Rigon, Angela Roche, John Ronayne, Christopher Rowell, Martin Royalton-Kisch, David Scrase, Lisa Shakespeare, Andrew Smart, Simon Smith (Peter Owen Ltd, London), Sonia Solicari, Nino Strachey, Dora Thornton, Julia Triolo, Amanda Turner, Paolo Vian, Leslie Webster and Jane Whannel. I am very grateful to Steve Wharton, whose Conservation Gallery display, 'The Art of the Potter', about the making of maiolica in sixteenth-century Italy, takes its inspiration from his doctoral research into Cipriano Piccolpasso's manuscript treatise, *Li tre libri dell'arte del vasaio*, and provides a fascinating complement to the exhibition. I must also thank Mohamed Hamid for his contribution to this display.

Special thanks are due to Bruno Brunetti and his research team of scientists from the University of Perugia, working with the MOLAB (MObile LABoratory) access programme within EU-Artech, who have helped clear up a notable problem concerning the inscriptions on cat. 20. Like all who have studied the life and work of Francesco Xanto Avelli I must acknowledge deep indebtedness to Francesco Cioci, who first provided a complete text of Xanto's sonnets and whose book, *Xanto e il Duca di Urbino*, has been the basis of all subsequent studies. I must also express deep gratitude to the John Paul Getty Foundation for the three months' research scholarship they awarded me, of which the present publication is one of the fruits.

In addition to staff at the Wallace Collection mentioned above, I am indebted there also to Gino Brignoli, Sophie Carr, Stephen Craig, Danielle Cunningham, Stephen Duffy, David Edge, Emma Garner, Andrea Gilbert, Melanie Oelgeschläger, Cassandra Parsons, Anita Richardson, Eleanor Tollfree and Rebecca Wallis as well as to interns Leda Cosentino, Aurélien Joudrier, Lily Mayer, Paul Somers and Dhikshana Turakhia.

I have omitted from the above paragraphs the name of Timothy Wilson, because my indebtedness to him is immeasurable. It is fair to say that without his moral support, even when our opinions have diverged, without his generosity in keeping me abreast of the rapidly expanding bibliography of the subject, I would not, after retirement from the Victoria and Albert Museum, have persisted with the study of Italian maiolica. To him this catalogue is dedicated.

J.V.G. MALLET

# Xanto: Pottery-painter, Poet, Man of the Italian Renaissance

J.V.G. MALLET

## INTRODUCTORY

There are many reasons for devoting an exhibition at the Wallace Collection to the work of Francesco Xanto Avelli, who spent most of his career at Urbino: firstly the beauty of the maiolica he decorated, which influenced contemporary potters and has fascinated collectors ever since; secondly the fact that so many key examples, especially for his early years, are in Great Britain, and that those in the Wallace Collection itself may not be lent elsewhere; thirdly that we know more about Xanto (though still not much) than we do about any other Renaissance decorator of maiolica; fourthly, Xanto's sonnets and the inscriptions on his maiolica open a window on his literary and political interests, and tempt us to explore the history of the violent but artistically gifted age we call the Italian Renaissance; finally, many matters concerning the life, pottery and poetry of Xanto remain controversial and, if the present exhibition cannot hope to resolve all uncertainties, it may at least draw attention to them.

The technique of maiolica differs in no important respect from that of the tin-glazed wares known as 'faïence' or 'delftware', the difference in name being largely a matter of historical context. Today the word 'maiolica' describes a soft-bodied, brownish or yellowish earthenware made suitable for polychrome decoration by a covering of lead-glaze opacified and whitened with tin-oxide, though in Xanto's lifetime the word was not yet universally understood in this sense.

The first tin-glazed earthenwares had originated in the Islamic lands of the Near East, probably in ninth-century Mesopotamia, spreading to Egypt and along North Africa to Islamic Spain, reaching Italy, perhaps from more than one source including North Africa, by the late twelfth and early thirteenth centuries. In the fifteenth century, when tin-glazed ware with iridescent lustre decoration was being imported in quantity to Italy from Spain, the name 'maiolica', probably derived from the Valencian *obra de Mallequa* (Malaga ware), was used to describe it, but this name soon became confused by Italians with their name for the island of Majorca.[1] In Cipriano Piccolpasso's mid-sixteenth century treatise on the potter's art, red lustre is still called *rosso di maiolica*, but a century earlier a technical recipe-book that shows knowledge of lustre techniques used the term *biancho di maioricha* for tin-glaze,[2] and by the early sixteenth century, as imports of lustred pottery from Spain dwindled, the word 'maiolica' was coming to be used of all tin-glazed ware, whatever its origins and whether lustred or not.

Piccolpasso's treatise explains that "Painting on pottery is different from painting on walls, since painters on walls for the most part stand on their feet, and painters on pottery sit all the time."[3] Piccolpasso illustrates this with a scene (fig. 1, p. 11) that would have been familiar, a decade or two earlier, to Xanto. Four painters sit in a circle with drawings or prints pinned to the peeling plaster wall behind them. They hold their work on their knees, fine plates such as those that concerned Xanto having the still unfired glaze protected by being cradled in soft tow within a wooden container. The brushes (fig. 2, p. 11) were of varying thickness depending on the use envisaged, and made with select hair from goats or donkeys. Piccolpasso adds that for exceptionally fine brushes such as were used for *istoriato* wares, whiskers of mice could be added.

The range of colours that could be fired to the necessary temperature of about 950 degrees centigrade was more restricted than that available to painters in tempera, fresco or oils, being limited to metal-based pigments that fired blue, green, yellow, ochre-brown, dark brown, manganese-purple, black and white. The addition of iridescent metallic lustre pigments to otherwise completed ware demanded treatment and firing that was normally only carried out by specialist workshops such as that of Maestro Giorgio Andreoli at Gubbio, of whom more later.

Towards the very end of the fifteenth century there arose in Italy a style of pottery-decoration known as *figurato*, with figure-subjects, or *istoriato*, 'storied' ie. 'narrative' ware. We cannot be sure where this style first evolved. Very probably the same causes – demand created by material wealth, the wide dispersal of visual images through prints, the technical perfection that maiolica had attained – produced similar results almost simultaneously in a number of Italian centres.[4] By the 1520s potters in the Marches, particularly in the lands ruled by the Dukes of Urbino, had assumed the leading role in the development of *istoriato*

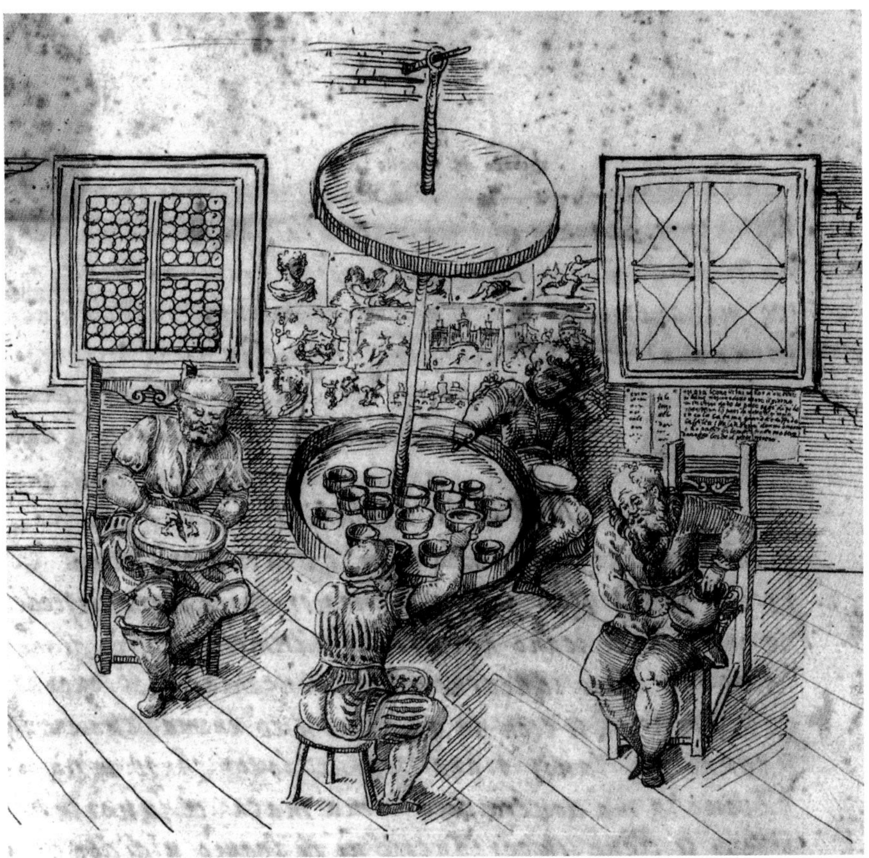

Fig. 1. Cipriano Piccolpasso ( 1524–1579), *Painters in their workshop*, from *Li tre libri dell'arte del vasaio*, *c*. 1557, manuscript, London, Victoria and Albert Museum, MSL/1861/7446, f. 57v

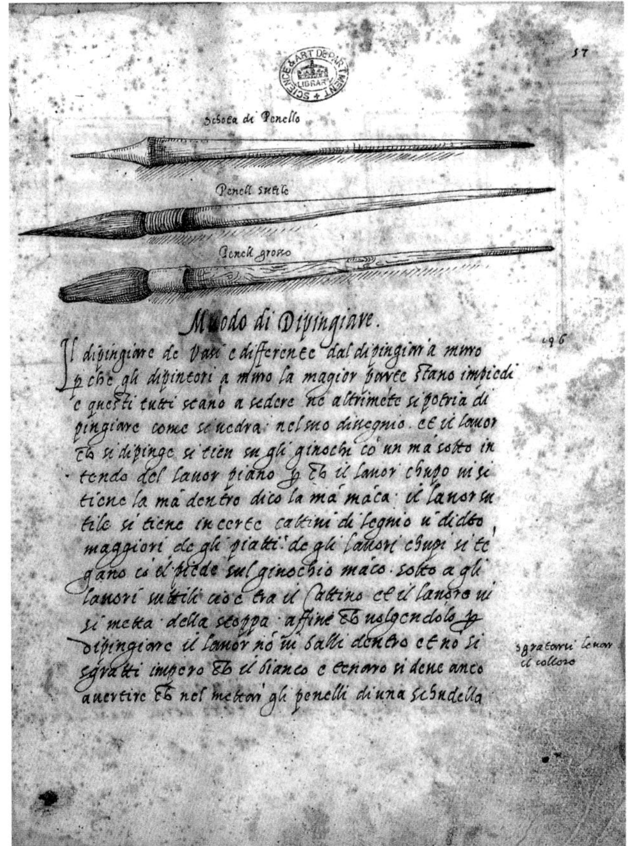

Fig. 2. Cipriano Piccolpasso, *A maiolica painter's brushes*, from *Li tre libri dell'arte del vasaio*, *c*. 1557, manuscript, London, Victoria and Albert Museum, MSL/1861/7446, f. 57r

maiolica. Though one would not think so from visiting collections of maiolica in Northern Europe, the findings of archaeologists indicate that *istoriato* wares, even at Urbino, constituted only a tiny minority of total production.

Why did this specialised branch of the maiolica industry, *istoriato* ware, become so centred round the town of Urbino? One might have thought Florence, with its influential school of draughtsmanship and painting, would have stimulated the potteries of Tuscany to produce what are, in effect, paintings on pottery; but though the Medici villa at Cafaggiolo, during the brief activity there around 1510 of a painter called 'Jacopo', produced a small group of truly outstanding early *istoriati*, the impulse soon waned. Alternatively Romagna, to the North of the Marches, possessed in the town of Faenza one of the most productive potting centres of the day, particularly noted for the fine technical qualities of its maiolica. However it is likely that the Faentine potters saw that a more reliable income was to be earned from utilitarian plates, bowls and drug-jars rather than by catering for the small clientele of the rich and powerful that showed interest in *istoriato* maiolica. The development of *istoriato* would seem to have

depended on a mere handful of patrons and potters. After the fall of the Manfredi family in 1501, Faenza, unlike the Duchy of Urbino, lacked a court.

The warlike Duke of Urbino, Francesco Maria I Della Rovere (1490–1538), may not have shown much interest in the arts, but in 1524 his wife, Eleonora Gonzaga (*c*. 1490–1550), daughter of Francesco, Marquess of Mantua, is known to have sent an *istoriato* service, thought to be the armorial one by Nicola da Urbino of which pieces survive, to her mother, Isabella D'Este.[5] Courtiers, diplomats and worldly clerics were potential patrons of *istoriato* ware, and the existence of a court acted as a magnet to artists and craftsmen. If Xanto claims in his sonnets to have been attracted to "high Urbino" by admiration for its Duke, we have to take his claim seriously.

For Xanto, as for his Urbino contemporaries who followed the same trade, a few scraps of information can be gleaned from the town's archives. That we know more about Xanto than about these contemporaries is because he himself has informed us. Around the year 1528 he began placing on the backs of his *istoriato* plates and dishes, in his distinctive handwriting, an inscription explaining the subject depicted. By 1531 he was dating and signing almost every piece. Another most unusual source of information on Xanto is a sequence of forty-four sonnets he wrote in praise of Francesco Maria I Della Rovere, Duke of Urbino (fully transcribed and translated here as *Appendix A*).[6] No maiolica painter contemporary with Xanto offers such a commentary not only on his own cultural aspirations but also on the turbulent political and military events of early sixteenth-century Italy.

Xanto frequently ended the signatures on his work either *da Rovigo* or *Rovigiese*, declaring his origin and probably his birth-place to have been in the North Italian town of Rovigo, on a tributary of the Adige. With one probably accidental exception,[7] legal documents at Urbino confirm Xanto's Rovigo origin. The fact that he often wrote his first name Frā̃ with a contraction sign over the letter 'a' has misled a few writers into calling him 'Fra Xanto Avelli' as though, like Fra Filippo Lippi, he had been a monk, but this is nonsense. The earliest recorded use by him on maiolica of the name 'Xanto' dates from around 1530, and this was perhaps a fashionably classicised version of the name 'Santo' or 'Sanctini' that occurs in some documents of the 1530s.[8] It has been pointed out that in the Veneto dialect Xanto would have spoken in early years, 'S' is pronounced as 'X' or 'Z'.[9] Though his father was presumably named Avello or Avelli, or perhaps Santo or Sanctini, no trace of such a family has so far been recorded among documents at Rovigo.[10] Even the exact year of Xanto's birth is disputed, the only evidence for it resting on statements of uncertain meaning contained in his sonnets.

In the late fifteenth and early sixteenth centuries the Polesine of Rovigo lay in the path of Venetian expansion on to the *terraferma*, and in 1482 Rovigo, previously governed by Ferrara, surrendered to Venice, a change formalised by a treaty sealed on 7 August 1484. If the citizens of Rovigo had hoped for better conditions and lighter taxes from their new masters, they were soon disappointed. Flooding from what Xanto was to describe in his Sonnet XXIX as the "haughty Adige" ensued in 1499 and 1502, while in 1503 the Po inundated the Southern Polesine.[11] These disasters were followed in 1507 by a famine and plague. In 1508 Pope Julius II linked France and the Emperor Elect Maximilian in the League of Cambrai against the Venetians, who were routed at Agnadello on 14 May 1509. The League allocated the Polesine, including Rovigo, to Alfonso d'Este of Ferrara, who seized his opportunity. Several years of conflict followed Ferrara's re-occupation of this scarcely defensible town and in October 1514 it was sacked, with all the horrors that involved. Finally, in May 1515, when the enemies of Venice abandoned the Polesine, they deliberately breached the banks of the Adige. These troubles, and the poverty, disease and political discords that accompanied them, substantially diminished the population of Rovigo and its district, so it would not be surprising if at some point Xanto sought his fortune elsewhere.[12]

We do not know exactly when he moved. In Sonnet III he tells us, in allegorical terms, that he was nurtured as a painter before he began also to write in praise of his hero and potential patron, the Duke of Urbino. He says nothing about pottery, and in any case such ceramics as Rovigo produced at the time would, if decorated at all, have had simple patterns incised through a coating of pale 'slip', a fluid mixture of clay and water; if Xanto did decorate tin-glazed ware before entering territory ruled by the Duke, he might conceivably have gained such experience at the court of Ferrara, about whose production of tin-glazed pottery we know little. We can only speculate as to where Xanto first acquired his literary interests, though Rovigo possessed a creditable school and good teachers.[13]

When we come to consider the controversial early stages of Xanto's development as a painter of maiolica it will be argued that he was at Urbino by around 1522, spent the years 1524–25 at Gubbio, was then probably in Urbino on a rather unsettled basis, before finally establishing a firm footing there by 1530. It is only at this point that archival documentation concerning him becomes available to us.[14]

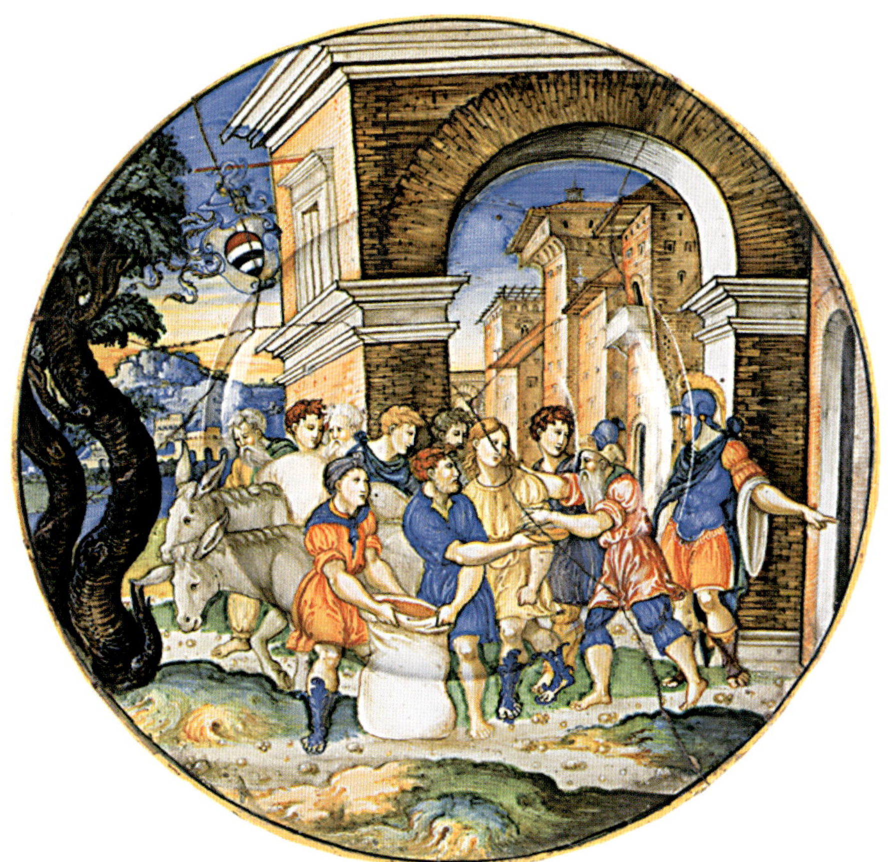

Fig. 3. Nicola da Urbino (active *c.* 1520–1537/38 ), *Joseph and his Brethren, c.* 1530, maiolica plate, 41.5 cm, Novellara, Collegiate church of Santo Stefano

Fig. 4. Reverse of fig. 3, detail showing inscription

The first document, dated 7 August 1530, relates to a dispute between master-potters and their skilled employees, listing *Franciscum de Ruigho* (Francesco da Rovigo) among the latter, while *Nicola Gabrielis* (Nicola di Gabriele Sbraga or Sbraghe, otherwise known as Nicola da Urbino), of whom we shall speak later, is included among the masters (figs. 3 and 4). The group of employees listed had made a secret agreement concerning their pay, and held out against returning to work even after a compromise offer of an increase in salary. The workshop owners listed in the document therefore agreed, on pain of a sizeable fine, not to employ any of the group of strikers without informing the other master-potters. We do not know on what terms the dispute was settled, but the names both of employers and employees (not all necessarily painters) are of great interest to historians of maiolica.[15]

The next document, of 28 January 1531, shows *Franciscus Sanctini* paying off a debt of fifty florins, which he was probably enabled to do out of money brought to him by Finalissa, a widow, to whom we now find him married.[16] This document shows him described for the first time as a master and as a citizen, not just an inhabitant of Urbino. No wonder that, on a plate of 1530 now in Milan, he appears to welcome the coming year, 1531, though in interpreting this plate we should remember that 1530 had

equally been something of an *annus mirabilis* for the Duke.[17] The document of 28 January 1531 is also the first time we hear of Francesco under a name, *Sanctini* or *Sanctino*, that approximates to the more humanist spelling, *Xanto*, he henceforth used for his signatures on maiolica. With his literary interests, even if he had no Greek, he probably knew that *Xanthos* meant yellow, perhaps alluding to blond hair such as a north Italian like Xanto is quite likely to have possessed.[18]

Though the New Year plate at Milan is signed with the initials *F.X.A.R.*, and though from 1531 onwards he often signs himself in full *Francesco Xanto Avelli da Rovigo*, sometimes adding *in Urbino*, it is not until 13 March 1534 that we find the name 'Xanto' spelt with an 'X' in a notarial document that confuses us by calling him *de Arimino* (from Rimini), probably in mistake for the less familiar town of Rovigo.[19] Signatures suggest independence, but as yet we have no clear evidence from legal documents that he possessed a workshop of his own, though these documents are mainly concerned with property deals and exchanges and cover the very years when Xanto was signing and dating his work. A dish last recorded when offered for sale with the Imbert Collection in 1911 was said to have been inscribed *FATA IN BOTEGA DI F.X R D URBINI 1532* but there is reason to suspect that, like many other pieces in that collection, the thing was spurious.[20] A particularly fine late dish, executed in 1541 for Ferrante Gonzaga, Duke of Ariano is, uniquely, inscribed as painted by Xanto in the workshop of another potter, Francesco da Silvano (figs. 26 and 27, p. 38). All Xanto's works, including the pieces signed *F.R.*, are of high technical quality, well thrown and immaculately fired; had he, all along, worked in reliable workshops run by others, or made arrangements to buy blanks from them, returning the ware for firing?

The last year in which we have archival information about Xanto, 1542, is also the year in which the sequence of his signed and dated maiolica comes to a halt. To judge by the number of surviving examples, in the previous five years or so his productivity had decreased. The desire he expressed in Sonnet XLI to accompany Duke Francesco Maria on the crusade to Constantinople being planned in 1538 suggests restlessness, perhaps even boredom with the trade of *istoriato* painting. The last known archival reference to Xanto, from 28 April 1542, does not show him hiring two assistants, as was once thought, but renting a second house of his to another inhabitant of Urbino, so it does not mean Xanto was moving away from Urbino.[21] So long as the date of his birth remains disputed, we do not know for certain how old he was at the time. It is possible he died soon afterwards or that increasing long-sightedness, such as afflicts many people from middle-age onwards, was making him unfit for the miniature-like work of *istoriato*-painting.

Probably by deliberate policy Xanto says nothing at all in his sonnets about pottery and never describes himself as a potter,[22] for which the words would have been *vasaio* or *figulo*. In the document just mentioned, of 28 April 1542, he is described as *vasarius et figulariae pictor* (potter and painter of pottery), and on a plate where he cites his own poem, he calls himself *F.X.A.R. pittor* (cat. 35). By his day a fair-sized workshop would have accepted considerable division of labour, and a highly skilled painter like Xanto would probably have been excused the drudgery of gathering and preparing raw materials, of throwing and glazing or, after he had contributed decoration, firing the results. His initial training was probably, at a provincial level, in painting frescoes or panel pictures, or perhaps he began as little more than a high quality house-painter, for there were always jobs to be done picking out decorative detail

on wooden ceilings or participating in the teamwork of decorating house facades. In making a case for the superiority of painting over sculpture, Vasari included among the numerous activities embraced by the former "painting glazed figures and, on vessels of clay, histories and other figure-subjects that resist water."[23] The devotional panels (cat. 15 and 21) and frieze-like panels of ancient history (cat. 51) in maiolica could be described as paintings, but no paintings by him other than on maiolica are known today. An altarpiece in the church of Schieti, to which Vitaletti referred, seems untraceable and may never have existed.[24]

A combination of military and literary prowess was commended to the ideal courtier by Baldassare Castiglione in the half imaginary discussions of his *Cortegiano*, first published in 1528 and supposed to have taken place some twenty years earlier in the Ducal Palace at Urbino.[25] As a craftsman, a practitioner of a 'mechanical art', Xanto's prospects at court would have been limited but, if he could be thought of as a devotee of the 'liberal art' of poetry, and a man willing to fight in a crusade, his probably undistinguished origins might to some extent have been overlooked. He could not realistically have hoped to gain acceptance as an intimate member of Francesco Maria's household, a *familiare* like Raphael's associate, Timoteo Viti, or the court painter, designer and architect Girolamo Genga;[26] yet there were in a Ducal entourage administrative posts of lesser prestige from which a literate man, even if not of gentle birth, might have drawn a secure income. If Xanto had been working to some such plan, the unexpected death of Francesco Maria in 1538 would have forced him to start all over again, and with a new Duke who continued and accentuated Francesco Maria's policy, already evident after 1522, of administering his dominions not from Urbino but from the more defensible coastal town of Pesaro.


THE LIFE AND TIMES OF FRANCESCO MARIA I, DUKE OF URBINO, AS REFLECTED IN XANTO'S SONNETS AND ON HIS MAIOLICA

Bramante, Raphael and Michelangelo all wrote verse. In the previous generation the court artist of the Duchy of Urbino, Giovanni Santi, Raphael's father, had composed a rhymed chronicle recounting the deeds of Duke Federigo da Montefeltro and digressing to enumerate the various painters of his day.[27] Among maiolica painters, however, Baldantonio di Paolo di Lamoli (Il Solingo Durantino), who left Castel Durante in 1548 and died at Pesaro in 1600, is the only poet who springs to mind apart from Xanto. Xanto composed a sequence of sonnets that was not published in his lifetime but survives in a single manuscript copy in the Vatican Library.[28] This manuscript (fig. 5), dedicated to Duke Francesco Maria I, was copied out by a professional

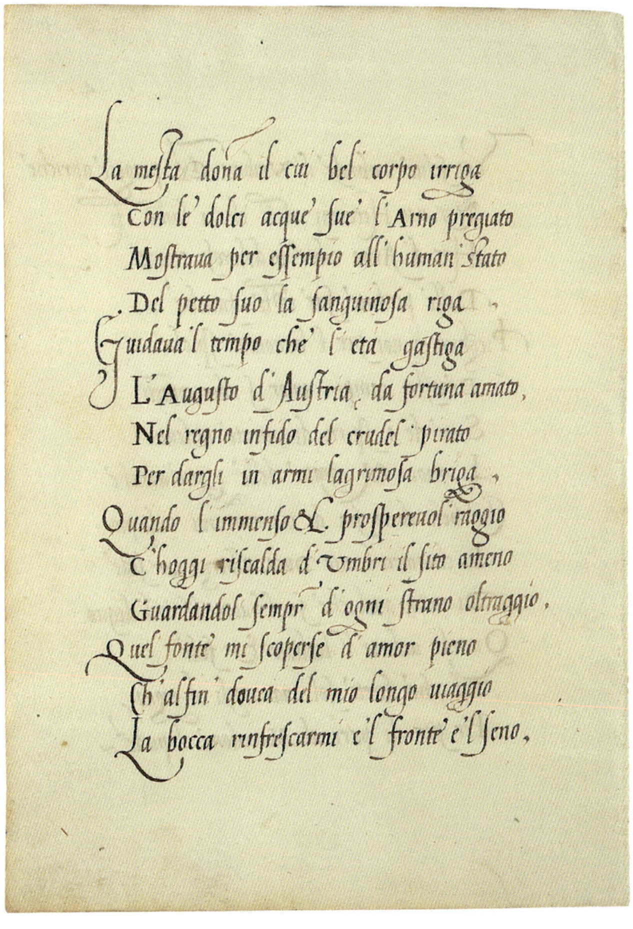

Fig. 5. Sonnet VIII from Xanto's sonnet sequence *Il Ritratto*, sixteenth century, manuscript, Biblioteca Apostolica Vaticana (Vatican), Urb. lat. 794, f.4v

scribe whose hand bears no relationship to Xanto's such as we know it from the backs of his maiolica dishes. It would appear to have been preserved by the Duke's heirs until the dynasty became extinct, after which it would have passed in 1658 to the Vatican Library with other material from the Fondo Urbinate. The sonnet-sequence is here transcribed as *Appendix A*, accompanied by Giovanna Hendel's English prose translation, which aims – no easy task – at service-ability without attempting to match the flowery and tortuous style of the original.

Sixteenth-century Petrarchan verse is especially difficult to render effectively in modern English prose. Lionello Venturi, who drew attention to the sonnets, said that to him they did not seem to have literary importance as such.[29] Vitaletti, who in 1918 published an unintention-ally incomplete version of the sonnet-sequence, disparaged Xanto's poems for windy, rhetorical repetitiveness and as unworthy to be set beside the works of the man's brush.[30] Cioci, writing more recently, seems inclined to treat at least some of the sonnets more leniently.[31] It is evident that our maiolica painter was no Ariosto, no Sannazaro, but something of an amateur and by no means so savagely inventive an amateur as Michelangelo. It is hard for one who does not possess the Italian language by birthright to judge Xanto's merits as a poet, but the heart beats faster when one turns from the Petrarchism of Xanto to two of Petrarch's own sonnets, printed here as *Appendix B* (also accompanied by Giovanna Hendel's translations) to give context to the inscriptions on cat. 39 and 47. What concerns us now is not the quality of Xanto's verse, but the light it throws on his maiolica, his life and his times.

The eulogistic tone adopted towards his Duke by Xanto may seem to us mere toadying, but the powerful men of that day were hungry for such praise not simply out of vanity, but as a means of legitimising their rule. In Sonnet III Xanto tells us that when he was not yet thirty, Love drew him to a golden oak, symbolic, we may be sure, of Duke Francesco Maria Della Rovere, since *rovere* is the Italian for oak and that tree appears gold (in heraldic terminology, *or*) on the Della Rovere coat of arms. Hence-forth Xanto determined to "write the Truth", that is to recount the real-life heroic deeds of Francesco Maria. Even the most principled courtiers did not refrain from tendering such praise, and the bulk of Xanto's sonnet-

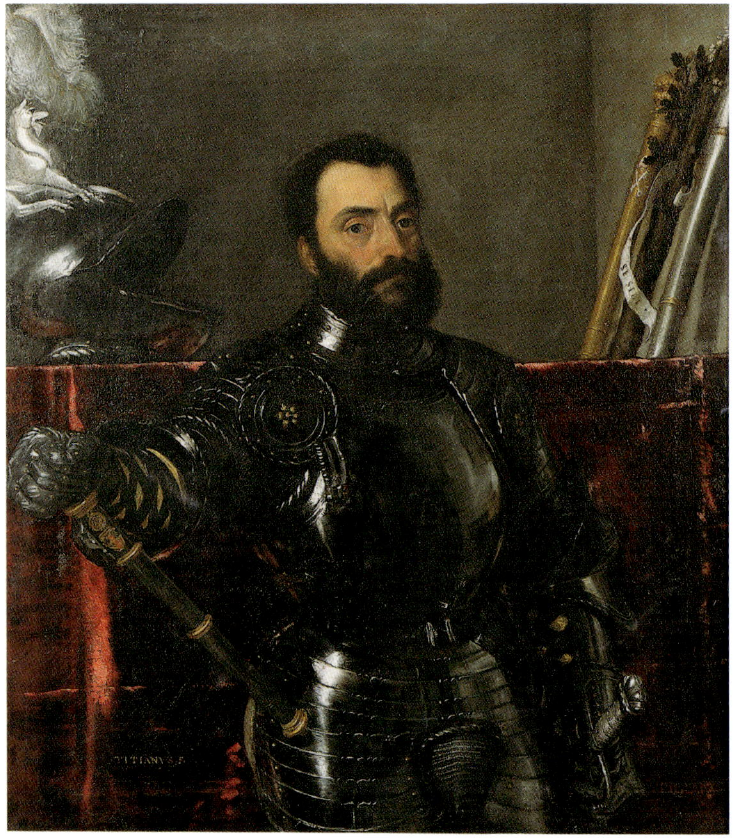

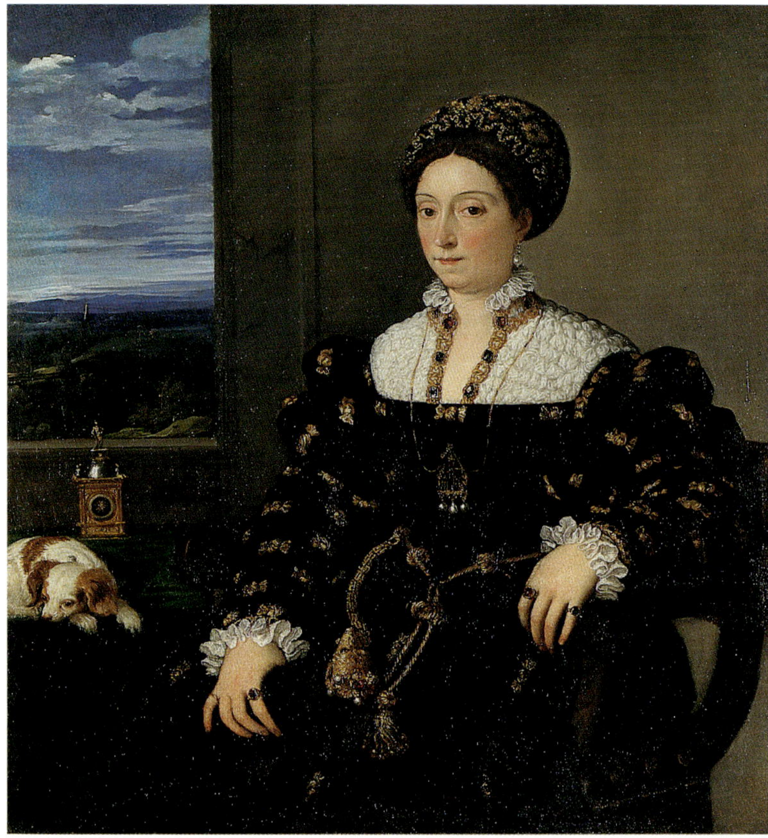

Fig. 6. Titian (*c.* 1488–1576), *Portrait of Francesco Maria Della Rovere*, 1536–37, oil on canvas, 114 cm × 103 cm, Florence, Galleria degli Uffizi, 1890: no. 926

Fig. 7. Titian, *Portrait of Eleonora Gonzaga Della Rovere*, 1536–38, oil on canvas, 114 cm × 103 cm, Florence, Galleria degli Uffizi, 1890: no. 919

sequence recounts the *Gesta* (deeds) of Duke Francesco Maria (fig. 6).

Xanto did well to express in Sonnet III a meritocratic view that great men were "today fitted by their *virtù* to rule", for despite the best efforts of Julius II, the right of his nephew, Francesco Maria, to the Duchy of Urbino was disputable in canon law.[32] In the Italy of Xanto's time *virtù* did not just mean 'virtue' in our modern sense, but embraced a range of manly skills in statecraft and war. The Duchy of Urbino was made up of vicariates belonging in theory to the Holy See, but in practice ruled by proxy. The Papacy was at a disadvantage in the game of dynastic marriages through which Renaissance rulers liked to enlarge and control their territories, since conclaves of cardinals were chary of electing, in succession, two popes from the same line. However, the Ligurian family of Della Rovere produced, with no great interval in between, two exceptionally forceful popes: Sixtus IV (1471–84) and his nephew Julius II (1503–13).

It was Sixtus who arranged the marriage between his brother and Giovanna da Montefeltro, daughter of Duke Federigo da Montefeltro, whose broken-nosed profile is familiar to posterity from Piero della Francesca's portraiture. When it became evident that Federigo's childless heir,

Duke Guidobaldo I, was unlikely to live long, Julius II seized the opportunity to have Francesco Maria Della Rovere, sole surviving son of the marriage set up by Sixtus, adopted as heir to the Duchy of Urbino (fig. 6). In 1508, when Duke Guidobaldo died, Francesco Maria Della Rovere succeeded him and it seemed that Urbino had been secured for the Della Rovere family. In 1505 this position was re-inforced by a dynastic marriage between Francesco Maria and Eleonora Gonzaga (fig. 7), daughter of Francesco II, Marquess of Mantua, and his wife, Isabella d'Este. Though the bride and bridegroom did not meet until 1508, and Julius II insisted on having the marriage solemnly reconfirmed at Rome in 1509, this dynastic alliance was to prove invaluable. Xanto refers to it and to the birth in 1514 of a son and heir, Guidobaldo, in Sonnet XII.

The politics of Italy during the years when Xanto was decorating maiolica were volatile in the extreme. The disunity of the states that made up the peninsula left them prey to the ambitions of larger European powers, in partic-ular to France, Spain and the Austrian Empire; in 1519 the Holy Roman Empire became, in the person of the Habsburg Emperor, Charles V, united to Spain. Ever since 1494, when Ludovico Sforza of Milan had called in Charles VIII of France, Italy had been riven by devastating wars that had culminated in 1525 with the defeat and capture of the French King, François Ier, at Pavia (cat. 46), and in the horrific Sack of Rome by Imperial troops in 1527 (cat. 28, 29). In the Eastern and Southern Mediterranean, too, the Ottoman Empire and the Barbary pirates were giving cause for anxiety.

It was against this background that in 1508 Francesco Maria received the baton of command over the papal forces and played a role in the anti-Venetian League of Cambrai, which successfully defeated Venice at the Battle of Agnadello in 1509. Conflict then entered a new anti-French and anti-Ferrarese phase, in which Francesco Maria incurred the Pope's wrath when, in 1511, Bologna opened its gates to the French, soon after which Francesco Maria killed with his own sword Cardinal Alidosi, the papal governor of Bologna, whom he believed to have acted treacherously. The young Duke of Urbino was summoned to Rome and stripped of all his titles while a committee of four cardinals, including the future Pope Leo X De' Medici, considered his case. Eventually Francesco Maria was forgiven and his ducal title, though not command of the papal armed forces, restored. Julius even handed to his nephew the vicariate of Pesaro, which had reverted to the papacy on the death of the last ruler of the Sforza line. Soon afterwards, on 21 February 1513, Pope Julius II died.

Julius was succeeded by a son of Lorenzo De' Medici of Florence, who took the name of Leo X (fig. 8) and who at first seemed favourable to Francesco Maria, confirming him as Prefect of Rome, Duke of Urbino and, on the usual annual basis, Captain General of the papal forces. It is

perhaps to Leo that Xanto refers, in the somewhat obscure passage that concludes Sonnet VI, as the very person on whom Francesco Maria thought he could rely, who yet turned against him. The fact is that Leo X developed dynastic hopes for his own family, lured by a vision of Medici rule extending over the Appennines, from coast to coast across Italy. As a first move, in 1515 Leo appointed his brother, Giuliano De' Medici, as Captain General of the papal forces, a slight perhaps designed to provoke Francesco Maria into the disobedience that would provide the Medici with a pretext for moving against him. Yet Giuliano's friendship towards Francesco Maria acted for a time as a brake on the Pope's further designs.

In February 1516, Giuliano died. Since Urbino and the adjacent vicariates were technically in the Pope's gift, Leo decided to appoint a nephew, Lorenzo De' Medici, as Duke of Urbino, depriving Francesco Maria of his vicariates and excommunicating him. Unable to resist the sudden assault by Leo and his allies, Francesco Maria sent his wife and young son to her relatives at Mantua, later himself escaping to join them there, probably the occasion alluded to in Sonnet XIV as having caused Xanto to suspend composition of his first poetic eulogy.

In 1517 Francesco Maria gathered a sufficient force to invade his former territories, which rose against the unpopular Florentines. Francesco Maria fought a brilliantly aggressive campaign, surprising his enemies in the vicinity of the Villa Imperiale outside Pesaro, and their Swiss auxiliaries at San Giuliano, near Rimini (Sonnet XVI). However, Florentine and Medici money proved too powerful. After all, the Pope was able to fund extravagances like the Urbino War and the rebuilding of St Peter's by such means as selling indulgences in Germany, and Leo was not to know that this practice would spark the Reformation. Having discredited his Medicean foes by an eight-month campaign, Francesco Maria was forced to retire with honour back to Mantua. In 1519 Lorenzo, the Medici Duke of Urbino, died, and would have remained a mere footnote in history had not he and Giuliano been immortalised by Michelangelo's enigmatic tombs in San Lorenzo, Florence. Meanwhile the appointment as Captain General of the Church of Federico II Gonzaga, Francesco Maria's brother-in-law, temporarily constrained the latter's hopes of another come-back.

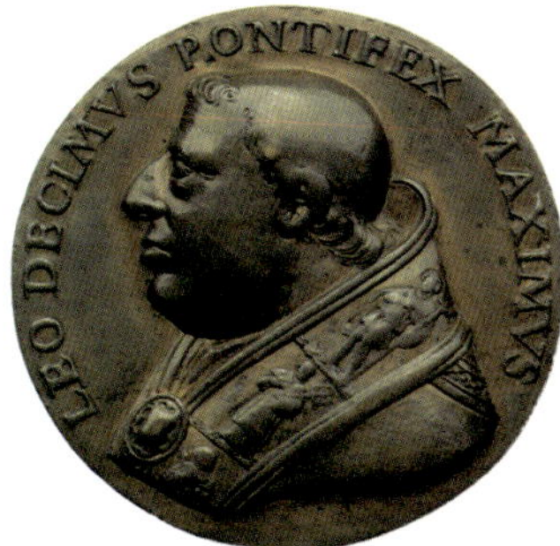

Fig. 8. Roman School, *Pope Leo X De' Medici*, 1521, bronze medal, 4.1 cm, Vienna, Kunsthistorisches Museum, Münzkabinett, 5,071 bß

On 2 December 1521, however, Pope Leo X unexpectedly died. Taking advantage of the confusion that ensued and of the surprise emergence as Pope Adrian VI of the Flemish candidate, Adrian Dedel, a former tutor of the Emperor Charles V, Francesco Maria crossed the rivers Rubicon, Isauro and Metauro (Sonnet XVIII) and repossessed himself of the Duchy of Urbino. He gained from Pope Adrian absolution from excommunication as well as reinvestment with his vicariates and ducal title.[33] Nothing better demonstrated Francesco Maria's political adroitness (*virtù*) than his conduct at this time when, in order to recoup his finances through a year's appointment as Captain General of the Florentines, he played on Cardinal Giulio De' Medici's hopes of succeeding the ailing Flemish pope.[34]

Francesco Maria had cause for anxiety when Adrian VI died on 14 September 1523 and on 18 November Cardinal Giulio De' Medici, who had been Leo X's right-hand man, was elected Pope, taking the name of Clement VII. However by this time, his year of command over the forces of Florence at an end, Francesco Maria had secured from the Venetians the post of Governor General, rising to be their Captain General in June 1524.[35] He thus secured Venetian protection against the Pope's attempts to deprive him of his Urbino vicariates, besides financial support and the wherewithal to provide extensive military employment to his subjects in the Duchy. His reputation at its height, Francesco Maria was appointed to command the combined forces of the Venetians and the Pope (Sonnet XX) when the League of Cognac was formed in May 1526 to counterbalance the predominance Charles V had established in Italy the previous year at the Battle of Pavia (cat. 46). It was as commander of the League's forces that Francesco Maria faced the Imperial armies as they began their campaign of 1527.

Duke Francesco Maria I of Urbino has received a largely unfavourable press from historians because of his role in the events that led to the calamitous Sack of Rome in 1527. Yet not all contemporaries seem to have judged him as harshly as the influential Florentine historian, Francesco Guicciardini, whose *History* was composed during enforced retirement from public events in which he and his elder brother had themselves both played controversial parts, encouraging Clement VII to contract the anti-Imperial alliance with France, Venice, Milan and Florence that had provoked the incursion by Charles's armies. Francesco's elder brother, Luigi Guicciardini, who was Gonfaloniere of Florence in that crucial year, considered Francesco Maria to have been motivated largely by hatred of the Medici, and judged Clement VII unwise "to have convinced himself that in Francesco Maria he would find that sense of responsibility and that respect that neither Pope Leo nor Lorenzo De' Medici nor indeed Clement himself had ever shown towards the Duke."[36]

Francesco Guicciardini who, at a council of war in September 1526, had been publicly and humiliatingly knocked down by the quick-tempered Francesco Maria for claiming precedence in command of the League's forces,[37] added to the accusation of anti-Medicean sentiment the rumour that Francesco Maria was obeying secret orders from the Venetians not to engage in battle with the Imperial armies.[38] The Duke, however, would have understood, without needing secret orders from the *proveditor in campo* of his Venetian paymasters, that their interest (which parallelled his own) was neither to increase the power of the Papacy by crushing the Imperial armies, nor to risk defeat in a pitched battle against a numerically superior force. Another contemporary, Paolo Giovio, added in excuse of the Duke's inaction that Clement had promoted the League of Cognac without subsidising sufficient troops to fight for it.[39]

To temporise, emulating the part of the Roman Fabius Cunctator, who had defeated Hannibal by delaying battle, seemed the obvious course. As the motley army of Germans, Spaniards and Swiss blundered south past Bologna and Florence, both of which bought off the invaders with indemnities, Francesco Maria hovered where he could not affect the outcome, no doubt expecting either that the Pope would agree an indemnity as had Bologna and Florence, or that the general of the Imperial armies, Duke Charles of Bourbon, would run out of the wherewithal to pay and feed his soldiers. Indeed it was a breakdown of discipline amongst the Imperial army's unpaid German mercenaries that left Bourbon little alternative to letting them loose on the immensely wealthy city of Rome.

What neither the Venetians nor the Pope nor Francesco Maria foresaw was the vulnerability of Rome to attack. During the crucial assaults by the Imperial army fog rendered the papal artillery useless. Charles de Bourbon was killed during the assault, leaving the Imperial armies virtually leaderless. Clement's commanders had taken no steps to destroy or defend the Ponte Sisto over the Tiber. The Pope scuttled along the overhead passageway from the Vatican to relatively safe refuge in the Castel Sant'Angelo.

From this vantage-point Clement could only watch impotently as the enemy ransacked the easy-going city over whose defence he had economised. Xanto summed up this situation on a plate, now lost, inscribed *Clemente in Castell chiuso & Roma langue* (Clement shut up in the Castello and Rome suffers).[40] Benvenuto Cellini tells us in his *Life* that one of his duties, in defending the Castel Sant'Angelo, was to light every evening three beacons and fire three cannons three times over to inform Francesco Maria, from whom help was forlornly expected, that the Castello had not surrendered.

Surrender, however, it eventually did, Clement negotiating and paying off the Imperial armies in part with gold melted down by Cellini from the treasury of St Peter's. At midsummer plague caused evacuation of the city by the Imperial troops, but they were back in September for six months of more methodical pillage.[41] By the time the troops finally moved out, in February 1528, they had been running amok for nine months. Some of the German adherents of Luther felt themselves agents of God's revenge on the City of Antichrist, and even Catholics saw the Sack as divine punishment, a view Xanto and his clients seem to have shared.[42] Rape and torture were daily occurrences and much damage had been done by fire to the city's fabric, while plague and hunger added to the death-toll.

Meanwhile Clement bargained and tricked his way out of the Castel Sant'Angelo, reaching Orvieto, the event perhaps alluded to on a plate in the British Museum inscribed *Vener' stratiata et il figliuolo in fuga* (Venus assaulted and her son in flight) followed by an admonitory *nota*. The figure of Venus has been identified as representing Rome, which is likely enough as Xanto had elsewhere used the same figures (from a print by Marco Dente after Bandinelli) to stand for Rome and an attacker. Although it has been suggested that the Cupids who walk away from the violent event relate to Francesco Maria, rather than to Clement, this seems unlikely, as it would be the only

known occasion on which Xanto criticised his Duke.[43]

It has been remarked that contemporary representations of the Sack of Rome are virtually unknown, and that none were created for some years.[44] The reason is clear: no-one had emerged from the event with credit, least of all Charles V, who had been in Spain at the time and, devout Catholic that he was, had been unable to control from that distance the actions of those who fought in his name. In view of the shortage of visual evidence concerning the Sack, the near-contemporary allegories painted on maiolica by Xanto have been strangely neglected by historians.

On plates and dishes by Xanto we are shown the Sack and related events represented as retribution for the lax morality of Rome and the avarice of its Pope (cat. 28); we see, among a pile of corpses, the two-headed imperial eagle with talons set on the rump of what may be a white papal horse or mule (cat. 29); on another plate a cherub bearing a Medici *pallone* looks the other way while an eagle-headed man representing the Empire butchers a woman symbolical of Rome;[45] another plate, inscribed *Cerco la monarchia per punir molti* (I am looking for the monarchy to punish many people), followed by the unusual explanation *immaginatione* and a flourish, shows a warrior with imperial eagle (Charles V) approaching an angel who rests a hand on an orb, symbol of temporal rule but also perhaps here alluding to the Medici *pallone* of Clement VII;[46] on a further piece Xanto painted Rome having the soles of her feet burnt as she lay prostrate *tra lascivi et scalci* (between lascivious persons and carvers);[47] on yet another, painted in 1534, she is chopped in half for her lasciviousness by the *buon Carlo quinto*, who was by this time seen as the innocent instrument of God's wrath.[48] Divine punishment is represented on another plate by flaming swords aimed respectively at the four great cities occupied by the Emperor – Genoa, Florence, Naples and Rome.[49] We should, however, beware of seeing every reference to the punishment of Rome as an attack on its Pope because, on Palm Sunday 1528, Clement himself "exhorted the cardinals and prelates to change their lives, because the scourge on Rome had come about because of these sins".[50]

Nowhere on the plates allegorical of the Sack does Duke Francesco Maria seem to appear, and Xanto's sonnets, which trumpet his appointment to lead the Venetian and

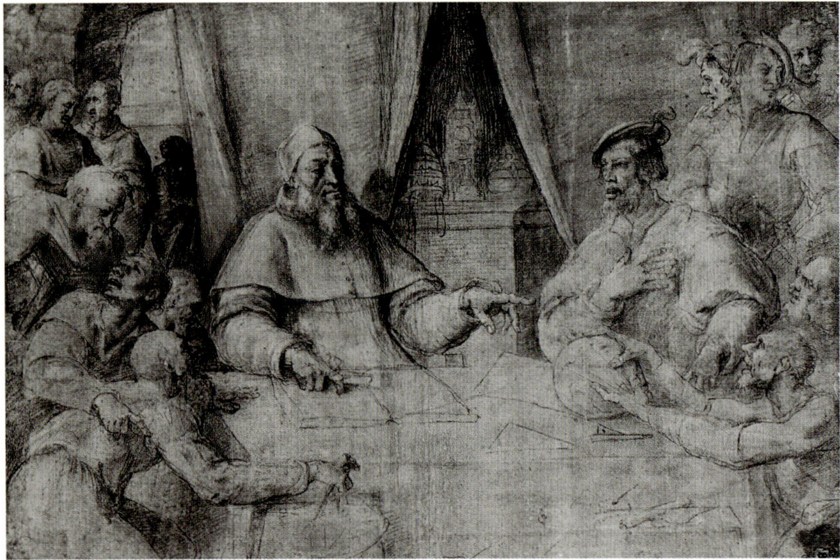



Fig. 9. Sebastiano del Piombo (1485–86–1547), *Pope Clement VII De' Medici and Charles V at the Congress of Bologna*, 1529–30, black and white chalk on grey prepared paper, 30.9 cm × 46.2 cm, London, British Museum, P&D 1955-2-12-1

Fig. 10. Nikolas Hogenberg, detail showing Francesco Maria Della Rovere, Duke of Urbino (at the far right on horseback) and others, from a sheet of the series illustrating the procession through Bologna after Charles V's Coronation by Clement VII as Holy Roman Emperor (Joannes Secundus, *Gratae et laboribus aequae posteritati Caesareas sanctique…*, The Hague, 1532 (?)), etching

Papal armies in 1526 (Sonnet XX), are silent about his role at the time of the Sack. Whatever Clement may have thought of Francesco Maria's behaviour, the Pope was in no position, immediately afterwards, to argue with a general who still commanded an army and enjoyed the protection of Venice. Though the relationship must on either side have involved humbug, Francesco Maria visited the Pope at the latter's temporary court at Orvieto in January 1528.[51] None the less in March 1529 rumours that Philibert, Prince of Orange, was acting for the Pope with a view to installing Ascanio Colonna as Duke of Urbino were sufficiently strong for Francesco Maria to have asked Venetian permission to move from Lombardy to the Duchy's defence.[52] The Venetians were evidently satisfied with Francesco Maria's behaviour at the time of the Sack and after, retaining him as Captain General until his death, despite a bid for his services from Charles V, who seems also to have been impressed by his generalship.[53] In the longer term, a full-length statue by Giovanni Bandini, of Francesco Maria with baton and *all'antica* armour, was allotted a niche in the Cortile Maggiore of the Doges' Palace, where it can be seen today.[54]

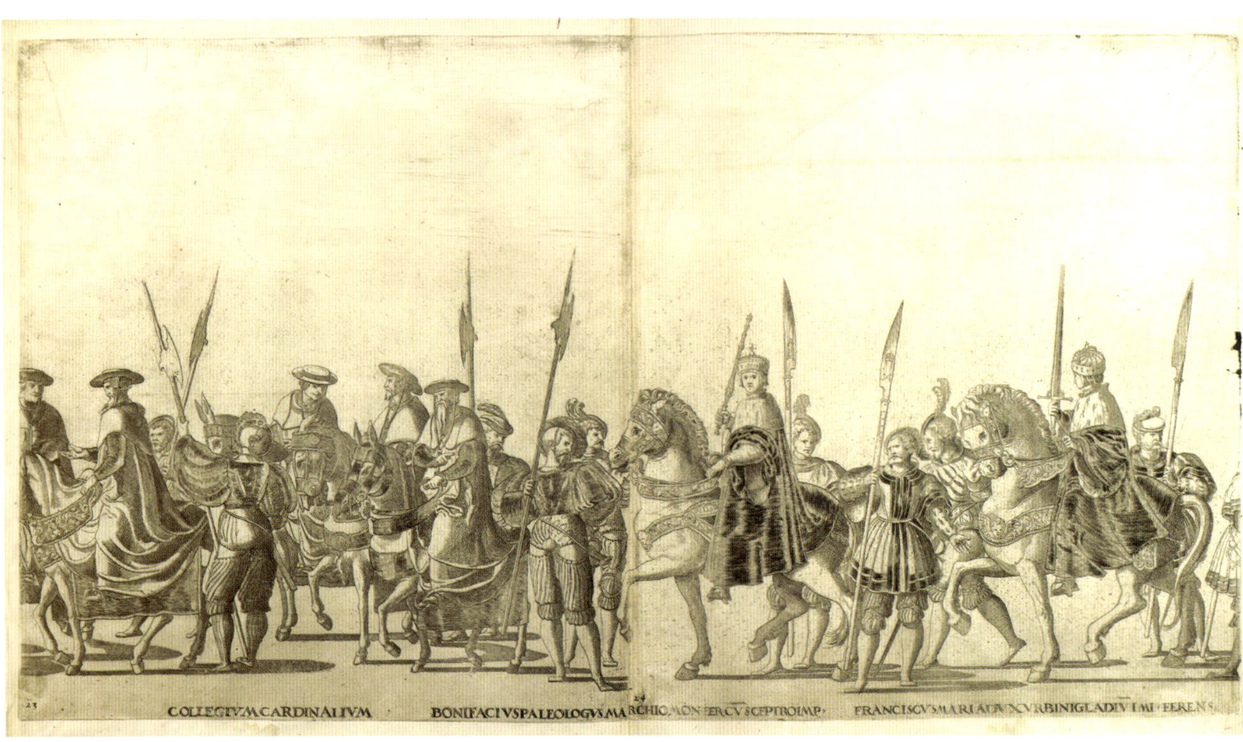

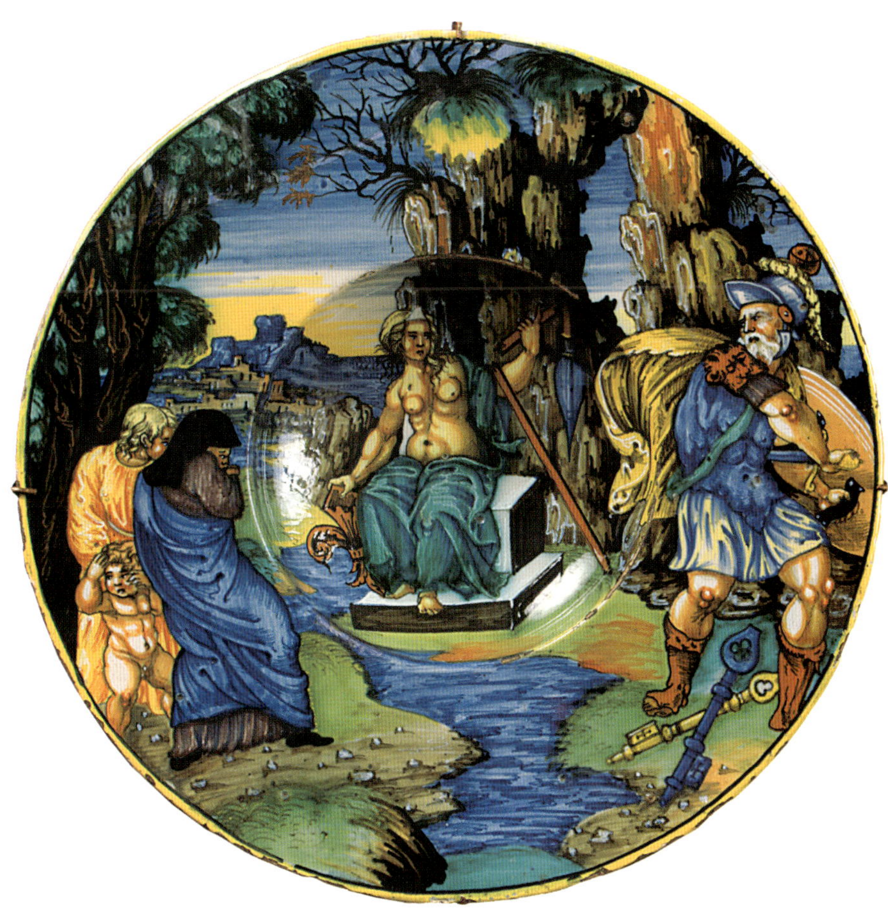

Fig. 11. Attributed to Giulio da Urbino (active
*c.* 1534–1541), *The Fall of Florence*, 1534,
maiolica plate, 26 cm, St Petersburg,
The State Hermitage Museum, F-1888

Francesco Maria's position must, however, have seemed precarious until, at the Congress of Bologna in 1529–30, the Venetians and the Emperor Charles V made it their business to protect him and have him confirmed by the Pope as Duke of Urbino. Sebastiano del Piombo's drawing of Clement VII and Charles V at the Congress (fig. 9, p. 20) has been interpreted as "Clement dominating the youthful emperor, a propagandistic reversal of the real balance of power".[55] Viewed in the light of Clement's priorities, among which the liberation of Italy from foreigners ranked well below reinforcement of Medicean power and papal authority, Sebastiano's perception may not have been wide of the mark.[56] Following the Emperor's coronation, Francesco Maria rode in the cavalcade through the streets of Bologna bearing the sword of state used by the Pope for the investiture (fig. 10, p. 20).[57] As a further sign of recognition Clement VII stopped off at Urbino, to visit the Duke, on his way back to Rome.[58]

Several other plates were painted and inscribed by Xanto in his manner of *c.* 1528–30 with political allegories that have not been conclusively explained. Such, for instance, is cat. 30 which is inscribed *fuggi Spagna: Marcho et francia. nota*, (flee, Spain: Venice and France, take note). This plate has by some writers been associated with a projected alliance against the Turks, though the early style of the dish means that it must have referred to an alliance proposed long before that of 1537–38.[59] A bowl at Padua with somewhat related imagery has been rather speculatively connected, by reason of a hound depicted in its centre, with the Battle of Pavia in 1525, at which the Imperial troops had been quartered at the Casa dei Levrieri (*levriero* means greyhound); alternatively the bowl has been associated with the League of Cognac of 1526. The piece bears the somewhat generalised inscription: *nota gli affanni tuoi misera Italia. pensa* (take note of your anguish miserable Italy. think). If the Battle of Pavia really was intended it is odd that the same hound appears on what seems to be a companion bowl inscribed *Mirare il tempo bell' ch'anoi ritorna* (marvel at the fine weather that is returning to us).[60] It must be admitted that some of Xanto's allegories, painted or written, are likely to prove impenetrable.

After the Coronation of the Emperor Charles V by Pope Clement, unfinished business remained at Florence, where the citizens had taken advantage of the Sack of Rome to throw off unpopular Medici rule. Clement had secured the Emperor's aid to effect his family's restoration. The Siege of Florence is depicted allegorically, on a plate of 1534 now in St Petersburg (fig. 11), by Xanto's close follower, Giulio da Urbino, complete with the thoroughly Xantesque inscription: "Florence assaulted by her very own

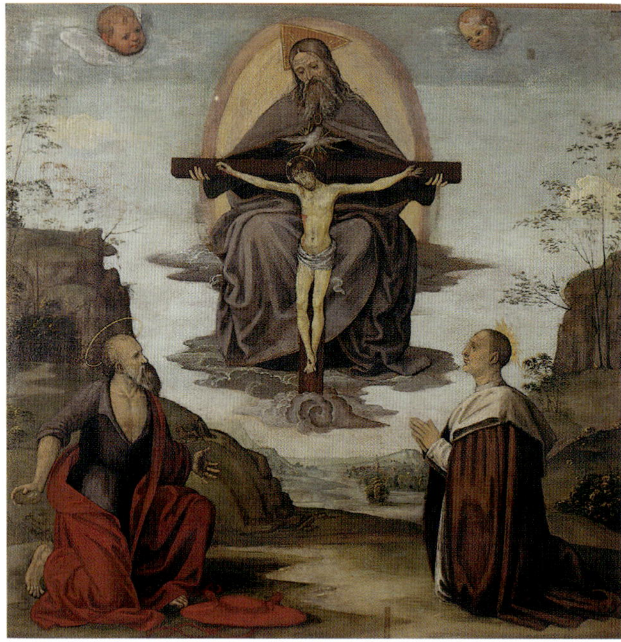

Fig. 12. Timoteo Viti (1469–1525), *St Jerome and the Beato Colombini adoring the Trinity*, *c*. 1520, oil on canvas, 147 cm × 144 cm, Urbino, Galleria Nazionale delle Marche, 1990 DE236

son".[61] We need not worry who is represented by the bearded warrior wielding a sword at the hapless Florence, because the Medici *pallone* on his helmet and the papal keys at his feet leave no doubt that, if not intended for Clement in person, it is that Pope's interest he serves. Indeed one of the more convincing conjectures identifies him as Alessandro De' Medici, the Duke installed after the Siege, who was by many believed to be an illegitimate son of Pope Clement.[62]

Cat. 31 in this exhibition, unsigned but indisputably from Xanto's hand, is probably connected with the Siege of Florence. Its inscription, *Nel anno de le tribulatio/ni de Italia/adi 26 de luglio/in Urbino* (In the year of Italy's tribulations, on 26 July, in Urbino), earned it, for reasons not fully explained, inclusion under 1530 in Ballardini's *Corpus* of dated wares.[63] Francesco Cioci has made an important connection between this dish and an altarpiece from about 1520 by Timoteo Viti (fig. 12).[64] Like the dish, Viti's altarpiece shows St Jerome twinned with a kneeling man whose head emits rays, a convention indicating a *beato*, or person who has been beatified but not canonised as a saint. The identity of this praying *beato*, the only known figure copied by Xanto directly from a painting, is revealed by the provenance of Viti's altarpiece which, until 1811, was in the Chiesa della Trinità dei Gesuati at Urbino. The Congregation of the Ingesuati, also known as *chierici di San Girolamo*, had been founded by the Beato Giovanni Colombini (1303–1367), so there can be little doubt that it is he, along with St Jerome, who is adoring the Holy Trinity in the altarpiece designed for Urbino's Chiesa della

Trinità.[65] We may rule out a suggestion that the praying man is Francesco Maria, and that the rays crowning his head represent the *sfavillanti rai* (shining rays) of the Duke's fame as described in Sonnet IX.[66] There would have been no reason for the Duke to wear monkish garb and it would have seemed blasphemous to adapt on a dish, still more so on an altarpiece, the iconography of a *beato* to represent a living and far from holy Duke.

A day and month are recorded on the back of the dish, but no year, though style and the presence, without signature, of an inscription in Xanto's writing suggest a date between 1527 and 1530. Which year between those dates was, by the month of July, best described as "the year of the tribulations of Italy"? 1527 was undoubtedly horrific but looks a bit early for the style of the piece and, besides, why associate the Beato Colombini with that year? 1528 represented a shocked lull as the Papacy and all Europe tried to recover from the trauma of the Sack. 26 July 1529 falls between the Treaty of Barcelona, agreed by Pope and Emperor and published on 29 June, and the League of Cognac, published on 5 August. Meanwhile the obvious trouble-spot in Italy was Florence, which was fortifying itself against assault by the Emperor, who was now intent on overcoming its republican government and restoring the Medici. The year 1530 began very well for the Duke of Urbino, with Francesco Maria confirmed in possession of his Duchy and Clement VII staying with him at Urbino on 6 April. At Florence the end of July represented the last days of Siege before capitulation, and the Florentines later suspected that underhand dealings took place on 25 July between their commander, Malatesta Baglioni, and the Imperial forces. In August 1530 Florence surrendered,[67] but 26 July seems to have had no particular significance and perhaps had no further meaning than as the day Xanto completed the dish.

If Xanto's dish had been painted for someone sympathetic to the Ingesuati, there were tribulations enough for the Florentine house of that order. Their beautiful convent, designed by Antonio di Giorgio da Settignano, is regretfully described by Vasari in his life of Perugino just because it no longer existed. This calamity, however, was effected not by enemy action in 1530 but by the Florentines themselves in a few days, from 7 October 1529, as they attempted under the direction of Michelangelo to fortify their city, necessitating the removal of those buildings outside the Porta a Pinti that might have provided cover for a besieging army.[68] Vasari relates that, unlike Perugino's frescoes in the Convent, which were destroyed along with the convent's structure,[69] three panel paintings were rescued. The Capitani di Parte Guelfa indemnified the Friars, who were re-housed at San Giovanni Battista della Calza, called, from 1531 to 1680, San Giusto e San Girolamo della Calza after the curious sock-shaped hood worn by the monks on their shoulders.[70] News of the destruction of the Florentine Ingesuati convent in 1529 would swiftly have reached the sister foundation *della Trinità* at Urbino.

One of the salvaged Perugino panels, dating from *c*.1485–1490, is described by Vasari as including a representation, at the foot of the cross, of the Beato Colombini, "the founder of the order", and this picture, which has sometimes been ascribed in whole or in part to Signorelli, is now in the Uffizi. In it Colombini stands with rays emanating from his head, a sock-like cap over his left shoulder, dressed in a white and brown habit not unlike those shown in Timoteo Viti's painting and on Xanto's dish.[71] It is probable, then, that Xanto painted Glasgow's dish in 1529 or 1530 for a client sympathetic to the Ingesuati, but whether the year of tribulation intended was 1529 or, as seems more likely, 1530, Xanto was already able by that time to mark his work *in Urbino*.

The continued interest in Florence of Xanto, or of the clients he served, is shown as late as 1538 by a lustred plate now in the Petit Palais at Paris, which has been associated with the execution of the anti-Medici leaders taken prisoner at Montemurlo in August 1537 by Alessandro Vitelli on behalf of the young Cosimo De' Medici.[72]

By 1532 Xanto felt able to celebrate the return of peace, commemorating this on the only plate bearing a reference to his own poetry (cat. 35). He inscribed the plate *Marte tornato in ciel, Venere contempla*, which a later generation might have paraphrased as "Mars makes love not war". He then gives a very precise reference to Canto XXV of a poem he calls *il Rovere Vittorioso, di F.X.A.R. pittore*. The implications of this for the composition of Xanto's sonnet sequence will be discussed below.

Despite the advent of peace, Xanto continued to comment from time to time on matters of passing interest. In 1531 he allegorised on a dish a flood that had occurred at Rome in October 1530, concluding his inscription with the word *historia*, as if recording a simple historical fact rather than wagging a reproving finger and hinting at divine retribution.[73] However, moral rebuke recurrs in Sonnet XXXVIII, whose position in the chronology of Francesco Maria's life makes it likely that a quarrel over the vicariate of Camerino explains Xanto's fulminations against *L'infetta Roma* (corrupt Rome), as he calls her, and *Donna caduta per furore insano/ d'avara ambizion*... (Oh woman fallen because of your insane frenzy of avaricious ambition). A plate by Xanto dated 1536,[74] inscribed *Di tua discordia Italia il premio hor hai* (For your discord, Italy, you now have the reward), has also rather convincingly been connected with the Camerino dispute, its inscription reading like an agonised cry of fear that Italy was once more about to be riven apart (cat. 50).[75]

At the time of his death in 1534, Clement VII had been resisting the marriage of Francesco Maria's heir, Guidobaldo, to Giulia Varano, heiress of the family that had ruled since the thirteenth century the vicariate of Camerino, quite close to the Duchy of Urbino.[76] Francesco Maria seized the opportunity offered by Clement's death to have his son's marriage to Giulia Varano celebrated with a speed that proved necessary because, on this occasion, the conclave chose a new pope the very same night it assembled. The other cardinals, Guicciardini tells us, were impressed by the age and apparent infirmity of Cardinal Farnese (fig. 13, p. 24) who, after being elected as Pope Paul III, belied his appearance and ruled with firmness and guile until 1549.[77]

One of the first things to engage the new Pontiff's attention was the Camerino marriage. The earliest biographer of the Duke, Giambattista Leoni, tells how Paul III sent at once to the young bride and her mother forbidding the alliance. Undeterred by the answer that the alliance had already been sanctified and apparently consummated, though Giulia was only twelve at the time, the Pope proceeded from threat to threat, right up to excommunication and dispatch of an army. On this occasion, as earlier, Francesco Maria was saved by the protection of Venice and of Charles V, who needed him to lead the fight against the Turks; on 8 May 1536, Paul III suspended the measures he had taken against Camerino, Giulia and Guidobaldo,[78] but when Francesco Maria died in 1538 Paul III snatched back

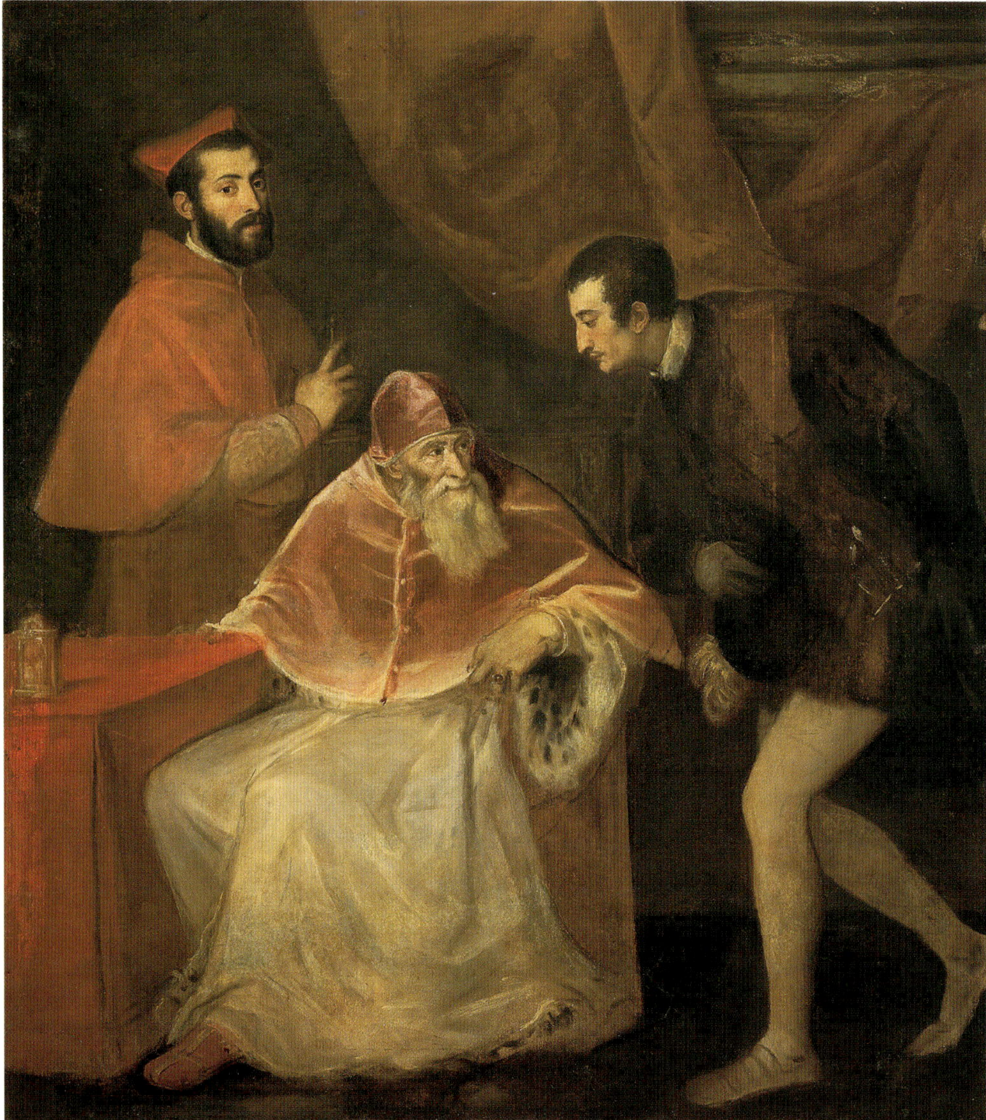

Fig. 13. Titian, *Paul III and his Grandsons*, 1545–46, oil on canvas, 202 cm × 176 cm, Naples, Museo Nazionale di Capodimonte, Q 129. Cardinal Alessandro Farnese is on the left, Ottavio Farnese on the right.

Camerino for Ottavio Farnese, the grandson who leans solicitously towards the Pope in Titian's triple portrait (fig. 13).[79]

We must beware of seeing political allegory where Xanto merely intended to illustrate a plain story, but it would be possible to list further pieces by him and his followers which, sometimes under the guise of classical history or myth, refer or seem to refer to events of his own time. An example of this ambiguity is a plate (fig. 14, p. 25) dated 1538 showing Hector and Achilles battling outside Troy in a stream whose river-god has, on his stomach, the inscription *XANTUS F*, which could be read either as "Xantus f[lumen]", the river Scamander in which Achilles slew Hector, or "Xantus f[ecit]", ie. "Xanto made it".[80] The date, 1538, is significant because the previous year Francesco Maria had been put in charge of combined land forces to fight the Turks. In Sonnet XLI Xanto tells

the Duke he hopes *Passar con teco insieme il sacro fiume / De' miei cognome, per dio vivo e vero* (to cross together with you the sacred river of my surname, for the living and true God). The crusade being planned was to have been directed towards Suleiman the Magnificent's capital, Constantinople, not too far from the Scamander river whose ancient name corresponded with Xanto's. The poet-potter's hopes are expressed in the present tense, so it is clear that at the time the Duke was still living.

In October 1538 Francesco Maria succumbed to a mysterious illness and died at Pesaro, thought by many to have been poisoned. The only other sixteenth-century *istoriato* painter known to have written poetry, the so-called Solingo Durantino, who worked mainly at Pesaro, made no bones about the matter and, in a poem published in 1565 about the Maltese War, declared that Francesco Maria, having been "made the general of Christianity / to arm

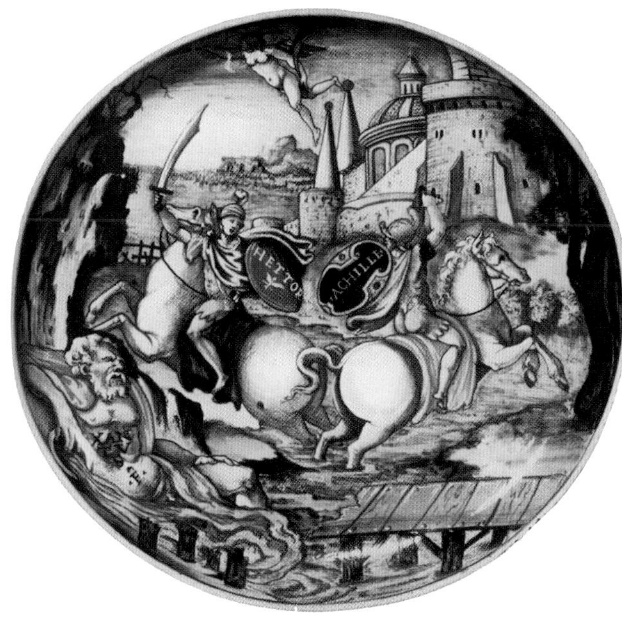



Fig. 14. Francesco Xanto
Avelli (*c.* 1486–*c.* 1542),
*Hector and Achilles fighting in
the River Xanthus*
(Scamander), 1538,
maiolica plate, 26 cm,
present location unknown

against those who have no baptism", had succumbed to poison administered by "the old enemy who never ceases to put evil in the way of good".[81]

It has been suggested that Xanto's concluding sonnets show a resigned awareness of the Duke's death,[82] yet the sequence, in the form in which it survives, makes no clear mention of such a traumatic occurrence, nor of the succession of Guidobaldo II to the Dukedom. To believe the sonnets were finalised after the Duke's death would be rather like supposing Petrarch to have forgotten to mention in his sonnets the demise of Laura, the object of his love. Although Giovanna Hendel's research suggests that the page bearing Sonnets XXXIX and XL was inserted after the rest of the manuscript had been copied, it seems safe to assume that the sonnets as we know them were completed before Xanto received news of the Duke's death, or he would have altered his dedication to the late Duke.

We may therefore deduce that Xanto's sonnets were completed before October 1538. However, as mentioned above, a plate dated 1532 (cat. 35) bears an inscription referring to "Canto" XXV of a poem called *Il Rovere Vittorioso*. This is a different title from the one that heads the Vatican's manuscript but, as Cioci has pointed out, it corresponds in subject-matter though not in actual wording to Sonnet XXV in the Vatican's *Il Ritratto*.[83] It therefore looks as though by 1532 the sonnet sequence existed in draft at least up to Sonnet XXV. At that time the focus of the sequence would have been on the Duke's victorious reconquest of the Duchy of Urbino and on the legitimisation of his rule, whereas by the time the Vatican's fair copy was made (passing over his failure to prevent the Sack of Rome, or his survival of the Camerino dispute)

a more general 'Portrait' would have been required of a Duke who was preparing to command a glorious crusade against the Turks.

In so far as the sonnets recount the life of Francesco Maria they follow a chronological order. However, from time to time the potter-poet allows himself to digress into reminiscence about his own life and the development of his poetic gift in the service of Francesco Maria. In such passages events are introduced out of sequence with the Duke's exploits, which are Xanto's main theme.

In Sonnet III Xanto says he was not yet thirty when he was encouraged to write poetry in praise of the Duke, seeming to imply that he had written about imaginary subjects until love for Francesco Maria led him to write about this real-life hero. In Sonnet XIV Xanto recounts how he was happily writing poetry in praise of the Duke, near the river Po, when he suddenly ceased, because his hero had been forced to seek safety at Mantua from a ferocious lion, the latter without doubt intended for Pope Leo X. This implies the date 1516 or, less probably, the occasion of Francesco Maria's second withdrawal from his Duchy in 1517. Sonnets III and XIV probably do not describe exactly the same moment, as I once assumed.[84] We do not know how long Xanto had been writing in praise of Francesco Maria before he was silenced by the Duke's expulsion, so my attempt to estimate Xanto's date of birth rested on less firm ground than I supposed. Were we to assume Xanto nearly to have attained the age of thirty by about 1516, he would have had to have been born by about 1486 or a little earlier, but if there was more of an interval between his first eulogies of the Duke and his silence following 1516–17, he would have to have been born earlier still. There is, then, uncertainty as to the exact year of Xanto's birth, but the date often given, about 1500, must be very considerably too late.[85]

Sonnet XXXI contains the words *assente ancor del tuo leggiadro aspetto, ti diei mia libertade …* (still absent from the cheering sight of you, I surrendered my liberty to you…), which probably means that Xanto began to write eulogies to the Duke even before settling in Urbino, thus confirming the statement in Sonnet XIV that he had been writing near the Po when news of the Duke's misfortunes silenced him. What he called, in Sonnet IX, his *sopita musa* (slumbering muse) is likely to have operated discontinuously.[86]

Very seldom, over the years, can the Duke and Xanto have been in the same place. As a military leader Francesco Maria spent most of his time with his troops. While he was Captain General of the Venetians, for instance, he had to stay within their territories. Even when he was in his Duchy we should not think of him as spending much time in the town of Urbino. He had learnt in 1516 just how indefensible that town was, and under Medici rule in 1519 it must have become even more open to attack when Cardinal Giulio De' Medici (the future Pope Clement VII) "had the walls of the city of Urbino, and of the other principal places of the Duchy, except those of Gubbio, thrown to the ground."[87] Furthermore, as Cecil Clough has pointed out to me, the retention of the precipitous fortress of San Leo by the Florentines left Urbino yet more open to sudden attack. On regaining most of his other territories in 1522, therefore, Francesco Maria made Pesaro his main residence,[88] and increasingly the centre of his administration. In his *Discorsi Militari* the Duke proudly describes the fortifications of Pesaro, which he himself had built at low cost, as superior to defences built *a pezzo a pezzo senza aver riguardo dell'insieme* (piece by piece without having regard to the whole).[89] Thus Xanto, even when he had settled at Urbino, can seldom have had sight of the Duke, however much he might lament the fact in Sonnet XXXII.

Sonnet VIII has given rise to the idea that Xanto only came to Urbino in 1530,[90] but that sonnet need imply nothing of the kind.[91] Xanto is there recalling, it seems to me, a time when he had received an important favour from the Duke. He describes this in confusingly allegorical terms by saying the Duke "uncovered that source of full love that eventually, after my long journey, would refresh my mouth, my brow and my bosom." Since the refreshing is obviously not to be taken literally, the journey, too, is probably allegorical of the journey of Xanto's life.

Xanto dates the occasion of his refreshment, whatever that was, by reference to the wounded state of Florence, which presumably means soon after that city's surrender to the Imperial troops in August 1530. He also dates it by saying that at the time Charles V, the "Augustus of Austria cherished by fortune", was engaged in the faithless (or infidel?) kingdom of a *crudel pirato* (cruel pirate) "to give him in arms tearful trouble". In 1530 Charles V was, at least in theory, reconciled with Clement VII and was restoring the Pope's family to power in Florence, so we may rule out the suggestion that Xanto blasphemously used the term "cruel pirate" to describe the Vicar of Christ. In one form or another the Turks or their North African ally, Barbarossa, are surely intended. The struggle with these Islamic powers was at the time perennial and, if the assault in 1530 by Charles's naval forces on the Barbary stronghold of Cherchell, near Algiers, be considered insufficiently important,[92] then the reference might be to the retreat of Suleiman the Magnificent from near Vienna in 1529. For our present purposes the identification of the "cruel pirate" is not very important because the date of Xanto's refreshment is sufficiently anchored to 1530 by reference to the Siege of Florence.

Sabine Eiche tells me that, judging from the Duke's correspondence, the Duke was in his Duchy, quite unusually, for much of 1530–31: he was at Pesaro on 3 January 1530, though back in Mantua by 6 February. On 24 February we know he attended the coronation of Charles V by Clement VII and took part in the subsequent cavalcade through Bologna (fig. 10, p. 20). A letter from his agent to the Duchess shows Francesco Maria to have been there on 15 March, though he planned to take leave of the Emperor and Pope the following day or the one after. He was in Urbino on 5 April, presumably to prepare for the Pope's arrival, in Murano on 13 April and again in Urbino on 19 April. Thereafter he was in Pesaro most of the time from 8 May 1530 until 20 May 1531, then at Fossombrone on 11 and 17 June before being at Urbino on 3 and 5 July 1531. On 14 July he was back in Pesaro, but in Urbino once again from 26 July to 31 August 1531; in Senigallia on 7 October, after which he returned to Pesaro by 13 October, remaining there until the end of the year. The years 1530 and 1531, then, offered rare opportunities for Francesco Maria to bestow in person some benefit on Xanto, possibly by granting him the citizenship of Urbino, though it is unlikely the Duke would have done so to a man who had not already lived a year or two in the town. Alternatively, the Duke may have adjudicated in favour of Xanto in the 1530 dispute over wages. In any case the sonnets give us no reason to suppose Xanto had not worked in Urbino before 1530, and I believe we shall find, when we consider his work, cause to believe he was there well before that date.

A letter sent on 7 July 1528 by the Duke of Urbino's representative, Giovanmaria Della Porta, to the Duchess Eleonora from the temporary court established at Viterbo by Pope Clement VII on his way to Rome from Orvieto after the Sack raises several matters of interest:

> Seeing Our Lord eat from *bianco sopra bianco* plates, I asked his steward why His Holiness (Clement VII) was not eating from ones painted with figures. I received the answer that he never ate off anything else, reserving the other kind for the use of cardinals, and that by obtaining some of that kind quickly, its arrival could not be better timed, as he has almost come to the end of one (ie. a service) similarly made that came to him from Faenza. And I was particularly told that he (the Pope) does not care for large or small bowls (*scotelle* or *scotellini*), nor candlesticks, nor much for flasks. What he really likes is to have lots of plates of the size I enclose, and of two smaller sizes of the same. Of larger dishes not more than two, two basins and ewers, saltcellars and other vessels as seems best to our Genga, but above all quickly, quickly, because the time is ripe, and to speed things more one could entrust the commission to two masters who would work concurrently.[93]

This letter tells us much about an order for a service of *istoriato* maiolica at a key moment of Xanto's career. That the Pope confined himself to simple pottery decorated in white on white was perhaps due to the state of mourning he still maintained for the previous year's disaster – he had even grown a beard, as Julius II had done after the loss of Bologna.[94] Della Porta was apparently surprised that, despite the difficult conditions in which the Pope had lived since quitting Rome, he did not use *istoriato* maiolica, but reserved that for the cardinals. *Istoriato* was, however, evidently used and not merely displayed on a *credenza* or sideboard as some ceramic historians have insisted.[95] Such plates would not long have survived use for cutting up meat with a knife, but the use of fingers for eating was more prevalent then than it is today. A newly fashionable dish, *insalata* (salad), might have suggested itself as one of several uses for which *istoriato* plates were suitable.[96] The practice of framing such plates and hanging them like pictures on a wall[97] is of later date and has not been traced back earlier than 1658, when a Palermo inventory listed two Urbino *istoriato* plates "mounted in wood with a gilded frame".[98] Use, even if only by cardinals and other grand folk, was clearly intended by those who commissioned or first owned *istoriato* ware.

At Urbino, it is interesting that the Duchess might be expected to consult the court artist, Girolamo Genga, as to what "other vessels" might please the Pope at this peculiarly delicate moment of his relationship with Francesco Maria. It is also fascinating to see that, in the interest of speed, collaboration between two pottery masters was recommended. It is precisely such collaboration that we can observe in some of Xanto's work, for instance in the case of the so-called 'Three Crescents' service, of which some pieces are by Xanto (cat. 25), and others by an anonymous hand now known as 'The Milan Marsyas Painter' (cat. 26).[99] This and another service with an unidentified coat of arms charged with an eagle, also divided between these two painters, are to be dated *c.* 1528–30, very close to the time of Della Porta's letter to the Duchess of Urbino.[100]

I have suggested elsewhere[101] an even earlier instance of Xanto's collaborating with another maiolica painter, Nicola da Urbino, who is recorded at Urbino from 1520 onwards and not known to have worked anywhere else.[102] As the two plates in question, cat. 17 and 18, each bearing the arms of the Florentine family of Bonzi, are unsigned, their attribution remains a matter of opinion rather than verifiable fact. They are shown with pieces bearing what is believed to be Xanto's early signature, *F.R.*, thought to stand for 'Francesco Rovigiese' (cat. 3, 13, 14 and 15), so there is an opportunity for visitors to the exhibition to make up their own minds. The Bonzi plate attributed to Nicola, with Perseus (cat. 18), shows all that painter's habitual fluency of line, especially in his drawing of the figures and the dragon-like Gorgon. Cat. 17, the plate here attributed to Xanto, is drawn with more rigid outlines and has a landscape background characteristic of the early pieces he signed *F.R.*. Within the development of Nicola's style and that of Xanto in his 'F.R.' phase, these plates seem datable *c.* 1525–27, which would make a case for Xanto having painted alongside Nicola at Urbino well before 1530.

Let us now return to the earliest works identified as Xanto's, among which cat. 1, with *Hercules and Omphale*,

bears the inscription *.OMNIA./VINCIT./AMOR./1522*. This
bowl was once attributed to the same hand as one in the
British Museum that bears on its underside the monogram
*BT* or *TB*.[103] Although this attribution has been rejected by
recent scholarship,[104] the resemblance is close enough to
suggest that both were probably produced in the same
workshop. Cat. 2, a fragmentary piece with *Samson rending
the Lion*, may be confidently assigned not just to the same
workshop, but to the same hand as the *Hercules and Omphale*.
It has been remarked that the surface of these three pieces
is uncharacteristically opaque, the colours lacking in
brilliance.[105] A recent reading of the *BT* monogram as
'Taviano di Berardino' would, if confirmed, show that the
three were made in Castel Durante,[106] close to Urbino, but
the comparisons next to be made argue for production at
Urbino rather than Castel Durante or (as used to be
thought) at Faenza.

A rosette pattern painted in *bianco sopra bianco* (opaque
white on the off-white tin-glaze) within the well of a
signed 'F.R.' bowl at Melbourne,[107] occurs in virtually
identical form on some of the earliest pieces attributed
to Nicola da Urbino: the seventeen plates comprising the
Correr Museum's service,[108] a plate at Berlin,[109] a dish
at Amsterdam[110] and a broad-brimmed bowl at Oxford
(fig. 15). On the last two are painted *The Calumny of Apelles*,
a composition seemingly derived from a fresco, now lost,
painted at Siena around 1509 by Luca Signorelli. Girolamo
Genga, who had collaborated on this Petrucci project, and
who returned to Francesco Maria's service soon after the
latter's recovery of his Duchy late in 1521, seems a likely
conduit through which knowledge of Signorelli's *Calumny*
could have reached Nicola; however, Signorelli's compositions are also known to have circulated by such means as
a book of designs signed by a certain Jacopo da Bologna.[111]
The *Calumny* subject was thought peculiarly appropriate
to the circumstances in which Francesco Maria had found
himself when accused and deprived of his Duchy by Leo X,
and Genga was later to supervise its depiction in fresco for
a room of Francesco Maria's Villa Imperiale at Pesaro.[112]
Nicola's plates with the *Calumny*, bearing the *bianco sopra
bianco* rosettes are, then, unlikely to have been painted
before the Duke's return in 1521, while their style and
palette dates them earlier than Nicola's Este-Gonzaga
set of 1524. For Xanto in his 'F.R.' phase to have known

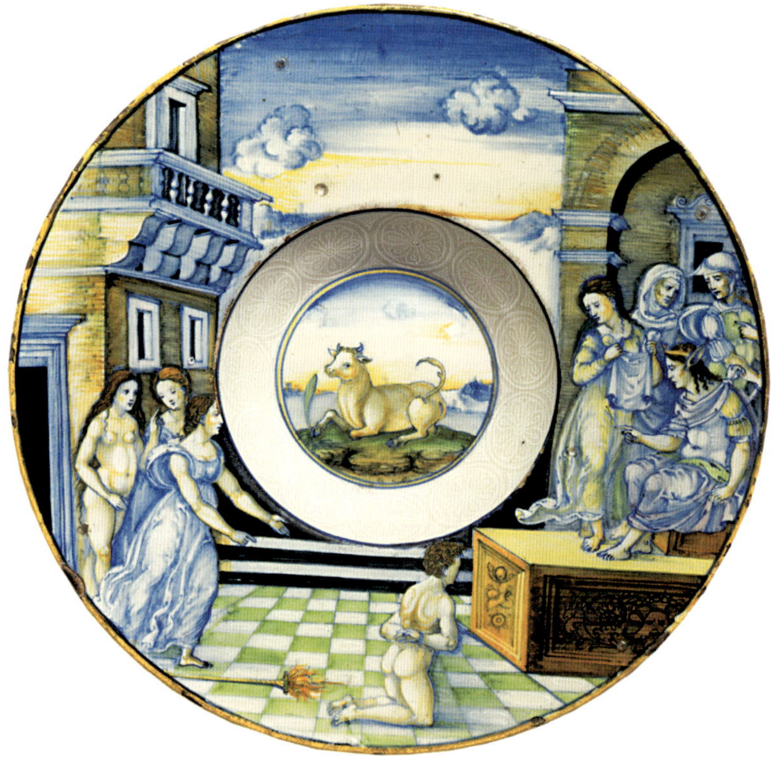

Fig. 15. Nicola da Urbino, *The Calumny of Apelles*, *c*. 1522, maiolica bowl,
27.9 cm, Oxford, Ashmolean Museum, WA1896.CDEF.C474

Nicola's rosette pattern, we should probably suppose
him in Urbino by 1521–23.

The earliest dated example of Nicola da Urbino's
work has been thought to be a bowl (fig. 16, p. 29) in the
Hermitage, St Petersburg, bearing on its underside a
fictive paper label with the name *NICHOL* in monogram,
and the date, 1521 (fig. 17, p. 29).[113] This is one of only five
works that bear various forms of Nicola's 'signature',
yet only one of the five has an inscription specifically
declaring Nicola its painter (figs. 3 and 4, p. 13). Unlike
Xanto at this time Nicola is likely to have been running a
workshop, so a name or monogram, unless accompanied
by some such word as *pinxit*, might be no more than a
workshop mark. Indeed one of the other four 'signed'
pieces on which our understanding of Nicola has been
based, admittedly of later date, is of such inferior quality
that even its inscription ending with *Nicola da .V.* in what

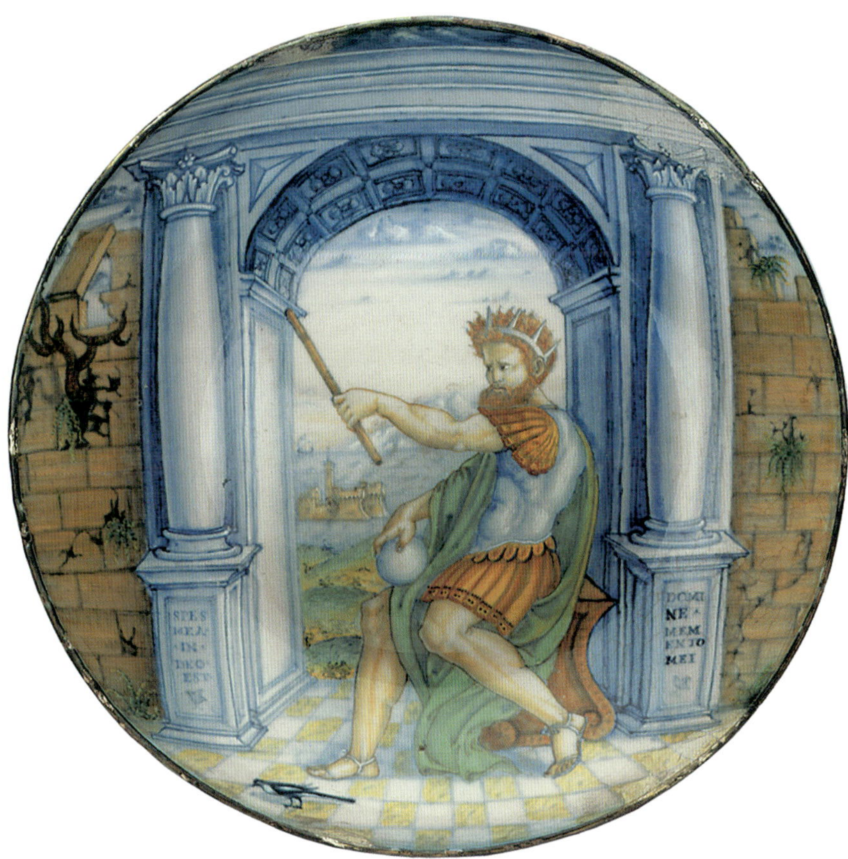

Fig. 16. Nicola da Urbino, *A Ruler*, 1521, maiolica bowl, 25.5 cm,
St Petersburg, The State Hermitage Museum, F-363

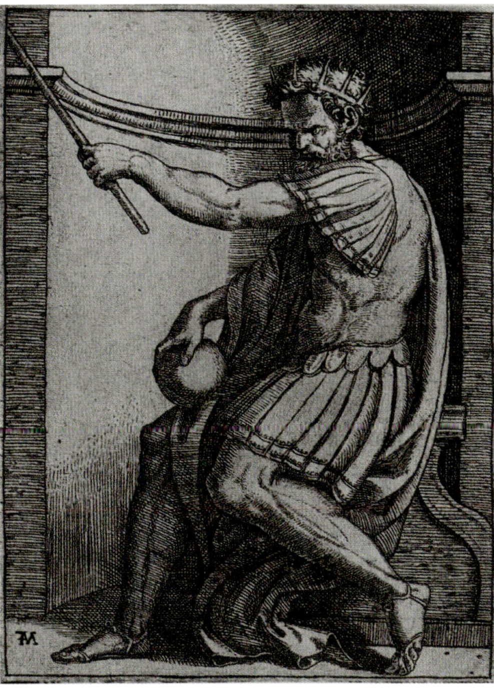

Fig. 18. Marcantonio Raimondi (*c.* 1470–82 – d. 1527–34) after
Raphael (1483–1520), *A Seated Emperor*, engraving, London,
British Museum, PG&D H.3.59

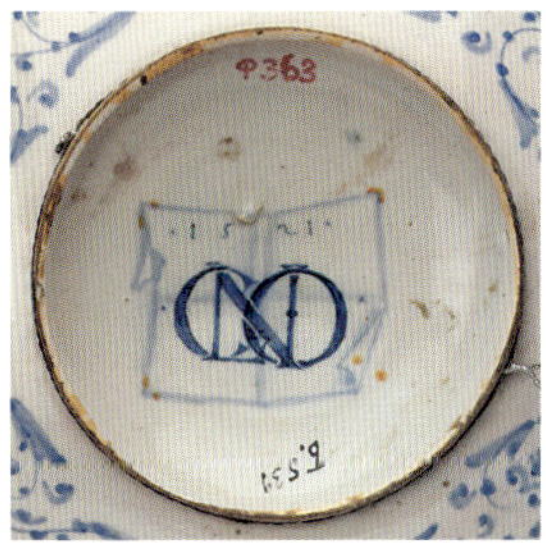

Fig. 17. Reverse of fig. 16,
showing a monogram that
can be read as *NICHOL* and
the date 1521

appears to be Nicola's handwriting fails to convince that
it is more than a product of his workshop.[114]

A good case has been made for the St Petersburg bowl
representing, in allegory, the return to his Duchy in 1521
of Francesco Maria, complete with a swallow to remind
us of his birth on the day of the Annunciation.[115] Political
allegory was more to Xanto's taste than to Nicola's[116] but,
whoever painted the Hermitage's bowl, the date on it,
1521, is quite likely to mark the Duke's restoration rather
than the date when the bowl was painted.[117] The contemporary Venetian diarist, Marino Sanuto, shows how very
close to the end of 1521 the events of Francesco Maria's
restoration followed one another: 1 December, Pope Leo X
died; 12 December, Urbino expelled the Florentines,
defenestrating the Governor; 22 December, the Duke
entered Pesaro in triumph.[118]

An exhibition at Faenza recently gave me the chance
to re-examine the Hermitage bowl in the original,[119] and
I was astonished to find in its figure-painting none of the
suppleness of line that study of Nicola's work, including
early work like the *Calumny* at Oxford (fig. 15, p. 28) or the
Correr service at Venice, had led me to expect. The quality
of the painting was not in doubt but I was left wondering
whether the Hermitage's bowl really could be by Nicola.
A Marcantonio print of *A Seated Emperor*, presumed to be
after Raphael (fig. 18), underlies its design. The
very same print furnished legs for Hercules on 'F.R.'/
Xanto's 1522 bowl (cat. 1) as well as on a 1528 piece (cat. 20)
and on a plaque of *c.* 1536 (cat. 51). This has left me
wondering whether Xanto might have participated,
within Nicola's workshop, in the painting of the
Hermitage's bowl.

The Hercules on the Xanto bowl of 1522 (cat. 1) seems
indeed to be a strange combination of two Marcantonio
engravings: the torso, in reverse, from a figure in his
print of *Two Nude Men* (fig. 29, p. 48), after Michelangelo's
*Drunkenness of Noah*;[120] the legs from those of the *Seated
Emperor* (fig. 18).[121] From the torso upwards the figure of
Omphale on the 1522 *Hercules and Omphale* bowl (cat. 1)
seems derived from a Marcantonio Raimondi engraving
(fig. 35, p. 74),[122] probably via a copy dated 1516 by Giovanni
Antonio da Brescia.[123] The sharing of engraved sources
for the figures on the 1522 bowl with those on a dish
of 1528 in Arezzo (cat. 20) and on a plate at Baltimore

(fig. 19)[124] is a strong argument for linking the 1522 bowl to those later works, which are attributed to Xanto.

It cannot be demonstrated that Xanto arrived promptly in the Duchy to welcome the return of the Duke in 1521, though the 1522 *OMNIA VINCIT AMOR* bowl makes it likely he was there soon after, probably, at the town of Urbino. The next stage in Xanto's life-history and development as a painter of maiolica is also likely to prove controversial. Once more many of the key pieces of stylistic evidence are assembled in the present exhibition in the hope that visitors may be tempted to form opinions of their own.

It would be odd if an artist as prolific as Xanto later proved to be had painted a mere handful of works during the early years when he is thought to have been signing with the initials 'F.R.'. This apparent gap in his production can be filled, as I have recently argued, by attributing to him a group of works painted and lustred between 1524 and 1525 at the maiolica workshop of Maestro Giorgio Andreoli in Gubbio.[125]

Like Xanto, Maestro Giorgio was a stranger from North Italy, but by the early 1520s he was a well-established

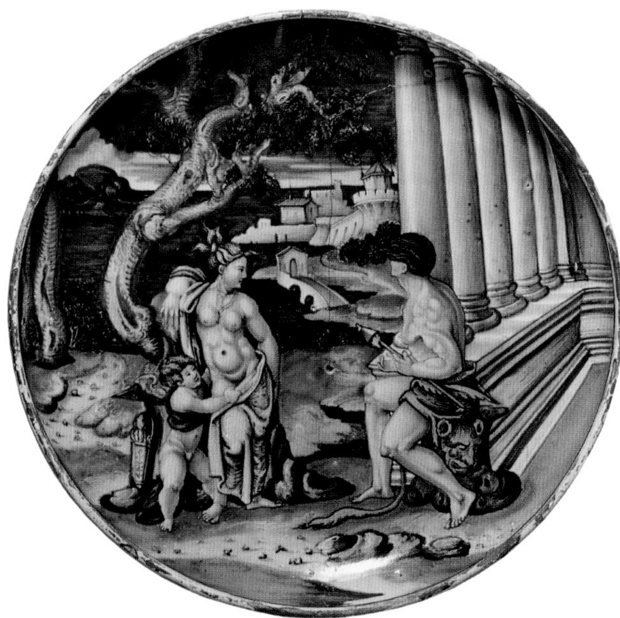

Fig. 19. Attributed to Francesco Xanto Avelli, *Hercules and Deianira* (in mistake for Omphale?), *c.* 1528–30, maiolica plate, 27.1 cm, Baltimore, Walters Art Museum, 48.1344

potter whose workshop at Gubbio had made a speciality of applying metallic lustre to tin-glazed pottery.[126] The technique of lustre required that ware should be given a final firing in a special kiln which, at a given moment, was starved of oxygen in order to create a 'reducing' atmosphere that developed the sheen and iridescence of the lustre pigments, whether golden or – something of a speciality of Giorgio's – ruby-coloured. Since all other pigments had to have been fired with the glaze before lustre was applied, there was no technical problem in acquiring completed ware from other workshops and enhancing its value by the addition of lustre. This later became common practice, but does not seem to have been done before *c.* 1525.

Remnants of a lustred service which we may call the 'S' service[127] (here represented by cat. 6–8) may be distinguished by an emblem (probably a sign of ownership) incorporating the letter 'S'. Some pieces from the 'S' service, with decorative borders and dated 1524 (cat. 6), must have been both made and lustred in Gubbio because the 'S' emblem is painted on the front in blue, a colour which had to be applied and fired before the addition of lustre. Others of the service bearing at the back in lustre pigments the 'S' emblem and the date 1525 (cat. 7 and 8) are decorated with *istoriato* subjects by an exceptionally able painter who is likely to have painted also the figures of children at the centres of the 1524 bowls with decorative borders. Two other lustred *istoriati* from 1524 (cat. 4 and 5) are surely by the same able painter and, since they share the same early nineteenth-century provenance, may originally have been considered part of the 'S' service. It is my contention that the talented painter who did most of the *istoriato* painting on the 'S' service, and on a whole group of other works lustred in Maestro Giorgio Andreoli's Gubbio workshop in 1524–25, is none other than Francesco Xanto Avelli.[128]

Let us be clear: the probability is that even when an artist such as Xanto worked within the Andreoli workshop at Gubbio, the application of lustre to his work would have been left to another hand. The evidence for this lies in the lustred inscriptions and decorative motifs on the reverse of ware, which seem to bear no correlation to the hands responsible for the polychrome decoration on the main surface. We know from a document of 1517 that Maestro

Giorgio was empowered to use his own name alone to stand for the family partnership, in other words a lustred inscription *M°. G°.* on the reverse of a piece is a trade-mark rather than a signature.[129] The same argument may be used also of the lustred inscription on cat. 10, or even of inscriptions in blue (hence added with the polychrome before the main firing) like that on a famous dish of 1520 with *The Judgement of Paris*.[130] The belief that the name *M° Giorgio* on the latter piece was a signature gave rise to the fallacious belief that Giorgio had himself painted some of the finest Gubbio *istoriati*, rather than being, as seems more likely, a prosperous business man and employer of artists and craftsmen. Had Giorgio really been a fine painter of narrative pottery it is inconceivable that his skill should not have declared itself both much earlier than 1520, the date on the Petit Palais dish, and later than 1525, the date on such pieces as cat. 9 and 10 for which Giorgio's authorship was also at one time proposed.[131]

The group of lustred maiolica attributable to the painter of the best *istoriati* of the 'S' service includes, like that service, pieces bearing the lustred dates 1524 and 1525 (cat. 4, 5, 9, 10 and 11).[132] A document dated 14 July 1525 shows that on that date a painter called Giovanni Luca da Castel Durante agreed to lodge with Maestro Giorgio for one year, and this has given rise to speculation that Giovanni Luca might be the painter of the fine work attributable to the painter of the best pieces of the 'S' service.[133] A serious, though not absolutely decisive objection to this identification is provided by the remarkable lustred dish in the Wallace Collection painted with bathing women (cat. 10) which has (if one excludes consideration of its border) been accepted as by the hand responsible for the best *istoriati* of the 'S' service. On the reverse of this dish is the inscription *Mastro Giorgio da ugubio a dj 6 daprile 1525*, more than three months before Giovanni Luca signed his agreement with Maestro Giorgio.

It is hard totally to disprove an attribution to Giovanni Luca, since no examples of his early work have been identified, though it has plausibly been suggested that he is a certain Giovanni Luca di Bartolomeo Baldi documented in 1520 at Castel Durante as an apprentice painter in the Picchi workshop.[134] In that case he seems to have been working in Urbino by 1527 and to have been involved in supplying a maiolica service, of which a flask in the Victoria and Albert Museum is probably a survivor, to Cardinal de Lenoncourt in 1550.[135] On the other hand arguments for an attribution to Xanto of the best work on the 'S' service, and of related Gubbio pieces from 1524 25, are very persuasive, resting partly on style, partly on a continuity in the use of certain prints as design sources.

The landscape backgrounds on the Gubbio pieces of 1524–25 that I attribute to Xanto deserve especial attention because they are usually independent of prints; the manner in which distant castles and towns are painted invites comparison with works signed *F.R.*, while some of the foregrounds, with what look like miniature cliffs, are a feature characteristic of some of the earliest works inscribed on the reverse in Xanto's handwriting (cat. 20).

As regards the use of prints, the maiolica here attributed to Xanto working at Gubbio in 1524–25 fits convincingly into a pattern of sources that accumulate as Xanto's career proceeds, beginning, as we saw, with the *AMOR VINCIT OMNIA* bowl of 1522 (cat. 1). A few of Xanto's earliest works were based on prints by Albrecht Dürer or on Italian copies of them (cat. 2),[136] but, as quickly as any contemporary *istoriato* painter, Xanto began to make use of Raphaelesque prints by Marcantonio Raimondi and engravers of his school. Borrowings from the border scenes of Marcantonio Raimondi's *Quos Ego* print (fig. 35, p.74) are particularly revealing of the links between two Gubbio *tondini* of 1525 in the Metropolitan Museum (both surely by Xanto)[137] and cat. 14, 20 and a *tondino* now at Melbourne that is signed by F.R.[138] All these are reversed with respect to Marcantonio's print, suggesting they were copied not from that original, but from the engravings of 1516 after that print's borders by Giovanni Antonio da Brescia.[139] Even in the early 1520s Xanto seems never to have based his figures on the rather crude, small-scale woodcuts from Venetian printed books that proved so satisfactory a stimulant to the imagination of Nicola da Urbino.

The flat plate or roundel in fig. 20, p. 32, which is dated 1525 in lustre, is not only derived from the same print as a plate from the 'S' service (cat. 7 and fig. 32, p. 60), but is very clearly by the same hand. The figures selected from the print are not, however, in all cases the same, and whereas all the warriors in fig. 20 are in the same relationship to one another as they are in the print, on cat. 7 the maiolica painter has adapted his design to the deep

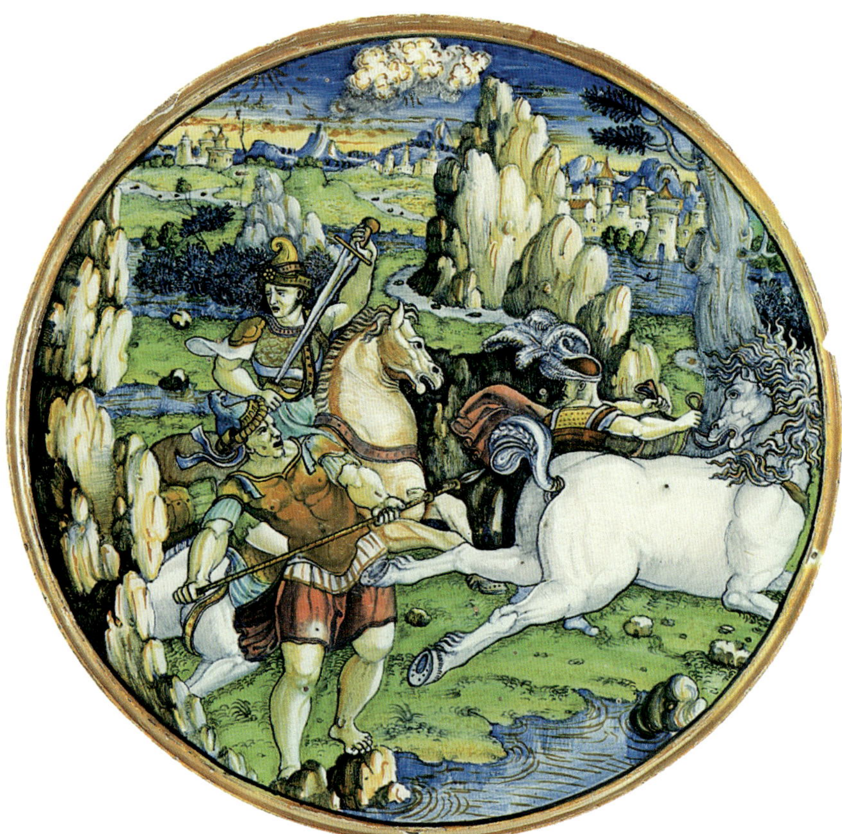

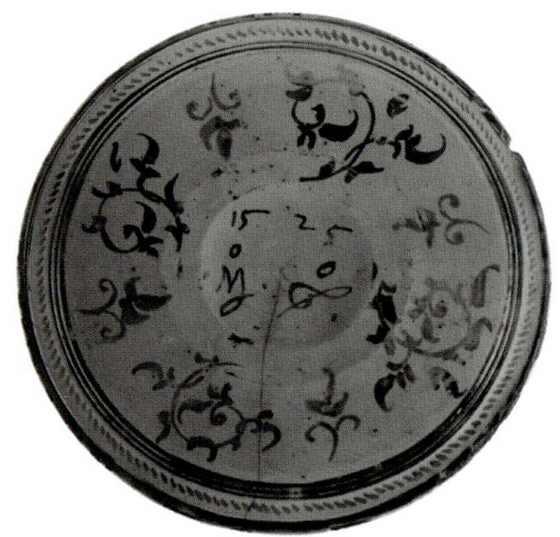

Fig. 20. Workshop of Maestro Giorgio Andreoli, Gubbio, the painting here attributed to Francesco Xanto Avelli, the lustre to another hand, also at Gubbio, *Battle Scene*, 1525, maiolica roundel, 30.3 cm, Washington, National Gallery of Art, 1942.9.334

Fig. 21. Reverse of fig. 20

centred bowl he was decorating, has used only three warriors from the extreme left and right of the print and has placed in the bowl's sunken centre a Cupid highly reminiscent of those in the centres of 1524 'S' service bowls like cat. 6. The use of figures from this *Battle Scene* print can be traced in later works by Xanto, the spearman, for instance, being used a number of times, as on cat. 54, to represent Metabus saving his child, Camilla, by hurling her over the river Amasenus.[140] Another link with Xanto is provided by the dancing Cupids after Marcantonio Raimondi on a lustred bowl of 1525 in the Pierpont Morgan Library[141] and on an unlustred dish at the Wallace Collection attributed to 'F.R.' (cat. 19). One of these putti appears on the *Hercules and Omphale* (or *Deianira*) plate at Arezzo (cat. 20).

Two plates from *c.* 1528–30, both representing *Leda and the Swan*, one from the 'Eagle' service, the other from the 'Three Crescents' service and both now generally accepted as by Xanto,[142] combine no less than three of the print-derived figures found on fine *istoriati* dated *1525* in Gubbio lustre: the spearman from the *Battle Scene* (fig. 32, p. 60), an *amoretto* from the *Dance of Cupids* (fig. 39, p. 84) and the seated woman from the extreme left of Marcantonio's *Judgement of Paris* (fig. 31, p. 56). Such shared combinations of print sources are surely more than coincidence.

An artist caught borrowing from a print may nowadays seem diminished by the fact,[143] but this was not always so. Vasari commended the practice of copying prints to *poveri artisti* ("poor", or perhaps "minor artists") who had little *disegno*,[144] a word that embraced both what we call 'drawing' and the wider concept we call 'design'. Where Xanto uses no prints, his imperfect grasp of anatomy and foreshortening are often exposed, but in this he was no exception among practitioners of the 'applied arts', which, during his lifetime, were becoming more consciously separated than had previously been the case from the increasingly learned Liberal Arts of Painting and Sculpture. Prints themselves were at that time not yet relegated to the status of mere reproductions from paintings, and they were also, as has been well demonstrated by the valuation of a Rome print-shop in 1525, fairly expensive.[145] It seems unlikely that Xanto owned examples of all the prints he copied, but he does seem to have made drawings or tracings of particular figures from them, which he could then have pricked for transfer onto his pottery. These figures he used with considerable skill in various combinations to build up whatever *istoria* he wished, sometimes reversing his stencil. We can see him developing this method of work in 1524–25, when I believe him to have worked at Gubbio for Maestro Giorgio Andreoli, though he was also quite capable of copying such figures freehand, and varying them in scale.[146]

The next group of works that may be considered as Xanto's consists of seven or perhaps six pieces inscribed on the front *F.R.*,[147] four of which are in the present exhibition (cat. 3 and 13–15), along with others that can be grouped with them (cat. 1–2 and 12). Since not one of the pieces inscribed *F.R.* is dated, and the only dated piece among those included in this category is the unsigned 1522 *Hercules and Omphale* bowl already discussed (cat. 1), it is hard to be sure which of them are to be dated before, during or after Xanto's experience with Maestro Giorgio.

We must, I think, exclude from the 'F.R.' category a strange dish dated 1536, painted with a head composed of phalluses (cat. 52).[148] Although this piece bears the initials 'F.R.' in blue on its reverse, they flank a symbol associated with the painter Francesco Urbini, who worked in the Andreoli workshop at Gubbio from about 1525 to 1537, by which year he had moved to Deruta.[149] Francesco Urbini made several crude copies after Xanto's *istoriati* (cat. 44) and even, in 1531, painted quite a good pastiche of a Xanto political subject,[150] though he was probably employed most of the time on decorative borders and the application of lustre, in which capacity he might have collaborated with Xanto at Gubbio in 1524–25. For lack of a better explanation of the initials 'F.R.' on the phallic head dish, I proposed the possibility that these initials are a claim not that the dish is by Xanto, but that it is of him, that is to say a caricature painted by a man long acquainted with Xanto.[151]

No piece signed *F.R.* is lustred, and it is my belief that Giorgio Andreoli would have discouraged anyone in his workshop from using a signature. Ever since 1517, as we have seen from a legal document,[152] he had been empowered to use his own name to stand for the Andreoli family firm, thereafter having the trade-mark, usually abbreviated to 'M° G°', painted in lustre under almost every piece, often accompanied by the date. It therefore seems likely that pieces marked *F.R.* were painted outside Giorgio's workshop, probably in Urbino but, if not, then conceivably in one of the other workshops at Gubbio.

For lack of dated pieces after 1522 we have nothing but style to help establish the sequence in which the marked and unmarked pieces of the 'F.R.' category were created.

A change that comes over the lustred work I take Xanto to have produced in Giorgio's Gubbio workshop in 1524–25 is the manner of painting rocks. On the 1522 bowl (cat. 1) these are represented almost like balls of wool marked with more or less concentric lines. The same characteristic can be noticed on cat. 2 and 3, and on a dish with St Jerome after Dürer that, uniquely, bears the initials in white.[153] I would consider it probable that all the pieces mentioned in this paragraph, like the 1522 bowl, were painted before Xanto worked for the Andreoli.

On two lustred *istoriati* of 1524 (cat. 4 and 5) the rocks begin to develop a more stratified appearance, a tendency that continues on pieces dated 1525 from the 'S' service (cat. 7 and 8). It is likely that influence was passing between Xanto and Nicola da Urbino at this time because the rocks in Nicola's Este-Gonzaga service, believed to be from 1524, show a similar change from the woolly-looking ones in his earlier Correr service. In parallel with developments in landscape style goes an increasing solidity and confidence in Xanto's handling of figures as more and more Raphaelesque prints came to his knowledge. These processes continue in what I take to be the later pieces in the 'F.R.' category (cat. 12–15), which show figures of increasing sophistication set against what are surely the most attractive landscape and architectural backgrounds Xanto was ever to paint. A characteristic of these landscapes is the way trees create dark blue, dagger-like reflections in pale blue lakes and inlets. It was these habitual reflections that first suggested to me the possibility that F.R./Xanto was responsible for one of the two plates with the arms of Bonzi (cat. 17), the other of which, certainly by Nicola, was presumably painted, at Urbino, around 1525–27 (cat. 18).

A plaque with *Christ Carrying the Cross*, cat. 15, after Marcantonio Raimondi's engraving from Raphael's *Spasimo di Sicilia* (fig. 36, p. 76), seems such an outsider to the group of pieces marked *F.R.* that, despite its mark, some have doubted its membership of the group at all. It is, however, painted on a pale blue *berettino* ground of exactly the same tint as that of cat. 14, which in other respects is typical of the 'F.R.' category. Unusually rigid adherence to a print-source makes identification of the hand difficult, but there is also a deliberate aping of mannerisms derived from prints, such as block-like foliage and stippled treatment of the foreground. Similar print-like mannerisms occur on some contemporary maiolica from Faenza and Forlì. Did Xanto make a brief visit to Romagna during his undocumented years around 1528–29? I have in the past found comparison with cat. 16, which bears on its reverse not only Xanto's handwriting, but also his signature in the rare form 'f.L.R.', persuasive for Xanto's authorship of the *Spasimo* plaque. Otherwise we must face the possibility that a second painter signing *F.R.* was active around the same time. When the plaque is compared to the print, the looping lines and oval forms on the former, absent from its engraved model, emerge as evidence of the painter's style. Such forms are uncharacteristic of Xanto and call to mind much more a group of pieces recently attributed to a Forlì artist who has been named the 'Painter of the Triumph of the Moon', none of whose pieces, however, is so carefully drawn.[154] If Xanto did effect the temporary transformation of his style needed to paint cat. 15, he slipped so rapidly back into alignment with Nicola's manner that any travels to Romagna are likely to have been of short duration;[155] more probably the *Spasimo* plaque is an interloper among Xanto's oeuvre.

The middle initial 'L' in the signature *f.L.R.* on cat. 16 has yet to be satisfactorily explained,[156] but these initials occur on two other pieces, one of which, at Budapest, bears lustre additions including the lustred date 1529.[157] I say "lustre additions" because there is nothing to suggest lustre was envisaged by Xanto when he painted the piece, and indeed the glinting metallic pigments that speck the drapery like measles and give the clouds a heavy, unatmospheric edging, can scarcely be considered an enhancement. Unlike the 'S' service and its contemporaries from 1524–25, this piece was probably painted outside Maestro Giorgio's workshop, and nothing prevents us supposing it was painted at Urbino, transported to Gubbio and there daubed with lustre pigments and given a final firing.

Cat. 20, the *Hercules and Omphale* dish from Arezzo, bears on its underside an inscription in Xanto's hand, perhaps mistakenly giving the subject as *De Hercule & Deianira*, followed by a flourish that has sometimes been likened to a 'y', sometimes to a Greek letter 'Φ'. It has often been said that this part of the inscription in Xanto's handwriting is, like the date 1528 above it and the *Mᵒ Giorgio da Ugubio*

trademark beneath it, in lustre pigment, thus proving Xanto to have painted the piece at Gubbio.[158] The present exhibition has provided an occasion to resolve the matter. Investigations by Professor Brunetti and his scientific team have shown Xanto's part of the inscription not to be in lustre but in the antimony yellow pigment that would have been fired with the rest of the decoration (see cat. 20). There is evidence that by 1525 ware painted in Urbino was sometimes lustred by Maestro Giorgio's firm,[159] so Arezzo's dish can no longer be used as evidence that Xanto was at Gubbio in 1528. The quantity of *istoriati* by Xanto lustred in the Giorgio workshop exceeds that of any other maiolica painter, suggesting that some understanding persisted between the parties even after 1525, when Xanto is likely to have left Gubbio.

Pieces from 1524–25 here attributed to Xanto working at Gubbio have no inscriptions by him on their reverses, and the reverses of wares signed 'F.R.' on the front are also uninscribed at the back.[160] However, around 1528–30 Xanto began inscribing his plates and dishes at the back to explain the subjects depicted at the front. He was not absolutely the first *istoriato* painter to do this – a Faenza plate of 1524 in the Louvre[161] informs us we are looking at a scene from the campaign of a Caesar – but Xanto was the first to add such inscriptions as a matter of course, and it was he who set the fashion.

The earlier-looking of Xanto's inscriptions are short and factual (cat. 20, 23), but around 1529 they assume the form of hendecasyllabic lines, often quoted or adapted from Petrarch.[162] A characteristic of these inscriptions is that they are followed, according to the nature of the subject-matter, by indicative words: *fabula* (for mythological subjects); *historia* (for historical fact or legend thought to be such); *nota*, or on one occasion *pensa* (where moral judgement is enjoined).[163] More rarely the combined injunction *fabula et historia* is found[164] and on a single occasion *sola vir[tus]*.[165] Cat. 34 has an inscription ending with the word *spere*, probably a reference to astrological spheres.[166] A plate in the Wallace Collection with the unedifying story of Phaedra and Hippolytus (cat. 24) is censoriously inscribed *Sporcizia* (Filth) while, as already mentioned, a plate painted not long after 1527 with an allegory of the Sack of Rome bears an inscription concluding with the word *immaginatione*.[167]

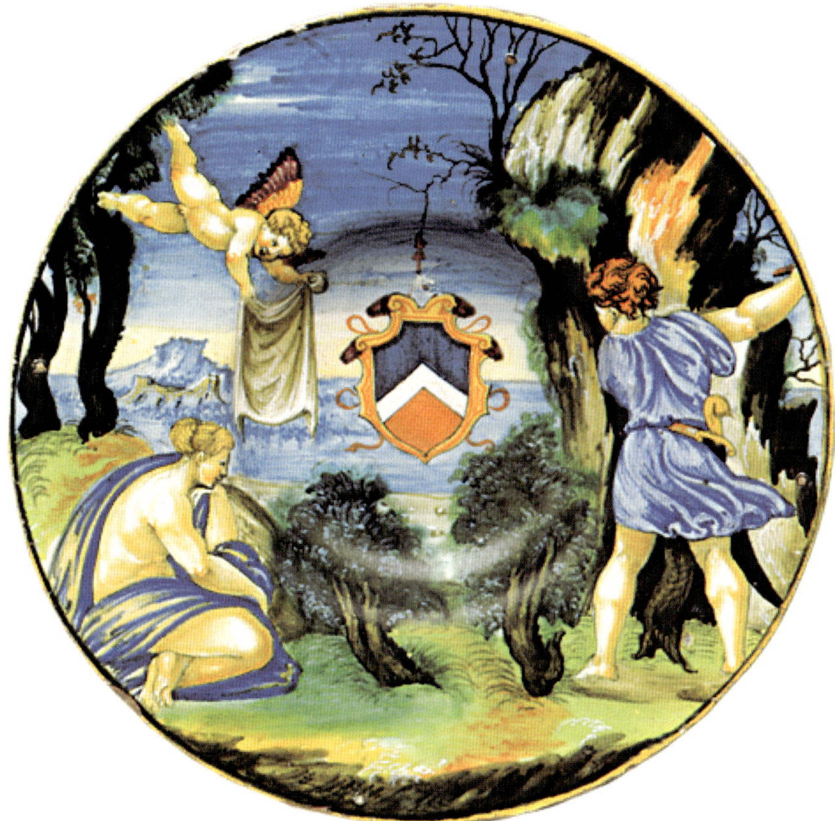

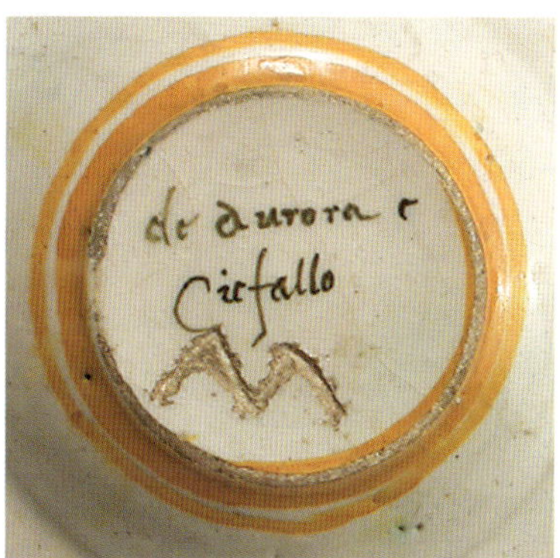

Fig. 22. Attributed to Francesco Xanto Avelli, *Aurora and Cephalus*, *c*. 1532, maiolica plate from the armorial Leonardi service, 20 cm, Pesaro, Museo Civico, C.A.S.155

Fig. 23. Reverse of fig. 22, with handwriting that appears to be by Nicola da Urbino

These admonitions are often followed, at least on the earlier and unsigned pieces, by a mark here described as the 'y/Φ' flourish, which has spawned over-ingenious interpretations, being variously read as a signature or other identification mark for Xanto or, if not that, then as a claim by him to authorship of the poetic lines it concludes.[168] All these suggestions seem invalidated because two of his closest followers, Giulio da Urbino and a painter 'L' who on occasion signed *Lu Ur*, also sometimes used this flourish, in each case to mean 'etc.'.[169] Xanto himself at least twice used the sign in this manner.[170] Julia Triolo has pointed out that such a flourish was often used in the notarial documents of the day to end the line of a formulaic part of a text.[171] At a time when punctuation was far from standardised, the 'y/Φ' appears often to have served where we should write a full-stop or 'etc.', and is significant only as a trait of handwriting used especially on his earlier inscriptions by Xanto, and not exclusively by him.

The earliest full signatures by Xanto date from 1530, and from 1531 onwards little of his work went unsigned, though as time went on he tended to use the initials 'F.X.R.' or simply 'X', placing no signature at all on a few of the very latest pieces like cat. 56, which is dated 1542. From 1531 until 1542, the last date we have on his work,

there is no difficulty in following his development year by year. Between 1528 and 1530 there are many pieces that reveal Xanto's authorship through a writing identical with that found on the signed wares that were to follow. The writing is energetic, impatient but legible, very different from that of his contemporary, Nicola da Urbino, whose elegant chancery hand, more seldom in evidence, hints at a difference from Xanto not only in temperament but also in education.[172] On some of Xanto's latest work the handwriting is executed in dark blue-black with a thick brush and can look very unlike earlier inscriptions.

Xanto's work shows little development in style between 1531 and 1542 but the palette from those years is dominated less by the sombre blues and dark greens that prevailed around 1528–30. Instead, yellow, yellowish green and ochre-brown set a warmer, paler tonality. Late works are often distinguishable by a broad, heavy touch and signs of waning invention, though a commission for an important client like Ferrante Gonzaga could still stimulate the painter to raise his game. His work is always of high technical quality, perhaps because he could rely on a studio for whose running he did not bear responsibility, as seems to have been the case when he painted Ferrante Gonzaga's dish in the Urbino workshop of Maestro Francesco da Silvano (figs. 26–27, p. 38).

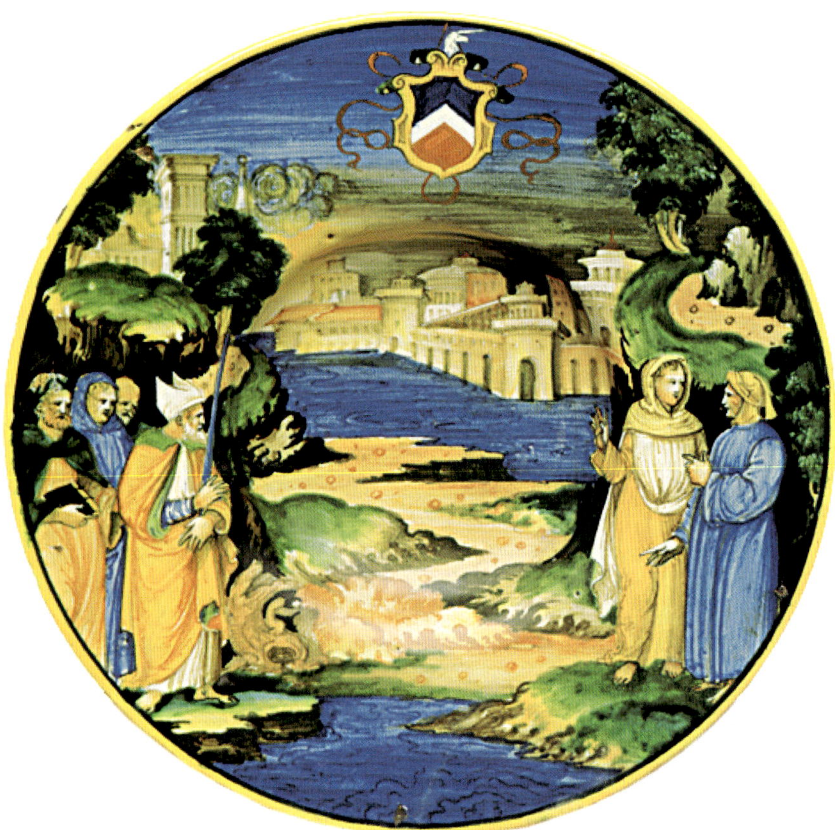



Poor painting can sometimes be explained in terms of Xanto's collaboration with a succession of pupils who, when they painted independently, seem to have been allowed or encouraged by Xanto to indicate their authorship by an initial.[173] Francesco Urbini probably painted borders for Xanto while the latter was (if I am right) at Gubbio from 1524–25, and thereafter perhaps took the opportunity to copy Xanto's *istoriati* (cat. 43) when they were sent up to Gubbio to have lustre added (cat. 44). The painter 'L' ('Lu Ur') was active alongside Xanto at Urbino around 1533–35; Lu Ur's clumsy work seems sometimes to have been improved by Xanto's own brush.[174] Most talented of all was Giulio da Urbino (cat. 47), whose early work often resembles Xanto's very closely. Giulio was active at Urbino from *c*. 1533–34 before moving to Rimini in 1535 (cat. 48) and thereafter to Verona, where he dated a plate in 1541.[175] One of Xanto's least competent assistants was the painter 'B', whose activity is traceable only in 1539.[176]

More intriguing is the painter 'S', probably identifiable as Sforza di Marcantonio, who later had a long career at Pesaro. Some of the earliest dated pieces attributable to him form part of the 'Teasel' service of 1538 (cat. 55), in whose production he seems to have been concerned alongside Xanto (cat. 54), copying with an accuracy that almost suppresses Sforza's own style, subjects such as *Metabus and Camilla* and *Hero and Leander*, for which Xanto had developed almost standardised treatments.[177] I have, however, found no clear signs of collaboration between Xanto and Sforza on individual plates. The earliest dated pieces to show Sforza's mature style, none of them signed, are from 1543,[178] the year after we lose track of Xanto, and by 15 May 1548, if not earlier, Sforza was in Pesaro.[179] It is not surprising, as he had copied inscriptions as well as compositions from Xanto's plates, that the older man's wording, such as *Leandro in Mare* . *& Hero Alla Finestra*, continued to haunt the maiolica Sforza painted at Pesaro as late as 1576.[180]

Nicola da Urbino, we know, was at least by 1530 head of a workshop, so management of production and sales probably took much of his time, perhaps explaining his work's scarcity in comparison with that of Xanto. Despite having been on opposite sides in the 1530 dispute over wages, by 1532, when an armorial service from which five pieces survive was made for a member of the Leonardi family of Pesaro, the two seem to have collaborated.[181] One piece from this service (fig. 22, p. 35), entirely typical of Xanto and made up of three stock figures he constantly used, bears on its reverse an inscription in what looks like Nicola's writing (fig. 23, p. 35). A large dish from the Leonardi service is both painted and inscribed by Xanto,[182] while the other pieces are painted neither by Xanto nor Nicola (fig. 24), yet some bear inscriptions in a chancery hand I take to be Nicola's. The large dish from the Leonardi service, which one would have thought demanded the greatest skill, was allocated to Xanto, who was also assigned one of the big dishes for the service of 1533 with the arms of Gonzaga impaling Paleologo beneath Duke Federico of Mantua's coronet (cat. 40), the smaller plates being by Nicola (cat. 41 and 42).[183] It almost looks as though Xanto may have been considered the better painter, though in fairness it must be admitted that a large dish by Nicola with Duke Federico's Olympus *impresa* may belong to the set.[184] In each case Xanto signed his large dishes, whereas Nicola placed neither signature nor workshop-mark on the plates.

The Leonardi service plate in fig. 24, p. 36 is a rare illustration on maiolica of a subject from Dante. So far as I know, Xanto himself never illustrated a Dantesque scene, though echoes of the *Divine Comedy* have been noted in the potter's sonnets. On five occasions Xanto is known to have illustrated scenes from the *Orlando Furioso* of Lodovico Ariosto (1474–1533), court poet of the Este Dukes of Ferrara, not far from Xanto's native Rovigo (cat. 36).[185] Petrarch (Francesco Petrarca, 1304–1374), whose popularity exceeded Dante's at the time, was the source most drawn on by Xanto both for his sonnets and for the inscriptions on his maiolica. The verse and the pottery are full of borrowings from Petrarch's *Trionfi* and *Canzoniere*, though on the maiolica the subjects are sometimes attributed to the classical authors from whom Xanto supposed the stories to originate: Ovid, Virgil, Trogus Pompeius (cat. 40 and 43) or Livy. Mythological subjects drawn from Ovid are the commonest on Xanto's maiolica, but subjects from classical history are not uncommon and probably owed their popularity to the Renaissance habit of drawing lessons for real life from Roman precedent. Except on devotional plaques, religious subjects are the exception in Xanto's work. Though he seems to have been an eager reader of the Italian poets esteemed in his day, there is no evidence that Xanto could read Latin, and his knowledge of the classics seems culled from digests and derivatives in his own tongue, so that his erudition was shallower than he would have had us believe.

To judge from Xanto's armorial services,[186] his clientele included some of the men and women most prominent in his time. Federico II Gonzaga, Duke of Mantua (1500–1540), brother-in-law of Francesco Maria Della Rovere, has already been mentioned (cat. 40), and to him we may add Federico's younger brother, Ferrante Gonzaga-Guastalla (1507–1557) (figs. 25–27, p. 38), a general in the service of the Emperor Charles V who, as a young man, had rescued his mother, Isabella D'Este-Gonzaga, during the Sack of Rome. There have been disagreements as to which member of the Pucci family owned the extensive service from 1532–33 that bears the arms of that prominent Florentine family beneath an *ombrellino* (cat. 36–37).[187] Two Venetian coats of arms have been associated with individuals, the first with Giacomo Michiel (1494–1551) who in 1512 married Laura Gritti (1533, cat. 39);[188] the second with Jacopo Pesaro (1464–1547), Bishop of Paphos (1535). In view of Francesco Maria's employment by the Venetians and his Venetian friend-ships, Gian Giacomo Leonardi (1498–1562), who served the Dukes of Urbino from 1530–1559 as ambassador to Venice, has been described as "an extremely strong candidate" as recipient of the 1532 service with the arms of Leonardi of Pesaro, "conceivably a gift from Francesco Maria della Rovere".[189] A recent identification of the arms on a service of 1531 (cat. 33) as those of a certain Eliseo Piani, an official of the Urbino Monte di Pietà, is interesting as a sign of local patronage.[190]

It is on armorial pieces and services that one would expect to find most evidence of the subject being, as it were, tailor-made for the client, but most attempts to demonstrate this seem inconclusive. In the case of the great dish (figs. 26 and 27, p. 38) with the arms of Ferrante Gonzaga-Guastalla, painted in 1541 by Xanto in Francesco da Silvano's workshop, the connection between subject and owner is clear. In 1535 Ferrante had been Charles V's general during the campaign, headed by the Emperor in person, when the Tunisian fortress of La Goletta was stormed: *L'alta Goletta inespugnabil tanto / Astretta, e presa con furor repente*…. (High Goletta, so untakeable snatched, and taken by sudden storm). The location of La Goletta, near the site of ancient Carthage, prompted the use of Marco Dente's print of the Romans assaulting that town (fig. 28, p. 39).

The arms on other services, including the so-called 'Three Crescents' service (cat. 25–26) and 'Teasel' service (cat. 54–55), remain unidentified. One intriguing if incon-clusive link with a patron has, however, emerged from archaeological investigation within the courtyard of the Palazzo della Cancelleria in Rome, where fragments of two

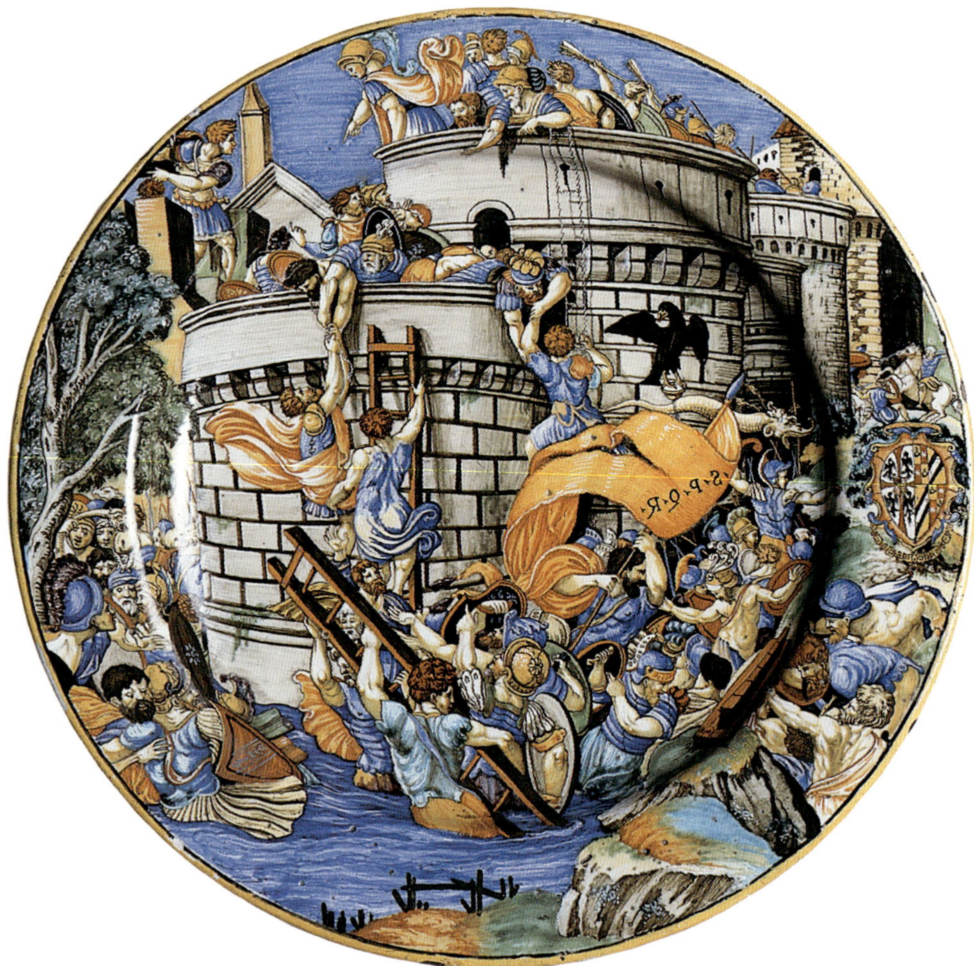

Fig. 26. Francesco Xanto Avelli, *The Storming of La Goletta*, with the arms of Ferrante Gonzaga-Guastalla, 1541, maiolica dish, 61 cm, France, private collection

Fig. 27. Reverse of fig. 26, detail showing inscription

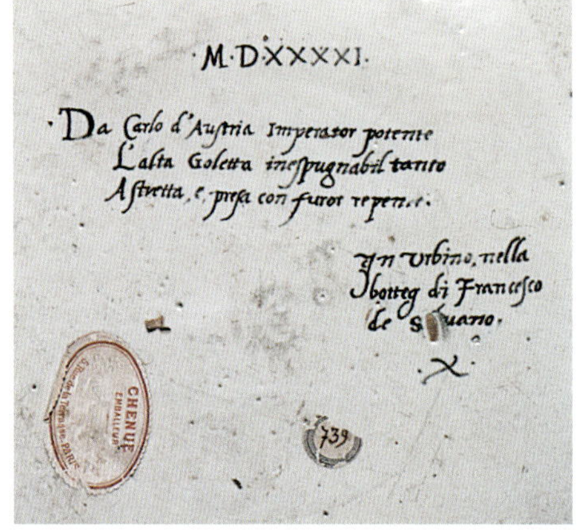

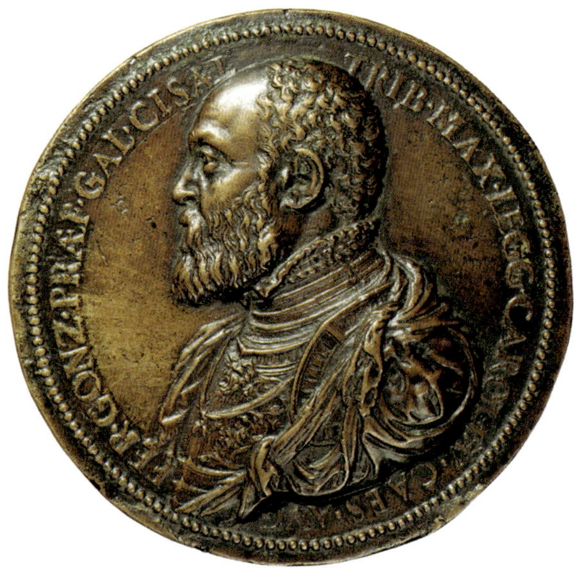

Fig. 25. Leone Leoni (*c.* 1509–1590), *Ferrante Gonzaga-Guastalla*, 1555, bronze medal, 7.4 cm, Vienna, Kunsthistorisches Museum, Münzkabinett, 6,868 bß

lustred plates have been unearthed, each representing a favourite Xanto subject: one with *The Death of Palinurus* bearing Xanto's signature; the other with the *The Dream of Astyages*, dated 1535.

If we could assume these are relics from a service belonging to the principal occupant of the Palazzo, that would still leave uncertainty because in 1535 Cardinal Ippolito De' Medici died and was succeeded by Cardinal Alessandro Farnese, a great patron in the making whose grandfather had the previous year become Pope Paul III (fig. 13, p. 24).[191] The site is at least indicative of ecclesiastical patronage at the highest level, even if there is nothing particularly edifying about the two classical subjects that found their way to the Cancelleria.

Biblical subjects are rare on Xanto's wares, and princes of the Church were as much in thrall to humanist culture as were secular princes; a few years later Cardinal Alessandro Farnese took delivery of that most overtly erotic painting, Titian's *Danaë*.[192]

It seems unlikely that a cardinal, in Rome, would have controlled the choice of subjects to have been painted on a maiolica service. Thought might be expended on the design and iconography of gold and silver plate, but the relatively cheap maiolica was scarcely an item of luxury,[193] being rather seldom considered worth listing in inventories. *Istoriato* plates were *cose da villa*, things suitable for informal life in the country, as Eleonora Duchess of Urbino wrote apologetically to her mother, Isabella D'Este, when sending to her in 1524 what we believe to be the magnificent Este-Gonzaga service painted by Nicola da Urbino, making no mention of the subjects depicted on it.[194] Customers were presumably willing to pay over the odds for lustred ware, as Piccolpasso tells us the number of successfully fired pieces could be as low as six in a hundred,[195] but the circumstances surrounding orders for lustre make it less, rather than more likely that the customer controlled the design.

It has been suggested above that a commercial understanding persisted between the Gubbio workshop and Xanto after he had left Maestro Giorgio's workshop in 1525. The proportion of Xanto's ware with lustre is particularly high, it has been noticed, between 1532 and 1535.[196] Between 1531 and 1533 the Andreoli workshop often tried to conceal beneath lustre scrolls the part of Xanto's inscriptions that informed the world of his name and, even more, of the town where he worked. This can hardly be because of a quarrel between Xanto and Giorgio, as I once thought, since trade between the two parties was at its height during these years. More probably the Andreoli were trying to circumvent the protectionism of the other Gubbio potters,[197] or to avoid payment of customs duties. Gubbio now forms part of Umbria, but in the sixteenth century it was a frontier town on the route across the Appenines to Florence or Rome, a vicariate attached to Urbino. During their brief occupation of the Duchy of Urbino the Medici had made Gubbio the Duchy's capital, exempting it from the destruction of defensive walls inflicted upon Urbino and other towns. Guicciardini comments that this was because Gubbio was less sympathetic than other centres of the Duchy towards Duke Francesco Maria, due to rivalry with Urbino,[198]

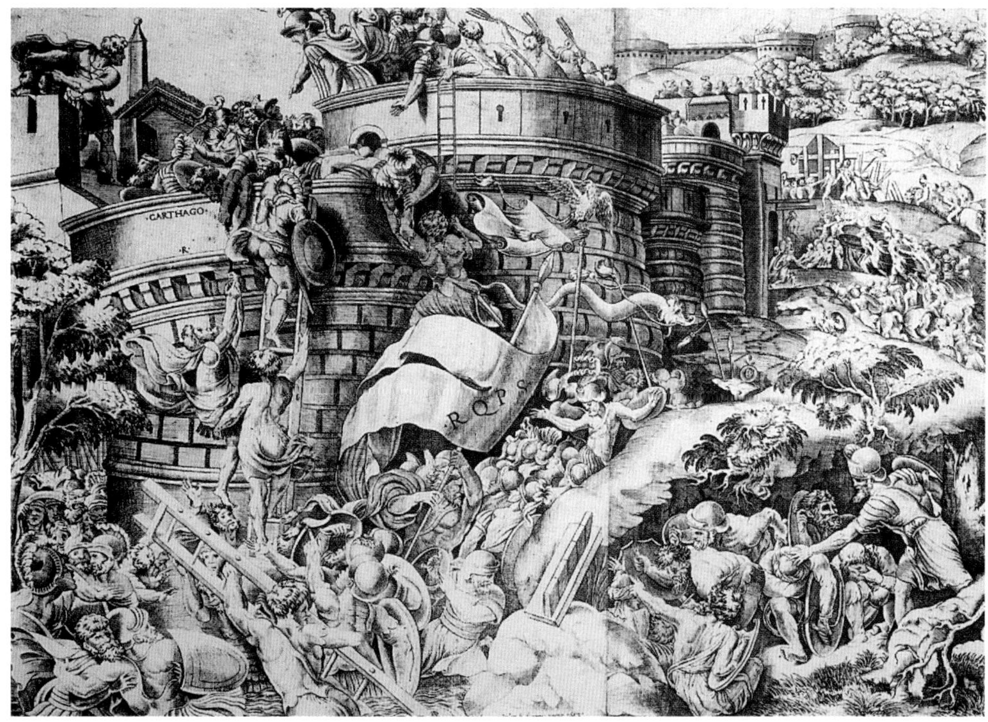

Fig. 28. Marco Dente (d. 1527) after Giulio Romano, *The Capture of Carthage*, engraving, *c.* 1521–23, Florence, Gabinetto Disegni e Stampe degli Uffizi, 748

a rivalry no doubt economic as much as political.

The discovery that in 1538 the widow of Nicola da Urbino leased her late husband's workshop for three years to Maestro Giorgio's son, Vincenzo,[199] has encouraged speculation that the Andreoli family established an Urbino outstation for adding lustre to that town's *istoriato* ware.[200] It might have made commercial sense for the Gubbio firm to establish a foothold in Urbino if that circumvented fiscal barriers against imports to Gubbio from Urbino.[201] However if a lustre workshop had existed at Urbino as early as 1531–33 it is hard to see why, between those years, the Andreoli thought it necessary to hide evidence of Urbino manufacture beneath lustred scrolls. A suggestion that the lustred initial 'N' found on some pieces might stand for 'Vincenzo', and that this might indicate application of lustre at Urbino, involves two assumptions, and does not explain why the lustred 'N' is found also on moulded ware with more abstract patterns thought typical of manufacture at Gubbio itself.[202]

The lustre applied to Xanto's maiolica after 1525 neither clarifies his subjects nor enhances his compositions, but mindlessly spangles work already complete without it. This can be seen by comparing two versions of the Actaeon myth, both dated 1533, one lustred (cat. 45), the other not (figs. 49 and 50, p. 138). Rather than imagining close contact between Xanto and a hypothetical Andreoli out-station in Urbino, such insensitivity seems consistent with the Andreoli buying Xanto's accumulated stock and carrying it off to be lustred at Gubbio. Lustre is applied to no greater purpose on armorial services, as in the case of the single lustred dish amongst thirty-seven survivors from the Pucci set. A suggestion that a lustred sun on this piece is symbolically placed behind the coat of arms[203] would carry more conviction were it not that exactly similar suns twinkle on plates with quite different subjects and, indeed, painted by quite other *maiolicari*. To gain an idea of Xanto's intentions we should imagine all lustred additions out of the way, since these are likely to have been added in circumstances outside his control. Even in 1524–25, when he was most likely at Gubbio, the lustre on his work was probably being added by another hand.

The Italian word *bottega* can mean either a 'workshop' or a 'shop', and the *bottega* of a sixteenth-century *maiolicaro* could probably be both sales outlet and place of production.

The premises let to Vincenzo Andreoli by Nicola's widow in 1538 contained, besides the tools of her deceased husband's trade, *doi credentie facte con le staggie da tenere vase conficate nel muro*, which sound like two structures with shelving to contain ware, attached to the wall, *una credenza o vero armario facto de tavole da tenere li vase* (a *credenza* or cupboard made with shelves to hold ware), *doi casse de noce usate da tenere drento vase* (two chests of walnut employed to hold ware inside) and *un altro casono vecchio de abeto da tenere vase* (another large chest, old, of spruce, to contain ware).[204] There were also *stagge dodice con li castagnoli per fare la credenza in piazza*, which sound like a dozen shelves with supports to erect a temporary display structure in the square (perhaps designed for outdoor sales, as at markets and fairs). Shelves, cupboards and chests, then, had been used by Nicola to display and store a stock of pottery. Is it not likely that Xanto also would have built up a stock of ware for sale in this way to passing customers?

We know little about how a man like Xanto may have sold his wares, except that in some cases a diplomatic agent like Giovanmaria Della Porta might negotiate a purchase. In August 1530 an agent nick-named *El Poeta* reported back from Pesaro to Federico II of Mantua that at Urbino he had seen ware of excellent quality painted "with landscapes, legends and historical subjects", but that the potters there were unable to quote a price "if they do not know the quality and quantity." Cost depended on the amount of workmanship involved, and at least at that preliminary stage of negotiations *El Poeta* was careful not to give away the name of the potential customer for fear of driving up the price.[205]

Such few indications as we have concerning distribution and sale of *istoriato* ware make me sceptical of suggestions that a lively interchange of ideas took place directly between Xanto and his customers. It has, for instance, been proposed that a highly intellectual scheme dictated the division of subjects allocated to the larger dishes of the Pucci service of 1532–33 into literary categories: epic; lyric; history.[206] It seems, however, unlikely that diners would have paused over their meal to reflect on where, in this scheme, each of the medley of subjects from Virgil, Ariosto, Ovid, Petrarch, Pliny, Valerius Maximus and Trogus Pompeius belonged. It has been suggested that this service was given to Cardinal Antonio Pucci by Francesco

Maria Della Rovere and that the Virgilian subjects on it
convey a variety of very personal messages understandable
to each.[207] It is impossible to prove or disprove suggestions
of this kind, yet I confess I feel happier with the idea that
the choice of subjects was in most cases left to the potter
who, even for the Pucci service, drew on images like
*The Death of Palinurus* that he had used or was to use on
other occasions. Xanto presumably knew what subjects
found a ready sale, but that does not mean he was closely
influenced by the taste of individual customers.

One theory has it that recipients of Xanto's maiolica
would have recognised his print-sources and have drawn
conclusions. In particular from about 1530 a number of
figures appear in Xanto's work that have been traced to the
notorious *Modi* of Giulio Romano (cat. 32, 35, 36, 43, 46, 49).
Giulio's audacious drawings from 1524 of heterosexual
couplings do not survive; however, they were promptly
engraved by Marcantonio Raimondi. Of Marcantonio's
engravings only a few cut-out fragments are known today,
but a pirated woodcut edition with sonnets by Pietro
Aretino that does in large part survive helps us understand
why the *Modi* must have given peculiar offence to the
authorities of papal Rome, because Aretino's verses imply
that the more outrageous sexual activities were favoured
by priests.[208] Since the prints were banned and an attempt
made to destroy the entire stock, even if Xanto had access
to several sheets, few of his customers are likely to have
known counterparts and thus to have recognised Xanto's
supposedly sly borrowings. He himself may have enjoyed
a private joke when using the banned prints in his political
allegories, but it is pure speculation to suppose a purchaser
would have spotted, for instance, that the figure representing François Ier in cat. 46 was based on a female figure
in the *Modi*, disentwined from her lover and kitted out
with armour (fig. 52, p. 140).[209] Xanto often needed models
for foreshortened figures in athletic poses such as his *istorie*,
including simple classical myths, demanded. The prints
of *I Modi* would have supplied that need. It seems equally
unlikely that Xanto's clients would have recognised the
figures he appropriated from fig. 42, p. 108, Marco Dente's
print after Baccio Bandinelli, nor have interpreted their
use as comment on Bandinelli's pro-Medicean politics: this
*Massacre of the Innocents* print, just like Raphael's design of
the same subject, furnished Xanto with poses useful for his

compositions, and that was probably all there was to it. [210]

Towards the end of his career Xanto began using a
series of prints of the *Influences of the Planets*, issued by
Gabriele Giolito de' Ferrari of Venice in 1533.[211] The use
by Xanto and others of figures from these prints, which
show people in the costume of their own time, led the
ceramic historian, Bernard Rackham, up the false trail of
attributing a group of wares on grounds not of style but of
subject-matter, thus creating an illusory 'Painter of the
Myths in Modern Dress', amongst whose supposed works
he overlooked a fine unsigned plate from Xanto's last year
of activity (cat. 56) copied in reverse from the woodcut
of *The Planet Venus* (fig. 56, p. 160). It is odd that, like the
1522 bowl (cat. 1), the very first piece we can confidently
attribute to Xanto, this plate is inscribed *Omnia vincit Amor*.


CODA

Although after 1542 we lose trace of Xanto, his influence
lingered and spread. Giulio da Urbino (cat. 47, 48) is not
recorded after 1541, when he was at Verona, but a man
more loosely connected to Xanto, formerly known to
scholars as 'Mazo' though better renamed 'the Eloquence
Painter', seems to have taken to Venice a number of
Xanto's motifs before being absorbed into the world of
Venetian workshop practice.[212] In 1537 Francesco Urbini
took his own eccentric version of Xanto's style to Deruta,
where it was taken up by the painter known as *El Frate*.[213]
Pesaro in the time of Francesco Maria's heir, Duke
Guidobaldo II (1538–1578), attracted a number of painters
who transferred an Urbino style of *istoriato* painting to
the Duchy's new capital.[214] These included Sforza di
Marcantonio, one of Xanto's last collaborators at Urbino,
who continued to repeat Xanto's subject-matter and
compositions with their inscriptions, sometimes in
garbled form, as late as 1576.[215] Most *istoriato* painters, at
Pesaro or Urbino itself, retained descriptive titles at the
back of their plates and dishes, a habit that may surely
be credited largely to the literary-minded Xanto.

The abundance of dates on Xanto's maiolica, whether
inscribed by himself or added in lustre by the Andreoli,
provides the firmest chronology we have for studying the
rise of *istoriato* painting in the Marches. For the twenty

years of his known activity, between 1522 and 1542, Elisa Sani has listed in *Appendix C* no fewer than 421 pieces of his work, and there must once have been many more. Such productivity is approached among identifiable *istoriato* painters of Xanto's time perhaps only by his follower, Sforza di Marcantonio (cat. 55), or by Francesco Durantino in the years before that painter set up his own workshop near Perugia.[216] We may well wonder if this was due not just to hard work and speed of execution, but also to a freelance status that would have left him more time for painting than was available to others who were engaged also in running workshops.

Those who have written most about Xanto have too often laboured under preconceptions which excluded attribution to him of work painted before he began to sign in 1530. Bernard Rackham, in particular, set up Nicola and even the painter 'F.R.', whose work most scholars now accept as actually *by* Xanto, as altogether Xanto's superiors. "Like Xanto", Rackham wrote, "F.R. was also, in most of his works, dependent on engravings, but he handled his derivative designs in a far less perfunctory manner which seems to reflect a personality profoundly different and more serious." [217] It is true that much of Xanto's later work is repetitive, even a little unfeeling, but the need for rapid production took its toll also on the quality of Nicola's later works.

It is interesting to note how that brilliant Victorian connoisseur, J. C. Robinson, never doubted that pre-1530 maiolica could be attributed to Xanto: "The earliest date as yet observed on any of them", he wrote, "is 1530, but there are many pieces extant, undoubtedly by him, neither signed nor dated, which are obviously of an earlier period." Robinson, as organiser and cataloguer of the great Loan Exhibition at the South Kensington Museum, had opportunities, the like of which did not recur until modern times, to study Xanto's work. His summing up, therefore, merits attention: "...he certainly had a talent for the arrangement of his works in composition, nearly all his subjects being 'pasticci'; the various figures or groups introduced, being the invention of other artists, copied with adroit variations over and over again, and made to do duty in the most widely different characters. As an original artist, if indeed, he can be so considered, he may be classed with the more mannered of the scholars of

Raffaelle. . . . Xanto's execution, although dexterous, is monotonous and mechanical; his scale of colouring is crude and positive, full of violent oppositions; the only merit, – if merit it be, – being a certain force and brightness of aspect; in every other respect his colouring is commonplace, not to say disagreeable even; blue, crude opaque yellow and orange tints, and bright verdigris green, are the three dominant hues, and are scattered over the pieces in full unbroken masses, the yellow especially meeting the eye at the first glance." Robinson, however, relents a little from this unfavourable judgement in considering "the unsigned pieces before 1531", saying: "the glaze is better and more transparent, the execution more delicate, and the outline less hard and black than in the later specimens." [218]

It must be admitted that in castigating some of Xanto's later work Robinson had a case but, though he was aware of the 'F.R.' category, he never linked it to Xanto, so his highly favourable judgements of such pieces as cat. 3, which he called "unquestionably one of the most perfect specimens of the 'Majolica istoriata' extant", praising its variety and harmony of colouring, may be accepted as pleas in defence of Xanto's earliest known works. [219] The present exhibition and its catalogue attempt to draw a new and possibly controversial picture of our maiolica painter's development which embraces not only works signed *F.R.* but also a small but much admired class of ware painted at Gubbio between 1524 and 1525.

Supposing Xanto to have been born before 1486, as here argued, and not *c.* 1500, he would have been old enough on his arrival in the Duchy of Urbino in the early 1520s to be treated with a certain respect even by established *capi-bottega*. Premature dating of Nicola's Este-Gonzaga Service to *c.* 1519,[220] instead of to its now rather convincingly documented date of 1524,[221] had made Nicola seem a more lonely pioneer in developing the Urbino style of *istoriato* than he probably was. The new chronology, the new attributions, suggest that in developing this Urbino style Xanto and Nicola were running neck and neck.

Perhaps the present exhibition may provide an opportunity not merely to review the circumstances of Xanto's life and historical context, nor just to reconsider this or that attribution, but also to revalue both his influence and his quality as an artist.

1 For the confusion with the 'Isola di Maiolica' (Majorca) see Mallet 1998, p. 12; Spallanzani 2006, pp. 4–5, 34, 363, 372.

2 Seccaroni 2004 and Mazzucato 2004, pp. 208–09.

3 Piccolpasso 1980, II, pp. 100–01.

4 This subject has recently been discussed by Timothy Wilson (2005A).

5 See Wilson 2004A, pp. 203–04. The literature on the Isabella D'Este service is also well summarised by Wilson (*ibid.*, pp. 412–13) in connection with no. XII.42.

6 Published in full in Cioci 1987.

7 Negroni 1985, p. 46, note 53; Triolo 1996, pp. 390–92.

8 See the documents for 28 January and 22 December 1531 in Triolo 1996, Appendix C, pp. 389–90.

9 Talvacchia 1994, p. 122.

10 Traniello 1988, p. 26.

11 See Appendix A.

12 I have drawn heavily, for the history of Rovigo's troubles, on Traniello 1988.

13 Traniello 1988, p. 26.

14 The archival documents concerning Xanto are conveniently included as Appendix C in Triolo 1996, pp. 388–96.

15 Triolo 1996, pp. 388–89. In partially transcribing the document in 1828 Pungileone (1879) misread the date as 3 August, giving rise to the mistaken belief that a second document was issued on 7 August.

16 Triolo 1996, p. 389.

17 Triolo in Ausenda 2000, no. 207. For an interpretation of the symbolism of that plate see Cioci 1987, pp. 80–84.

18 Timothy Wilson has pointed out to me that the Paduan sculptor, Andrea Briosco, was called *Riccio* (Curly) presumably after his hair. Jeremy Warren tells me the name *Ulocrino*, also recorded at Padua, is a classicised version of the same name, and probably also refers to Briosco.

19 Triolo 1996, pp. 390–91. Cioci (1995, p. 242) discusses this reference and concludes that the word *Arimino* may well have been a slip of the pen. At the suggestion of Dora Thornton, Carmen Ravanelli Guidotti has kindly checked this document and assures us that, even if the notary made a mistake, at least the modern transcript as 'de Arimino' is correct.

20 Dubrujeaud 1911, no. 463; Wilson 1990, p. 322, note 4.

21 Archivio Notarile Urbino, Vanni Vincenzo, n. 351, A. 1541–1546, F. 66 r. This was published by Scatassa 1904, p. 199. The document is discussed and published in full by Triolo (1995, pp. 214–15).

22 Unless, as Cioci (1987, p. 101) suggests, the *vaso lucido e repleto* referred to in Sonnet V is intended as an allegorical reference couched in ceramic terms, though this seems to the present writer unlikely.

23 The passage is little altered in the 'Proemio' to the first and second editions of Vasari's *Vite*.

24 Vitaletti 1912, p. 19: "All'Avelli fu anche dato l'incarico di dipingere una pala d'altare per la chiesa di Schieti, come gentilmente mi comunica il Prof. Ercole Scatassa" (To Avelli was also entrusted the commission of painting an altarpiece for the church of Schieti, as Prof. Ercole Scatassa kindly tells me). At my suggestion both the late Professor Giuseppe Liverani and Julia Triolo have enquired after this supposed altarpiece, but in each case without result. For the reliability of Vitaletti's statement see Wilson 2004–2005, p. 159.

25 Baldassare Castiglione, *Il Libro del Cortegiano*, Venice, 1528 and later editions. The view that poetry as well as military prowess was desirable in a courtier is put by Castiglione into the mouth of his kinsman, Count Ludovico of Canossa, in Book I.

26 Warnke 1993, p. 116.

27 Santi 1893.

28 Urb. lat. 794. Venturi 1914, pp. 471–72; Vitaletti 1918, 1, pp. 11–15 and 2, 41–44 in a version from which two sonnets were accidentally omitted. To Francesco Cioci goes the credit for restoring the missing sonnets, first in Cioci 1979, then in Cioci 1987. See also Cioci 1988.

29 Lionello Venturi in Adolfo Venturi (ed.), *L'Arte*, Anno XVII, Fasc. V–VI.

30 Vitaletti 1918, p. 13.

31 He singles out Sonnets XVI and XVIII for especial praise. See Cioci 1987, p. 137.

32 Clough 2002, I, pp. 35–62.

33 Clough 2005, p. 99.

34 Clough 2005, pp. 96–97.

35 Clough 2005, p. 99–100.

36 L. Guicciardini 1993, p. 104.

37 Clough 2005, p. 76.

38 F. Guicciardini 1561, Book XVII, Ch. 3.

39 Clough 2005, p. 76. For a comparison of the judgements on Clement of Francesco Guicciardini and Paolo Giovio, each of whom knew Clement well, see Price Zimmermann 2005, pp. 19–27.

40 Formerly in the Museo Internazionale delle Ceramiche, Faenza, destroyed in World War II. Ballardini 1938B, pp. 123–24, pls. XXVIa and XVIIIa. See Cioci 1987, p. 33. A similar moral is drawn on a plate formerly in the Sackler Collection, inscribed *Di Clemente al conspetto Roma langue* (in the presence of Clement Rome languishes), illustrated in Mallet 1988, p. 99, figs. 13 and 13R.

41 Chastel (1983, p. 91) quotes a contemporary account by an Austrian *Landsknecht* as summarising very well the three phases of the Sack.

42 See comments by Cioci (1987, pp. 48–49), citing Petrarch, on a dish in the Louvre, made for the Florentine family of Pucci.

43 Thornton and Wilson 2007, no. 157; Cioci (1991A, pp. 32–35) makes a good case for the female figure in that plate representing Rome, as is likely enough since the same figures were used for Rome assaulted by Charles V on a piece from the 'Three Crescents' service illustrated, for instance, by Vossila (2002, pp. 107–09, figs. 8, 10 and 11).

44 Chastel 1983, p. 41.

45 Cioci 1987, pp. 37–38.

46 Fiocco *et al.* 2001, no. 151.

47 Cioci 1987, p. 38; Hausmann 2002, no. 66.

48 Cioci 1987, p. 39; Kube 1976, no. 76.

49 Triolo in Ausenda 2000, no. 212. See also Cioci 1987, pp. 50–51.

50 Reynolds 2005, p. 160.

51 Clough 2005, p. 105.

52 Dennistoun 1909, III, p. 40.

53 Clough 2005, p. 106.

54 Dal Poggetto 2004, p. 106, fig. 1; p. 162.

55 Chapman 2006, p. 167.

56 McClung Hallman 2005, pp. 29–40.

57 Leoni 1605, p. 12.

58 Clough 2005, p. 107.

59 For different interpretations of this allegory see Borenius 1930, no. 42; Rackham 1957, 5, p. 105, no. 9 and note 22; Cioci 1987, pp. 56–57 and 59; Poole 1995, pp. 322–26, no. 385.

60 Munarini 1990, pp. 26–28; Munarini and Banzato 1993, pp. 307–09, nos. 294–95.

61 For Giulio da Urbino see Rasmussen 1980, pp. 81–96, the Hermitage's allegory of the Siege of Florence, p. 90 and fig. 10; Mallet 1988, pp. 76–78, the Hermitage's allegory of the Siege of Florence illustrated fig. 18 and 18R.

62 Kube (1976, no. 78) identifies the bearded warrior as Malatesta Baglioni; Cioci (1987, pp. 52–53) suggests Charles V; Vossila (2002, pp. 112–15) proposes Alessandro De' Medici.

63 Ballardini 1933, 253, 233, 357R. At the 1980 Xanto seminar in Rovigo the present writer appealed for suggestions. Mallet 1988, p. 68 and p. 91, figs. 1 and 1R.

64 Cioci 1987, p. 35 and pp. 113–15.

65 Ferriani 1983, pp. 318–19, no. 97; Dal Poggetto 2003, p. 186.

66 Cioci 1987, p.112 and pp. 113–14, note on lines 5–6; Cioci 2004, p. 217.

67 Varchi, ed. Arbib, II, pp. 456–66. I owe this reference to Caroline Elam.

68 Vasari, ed. Milanesi, III, p. 570.

69 *per l'assedio di Firenze, insieme con tutta la fabrica, gettate in terra, loc. cit.* note 68.

70 Richa and Zocchi 1754, IX, 98ff; Paatz and Valentiner Paatz 1952, II, pp. 272ff. I owe these references to Caroline Elam.

71 Scarpellini 1984, no. 41 and pls. 58 and 62.
The habit there shown does not correspond
exactly with that in Viti's painting and
Xanto's dish, but on all three the defining
sock-like cap is shown on the left shoulder.
There may, however, have been some varia-
tion in the Order's dress, since Cioci (1987,
p.113) describes a differently coloured habit.

72 Cioci 2003.

73 Triolo in Ausenda 2000, no. 209.

74 Rackham 1940, no. 636.

75 Cioci 1987, pp. 63–66.

76 Cioci 1987, pp. 63–65; Cioci 2004, pp. 409–10,
cat. entry XII. 37.

77 F. Guicciardini 1561, Book 20, Ch. 2: *E
concorsero i cardinali più volontieri ad eleggerlo,
perchè essendo già quasi settuagenario, e riputato di
complessione debole, e non ben sano (la quale opinione
fu aiutata da lui con qualche arte) sperarono avesse ad
essere breve il suo pontificato.*

78 The Camerino succession, its antecedents
and consequences are well described in Law
2002. Law (ibid., p. 31 and note 89) suggests
that a maiolica *istoriato* dish with the arms
of Varano was part of a service probably
commissioned to celebrate the marriage, but
this seems unlikely because the piece is dated
1537 and bears only the arms of Varano. See
Giacomotti 1974, no. 994. The Paris piece is
probably by the anonymous painter of a dish
at Princeton dated 1536 and inscribed *In Castel
Durante*. See Wilson 2002A, pp. 132–33 and
figs. 13–14.

79 Law 2002, pp. 31–32.

80 Mallet 1988, p. 80, fig. 23. A plaque in the
Hermitage with this same subject is inscribed
*passando Hettorre il bel fiume di Xanto Fu dal superbo
Achill' per forza ucciso.* followed by an ampersand
and the y/Φ flourish, the latter causing Elena
Ivanova (2003, p. 78, no. 48) to date the piece
before 1531. However the style of the piece
suggests a dating in the mid-1530s, perhaps
as late as 1538 (see cat. 51).

81 Baldantonio di Paolo da Lamoli detto il
Solingo Durantino, *Narratione de gli gran fatti
della guerra di Malta; Le cagioni che mossero il gran
Turco ad armare; Co'l nome delli Bassa, & di molti
famosi corsari. Con altre cose appartene[n]ti al sugetto,
il quale comprende quanto è successo dalla perdita
de Rodi infino al fine della guerra di Malta.* Pesaro,
1565. A copy of this poem is in the Biblioteca
Oliveriana at Pesaro, Fascicolatura A-F4 (24 cc.);
in 8° (cm 15).

82 Cioci 1987, pp. 191 and 197.

83 Cioci 1987, pp. 60–61, 63 and 78.

84 Mallet 1984, pp. 398–402.

85 The implications for our understanding of
Xanto's biography are discussed by Triolo
(1996, pp. 104–07).

86 Mallet 1984, p. 400.

87 F. Guicciardini 1561, Book XIII, Ch. 4.

88 Dennistoun 1909, II, p. 404; Eiche 1986,
pp. 34–37; Eiche 2001, pp. 232–36.

89 Valazzi 2004, p. 164.

90 Cioci 1987, p. 34 and p. 109, makes the
assumption that this was also the occasion
mentioned in Sonnet III, when Xanto, not
yet thirty, first took up poetic praise of
the Duke.

91 For discussion of the evidence of the Sonnets
for Xanto's date of birth see Mallet 1984;
Triolo 1996, pp.77–79, p. 97 and pp.104–07;
Mallet 2004, pp. 48–51.

92 The suggestion of Cherchell is due to Triolo
(1996, p. 106 and p. 115, note 39).

93 Spallanzani 1994, p. 129.

94 Reynolds 2005, pp. 143–61.

95 On the question of the use of *istoriato* maiolica
see Mallet and Dreier 1998, pp. 33–37.

96 Hollingsworth 2004, pp. 19–21.

97 Higgott 2003, pp. 76–77.

98 Mazzola 1993, p. 11. I am indebted to Timothy
Wilson for this reference.

99 Mallet 1988, pp. 69–73 and pls 2–4.

100 For the 'Eagle' service and the 'Three
Crescents' service see Triolo 1996, pp. 253–78.
A single piece from the 'Three Crescents'
service is dated 1530.

101 Mallet 2004, p. 45 and figs. 15 and 16.

102 Negroni cites a mention of him dated 3
September 1520 as in Urbino (1985, p. 17 and
note 26).

103 Rackham and Ballardini 1933, pp. 395–96 and
figs. 1 and 2; Rackham 1940, I, pp. 260–61,
no. 793.

104 Wilson 1987, pp. 52–53 and nos. 66 and 67;
Thornton and Wilson 2007, no. 142,
Rackham 1940, no. 793.

105 Rackham and Ballardini 1933, pp. 395–96.

106 Balzani and Regni 2002, pp. 52–53.

107 Mallet 1976, p. 17.

108 Pieces from the Correr service are illustrated,
for instance, in Conti 1980, pls. 187–90.

109 Hausmann 1972, no. 170.

110 Wilson 1987, no. 50.

111 For the book of designs at Lille see Jestaz 1972,
pp. 217–222; Faietti and Oberhuber 1988,
pp. 311–15.

112 Massing 1990; Massing 1991.

113 Kube 1976, no. 58; Ivanova 2003, no. 29.

114 Wilson 1987, no. 63; Thornton and Wilson
2007, no. 148. The attribution to Nicola of
this inscribed piece seems first to have
been doubted by Burr Wallen (1968, p. 100,
note 2).

115 Cioci 2002A, IV, pp. 67–88.

116 It is hard to share Cioci's view that the subject
of Paris shooting Achilles in the heel, painted
a number of times by Nicola, should be
regarded as a political allegory. See Cioci 1997A.

117 Cioci 2002A, p. 71.

118 Marino Sanuto, *I Diari*, Venice 1879–1903.

119 Ivanova 2003, no. 29.

120 *Ill. Bartsch* 27, p. 134, 464 (345).

121 *Ill. Bartsch* 27, p. 119, 442 (332).

122 From the border of the *Quos Ego* print,
*Ill. Bartsch*, 27, p. 49, 352-I (264).

123 *Ill. Bartsch* 25 (Commentary), pp. 347–49, .025.
For the use of this print on a broad-bordered
bowl signed *F.R.* see Mallet 1976.

124 Prentice Von Erdberg and Ross 1952, no. 48
and pls. 31 and 60.

125 Mallet 2004.

126 For a recent summary of Maestro Giorgio's
activities see Biganti 2002A, p. 50.

127 Wilson 2002B. Though I have differed from
Wilson in my conclusions, I have profited
greatly from this paper. I first brought the
'S' service into the argument in Mallet 1976,
pp. 11 and 14.

128 For the group of maiolica that can be grouped
around the better *istoriati* of the 'S' service
(sometimes confused with the painter of a
dish with *The Judgement of Paris*, in the Petit
Palais at Paris, Join-Dieterle, I, 1984, no. 54)
see Mallet 2004, pp. 41–42.

129 Mallet 1979, p. 279.

130 Join-Dieterle 1984, no. 54.

131 Falke 1934, p. 328; Rackham 1940, pp. 223–24.

132 I provided a list of such works, though with
no pretensions to completeness, in Mallet
2004, p. 42.

133 Fiocco and Gherardi 1989, pp. 422–23; Fiocco
and Gherardi 1995, pp. 33–34 and p. 36;
Wilson 2002B, pp. 121–22.

134 Balzani and Regni 2004, pp. 14–15.

135 Gardelli 1999, pp. 277–79; Wilson 2004B,
pp. 119–20.

136 Other early pieces attributable to Xanto
working after Dürer prints or Italian copies
of them are a dish signed *F.R.* sold Sotheby's,
10–11 May 1962, lot 34; a plate, dated 1525
in lustre, of *The Prodigal Son*, in the
Metropolitan Museum, New York
(Rasmussen 1989, no.119).

137 Wilson 2002B, p. 120, figs. 20 and 21.

138 Mallet 1976, cover illustration and p. 4, fig. 1.

139 *Ill. Bartsch* 25 (Commentary), pp. 345–49.

140 Eg. Ballardini 1933, 43, 46 (1532); 86, 90 (1533);
138, 144, 313R (1534); 139, 145, 314R (1534).

141 Wilson 2002B, p. 119, fig. 19. The print
underlying both pieces is Marcantonio
Raimondi's *Dance of Cupids* (*Ill. Bartsch* 26,
p. 215, 217–1 (177).

142 Triolo 1996, p. 256, no. 2A.3, Sotheby's,
London, 11 March 1980; Triolo 1996, p. 266,
3A.7, now in the George Gardiner Museum
of Ceramic Art, Toronto, acc. no. G83 1.0387.

143 Bertrand Jestaz laid almost excessive stress
on the identification of prints used by
maiolica painters. However, his useful articles
were generated by research towards a catalogue
where consideration of attribution, which

necessarily concentrates the eye on questions of quality, was the responsibility of his colleague, Jeanne Giacomotti. See Jestaz 1972, pp. 215–17 and 237–38.

144 Vasari, ed. Milanesi, V, p. 415. The implications of this for maiolica are discussed by Patricia Collins (1987, pp. 222–35).

145 Landau and Parshall 1994, pp. 295–97.

146 Wilson 2002B, p. 121.

147 Cat. 52 is excluded from this number for reasons to be explained in the next paragraph.

148 Wilson 2005B.

149 Mallet 1979.

150 Giacomotti 1974, no. 847; Mallet 1979, p. 291, no. 5; Cioci 1987, p. 55. My tentative attribution to Francesco Urbini has since been all but conclusively confirmed by publication of a dish with the same arms and much more securely attributable to Francesco Urbini in Barral 1987, no. 11.

151 Mallet 2004, p. 53.

152 Filippini 1942, pp. 76–78; Biganti 2002B, p. 45.

153 Sotheby's, London, 10 May 1962, lot 34. This must be the dish previously sold from the Fountaine Collection, 16 June 1884, lot 20.

154 Fiocco and Gherardi 2002A; Thornton 2003; Fiocco and Gherardi 2004, pp. 16–23; I confess I have been resistent to the idea, put to me by Carola Fiocco and Gabriella Gherardi, that the *Spasimo* plaque might be *Romagnol*, but comparison with the print-source has now shaken my belief in Xanto's authorship.

155 Francesco Cioci 1993, p. 34, mentions an outbreak of plague in Faenza in 1528 as a possible cause why Xanto might have fled the town.

156 See Mallet 2004, pp. 50–51.

157 Illustrated, for instance, by Ballardini (1933, 205, 235, 345R) or, for good colour, by Cioci (1993, figs. 5–6). The other piece marked *F.L.R.* is a fragment in the Bargello at Florence illustrated, for example, by Conti (1971, no. 41 and cover-illustrations).

158 This point is discussed in Mallet 2004, p. 48.

159 The *St Jude* dish at Pesaro (cat. C.A.S.: 1, Mancini della Chiara 1979, no. 146) which can surely only be by Nicola da Urbino, who is not known to have worked outside Urbino, has a lustred background and bears on its reverse 1525 and the 'Mᵒ. Gᵒ.' mark. See Ballardini 1933, pl. XX, 178, 313R.

160 I make an exception of the Ashmolean's phallic plate of 1536 (cat. 52 here), since, as explained above, I do not consider the initials on this a true signature of F.R./ Xanto.

161 Giacomotti 1974, no. 337.

162 Holcroft 1988. Xanto's use of Petrarch is also extensively discussed in Cioci 1987.

163 For *Pensa* see a *tondino* at Padua (Munarini and Banzato 1993, no. 294).

164 On Glasgow's *Apollo and Daphne* plate (cat. 25 here) and Milan's *Euridice* Ausenda 2000, no. 210.

165 F. Liverani 1979, pp. 33–36, no. 8; Cioci 1987, pp. 70–73.

166 Timothy Wilson tells me he owes this suggestion, a correction of his previous reading as "hope", to a private communication from Francesco Cioci.

167 See above, p. 19 and note 46.

168 Cioci 1987, p. 44.

169 For the Giulio piece see cat. 47 here. The 'Lu Ur' piece, dated 1533, represents Charles V stripping Rome bare, and is signed *In Urbino /L*. It was in the Sackler collection when illustrated in Mallet 1988, p. 99, figs. 14 and 14R.

170 Rasmussen 1984, no. 123 and Pl. XI; Lessmann 1979, no. 143.

171 For her useful discussion see Triolo 1996, pp. 75–76 and fig. 192. I have retained the description 'y/Φ' flourish despite her suggestion that "the Greek letter 'phi' should be henceforth eliminated", because I can see no better reason to retain the description 'y'.

172 Francesco Liverani (1991, p. 46) has touched on this contrast between Xanto and Nicola.

173 Mallet 1988.

174 Wilson 1993A.

175 Rasmussen 1980; Mallet 1988, pp. 76–78; Gresta 2002; Houkjaer 2005, pp. 184–85, no. 157.

176 Mallet 1988, p. 80.

177 Wilson 1993B, pp. 210–14; 1942.9.337 (C-62); Fiocco and Gherardi 1996.

178 Dish on low foot with *Diana and Actaeon* (Gardelli 1987, p. 104, no. 41); plate with *The Vision of Constantine*, formerly in the H.A. Cann collection.

179 Bonali and Gresta 1987, p. 37, note 54.

180 Lessmann 1979, no. 496.

181 Triolo 1996, pp. 292–96. To this may be added a plate, 22.5 cm in diameter, inscribed *Chomo paris amaz'/ achille al tempio de apolo*, formerly in the Oscar Bondy Collection, Vienna, illustrated in *Salon International*, Paris, 1927, p. 78

182 Ballardini 1938, pl. V, 41, 258R.

183 The parallel of the Leonardi service makes me more confident than I was at the time of the Victoria and Albert Museum's *Splendours of the Gonzaga* exhibition that cat. 40 here really does belong to the same service as the smaller, undated Nicola pieces that bear the same arms (cat. 41 and 42 here). See Mallet 1981, p. 199, nos. 194–96. A large dish (ibid. no. 197) and a plate bearing Federico II's Olympus device, both by Nicola, may not have belonged to the same service.

184 Rackham 1940, no. 575.

185 Wilson 1990. Ravanelli Guidotti 1994A.

186 Xanto's armorial services have been admirably studied by Julia Triolo (1996, where they are catalogued on pp. 245–376).

187 Van de Put and Rackham 1916, p. 105; Wilson 1993B, pp. 205–09; Cioci 1997B, pp. 195–205; Spallanzani 1999, pp. 71–83; Cioci 2002B; Cioci 2006.

188 Cioci 1987, pp. 204–06.

189 Triolo 1996, pp. 137–38.

190 Paciaroni 2002, p. 175; Poole 2003.

191 Palmer 1991, pp. 181–82; Triolo 1996, pp. 136–37 and p. 151, note 3.

192 For Alessandro's taste see Robertson 1992.

193 Goldthwaite 1989/97, p. 191.

194 Palvarini Gobio Casali 1987, pp. 211–12, note 29.

195 Piccolpasso 1980, II, p. 90.

196 Triolo 2002, p. 126.

197 Mallet 2004, pp. 52–53. For my earlier explanation see Mallet 1988, pp. 68–69.

198 F. Guicciardini 1561, Book 18, Ch. 4; Ugolini 1859, II, p. 222; Biscarini 2002, p. 35 and p. 43, note 66.

199 Negroni 1985, no. 1, pp. 19–20.

200 Fiocco and Gherardi 1989, p. 429.

201 For evidence of protectionist policies at Urbino see Wilson 2003A, pp. 153–56. For evidence of protectionism at Gubbio see Mallet 2004, p. 53.

202 Fiocco and Gherardi 1989, p. 419.

203 Cioci 2002B, pp. 78–79, pl. VI and figs. 22–23

204 Negroni 1985, p. 19, note 43.

205 Braghirolli 1878, p. 25. Amongst the effects left by Iohannes Franciscus Aquilini called *el Poeta*, when he died in 1539, *doi piatti* were thought worth listing. See Albarelli 1986, pp. 369–70, no. 1641.

206 Triolo 1991.

207 Cioci 2002B.

208 Lawner 1988.

209 For an ingenious attempt to identify shared jokes of this kind, see Talvacchia 1994.

210 Vossilla 2002.

211 For these engravings see Lippmann 1895.

212 Mallet 1988, pp. 81–82; Alverà Bortolotto 1988, pp. 38–40 and 63, no. 26; Wilson 1987, p. 69, no. 100.

213 Fiocco and Gherardi 1988, pp. 110–136.

214 Berardi 1984, pp. 169–191; Bonali and Gresta 1987

215 Lessmann 1979, no. 496.

216 Wilson 2004B.

217 See, for instance, Rackham 1957, p. 99; Mallet 1992, pp. 142–43 and Appendix, pp. 152–54.

218 Robinson 1863, pp. 422–23.

219 Robinson 1856, pp. 13–14, no. 11.

220 E.g. in Rackham 1940, no. 547.

221 Palvarini Gobio Casali 1987, pp. 180–82, notes 27 and 29.

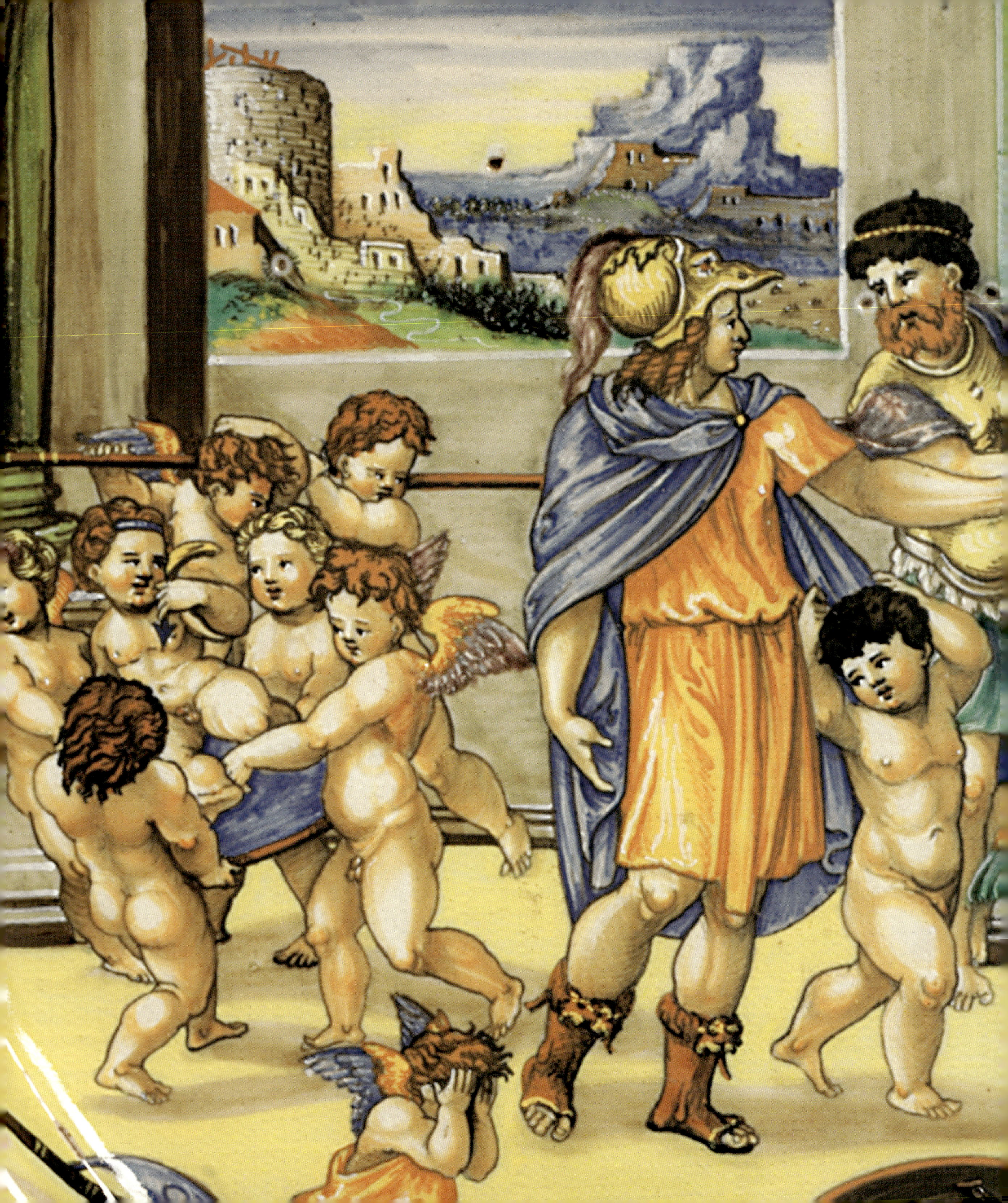

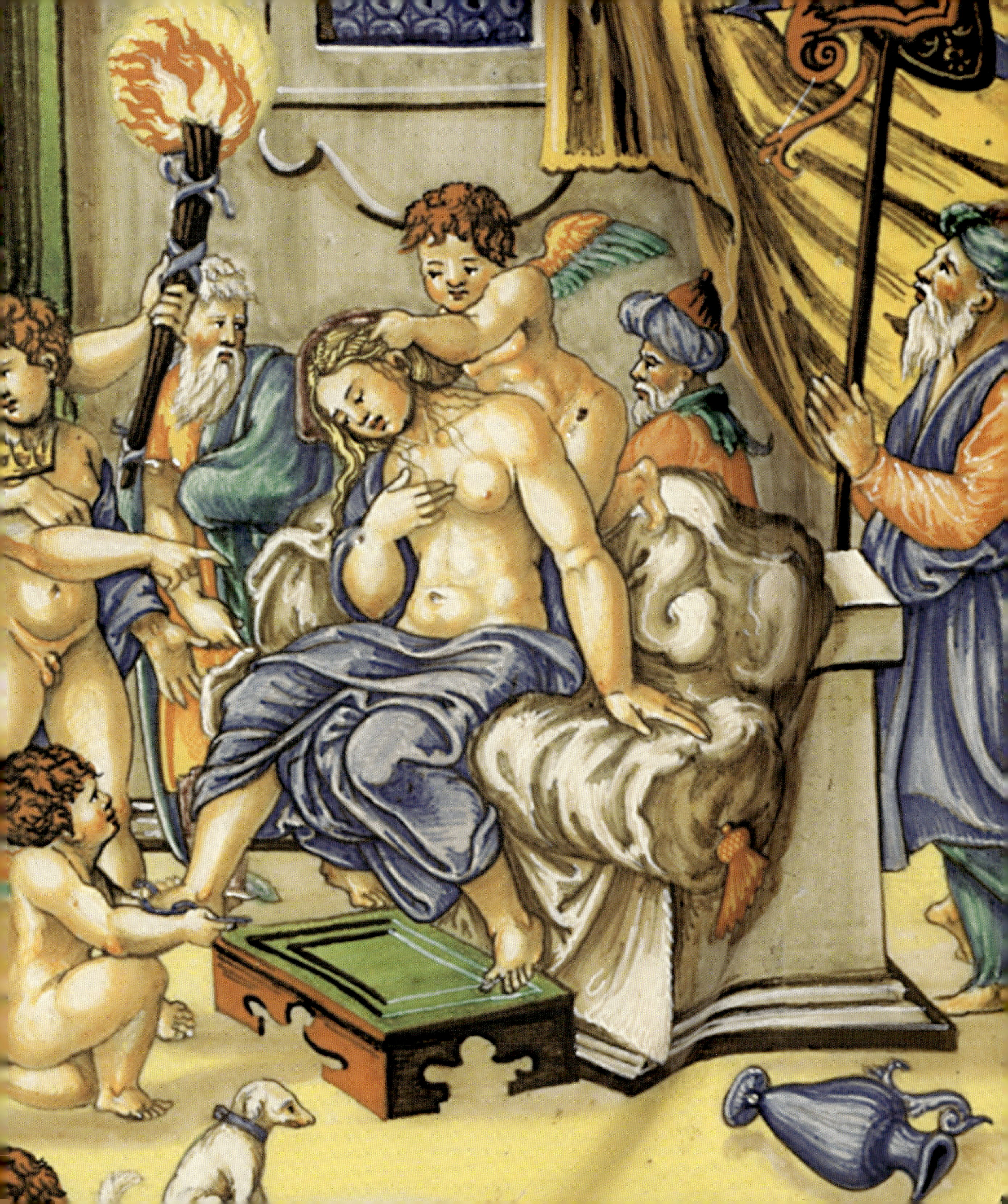

1. # Bowl with broad border (*Tondino*): *Hercules and Omphale*

Attributed to Francesco Xanto Avelli, Duchy of Urbino (Urbino?), dated 1522

D: 30.0 cm
London, Victoria and Albert Museum, 2542-1856

PROVENANCE

Bought 1856, apparently from "Arondel, 26 Rue Bonaparte, Paris"
(V&A Departmental Register).

BIBLIOGRAPHY

Fortnum 1873, p. 534 (as Faenza?); Solon 1907, fig. 38 (as Urbino); Rackham and Ballardini 1933, pp. 394–95, fig. 2 (as 'F.R.' at Faenza); Rackham 1933, p. 34, pl. 18A (as 'F.R.' at Faenza); Ballardini 1933, 115, 120 (as Faenza, monogrammist *F.R.*); Rackham 1940, no. 793 (as F.R. at Faenza); Chompret 1949, II, 493 (as Faenza); Mallet 1971A, p. 170 (as by 'F.R.' who was possibly Xanto); Mallet 1976, p. 9 (as *F.R.*, probably Xanto, Duchy of Urbino); Wilson 1987, no. 67 (as 'F.R.', Urbino district); Mallet 2004, fig. 1. (as Xanto, probably at Urbino).

NOTES

1. *Ill. Bartsch* 27, p. 49, 352-I (264).
2. *Ill. Bartsch*, 25 (Commentary), pp. 347–49, .025
3. Wilson 1987, no. 67; also Fuchs 1993, p. 206, no. 144.
4. *Ill. Bartsch* 27, p. 119, 442 (332).
5. *Ill. Bartsch* 27, p. 134, 464 (345).
6. Rackham and Ballardini 1933, pp. 393–407.
7. Wilson 1987, no. 66.

Polychrome. Left, Omphale seated, Cupid at her feet; right, Hercules seated, with distaff; foreground, a tablet inscribed ·OMNIA·/·VINCIT·/·AMOR· 1522·; the well plain; centre, a circular panel with buildings on an island.
Reverse: plain.
Broken in a number of pieces but essentially complete.

From the waist upwards Omphale derives (in reverse) from a figure of Dido receiving Aeneas in the border panel of Marcantonio Raimondi's *Quos Ego* (fig. 35, p. 74)[1], or from the reversed detail by Giovanni Antonio da Brescia.[2] This figure of Dido was more closely copied (unreversed) on cat. 20 where the Hercules is also replicated. No single print source has been identified for the Hercules figures but, as suggested by Wilson,[3] the legs seem adapted from Marcantonio's *A Seated Emperor* (fig. 18, p. 29),[4] the head and shoulders by reversing a nude man engraved by Marcantonio (*Two Nude Men*, fig. 29)[5] from Michelangelo's *Drunkenness of Noah*.

The tag *Omnia vincit Amor*, "Love conquers all", (Virgil, *Eclogues* 10, 69) here refers to the way Cupid so subjugated Hercules to Omphale, Queen of Lydia, that he became effeminate and spun yarn. The same words occur on the reverse of cat. 56, which is dated 1542, the last year in which work is attributable to Xanto.

Cat. 1 is the only dated piece now accepted as belonging to the group of works signed 'F.R.' whose work was first defined by Rackham and Ballardini, but erroneously attributed to Faenza.[6] It is now generally accepted that the initials 'F.R.', absent from cat. 1 but found on some others of the group (eg. cat. 3 and 13–15), stand for 'Francesco Rovigiese' or simply for 'Francesco'. The *tondino* has been compared with one in the British Museum marked at the back with the monogram *BT* or *TB*. These two are not a pair and do not seem by the same hand,[7] but it is likely they were painted in the same workshop, wherever that was.

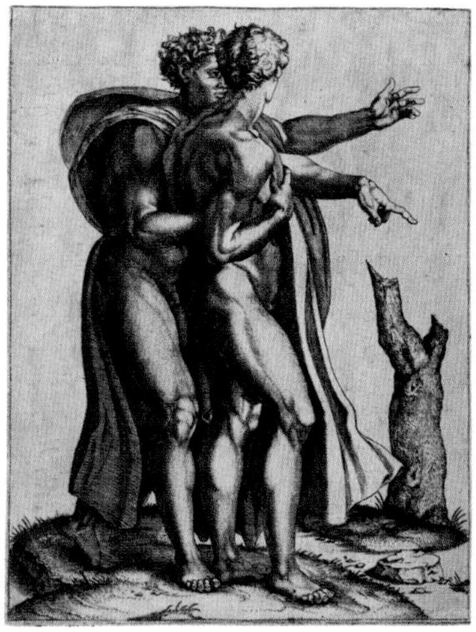

Fig. 29. Marcantonio Raimondi
(*c.* 1470–82 – *c.* 1527–34) after Michelangelo
(1475–1564), *Two Nude Men*, engraving,
London, British Museum, PG&D H.3.72

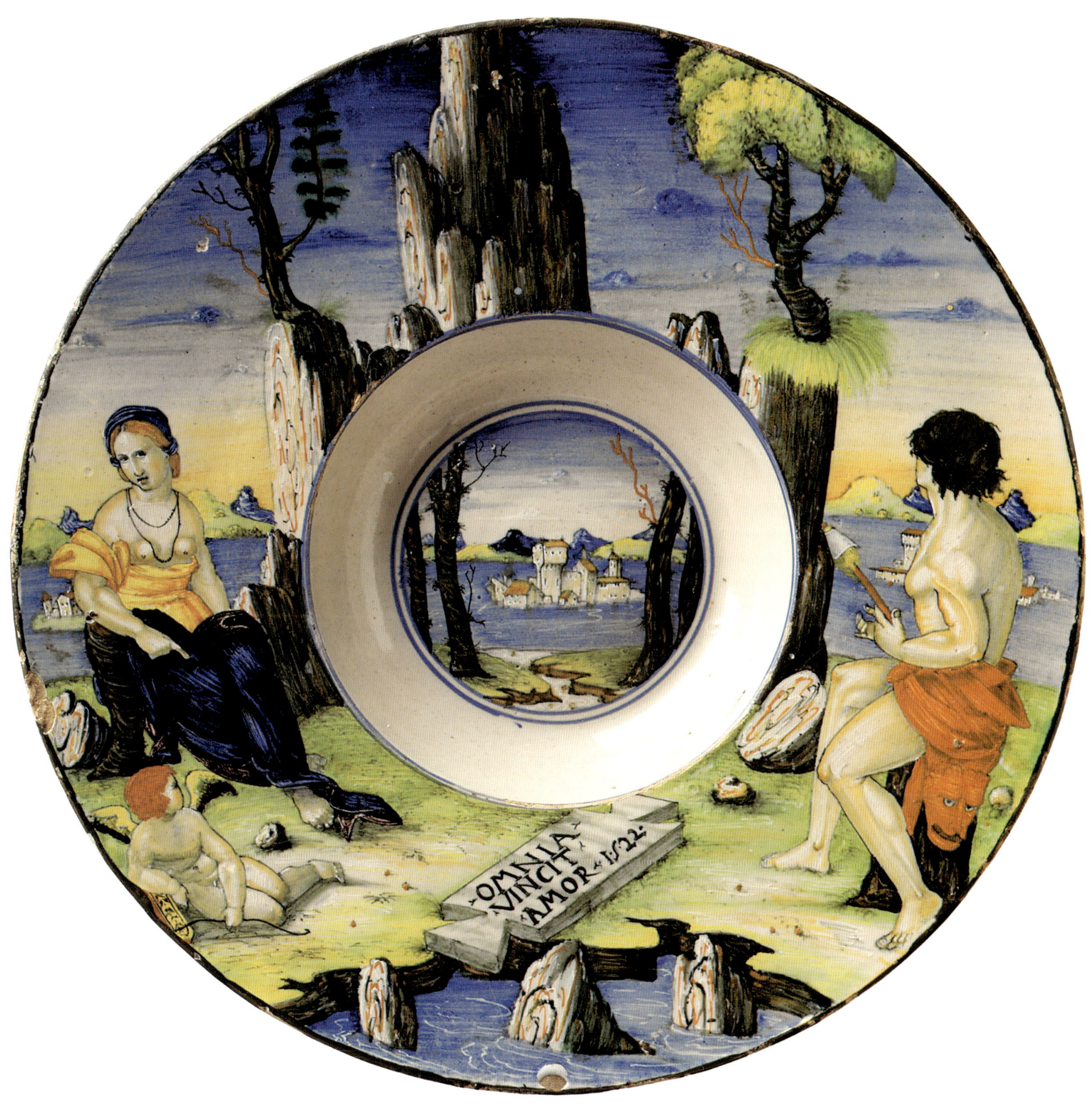

OMNIA
VINCIT
AMOR · 1522

## 2.  Fragment from centre of a dish:
### *Samson rending the Lion*

Attributed to Francesco Xanto Avelli, Duchy of Urbino (Urbino?), *c*. 1522

Largest measurement: 23.5 cm
London, Victoria and Albert Museum, 658-1884


PROVENANCE

Alessandro Castellani collection.

BIBLIOGRAPHY

Castellani sale, Rome, 17 March-10 April
1884, lot 58 (as Cafaggiolo); Solon 1907,
fig. 22 (as Cafaggiolo); Rackham and
Ballardini 1933, p. 395,
fig. 3 (as F.R. at Faenza); Rackham 1933,
p. 34 (as F.R. at Faenza); Rackham 1940,
no. 794 (as 'F.R.' at Faenza); Mallet 2004,
p. 51 (not illustrated but assigned to
Xanto, before 1524).

NOTE

1. *Ill. Bartsch* 10 (Commentary), p. 244, .202;
   Bartrum 2002, p. 120, no. 51.


Polychrome. Samson, bearded, forces apart the jaws of the Lion; in the background a rocky, mountainous landscape with two castles.
Only an approximately oval portion from near the centre of the dish survives. A low foot has been ground away from the underside.

The figure subject is quite closely copied from the woodcut by Albrecht Dürer (fig. 30).[1]

The popularity of Samson and the Lion (*Judges* 14, 5–6) as a subject for art developed in the Middle Ages because the incident was seen as prefiguring Christ's struggle with the Devil on behalf of mankind.

The rather primitive style of the landscape and the tentative outline of the drawing is particularly close to cat. 1 and suggests a similar dating, *c*. 1522. Samson's ruddy face and dark mane of hair may be compared with the more sophisticated (and hence perhaps slightly later) handling of some of the heads on the dish with *The Israelites gathering Manna* (cat. 3), which bears the initials *F.R.*.

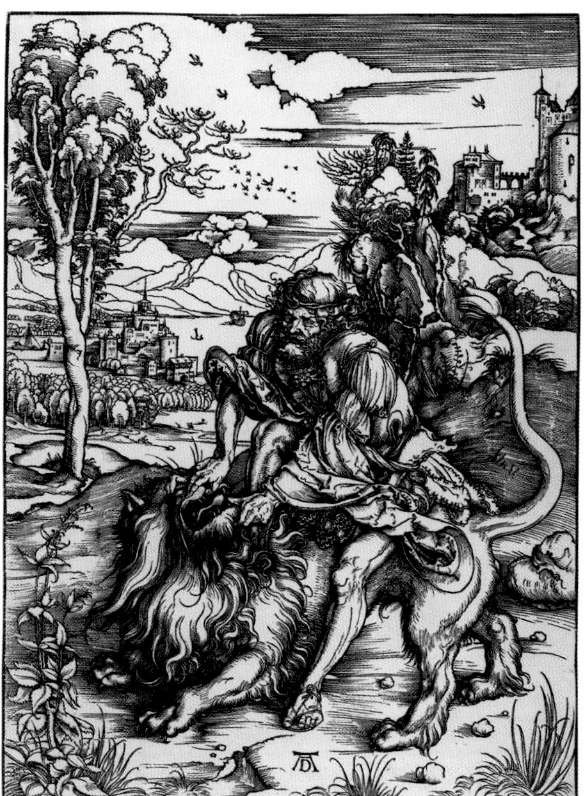

Fig. 30. Albrecht Dürer (1471–1528), *Samson and the Lion*, *c*. 1497–98, woodcut, London, British Museum, PG&D 1895-1-22-663

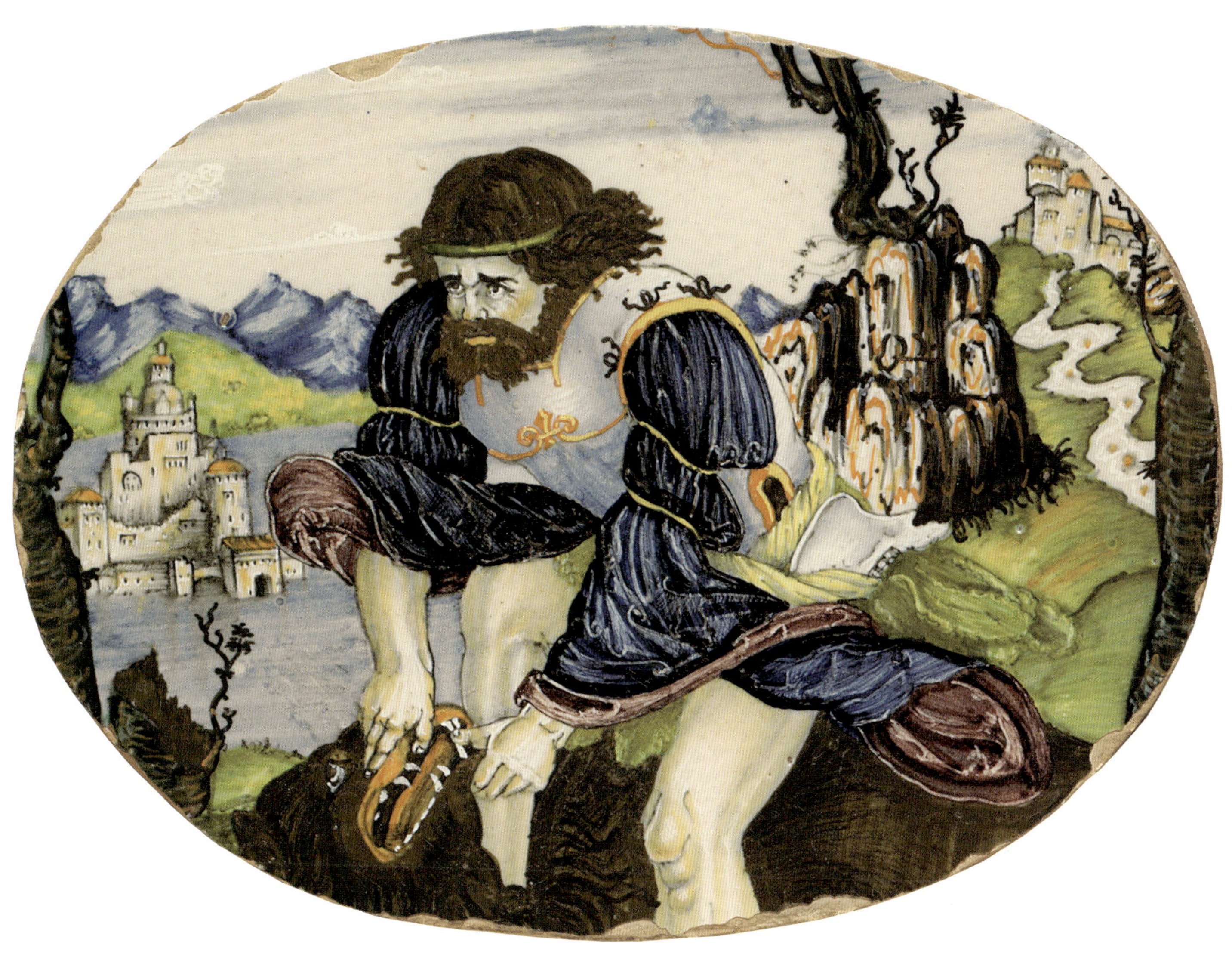

3. Dish on low foot (*Coppa*):
## *The Israelites gathering Manna*

Attributed to Francesco Xanto Avelli, Duchy of Urbino,
signed .F.R., *c*. 1522–25

D: 41.0 cm
London, Victoria and Albert Museum, 7680-1861


PROVENANCE

Soulages Collection.

BIBLIOGRAPHY

Robinson 1856, pp. 13–14, no. 11 (as Faenza
and grouped with other pieces bearing the
same initials which, however, he read
as F.B.); Fortnum 1873, p. 534 (as Faenza,
and by an artist distinct from the painter
of cat. 15 and others with a pale blue,
*berettino* ground); Fortnum 1896, p. 267
(as Faenza or Castel Durante, but not to
be confounded with "an artist associated
with the Casa Pirota" known as "the green
man"); Rackham and Ballardini 1933,
p. 400, fig. 13 (as Faenza); Rackham 1940,
no. 796 (as Faenza); Mallet 1976, p. 11 (as
Castel Durante or Urbino and comparable
to the .f.L.R. lion-hunt dish, cat. 16)

NOTE

1. *Ill. Bartsch* 26, p. 17, 8 (10).


Polychrome. Moses stands somewhat to the left, among a throng of
Israelites, pointing with his rod; in front of him men and women gather
manna into baskets and urns; trees and buildings in the background.
In the foreground, right, the blurred initials .F.R..
Reverse: plain.
Broken into about six pieces but virtually complete. Many holes left by
former rivets have been filled.

Quite closely copied from Agostino Veneziano's print of the subject after
Raphael,[1] but omitting figures to the right hand side of the print.

The incident of the gathering of manna occurred when the Israelites,
facing starvation in the wilderness, had begun to murmur against Moses
and Aaron. God provided for them and during the night a small round
substance fell, which the Israelites named 'manna' and gathered up,
since it proved excellent to eat (*Exodus*, 16, 11–36 and *Numbers*, 11, 7–9).

The print copied on cat. 3 is based on one of the scenes on the vault of
the *Logge* painted in the Vatican by Raphael and his pupils in 1516–19. Its
design would thus have retained much of its novelty when used by 'F.R.'
on maiolica *c*. 1523–25.

For the initials 'F.R.' and their implications see cat. 13 and Introduction,
pp. 27–28 and 33–34.

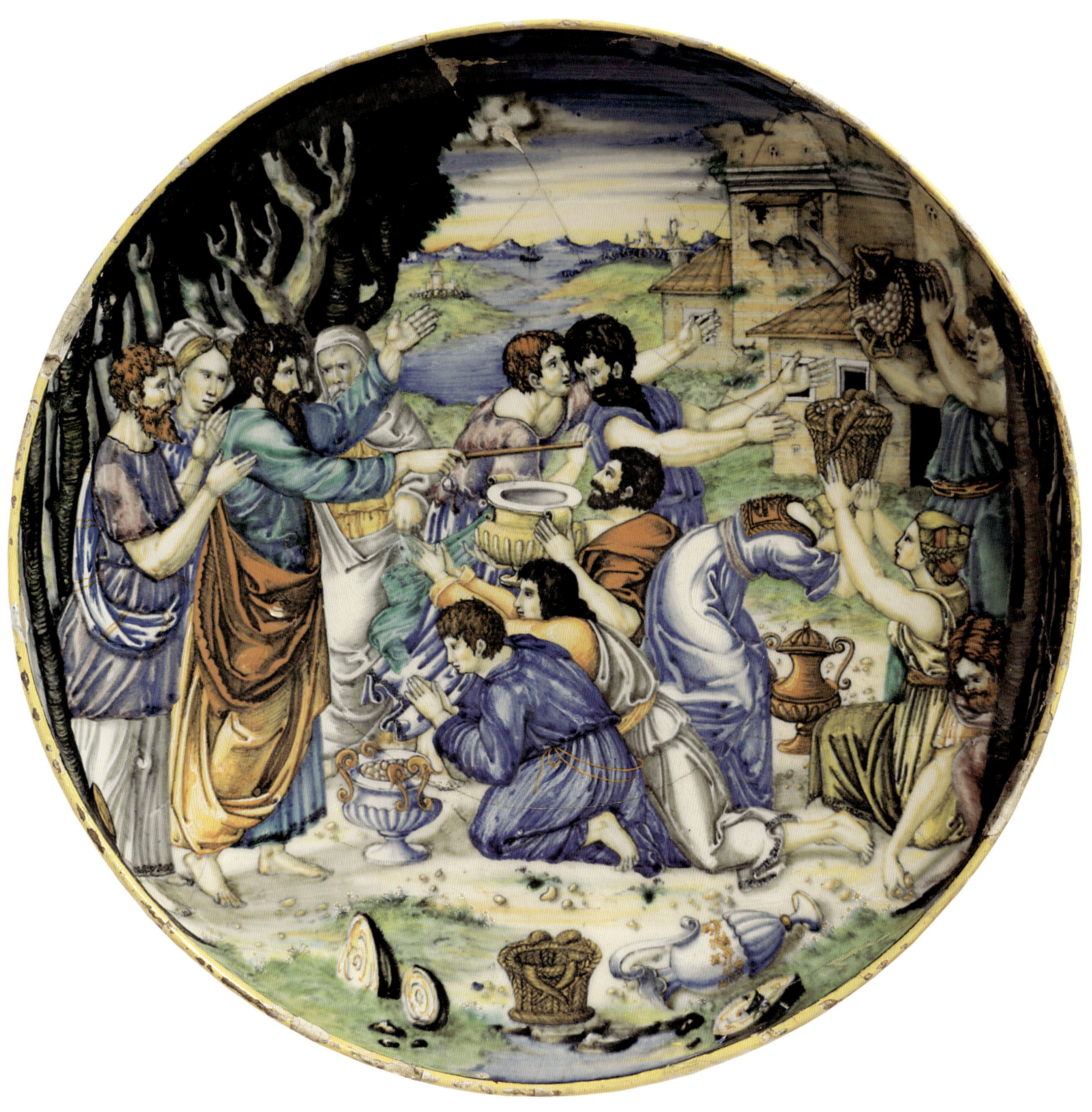

### 4. Plate with broad border :
*A River God in a Landscape*

Attributed to Francesco Xanto Avelli, Gubbio, in the workshop of
Maestro Giorgio Andreoli, and lustred there by another hand; dated 1524

D: 24.0 cm
London, British Museum, PG&E 1851, 12-1, 7


PROVENANCE

Acquired in 1851 from the Abbé Hamilton's
collection via a London dealer.

BIBLIOGRAPHY

Solon 1907, fig. 33 (as Gubbio, date
misread as 1527); Ballardini 1933, 139, 152,
296R (as Faenza, monogrammist F.R.?);
Rackham 1940, p. 223 (Gubbio, grouped
with cat. 9); Rackham 1957, p. 108 (as
not by F.R. but by the painter of cat. 9);
G. Liverani 1968, pp. 695–98 and fig. 11 (as
"Faenza, monogrammista F.R. e lustro di
Mastro Giorgio, 1524,", F.R. being considered the master of Xanto, or possibly the
same person before his supposed move
from Faenza to Urbino); Wilson 1987, no.
163 (as lustred in the workshop of Maestro
Giorgio, Gubbio 1524; perhaps painted by
F.R.); Wilson 2002B, p. 122 and pl. xxxii
(as Gubbio, Maestro Giorgio workshop,
1524); Mallet 2004, pp. 41–42, 44 and fig.7,
where the photograph was regrettably
reversed (painted by Xanto in Maestro
Giorgio's workshop at Gubbio, and there
lustred); Thornton and Wilson 2007,
no. 298.

NOTES

1. *Ill. Bartsch* 26, p. 242, 245- I (197).
2. *Ill. Bartsch* 26, p. 214, 214 (176).
3. Wilson 1993B, pp. 202–04.
   Inv. 1942.9.349 (C-74).


Painted in polychrome and lustre. A landscape with, centre, a reclining
nude river god holding palm branch and rudder.
Reverse: floral scrolls and the inscription *1524 / M⁰. G⁰.*, all in lustre.

The river god derives either (in reverse) from Marcantonio's print of
*The Judgement of Paris* (fig. 31, p. 56)[1] or (in same direction) from Agostino
Veneziano's engraving in which this figure appears alone.[2]

The figure used for the river god appears, in reverse, on cat. 5, but also
on the *Conversion of Saul* in the National Gallery of Art, Washington, which
Wilson and others accept as by the painter 'F.R.'.[3] The landscape, with
the cliff-like foreground characteristic of Xanto in his early phase, is an
independent creation.

This plate and cat. 5 were among twenty-one pieces acquired in 1851
from the Abbé James Hamilton collection. As they share this provenance
with six of the British Museum's seven pieces from a service (cat. 6–8) with
an emblem incorporating the letter 'S', dated 1524 and 1525, seemingly
largely by the same hand as cat. 4 and 5, there is a good chance the latter
two had always been with that service and may from the start have been
considered part of it.

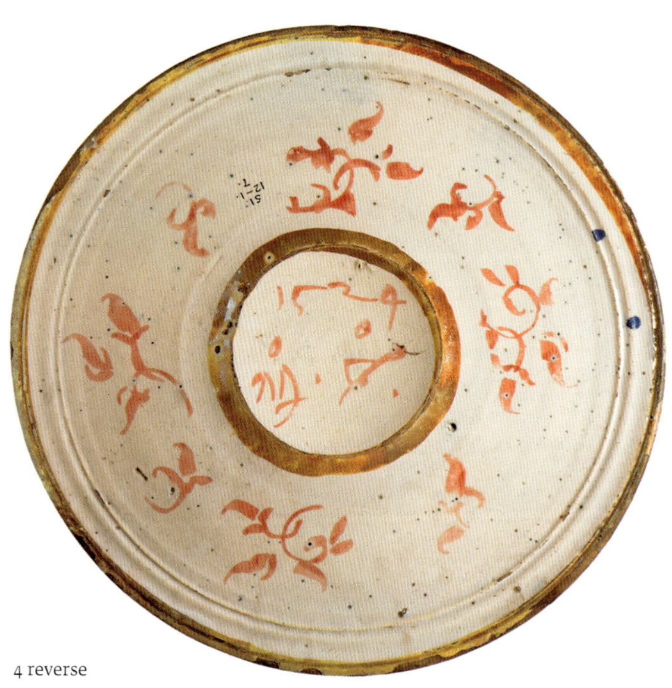

4 reverse

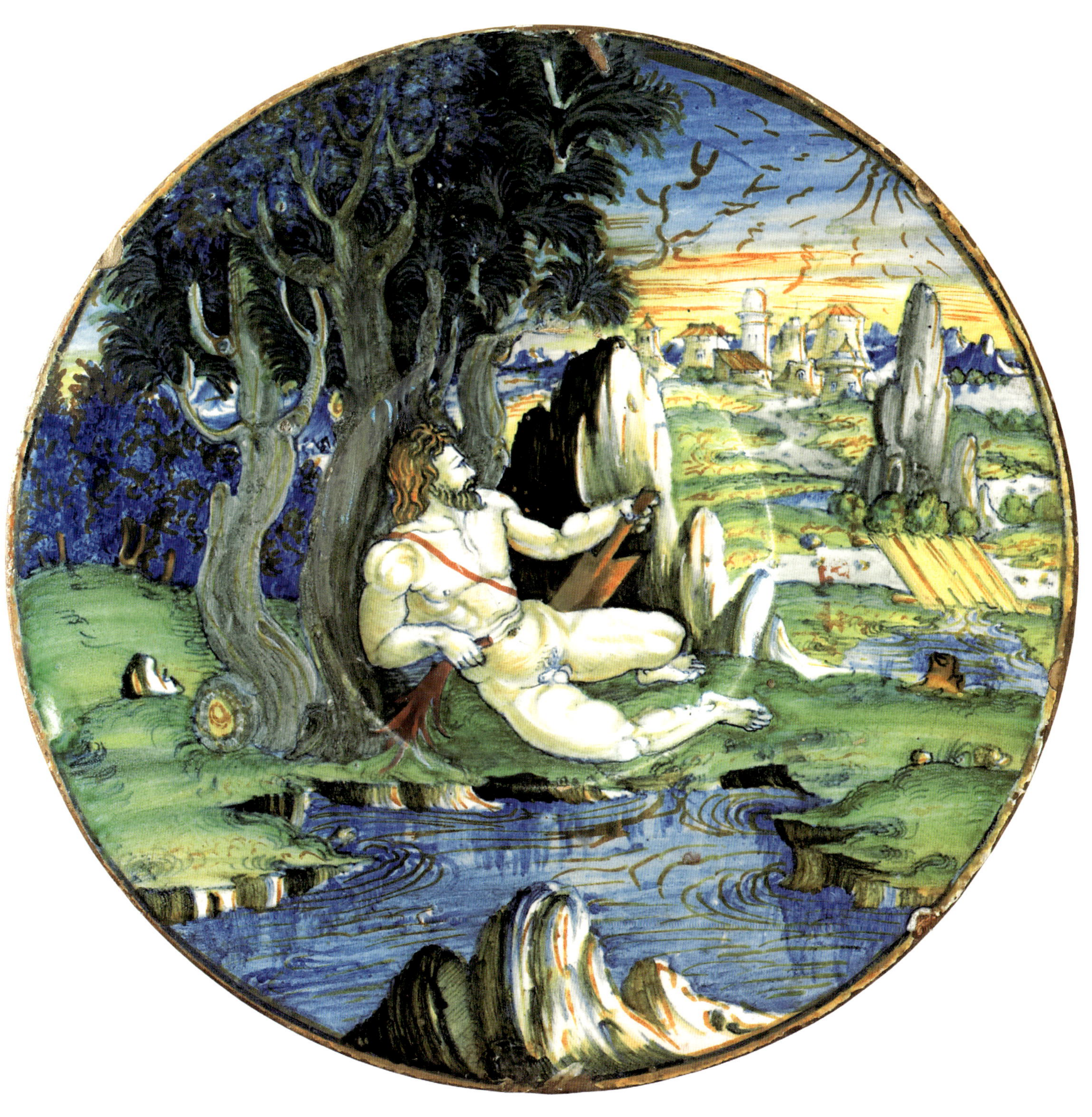

55

5. Bowl with broad border (*Tondino*):
*The Judgement of Paris*

Attributed to Francesco Xanto Avelli, Gubbio, in the workshop of
Maestro Giorgio Andreoli, and lustred there by another hand; dated 1524

D: 26.5 cm
London, British Museum, P&E 1851, 12-1, 8

PROVENANCE

Acquired in 1851 from the Abbé James
Hamilton's collection via a London dealer.

BIBLIOGRAPHY

Ballardini 1933, 138, 151, 394R (as Faenza,
monogrammist F.R.?); Rackham 1957,
p. 108 (as not by F.R. but by the painter of
the V&A's *Three Graces* roundel, here cat. 9);
Wilson 1987, no. 68; Wilson 2002B, p. 122
and pl. xxxiii, (as Gubbio, Maestro Giorgio
workshop, 1524); Mallet 2004, pp. 41–42, 44
and fig. 8 (as painted by Xanto in Maestro
Giorgio's workshop at Gubbio, and there
lustred); Thornton and Wilson 2007,
No. 299.

NOTES

1. *Ill. Bartsch* 26, p. 242, 245-I (197).
2. *Ill. Bartsch* 26, p. 214, 214 (176).
3. Wilson 1987 suggests rather uncon-
   vincingly that the goddesses echo an
   earlier treatment by Marcantonio of
   *The Judgement of Paris*, *Ill. Bartsch* 27,
   p. 34, 339 (254).

Polychrome and lustre. Left, the three nude goddesses, Juno, Minerva and
Venus; right, reclining, the nude Paris proffering the golden apple; centre,
on a smaller scale, Mercury holding his caduceus; the well decorated with
gold lustre.
Reverse: in lustre, plant-scrolls and the inscription 1524 / *M⁰. G⁰*.

Paris derives either from the river god to the right in Marcantonio
Raimondi's *The Judgement of Paris* (fig. 31)[1] or (reversed) from an engraving
in which this figure appears alone.[2]

Though isolated from the scene on the border, the small central figure
of Mercury plays his part in the narrative, as it was he who handed to Paris
the golden apple to be awarded to the most beautiful of the three goddesses,
Juno, Minerva and Venus. Paris awarded the prize in this dangerous beauty
contest to Venus, initiating a chain of disastrous consequences that led to
the Trojan War.

The three rather crudely drawn figures of goddesses and the figure of
Mercury appear to be original to Xanto,[3] and reveal the limitations of his
draughtsmanship when unsupported by an engraved source. This could
suggest Xanto used the engraving in which the river god alone appears,
not the complete engraving of *The Judgement of Paris*, from which one would
have expected him to have used Marcantonio's figures of the goddesses,
as he did on cat. 10 and some later pieces. The reclining Paris is shared
with cat. 4 but, characteristically, the painter has there chosen to use it
the other way around.

Perhaps originally part of the 'S' service which shares its provenance.
See cat. 4.

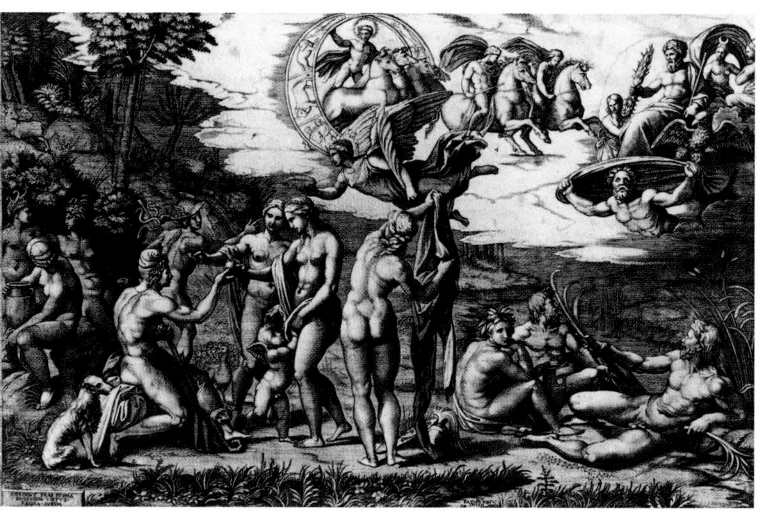

Fig. 31. Marcantonio Raimondi after
Raphael, *The Judgement of Paris*, engraving

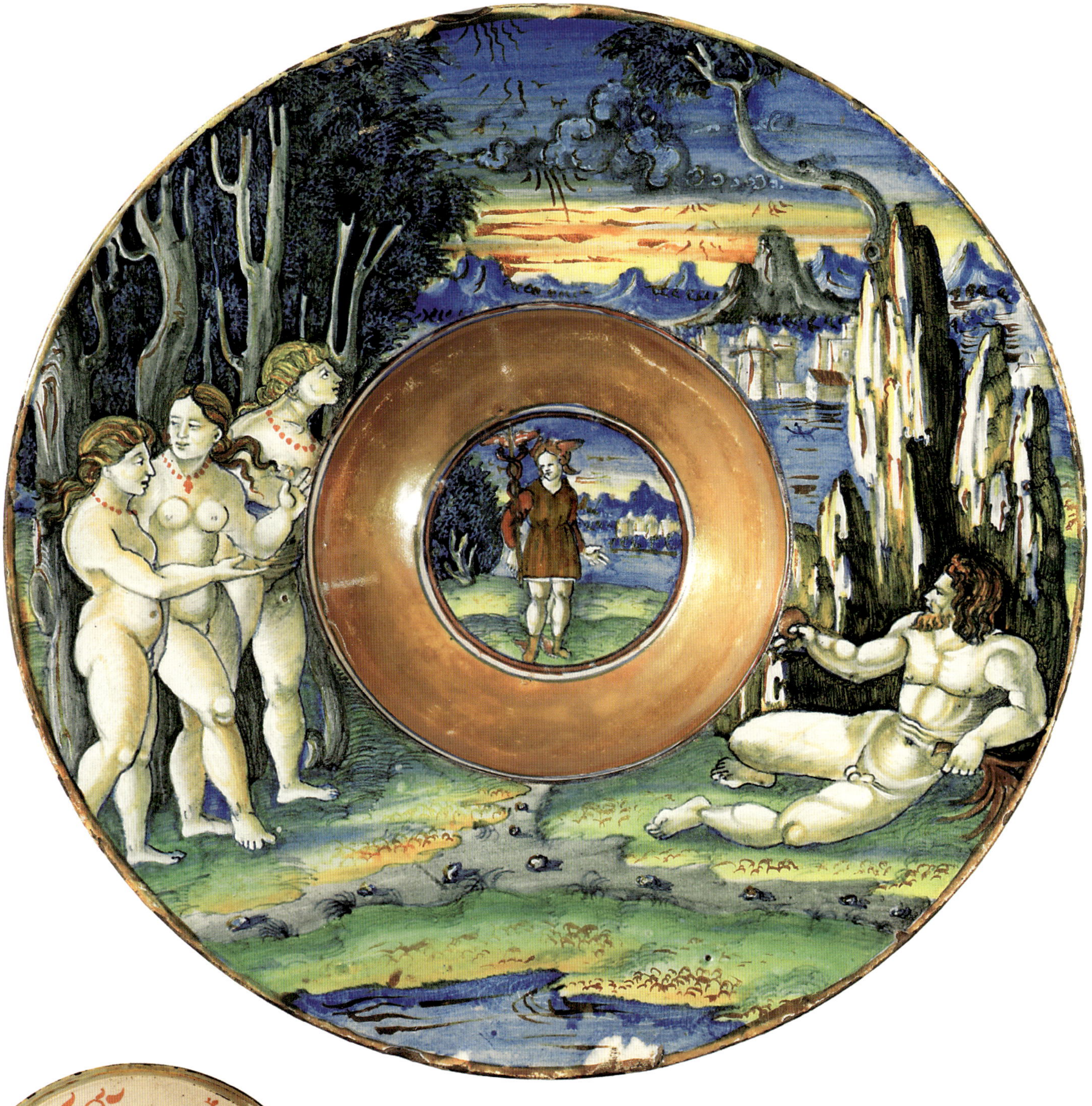

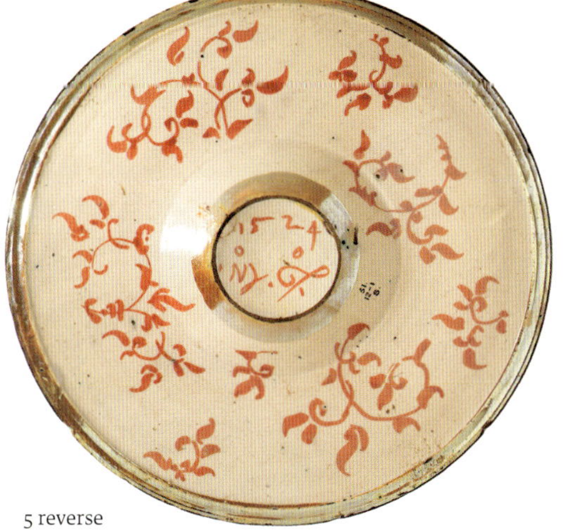

5 reverse

6. Bowl with broad border (*Tondino*):
*Cupid at an Altar, Border with Trophies*

Centre probably by Francesco Xanto Avelli, Gubbio, in the workshop of
Maestro Giorgio Andreoli; the border and lustre pigments painted there
by another hand or hands; dated 1524

D: 20.8 cm
London, British Museum, PG&E 1851, 12-1, 13


PROVENANCE

Acquired in 1851 from the Abbé James
Hamilton's collection via a London dealer.

BIBLIOGRAPHY

Ballardini 1933, 142, 141, 292R (as Castel
Durante style, lustred by Maestro
Giorgio); Wilson 1987, no. 164 (as lustred
and perhaps painted in the workshop of
Maestro Giorgio, Gubbio); Fiocco and
Gherardi 1989, p. 416, fig. 116 and p. 424
(Gubbio, workshop of Maestro Giorgio, the
'S' sign perhaps that of a noble family);
Wilson 2002B, pp. 114–20 and figs. 7 and 8
(as Giorgio workshop, border and centre
by different hands); Thornton and Wilson
2007, no. 305.

NOTES

1. Fortnum 1873, pp. 197–98.
2. For fuller discussion of the 'S' service
   see Wilson 1987, no. 164; Wilson 2002B,
   pp. 114–20.
3. Mallet 2004, pp. 39–42.


Polychrome and lustre. Centre, Cupid seen from behind, approaching
an altar on which is, in blue, an owner's emblem incorporating an 'S';
the border with military trophies and the letter 'S', the well in gold lustre.
Reverse: in lustre, plant-scrolls and, centre, *.1524. M⁰. / G⁰.*
Chipped at the rim.

The emblem painted in blue on the altar at the centre is repeated in lustre
on the reverses of several *istoriato* pieces including cat. 7 and 8, which are
dated 1525, whence the name the 'S' service. The 'S' emblem is most likely
a mark of ownership by a person, a monastery or other institution, though
Fortnum says it is "seen on some of the coins of Perugia".[1] Since on the
present bowl and on another in the British Museum also dated 1524 the
emblem is painted in blue, it has been pointed out that these pieces were
presumably painted at Gubbio and not just lustred there, and that the same
is probably the case with the *istoriati* from the 'S' service. Six of the seven
pieces from the 'S' service in the British Museum share a provenance, as also
do cat. 4 and 5, from the collection of the Abbé Hamilton, who had lived in
Rome from 1841–51.[2] The attribution to Xanto of the best painting on the
*istoriato* plates from the 'S' service and of the winged *putto* on the present
piece remains controversial, but if that attribution be accepted it would
seem to follow that Xanto worked at Gubbio during 1524–25, probably in the
workshop of Maestro Giorgio.[3]

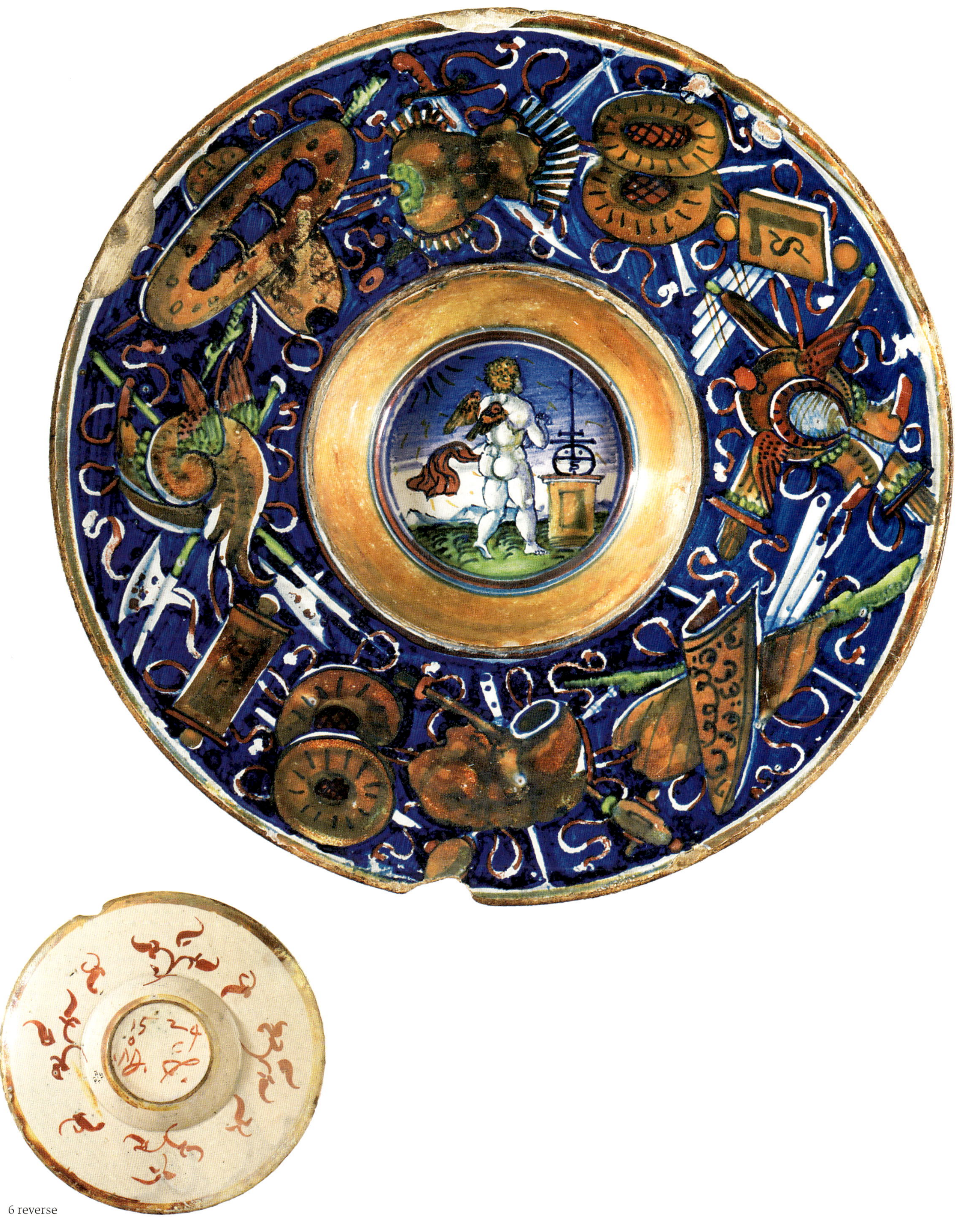

### 7. Bowl with broad border (*Tondino*): *Battle Scene*

Attributed to Francesco Xanto Avelli, Gubbio, in the workshop of
Maestro Giorgio Andreoli, the lustre pigments added there
by another hand; dated 1525

D: 20.8 cm
London, British Museum, PG&E 1851, 12-1, 10


PROVENANCE

Acquired in 1851 from the Abbé James
Hamilton's collection via a London dealer.

BIBLIOGRAPHY

Ballardini 1933, 164, 168, 301R (as Faenza,
monogrammist F.R.? lustred by Maestro
Giorgio); Wilson 1987, no. 167 (as lustred,
and perhaps painted, in the workshop
of Maestro Giorgio); Wilson 2002B,
pp. 118–22, pl. xxi and fig. 10 (as Gubbio,
Giorgio's workshop, possibly by Giovanni
Luca da Castel Durante); Mallet 2004,
pp. 42–44 (as painted by Xanto in Maestro
Giorgio's workshop at Gubbio, and there
lustred); Thornton and Wilson 2007,
no. 301.

NOTES

1. *Ill. Bartsch* 27, p. 108, 420 (316).
2. Wilson 1993B, pp. 180–83. 1942.9.334
   (C-59).
3. Barral 1987, no. 12, there over-cautiously
   ascribed to Xanto's studio and dated
   *c.* 1534, which is surely too late.
4. Ballardini 1938A, nos. 43, 46; 86, 90,
   277R; 138, 144, 313R; 139, 145, 214R.
5. Munarini and Banzato 1993, no. 296.


Polychrome and lustre. Left, a horseman unsheathing his sword and a
foot-soldier jabbing with his lance; right, a man hurls a boulder, all in
a rocky landscape. In the centre stands a blindfolded Cupid; the well with
gold lustre.
Reverse: in lustre, plant-scrolls, *M⁰. G⁰ / 1525* and an emblem incorporating
the letter 'S'.

The figures derive from those on the extreme left and right of the *Battle
Scene* print probably by Marco Dente after Raphael or Giulio Romano
(fig. 32).[1]

The *Battle Scene* print was more extensively used on a lustred flat plate
(fig. 20, p. 32), very evidently by the same hand and bearing the same date,
in the National Gallery of Art, Washington.[2] The repeated use of figures from
this print until the very end of Xanto's career reinforces the view here argued
that the 'S' service was painted, at least in part, by Xanto. See, for instance,
the boulder-thrower on a dish at Dijon, attributable to Xanto *c.* 1528–30.[3]
For examples of Xanto's frequent use of the spearman to the left in the print
see cat. 25, 45 and 54. The use of this spearman, as in cat. 54, to represent
Metabus hurling his daughter Camilla to safety over the River Amasenus,
was repeated by Xanto a number of times,[4] the latest being on an unsigned
plate at Padua dated 1542.[5]

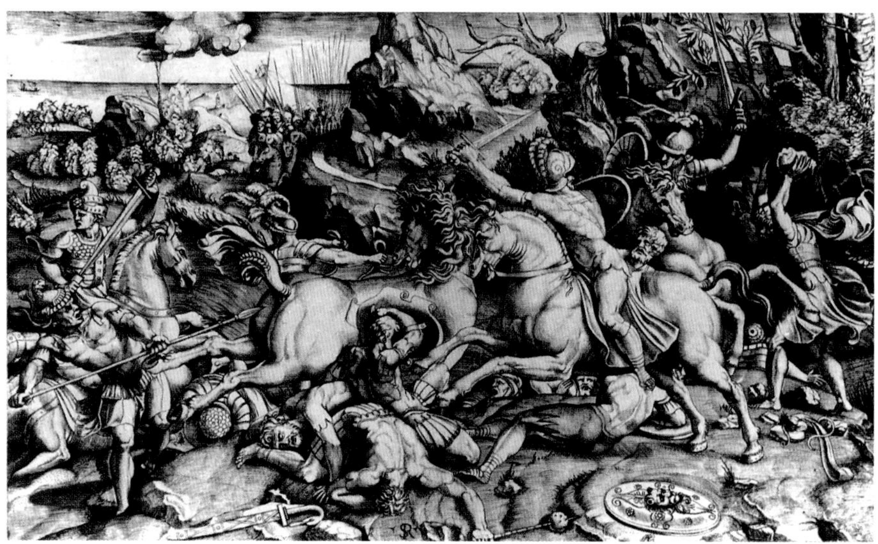

Fig. 32. Marco Dente after Raphael or
Giulio Romano (1499–1546), *Battle Scene*,
engraving

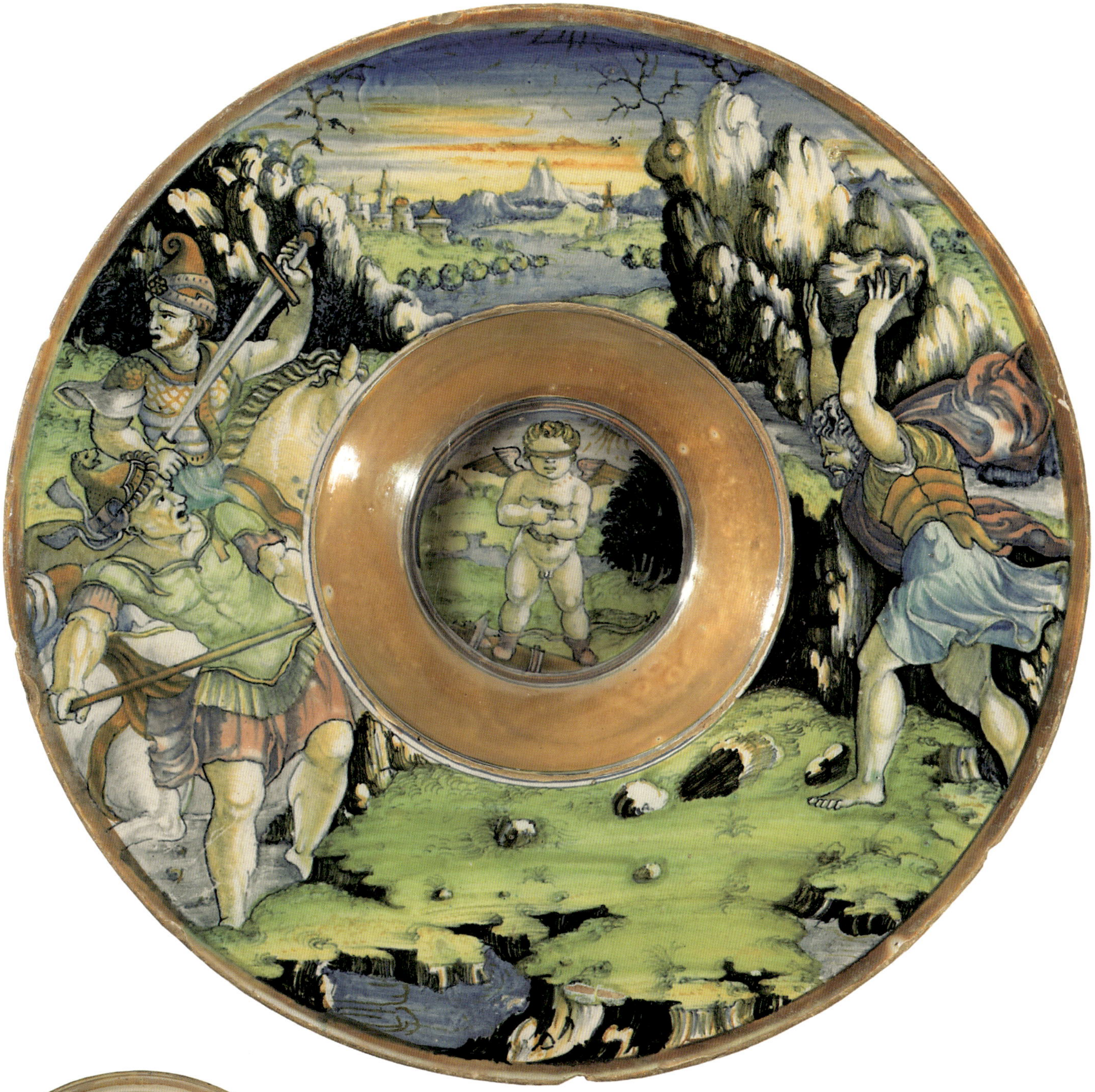

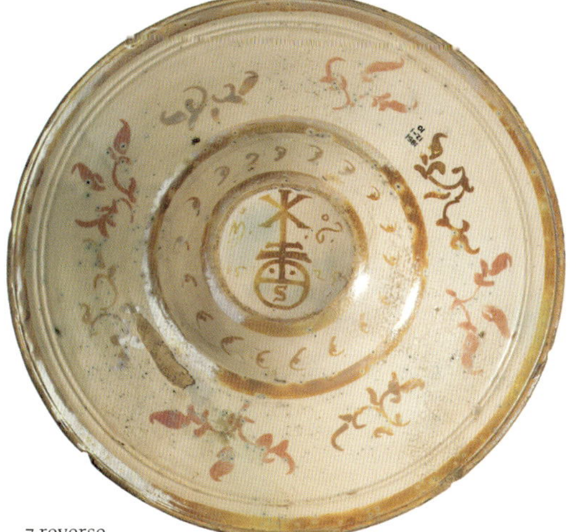

7 reverse

## 8.  Plate: *Horseman holding a Standard*

Attributed to Francesco Xanto Avelli, Gubbio, in the workshop
of Maestro Giorgio Andreoli; the lustre pigments added there
by another hand; dated 1525

D: 25.4 cm
London, British Museum, PG&E 1851, 12-1, 12

PROVENANCE

Acquired in 1851 from the Abbé James
Hamilton's collection via a London dealer.

BIBLIOGRAPHY

Fortnum 1873, pp. 197–98; Ballardini 1933,
163, 167, 300R (as Faenza, Monogrammist
F.R.? lustred by Maestro Giorgio); Wilson
1987, no. 168 (as Gubbio, lustred and
perhaps painted in the workshop of
Maestro Giorgio); Fiocco and Gherardi
1989, pp. 422–25 and figs. 126–27 (as
Gubbio, workshop of Maestro Giorgio);
Wilson 2002B, pp. 118–22, pl. xxii and
fig. 11 (as Gubbio, Maestro Giorgio's
workshop, possibly by Giovanni Luca da
Castel Durante); Mallet 2004, pp. 42–44
and fig. 4 (as painted by Xanto in Maestro
Giorgio's workshop and there lustred);
Thornton and Wilson 2007, no. 302.

Polychrome and lustre. A man holding a standard and riding a grey
horse from left to right across a landscape background with trees, rocks
and buildings.
Reverse: in lustre, leafy scrolls and 'S' emblem flanked by *1525 / Mº. Gº*.

No engraved source has been identified for this plate and it is not clear
whether a particular person or incident is represented.
    For discussion of the 'S' service, to which this plate belongs, see cat. 6.

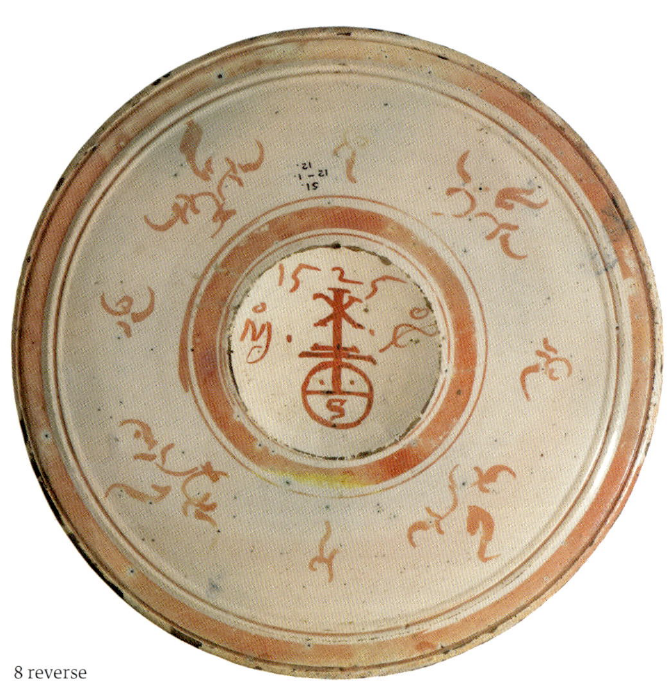

8 reverse

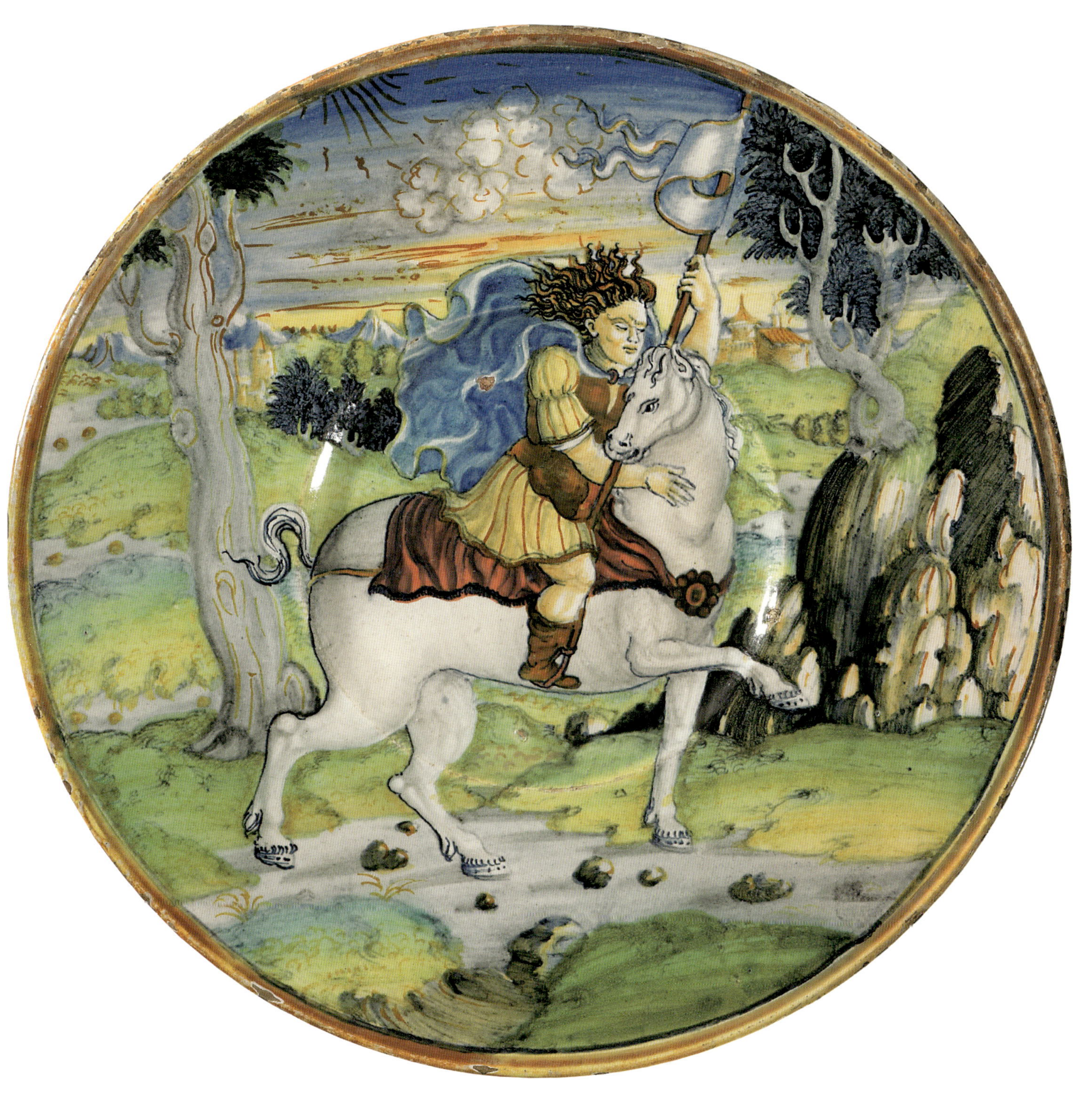

9. Flat plate: *The Three Graces*

Attributed to Francesco Xanto Avelli at Gubbio, in the workshop
of Maestro Giorgio and there lustred and dated 1525

D: 30.5 cm
London, Victoria and Albert Museum, 175-1885


PROVENANCE

First recorded as at Rome, 1849, and
bought two years later by Roussel,
according to a note by J. C. Robinson,
from a shop near S. Andrea della Valle;
Lord Amherst of Hackney, who sold it to
his uncle, Andrew Fountaine; purchased
at the Fountaine sale by Beckett Denison
at whose sale it was bought by the dealer
Whitehead and passed to the Victoria
and Albert Museum.

BIBLIOGRAPHY

Delange 1853, p. 183; Waring 1858, p. 17;
Darcel and Delange 1867–69, p. 34 and pl.
lxvi; Fountaine sale 1884, lot 372; Beckett
Denison sale, Christie's, London, 6 June
1885, lot 804; Rackham 1940, no. 673 and
pp. 223–24 (further bibliography cited);
Fiocco and Gherardi 1989, p. 328; Wilson
1993B, pp. 171 and 180–82; Fiocco and
Gherardi 1998, p. 29 and pl. 4; Mallet
2004, p. 41.

NOTES

1. *Ill. Bartsch* 27, p. 35, 340 (255) or p. 36, 341
   (356) respectively.
2. See Bober and Rubinstein 1986,
   pp. 95–97, no. 60.
3. Wilson 2002B, pp. 120–21 and p. 20,
   pl. xxi.
4. Fountaine sale 1884, lot 372.
5. Rackham 1940, no. 673 and pp. 223–24;
   Falke 1934, p. 328.


Polychrome (including opaque white) and lustre. The three naked Graces,
standing with arms resting on one anothers' shoulders, between two
streaming urns in a landscape with palms and other trees; buildings in
the background.
Reverse: in lustre, leafy scrolls within a zig-zag at the border; in the centre,
in red lustre, the workshop mark *1525 / M⁰ G⁰* below the date.

Based on Marcantonio Raimondi's engraving (fig. 33) or Marco Dente's
repetition,[1] after a Roman marble copy of a Hellenistic original.

   The Graces, daughters of Jupiter and Eurynome, personified grace,
beauty and benificence. Antique versions of the three interlaced figures
copied by Marcantonio survive in painting and mosaic as well as in sculpture, both in the round and in relief. The three-dimensional Roman marble
version in the Piccolomini Library at Siena Cathedral was perhaps the one
most copied in Renaissance times.[2] The urns and palms are included in the
engraving, and were perhaps Marcantonio's inventions, but the landscape
was added by the maiolica painter. As noted by Wilson,[3] a Gubbio dish at
Cleveland, of the same design but with a decorative border, is weaker in
figure-drawing. It may, none the less, be in part by Xanto.

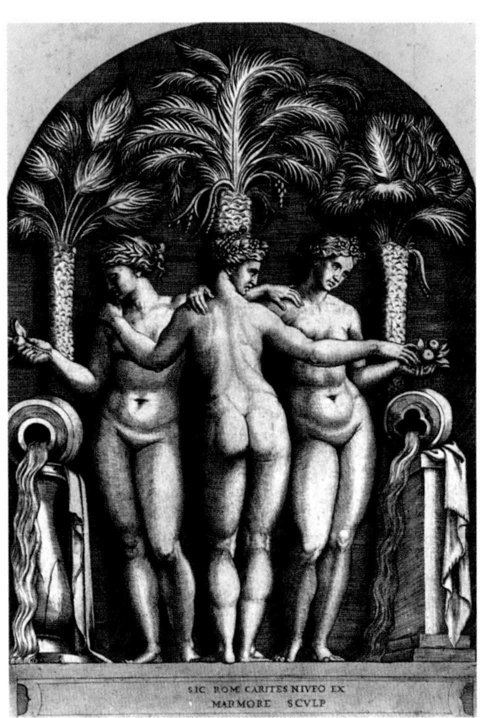



Fig. 33. Marcantonio Raimondi
after an ancient bas-relief,
*The Three Graces*, engraving

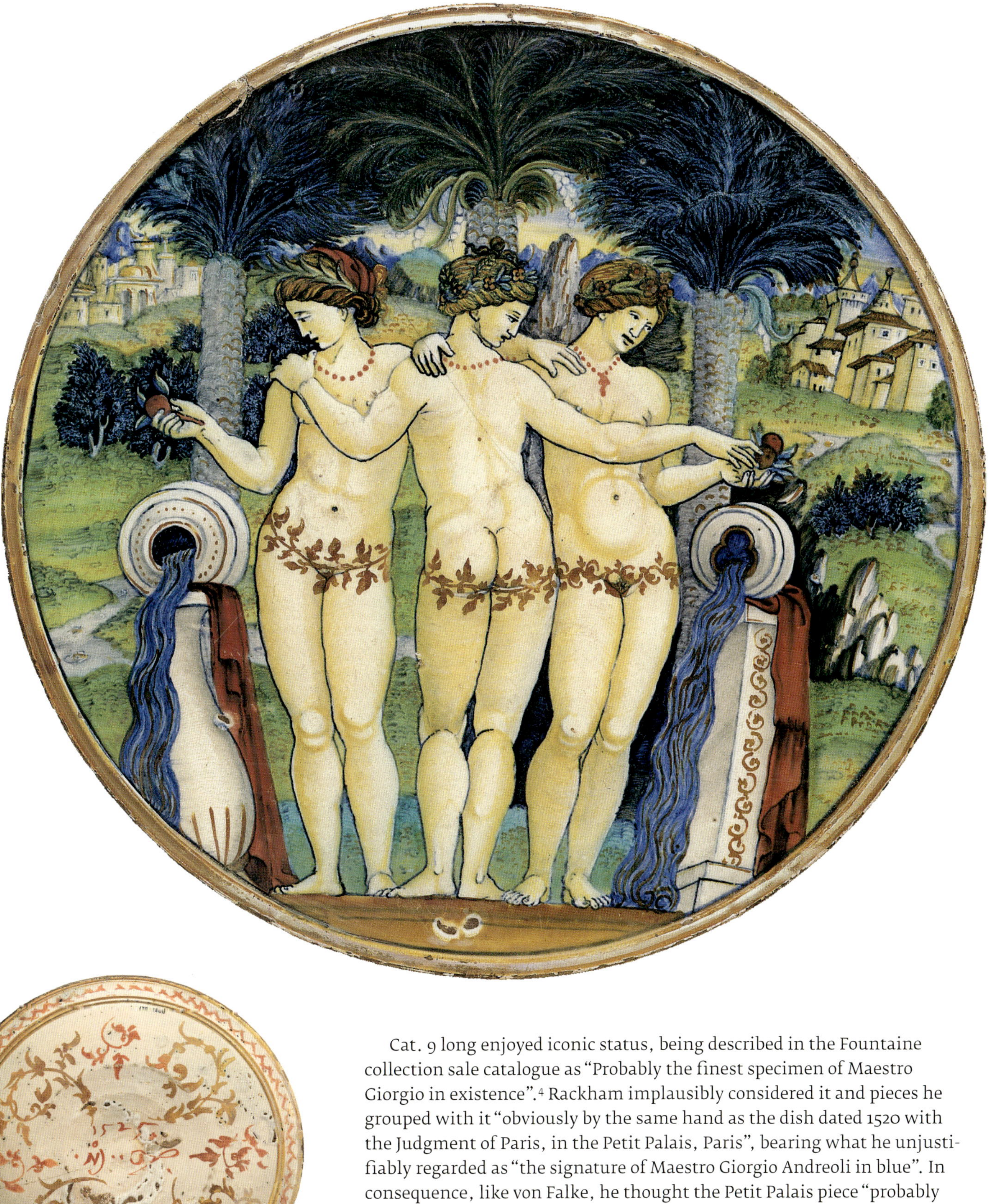

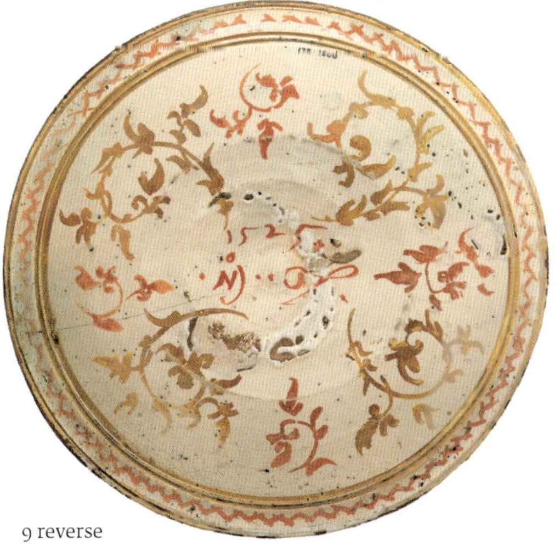



Cat. 9 long enjoyed iconic status, being described in the Fountaine collection sale catalogue as "Probably the finest specimen of Maestro Giorgio in existence".[4] Rackham implausibly considered it and pieces he grouped with it "obviously by the same hand as the dish dated 1520 with the Judgment of Paris, in the Petit Palais, Paris", bearing what he unjustifiably regarded as "the signature of Maestro Giorgio Andreoli in blue". In consequence, like von Falke, he thought the Petit Palais piece "probably entirely painted by the master himself, not merely lustred by him."[5] These misunderstandings invalidate much that Rackham and some later authors have written about this composite 'Painter of the Three Graces'.

## 10.  Large dish without foot ring: *Women Bathing*

Attributed to Francesco Xanto Avelli, Gubbio, in the workshop of Maestro Giorgio Andreoli; the border and pattern on the cistern painted at Gubbio, probably by Francesco Urbini; lustre added there by a hand other than Xanto's; dated 1525

D: 44.6 cm
London, Wallace Collection, C66


PROVENANCE

Prince Bandini Giustiniani collection, Rome; Baron de Parpart, Schloss Hunegg, Switzerland; purchased in 1872 by Sir Richard Wallace from A. Beurdeley, Paris.

BIBLIOGRAPHY

Darcel and Delange 1867–69, p. 34 and pl. lxv; Fortnum 1896, p. 167; Norman 1976, no. C66, (further bibliography cited); Fiocco and Gherardi 1998, p. 20, pl. v; Wilson 2002B, p. 120, pl. xxv and fig. 18; Mallet 2004, pp. 41–42 and pls. 9 and 10.

NOTES

1. *Ill. Bartsch* 27, p. 35, 340 (255) or p. 36, 341 (256). See also cat. 9.
2. *Ill. Bartsch* 26, p. 242, 245-I (197). See also cat. 4 and 5.
3. *Ill. Bartsch* 25, p. 75, 2 (249).
4. Rackham 1913, pp. 196 and 203.
5. Fiocco and Gherardi 1998, p. 29; Wilson 2002B, pp. 121–22; against this view see Mallet 2004, p. 41.
6. Mallet 1987, p. 332.


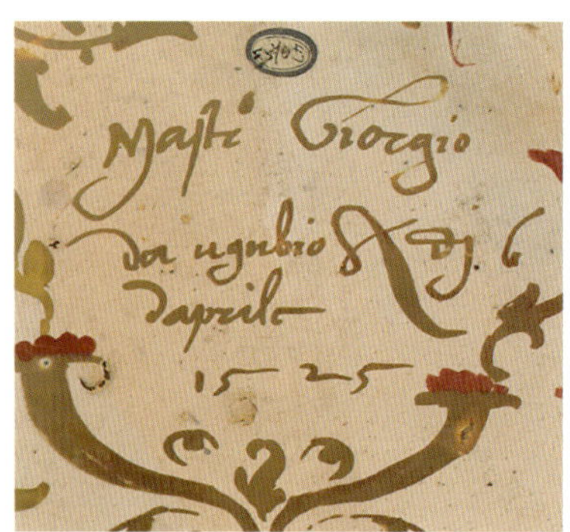

10 reverse (detail)

Polychrome and lustre. Centre, fourteen nude women bathing in a cistern set in a wooded landscape. The border of the dish painted on a dark blue ground with grotesques including animal and vegetable motifs, cornucopiae and military trophies. The date 1525 in blue is incorporated in the right-hand side of the border, and on a scroll are the words *ama la virtu* (love virtue), written in blue by a hand that is not Xanto's and is probably that of the painter responsible for the border.
Reverse: in red and gold lustre, running scrolls at border and leaf-scrolls centred by the inscription: *Mastro Giorgio / da ugubio adj 6 / daprile / 1525*, above twinned cornucopiae.

Centre, three women from Marcantonio Raimondi's print, *The Three Graces* (fig. 33, p. 64);[1] left, two foreground figures from Marcantonio's *Judgement of Paris* (fig. 31, p. 56);[2] right, three foreground figures from a woodcut of *Diana and Actaeon* by the engraver signing 'I.B.' with a bird (Giovanni Battista Palumba), whose engraving seems also to have suggested the trees in the middle distance.[3] As pointed out by Rackham, who first identified these design sources, the heads of the women in the second row were invented by the maiolica painter to fill gaps between the foreground figures.[4]

Long agreed to be by the same painter as cat. 9, this dish has shared the latter's critical fortune, being at one time implausibly attributed to the hand of Maestro Giorgio Andreoli himself. The pieces most securely by the hand responsible for cat. 9 and 10 are dateable to 1525 or, in a few cases, 1524, suggesting instead a talented painter working for the Andreoli under contract for perhaps no more than a year. This painter is not likely, as some authors have been tempted to suggest,[5] to be the painter Giovanni Luca da Castel Durante who agreed a one-year contract with Giorgio on 14 July 1525, because that was some three months after the date lustred on cat. 10.

The decorative polychrome border-pattern shows a command of flat pattern alien to Xanto's style; I have elsewhere proposed that Francesco Urbini may already at this time have been painting border-patterns at Gubbio.[6] The lustred handwriting on the reverse is certainly not Xanto's, so the addition of lustre is unlikely to have been done by him.

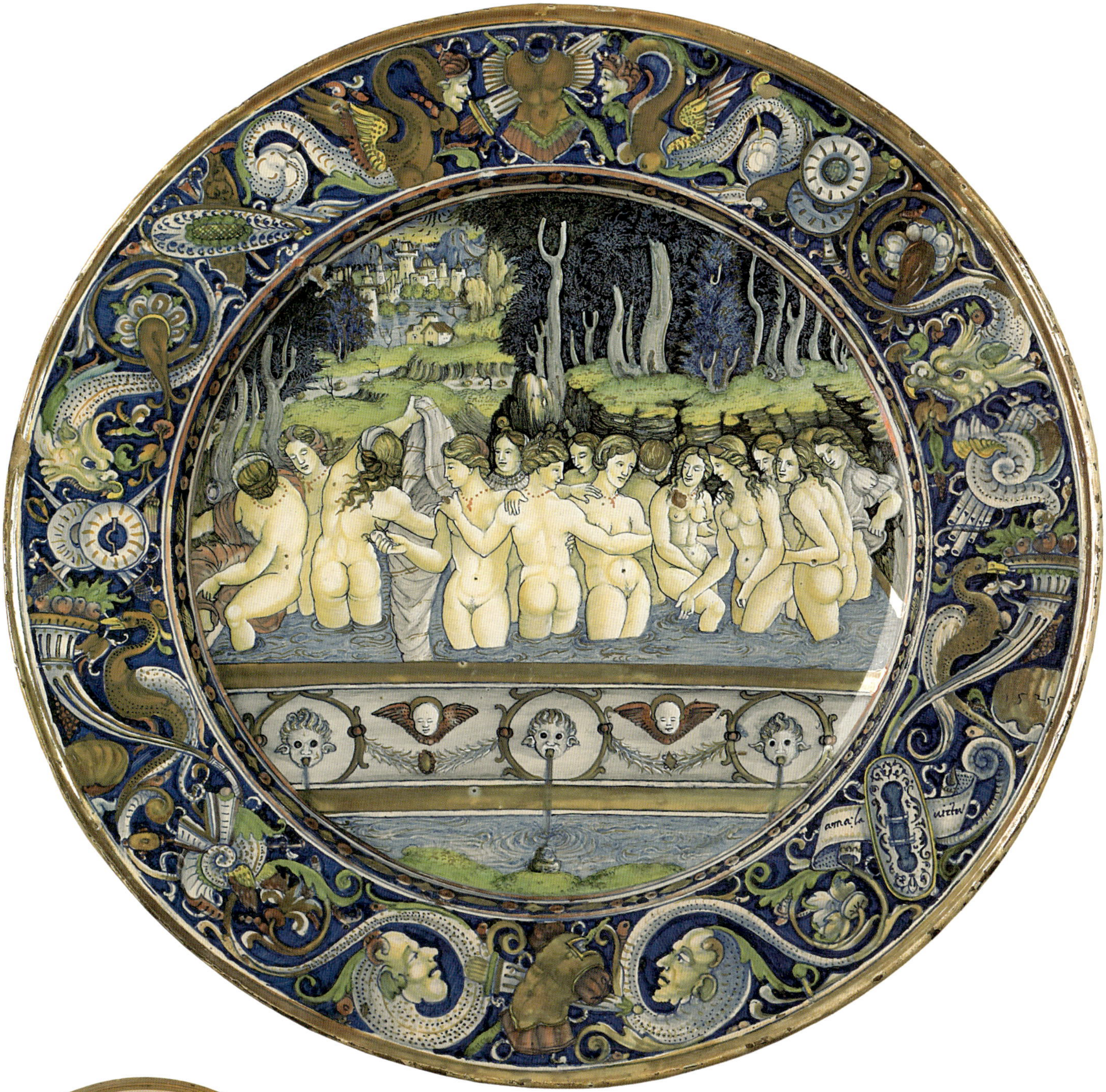

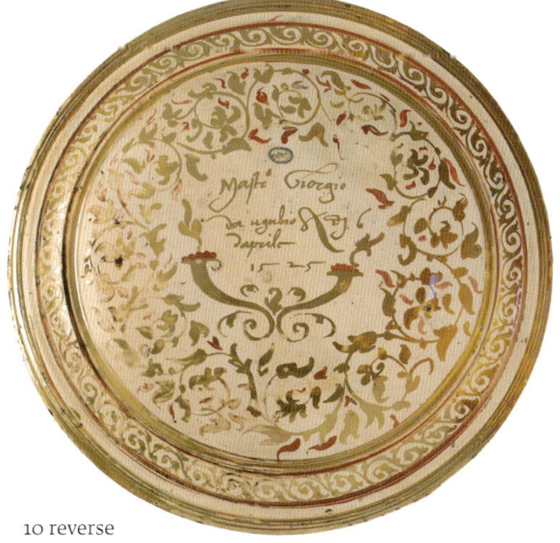

## 11.  Dish without foot ring: *An Allegory of Envy*

Attributed to Francesco Xanto Avelli, Gubbio, in the workshop of
Maestro Giorgio, the border and lustred decoration added there by another
hand or hands. Dated 1525

D: 40.5 cm
London, Victoria and Albert Museum, C.2200-1910



BIBLIOGRAPHY

Passeri 1857, p.43; Bohn 1876, lot 1926;
Fountaine sale 1884, lot 374; Falke 1934,
p. 332, fig. 7 (as by Giorgio); Rackham
1940, no. 674 (further bibliography cited);
Wilson 2002B, p. 120 and note 61 (grouped
with the larger 'S' service pieces).

NOTES

1. *Ill. Bartsch* 25, p. 298, 24 (405).
2. 8938-1863; Rackham 1940, no. 675.

Polychrome and lustre. Centre, an older woman gazing enviously at a young
couple seated to the left, a child at their feet; to the right, another young
couple stand embracing; in the background a road leads to a fortified town;
the well with a bead-like pattern; the border with a running pattern of
foliage and berries.
Reverse: in lustre, an ewer, leafy sprays and *1525 / Mº Gº*.
Slight restorations.

Quite closely copied from an engraving, *Old Woman and Two Amorous Couples*
(*Allegory of Envy?*), by Cristofano Robetta (fig. 34).[1]

   This dish bears the same lustred date, 1525, as cat. 7–10, and has correctly
been grouped with these. The landscape in particular invites comparisons
with such pieces from the 'S' service as cat. 7 and 8. By the same hand –
Xanto's, as argued here – is another version of this subject after Robetta
painted, without any border, on a low-footed dish, also in the Victoria and
Albert Museum.[2]

   The lustred representation, on the underside, of an ewer described by
Passeri (who owned this dish in Pesaro in the eighteenth century) as *un
boccaletto all'uso antico* (a little jug in antique style), is unique to this piece.
Possibly it indicates that the dish was a basin on which such an ewer was
meant to be placed.

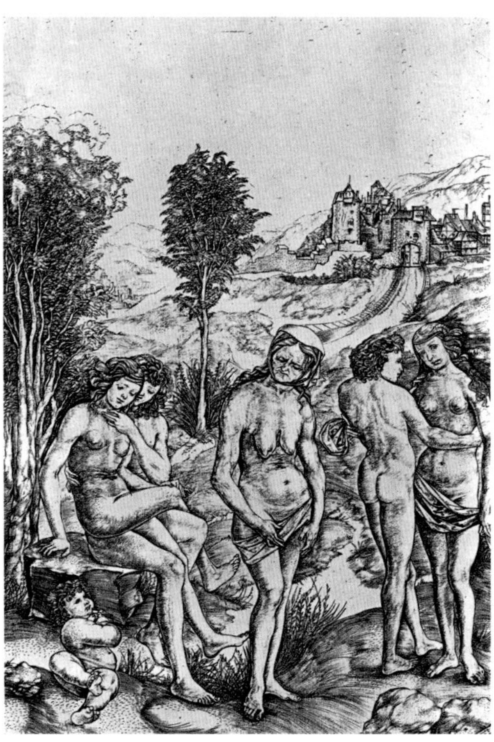

Fig. 34. Cristofano Robetta (*c.* 1462–
d. after 1534). *Old Woman and Two
Amorous Couples*, engraving

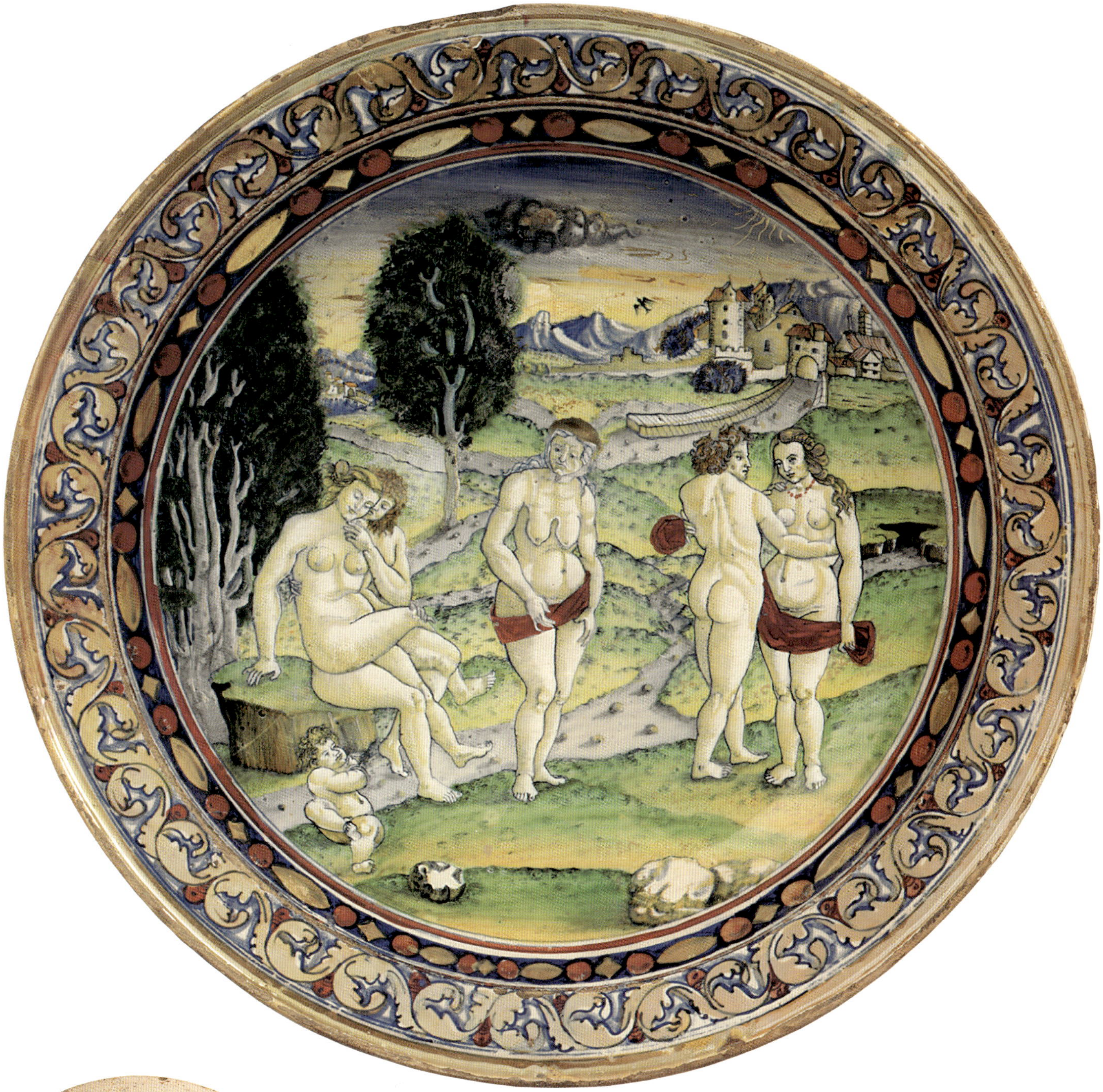

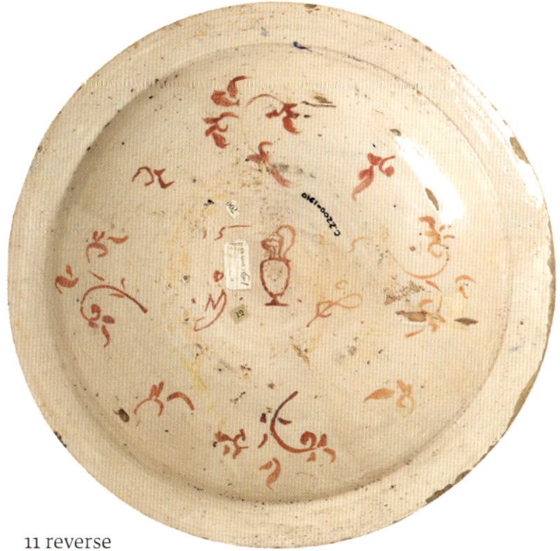

12. Bowl with broad border (*Tondino*):
 *Narcissus at the Fountain of Love*

Attributed to Francesco Xanto Avelli, Duchy of Urbino, *c.* 1525–26

D: 27.6 cm
London, Wallace Collection, C47


PROVENANCE

It is not known where Sir Richard Wallace acquired this piece, but he exhibited it at Bethnal Green.

BIBLIOGRAPHY

Bethnal Green 1872–75, no. 1486; Rackham 1957, 5, p. 102 (as *The Fountain of Love*); Norman 1976, no. C47 (further bibliography cited).

NOTES

1. Ovid, *Metamorphoses*, Book III, lines 339–510.
2. Ballardini 1938A, 89, 95, 276R.
3. Rackham and Ballardini 1933, pp. 393–407, no. 6, fig. 5.


Polychrome. Centre, Narcissus seated, leaning over the lower basin of a fountain at the summit of whose upper basin balances a blindfolded Cupid shooting with his bow; to the left the nymph, Echo, to the right five other lovelorn nymphs; rocky landscape with trees and a distant sea.
Reverse: plain white.
Broken in the upper left-hand side and repaired.

The design appears to be original to the maiolica painter.

According to Ovid,[1] Narcissus, son of the river god Cephisus and the nymph, Liriope, rejected the advances of the nymph, Echo, instead falling in love with his own image reflected in the waters of a spring, as a result of which he was changed into the flower that bears his name. A version of the same subject formerly in the Schlossmuseum, Berlin, dated 1533,[2] at a time when Xanto had become more dependent on prints, lacked the freedom of invention with which the story is told on cat. 12.

Ever since Rackham and Ballardini defined the painter 'F.R.', cat. 12, though unsigned, has been accepted as his.[3] In his catalogue, Norman accepted as by Xanto the 'F.L.R.' pieces like cat. 16 and pieces with the y/Φ flourish like cat. 24, but felt "the differences between the style, colour and drawing of the works signed *F.R.* and of those signed *F.L.R.* seem so great as to make it unlikely that only one hand was involved." He therefore retained for the present piece an attribution to Faenza. The problem is discussed in the Introduction, pp. 33–34 and under cat. 13, but it may here be pointed out that the stylistic gap pinpointed by Norman is more readily bridged if Gubbio pieces from 1524–25, such as cat. 4–11, are accepted as by F.R./Xanto. The figure of Echo on cat. 12 is not far removed in style from the Phaedra to the left on cat. 24, and the geology of the foreground can be compared with that of, for instance, cat. 1, 4 and 7.

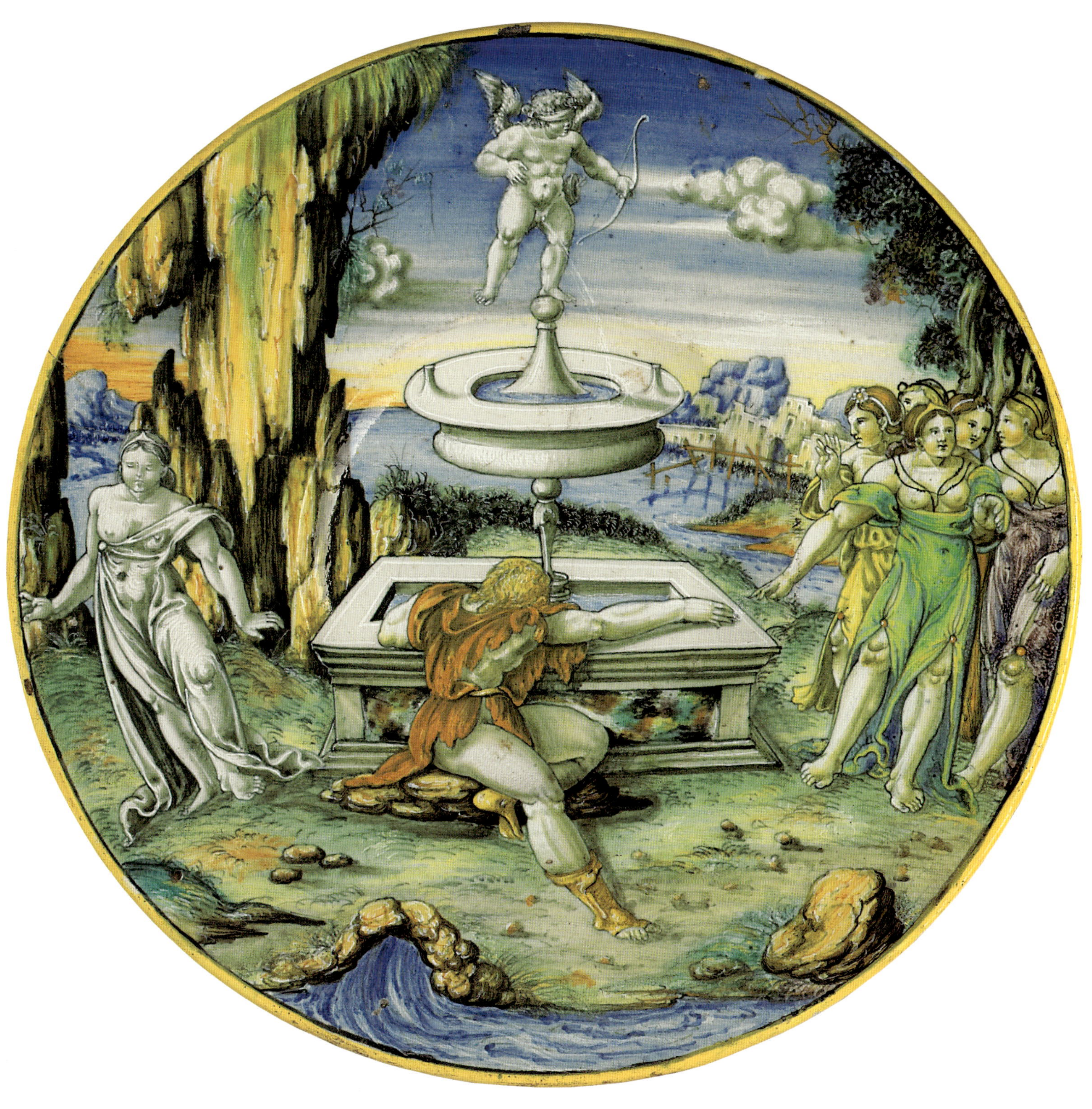

## 13. Dish on low foot (*Coppa*): *Solomon building the Temple*

Attributed to Francesco Xanto Avelli, Duchy of Urbino,
signed F.R., *c*. 1525–27

D: 27.8 cm
London, British Museum, PG&E 1855, 12-1, 102

PROVENANCE

Ralph Bernal.

BIBLIOGRAPHY

Bernal sale 1855, Bohn 1876, lot 2047;
Wilson 1987, no. 69 (further bibliography
cited); Thornton and Wilson 2007, no. 154.

NOTES

1. Robinson 1856, p. 13.
2. Rackham and Ballardini 1933,
   pp. 393–407.
3. Ballardini 1938B, pp. 123–24; Rackham
   1957, 5, pp. 99–113; Mallet 1992,
   pp. 142–43.
4. Mallet 1971A, pp. 170–183; Mallet 1976,
   pp. 4–19; Mallet 2004, pp. 37–54.

Polychrome. Left, a group of four men centred by a bearded man (Solomon?)
watch the construction of a building, right; in the background a castle
seen across a lake; in the foreground a seated black and white dog.
Signed, lower right, *F.R.*
Reverse: plain
Restorations to rim.

Like cat. 12 this composition appears to be original to the painter.

Solomon's building of the Temple (I *Kings*, Ch. 6; II *Chronicles*, 2–3) is rare on maiolica.

This and cat. 3, 14 and 15 are four of only six known pieces signed by the painter 'F.R.', already mentioned (as Faenza) by J.C. Robinson in 1856,[1] and in 1933 made the subject of an important study by Ballardini and Rackham, who assembled other, unsigned, pieces round them, believing 'F.R.' worked at Faenza. The attribution to Faenza followed from a belief (no longer held) that a dish marked as from the Casa Pirota workshop in Faenza was by the same hand, and seemed supported by the fact that two pieces (cat. 14 and 15) were painted on pale blue *berettino* grounds such as were commonly used at Faenza.[2] Later Ballardini, but not Rackham, came to believe 'F.R.' might after all be an early signature of Xanto ('Francesco Rovigiese').[3] The present writer queried the Faenza attribution and has come round to the view that 'F.R.', after a spell working for Maestro Giorgio at Gubbio from 1524–25, developed into the painter whose inscriptions often terminate with a flourish resembling a 'y' or a 'Φ', and who, around 1530, began to sign in full as Francesco Xanto Avelli.[4] See Introduction, pp. 34–35.

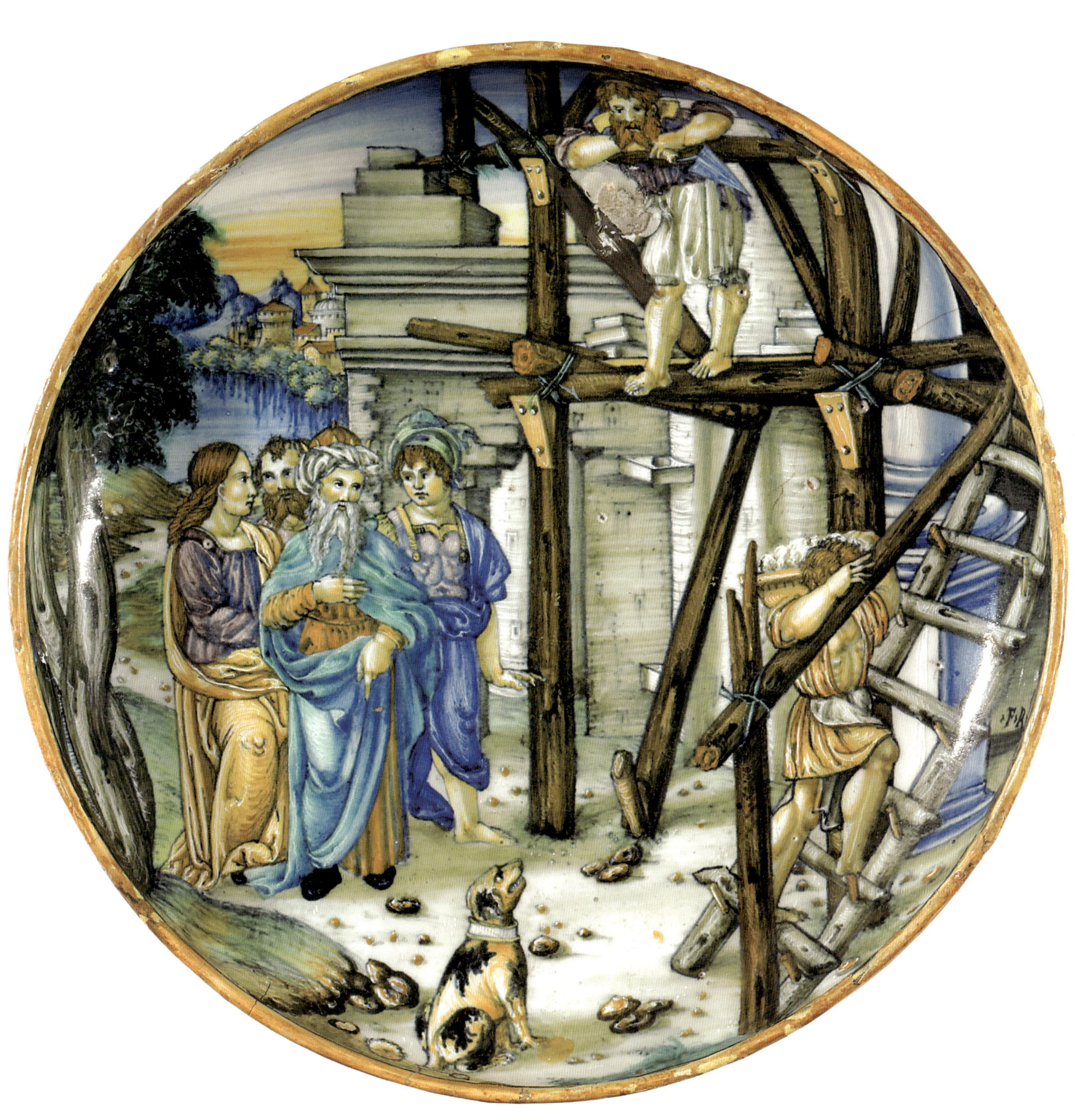

## 14. Plate with broad border (*Tondino*): *Dido entertaining Aeneas*

Attributed to Francesco Xanto Avelli, Duchy of Urbino, signed *F.R.*, *c*. 1525–26

D: 25.5 cm
London, Victoria and Albert Museum, C.2117-1910

PROVENANCE

Madame d'Yvon; George Salting, by whom bequeathed in 1910.

BIBLIOGRAPHY

Darcel and Delange 1867–69, pl. lxxvii (as possibly by the itinerant Xanto, probably at Forlì or Fabriano); D'Yvon sale 1892, lot 56; Rackham and Ballardini 1933, p. 399 and fig. 11 (as Faenza, not by Xanto); Rackham 1940, no. 795 (further bibliography cited); Mallet 1976, p.18 and fig. 4.

NOTES

1. *Ill. Bartsch* 27, p. 49, 352-I (264).
2. *Ill. Bartsch* 25 (Commentary), p. 349, .026; pp. 347–49, .025.
3. Mallet 1976, cover-illustration and figs. 1 and 3.
4. Wilson 2002B, p. 120, figs. 20 and 21.

Polychrome on a pale blue (*berettino*) ground. Right, seated next to Aeneas at a round table, Dido embraces Cupid disguised as Ascanius; centre, a harpist and other attendants; left, further attendants approach carrying precious vessels. On masonry in the foreground are the initials .F.R. in black. Reverse: plain pale blue.

Derived from a scene at the bottom right of Marcantonio Raimondi's *Quos Ego* print (fig. 35),[1] which represents scenes from Virgil's *Aeneid*. Since the scene is in reverse, however, it is likely to have been copied from Giovanni Antonio da Brescia's copy,[2] a conclusion also encouraged by the fact that another plate signed by 'F.R.', showing Dido receiving Aeneas at Carthage,[3] is not only reversed from Marcantonio's print, but also accords with the Giovanni Antonio copy in its spelling of the name *Cartagine* without an 'h'. Two lustred plates dated 1525 in the Metropolitan Museum,[4] both surely by Xanto, are reversed from the upper scenes on the *Quos Ego*.

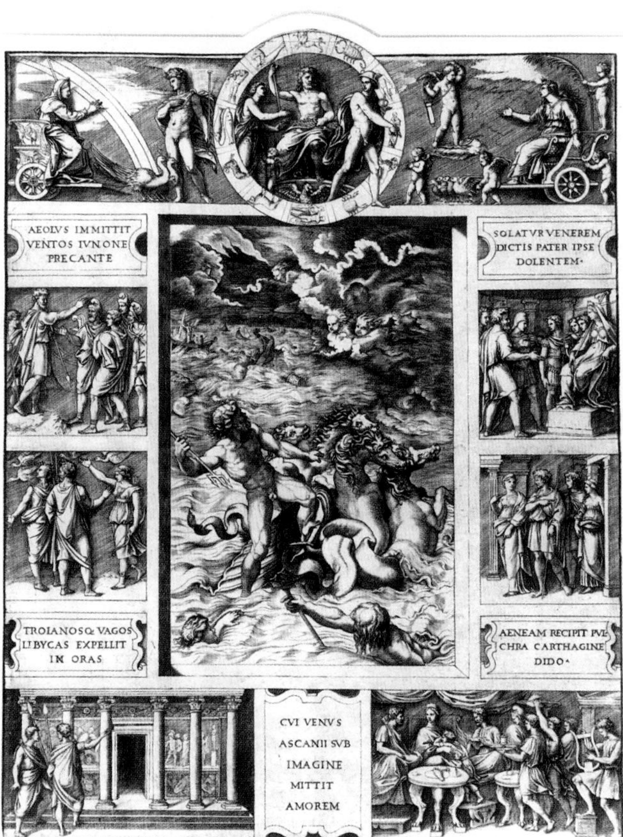


Fig. 35. Marcantonio Raimondi after Raphael, *Quos Ego* (*Neptune calming the Tempest which Aeolus raised against Aeneas' Fleet*), engraving

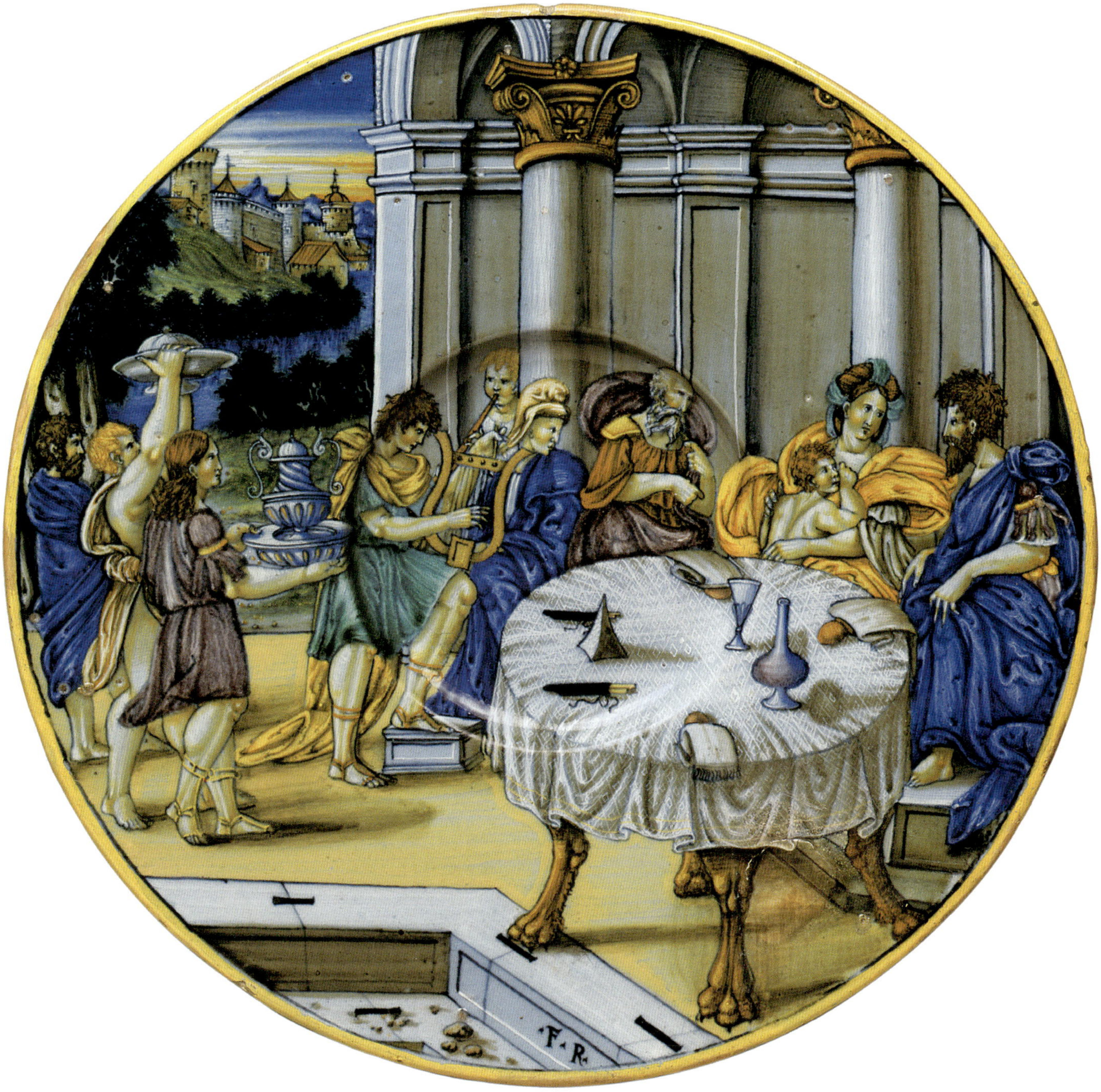

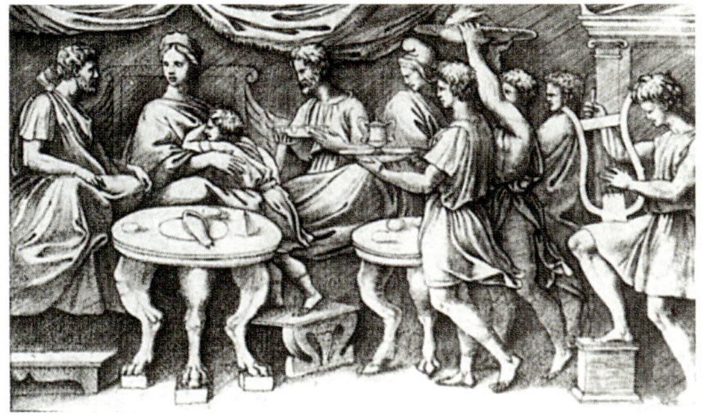

Detail from border of fig. 35

Cupid, disguised as Ascanius, infant son of Aeneas, wins the heart of Queen Dido of Carthage.

For the signature 'F.R.' see cat. 13 and Introduction pp. 27–28 and 33–34.

This plate, painted on a pale blue ground that exactly matches the tint of cat. 15, was considered strong evidence that F.R. worked at Faenza, where such blue ground-colours were often used. However there is no technical difficulty in adding blue pigments to a tin-glaze, and if one supposes Faentine influence necessary to have suggested the idea, it is worth remembering that one of Xanto's fellow strikers at Urbino in 1530 was a certain Michele da Faenza.

## 15.  Plaque: *Christ carrying the Cross*

Possibly by Francesco Xanto Avelli, at Urbino or in the Marches,
or else by the 'Painter of the Triumph of the Moon', working at Forlì.
Signed *F.R.*, *c*. 1525–28

H: 51.0 cm; W: 33.0 cm
London, Victoria and Albert Museum, 4351-1857


PROVENANCE

Purchased 1857.

BIBLIOGRAPHY

Fortnum 1873, pp. 479 and 516–17; Rackham
and Ballardini 1933, p. 404; Rackham
1940, no. 799 (further bibliography cited);
Rackham 1957, p. 99.

NOTES

1. *Ill. Bartsch* 26, p. 44, 28-I (34) or p. 45,
   28A-I (34) respectively.
2. Mallet 2004, p. 46, fig. 13.
3. Fortnum 1896, p. 261.
4. Rackham and Ballardini 1933, p. 404;
   Rackham 1957, p. 99.
5. Mallet 1994, pp. 50–55.
6. Fiocco and Gherardi 2002A, pp. 77–83 and
   pp. 97–98; *eaedem*, 2004, pp. 19–24.
7. Robinson 1863, p. 405, no. 5173.


Polychrome on a pale blue (*berettino*) ground. Centre, Christ, stumbling under
the Cross and gazing backwards at the Virgin Mary who extends her arms;
the two other Maries follow among a throng of soldiers both mounted and
on foot; in the background a road leads past some trees towards Golgotha.
In the foreground, right, is a square stone marked .F.R..
Reverse: unglazed body .

From Marcantonio Raimondi's engraving *The Bearing of the Cross* (fig. 36) (or
Francesco Villamena's copy) after the painting by Raphael known as the
*Spasimo di Sicilia*, in the Prado, Madrid.[1] The maiolica painter has cropped
the top of the printed image.

For the painter signing 'F.R.' see cat. 13 and Introduction, p. 27–28 and
33–34. Were it not for the initials .F.R. in its foreground cat. 15 might never,
due to its difference in style, have been grouped with the other 'F.R.' pieces.
However its *berettino* blue ground is a good match to that of cat. 14, a more
typical work of 'F.R.', while being, for instance, different in colour from that
of a fragment at Berlin attributable to 'F.R.'.[2]. Attribution of the *Spasimo*
plaque to the early Xanto involves supposing that on this occasion Xanto
modified his style to mimic that of the print he was copying, adopting a
print-like manner of hatching and stippling.

On the other hand Fortnum long ago made an association of the whole
'F.R.' category with a dish in the Rothschild Collection at Waddesdon Manor,
in the foreground of which is a stone inscribed .F.[3] Not without hesitation
Rackham and Ballardini included the *Spasimo* panel among works by 'F.R.',
though Rackham later confessed to uncertainty.[4] Though far less sophisticated than the *Spasimo* plaque, the Waddesdon dish shares with it a number
of mannerisms not otherwise found on 'F.R.' pieces nor on Xanto's later
work, notably a looping line for draperies, a block-like handling of foliage
and a speckled treatment of the foreground. In writing of the Waddesdon
dish I took its letter 'F.' to be part of an inscription *ANEA AN*, referring to that
dish's subject, the boyhood of Aeneas with his father, Anchises,[5] in which
case the .F., though somewhat distanced from the rest of the inscription,
might stand for 'Filius', that is 'son of Anchises'.

Fiocco and Gherardi have recently brought the Waddesdon dish into
relationship with work attributable to a painter they name 'The Painter of
the Triumph of the Moon', whose work they convincingly trace to Forlì.[6]
Possibly the *Spasimo* plaque, which shares some of this painter's mannerisms,
should be assigned to him and not to Xanto. It is interesting that already
in 1863 J. C. Robinson proposed that the Waddesdon dish and the *Spasimo*
plaque were by the same hand.[7]

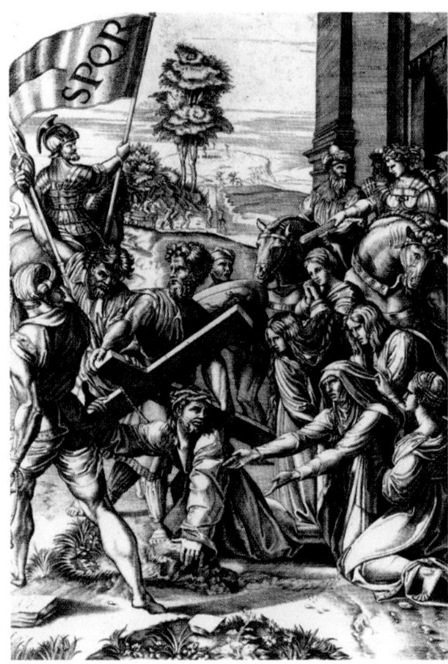

Fig. 36. Marcantonio Raimondi after
Raphael, *The Bearing of the Cross*, engraving

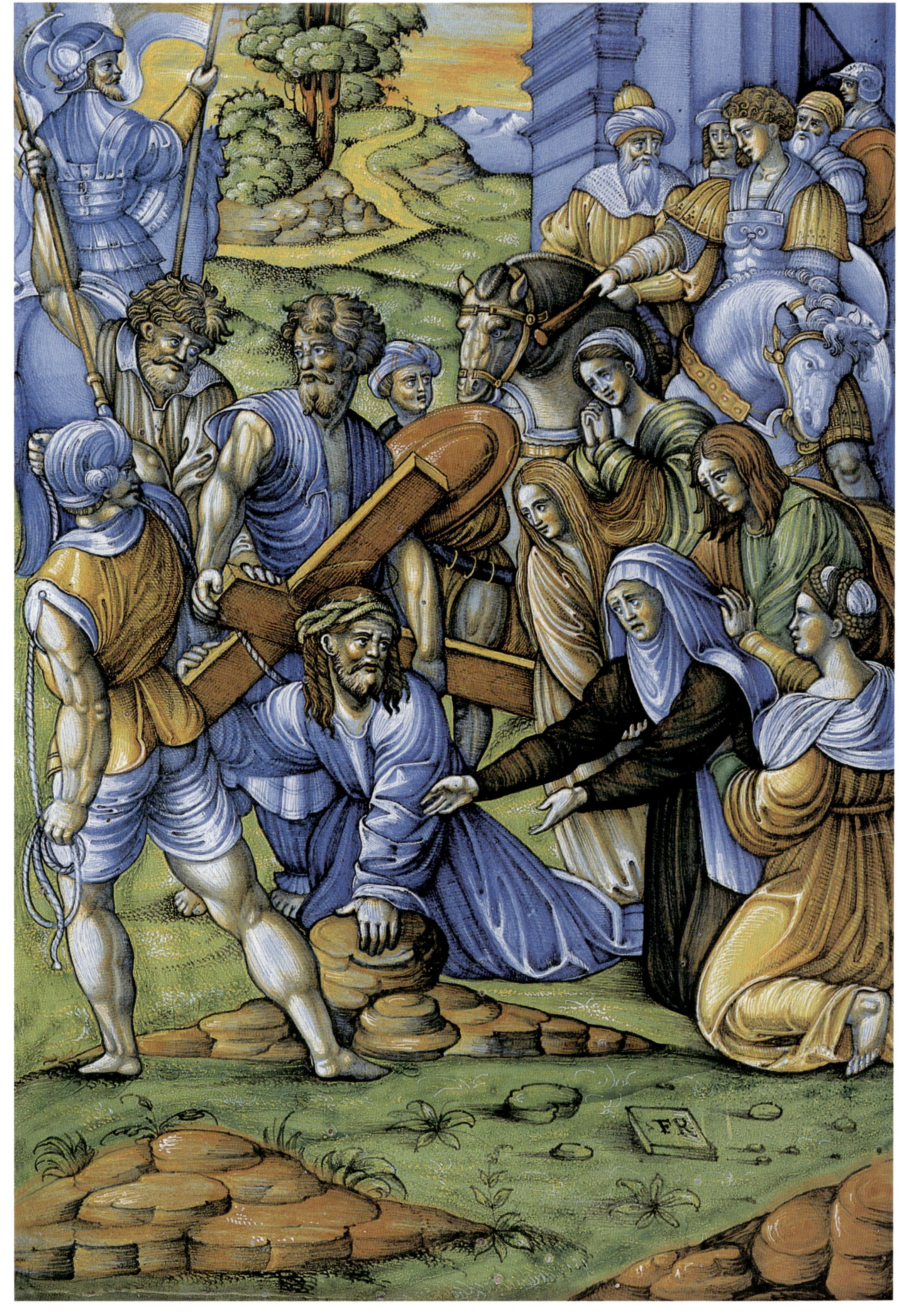

## 16.   Large dish on low foot: *A Roman Lion-Hunt*

Attributed to Francesco Xanto Avelli, Duchy of Urbino (Urbino?);
signed *.f.L.R.*, *c*. 1529

D: 38.0 cm
London, British Museum, PG&E 1970, 12-11, I

PROVENANCE

The Rev. Thomas Berney; Fernand Adda.

BIBLIOGRAPHY

Robinson 1863, no. 5240 (as an early and
fine work of Xanto, painted before 1530);
Rackham and Ballardini 1933, pp. 402–03
and p. 404, fig. 19 (as Faenza, by 'F.R.');
Rackham 1959, no. 297 (further bibliography cited); Tait, 1976, pp. 3–6; Wilson
1987, no. 70; Thornton and Wilson 2007,
no. 155.

NOTES

1. *Ill. Bartsch* 27, p. 110, 422 (317); Bober
   and Rubinstein 1986, pp. 232–33, 199
   and 199a.
2. Rackham and Ballardini 1933, p. 402,
   figs. 16 and 17; Conti 1971, front-cover
   illustrations.
3. Ballardini 1933, 205, 235, 345R; Cioci
   1993, pp.35–36, figs. 5 and 6.

Polychrome. In the foreground a lion-cub leaps between the legs of a
huntress and over a dead stag to attack a seated woman; right foreground,
a larger lion is speared by horsemen; in the background, turbaned Orientals
and others, an arch, trees and distant hills.
Reverse: white with, towards the rim, blue plant-scroll. The foot outlined
in yellow; within the foot a dark blue inscription: *Que stabant vix hospitibus
spectanda sepulchra; Quellibet arbitrio iam videt. illa suo. .f.L.R.*

Copied from Marcantonio Raimondi's engraving (fig. 38) after a Roman
sarcophagus of the mid-third century A.D., formerly in the atrium of old
St Peter's (fig. 37).[1] During the seventeenth century the relief was moved to
the facade of the Casino of the Palazzo Rospigliosi in Rome and is now in the
Palazzo Rospigliosi. The dog-Latin inscription, derived from the print, may
be translated as: "the sarcophagi which used to stand almost out of sight
of visitors are now seen and judged by whoever wishes."

The oblong Roman marble relief underwent a double transformation,
from sculptural relief to engraving, to circular maiolica dish. Marcantonio
'restored' the missing head of a hound, misunderstanding it as a small lion,
a mistake followed by the maiolica painter. The deceased is shown twice on
the sarcophagus: left, about to mount his horse; centre, with spear raised
to kill the lion.

The signature 'F.L.R.' is recorded on only two other pieces, always on
the reverse: one, a fragment in the Bargello at Florence, is inscribed *Nosce te
ipsum.*;[2] the other, at Budapest, is lustred and bears the lustred date 1529,[3]
earlier than any date found on pieces fully signed by Xanto. No interpretation
of the letter 'L' has yet been generally acccepted, but 'F.L.R.' is thought to be
a signature intermediate in time between *F.R.* and *Francesco Xanto Avelli*.

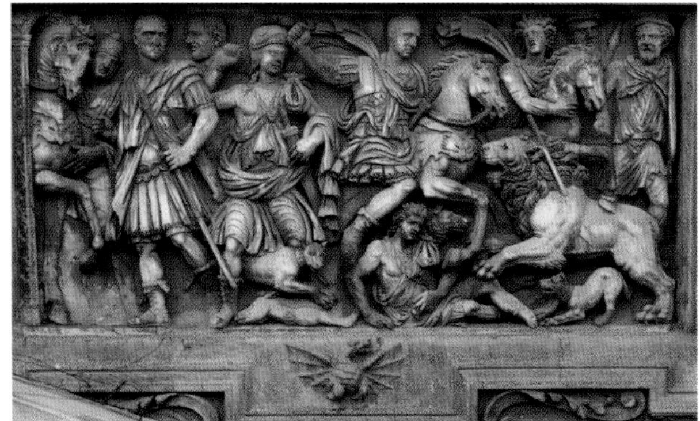

Fig. 37. Roman sarcophagus, detail showing a lion-hunt,
mid-third century A.D., marble, Palazzo Rospigliosi, Rome

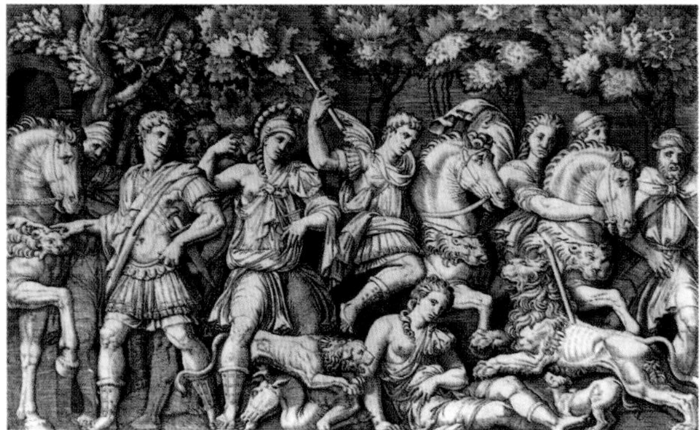

Fig. 38. Marcantonio Raimondi after an ancient sarcophagus,
*The Lion-Hunt*, engraving

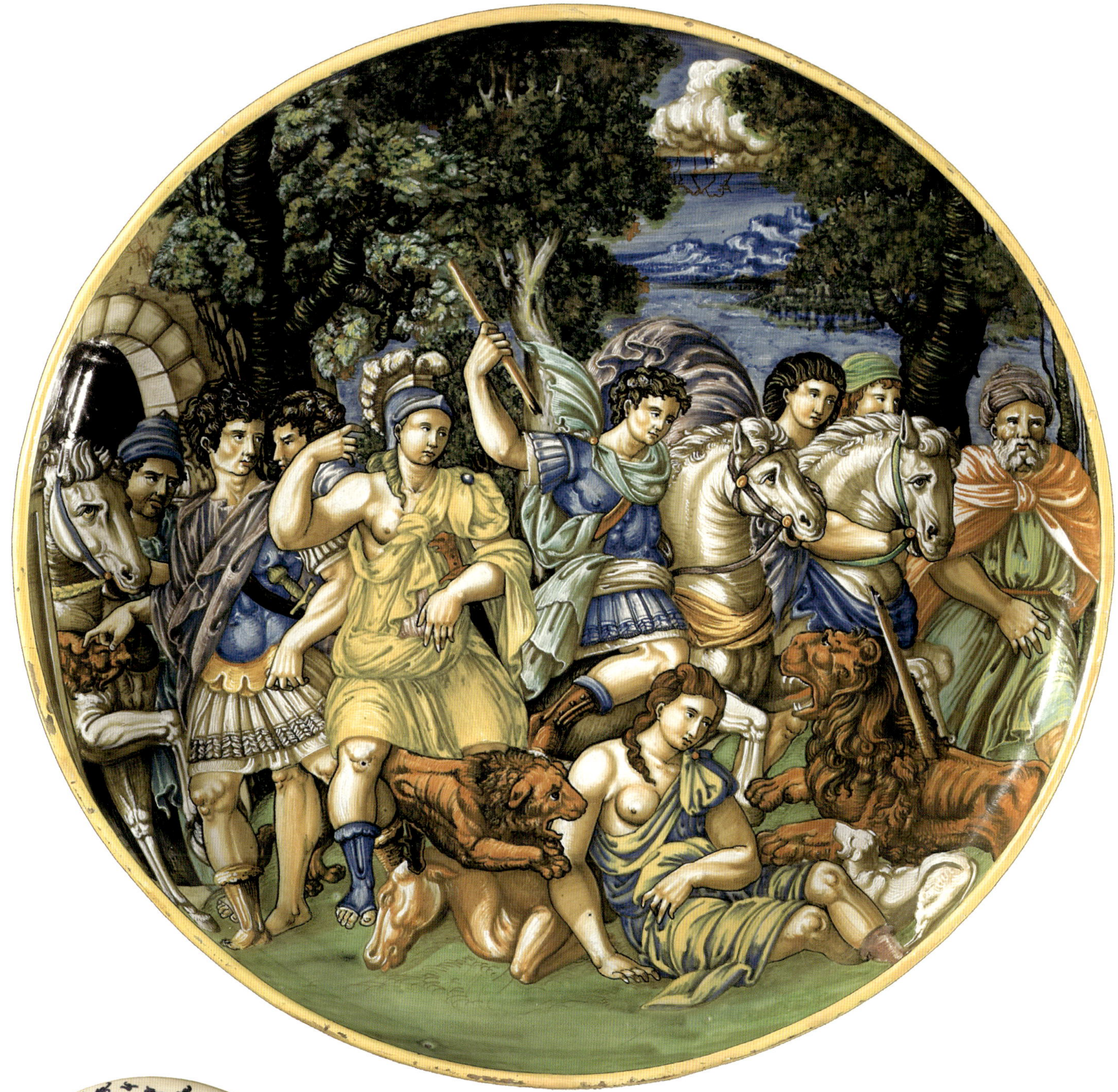

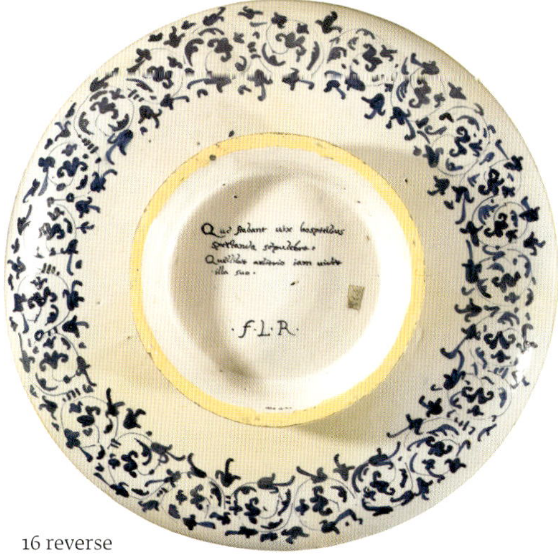

17.  Plate: *The Metamorphosis of Callisto*

Attributed to Francesco Xanto Avelli, Urbino, *c.* 1525–27

D: 27.5 cm
London, Victoria and Albert Museum, C.19-1922

PROVENANCE

Montferrand collection; Morland
collection; Alexander Nesbitt collection;
given in 1922 through the National Art
Collections Fund to the Victoria and
Albert Museum by Henry Oppenheimer.

BIBLIOGRAPHY

Rackham 1922 (as by Nicolò Pellipario or,
as we would now say, Nicola da Urbino);
Rackham 1940, no. 548 (as by Pellipario,
further bibliography given); Mallet 2004,
p. 45 and p. 47, fig. 16 (as by Xanto
working at Urbino in close contact with
Nicola).

NOTES

1. Rackham 1922.
2. Mallet 1976.
3. Mallet 2004, p. 45 and p. 47, figs. 15
   and 16.

Polychrome. Foreground right, Arcas holds three hounds on the leash
while he raises his spear; foreground left, a white hound attacks Callisto
in the form of a bear; background, a landscape with trees, buildings and
mountains seen across a lake; in the sky is a star. Suspended from a tree
is a shield of arms (Bonzi of Florence), *Azure, a bend sinister, or, between three
gimlets, 2 and 1 of the second and in chief three fleurs de lys or between the points of a label
of four gules.*
Reverse: plain white.

No engraved source has been identified for this plate.

According to Ovid (*Metamorphoses,* II, 466–507) the nymph Callisto had had
an affair with Jupiter, whose wife, Juno, took her revenge by turning Callisto
into a bear. Callisto's young son, Arcas, encountered this bear one day while
out hunting and, not recognising her as his mother, was about to spear her
when Jupiter stayed his hand, installing mother and son in the heavens as
adjacent stars, known as 'the Bear'.

In 1922, when this Callisto plate was re-united in the Victoria and Albert
Museum with cat. 18, the only other known piece bearing the Bonzi arms,
the two were not unnaturally given the same attribution.[1] Since cat. 18 is a
fine and characteristic work of Nicola da Urbino (then mistakenly identified
as Nicolò Pellipario), Bernard Rackham assumed the Callisto plate must also
be by him. Rackham dated both plates *c.* 1520, some five years earlier than
now seems likely (see cat. 18). When cat. 17 and 18 are examined together it
will be noticed how well they match one another in colours, balance of tone
and certain mannerisms in handling clouds and trees. However a harder
look reveals underlying differences in draughtsmanship: the figure of Arcas
lacks the suppleness of line with which Andromeda and Perseus are drawn
on cat. 18; the hounds on cat. 17 resemble those on cat. 13 and on a dish
at Melbourne,[2] both signed F.R.; the dagger-like reflections in the lake on
cat. 17 resemble those on several 'F.R.' pieces, including cat. 13. I therefore
recently suggested Xanto, in his 'F.R.' phase, as author of cat. 17, very
evidently working alongside Nicola.[3] Since Nicola is not known to have
worked outside Urbino, this implies that Xanto was in Urbino around 1525
or soon after.

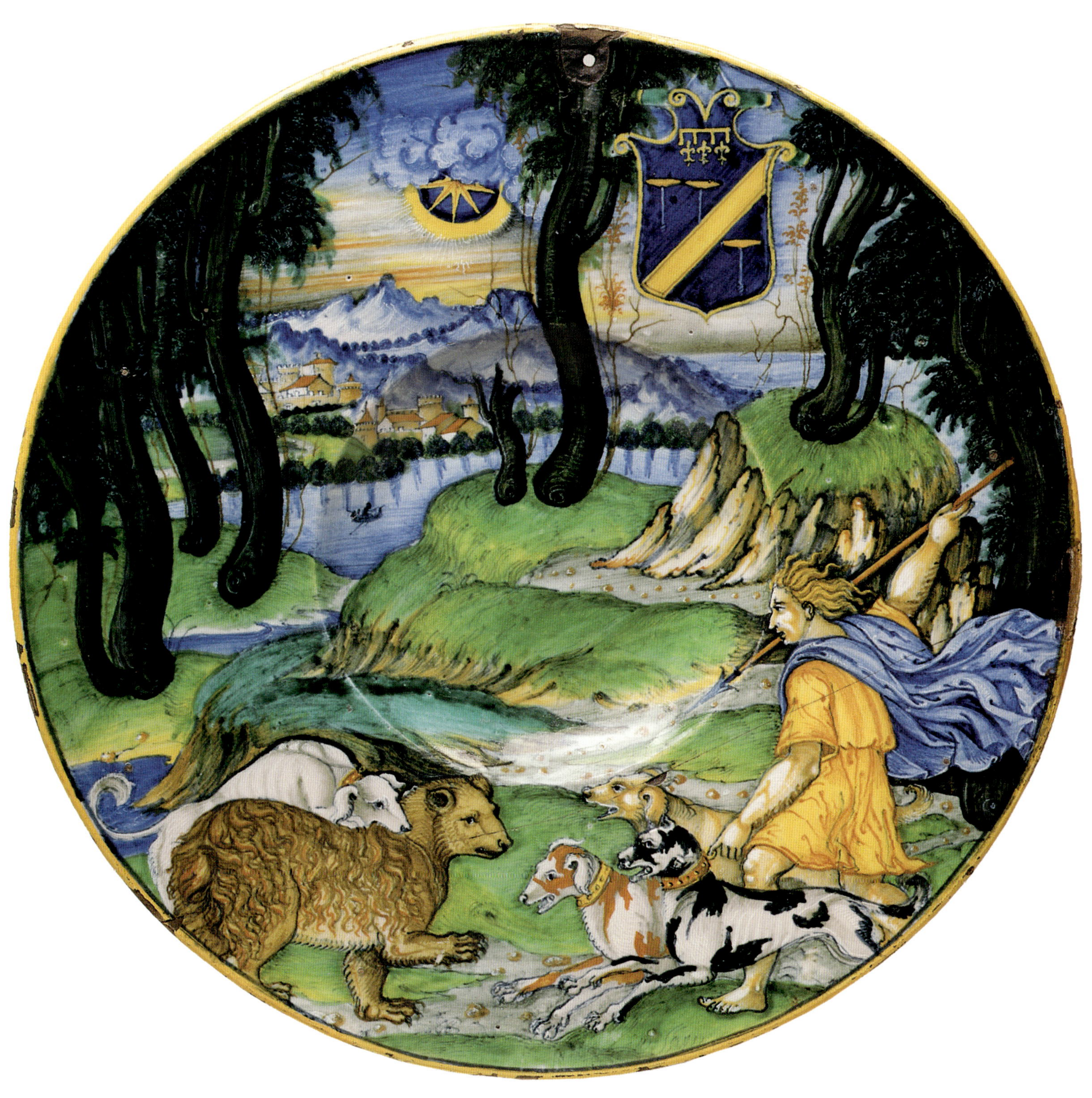

## 18.  Plate: *Perseus and Andromeda*

Attributed to Nicola da Urbino, Urbino, *c.* 1525–27

D: 27.0 cm
London, Victoria and Albert Museum, C.2227-1910

PROVENANCE
George Salting Bequest, 1910.

BIBLIOGRAPHY
Burlington Fine Art Club 1887, no. 197;
Rackham 1922; Rackham 1940, no. 549
(further bibliography cited); Mallet 2004,
p. 45 and p. 47, fig.15.

NOTES
1. Illustrated in Rasmussen 1989,
   Appendix 1, p. 249, 67.10.
2. Curnow 1992, no. 64.

Polychrome. Left, the naked Andromeda bound to a rock; foreground, a dragon-like monster emerges from a pool while, right, Perseus descends in a cloud, with cutlass raised to protect her. In the background a lakeland landscape with walled town and mountains. From a tree, centre, hangs a shield bearing the arms of Bonzi of Florence (see cat. 17).
Reverse: plain white.
Slight restoration at the top, running through part of the shield of arms.

The iconography, more than the composition, seems adapted from a woodcut of the subject contained in *Ovidio Metamorphoseos Vulgare*, an Italian language digest of Ovid's *Metamorphoses*, issued at Venice in a number of editions from 1497 onwards.

According to Ovid (*Metamorphoses*, IV, lines 663–739) Andromeda, the innocent daughter of an Ethiopian king, had been chained to a rock as a sacrifice to a sea-monster to pay the penalty for some words her mother had spoken. Perseus, son of Jupiter and Danae, was flying by with the aid of his winged hat and sandals when he saw her and fell in love. He killed the monster and was rewarded with the hand of Andromeda in marriage. Nicola da Urbino painted this subject with considerable variations at least twice: on the Este-Gonzaga service[1] and on the Calini service.[2] In those cases, unlike cat. 18, Nicola included an incident represented in the Venetian woodcuts but not in Ovid, where Perseus arrives on the winged horse, Pegasus, bearing the decapitated head of the Gorgon.

The case for attributing this plate to Nicola rests on its close similarity in style to the Este-Gonzaga service and the Calini service, both of which have long been accepted as fully autograph works by Nicola. Though cat. 17, which bears the same arms, was accepted by Rackham and other authors until recently as also painted by Nicola, in the opinion of the present writer cat. 17 should be attributed to Xanto during the period when he was signing as 'F.R.'.

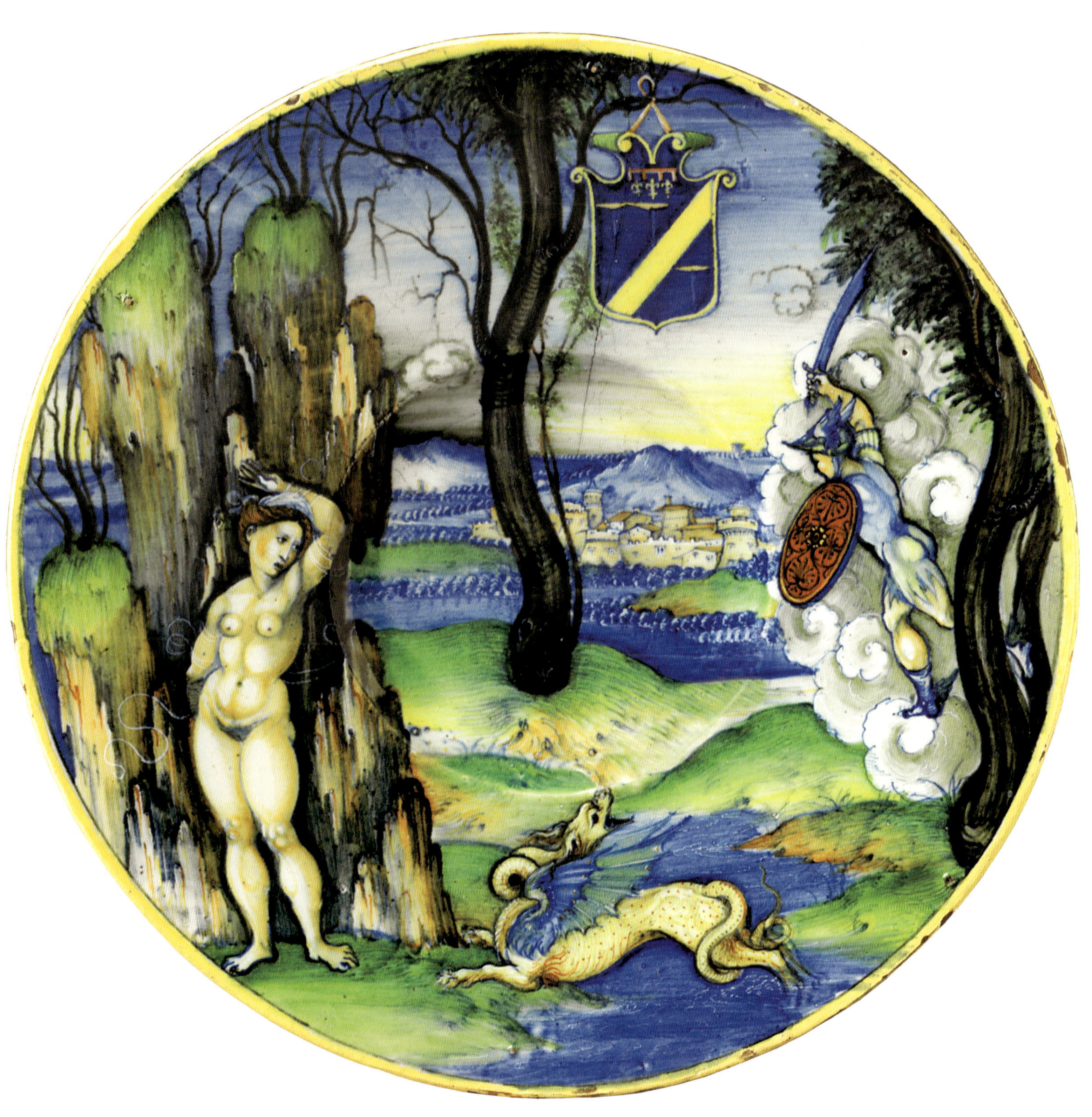

# 19.  Large dish on low foot (*Coppa*): *Dance of Cupids*

Attributed to Francesco Xanto Avelli, Urbino, *c*.1527–28

D: 26.9 cm
London, Wallace Collection, C46

PROVENANCE

Isaac Falcke.

BIBLIOGRAPHY

Robinson 1863, no. 5211 (grouped with
pieces now recognised as by 'F.R.'/
Xanto and attributed to Faenza or Forlì,
*c*. 1520–30); Rackham and Ballardini 1933,
p. 401 and p. 403, fig. 18 (as by 'F.R.'
working at Faenza); Norman 1976, no. C46
(as by 'F.R.' working at Faenza; further
bibliography cited).

NOTES

1. *Ill. Bartsch* 26, p. 215, 217-I (177); p. 216,
   217A (177); p. 216, 217C (177).
2. Wilson 2002B, p. 120 and p. 119, fig. 18.

Polychrome. Across the dish's centre winged, naked Cupids and wingless *putti*
link hands and dance in a ring. In the background is an arched doorway
flanked with garlands, through which appears a landscape with distant hills;
above the arch and down the sides of the dish are draped dark blue curtains.
Reverse: plain.
The foot ground away. Broken diagonally from two to eight o'clock;
a small area missing at the upper end of the break and replaced in plaster.

The dancing Cupids are closely copied from one or other version of
Marcantonio Raimondi's engraving (fig. 39), or from the copy attributed
to Marco Dente da Ravenna.[1]

   This unsigned dish was in 1933 classified by Rackham and Ballardini as
by the hand of the painter signing 'F.R.' (see cat. 13), an attribution later
accepted by Norman, along with the now unacceptable allocation of the
'F.R.' category to Faenza, in his catalogue of the Wallace Collection's
maiolica. Cat. 19 should probably be ranked either as a very late example of
Xanto's work during the years when he used the initials 'F.R.', or else as an
early example of the manner he employed around 1527–30 on pieces whose
inscriptions he terminated with a flourish resembling a 'y' or a Greek letter
'Φ'. The architectural background, for which Marcantonio Raimondi's
print provided no model, looks quite late.

   Xanto later made rather frequent use of figures from the *Dance of Cupids*
print, as on cat. 20, 28 and 39. Use of the *Dance of Cupids* print is also a link
between such pieces and a Gubbio *tondino* in The Pierpont Morgan Library,
New York,[2] dated 1525 in lustre like several other Gubbio pieces here
attributed to Xanto.

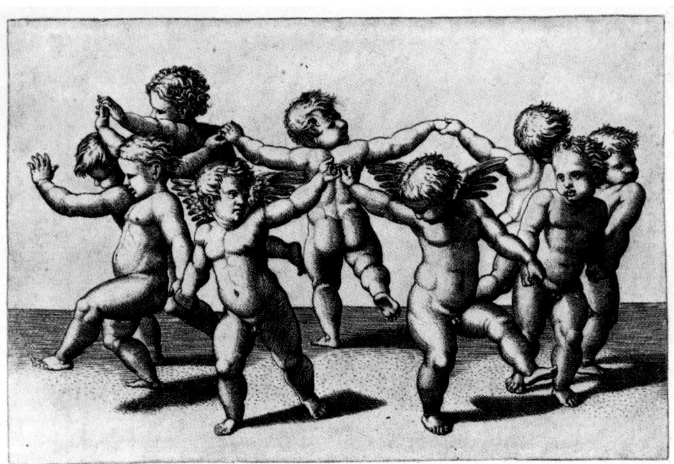

Fig. 39. Marcantonio Raimondi after
Raphael, *Dance of Cupids*, engraving

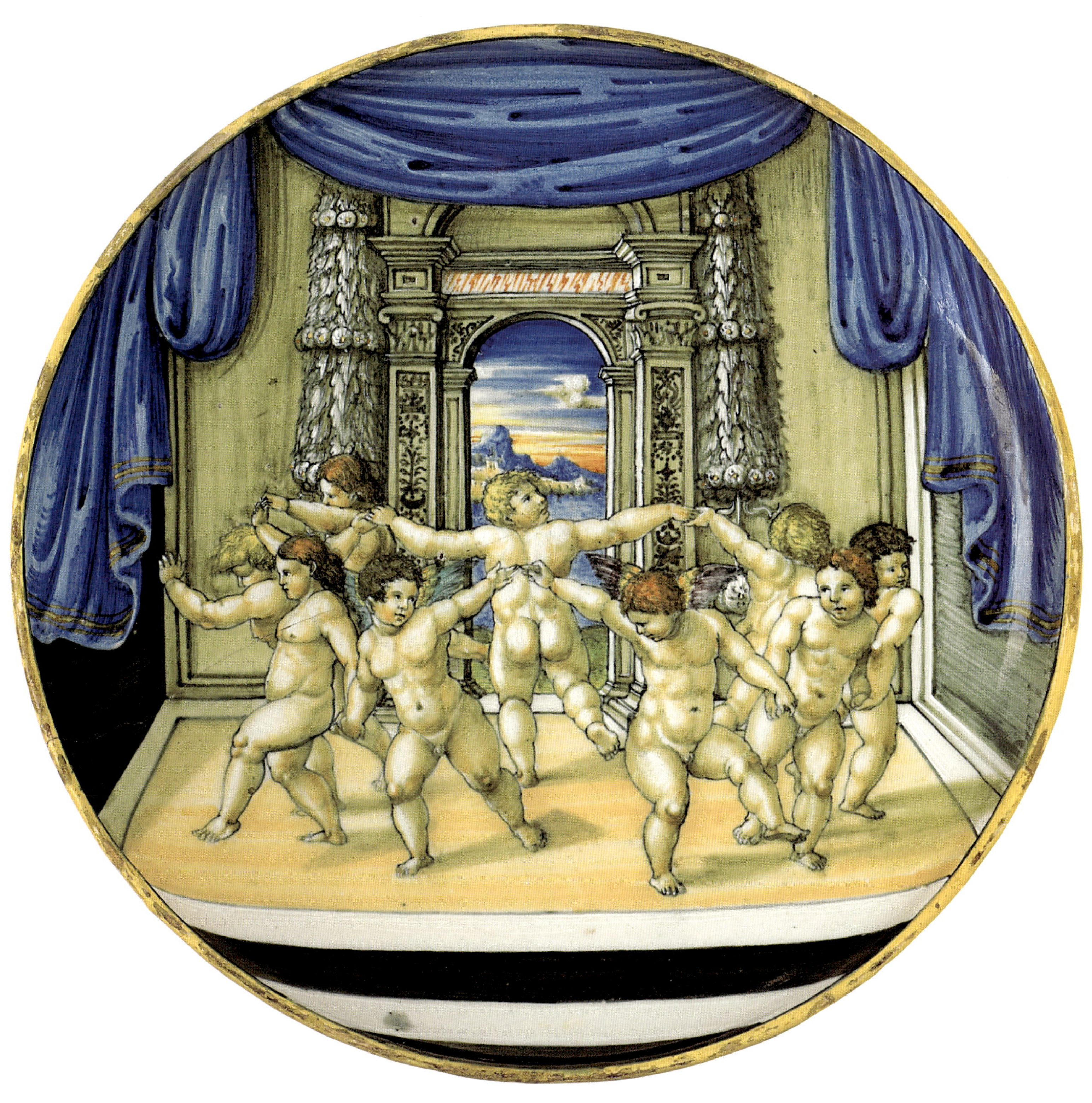

## 20.  Dish on low foot (*Coppa*): *Hercules and Deianira (Omphale?)*

Attributed to Francesco Xanto Avelli, probably working at Urbino; lustre, including the date, 1528, added in the workshop of Maestro Giorgio Andreoli at Gubbio

D: 27.2 cm
Arezzo, Museo Statale d'Arte Medievale e Moderna, no. 14582


PROVENANCE

From the collection of the Fraternita dei Laici, Arezzo; transferred to the museum in 1933.

BIBLIOGRAPHY

Ballardini 1933, 217, XXVII, 339R (as Monogrammist 'F.R.', Phi series, Faenza, lustred by Maestro Giorgio); Rackham 1957, p. 105 (as by 'F.R.', not Xanto, Faenza, "with added Gubbio lustre enrichment"); Fuchs 1993, no. 144 (as by Xanto, lustred by Maestro Giorgio at Gubbio; further bibliography cited); Fiocco and Gherardi 1989, pp. 427–29 and 445, pl. l (as painted and not just lustred at Gubbio); Cioci 1993 (as by Xanto working at Gubbio); Fiocco and Gherardi 1998, p. 35, pl. 12 and pp. 40–42 (as Gubbio? by Xanto); Mallet 2004, p. 44, figs. 11 and 12; p. 48 (as by Xanto working at Urbino, the lustre added by the Andreoli at Gubbio).

NOTES

1. *Ill. Bartsch* 27, p. 49, 352-I (264), here shown in the same sense as on Marcantonio's original, though on cat. 1 the image is reversed and perhaps derived from Giovanni Antonio da Brescia's copy *Ill. Bartsch* 25 (commentary pp. 347–49, .025.

2. *Ill. Bartsch* 27, p. 134, 464 (345) and p. 119, 442 (332).

3. For this iconographical conundrum see Montagu 1968.

4. Rackham and Ballardini 1933, p. 396 and fig. 6.

5. Rackham 1957, p. 105.


Polychrome and lustre. Right, Hercules sits with a distaff; centre, Omphale looks and points at him; left, Cupid tugs her away; background, a town on an island.

Reverse: antimony yellow decoration inside the rim and outside the foot, and between these zones a band of running plant-scroll in gold and red lustre; inside the foot ring is the inscription in Xanto's handwriting, in antimony yellow: *De Hercule / & Deianira* followed by a flourish resembling the letter 'y' or Greek letter 'Φ'. A further inscription in another hand, in red lustre, reads: *1528 / Mᵒ. Giorgio / da ugubio*.

Broken through from seven o'clock to one o'clock; some areas of the rim restored. In old photographs the piece is shown in a gilt frame, apparently of some age.

Cupid derives from Marcantonio Raimondi's *Dance of Cupids* (fig. 39, p. 84); Deianira (or Omphale) combines elements of the figures of Dido and Aeneas in the border scene of Dido receiving Aeneas at Carthage from the same engraver's *Quos Ego* print (fig. 35, p. 74);[1] Hercules, as on cat. 1 and a dish at Baltimore (fig. 19, p. 30), seems derived from a combination of a head and torso from Marcantonio's print, *Two Nude Men* (fig. 29, p. 48) after Michelangelo's *Drunkenness of Noah*; the legs from those of the same engraver's *Seated Ruler* (fig. 18, p. 29).[2]

Xanto's inscription confuses the legend of Hercules and Omphale, or perhaps Hercules and Iole, with that of Hercules and Deianira. The idea that, like Omphale, Deianira enslaved Hercules and rendered him effeminate through the power of love, seems to lack classical authority and may derive from Boccaccio.[3]

In 1933 Rackham and Ballardini considered cat. 20 a key link between work signed 'F.R.' or 'F.L.R.', and the category with inscriptions often terminating in a y/Φ flourish but no signature.[4] Rackham later emphasised and perhaps exaggerated the importance of the flourish, often seen *c.* 1527–30 and only occasionally later.[5] On cat. 20 the flourish and Xanto's handwriting have by some authors been thought to be in yellow lustre, and not in antimony yellow, as the report accompanying this catalogue entry, by Professor Brunetti, has recently shown them to be (fig. 40, p. 88). The inscription on cat. 20 cannot, therefore, any longer be used as evidence that the piece was painted, and not merely lustred, at Gubbio.

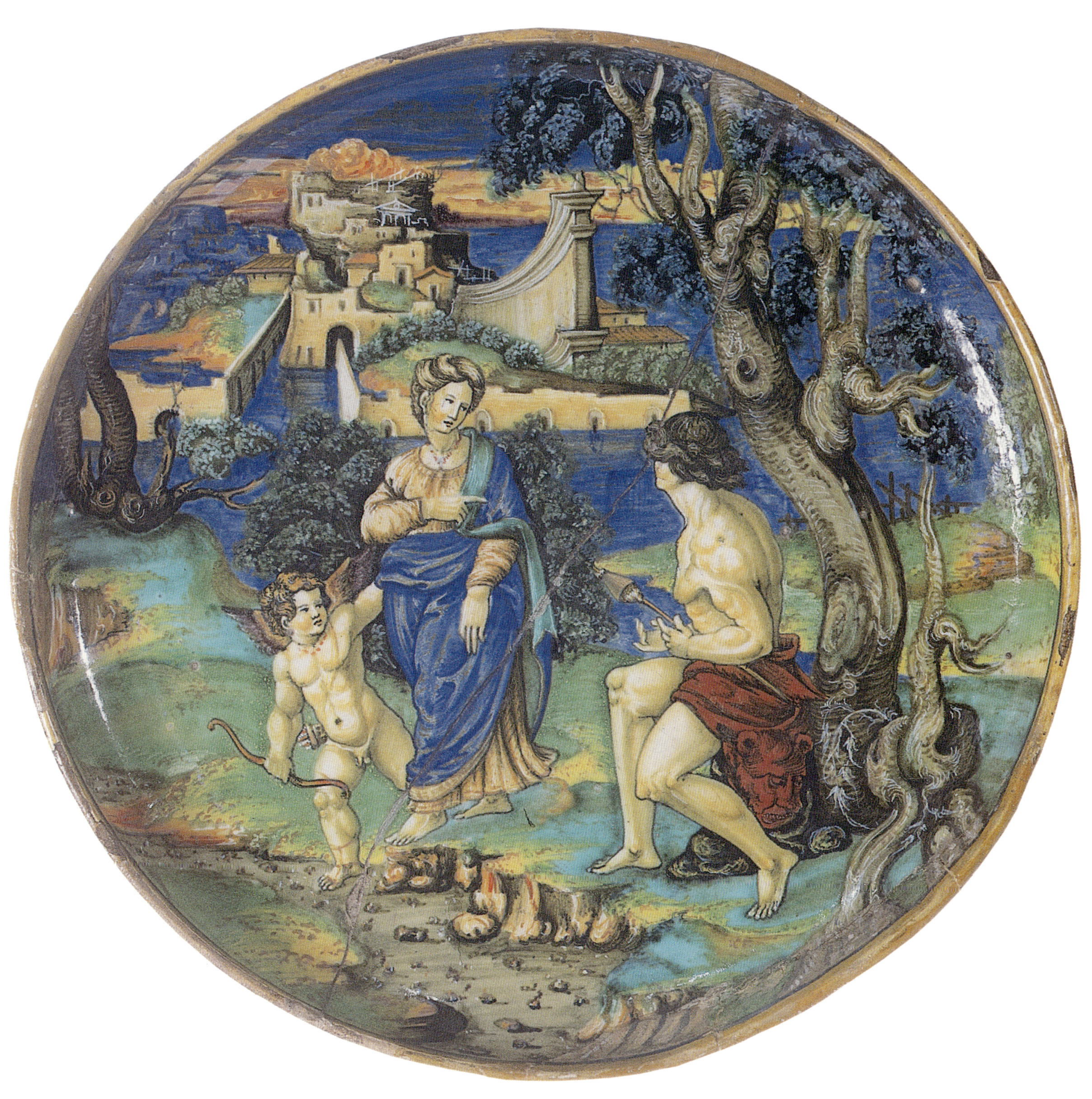

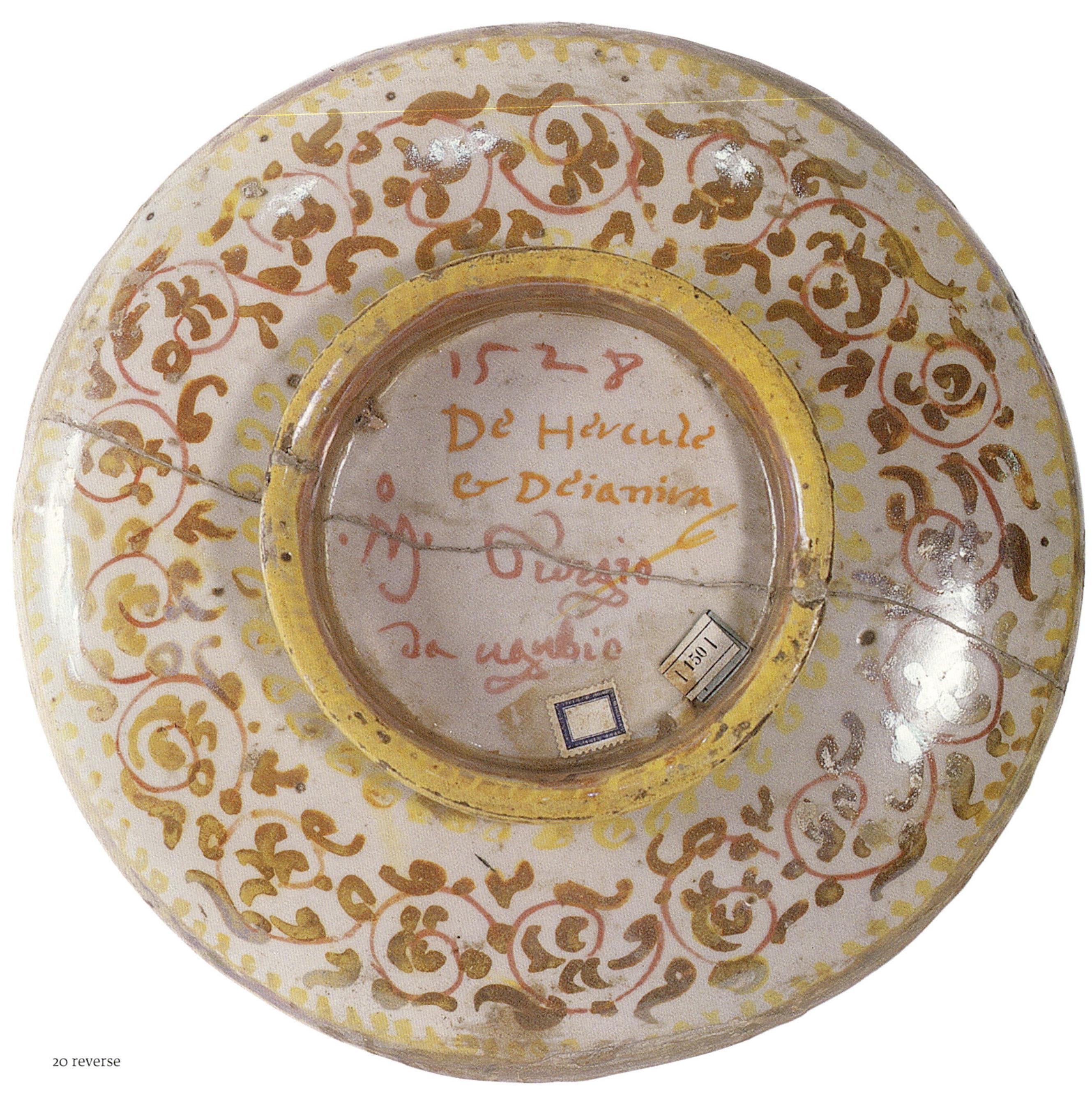

20 reverse

# MOLAB Laboratory* report on the non-destructive investigation of the *Hercules and Deianira (Omphale)* dish in the Museo d'Arte Medievale e Moderna, Arezzo

The MOLAB mobile laboratory recently undertook a non-destructive investigation of the *Hercules and Omphale* dish at the Museo d'Arte Medievale e Moderna in Arezzo. Analysis by X-ray fluorescence (XRF), UV-visible reflectance spectroscopy (UV-vis) and fibre optic micro-Raman was carried out using advanced portable equipment. In addition to a complete characterisation of the polychrome and lustre decoration on the front, the analysis led to the identification of the techniques used to produce the inscriptions and geometrical decorations on the reverse.

As expected, Maestro Giorgio's monogram proved to be inscribed in red lustre, identified by UV-vis spectroscopy through the typical surface plasmon resonance at 560 nm related to the optical absorption of Cu nanoparticles, typical of red lustre. By contrast, on the yellow inscriptions, UV-vis spectra did not show any feature attributable to the possible presence of Ag nanoparticle, typical of gold lustre. In addition, XRF spectra revealed that the inscriptions are made from a yellow pigment containing Pb and Sb, definitely identified as lead antimonate (or Naples yellow) by micro-Raman spectroscopy. Lead antimonate was also found on the rim and on several yellow decorations on the reverse.

*A Transnational Access service of the European Community, through the Eu-ARTECH project of the 6th Framework Programme – RII3-CT-2004-506171.

1. This investigation was carried out at John Mallet's request by Bruno Brunetti, Professor of General and Inorganic Chemistry at the University of Perugia, Italy. Professor Brunetti kindly provided this report and the accompanying illustration.

Fig. 40. Reverse of 20, annotated to indicate results of pigment analysis

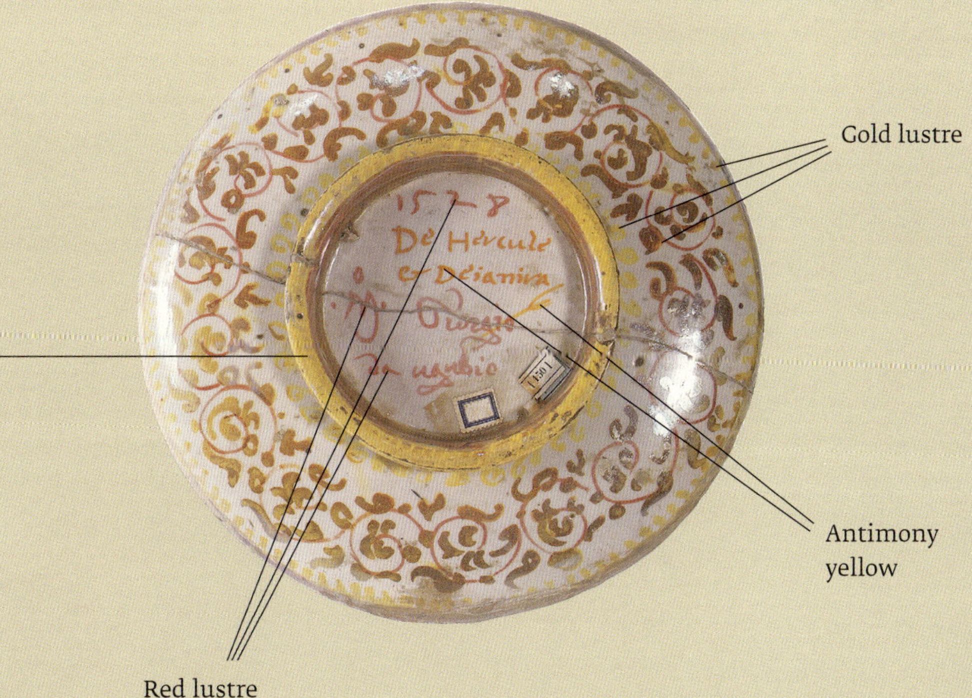

# 21.  Plaque: *St Sebastian and St Roch*

Attributed to Francesco Xanto Avelli, Urbino, dated 1528

H: 15.5 cm; W: 13.0 cm
London, Victoria and Albert Museum, C.2253-1910

PROVENANCE

George Salting Bequest, 1910.

BIBLIOGRAPHY

Ballardini 1933, 200, 229; Rackham 1940,
no. 628.

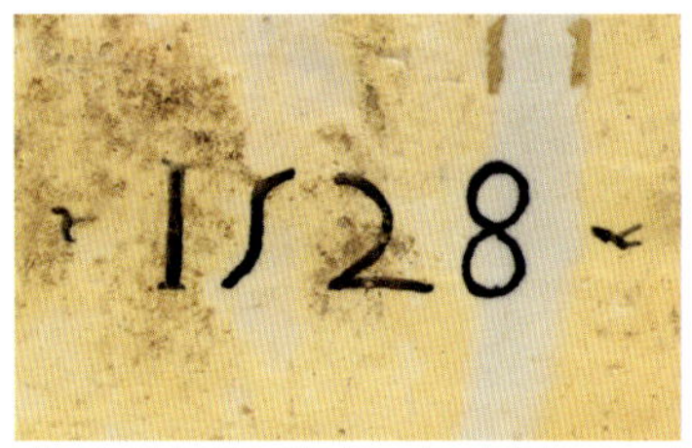

21 reverse (detail)

Polychrome. Left, St Sebastian tied to a column, his body pierced with arrows; right, St Roch, dressed as a pilgrim with a staff, indicates a plague-spot on his thigh. In the background a fortress on a hill. The panel edged with black.
Reverse: plain except for the date 1528 written in black.

No design sources have been traced.

The small size of the panel suggests it would have been used for private devotions, and the black border would perhaps have been hidden under a frame. The two saints depicted are often twinned in Renaissance art, and were invoked most particularly to ward off plague and other illness. Saint Sebastian was said to have been a Roman officer in the Praetorian Guard at the time of the Emperor Diocletian, in the third century AD. Secretly a Christian, he came forward in support of two companions who had been condemned to death for their belief. He was condemned to be shot to death with arrows and was left for dead, but survived. According to one legend he then confronted the Emperor with a renewed avowal of his faith, and for this was beaten to death with clubs. St Sebastian's association with sickness may have arisen because, in Greco-Roman culture, disease was thought to be caused by the arrows of Apollo. St Roch (1293–1327) was born at Montpellier in France and travelled Europe tending victims of the plague, which he himself eventually caught. Because he journeyed to Rome he is usually shown, as here, dressed as a pilgrim. He points to a dark spot on his thigh, where the plague often first manifested itself. St Roch survived the disease but it left him so ravaged that his fellow citizens at Montpellier failed to recognise him and cast him into prison, where he died. St Roch's remains were removed in 1485 to Venice, where the Scuola Grande di San Rocco, a confraternity especially concerned with care of the sick, was founded.

Though both Ballardini in his *Corpus* of dated maiolica, and Rackham in his Victoria and Albert Museum *Catalogue*, qualify their attributions of this unsigned plaque to Xanto, that was probably because they were trying to draw a non-existent distinction between 'F.R.' and Xanto. When compared to works from the same phase of Xanto's development, such as cat. 20 and 22–24, there no longer seems room for doubt that this plaque is by Xanto. The plaque had its date fired with the rest of its decoration and, since the piece bears no lustre, there is no reason to associate it with Gubbio. It seems likely to have been painted entirely at Urbino.

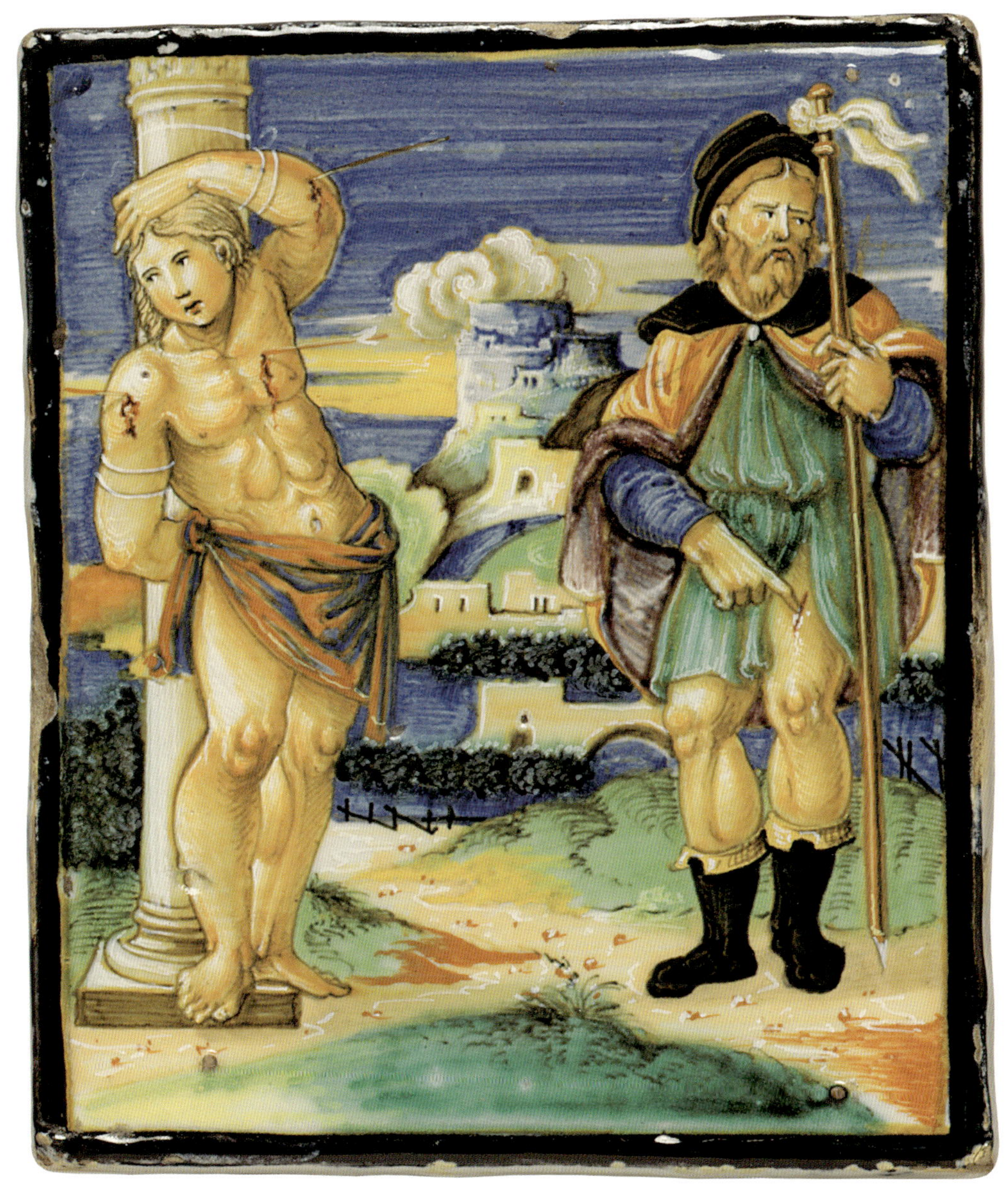

## 22.  Dish on low foot (*Coppa*): *Charity*

Attributed to Francesco Xanto Avelli, Urbino, *c.* 1527–30

D: 26.3 cm
National Trust, Polesden Lacey, Pol/C/17

PROVENANCE

Bequeathed to the National Trust by
the Hon. Mrs. Ronald Greville in 1942.

BIBLIOGRAPHY

Mallet 1971A, pp. 171–73 and figs 1–3;
Mallet 1971B, no. 20.

NOTES

1. *Ill. Bartsch* 27, p. 78, 386 (294).
2. *Ill. Bartsch* 26, p. 239, 242 (194).

Polychrome. Centre, Charity personified as a woman holding a child in her arms and another by his hand, while two further children flank the group. To the right, what appears to be an altar; behind the group dark blue curtains half conceal the architectural setting.
Reverse: plain.
Recent conservation: two cracks consolidated, chipping at the rim partially filled and repainted.

The central group of Charity and two children is quite closely copied from Marcantonio Raimondi's engraving of *Charity*;[1] the two outer boys derive from Marco Dente da Ravenna's *Bas-Relief with Three Cupids* (*Throne of Neptune*), engraved after the antique relief  still today in the church of San Vitale, Ravenna, the engraver's native town (fig. 41).[2]

The modern English word, Charity, narrowly connected with almsgiving, reflects little of the scope of Christian *Caritas*, the greatest of the three theological virtues. St Paul is eloquent on the subject in Ch. XIII of his first Epistle to the Corinthians: "Though I speak with the tongues of men and of angels, and have not charity, I am become *as* sounding brass, or a tinkling cymbal", concluding: "And now abideth faith, hope, charity, these three; but the greatest of these *is* charity." The virtue of *Caritas* is sometimes rendered in English as 'Love', which does at least convey one essential characteristic of the virtue: a warmth of feeling for God and for one's fellow human beings. By the sixteenth century Charity was usually represented as a woman with two children at her breast and sometimes, as here, with further children at her feet.

The sombre tones in which the Polesden Lacey *Charity* is painted are characteristic of this phase in Xanto's art. The lack of an inscription tends to support an early dating to, say, *c.* 1527–29.

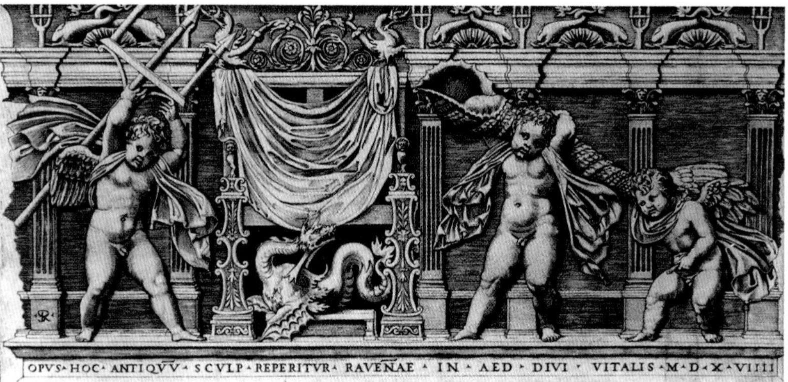


Fig. 41. Marco Dente da Ravenna after the antique bas-relief in the church of San Vitale in Ravenna, *Bas-Relief with Three Cupids* (*The Throne of Neptune*), engraving

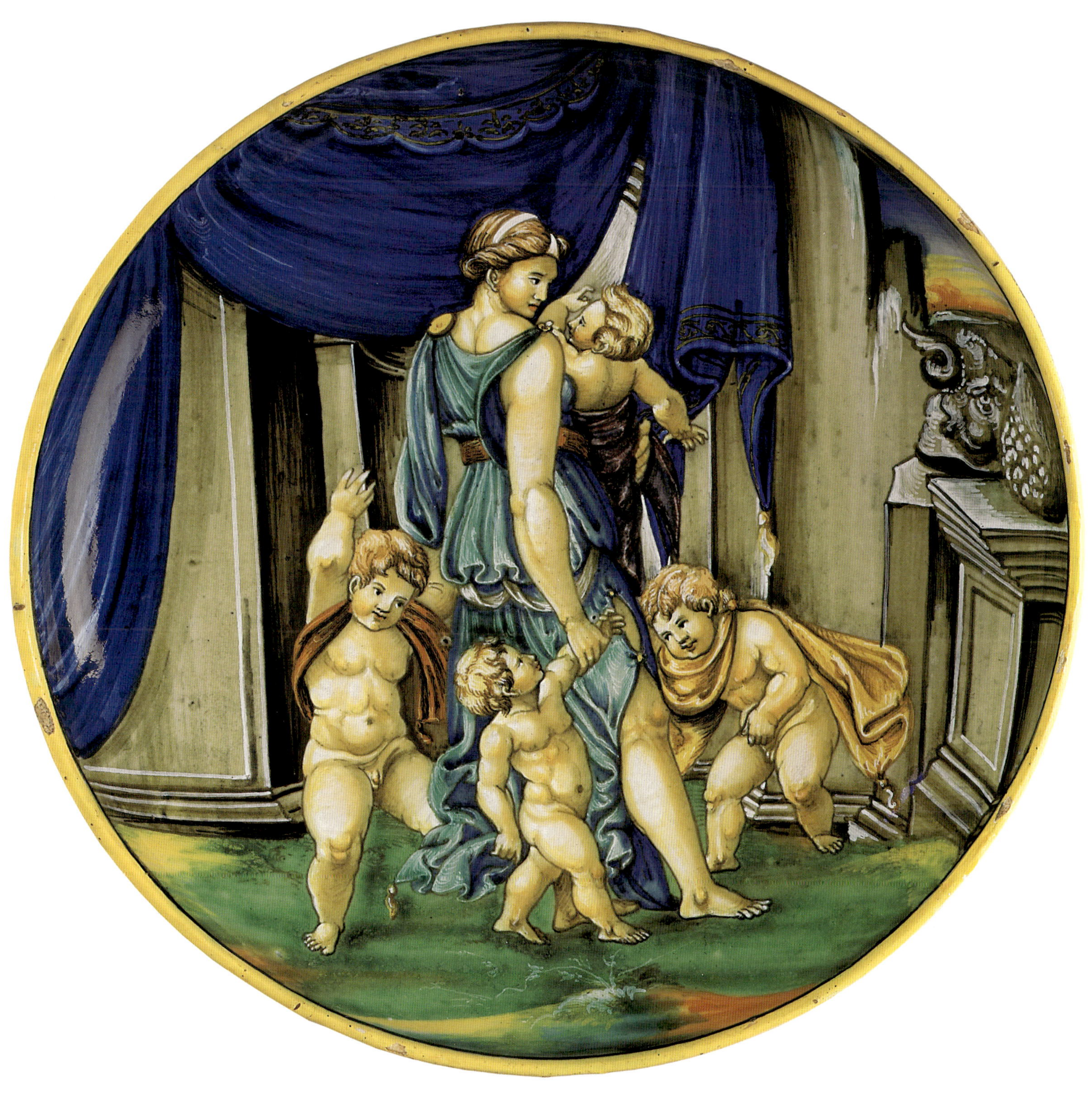

23. # Bowl with broad border (*Tondino*):
## *Phrixus escaping on the Ram and sacrificing it to Mars at Colchis*

Attributed to Francesco Xanto Avelli, Urbino, *c.* 1526–28

D: 26.9 cm
Oxford, Ashmolean Museum, Barlow Loan, LI180.3


PROVENANCE

Henry Pfungst (?); Basil Barlow.

BIBLIOGRAPHY

Pfungst 1890 (possibly the piece here described); Wilson 2002B, p. 121 and figs. 22–23; Mallet 2004, p. 45 and p. 49, figs. 18–19.

NOTES

1. *Ill. Bartsch*, 26, p. 13, 4 (6).
2. Triolo 1996, p. 266–67.
3. Triolo 1996, p. 266, 3A.8, and p. 454, fig. 15.
4. Pfungst 1890, no. 27.


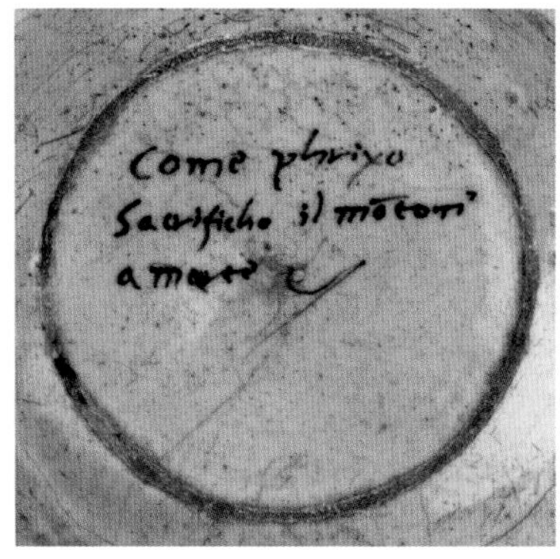

23 reverse (detail)

Polychrome. Left foreground, Phrixus kneels on the island of Colchis to sacrifice the ram with the golden fleece to Mars; above right, Mars descends from heaven to accept the gift; right foreground, Mars hangs the fleece on a tree. In the background an island with a natural arch.
Reverse: inscribed *Come phrixo / Sacrificho il montone / a marte* (Phrixus sacrificed the ram to Mars), followed by a y/Φ flourish; otherwise plain.
A small piece is missing and replaced at eight o'clock on the rim.

The figure of Phrixus may be a partial memory of Marco Dente's *Noah's Sacrifice*.[1]

Ovid (*Metamorphoses,* VII, line 7) gives a mere passing reference to the *Phrixia vellera* (the Phrixian fleece), but possibly Xanto took the legend not directly from a classical source but from Zoppino's Italian version, published in 1522.[2] As related by Zoppino, King Athamas had two sons, Phrixus and Helle. Their mother Nephele gave them a ram with a golden fleece, telling them to mount it without fear. While they were passing over the sea Helle fell off and was drowned. Reaching the Island of Colchis, Phrixus sacrificed the ram to Mars, who was so pleased that he hung the fleece on a tree.

An unsigned version of this rare subject, attributable to Xanto and forming part of the 'Three Crescents' service, was sold from the Kunstgewerbemuseum, Cologne, in 1931.[3] A version by Xanto, formerly in the Henry Pfungst collection, London, may perhaps have been the present piece.[4]

This is surely one of the earliest pieces on which Xanto's handwriting, followed by the y/Φ flourish, can be recognised. The green tonality of the piece and its unusually adventurous landscape may be due to the experience of working closely with Nicola da Urbino, as suggested by the Bonzi armorial plates (cat. 17 and 18). The figure-drawing may also be compared with that of, for instance, cat. 8, from the 'S' service.

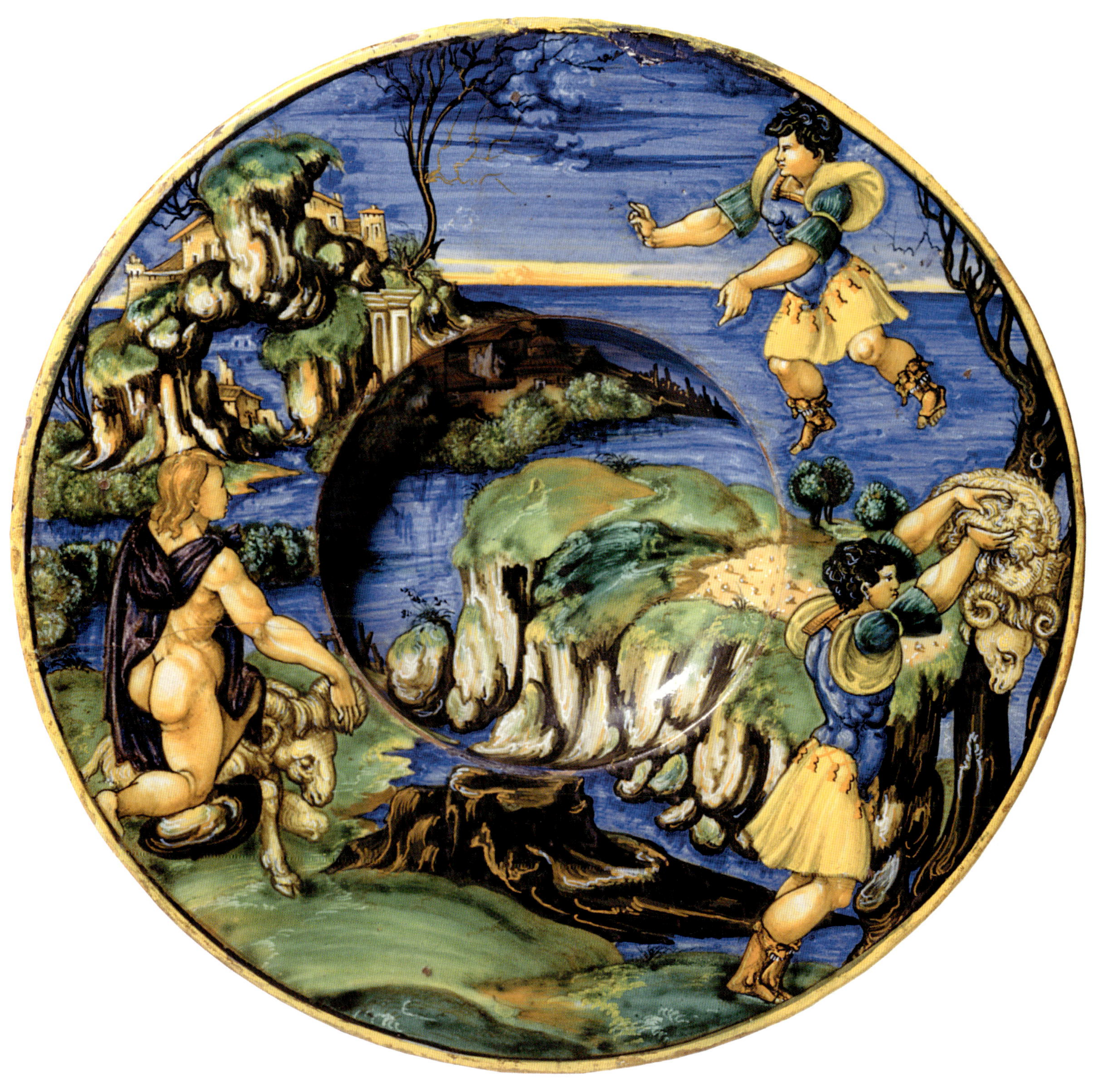

## 24. Bowl with broad border (*Tondino*):
## *Hippolytus escaping from the Wrath of Theseus*

Attributed to Francesco Xanto Avelli, Urbino, *c.* 1527–28

D: 27.1 cm
London, Wallace Collection, C86

PROVENANCE
Prince Napoleon.

BIBLIOGRAPHY
Prince Napoleon sale 1872, lot 249; Norman 1976, no. C86 (as Urbino, circle of Xanto, *c.* 1530).

NOTE
1. *Metamorphoses*, XV, 497–546; *Fasti*, VI, 734–45.

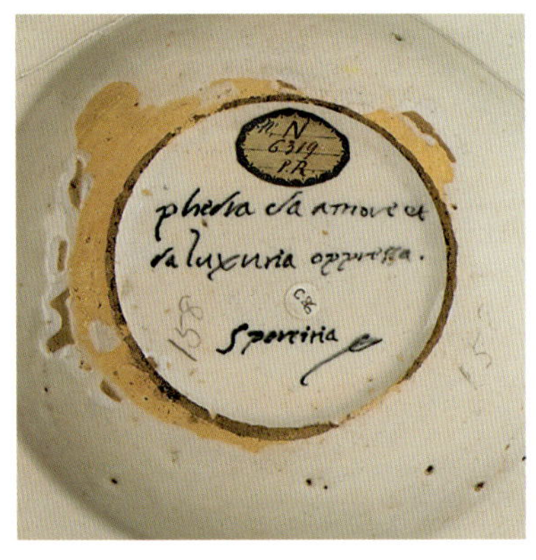

24 reverse (detail)

Polychrome. Left, Phaedra, naked except for a cloak thrown over a shoulder, looks on as Theseus, centre, with falchion and target, pursues the scantily draped Hippolytus, right, who springs into a chariot standing at the edge of the sea, the hindquarters of one of the horses visible near the bowl's outer rim.

Reverse: within the foot, inscribed in dark blue: *phedra da amore et/ da luxuria oppressa./ Sporcitia* followed by a y/Φ flourish. (Phaedra overcome by love and by lust. Filth).

Three pieces broken out of the lower edge of the border and reinstated. Phaedra's left hand recently retouched after removal of old overpaint.

No close engraved source has been identified.

Phaedra, wife of Theseus, fell in love with her step-son, Hippolytus and, out of spite at rejection, or from fear of discovery, denounced him to her husband. Theseus pursued Hippolytus, who escaped in a chariot which was, however, overturned when a sea-monster alarmed the horses. Hippolytus was killed, though he was subsequently brought back to life by Aesculapius. Ovid relates elements of the story in his *Metamorphoses* and *Fasti*,[1] and it provided the plot for plays by Euripides and Seneca. The reproving word, *Sporcitia* (Filth), that concludes the inscription is not otherwise recorded on Xanto's work.

The free composition of this bowl, and the flexibility of limb shown by the figures, suggest influence from Nicola da Urbino. One of the earlier-looking pieces inscribed in Xanto's handwriting, the *tondino* was probably painted not long after Xanto had collaborated with Nicola over the Bonzi service (cat. 17 and 18).

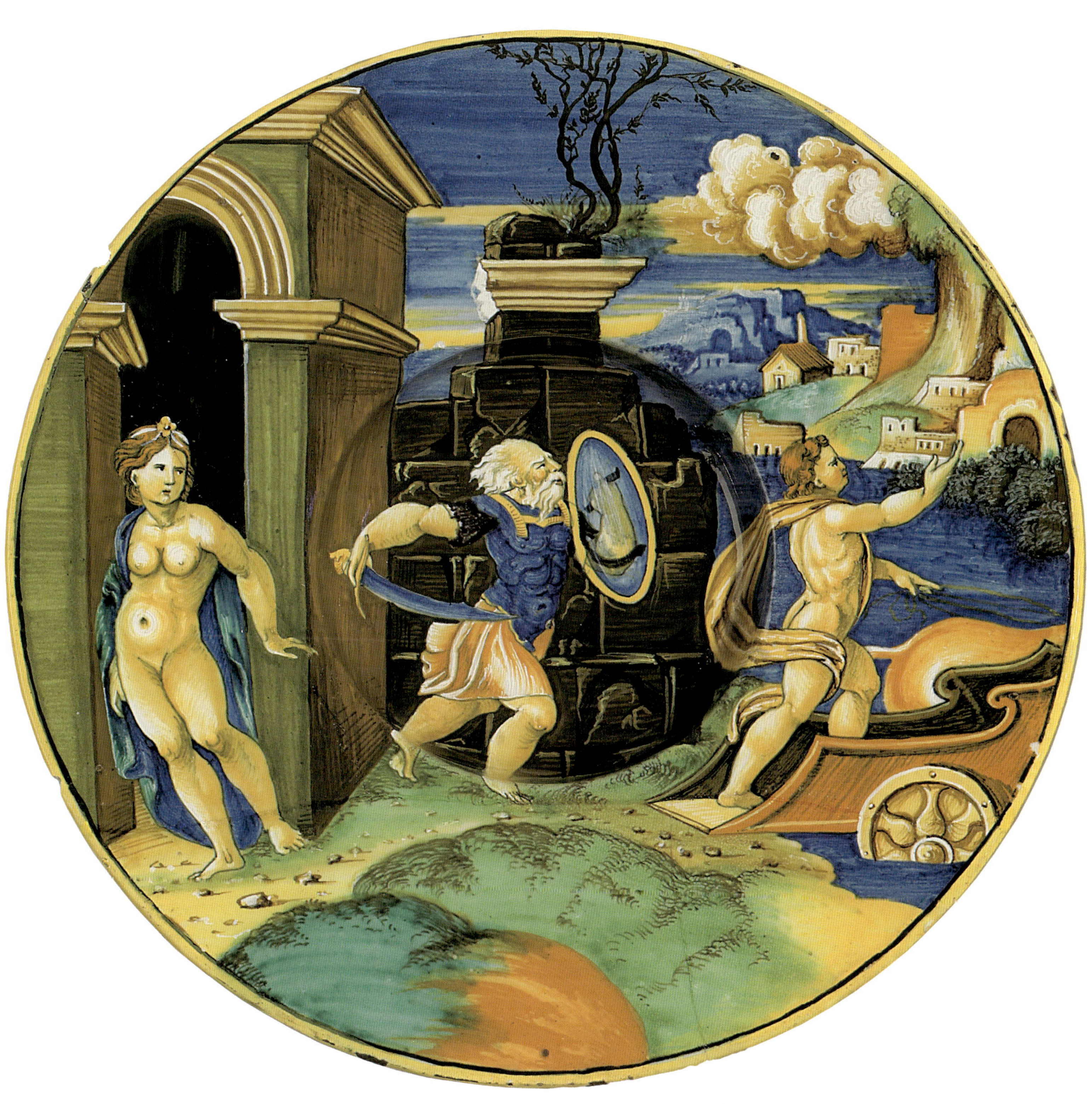

# 25. Plate: *Apollo and Daphne*

Attributed to Francesco Xanto Avelli, Urbino, *c.* 1530

D: 26.0 cm
Glasgow City Council (Museums), 1893.93.a

PROVENANCE

Frédéric Spitzer collection.

BIBLIOGRAPHY

Molinier 1892, no. 41; Spitzer sale 1893, lot 1082 (as workshop of Francesco Xanto, "vers 1535"); Rackham 1957, p. 106, note 24; Mallet 1988, p. 69 and p. 92, figs 3 and 3R; Cioci 1987, p. 47; Cioci 1993, pp. 38–39 and figs. 8–9; Triolo 1996, pp. 258–77; Wilson 1996, no. 84; Triolo 2001, p. 58 and fig. 9; Manara 2002.

NOTES

1. *Ill. Bartsch* 27, p. 108, 420 (316), also used on cat. 7, 45 and 54.
2. *Ill. Bartsch* 27, p. 15, 323 (243).
3. *Ill. Bartsch* 28, p. 192, 53 (89).
4. *Metamorphoses*, I, lines 452–567.
5. Rasmussen 1989, nos. 75–76.
6. Cioci 1987, p. 46, note 4; 1993, pp. 38–39. Xanto's only recorded comparable inscription, ending *fabu. hist.*, is on a plate in Milan also with a seemingly unpolitical subject, Orpheus and Eurydice. For Julia Triolo's interpretation of the double description, see Triolo 2000, no. 210.

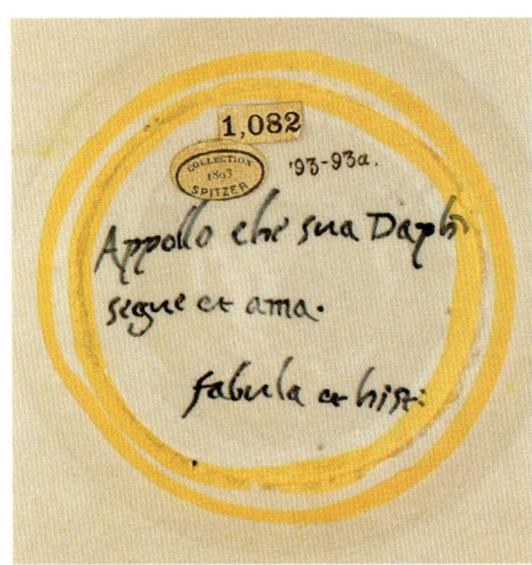

25 reverse (detail)

Polychrome. Left, Apollo pursues Daphne, right, who is turning into a laurel-tree; in the centre reclines Daphne's father, the river god Peneus. In the background is a landscape with, suspended from a rock, a shield of arms: *azure, three crescents addorsed, argent* (two above and one below). Reverse: concentric yellow lines; within the foot ring is the inscription: *Apollo che sua Daph[ne]/ segue et ama./ fabula et hist:* (Apollo who follows and loves his Daphne./fable and history).

Apollo derives from a spearman in the *Battle Scene* engraved after Raphael or Giulio Romano(fig. 32, p. 60);[1] the river god, Peneus, derives from Marco Dente's *The Birth of Venus* (fig. 46, p. 126);[2] the Daphne is reversed from a figure in Gian Giacomo Caraglio's *The Muses and Pierides* after Rosso Fiorentino (fig. 43, p. 114 ).[3]

According to Ovid,[4] Daphne was Apollo's first love. He pursued her until, to escape his embrace, she appealed to her father, the river god Peneus, and was changed into a laurel.

The so-called 'Three Crescents' service has caused perplexity not only because of uncertainty over the identification of the coat of arms, but also because pieces with a variant of the arms with one crescent up and two below are attributable to a different hand (see cat. 26), now known as 'The Milan Marsyas Painter'. Rasmussen argued that these pieces constituted a separate service,[5] but it is far more likely they resulted from the splitting of a large commission between two painters, as recommended in 1528 by Giovanmaria Della Porta (see Introduction, p. 27) and that these two failed to coordinate their treatments of the arms, besides duplicating the subject of Apollo and Daphne. Rasmussen, indeed, contended that the three crescents should not be considered regular coats of arms, but were informal devices or *imprese*, in the case of Xanto's pieces the *impresa* of the Vitelli of Città di Castello, in the case of 'The Milan Marsyas Painter', of Manetti of Florence. Proposed armorial identifications have included the Strozzi, Buoncristiani and Cosi families, all of Florence.

The approximate date of the Xanto pieces, at least, is established by the inscription, *1530*, unaccompanied by a signature, on the piece in the Lehman collection. The conclusion of the inscription on the present piece, *fabula et historia*, is most unusual, as though Xanto could not decide whether the event depicted were myth or fact. Cioci, indeed, has suspected that some political reference may be concealed by the myth.[6]

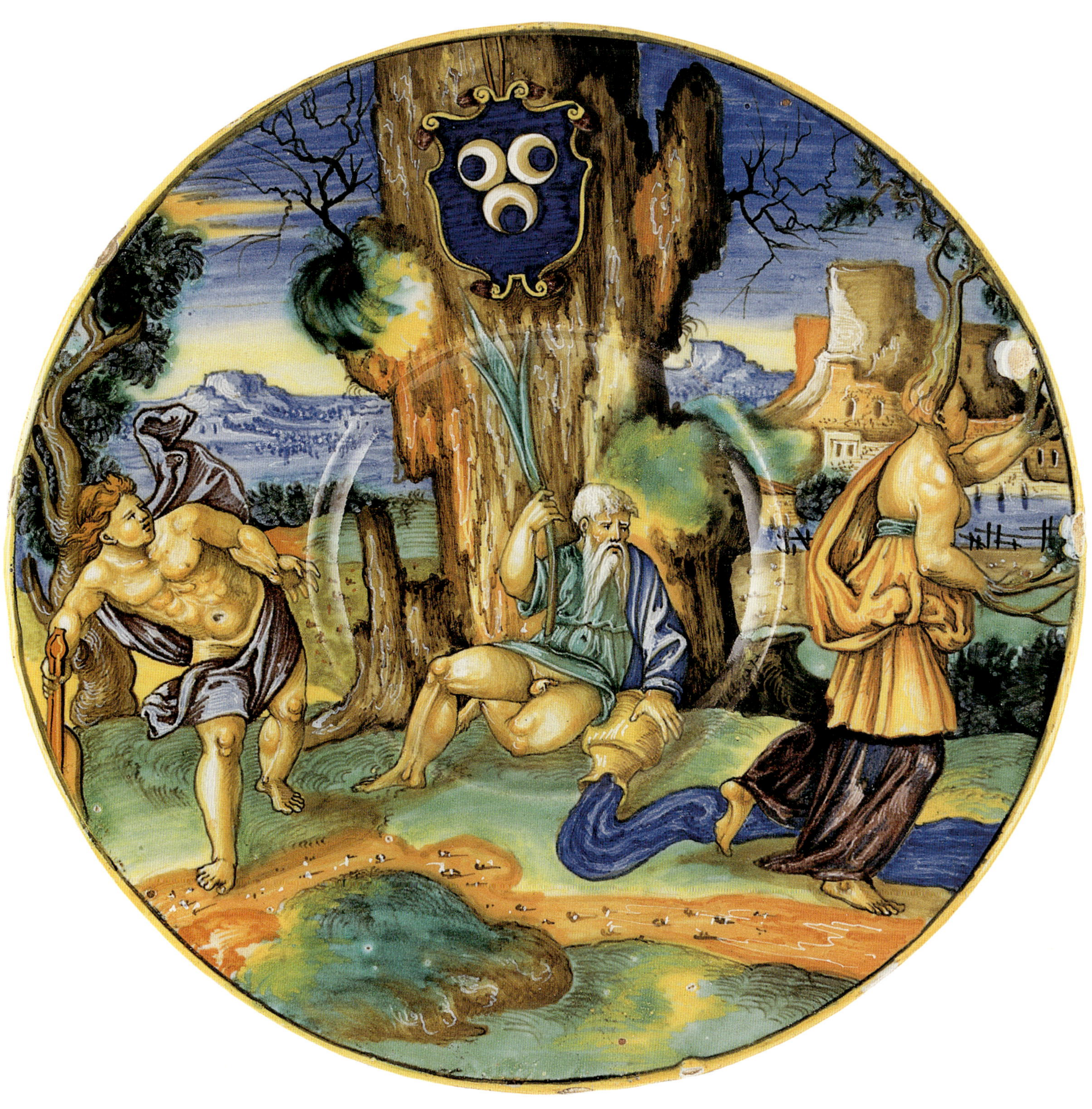

## 26. Bowl with broad border (*Tondino*): *The Hunting of the Calydonian Boar*

Attributed to 'The Milan Marsyas Painter', Urbino, *c.* 1530

D: 19.3 cm
Cambridge, Fitzwilliam Museum, C.132-1933

PROVENANCE

Alfred De Pass collection, by whom given in memory of his son, Crispin, in 1933.

BIBLIOGRAPHY

Rackham 1934; Mallet 1988, p. 93 and pl. 4; Poole 1995, no. 380.

NOTES

1. *Metamorphoses*, VII, lines 270–430.
2. Mallet 1988, pp. 69–73 and figs. 6 and 6R.
3. Wilson 2000, nos. 199–203 and no. 206. no. 204, also from the Bossi collection, might also have belonged to this set.

Polychrome. Left, Meleager draws his bow at (right) a boar which is already wounded with an arrow. In the background a landscape with trees and distant hills. From a bough at the top is suspended a shield of arms: *azure, three crescents addorsed argent* (one above and two below).
Reverse: white.
Three small chips on the outer rim.

No close print-source has been identified for this design.

The citizens of Calydon had offended the goddess Diana, who sent a large and ferocious boar to terrorise them. Meleager gathered a band of young people including the beautiful Atalanta, with whom he fell in love, to hunt the boar. Far from shooting the boar with an arrow, as shown on the present bowl, Ovid relates that Meleager killed him with spears, giving the skin and head of the beast to Atalanta.[1]

Though by different painters and with variants of an unidentified coat of arms, both this bowl and cat. 25 probably belong to the same armorial set and can be dated accordingly. The painter of the present bowl may be identified as the anonymous maiolica painter named 'The Milan Marsyas Painter' after a *tondino* in the Castello Sforzesco in Milan.[2] In adopting this name I had not fully appreciated that the Marsyas *tondino* probably forms a set with five other pieces in the Castello Sforzesco at Milan which share its early provenance from Giuseppe Bossi's collection. I now have severe doubts as to whether the inscriptions on the backs of these are by the hand of their painter who, as Wilson points out,[3] did not normally inscribe his work.

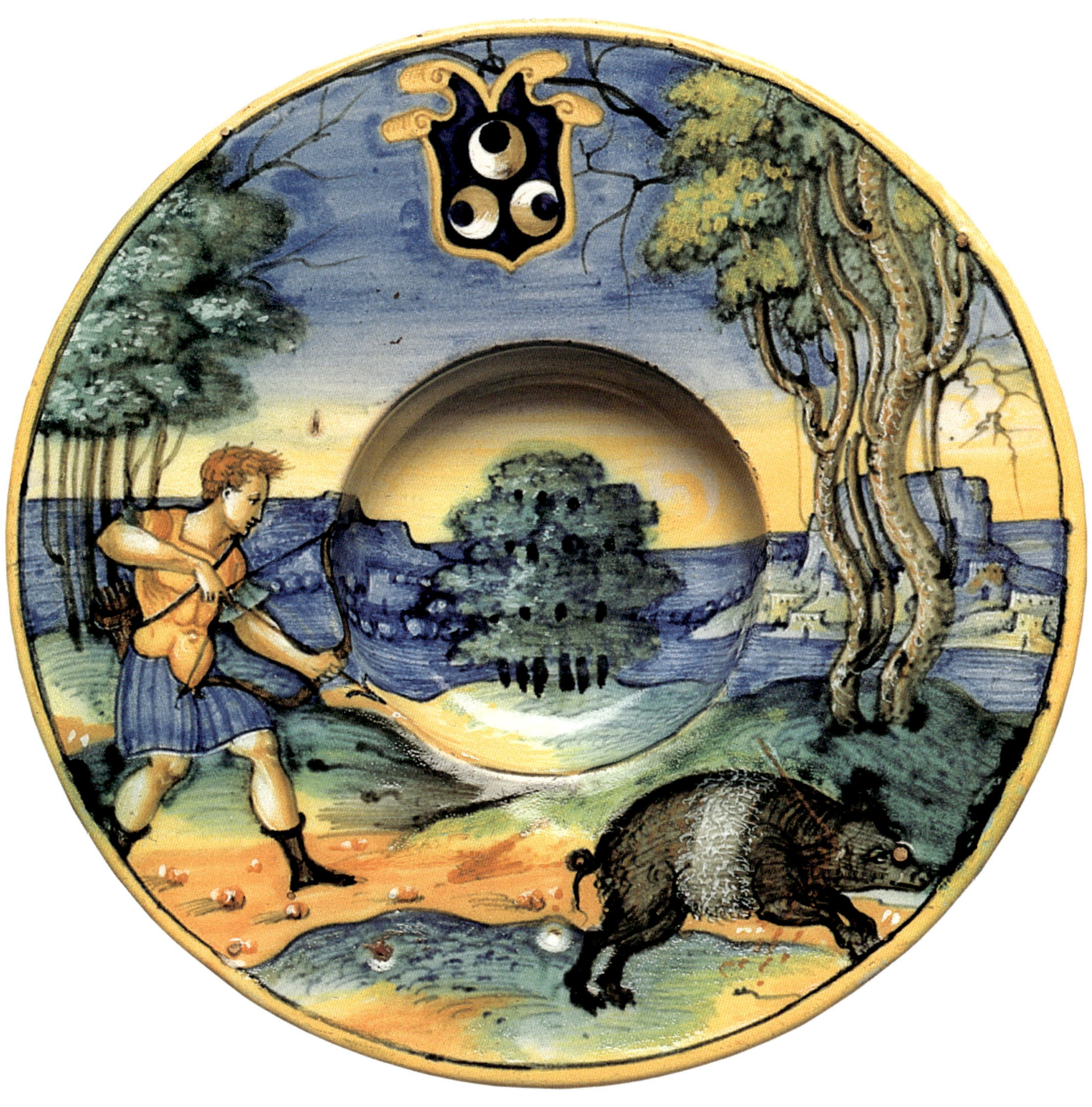

## 27. Bowl with broad border (*Tondino*): *An Allegory*

Attributed to Francesco Xanto Avelli, Urbino, *c.* 1528–30

D: 20.0 cm
Glasgow City Council (Museums), 1896.76.b

PROVENANCE

Bought in 1896 from Thomas Lawrie and
Son, 88 Vincent Street, Glasgow.

BIBLIOGRAPHY

Tennent 1982; Mallet 1988, p. 68 and p. 92,
figs. 2 and 2R.

NOTES

1. *Ill. Bartsch* 27, p. 15, 323 (243).
2. Watson 1986, no. 50. Cioci (1991B,
   pp. 5–11) proposes a plausible
   interpretation of *Mech, Moch*. It may be,
   though, that Rome, rather than Pope
   Clement VII, was the intended target
   of that allegory.
3. Bressan 1857, p. 26.

Polychrome. Two children, left, walk away holding toy windmills or
pin-wheels; right, a bearded man or river god reclines holding a standard
topped by a crescent moon; centre, a landscape with buildings and hills.
Reverse: a single yellow line at the outer rim; inscribed within the foot:
*Tich, Tach./ nota* followed by the y/Φ flourish.
Broken in three pieces; glaze and body chipped at edges of the breaks and
at the rim.

The two children appear frequently in Xanto's work, but no engraved source
has yet been identified. The reclining man is taken from Marco Dente's
*The Birth of Venus* (fig. 46, p. 126).[1]

The crescent moon on the bearded man's standard may indicate a connection
with the unidentified possessor of the 'Three Crescents' service (see cat. 25)
and might connect the *tondino* to some particular historical incident. The
inscription is reminiscent of *Mech, Moch./ leggi* inscribed on a *tondino* in the
Corcoran Gallery.[2] In both cases an imitation of noise is probably intended –
the rattling wheels of the cart on the Corcoran *tondino*, the clack-clack made
by the revolving sails of the toy windmills on the Glasgow one. Alternatively,
as Patricia Collins has suggested to me, the ticking-by of time may be
implied, indicating that the carefree children will age like the man on the
right. The terminating word *nota* suggests the subject on the present bowl
was intended to point a moral. This may have alluded to some popular saying
about the cyclical nature of events such as the Vicentine, Luigi Da Porto,
quoted in 1509 in connection with the woes of Venice: "So I have always
heard it said that peace makes prosperity; prosperity makes pride; pride
makes anger; anger makes war; war makes poverty; poverty makes
humanity; humanity makes peace; and peace, as I said, makes prosperity:
and thus the affairs of the world revolve." (*Perciocchè io sempre ho udito dire, che
la pace fa ricchezza; la ricchezza fa superbia; la superbia fa ira; la ira fa guerra; la guerra fa
povertà; la povertà fa umanità; la umanità fa pace; e la pace, come dissi, fa ricchezza: e così
girano le cose del mondo*).[3] The Italian word for a child's windmill is *girandola*.

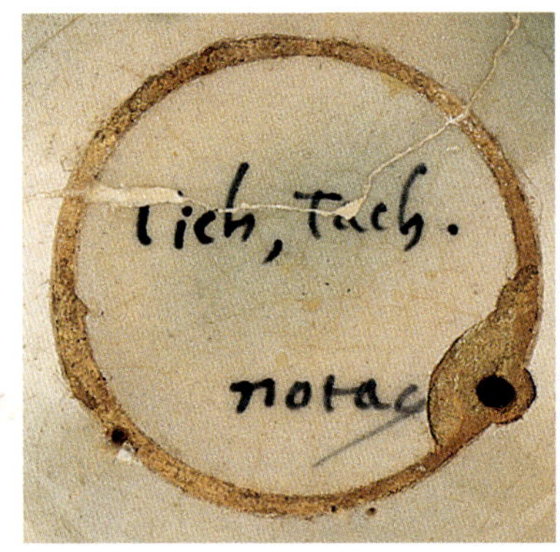

27 reverse (detail)

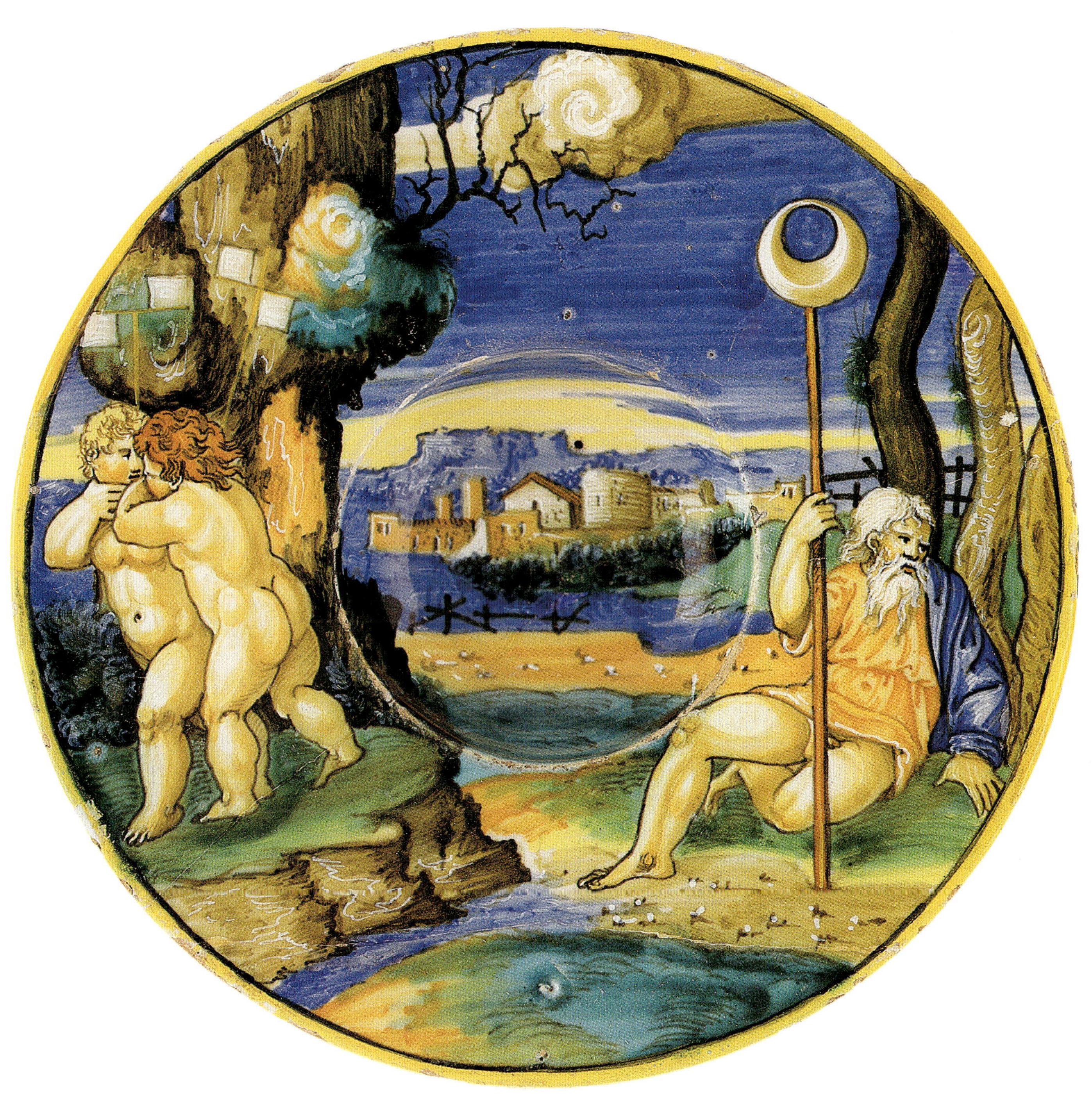

28. Bowl with broad border (*Tondino*):
*An Allegory of the Sack of Rome*

Attributed to Francesco Xanto Avelli, *c*. 1528–30

D: 27.0 cm
National Trust, Polesden Lacey, Pol/C/18

PROVENANCE

Bequeathed to the National Trust by the
Hon. Mrs. Ronald Greville in 1942.

BIBLIOGRAPHY

Mallet 1971A, pp. 173–74 and figs, 4 and 12;
Mallet 1971B, p. 37, no. 10; Cioci 1987,
pp. 36–37.

NOTES

1. *Ill. Bartsch* 26, p. 215, 217-I (177).
2. Wilson 2002B, pp. 119–20 and fig. 19.
3. *Ill. Bartsch* 26, p. 242, 245-I (197).
4. For the *pallone* symbol see Norman 1969,
   pp. 447–48; Mallet 1971A, p. 173 and fig. 4;
   Mallet 1974, pp. 12–13 and pls. xiii–xiv.
5. Ballardini 1938B, pl. xxiiia; Mallet 1988,
   pl. 13; Emma Budge sale, Berlin, 4–6
   October 1937, lot 316.
6. Cioci 1987, pp. 36–37.

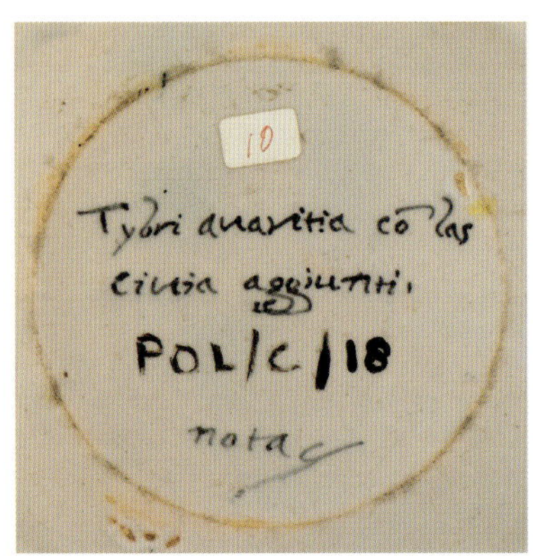

28 reverse (detail)

Polychrome. Left, a nude river god reclines holding a cornucopia, his right
hand resting on a *pallone*, or pneumatic ball; in the centre Cupid waves in
the direction of a nude woman who is seated holding an open sack in front
of a yellow curtain.

Reverse: inside the foot, in dark blue: *Tybri avaritia co[n] las/ civia aggiunti./ nota*
(the avarice of the Tiber combined with lasciviousness. Take note.), followed
by the y/Φ flourish.

Small chips to rim.

No graphic model has so far been identified for the relatively well drawn
figure that symbolises the Tiber. The Cupid is taken from Marcantonio
Raimondi's *Dance of Cupids* (fig. 39, p. 84).[1] The same Cupid was chosen from
this print for cat. 20. The print was used for a *tondino* in The Pierpont Morgan
Library[2] that I believe to have been painted by Xanto at Gubbio in 1525. The
seated woman derives from a figure at the extreme right of Marcantonio
Raimondi's *The Judgement of Paris* (fig. 31, p. 56),[3] the same figure that was
inserted into a number of other pieces with inscriptions terminating in
y/Φ, but also into cat. 10, the Wallace Collection's 1525 Gubbio dish with
*Women Bathing*.

The allegory appears concerned with the causes of the Sack of Rome. The
loose morality of the woman holding an open sack invites divine punishment. The River Tiber holds a cornucopia, emblem of prosperity, resting his
other hand on a *pallone*, thought to be associated with the Medici, and hence
with Pope Clement VII.[4] The *Pallone* emblem was used by Xanto on three other
political allegories: formerly at Faenza (destroyed); formerly in the Spero
and Sackler collections; formerly in the Budge collection.[5] It also alludes to
Clement VII's papacy on cat. 47, by Xanto's close follower, Giulio da Urbino.
Francesco Cioci has suggested that the curtain is about to be pulled back
to reveal the horrible sequel but, as on other Xanto pieces of this period,
it could equally be a purely decorative feature.[6]

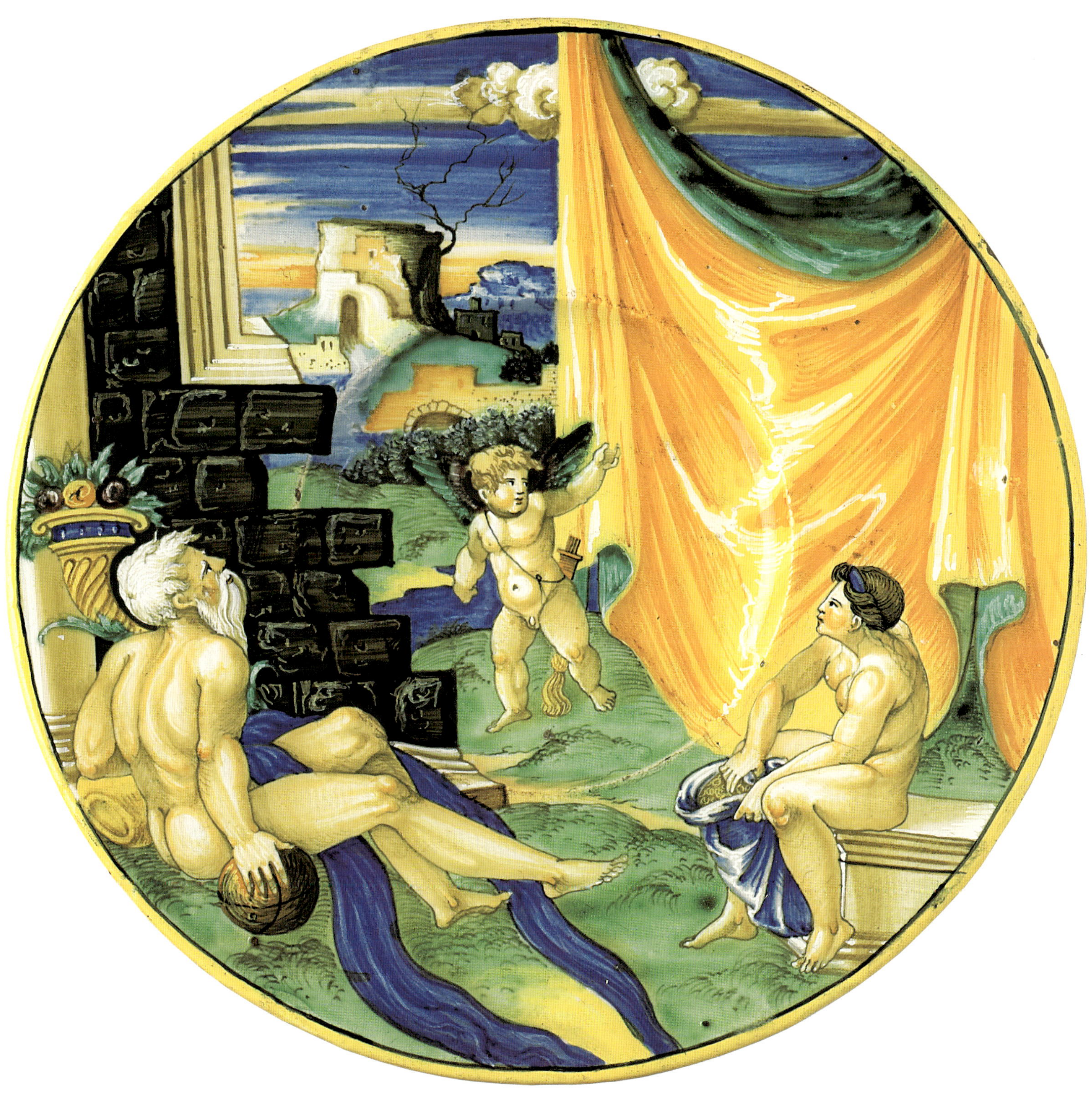

## 29.  Plate: *Allegory of the Triumph of Germany*

Attributed to Francesco Xanto Avelli, Urbino, *c.* 1528–30

D: 26.6 cm
London, Wallace Collection, C87

PROVENANCE

Prince Napoleon.

BIBLIOGRAPHY

Prince Napoleon sale 1872 (bought by Davis
for 15 guineas); Bethnal Green 1872–75,
no. 1421; Norman 1976, no. C87 (as in a
style similar to that of Francesco Xanto
Avelli da Rovigo, about 1530–40); Cioci
1987, pp. 40–41.

Polychrome. In the foreground an eagle perches on the saddle of a white
horse or mule, surrounded by a heap of the dead or dying. In the background
are classical buildings.
Reverse: plain.
Broken into several pieces and reassembled.

The figures on this plate do not seem to be taken from any known
graphic source.

Since the piece lacks an inscription it is hard to tell whether the allegory
alludes to anything more specific than the dominance of the Emperor
Charles V and the disasters consequent on the Sack of Rome in 1527.

    Norman's cautious attribution merely to a painter working in a style
similar to Xanto's must be understood in the light of doubts that still
persisted in 1976 as to whether 'F.R.' and Xanto were one and the same
person, and as to whether 'F.R.' should be considered as working in Faenza.
When this plate is seen in the context of pieces bearing inscriptions in
Xanto's handwriting and dateable *c.* 1527–30, little doubt can remain that
the present piece should be grouped with those.

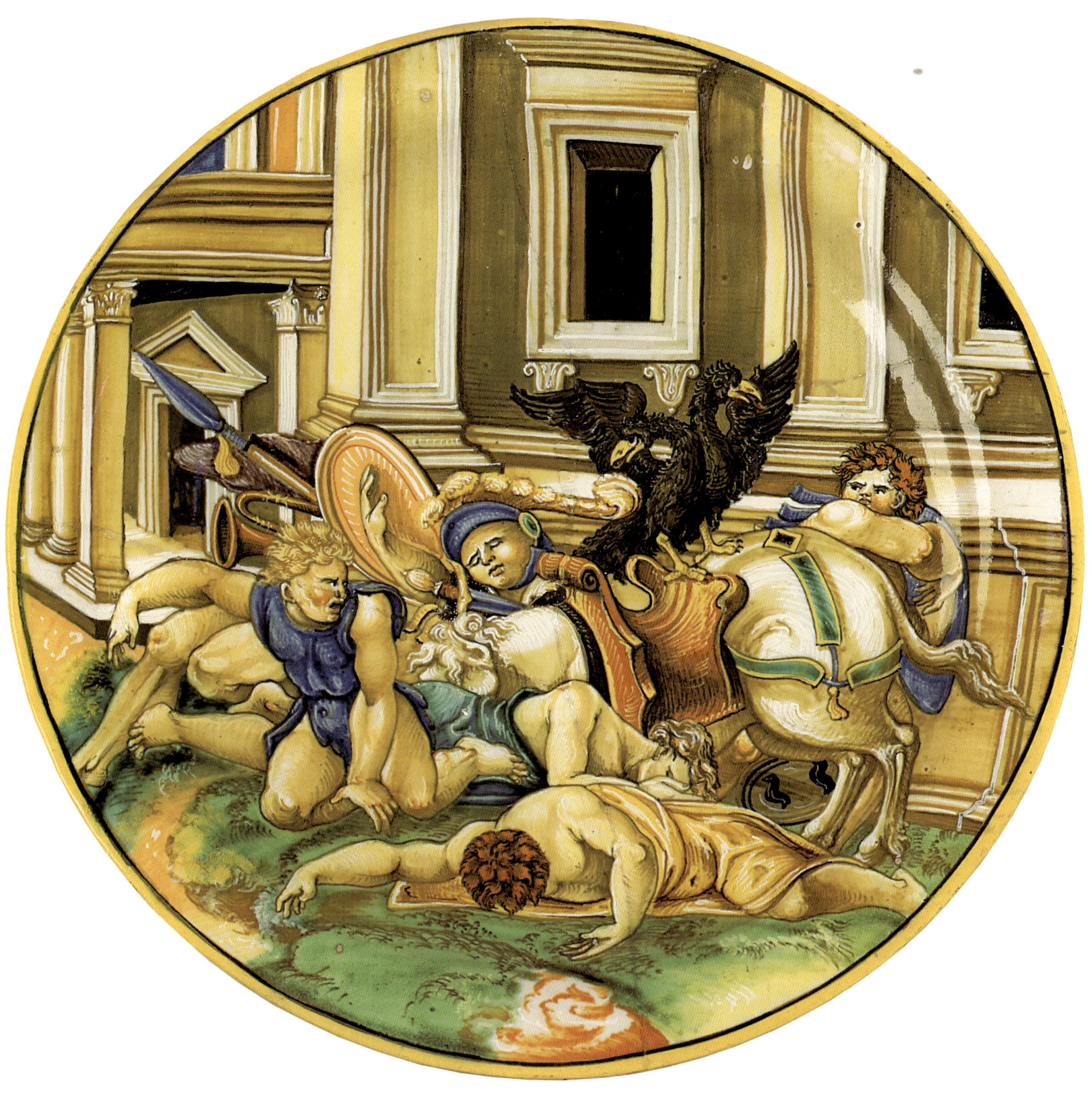

## 30.  Bowl with broad border (*Tondino*): *A Political Allegory*

Attributed to Francesco Xanto Avelli, Urbino, *c*. 1528–30

D: 27.0 cm
Cambridge, Fitzwilliam Museum, C. 14–1953

PROVENANCE

Henry Harris; Alfred Spero; Marmaduke
Langdale Horn, by whom bequeathed in
1953 to the Fitzwilliam Museum.

BIBLIOGRAPHY

Borenius 1930, no. 42, pl. xiiic; Henry
Harris sale, London, Christie's, 20 June
1950, lot 110; Rackham 1957, p. 105, no. 9,
and note 22 (as by F.R. as distinct from
Xanto); Cioci 1987, pp. 56–57 and 59; Poole
1995, no. 385.

NOTES

1. *Ill. Bartsch* 26, p. 29, 18-I (19), or a copy.
2. *Ill. Bartsch* 26, p. 33, 21 (24).

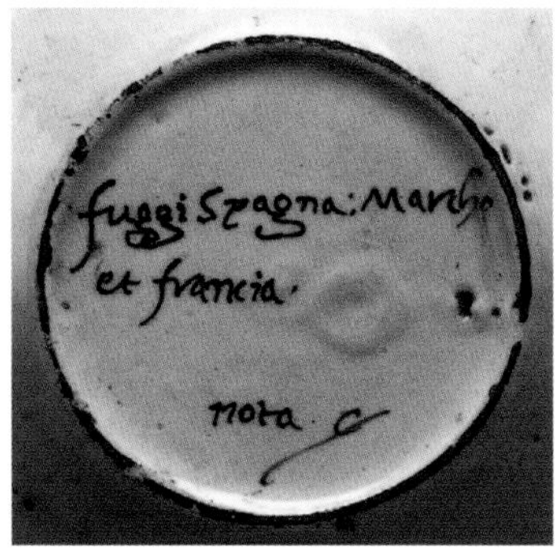

30 reverse (detail)

Polychrome. Left, a bearded man with a trident, a white horse, a cock; right,
a man, nude except for a billowing cloak, appears to retreat as he raises a
curved scimitar. In the background a landscape with hills and fortifications.
Reverse: plain except for an inscription in dark blue within the foot: *fuggi
Spagna: Marcho/ et francia./ nota*, (Flee Spain: Mark and France. Take note.)
followed by a y/Φ flourish.
The rim worn. There is a three-piece repair near the rim between twelve
and two o'clock.

The nude man is taken from Marcantonio Raimondi's engraving after
Raphael of *The Massacre of the Innocents*.[1] The bearded man to the left seems
copied (with the addition of *all'antica* armour) from a figure to the left
in Marco Dente's engraving or Beatrizet's copy of the same subject after
Baccio Bandinelli (fig. 42).[2]

    The meaning of this allegory is unclear. The style of painting and the
presence of an inscription without signature suggest production around
1528–30. The man with the trident presumably represents the maritime
power of Venice, whose patron saint was Mark. The cock stands for France
and the horse has been thought to stand for Spain. This leaves open the
question of whom the nude man with the scimitar may represent.  The only
alliance of France and Venice against Spain within our period was the League
of Cognac which, by the time this bowl is likely to have been painted, had
already ended in disaster for Spain's enemies with the 1527 Sack of Rome by
the Imperial troops. An alternative explanation by Francesco Cioci identifies

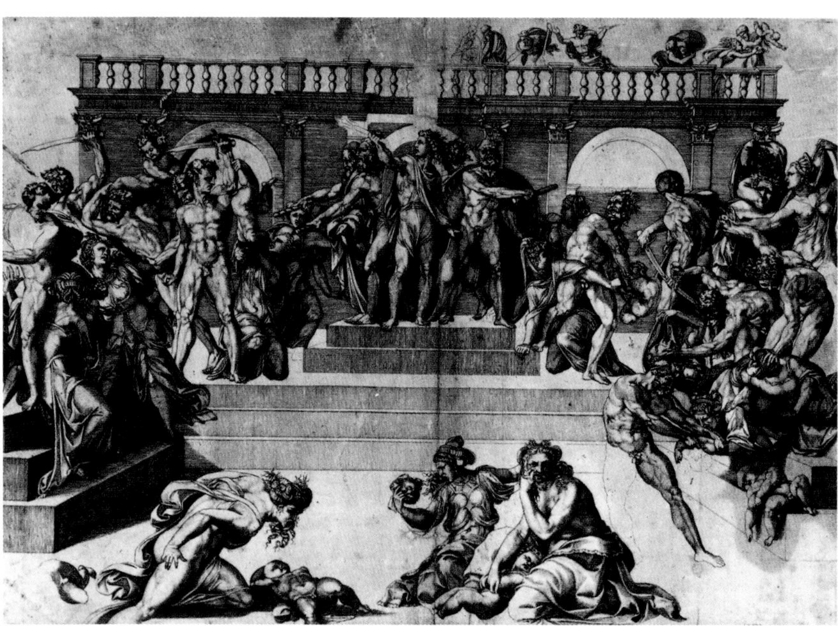

Fig. 42. Marco Dente after Baccio
Bandinelli (1488–1560) or a copy by
Nicolas Beatrizet (1507 or 1515–*c*. 1565),
*The Massacre of the Innocents*, engraving

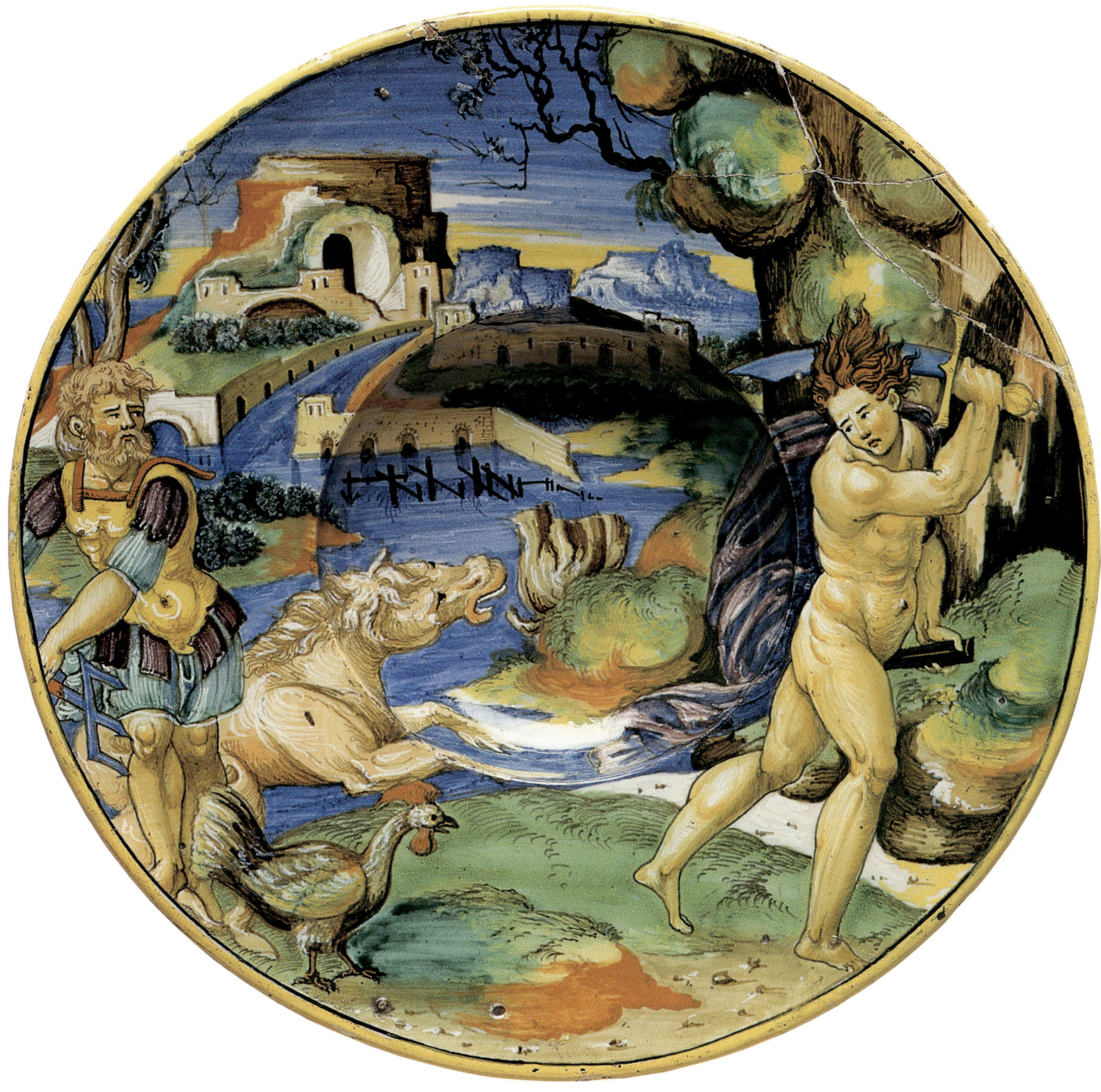


the subject as a league of Christian powers against the Turks: the bearded
man wielding the trident on behalf of St Mark being Francesco Maria in
his capacity as Captain General of Venice, the Turk being represented as the
fleeing nude man wielding a sword. That interpretation fits the disposition
of the figures on the plate and is not excluded by the early date, since a
crusade was in the air at the time of the Congress of Bologna in 1530. The
punctuation of the inscription, however, makes it a little hard to interpret
its words as "Fly from Spain, Mark and France".

# Dish on low foot (*Coppa*):
## *St Jerome and the Beato Colombini at Prayer*

Attributed to Francesco Xanto Avelli, Urbino, *c.* 1528–30

D: 26.0 cm
Glasgow City Council (Museums), 1893.93.b


PROVENANCE

Frédéric Spitzer collection.

BIBLIOGRAPHY

Molinier 1892, p. 34, no. 50 (as Urbino, Francesco Xanto); Spitzer sale 1893, lot 1087 (as Urbino. Francesco Xanto); Ballardini 1933, 233, 253, 358 R (as Urbino, 1530?); Olding 1982, no. 44 (as probably by Xanto); Mallet 1988, p. 68 and p. 91, figs. 1 and 1R (as by Xanto, *c.* 1527–30); Cioci 1987, p. 35 and pp. 113–15 (as Xanto, probably 1530); Cioci 2004, p. 217 (as probably 1530 and representing Francesco Maria I with the *sfavillanti rai* mentioned in Sonnet IX).

NOTE

1. Cioci 1987, p. 35 and pp. 113–14.


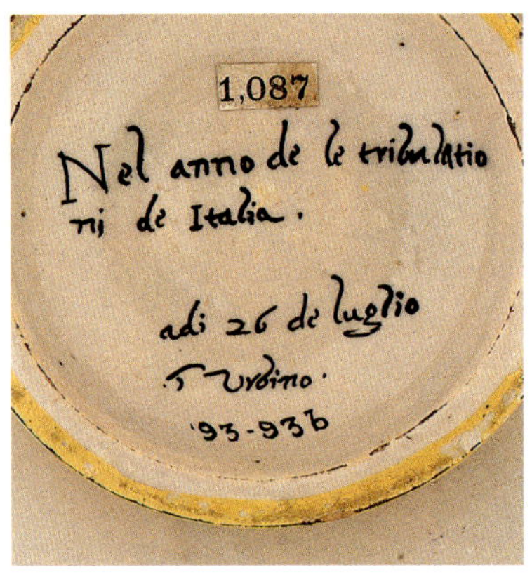

31 reverse (detail)

Polychrome. Left, St Jerome, with halo, in the wilderness with his lion; right, a *Beato* with rays surrounding his head, at prayer in monk's habit. Reverse: a yellow line round the exterior of the foot; inscribed inside the foot: *Nel anno de le tribulatio/ni de Italia./adi 26 de luglio/i Urbino* (In the year of the tribulations of Italy. On the 26th day of July, in Urbino). Two sections broken off at the rim and re-bonded.

The figure of the kneeling man in a monk's habit is evidently copied, as Francesco Cioci first pointed out, from a similar kneeling figure in Timoteo Viti's painting of *St Jerome and the Beato Colombini adoring the Trinity* (fig. 12, p. 22).[1]

The rays surrounding the head of the praying monk, both in Viti's painting and on Xanto's dish, indicate that, though not a canonised saint, he was beatified. Since Viti's painting was in the Church of the Trinità dei Gesuati at Urbino until 1811, it seems certain that the figure represents the Blessed Giovanni Colombini (1303–1367), founder of the Community of the Ingesuati, known also as 'Chierici di San Girolamo', which would explain the choice of that saint to accompany Columbini. The monkish figure copied from Viti's altarpiece onto cat. 31 was surely also intended by Xanto to represent Colombini and not, as suggested by Cioci, Duke Francesco Maria I of Urbino. The inscription probably refers to the disasters overtaking Florence in 1529–30. On 26 July 1530, Florence was on the point of having to surrender to the forces of the Holy Roman Emperor, Charles V. It is however likely that the Beato Colombini is portrayed on the dish out of sympathy for the Ingesuati of Florence, who in 1529 had to move inside the city when their convent, outside the walls was destroyed by the Florentines themselves as a defensive measure against the besiegers. For further discussion see Introduction, pp. 22–23.

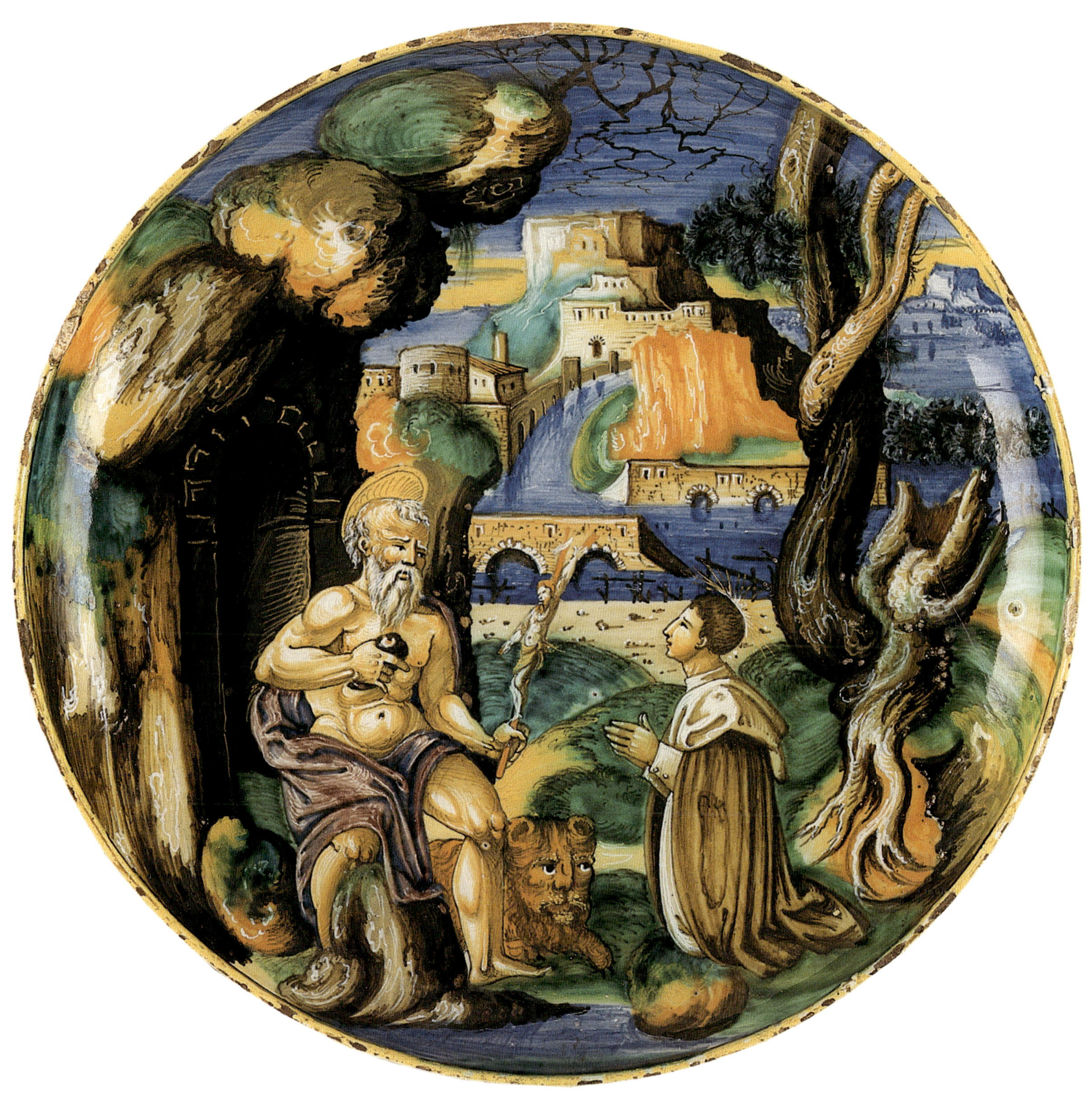

# 32.  Broth-Bowl (*Scodella*): *The Birth of Hercules* (?)

Attributed to Francesco Xanto Avelli, Urbino, *c.* 1530

D: 16.5 cm; H: 7.0 cm
London, Victoria and Albert Museum, C.2241-1910

PROVENANCE

Fountaine collection; George Salting,
by whom bequeathed in 1910.

BIBLIOGRAPHY

Fountaine sale 1884, lot 221; Ballardini
1938A, 194–95, 201 (wrongly described as
dated 1535); Rackham 1940, no. 629.

NOTES

1.  Piccolpasso 1980, I, pp. xxxiii–xxxvii;
folios 28–29; II, pp. 30–31.
2.  Ballardini 1933, 228, 252; Petruzzellis-
Scherer 1988, p. 123, no. 1 and p. 135,
figs. 1–2.
3.  Lawner 1988, pp. 78–79, no. 9.
4.  *Ill. Bartsch* 26, p. 244, 247 (200).
5.  Falke 1994, no. 258.

Polychrome. The inside with a birth-scene, left, the child, a boy, is held
on the lap of a woman who sits on a chair holding in her right hand what
appears to be a swaddling band; centre, the mother reclines on a bed; right,
a third woman sits warming a cloth before a fire. Outside, a symmetrical
design, set against a blue ground, of paired Cupids with baskets of fruit
instead of heads, with dolphins, pan-pipes and two labels, one inscribed
*M.X.A.R.*, the other *.M.A.XX.*; the vessel's stem painted with fruit; the foot
with a wreath.

The other pieces of what would have been a five-piece accouchement set,
presented to a mother at the birth of a child, are lacking.

No sixteenth-century accouchement set appears to have survived complete.
Piccolpasso illustrates the five parts of such a set and explains their uses
when brought to the bedside of a mother after a birth.[1] A *scodella* (broth-bowl)
like the present one would have stood at the base of the pile of vessels, its
lip being covered by an upturned *tagliere* or trencher-plate such as survives
for a closely related *scodella* in the Correr Museum at Venice. On the *tagliere*
would have stood an upturned *ongaresca* or bowl, within whose foot would,
in turn, have stood a salt-cellar with cover.

On the Correr Museum's *scodella*[2] and the present one the figure
of the mother is freely derived from one of the notorious *Modi* prints by
Marcantonio Raimondi after Giulio Romano (fig. 45, p. 118).[3], while
the two other women are adapted from the Muses Calliope and Erato in
Marcantonio's *Parnassus* after Raphael (fig. 44, p. 116).[4]

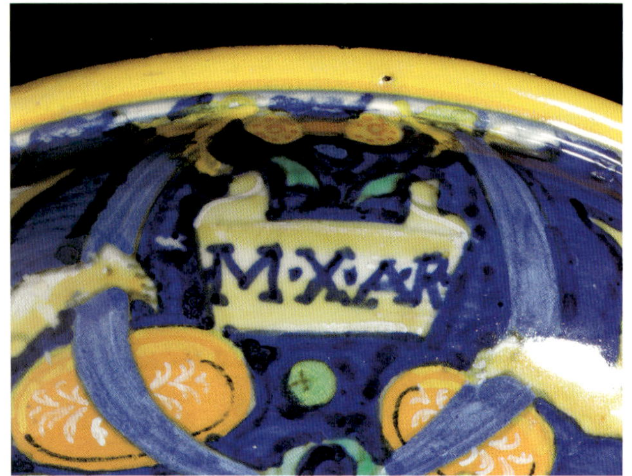 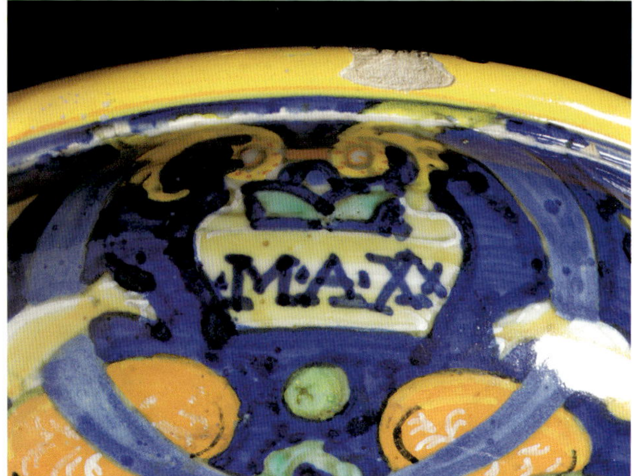

32 exterior (details)

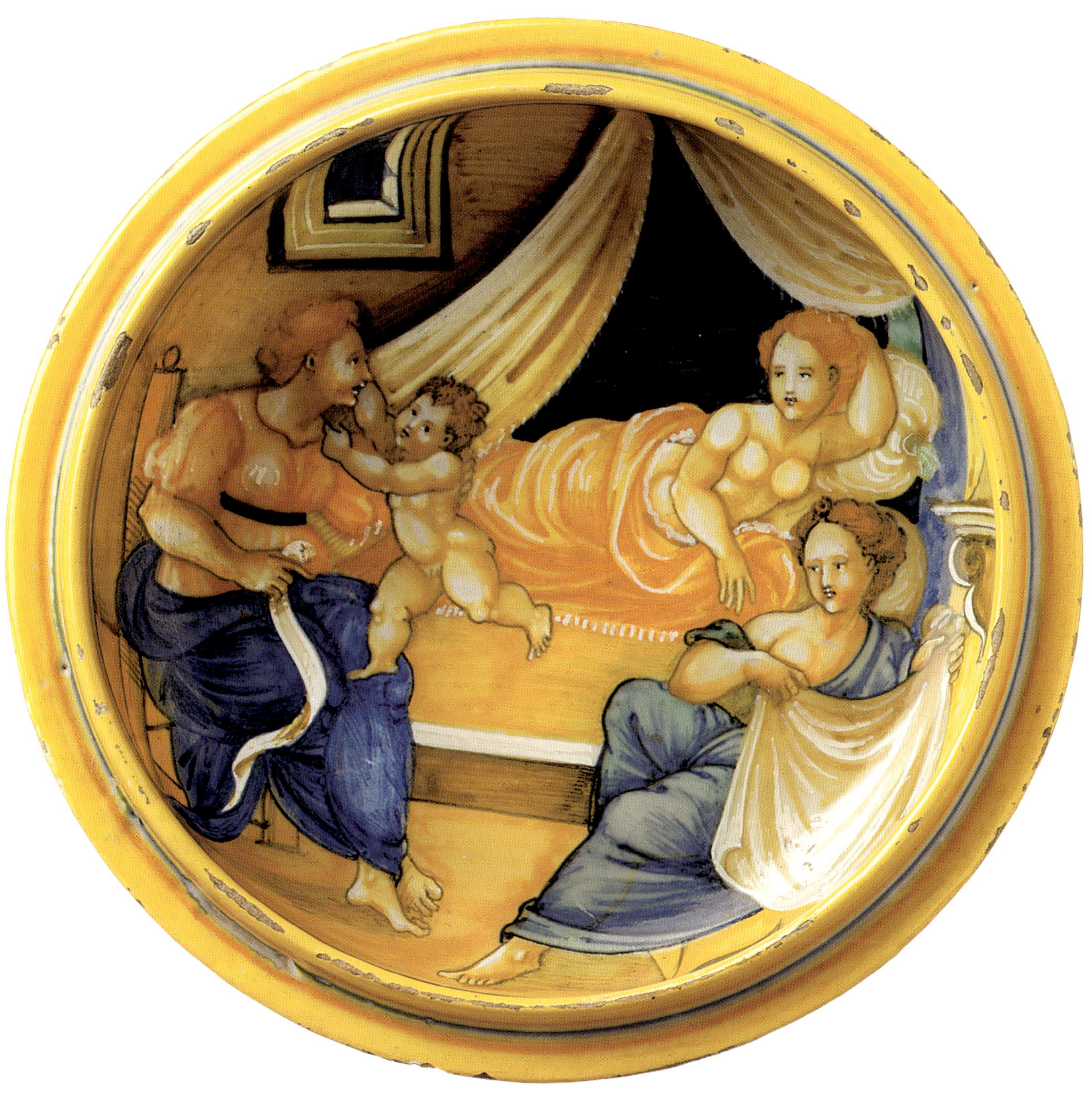

Since the child is a boy the scene cannot represent *The Birth of the Virgin*, nor can *The Nativity of Christ* be intended since the scene is in a well-appointed bedroom, not a cattle-stall. Rackham describes the scene as representing an ordinary birth but, although painted as if from real life, *The Birth of Hercules* may have been intended.

Apart from the Correr Museum's closely related *scodella*, another in similar style formerly in the Pringsheim collection was signed *F.X.A.R.* and dated 1530 or 1531, the confusion in the way the date was written being repeated on the Correr piece.[5] The inscriptions on the Victoria and Albert's *scodella* have also caused perplexity, *M.X.A.R.* having sometimes been interpreted as 'Maestro Xanto Avelli Rovigiese', though that would still leave the other inscription .*M.A.XX.* unexplained.

## 33.  Dish on low foot (*Coppa*): *The Judgement of Paris*

By Francesco Xanto Avelli, signed as painted in Urbino, dated 1531

D: 26.0 cm
Cambridge, Fitzwilliam Museum, C.86-1961

PROVENANCE

Probably Girolamo Talpa and Cardinal
Filippo Antonio Gualtieri collections;
Fountaine collection (bears diamond-
engraved collection mark and *30*), possibly
since the time of Andrew Fountaine I
(1676–1753); M. Colnaghi; Stephenson
Clarke; Louis C.G. Clarke, by whom
bequeathed in 1960.

BIBLIOGRAPHY

Fountaine sale 1884, lot 175; Moore 1988,
pp. 435–47; Poole 1995, no. 388; Triolo 1996,
pp. 279–81 and pp. 463–64, figs. 32–33a;
Paciaroni 2002; Poole 2003.

NOTES

1.  *Ill. Bartsch* 28, p. 192, 53 (89).
2.  *Ill. Bartsch* 26, p. 244, 247 (200).
3.  Poole 2003. The ewer was shown at
    the International Ceramics Fair,
    London, 1989.

Polychrome. Left, Juno and Minerva scantily clad, watch while Venus,
accompanied by Cupid, receives the golden apple from Paris, seated, right.
In the background a landscape with trees, a natural rock-arch and buildings
on a hill. From a branch, top, hangs a shield of arms: *vert, a fess or, a chief party
per pale gules* (shown as orange) *and argent two rosettes counterchanged* flanked by
*Eli* and *PYA*.
Reverse: white, inscribed in dark blue within the foot: *.1531./ Per cui Troia
superba fù/ combusta./.Favola.* (For whom proud Troy was burnt. Myth.),
followed by the signature: *Fra[n]cesco Xanto, Avelli da/ Rovigo, i[n] Urbino/ pi[n]se.*
Outside the foot, between two trefoils and forming an arc parallel to the
rim is the further inscription: *. IUDITIUM PARIDIS . MANET ALTA MENTE
REPOSITUM.* (See below).
The rim worn, with a chip at four o'clock and repaired breaks between five
and seven o'clock.

The goddesses are adapted from Gian Giacomo Caraglio's *The Muses and
Pierides*, after Rosso Fiorentino (fig. 43);[1] Paris derives from the Apollo
in Marcantonio Raimondi's *Parnassus* after Raphael (fig. 44, p. 116), and
Cupid is taken from the same print, though revolved to stand upright
rather than flying parallel to the ground.[2]

The beauty contest between the three goddesses that resulted in the
Trojan War was treated a number of times by Xanto including, if the
attribution here proposed is correct, on cat. 5. Xanto has chosen not to use
Marcantonio Raimondi's engraving of the subject (fig. 31, p. 56), though on
other wares he had appropriated figures from that source. The commentary,
unusually added inside the rim of the reverse, quotes Virgil, *Aeneid* I, lines

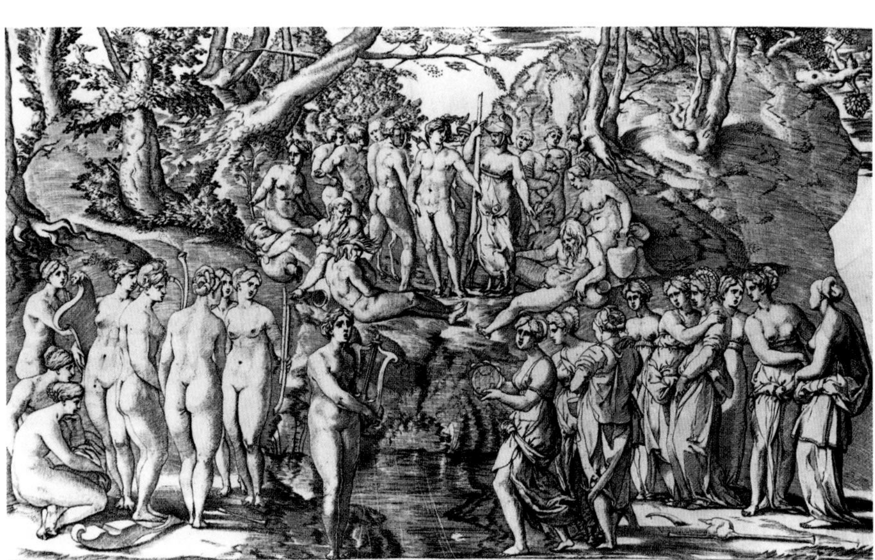

Fig. 43. Gian Giacomo Caraglio
(*c*. 1500–1565) after Rosso Fiorentino
(1494–1540), *The Muses and the Pierides*,
engraving

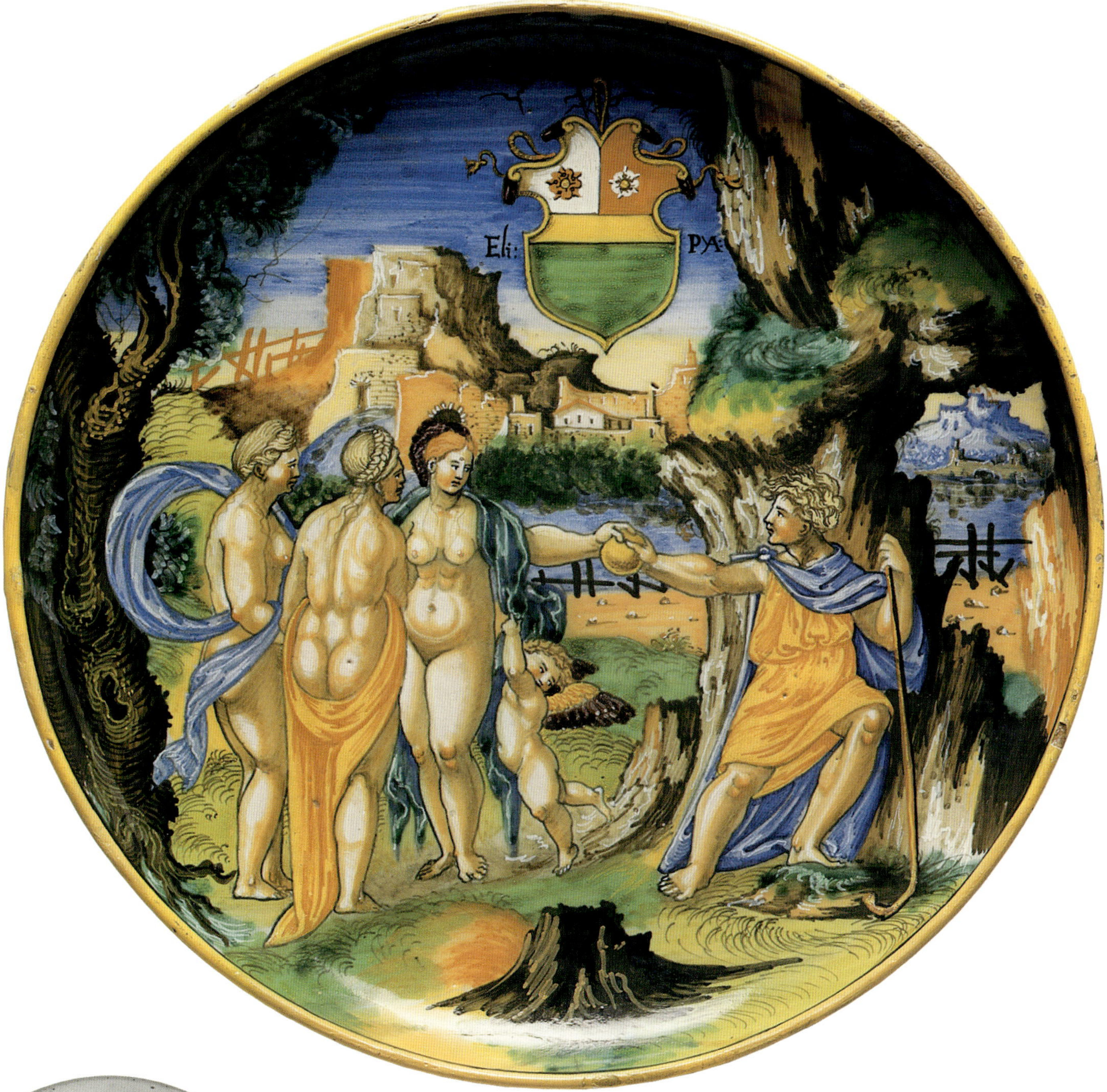

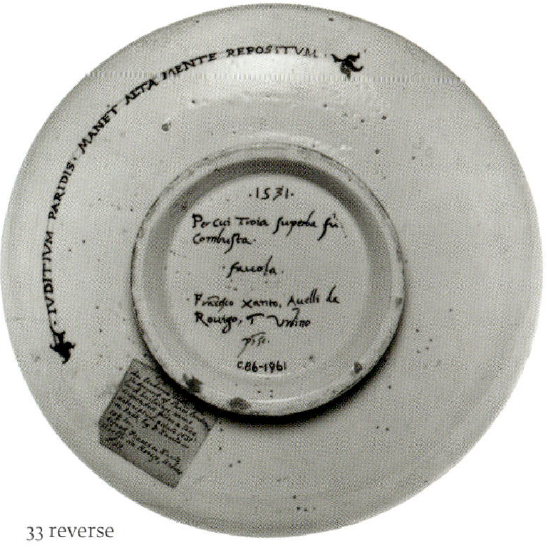

33 reverse

26–27: "Deep in her [Juno's] mind rankle the judgement of Paris, the insult of having her beauty scorned; hatred of Troy's origins; Ganymede abducted and made a favourite."

The coat of arms, which appears also on a trencher-plate (*tagliere*) in the Fitzwilliam Museum, formerly in the Casa Beni at Sanseverino, has recently been identified as that of Eliseo Piani, an official of Urbino's local Monte di Pietà, the charitable institution that lent money to citizens. The present plate is probably the piece described in an inventory of maiolica sold in 1712 by Girolamo Talpa (1654–1739) of Sanseverino to Cardinal Filippo Antonio Gualtieri (1660–1728) of a noble Orvieto family. It has been suggested by Julia Poole that an ewer by a different hand, with a slight variant of the arms but also inscribed *ELI/PYA*, might be a *bucale* described in Talpa's 1712 inventory.[3]

115

## 34. Plate: *Mars and Venus*

By Francesco Xanto Avelli, signed as painted in Urbino, dated 1531

D: 27.4 cm
London, Ranger's House, English Heritage, Wernher Foundation, 218-127

PROVENANCE

George Schultz collection; Sir Julius Wernher (probably not acquired before 1900); Sir Harold Wernher; the Wernher Foundation.

BIBLIOGRAPHY

Wilson 2002c, p. 36 and note 10; p. 39, fig. 9.

NOTES

1. *Ill.Bartsch* 27, p. 108, 420 (316).
2. *Ill. Bartsch* 29, p. 174, 17 (195).
3. *Ill. Bartsch* 26, p. 244, 247 (200).
4. Ausenda 2000, nos. 207, 208 and 213.

Polychrome. Left, Mars reclines on a cloud with shield and spear; centre, a lion lies down with two doves; right, Venus sits on further clouds holding a dart; above fly two Cupids with torches. Within the yellow rim is a circle of coiled clouds.
Reverse: off-white with, inside the foot ring, the dark blue inscription: *.1531./ Stan[n]osi i[n] pace Vene[re]/ bella & Marte./ Spere./ fra[ncesco]: Xa[n]to Ave: Ro/ vigiese pi[nse]: i[n] Urbino* (Beautiful Venus and Mars are at peace. Spheres. Francesco Xanto Avelli painted this in Urbino).
Cracked or broken across from one to seven o'clock; some areas of the adjacent decoration retouched; some chips at rim.

Mars seems to be adapted from the spearman in Marco Dente's *Battle Scene* (fig. 32, p. 60)[1] but with the lower part of the body and legs, though not the torso and head, reversed – hence the awkwardness of the pose. Venus is more straightforwardly derived from *Envy Driven from the Temple of the Muses* by the Master of the Die after Baldassare Peruzzi.[2] The flying Cupids are taken from Marcantonio Raimondi's *Parnassus*, after Raphael (fig. 44).[3]

Around the years 1530–31 Xanto painted several plates with the gods disporting themselves among clouds. Apart from cat. 35, there are three

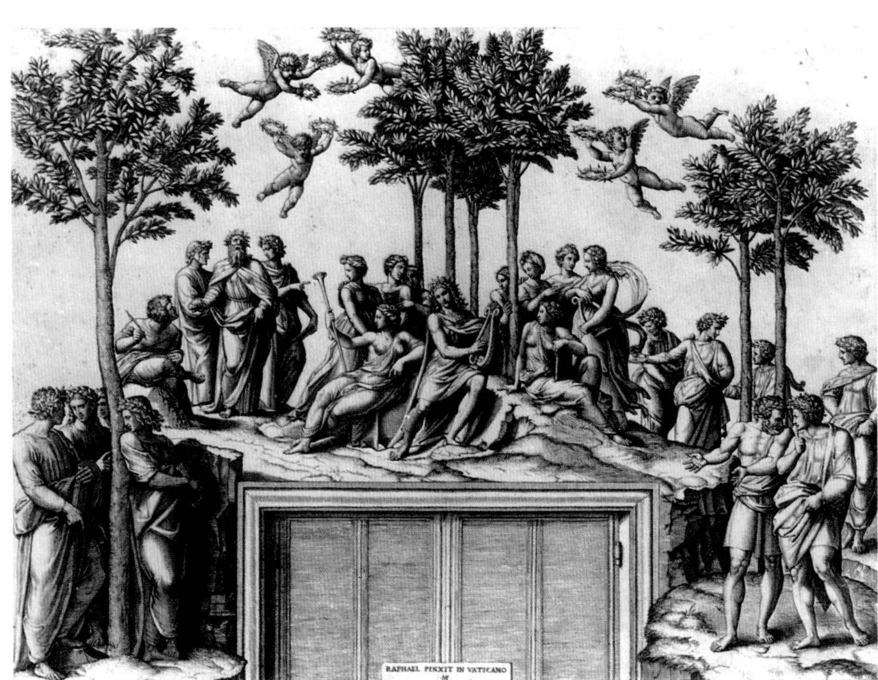

Fig. 44. Marcantonio Raimondi after Raphael, *Parnassus*, engraving

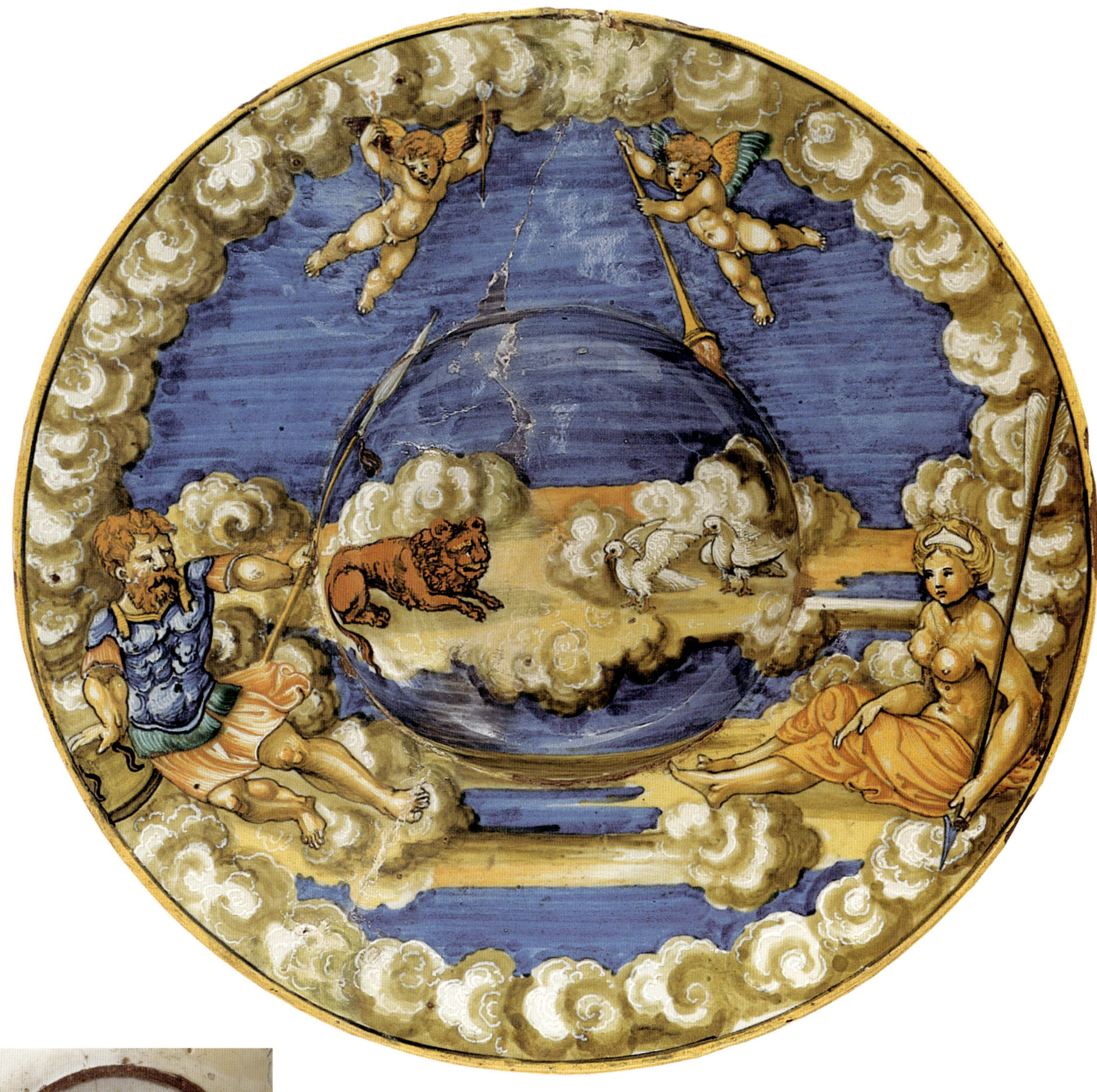

34 reverse (detail)

in the Castello Sforzesco at Milan.[4] Some of these may have been intended to bear an astrological meaning. Francesco Cioci has pointed out to Timothy Wilson that the unusual word used in conclusion of the inscription should probably be understood as *sfere*, the heavenly spheres, not as some part of the verb *sperare*, to hope. The plate no doubt expresses a wish that peace is at hand.

## 35.  Dish on low foot (*Coppa*): *Mars, Venus and Cupid*

By Francesco Xanto Avelli, signed as painted in Urbino, dated 1532;
lustred in Maestro Giorgio's workshop, probably at Gubbio

D: 26.2 cm
London, British Museum, PG&E 1855, 3-13, 12

PROVENANCE

Given by A.W. Franks in 1855.

BIBLIOGRAPHY

Fortnum 1873, pp. 345–46 and 363, mark
no. 21; Ballardini 1938A, 61, 64, 262R;
Ballardini Napoletani 1940, pp. 905–22;
Mallet 1984, p. 100, pl. cxiii; Cioci 1987,
pp. 60–63; Mallet 2004, p. 50. Thornton
and Wilson 2007, no. 164.

NOTES

1. *Ill. Bartsch* 28, p. 189, 50-II (86).
2. *Ill. Bartsch* 26, p. 244, 247 (200).

Polychrome and lustre. Left and centre, Venus reclines among the clouds
with a child in her embrace; right, Mars raises a curtain to reveal her;
above flies a Cupid holding a basket of fruit above his head.
Reverse: within the foot ring, in dark blue, is the inscription: *.1532./ Marte
tornato i[n] ciel,/ Venere contempla./ Nel XXV canto dil Rovere/ vittorioso, di .F.X.A.R.
pittor./ .fra[ncesco]:Xanto .A. da Rovigo,/ i[n] Urbino pi[nxit]:* (1532, Mars returned
to heaven, contemplates Venus. In Canto XXV of *the Victorious Rovere*, by
F.X.A.R., painter. Francesco Xanto A. da Rovigo painted it in Urbino).
The signature and place of production covered in lustre scrolls, the
off-white tin-glaze of the area outside the foot ring decorated with
spiralling leaf-scrolls.
Broken and repaired at five o'clock; some wear at the rim.

Venus is adapted from a figure in Marcantonio Raimondi's engraving
from *I Modi*, probably from an original print since the surviving Venetian
woodcut copy (fig. 45) is reversed. Mars is taken from Gian Giacomo
Caraglio's *Mercury carrying Psyche to Olympus*,[1] and Xanto has even forgotten
to remove Mercury's wings from the helmet. The Cupid in the sky is from
Marcantonio Raimondi's *Parnassus* after Raphael (fig. 44, p. 116).[2]

This is the only known piece of maiolica on which Xanto quotes his own
poetry (See Introduction, pp. 14 and 25). The immediate meaning of the
allegory,  which like cat. 34 may bear some relationship to astrology, must
concern the return of peace.

   The lustre, though giving a surface sparkle that presumably appealed
to contemporaries, is poorly integrated with the design and was clearly not
added under Xanto's control. In judging Xanto's style or interpreting his
allegories on work dated between 1528 and 1542, one should discount all
lustre additions. There is no evidence that a lustre kiln was operating at
Urbino before 1538, if then, so it is likely that Xanto's *istoriati* were sent to
Gubbio for lustre enrichment. Possible reasons why, between 1531–33, the
names 'Urbino' and 'Xanto' were partially obscured in lustre are discussed
in the Introduction, pp. 39–40.

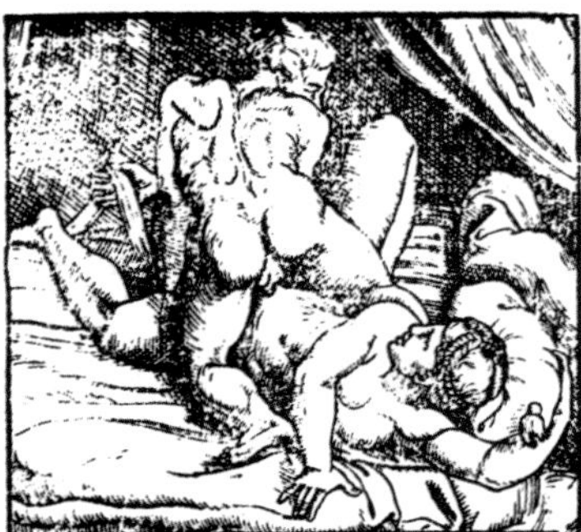

Fig. 45. Anonymous, after Marcantonio
Raimondi from Giulio Romano, *I Modi*,
illustration to Sonnet 9, *c.* 1527, woodcut

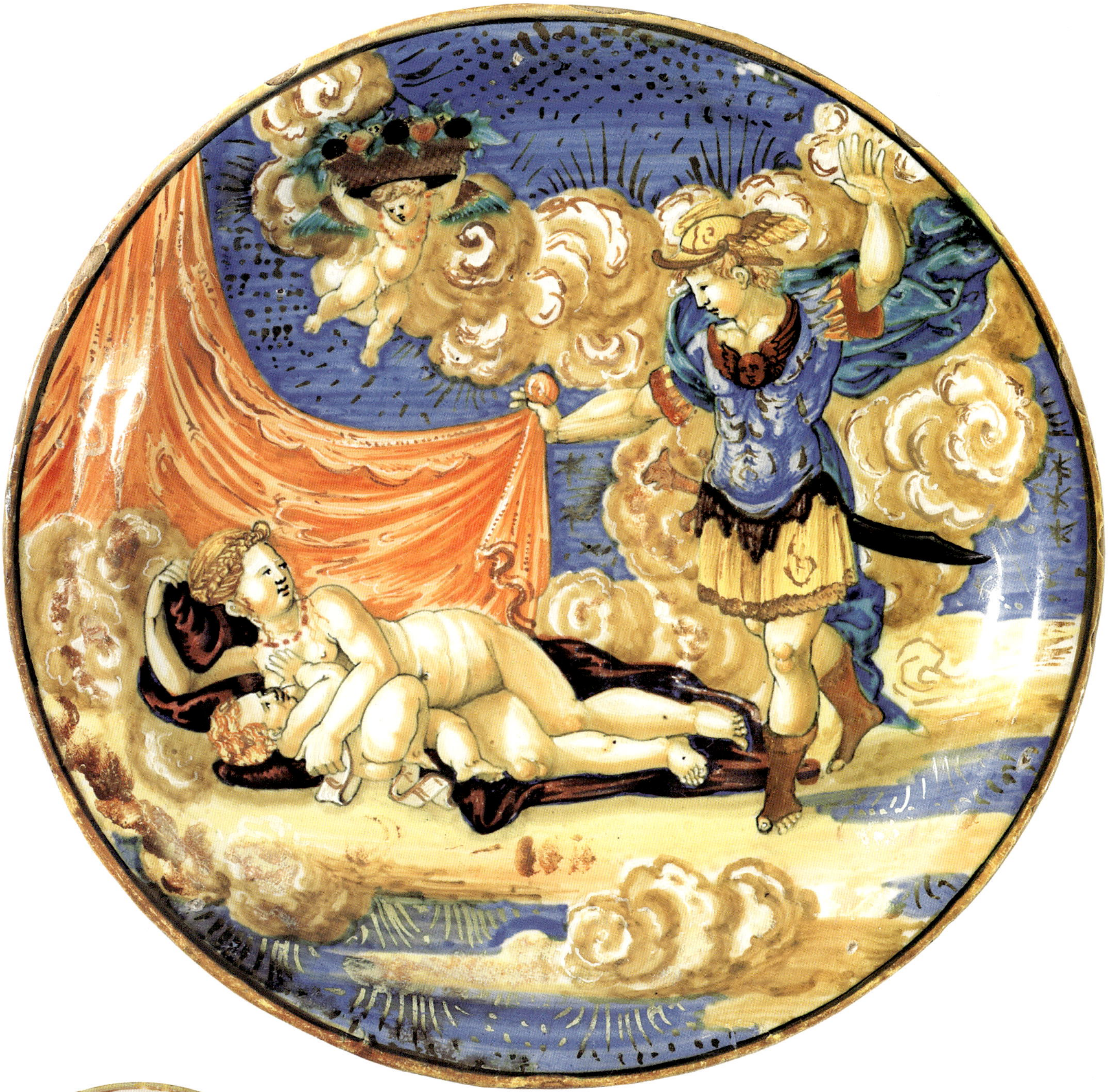

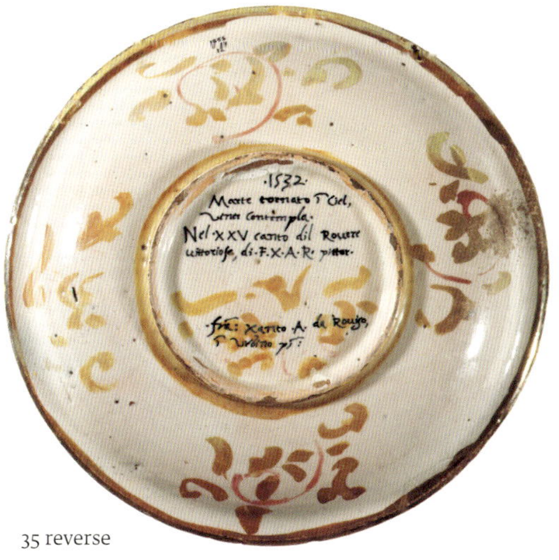
·1532·
Marte tornato 'l Ciel,
Venra contempla.
Nel·XXV canto dil Rouere
uittoriose, di·F·X·A·R· pittor·

frà: Xanto A. da Rouigo
'n Urbino pi:

## 36. Plate: *Astolfo in the Land of Women*

By Francesco Xanto Avelli, signed as painted in Urbino, dated 1532

D: 26.1 cm
London, British Museum, PG&E 1913, 12-20, 121


PROVENANCE

A.H.S. Barwell Bequest, 1913.

BIBLIOGRAPHY

Ballardini 1938A, 50, 53, 252R; Ballardini Napoletani 1940, p. 919; Wilson 1987, no. 222; Collins 1987; Triolo 1988, pp. 240–41, no. 7 and pl. xxxiii a, b; Wilson 1990; Triolo 1996, pp. 308–09, no. 7.9 and p. 484, figs. 56 and 56a; Ravanelli Guidotti 1994A; Thornton and Wilson 2007, no. 161. For the Pucci service as a whole, see Bibliography to cat. 37.

NOTES

1. Respectively from Lawner 1988, pp. 76–77, no. 8 and pp. 78–79, no. 9.
2. *Ill. Bartsch* 26, p. 153, 117 (104).
3. *Ill. Bartsch* 26, p. 223, 226-I (183).
4. *Ill. Bartsch* 26, p. 135, 104-I (89).
5. Wilson 1987, no. 222; Wilson 1990, pp. 323 and 326.


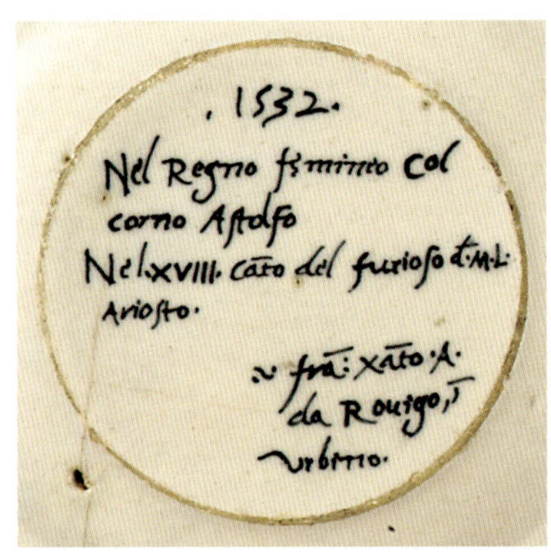

36 reverse (detail)

Polychrome. Left, Astolfo on horseback blows his magic horn; five terrified male figures and a horse make their escape. From a cornice of the architectural background, top right, hangs a shield of arms: *Argent, a moor's head proper wearing a headband Argent charged with three hammers Sable. Behind the shield, an ombrellino*.
Reverse: within the foot is written in dark blue: *.1532./ Nel Regno femineo col/ corno Astolfo/ Nel XVIII ca[n]to del furioso di .M.L./ Ariosto./ di [?] fra[ncesco]: Xa[n]to .A./ da Rovigo, i[n]/ Urbino.* (1532. Astolfo with his horn in the realm of the women in the 18th canto of Orlando Furioso by L. Ariosto, by Francesco Xanto A. da Rovigo in Urbino)
A crack extends inward from the rim.

Astolfo and the man on his knees, foreground, left, are adapted from Marcantonio Raimondi's *I Modi* after Giulio Romano (fig. 45, p. 118).[1]
The man with raised sword escaping, centre, derives (in reverse) from Raimondi's *The Martyrdom of St Felicity* after Raphael.[2] The bearded man fleeing, right of centre, derives from *A Naked Man pursuing a Naiad* (fig. 54, p. 146).[3]
The man in a blue cloak in the doorway, right, derives from *The Martyrdom of St. Lawrence* by Marcantonio Raimondi after Baccio Bandinelli.[4]

In the definitive 1532 edition of Lodovico Ariosto's *Orlando Furioso* the incident here shown by Xanto corresponds not with Canto XVIII, as inscribed on the plate, but with Canto XX,[5] so Xanto evidently consulted an earlier edition of the poem, first printed in 1516. Xanto has illustrated the scene where Astolfo enters a land ruled by women who put to death any man who does not, in a single night, kill ten men and make love to ten women. Rather than attempt this exhausting feat, Astolfo blows on a magic horn which has the power of terrifying all humans, women included. Strangely, Xanto has depicted no women, and the men who flee from the horn are presumably his own followers.

The arms are those of the Pucci family of Florence. Two of Xanto's five plates illustrating Ariosto's *Orlando Furioso* belong to the Pucci service: the other one from the set, at Cambridge, shows *Orlando and Friends finding Ruggiero's Arms*. For further discussion of the Pucci service see cat. 37.

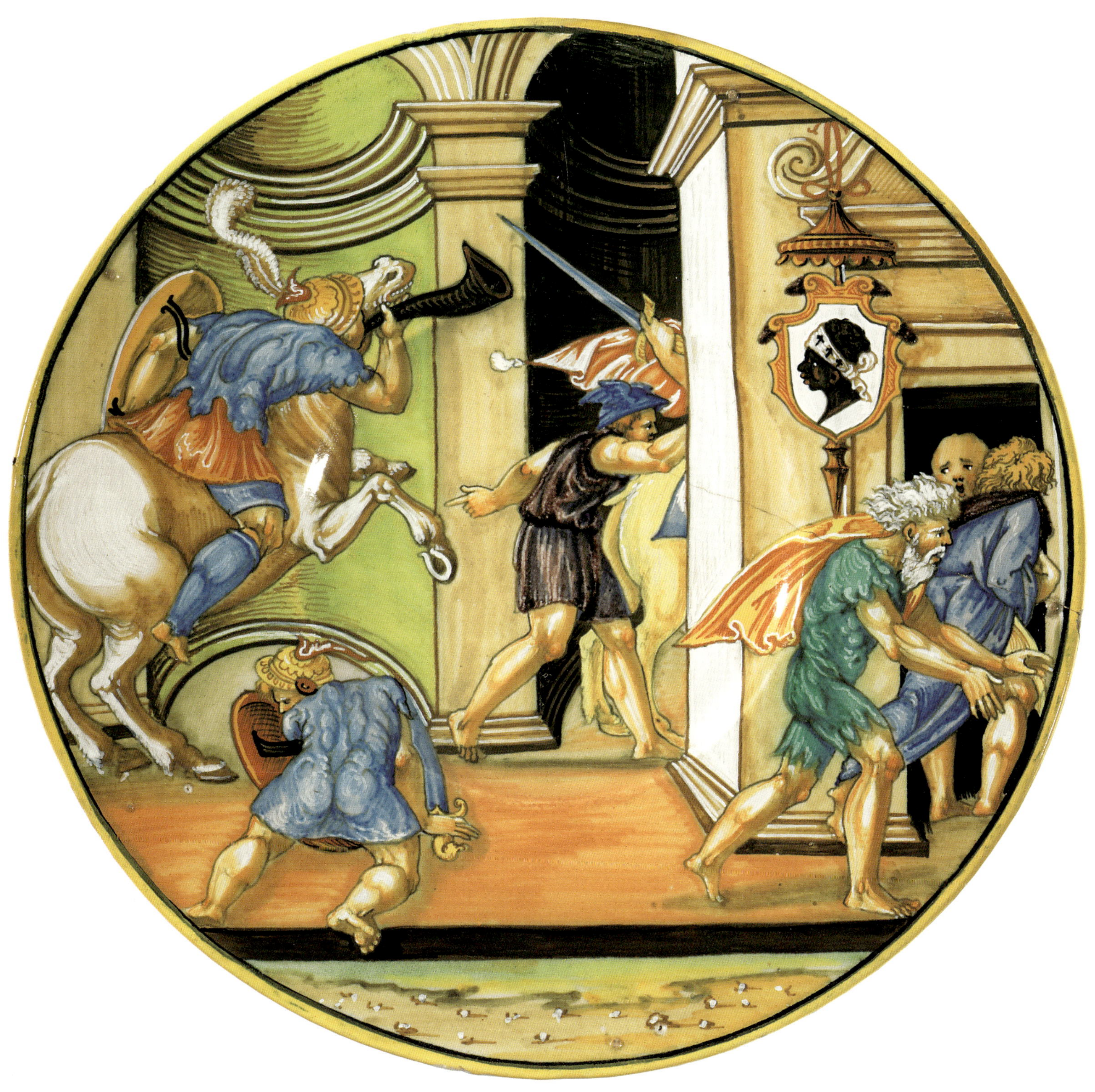

## 37. Triangular Salt Cellar:
### *Pucci Arms, Cupids and Ornament*

By Francesco Xanto Avelli, Urbino, signed and dated 1532;
the sides perhaps by an assistant

Largest measurement: 15.7 cm
London, British Museum, PG&E 1855, 12-1, 110

PROVENANCE

Ralph Bernal.

BIBLIOGRAPHY

Bernal sale 1855, lot 2081;
Ballardini 1938A, 57, 60; Wilson 1987,
no. 74; Triolo 1988, pp. 281–82, no. 37 and
pl. lxi a, b; Rasmussen 1989, Appendix I,
no. 80.3; Triolo 1992, p. 89; Triolo 1996, pp.
340–41, no. 7.37 and p. 505, fig. 82;
Appendix I, no. 80.3; Thornton and
Wilson 2007, no. 162.

NOTES

1. Hausmann 1972, no. 198.
2. Chicago Art Institute, Elizabeth R.
Vaughn Fund, 1964.140. Triolo 1996,
p. 278, 3B.9 and p. 462, fig. 31.
3. Triolo 1988; Triolo 1991; Triolo 1992,
pp. 87–89; Triolo 1996, pp. 297–341;
Triolo 2002.
4. Rasmussen 1989, pp. 252–57.
5. Cioci 1997B; Cioci 2002B.
6. Spallanzani 1999; Cioci 2006.

Polychrome. Of shaped triangular form; the lower corners moulded as foliate dolphin-masks; the depression for the salt decorated in white on white and in yellow with a daisy and inscribed: *Fran: Xanto. A. Rovi:* the upper surface with three shields with the arms of Pucci beneath an *ombrellino* supported by Cupids, all on a dark blue ground; the sides with cornucopiae and floral motifs on a black ground incorporating the date *1532*.
A copper mount of later date covers damage to the edge.

Two comparable triangular salt cellars are known, but both have chamfered corners: the first, in Berlin,[1] is signed F.X.; the second, at Chicago,[2] bears the 'Three Crescent' arms but in the form with one crescent uppermost and two below, and is therefore attributable not to Xanto but to 'The Milan Marsyas Painter' (cat. 26). This triangular form of salt, difficult to make in pottery, probably derived from bronze prototypes.

Thirty-seven pieces from the Pucci service are recorded, making it the largest set by Xanto to survive. It has been extensively studied by Julia Triolo.[3] Thirty-two pieces are illustrated in Rasmussen's catalogue of the Lehman Collection.[4] For which member of the Florentine Pucci family the service was commissioned has been the subject of debate but if, as seems the case, the umbrella-like symbol (*ombrellino*) is the *gonfalone* of a *Cardinale Penitenziere Maggiore*, an ecclesiastical office second only to that of the Pope, then in 1532–33 Cardinal Antonio Pucci (1485–1544) is the only possible candidate.[5] Cardinal Antonio's pro-Imperial politics would have been congenial to Francesco Maria and hence to Xanto. In order to accept Cardinal Antonio as the service's first owner it is necessary to explain why the Moor's head is not combined, as it normally was on his arms, with the Medici *palle* of both Leo X, who appointed him Bishop of Pistoia in 1518, and Clement VII, by whom he was raised to the purple in 1531. There must also be an explanation as to why, unusually, the *ombrellino* is shown in place of a cardinal's hat.[6]

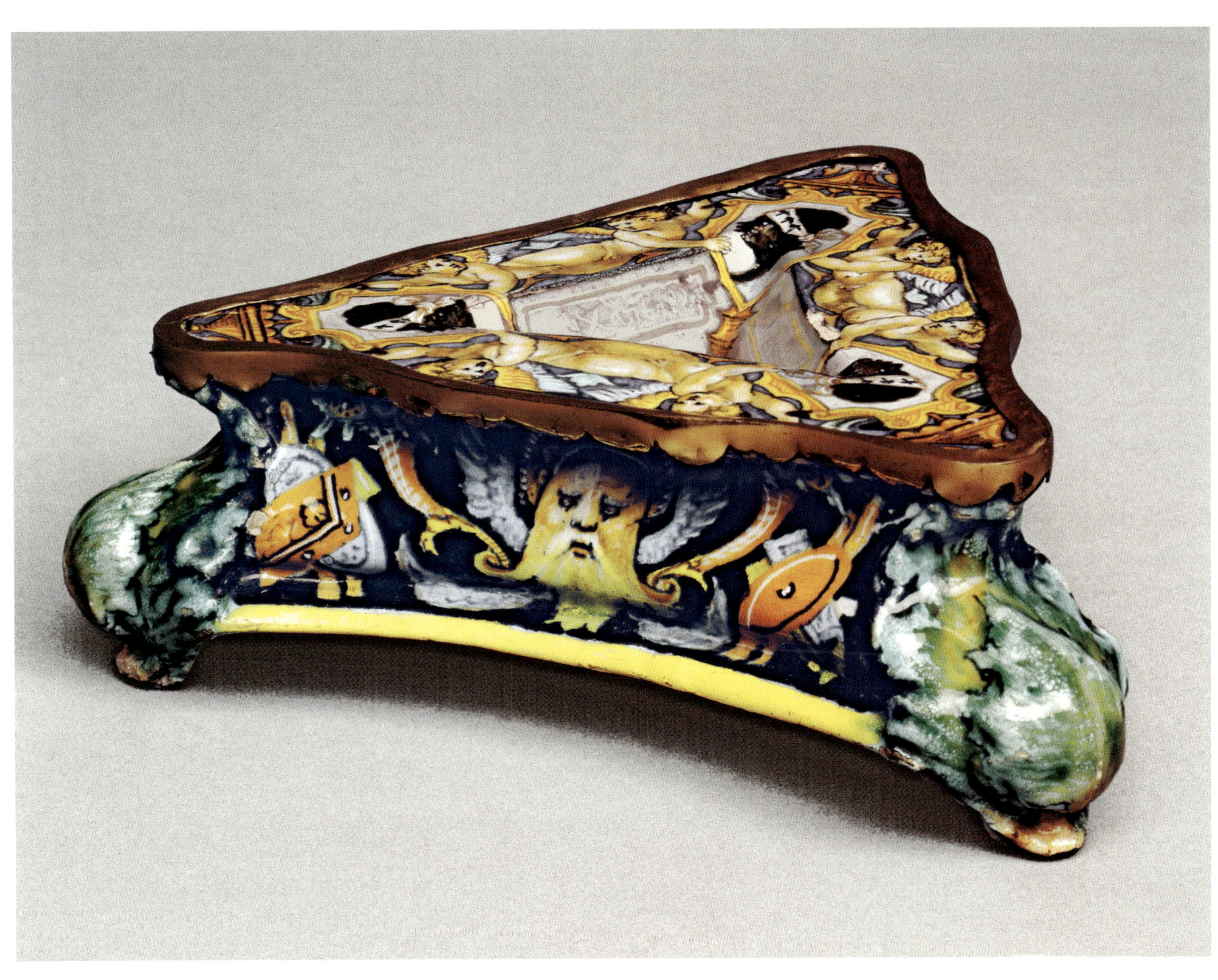

38.  Bowl with broad border (*Tondino*):
*The Descent of Orpheus into Hades*

By Francesco Xanto Avelli, signed as in Urbino, dated 1532
Lustred in Maestro Giorgio's workshop, probably at Gubbio

D: 26.5 cm
London, Wallace Collection, C88

PROVENANCE
Possibly Pourtalès-Gorgier collection;
possibly Basilewsky collection; Prince
Napoleon collection. For further detail
see Norman 1976, no. C88.

BIBLIOGRAPHY
Pourtalès-Gorgier sale, lot 1697; Prince
Napoleon sale, lot 251; Bethnal Green
1872–75, no. 1504; Ballardini 1938A, 60, 63,
256R; Norman 1976, no. C88.

NOTES
1. *Ill. Bartsch* 27, p. 108, 420 (316).
2. *Ill. Bartsch* 16, p. 70, 14 (304).
3. *Ill. Bartsch* 26, p. 135, 104-I (89).

Polychrome and lustre. Left, Orpheus plays a *lira da braccio*; centre, Charon rows his ferry across the Styx; centre foreground, a reclining, white haired male figure; right, a figure with a head like a crane's faces outward, while Cerberus, with the heads of three hounds, faces inwards towards the bowl's centre. The background with trees and rocks.
Reverse: somewhat discoloured off-white tin-glaze decorated with three groups of spiralling plant-scroll. Within the foot, the inscription in dark blue: *.1532./ Alla Caro[n]thea Cimba arri/ va Orpheo/ Nel .XL. L. d[i] Ovidio Meth:/ fra[ncesco] Xa[n]to A/ da Rovigo, i[n]/ Urbino.* (Orpheus arrives at the bark of Charon. In Book 40 of Ovid's *Metamorphoses*. Francesco Xanto A. from Rovigo, in Urbino). Xanto's name and that of the town have been deliberately obscured with lustre.
Broken in three pieces and restored.

No print sources have been traced for Orpheus or Cerberus; the reclining figure in the foreground derives (in reverse) from one of the versions of the *Battle Scene* print (fig. 32, p. 60);[1] Charon is taken from the print of *Sol* by Master I.B. (Georg Pencz);[2] the body of the crane-headed man is from a figure in the background, centre, of Marcantonio Raimondi's *The Martyrdom of St Lawrence* after Baccio Bandinelli.[3]

In referring to the *Metamorphoses* of Ovid, Xanto presumably misread his reference as 'XL' instead of 'XI', as it is in Books X and XI that Ovid tells the story of Orpheus, a famous Thracian poet who, disconsolate at the death of his wife, Eurydice, descended into Hades in an attempt to release her. Orpheus failed in this because he could not resist looking back at her before regaining the upper world, breaking the terms of the bargain he had made with Pluto, god of the underworld. Thereafter Orpheus despised women, which so infuriated the maenads of Ciconia that they tore him to pieces. His shade, however, returned to Hades and was reunited with that of Eurydice. Xanto's plate probably represents this return to Hades. The personalities of Orpheus with his lyre, Charon, the ferryman to Hades and of Cerberus, the three-headed guardian dog, are recognisable; possibly the reclining man represents Tityus, temporarily released from torment by the power of Orpheus's music. The bird-headed man seems harder to identify.

For attempts to hide Xanto's name and that of Urbino under lustre, see Introduction, pp. 30–40.

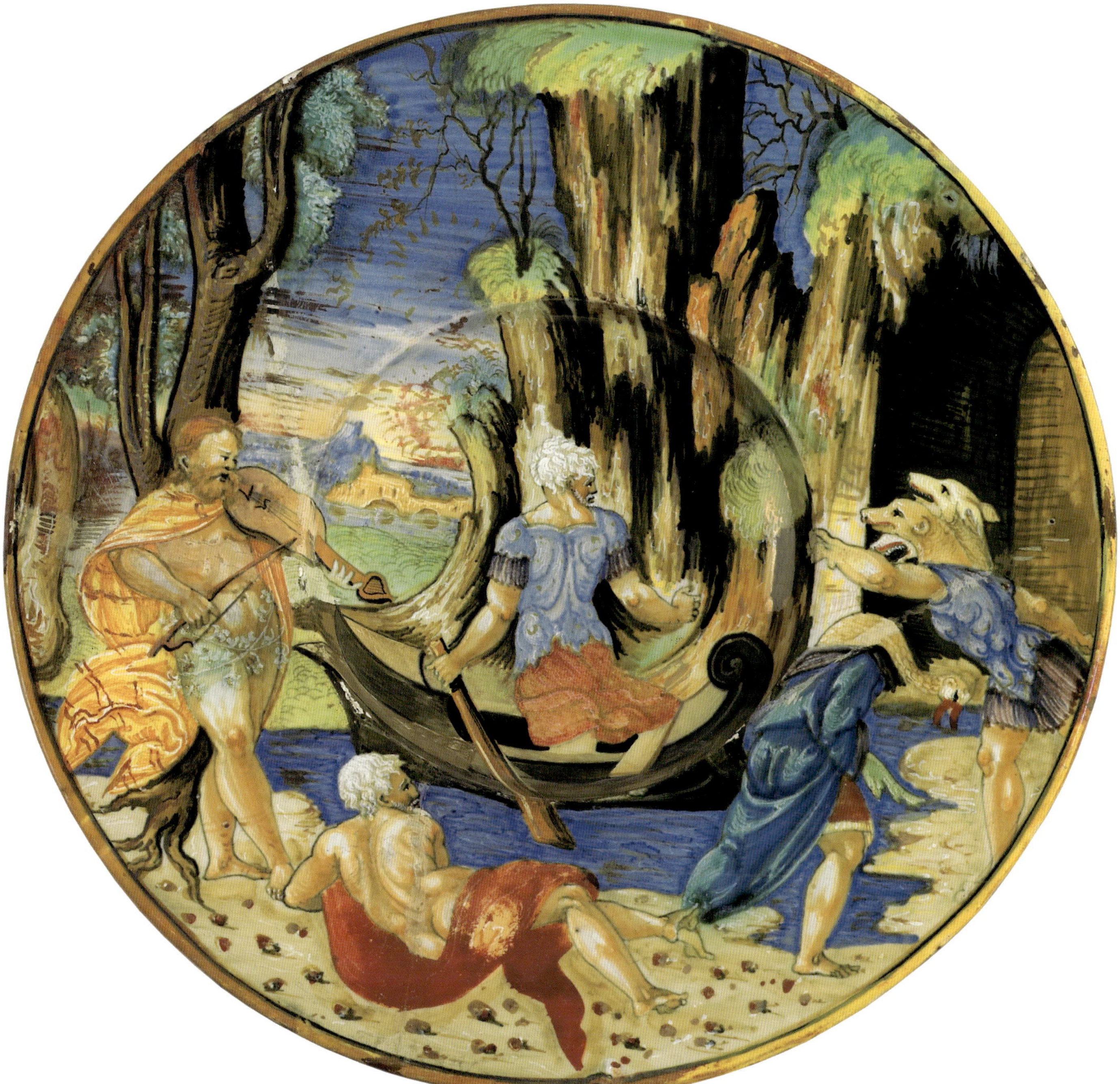

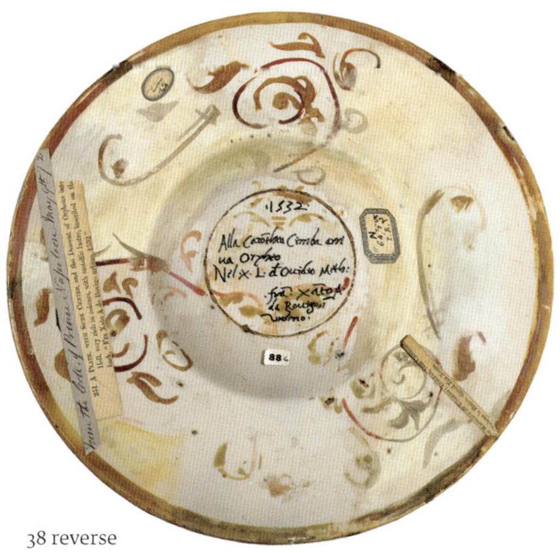

# 39.  Dish: *The Triumph of Neptune and Venus*

By Francesco Xanto Avelli, signed as painted in Urbino, dated 1533

D: 48.0 cm
London, Wallace Collection, C89

PROVENANCE

A. Joseph.

BIBLIOGRAPHY

Robinson 1863, no. 5242, as belonging to
A. Joseph; probably Bethnal Green 1872-75,
no. 1469; Ballardini 1938A, 83, 89, 275R;
Norman 1965; Norman 1976, no. C89; Cioci
1987, pp. 200–07; Triolo 1996, pp. 347–49;
Cioci 1997A; Syson and Thornton 2001,
pp. 251–54; Higgott 2004.

NOTES

1. *Ill. Bartsch* 27, p. 15, 323 (243).
2. *Ill. Bartsch* 28, p. 189, 50-II (86).
3. *Ill. Bartsch*, respectively 28, p. 183, 44-I
   (85); 26, p. 33, 21 (24); 26, p. 223, 226-I
   (183); 26, p. 135, 104-I (89); 27, p. 47, 350
   (262); 26, p. 244, 247 (200); 28, p. 201, 62
   (95); 26, p. 215, 217-I, (177); 26, p.239, 242
   (194); 26, p. 212, 213 (173).
4. Cioci 1987, pp. 200–07. The two plates he
   cites are one dated 1533 (Borenius 1930,
   no. 37) and one dated 1534, formerly at
   Brunswick (Lessmann 1979, p. 564, VI).
5. Francesco Petrarca, *Rime*, XXXIII, 1–2;
   *Trionfo della Fama*, I, 10–13.
6. Robinson 1863, no. 5253; now
   Los Angeles County Museum, Randolph
   Hearst Collection, inv. 50.9.17.
7. Higgott, 2004, pp. 63–67 and figs. 12, 14,
   15, 22 and 23.

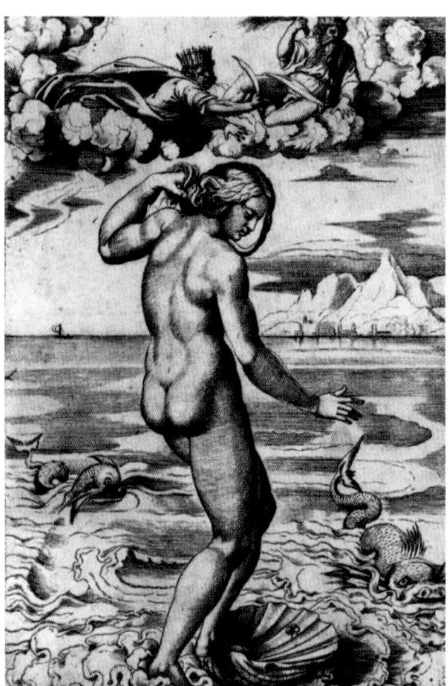

Fig. 46. Marco Dente after Raphael,
*The Birth of Venus*, engraving

Polychrome. Centre, Venus, nude, steps onto a scallop-shell, surrounded by marine deities, including Neptune, Cupids and dolphins; in the sky, top left, the Planet Venus and, top right, a coat of arms: *argent, six bars azure charged with besants, five, four, three, two and one, impaling argent, on a chief azure a cross patty of the first.* Reverse: yellow concentric lines round the rim and well; under the dish's centre are four small blue leaves and the dark blue inscription: *M.D.XXXIII/ Triompha qui Nettu[no] nelle salse onde, / Su le qual gode l'amorosa Stella / Ignuda frà suoi figli, e, vaga, e, bella / Vien coronata di fioretti, e, fronde.* (Here triumphs Neptune in the salt waves on which rejoices the amorous star, naked amongst her sons, and fair and lovely as she comes crowned with blossom and leaves).

Venus is from Marco Dente's engraving (fig. 46) after the fresco by Raphael and pupils in Cardinal Bibbiena's bathroom in the Vatican;[1] Neptune is reversed from the print, probably by Caraglio, of *Mercury Carrying Psyche to Olympus* after Raphael's fresco in the Villa Farnesina.[2] Other figures have been traced to the following: Caraglio after Rosso Fiorentino, *Hercules killing Cerberus*; Marco Dente after Baccio Bandinelli, *The Massacre of the Innocents* (fig. 42, p. 108); Raimondi after the Antique, *A Naked Man Pursuing a Naiad* (fig. 54, p. 146); Raimondi after Bandinelli, *The Martyrdom of St. Lawrence*; Raimondi after Raphael's fresco in the Villa Farnesina, *The Triumph of Galatea*; Raimondi after Raphael, *Parnassus* (fig. 44, p. 116); Marco Dente or Caraglio after Raphael, *Alexander and Roxana* (fig. 47, p. 128); Raimondi after Raphael, *Dance of Cupids* (fig. 39, p. 84); Marco Dente after an antique relief in San Vitale, Ravenna (reversed), *Bas-relief with Three Cupids (The Throne of Neptune)* (fig. 41, p. 92) and possibly Raimondi's *Roman Triumph*.[3]

Cioci has shown that on signed plates of 1533 and 1534[4] Xanto quoted Petrarch's lines: *Già fiammeggiava l'amorosa stella / Per l'oriente…* (Appendix B, Sonnet XXXIII) and that the Planet Venus, which precedes the dawn, was again unambiguously described as *l'amorosa stella* by Petrarch in his *Trionfo della Fama*.[5] Indeed there is a further Xanto plate of 1533 inscribed: *dil terzo cielo l'amorosa stella*,[6] identifying the third heaven in which, according to pre-Copernican astronomy, the planet of Venus revolved. Venus, goddess of love, and not the Pleiad Alcyone suggested in Norman's catalogue, must therefore be the 'amorous star' intended by Xanto. When Xanto appropriated Petrarch's expression *l'amorosa stella* in his own Sonnet XXIV he clearly meant Venus, the morning star. The primary subject of the dish under consideration, then, is *The Triumph of Neptune and Venus*. Since the coat of arms relates to Laura Gritti and Giacomo Michiel, members of two influential Venetian families who had married in 1513, allusions to maritime Venice or even to their twentieth wedding anniversary are likely enough. Although Neptune's trident and the scallop-shell of Venus are the only clear identifying emblems, Higgott, who illustrates the dish in its nineteenth-century frame, suggests identifications for the minor participants in the *Triumph*.[7]

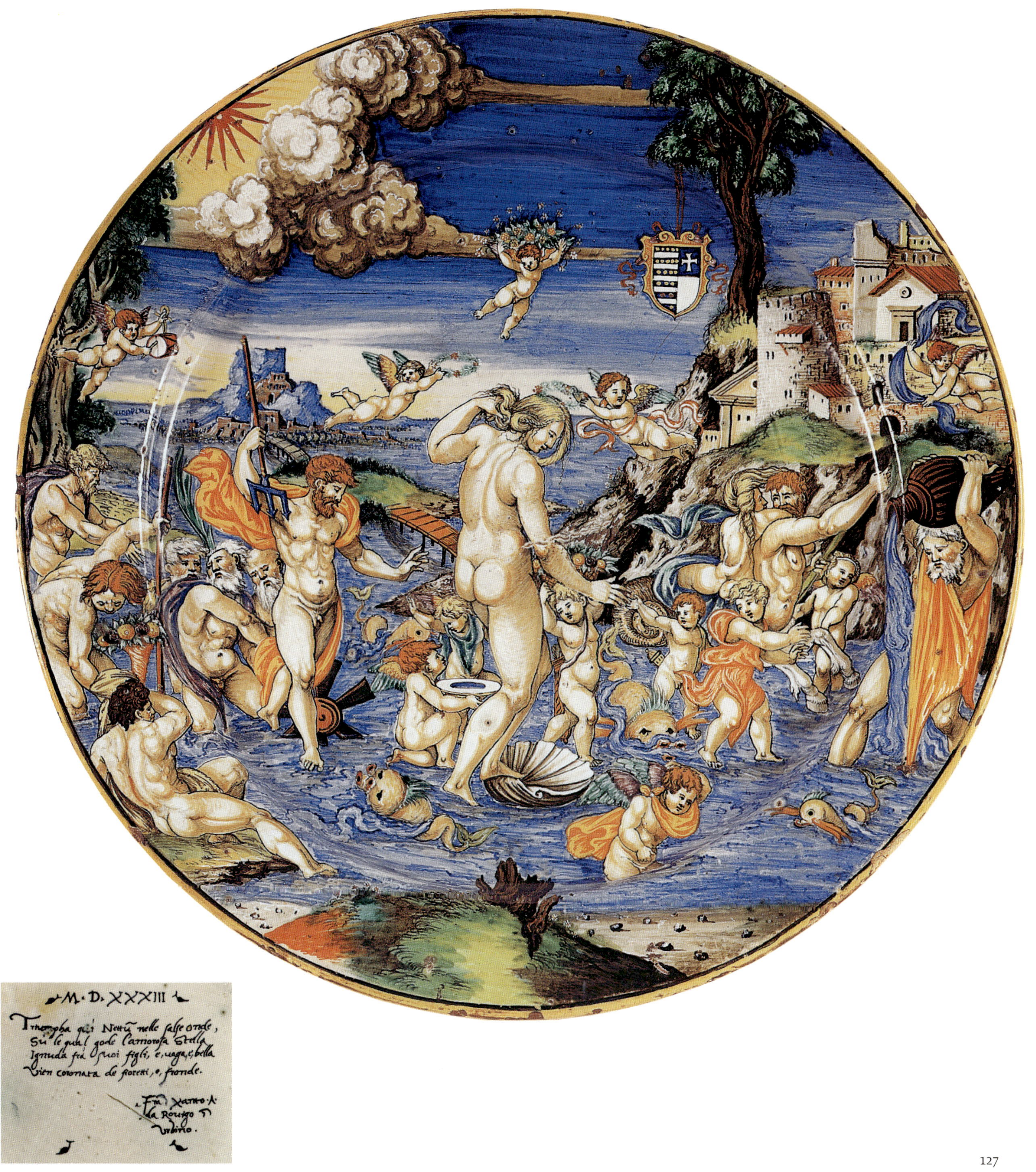



39 reverse (detail)

# 40.  Dish: *The Marriage of Ninus and Semiramis*

By Francesco Xanto Avelli, signed as painted in Urbino and dated 1533

D: 46.5 cm
London, Victoria and Albert Museum, 1748-1855

PROVENANCE
Ralph Bernal.

BIBLIOGRAPHY
Bernal sale, lot 1938; Fortnum 1873,
pp. 396–97; Rackham 1940, no. 632
(further bibliography cited); Mallet 1981,
no. 196; Triolo 1996, pp. 342–44 (further
bibliography cited).

NOTES
1. *Ill. Bartsch* 28, p. 201, 62 (95).
2. *Ill. Bartsch*, respectively 26, p. 210, 211
   (171); 26, p. 15, 6-I (7); 26, p. 194, 198
   (161); 26, p. 135, 104-I (89); 26, p. 13, 4
   (6); 26, p. 37, 23-I (29).
3. Holcroft 1988.

Polychrome. Ninus, centre, surrounded by Cupids and courtiers, one bearing a torch, offers Semiramis a crown, as she sits on a throne modestly revealing her torso, while behind her a Cupid dresses her hair. In the foreground is a weeping Cupid. At the extreme right, behind the throne, are Orientals. At the extreme left warriors approach casting glances over their shoulders, and a seated man holds a shield inscribed:.X.H.A.. An opening in the architectural background reveals a hilly landscape with a fortress. At the top hang a curtain and a shield of arms: *Gonzaga impaling Paleologo, Quarterly of six, 3 and 3: 1, gules a double-headed eagle displayed or (Byzantium); 2, argent a cross potent between four crosslets or (Jerusalem); 3, or three pales gules (Aragon); 4, barry gules and or (Hungary); 5, azure, two barbels or (for Bar); 6, gules a cross cantonned by four B's or; over all an escutcheon per fesse gules and argent (for argent a chief gules - Montferrat).*
Reverse: yellow line at the rim; in blackish-blue: *.M.D.XXXIII./ Hor vedi la magnanima Reina/ chuna treccia rivolta, e, laltra sparsa/ Corse alla, Babilonica ruina./ Nel .I. libro di Trogo Pompeio./ .Fra[ncesco]: Xa[n]to .A./ da Rovigo. i[n]/ Urbino.* (Now see the noble queen who ran, with one tress bound up and the other loose, at the ruin of Babylon. In the first book of Trogus Pompeius.).

The central group derives from Caraglio's print of *Alexander and Roxana* after Raphael (fig. 47), an attempted reconstruction of Aëtion's lost Greek painting of Alexander and Roxana as described by Lucian.[1] Other prints used to extend the composition include: Marco Dente (?), *Battle with a Cutlass*; Agostino Veneziano after Raphael, *Isaac blessing Jacob*; Agostino Veneziano after Raphael (?), *Cleopatra*; Raimondi after Bandinelli, *The Martyrdom of St. Lawrence*; Marco Dente after Raphael, *Noah's Sacrifice*; Marcantonio Raimondi, *Christ at the Table of Simon the Pharisee*.[2]

Despite Xanto's citation of Trogus Pompeius the lines he quotes are, with minor discrepancies, from Petrarch's *Trionfo della Fama* and must refer not to Alexander and Roxana, like the print that is his source for the dish's central

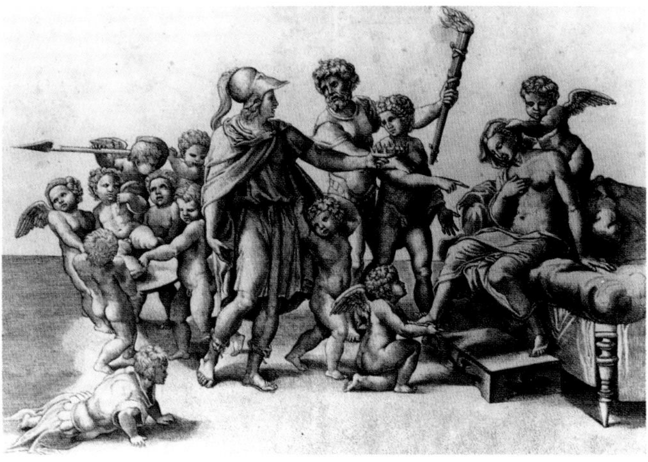

Fig 47. Gian Giacomo Caraglio after
Raphael, *Alexander and Roxana*, engraving

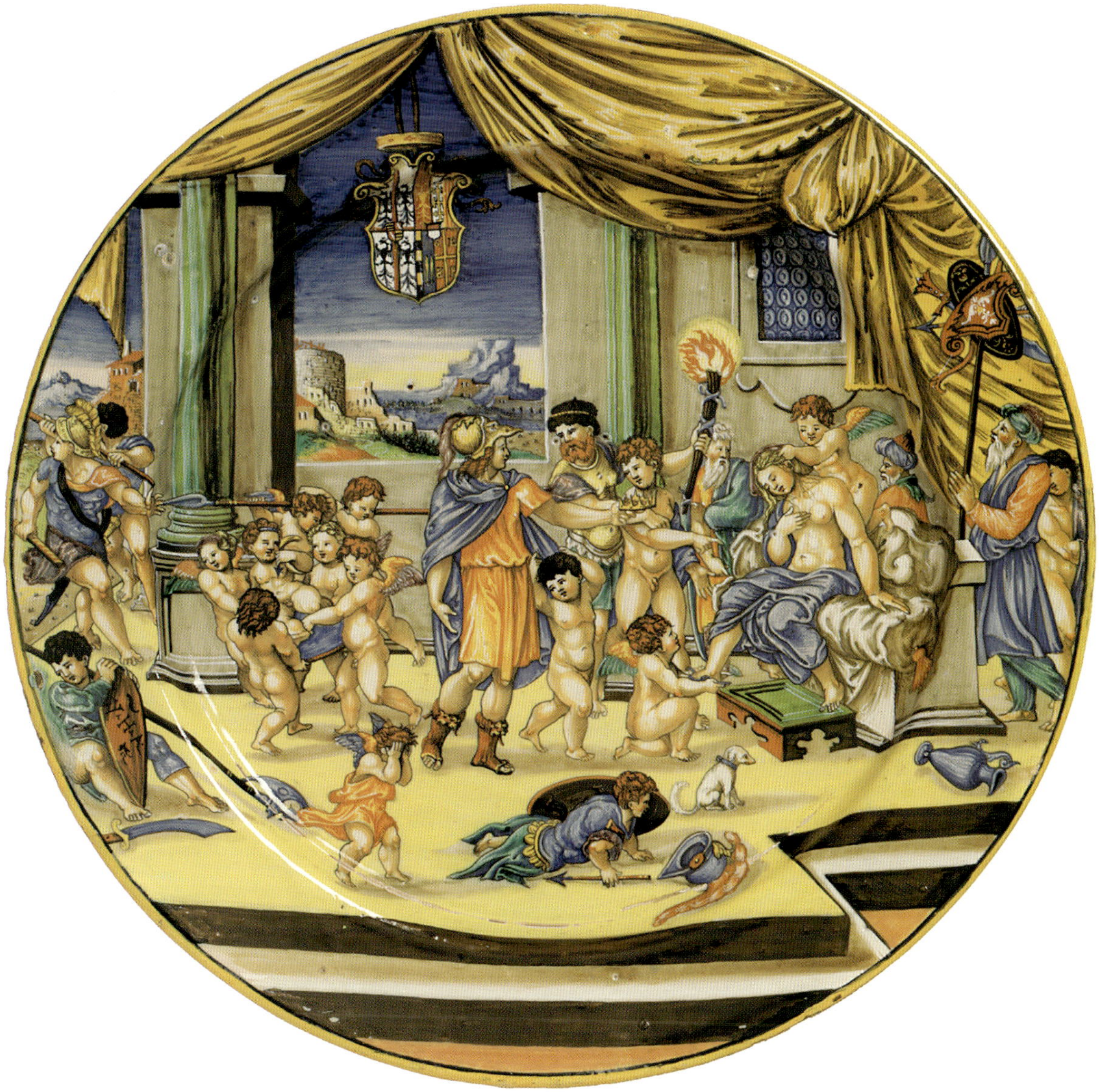

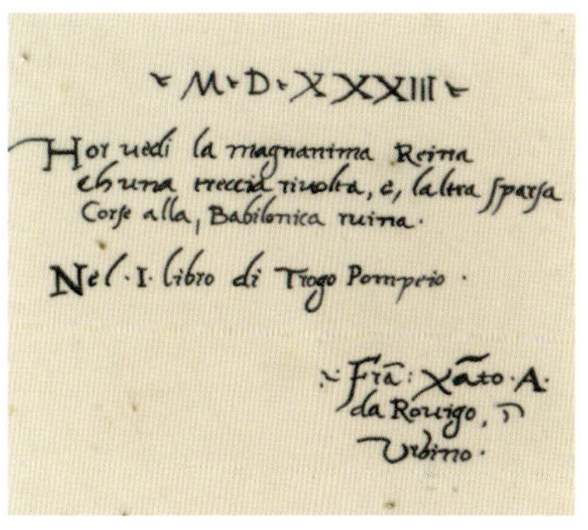



40 reverse (detail)

group, but to Queen Semiramis. Alison Holcroft, who has given more thought to the matter than other writers, recounts various legends concerning Semiramis and concludes that one told by Diodorus Siculus best fits the painting. Diodorus recounts that Semiramis was married to Onnes, a councillor to Ninus, King of Babylon. Onnes took her with him on a campaign, where her beauty and military prowess so impressed Ninus that he sought her in marriage. Onnes killed himself, leaving the way open for Ninus. If this is the story represented, it is clear why Ninus offers a crown to Semiramis, but the quotation from Petrarch has to be explained away as serving "merely to identify the protagonist, not the content of the picture."[3] The quotation and the way warriors running from the left look apprehensively over their shoulders are better explained by the story Valerius Maximus tells, that Semiramis, who had gained the throne of Assyria after the death of Ninus, was having her hair dressed when she learned of the revolt of Babylon. She seized her weapons and only resumed her coiffure when the revolt had been suppressed. Knowingly or not, Xanto has combined the marriage of Semiramis to Ninus with events that followed the latter's death.

The arms are those of Federico Gonzaga and his wife, Margherita Paleologo. See cat. 41.

## 41. Plate: *The Chariot of Juno*

Attributed to Nicola da Urbino, Urbino, *c.* 1533

D: 27.4 cm
London, Wallace Collection, C92

PROVENANCE
Alessandro Castellani.

BIBLIOGRAPHY
Castellani sale 1871, lot 120; Bethnal Green 1872-75, no. 1440; Norman 1976, no. C92.

NOTES
1. Norman 1976, no. C92, citing Rackham 1940, no. 573.
2. Mallet 1981, no. 194.
3. G. Liverani 1938; Rackham 1940, no. 575; Munarini 1990, p. 18 and fig 10; Ivanova 2003, no. 36.

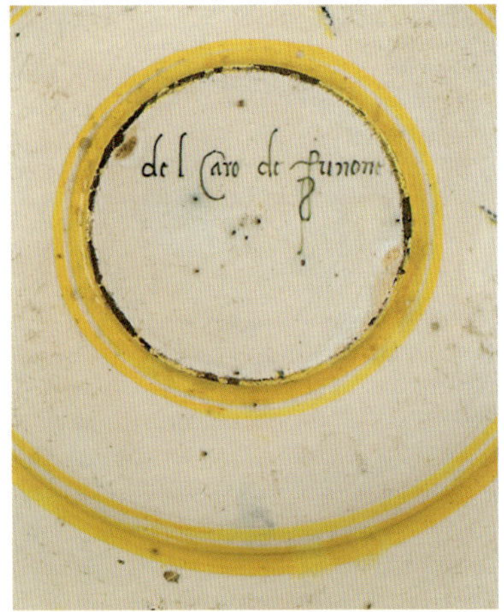

41 reverse (detail)

Polychrome. Right, Juno sits among clouds in her chariot which is drawn, left, by two peacocks; centre, a winged Cupid offers Juno a dish; in the clouds above, left, stands a Cupid with a quiver of arrows and, right, a third Cupid rests against a helmet; top centre, a coat of arms for Gonzaga and Paleologo of Montferrat, roughly as on cat. 40 and 42.
Reverse: concentric yellow lines. Within the foot ring, in grey, is painted the inscription: *del Caro de Junone*, (of the chariot of Juno).

As Norman noticed, Rackham's suggestion that Juno in her chariot is derived from an engraving of 1533 published by Gabriele Giolito seems incorrect; the design would not have been beyond Nicola's unaided powers of invention.[1]

Cat. 41 seems designed almost as a pair to a plate now at Faenza, with the same arms of Gonzaga and Paleologo and painted by Nicola with the Chariot of Mars, god of war.[2] Juno was the much deceived and vengeful wife of Jupiter but she was also the protectress of women, watching over marriage and childbirth, which may have made her a suitable subject for this plate if it was made on the occasion of or not long after the marriage of Federico Gonzaga, Duke of Mantua, to Margherita, daughter of Guglielmo Paleologo, Marquess of Montferrat.

This dynastic marriage took place in 1531 against the wishes of the Emperor Charles V and was indeed to cause headaches for the Gonzaga, since the territory of Monferrato was separated from Mantua by a wide swathe of land controlled by the rulers of Milan. Cat. 41 and 42 cannot pre-date preparations for the marriage and if, as seems rather likely, cat. 40, the large dish by Xanto, may be considered part of the same set, then both the smaller plates by Nicola displayed here must presumably share its date, 1533. It is also likely enough that other wares by Nicola bearing the simple Paleologo arms, and those with the Olympus *impresa* of Duke Federico, were commissioned at the same time.[3] The present plate, though a late work for Nicola, who was to die around 1538, still has a certain liveliness that is almost wholly lacking in cat. 42.

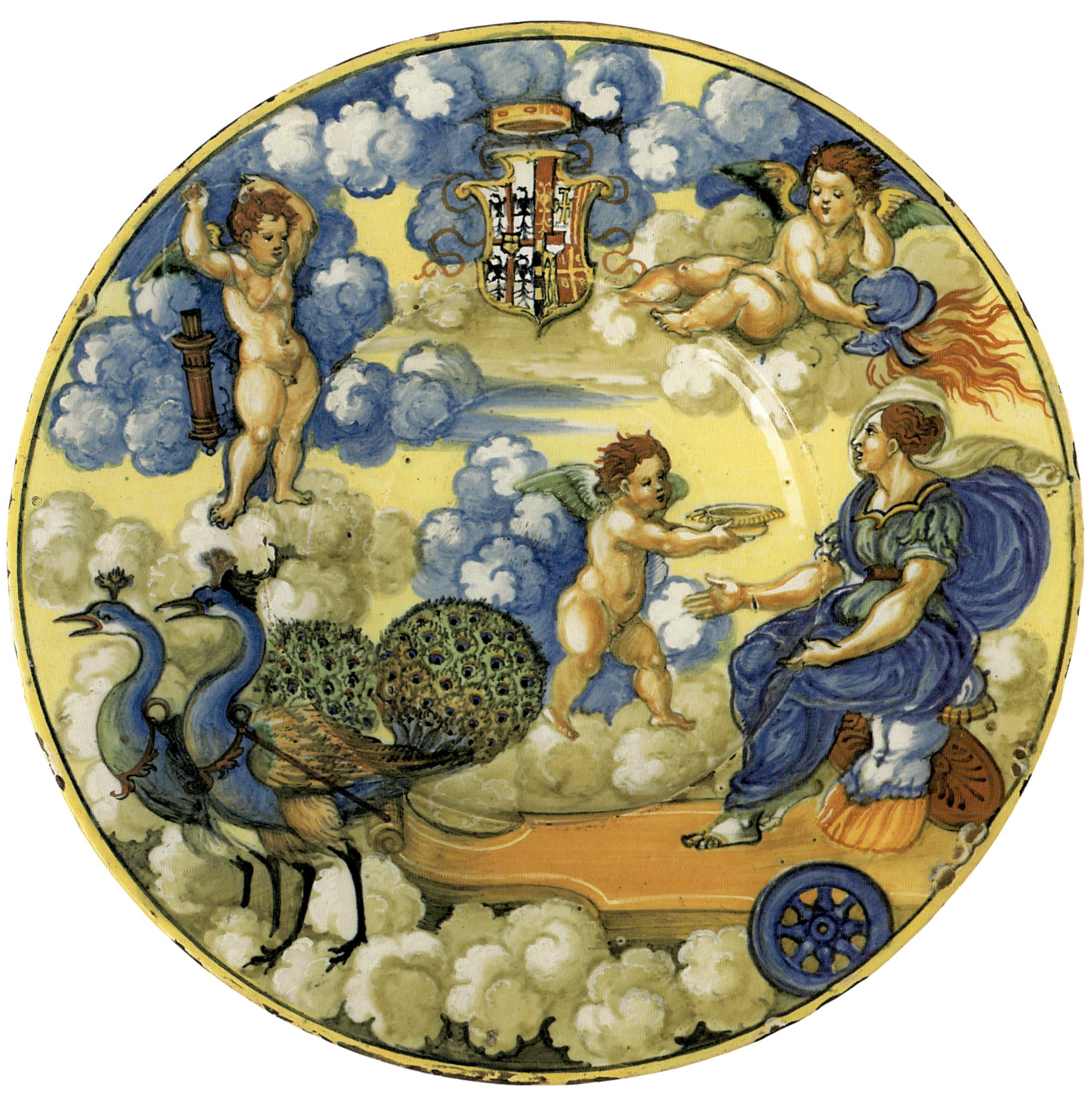

# 42.  Plate: *The Council of Apollo and Minerva*

Attributed to Nicola da Urbino, Urbino, *c.*1533

D: 27.5 cm
London, British Museum, PG＆E 1855, 12-1, 55

PROVENANCE

Ralph Bernal.

BIBLIOGRAPHY

Bernal sale 1855, lot 1809 (unattributed);
G. Liverani 1938, p. 345 (wavering between
attributions to 'Pellipario' – as Nicola
was then wrongly called – or to Xanto);
G. Liverani 1955 (the service given firmly
to 'Pellipario'); Mallet 1981, no. 195;
Wilson 1987, no. 64; Thornton and
Wilson 2007, no. 147.

NOTES

1. *Ill. Bartsch* 28, p. 192, 53 (89).
2. G. Liverani 1955, p. 12.

Polychrome. Left, two river gods; right, standing figures of Apollo, Mercury,
Minerva, Diana and Venus; background, a landscape with ruins and,
hanging from a tree, a shield with the arms of Gonzaga and Paleologo of
Montferrat, roughly as on cat. 40 and 41.
Reverse: concentric yellow rings and, inside the foot, the inscription:
*del Chonsiglio de/ A pollo .e. minerva.* (concerning the council of Apollo and
Minerva).

The figures of river gods in the foreground are adapted, one in reverse,
from figures in the engraving by Caraglio after Rosso Fiorentino of
*The Muses and the Pierides* (fig. 43, p. 114).[1] The figures of Apollo and of the
goddesses are also adapted and redistributed from the same print.

It will be noticed that Nicola's use of the *Pierides* print is freer than was the
normal practice of Xanto, who also often used this engraved source. It is
not clear whether the gods are conferring about some particular matter, or
whether a generalised scene is intended. Though there is no need to doubt
that this piece is fully autograph as one would expect for such an important
client, it betrays a falling-off in Nicola's artistry from his work in the 1520s.
Characteristic of Nicola's late style are the rust-coloured shadows much
used for flesh. Recent writers on maiolica have not lent even the degree of
credence that Liverani did to a label on the old wooden frame of the Gonzaga
Paleologo plate in the Museo delle Ceramiche at Faenza, which claimed
that Giulio Romano drew or designed that piece in 1536.[2] By the seventeenth
century, when the fashion for framing *istoriato* maiolica arose, wild and
unfounded attributions to Raphael and pupils of his such as Giulio Romano
were rife.

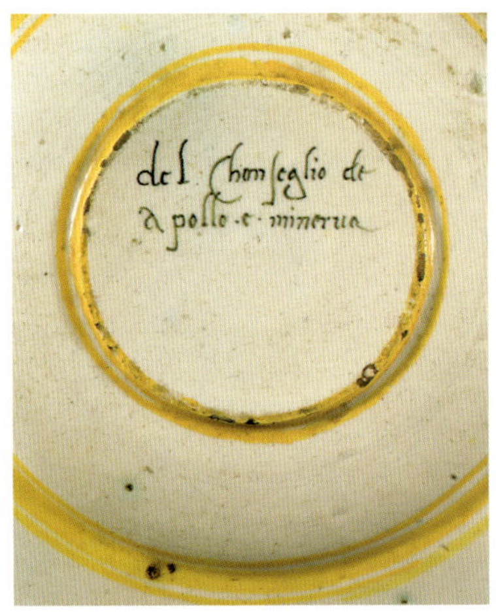

42 reverse (detail)

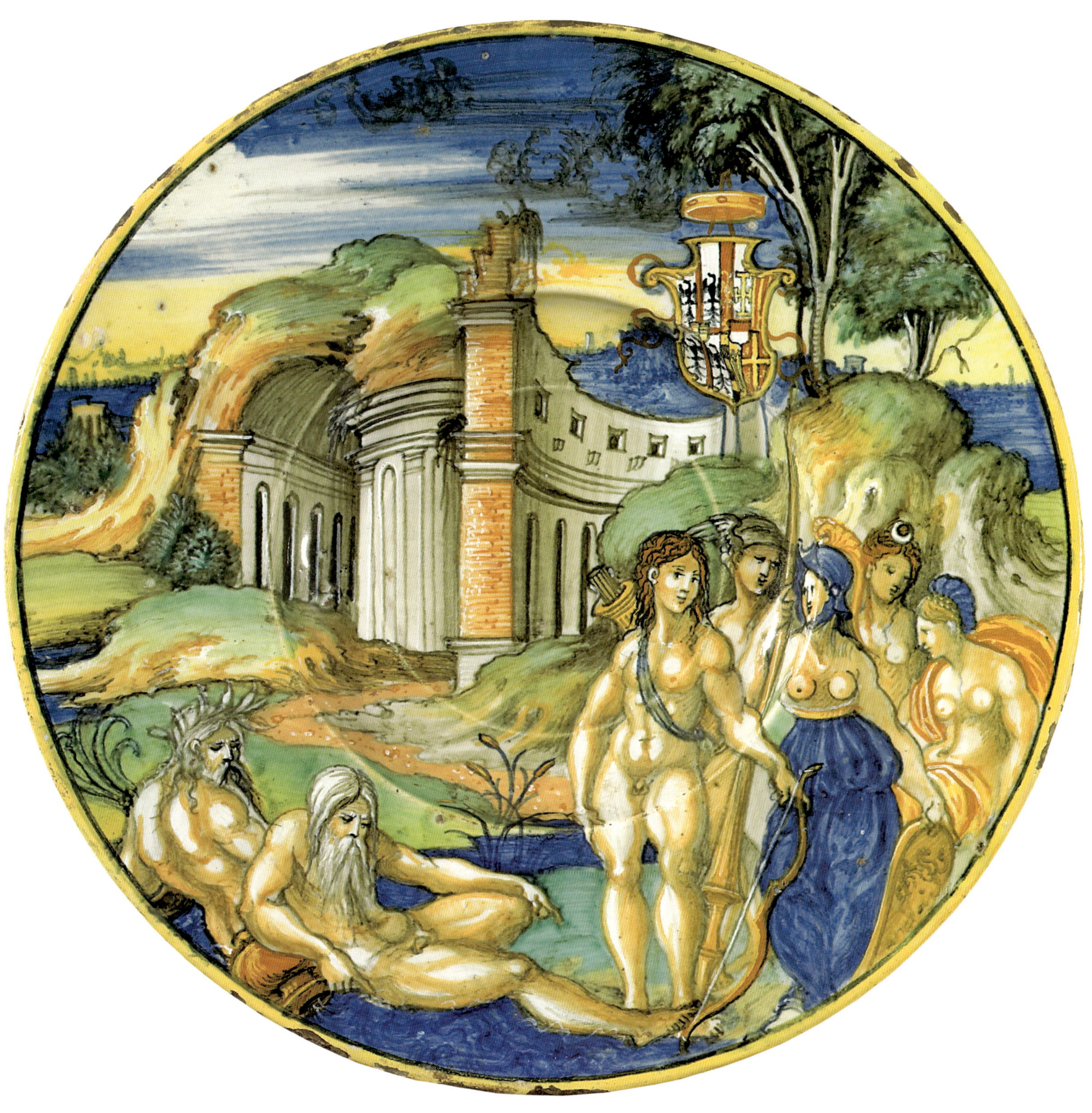

<h1>43. Plate: *Romulus and Remus suckled by the She-Wolf*</h1>

By Francesco Xanto Avelli, signed as painted in Urbino and dated 1533

D: 26.5 cm
London, British Museum, PG&E 1854, 2-13, I

PROVENANCE

Thought by Thornton and Wilson to be probably identifiable in the Préaux sale catalogue, Paris, 1850, and perhaps from the Baron collection, Paris.

BIBLIOGRAPHY

Préaux sale, Paris, 9–11 January 1850, lot 178; Wilson 1987, no. 76; Holcroft 1988, p. 233, note 61; Syson and Thornton 2001, pp. 260–61 and fig. 214: Thornton and Wilson 2007, no. 165 (further bibliography to be cited).

NOTES

1. Lawner 1988, pp. 76–77, no. 8
2. Wilson 1996, no. 85; Royer 2003, p. 123 and pl. I.
3. Robinson 1856, p. 26, no. 34.

Polychrome and lustre. Left, a man carries the swaddled babies to the river Tiber; centre, a she-wolf suckles Romulus and Remus; right, the river god, Tiber, pours a stream from a jar. Up a tree on the right is a bear with what seems to be a snake round its neck.

Reverse: the rim and foot emphasised with gold lustre bands; a stylised scroll-pattern in red and gold lustre; within the foot, in blue: *.1533./ De Marte i figli/ alla pietosa Lupa./ Nel. XLIII. Lib[ro]: de Trogo po[m]/peio./ .fra[ncesco]: Xanto/ .A. da Rovigo/ i[n] Urbino.* (1533, The sons of Mars at the compassionate she-wolf. From Book 43 of Trogus Pompeius. Francesco Xanto A. from Urbino, in Urbino). Also marked N in gold lustre.

The man carrying the two babies is derived from engraving No. 8 of *I Modi*, by Marcantonio Raimondi after Giulio Romano (fig. 48) and, as usual with Xanto, reversed from the surviving woodcut version, which means it would have been the same way round as the original engraving.[1]

Romulus, legendary founder of the city of Rome, was born with his twin brother Remus to a Vestal Virgin, who excused her pregnancy by claiming to have been violated by Mars. The babies were ordered to be drowned in the Tiber but survived and were reared by a she-wolf before being discovered by a herdsman called Faustulus. The man approaching from the left of the plate carrying the babies cannot, however, be Faustulus since they are still swaddled and hence younger than when represented with the she-wolf. The significance of the bear and snake, which do not feature in another version, is unclear.

Xanto's other surviving version of the subject, dated 1531, formerly in the Pasolini and Sprovieri collections,[2] may have inspired cat. 44. In 1856 J.C. Robinson hazarded the mildly implausible guess that the lustred mark N might stand for Vincenzo Andreoli, son and partner of Maestro Giorgio: "It has more than once occurred to the author of this catalogue, that the N may in reality be the monogram of Cencio (Vincentio), containing as it does the three letters VIN.".[3]

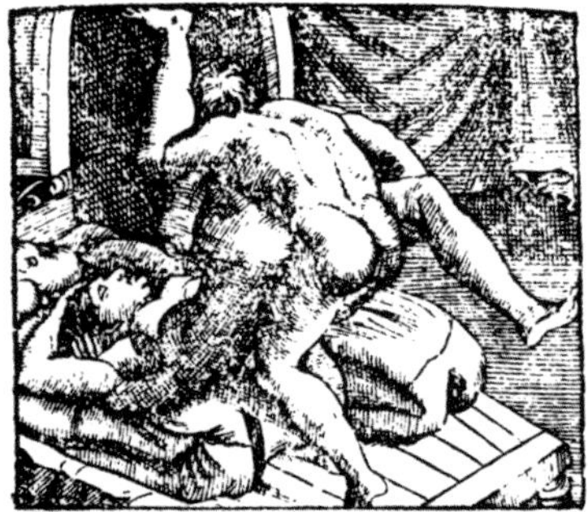

Fig. 48. Anonymous, after Marcantonio Raimondi from Giulio Romano, *I Modi*, illustration to Sonnet 8, *c.* 1527, woodcut

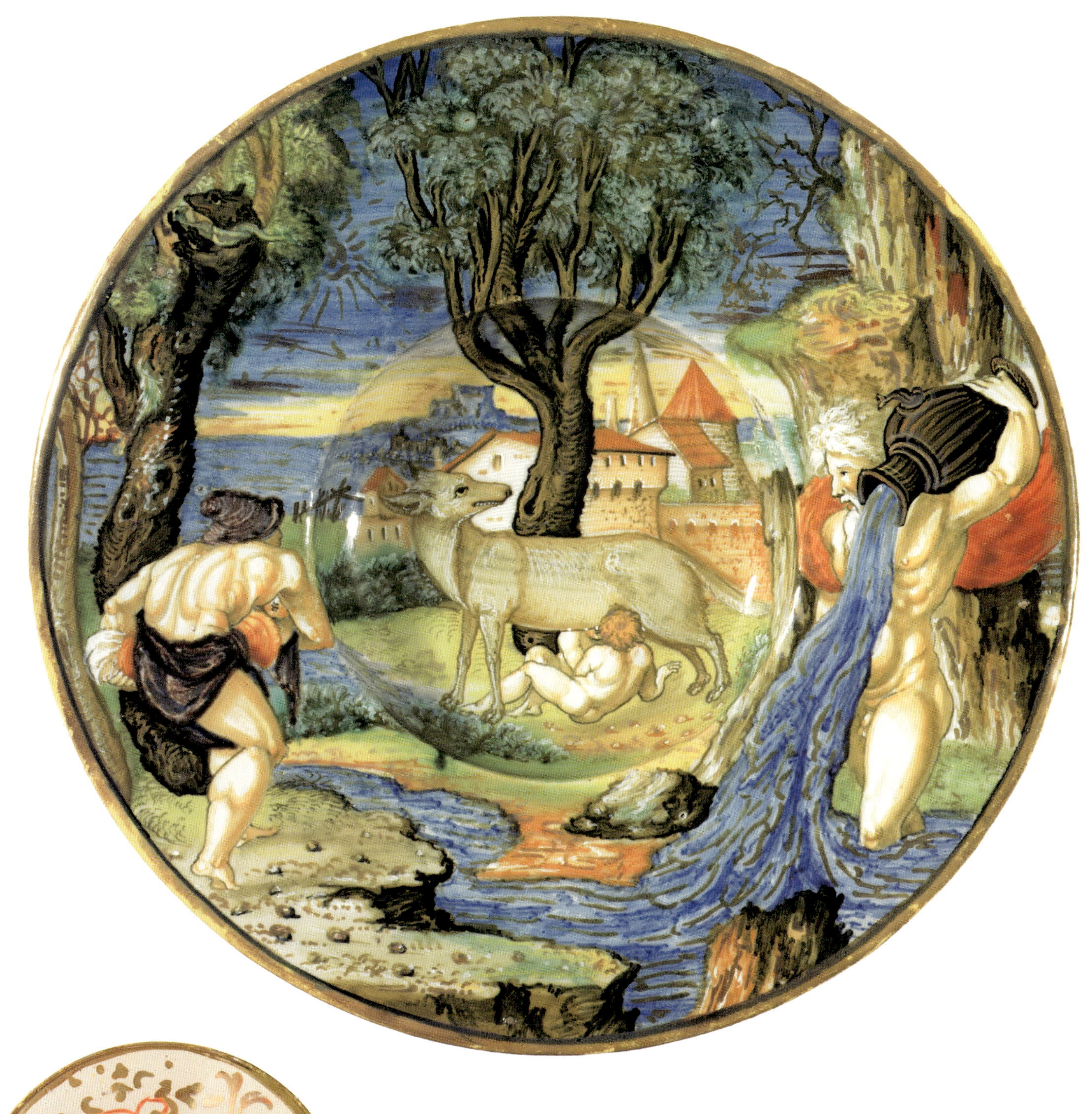

44. Plate: *Romulus and Remus suckled by the She-Wolf*

Attributed to Francesco Urbini, at Gubbio, 1531 (?)

D: 27.0 cm
London, Victoria and Albert Museum, 1705-1855


PROVENANCE

Ralph Bernal.

BIBLIOGRAPHY

Bernal sale 1855, lot 1818; Fortnum 1873,
p. 273 (as lustred, and perhaps painted, at
Gubbio, *c*.1530–40); Borenius 1928, pp. 5–7;
Rackham 1940, no. 740 (as by Francesco
Urbini, probably painted at Urbino);
Mallet 1979, p. 282 and p. 290, no. 3 (as
Francesco Urbini at Gubbio); Mallet 1988,
pp. 73–75 and fig. 12.

NOTES

1. *Ill Bartsch* 26, p. 194, 198 (161).
2. Mallet 1979, pp. 282 and 290, no. 2;
   pl. xciva.
3. Borenius 1928, pp. 5–7 and fig. 10;
   Rackham 1940, no. 778; Mallet 1979,
   and pl. xcvii a and b; Battini 1974, p. 218,
   illustrates, without giving its location,
   an apparently unsigned piece with the
   *Death of Aeschylus*, marked Deruta and
   dated 1537.
4. Mallet 1979, pp. 286–87, pp. 292, no. 9
   and pl. xcv a and b; Fiocco and Gherardi
   1989, p. 430 and p. 447, pls. lii a and b;
   Fiocco and Gherardi 1998, p. 23, pl. 8
   and pp. 61 and 82, no. 18.
5. Ballardini 1940, pp. 105–08, pls. xxvii a
   and b. Destroyed in World War II.
6. Rackham 1940, no. 779.


Polychrome and lustre. Left, a man carrying the two babies and accompanied by a woman approaches the Tiber, on whose waters float the swaddled babes in a cradle; in the centre stands the she-wolf suckling the two boys; to the left stands a herdsman with a stick, probably Faustulus. In the background rises the city of Rome.
Reverse: three leafy scrolls and the indistinct date *1531* all in lustre.

The man carrying the babies bears a relationship to the figure copied from *I Modi* on cat. 43 (fig. 48, p. 134) and on Xanto's similar plate of 1531, but Francesco Urbini has misunderstood the posture, which he probably knew only from copying a plate by Xanto. The boy standing beneath the wolf also appears copied, in reverse, from a favourite figure of Xanto's, Cupid hiding his head and weeping before the dying Cleopatra in Agostino Veneziano's print.[1]

In their catalogues both Fortnum and Rackham overlooked the indistinct lustred date, probably 1531 by comparison with a plate with the same subject and by the same hand at Göteborg which is inscribed in lustre: *1531/ Mᵒ Gᵒ da Ugubio*.[2] As Borenius first proposed, the painter's name is revealed by an unlustred dish signed *fran[ces]co, Urbini,/ i[n] deruta*.[3] All the more typical works attributed to Francesco Urbini are lustred in the manner of the Andreoli workshop at Gubbio and several bear that firm's mark, *Mᵒ Gᵒ* in lustre. Two bear inscriptions in blue ending: *i[n] Gubio*, and the date 1534.[4] A single unlustred piece, the colouring of which suggests a date *c.*1525, bears a blue hieroglyph also found in blue under four pieces dated 1536 that are attributable to Francesco. On a fifth piece, cat. 52, this same hieroglyph is puzzlingly flanked by the initials *F.R.*, while on a sixth, a moulded Gubbio dish or *coppa baccellata*,[5] it was found in lustre, suggesting that Francesco Urbini sometimes did decorative lustre work. His *istoriati* are unskilful, but he had a talent for flat pattern which I believe can be discerned on the borders of some Gubbio dishes from *c.*1524–36, including cat. 10 and perhaps cat. 11, besides some of the 'S' service *tondini*. It is worth comparing the border of cat. 10 with that of a Deruta dish attributed to Francesco Urbini by Rackham.[6] See also cat. 52.

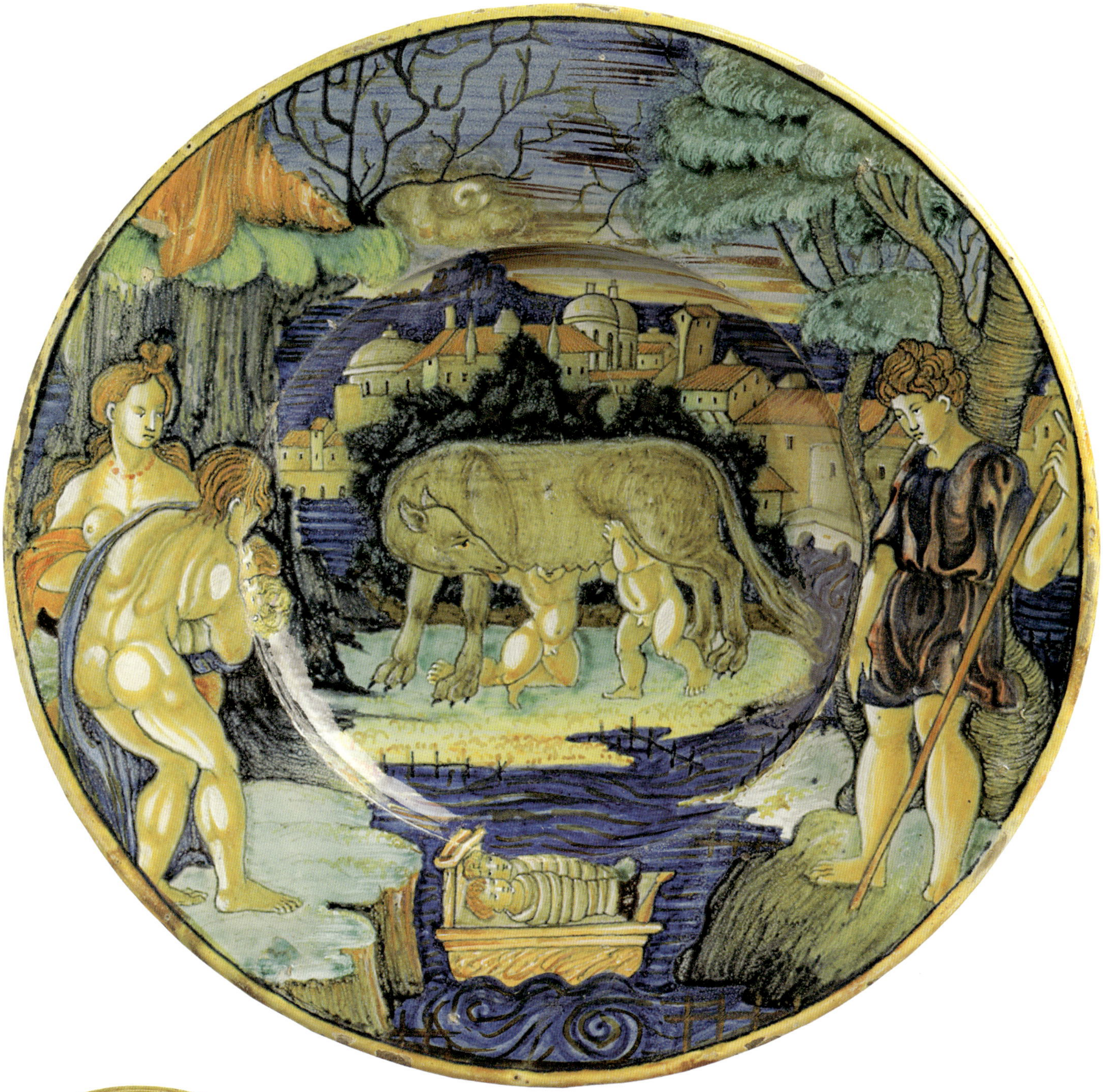

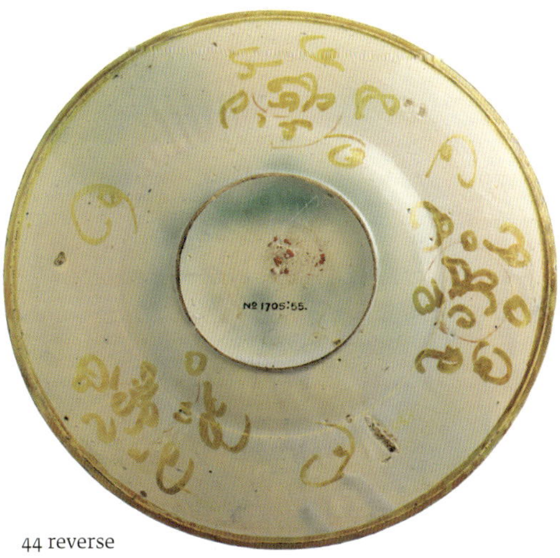

# 45. Plate: *Actaeon changed by Diana into a Stag*

By Francesco Xanto Avelli, signed as painted at Urbino and dated 1533

D: 26.0 cm
London, Victoria and Albert Museum, C.2206–1910



Polychrome with lustre. Right, Diana and her nymphs bathe in a cistern; left, Actaeon is shown with his head already turned into that of a stag, while his hounds turn on their master. In the well of the plate Cupid stands weeping. In the background is a town.

Reverse: leafy scrolls in lustre. Inside the foot, in blue, is the inscription: *.1533./ Il misero Atteo [n] co[n]/verso i[n] cervo./ Nel. III .L. de Ovidio. M./ fra [ncesco] Xanto A./ da Rovigo i[n]/ Urbino.* (The wretched Actaeon changed into a stag. In Book III of Ovid's *Metamorphoses*. Francesco Xanto A. da Rovigo in Urbino).

Actaeon (except for the head) derives from the spearman in the *Battle Scene* print by Marco Dente after Raphael or Giulio Romano (fig. 32, p. 60),[1] much used by Xanto, eg. for cat. 7, 25 and 54. The bathers are from *The Muses and the Pierides*, by Caraglio after Rosso Fiorentino (fig. 43, p. 114);[2] Cupid is from Agostino Veneziano's *Cleopatra*.[3]

According to Ovid[4] Actaeon, when hunting in a forest, stumbled upon Diana and her nymphs while they were bathing. For this the chaste goddess punished him by turning him into a stag; not recognising him, his own hounds pursued and killed him.

This plate is very similar in design to an unlustred plate of the same year (figs. 49 and 50),[5] though the figures of Actaeon and Cupid are of different derivation and Diana is centrally placed. The similarity offers a chance to assess the way lustred additions alter the appearance of an *istoriato* plate, in ways of which Xanto can surely not have approved, assuming he saw the result. No gaps were left in the colouring of pieces like cat. 45 expressly for

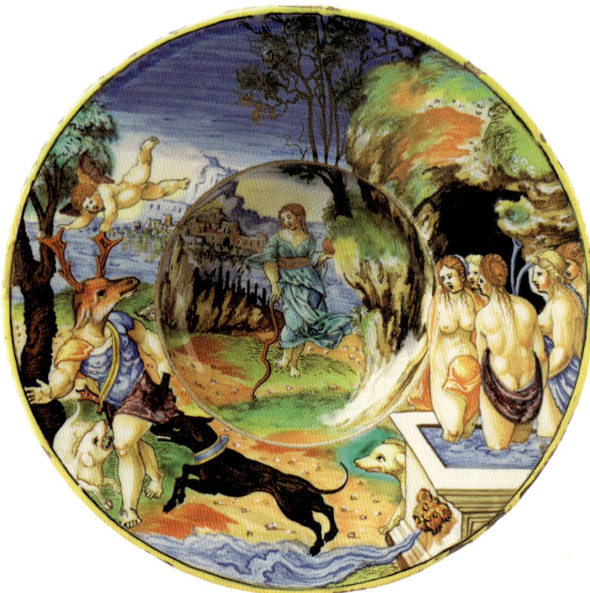

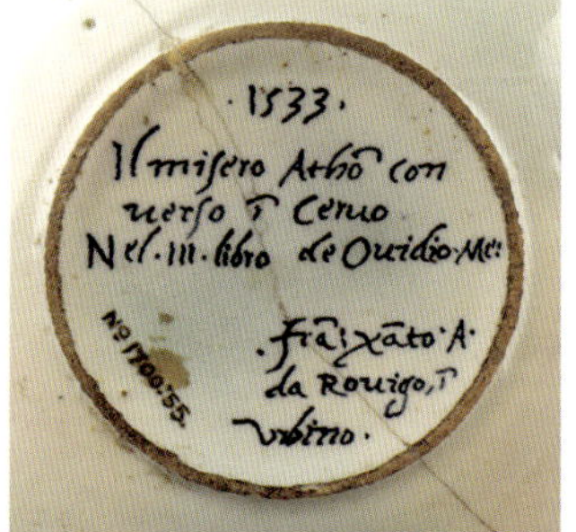

Fig. 49. Francesco Xanto Avelli, *Diana and Actaeon*, 26.0 cm, maiolica plate, London, Victoria and Albert Museum, 1700-1855

Fig. 50. Reverse of fig. 49 (detail)

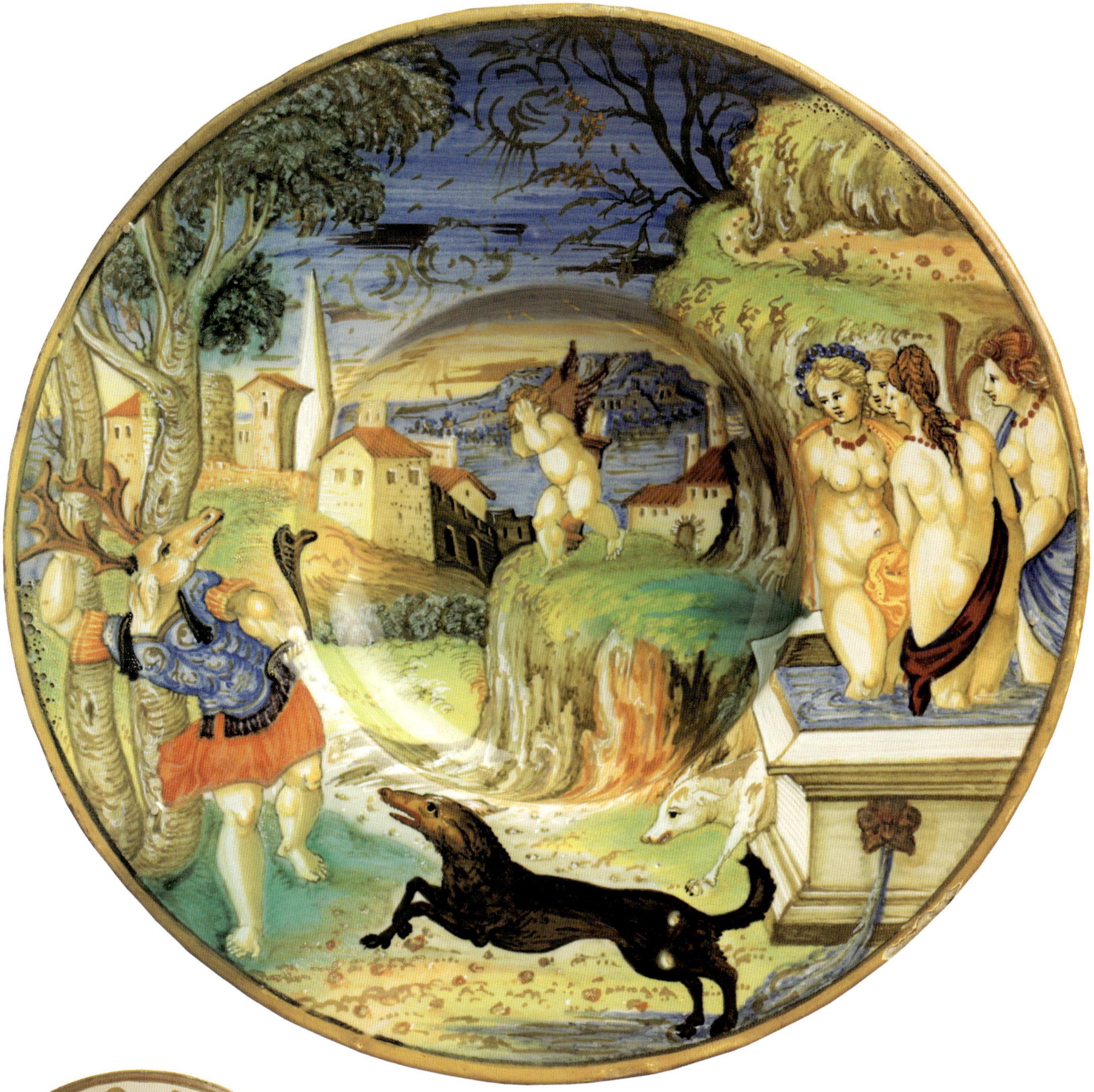

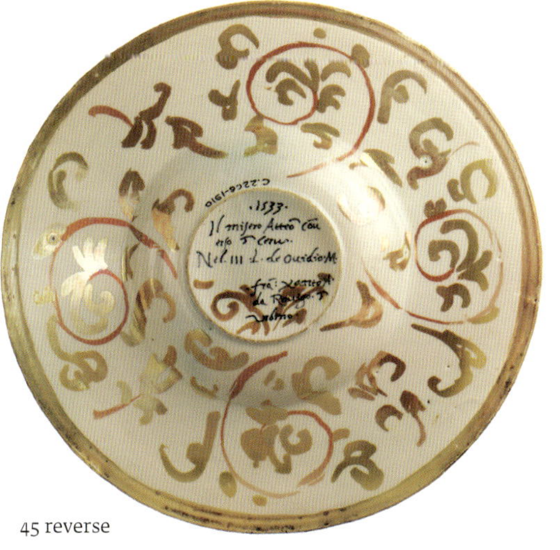



the application of lustre at a subsequent firing, as seems sometimes to have been the practice with pieces here attributed to Xanto working at Gubbio in 1524–25. The discovery that in 1538 Maestro Giorgio's son, Vincenzo, took a five year lease on the workshop in Urbino of the recently deceased Nicola di Gabriele (Nicola da Urbino), has encouraged speculation that the Gubbio firm may have been applying lustre at an Urbino outstation even before that, but to date there is no hard evidence for this theory.

## 46. Plate: *The Battle of Pavia*

By Francesco Xanto Avelli, working at Urbino and possibly assisted by
'Lu. Ur.' or Sforza di Marcantonio; signed *F.X.* and dated 1534; almost
certainly lustred in the Andreoli workshop at Gubbio

D: 28.3 cm
London, British Museum, P&E 1855, 3-13, 11


PROVENANCE

Given by A.W. Franks.

BIBLIOGRAPHY

Fortnum 1873, p. 347; Wilson 1987, no. 220;
Syson and Thornton 2001,  p. 257 and
fig. 212; Cioci 2004; Thornton and Wilson
2007, no. 167.

NOTES

1. *Ill. Bartsch* 26, p. 208, 209 (170).
2. Lawner 1988, pp. 62–63, no. 1.
3. *Ill. Bartsch* 26, p. 135, 104-I (89).
4. Quoted from Wilson 2003c, p. 7.
5. Cioci 2004, pp. 218–19.
6. F. Guicciardini 1561, Book XV, Ch. 5.


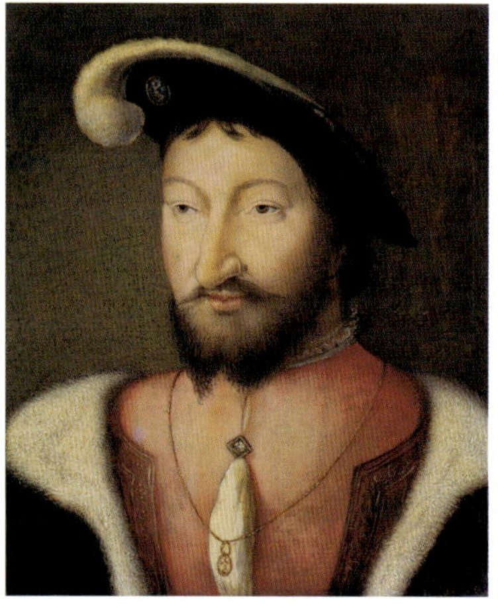

Fig. 51. After Joos van Cleve
(*c.* 1480–1540/1), *François Ier*, oil on
walnut (?) panel, 16.4 × 13.4 cm,
London, Wallace Collection, P551

Polychrome with lustre. Left, a warrior runs to another warrior, helmeted,
who lies prostrate in the foreground, a sceptre behind him; centre, a
horseman breaks through a wall; right, a shepherdess (?), stands on a ball,
leaning on a rustic crook; background, a classical building with a curtain
and a landscape with a lustred sun.
Reverse: lustred scrolls; within the foot, lustred *fleurs-de-lys* and in blue: *.1534./
Caddette il Re Cristia[n]/sotto Pavia./.F.X.* (1534. The Christian King fell below
Pavia. F.X.).
Broken, cracked between eight o'clock and three o'clock, and at ten o'clock,
and repaired, with some retouching especially on the heads of the horse and
the shepherdess.

The man to the left and the horseman are both from Marcantonio
Raimondi's *Abduction of Helen* after Raphael;[1] the François Ier seems to be a
dressed up rendering of an engraving from Giulio Romano's *I Modi* (fig. 52,
Introduction, p. 41);[2] the right-hand figure is from Marcantonio Raimondi'
*Martyrdom of St Lawrence* after Baccio Bandinelli.[3]

Xanto's inscription identifies the Battle of Pavia. The 'Most Christian
King' (a counter-claim by France to the pretensions of the 'Holy Roman
Emperor') was François Ier (fig. 51), who on 24 February 1525 suffered severe
defeat and capture by the Imperial forces outside Pavia. The fallen monarch
is unmistakable, the remaining figures less easily identified. Accounts
conflict, but it appears that François, unhorsed and slightly wounded, was
captured by troops who failed to recognise him. The Nuncio Bernardino
Castellaro reported the day after the battle: "the Viceroy of Naples ran to the
noise and took charge of him with respect, keeping away those around him."[4]
Francesco Maria and the Venetians heard a similar account but with *monsignor
de La Mota* as the King's rescuer and capturer. The man running towards the
King may thus be intended for Charles de Lannoy, Viceroy of Naples, or for a
less well known officer. The horseman might represent the Marquess del Vasto
or the Marquess of Pescara, Imperial commanders who initiated the battle by
breaching the walls into the Barco of Pavia where part of the besieging

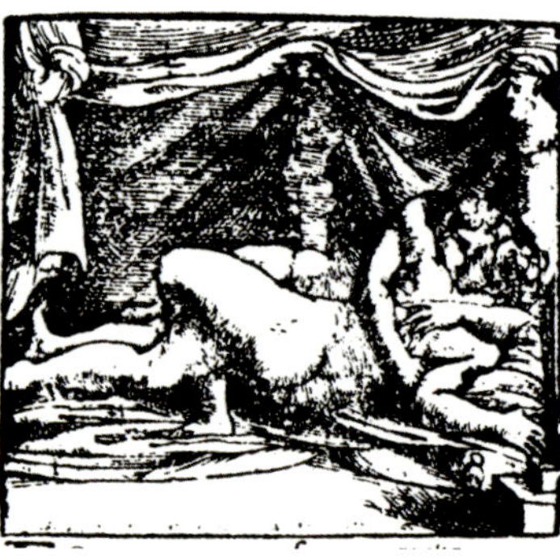

Fig. 52. Anonymous, after Marcantonio
Raimondi from Giulio Romano, *I Modi*,
illustration to Sonnet 1, *c.* 1527, woodcut

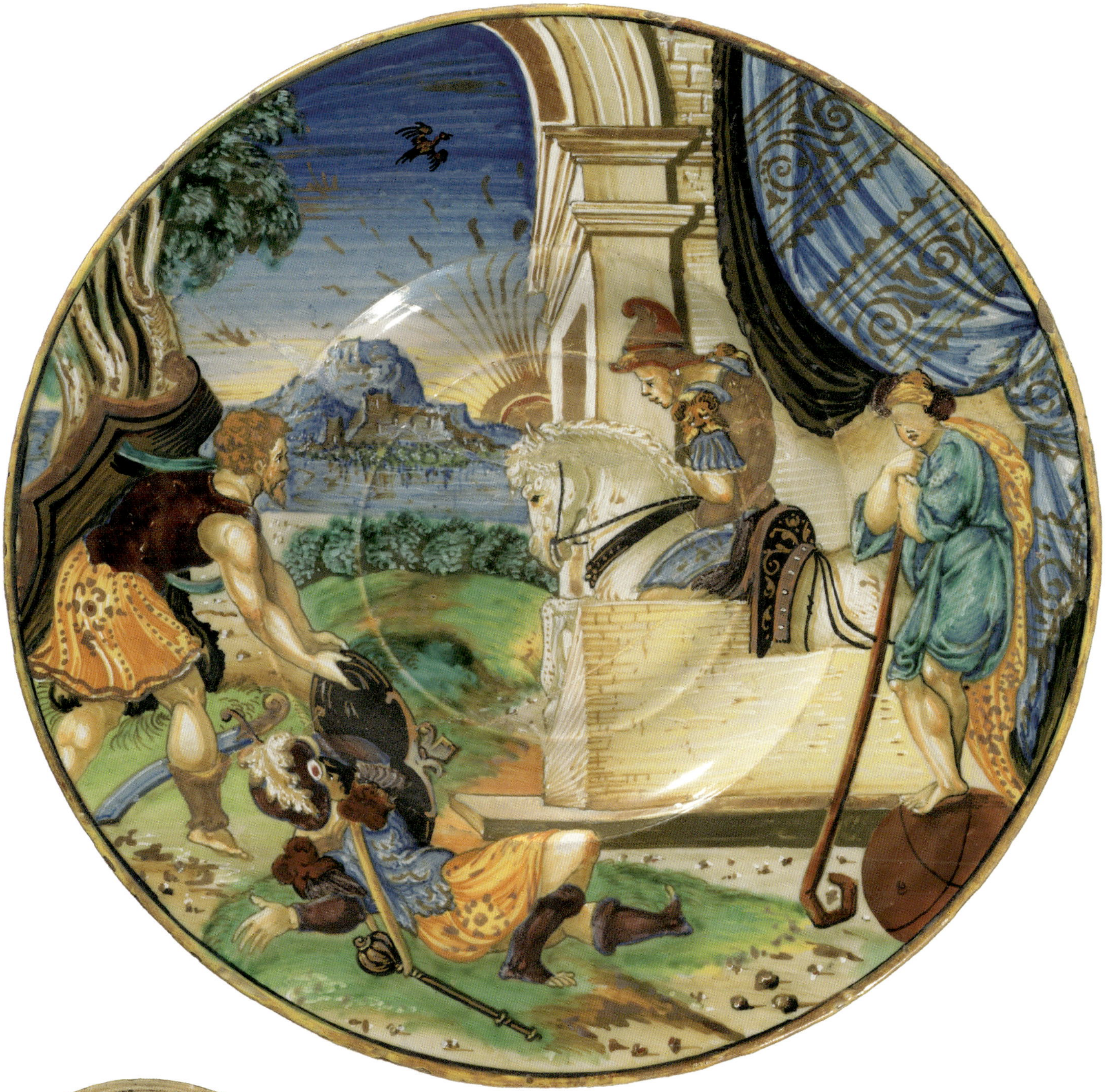

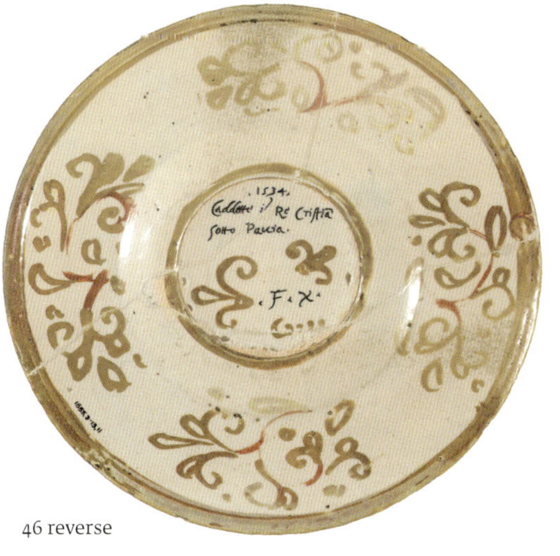





French army was encamped; but Cioci is probably right in supposing that here, as on cat. 30, the white horse represents Spain.[5] The figure to the right balances like *Fortuna* on a sphere which could also be the emblem for Clement VII – a *pallone* or ball in allusion to the Medici arms – while the stick looks like a rustic pastoral crook. If this figure is female, she could also personify Rome. François was encouraged to persist with the campaign that culminated in his siege of Pavia, with its crushing consequences, by support from the Pope, albeit promised secretly at first, and in any case inactive and ineffective.[6] The plate thus seems part allegory, part representation of an historical event. Unevenness in draughtsmanship might indicate participation by an assistant, possibly 'Lu. Ur.' or Sforza.

## 47. Dish on low foot (*Coppa*):
### *An Allegory of Rome and the Medici*

By Giulio da Urbino, working in Urbino, signed and dated 1534

D: 27.6 cm
London, British Museum, PG&E 1997, 4-I, 1


PROVENANCE

Charles Loeser, Florence.

BIBLIOGRAPHY

Trinity Fine Art 1994, no. 40; Thornton
1999; Gresta 2002; Cioci 2002c; Thornton
and Wilson 2007, no. 171.

NOTES

1. *Ill. Bartsch* 26, p. 33, 21 (24).
2. *Ill. Bartsch* 26, p. 239, 242 (194).
3. *Ill. Bartsch* 28, p. 187, 48-I (86).
4. Ravanelli Guidotti 1985, no. 80.
5. Mallet 1988, pp. 76–78 and p. 102,
   fig. 20 and 20R, points out that the
   way Giulio dots his numeral '1' makes
   it certain the date should be read as
   1541, not 1547.
6. Gresta 2002.
7. Thornton 1999.
8. Cioci 2002C.
9. Dennistoun 1909, II, pp. 418–20; III,
   pp. 43–44 and 53.


Polychrome and lustre. Centre, a Cupid holds a pneumatic ball while, left, a man tugs at his wing. Right, three nude women dance, holding cornucopiae and ears of corn. In the background is a broken wall, a tower and a town. Reverse: leafy scrolls in red and gold lustre. Within the foot, the inscription in dark blue: *.1534./ D'amorosi pe[n]sieri gli animi/ in gombro:/ Nel. .& [y/Φ]:/ Giulio da./ urbino:* (with amorous thoughts I encumber souls. In & [y/Φ flourish]. Giulio da Urbino).
Small repair to rim at three o'clock, over-painted; hairline crack visible between seven o'clock and three o'clock.

The man to the left derives from *The Massacre of the Innocents* by Marco Dente da Ravenna after Baccio Bandinelli (fig. 42, p. 108);[1] the Cupid is from *Bas-Relief with Three Cupids (The Throne of Neptune)* by Marco Dente da Ravenna after an antique relief (fig. 41, p. 92);[2] the three nude women are from *Hercules defeating the River God Achelous in the Form of a Bull* by Gian Giacomo Caraglio after Rosso Fiorentino.[3]

The present dish of 1534 and a jug of 1535 at Bologna inscribed as painted in the workshop of a *mastro alisandro a rimino*,[4] are Giulio's only signed pieces. Others dated 1535 and attributable, like cat. 48, to Giulio, are inscribed as painted in Rimini. A dish bearing his handwriting is dated 1541 *in verona*.[5] Giulio never marked his work *in Urbino*, but his earliest identifiable pieces, dated 1533–34, share Xanto's print sources, style and manner of inscribing, suggesting a close working relationship about which Gresta has written interestingly but speculatively.[6] After moving in 1535 to Rimini, Giulio ceased using Xanto's print-sources, never again attempting political allegory. Thornton's interpretation of the present allegory as Charles V punishing Clement VII's lascivious and wealthy Rome in 1527,[7] seems more convincing than Gresta's idea that Giulio has represented the return of Francesco Maria to the State of Urbino, or Cioci's that the warrior represents that Duke in his continuing tussle with the Medici over possession of Urbino.[8] Thornton showed the inscription to be a modified quotation from Petrarch's sonnet, No. X in the *Canzoniere* (see *Appendix B*). This alludes to a friend and patron of Petrarch's from the Colonna family, which had humiliated Pope Boniface VIII at Anagni in 1303, an event Giulio may have seen as an historical parallel to Clement's humiliation in 1527, which had been preceded by an uprising of the Colonna. Yet by 1529 Clement had repaired his relationship with the Colonna family sufficiently for it to be rumoured that he was planning the replacement of Francesco Maria as Duke of Urbino by Ascanio Colonna; despite that, the following year Ascanio was welcomed by Francesco Maria as a guest in the Duchy.[9]

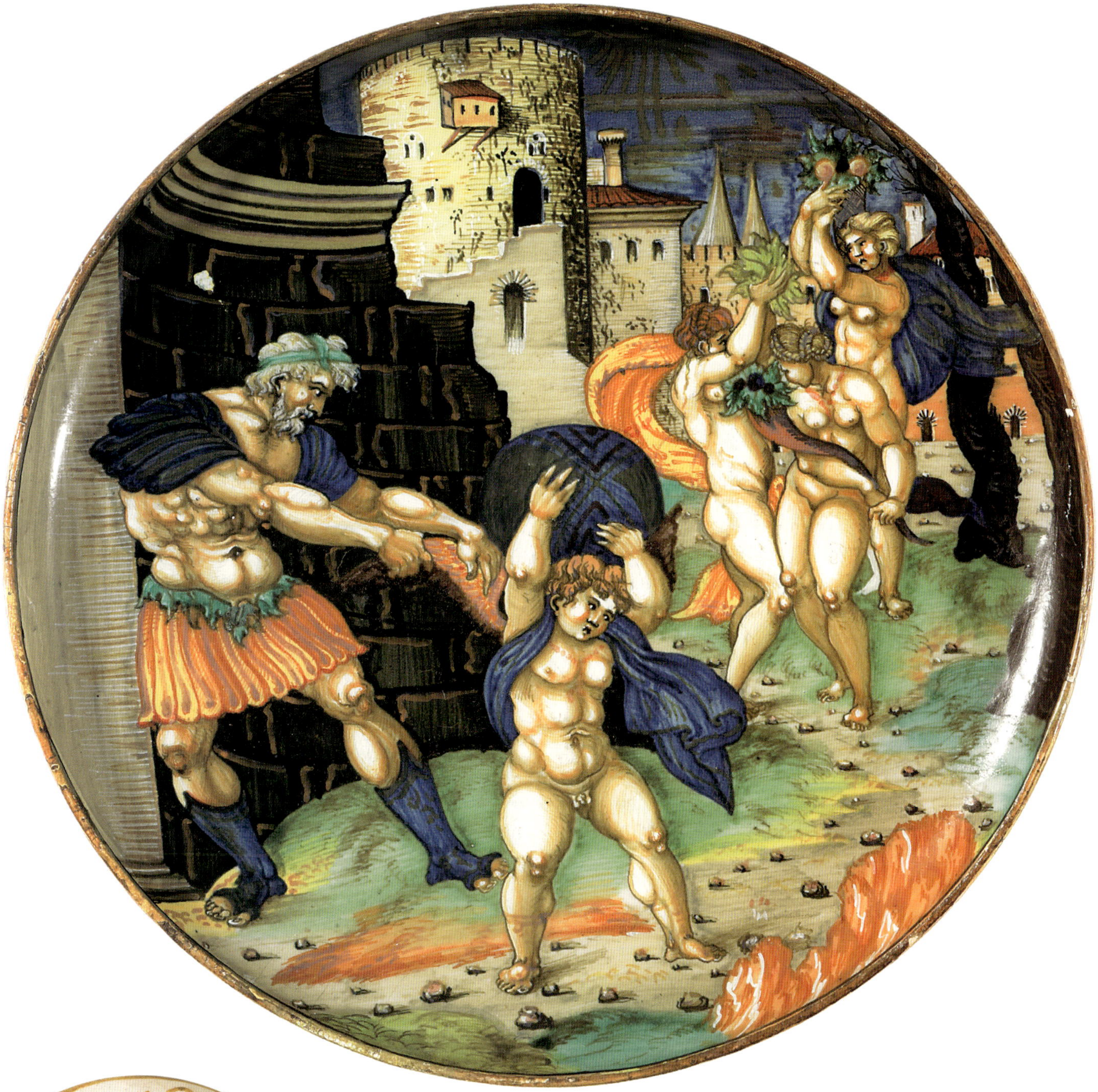

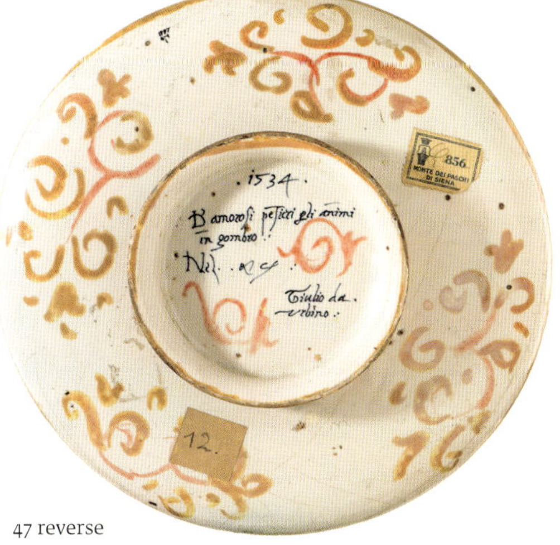

47 reverse

143

48. Dish on low foot (*Coppa*): *Cicero declaiming to Octavian, the future Emperor Augustus*

Attributed to Giulio da Urbino, in the workshop of Maestro Alessandro; inscribed as painted in Rimini and dated 1535

D: 26.5 cm
London, Wallace Collection, C74

PROVENANCE

Unknown; not identifiable in Bethnal Green 1872-75.

BIBLIOGRAPHY

Ballardini 1938A, 175, 184, 335R; Rackham 1940, p. 309; Norman 1976, no. C74; Gresta 2002, p. 153, fig. 17.

NOTES

1. Delucca 1998.
2. Ravanelli Guidotti 1985, no. 80.

Centre, the middle-aged Cicero sits on a cylindrical pedestal addressing a younger man, presumably Octavian, who stands to the right; left, two further young men stand in conversation; in the background, an arched recess.
Reverse: inscribed within the foot: *.1535./De gaio otaviano/ecicerone: –/In rimino:* (Concerning Gaius Octavianus and Cicero. In Rimini).
Broken rim formerly concealed by a gilt-wood frame.

In his choice of subject, as in his abandonment of reliance on prints as models for his figures, Giulio shows his new independence from Xanto's influence. This dish seems to represent Cicero, defender of republican rule in Rome, attempting to win the mind of the young Octavian, adopted heir to Julius Caesar. The attempt, prompted by Cicero's even greater mistrust of Mark Anthony, failed. Cicero was proscribed and killed and Octavian emerged, under the name of Augustus, as Emperor. Such a subject might have appealed to republican Florentines in flight from the vengeful Medici, now restored to power.

Giulio's presence in Rimini is recorded both in a document of 18 March 1535[1] and by an inscription of the same year on a jug from which we learn that he was working in the *bottega* of Maestro Alessandro.[2] The present dish lacks something of the assurance of throwing and glazing on which Giulio had been able to rely when working at Urbino (see cat. 47). The underside, for instance, is stained and sanded. Though Giulio's handwriting is immediately recognisable, the style of his painting changed when he was no longer working closely with Xanto. Lacking access to the prints he had shared with the latter, he paints more freely and independently; but the removal of competitive stimulus makes his draughtsmanship less rigorous. While some of the work Giulio may be assumed to have painted in Urbino in 1533–34 bears lustred enrichment, this is not the case with any work of his marked as painted in Rimini.

48 reverse (detail)

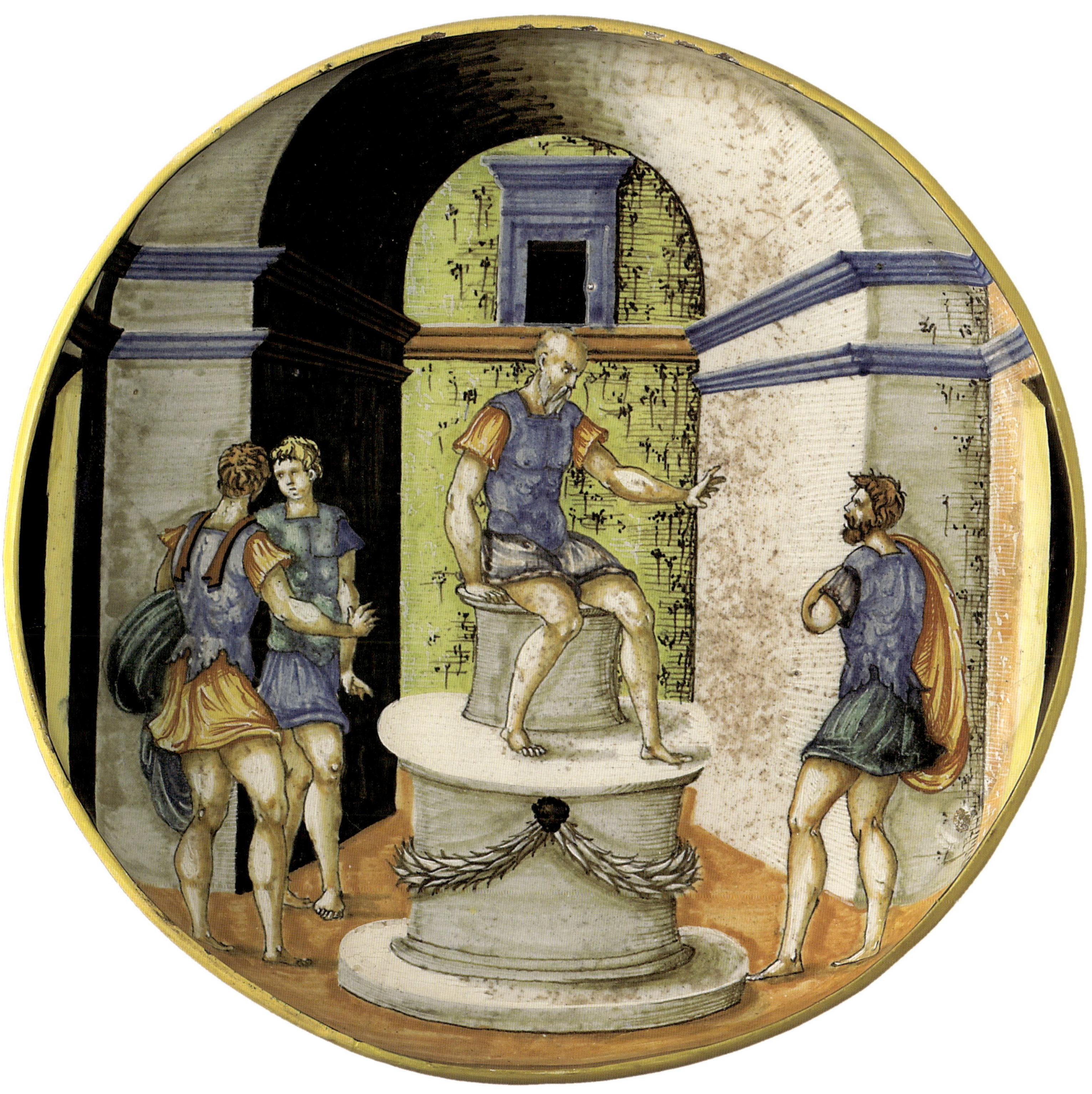

## 49. Plate: *Glaucus and Scylla*

By Francesco Xanto Avelli, Urbino, signed and dated 1535

D: 25.4 cm
London, Wallace Collection, C91


PROVENANCE

Probably comte de Pourtalès-Gorgier;
A. Basilewsky; Prince Napoleon.

BIBLIOGRAPHY

Probably the plate in the Pourtalès-Gorgier
sale, 1865, lot 1699; Musée Rétrospectif
1865, no. 2774; Prince Napoleon sale 1872,
lot 252; Bethnal Green 1872-75, no. 1494;
Ballardini 1938A, 179, 189, 344R; Tervarent
1951, fig. 25; Norman 1976, no. C91;
Gresta 2002.

NOTES

1. Lawner 1988, pp. 88–89.
2. *Ill. Bartsch* 26, p. 33, 21 (24).
3. *Ill. Bartsch* 26, p. 223, 261-I (183).
4. *Ill. Bartsch* 28, p. 80, 4 (68).
5. Ovid, *Metamorphoses*, XIII, lines 900–68;
   XIV, 1–74.
6. Gresta 2002, pp. 151–52, pl. xlvi and fig. 14.


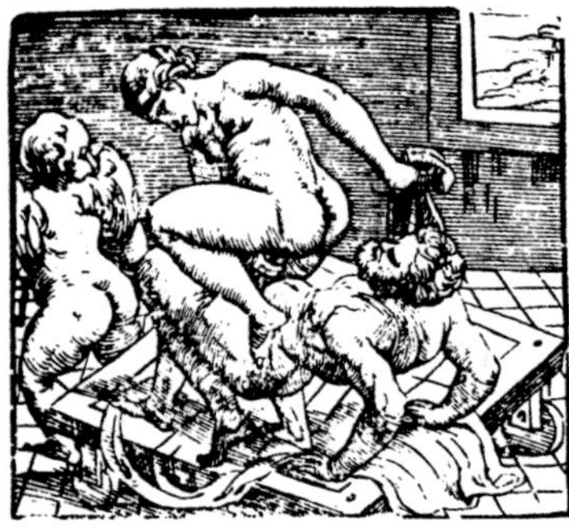

Fig. 53. Anonymous, after Marcantonio
Raimondi from Giulio Romano, *I Modi*,
illustration to Sonnet 14, *c*. 1527, woodcut

Polychrome and lustre. Centre, Scylla bathes in a cistern; right, Glaucus
lands a catch of fish in his net; left, Glaucus runs to the sea. In the background, in front of a town, sits a second woman, perhaps Circe. At the
horizon, a lustred sun.

Reverse: painted with leafy scrolls in ruby lustre. Within the foot, in black,
is inscribed: *.1535./ Scilla i[n] reo fo[n]te la[n]gue,/ e, Glauco i[n] pesce./ Fra[ncesco]:*
*X./ R .* (1535. Scylla languishes in the evil spring, and Glaucus [turned into a]
fish. Francesco Xanto Rovigese).

Broken in two and repaired.

The figure of Scylla derives from Marcantonio's engraving after Giulio
Romano for *I Modi*, no. 14 (fig. 53), of which the original engraving, no longer
extant, would have been the same way round as shown by Xanto;[1] Glaucus
with his net is (in reverse) from a figure in *The Massacre of the Innocents* by
Marco Dente after Baccio Bandinelli (fig. 42, p. 108);[2] the figure of Glaucus
on the left is (reversed) from *Naked Man pursuing a Naiad*, from an ancient
bas-relief (fig. 54);[3] the woman in the background, presumably Circe, is
derived from the Madonna in *The Adoration of the Shepherds* by Gian Giacomo
Caraglio after Parmigianino.[4]

Glaucus, a fisherman, had hauled in a good catch when he ate a grass
which metamorphosed him into a fish-like marine creature. He subsequently fell in love with the nymph, Scylla, who rejected him. Glaucus
appealed for help to Circe, the sorceress, but as she wanted Glaucus for
herself she put a poisoned charm in the pool where Scylla bathed, making
her rival repulsive to Glaucus.[5]

Gresta has suggested that Giulio da Urbino collaborated with Xanto on
this piece,[6] but the present writer sees no evidence of this. Giulio's representation of brickwork by marks that have been compared to notes of music
was presumably copied from Xanto, who also did this, for example on
cat. 13, 39, 43 and 50, so this trait is no *segno inconfondibile* (unambiguous
sign) of Giulio's handwork. For Giulio's move to Rimini by 18 March 1535,
see cat. 48.

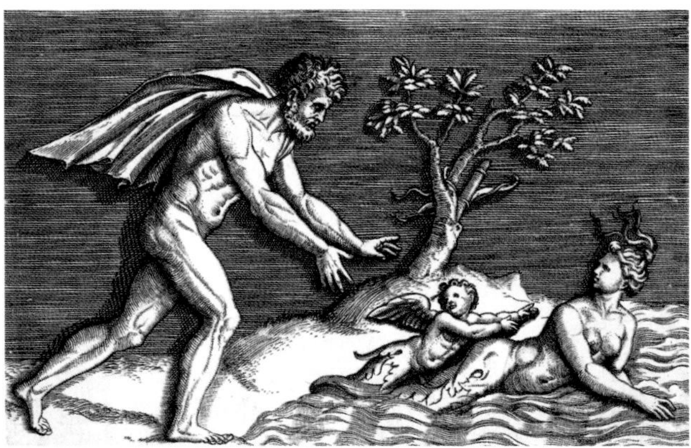

Fig. 54. Marcantonio
Raimondi, *Naked Man
pursuing a Naiad*, engraving

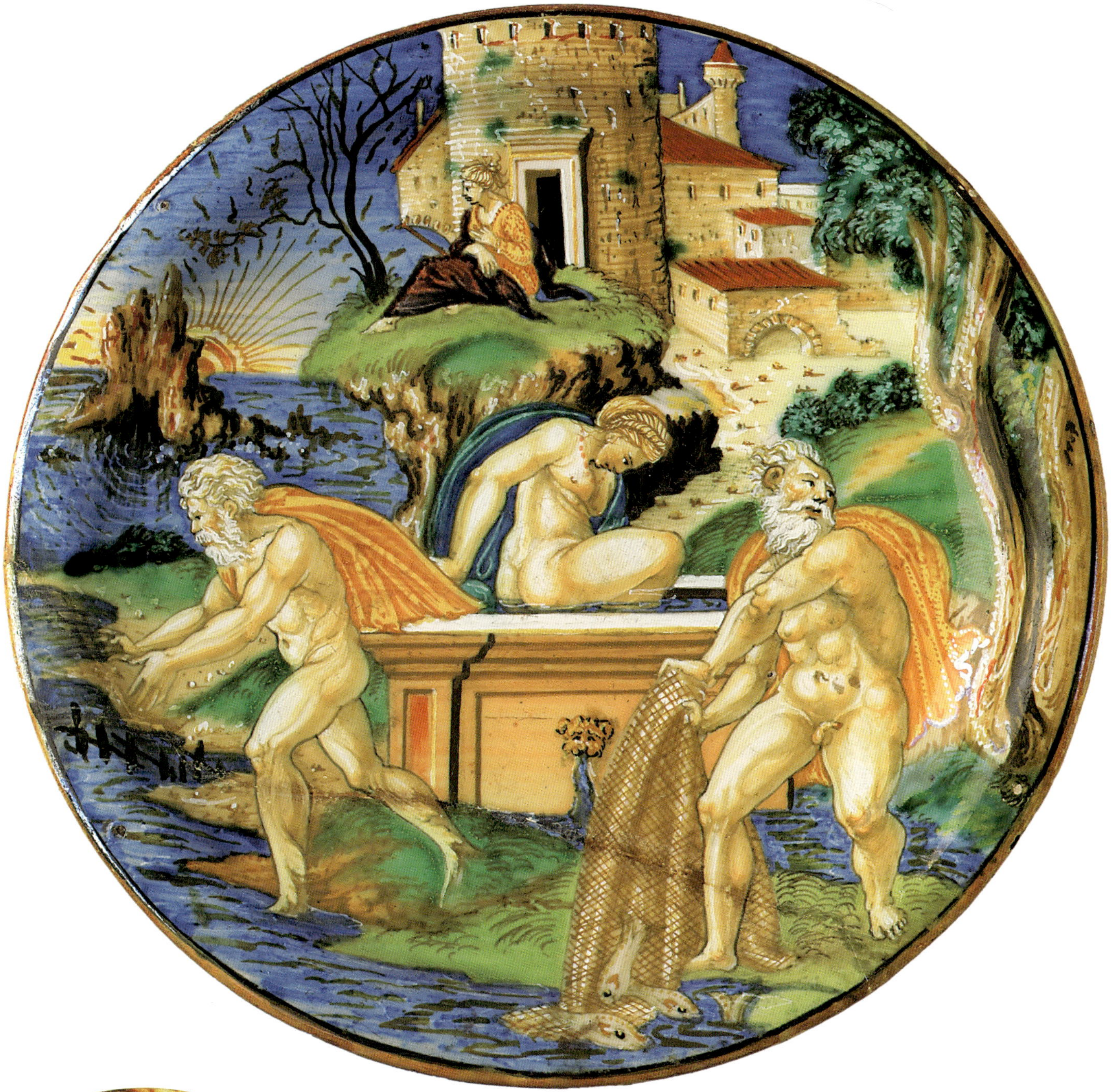

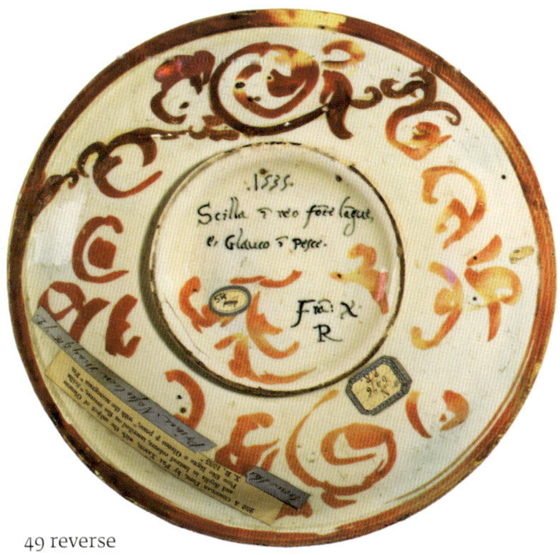
.1535.
Scilla ꝯ ẽo foce laqua,
e Glauco ꝯ pesce.
Fᵃ X
R

# 50. Plate: *Allegory of the Discords of Italy*

By Francesco Xanto Avelli, Urbino, signed and dated 1536

D: 26.0 cm
London, Victoria and Albert Museum, 1698-1855

PROVENANCE

Ralph Bernal.

BIBLIOGRAPHY

Bernal sale 1855, lot 1802; Fortnum 1873, pp. 398–99; Rackham 1940, no. 636; Cioci 1987, pp. 63–66.

NOTES

1. *Ill. Bartsch 27*, p. 64, 373 (284).
2. *Ill. Bartsch 28*, p. 201, 62 (95).
3. Cioci 1987, pp. 63–65; Law 2002.

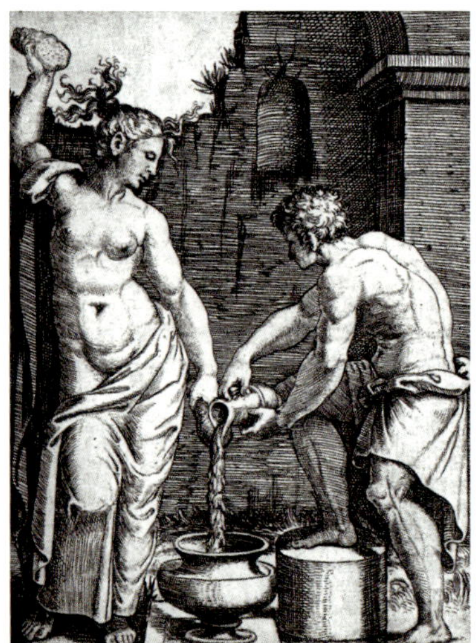

Fig. 55. Marcantonio Raimondi after Francesco Francia (*c.* 1450–1517), *Woman with Two Sponges*, engraving

Polychrome. Right, Italy, a semi-nude wounded woman with a torn shield at her feet, a broken lance held high in her right hand, stands among ruins; centre, Cupid, with bow and quiver, walks away from her; left, a bearded man and a woman sit in attitudes of despair.
Reverse: plain, with bluish tint. Inside the foot, in black: *.1536./Di tua discordia Italia/il. premio hor hai./F:co .X./Rov:* (Italy, you now have the reward for your discord. F[rances]co X. Rov[igiese]).

The figure of Italy is derived from Marcantonio Raimondi's *Woman with Two Sponges,* perhaps after Francesco Francia (fig. 55);[1] Cupid derives from *Alexander and Roxana* after Raphael (fig. 47, p. 128).[2]

The year 1536 began with potentially dangerous political events. Charles V returned via Naples and Rome from his North African campaign. Meanwhile François Ier had invaded Savoy and taken Turin. However, when fighting took place it was mainly in France. Cioci is probably right, therefore, in seeing the apprehensions expressed on this plate as concerned with the affair of Camerino. While the Papal See was vacant following the death of Clement VII, Francesco Maria Della Rovere had gained control of that vicariate of the Church by a marriage, rapidly concluded, between his heir, Guidobaldo, and Giulia, heiress to the Varano family which had ruled Camerino since the thirteenth century.[3] The moment Pope Paul III was elected, he set about trying to reverse this situation, excommunicating Francesco Maria and preparing to invade the Duchy of Urbino, being dissuaded from this only by the combined efforts of the Emperor Charles V and the Venetians. Cioci associates this plate with Xanto's Sonnet XXXVIII, seeing in the bearded old man of the plate the white-haired shepherd who, in the sonnet, inveighs against the miserly ambition of Rome.

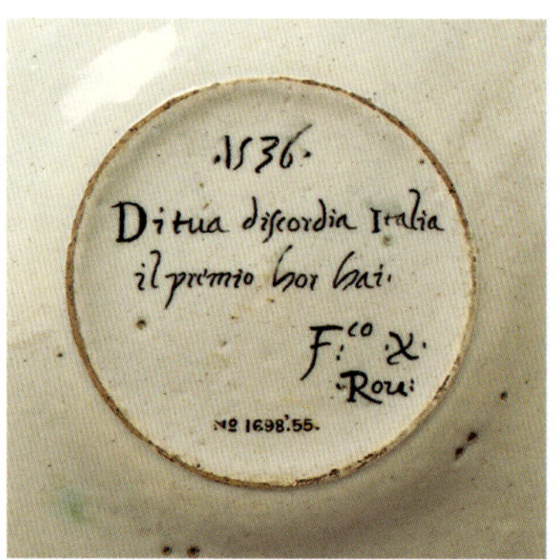

50 reverse (detail)

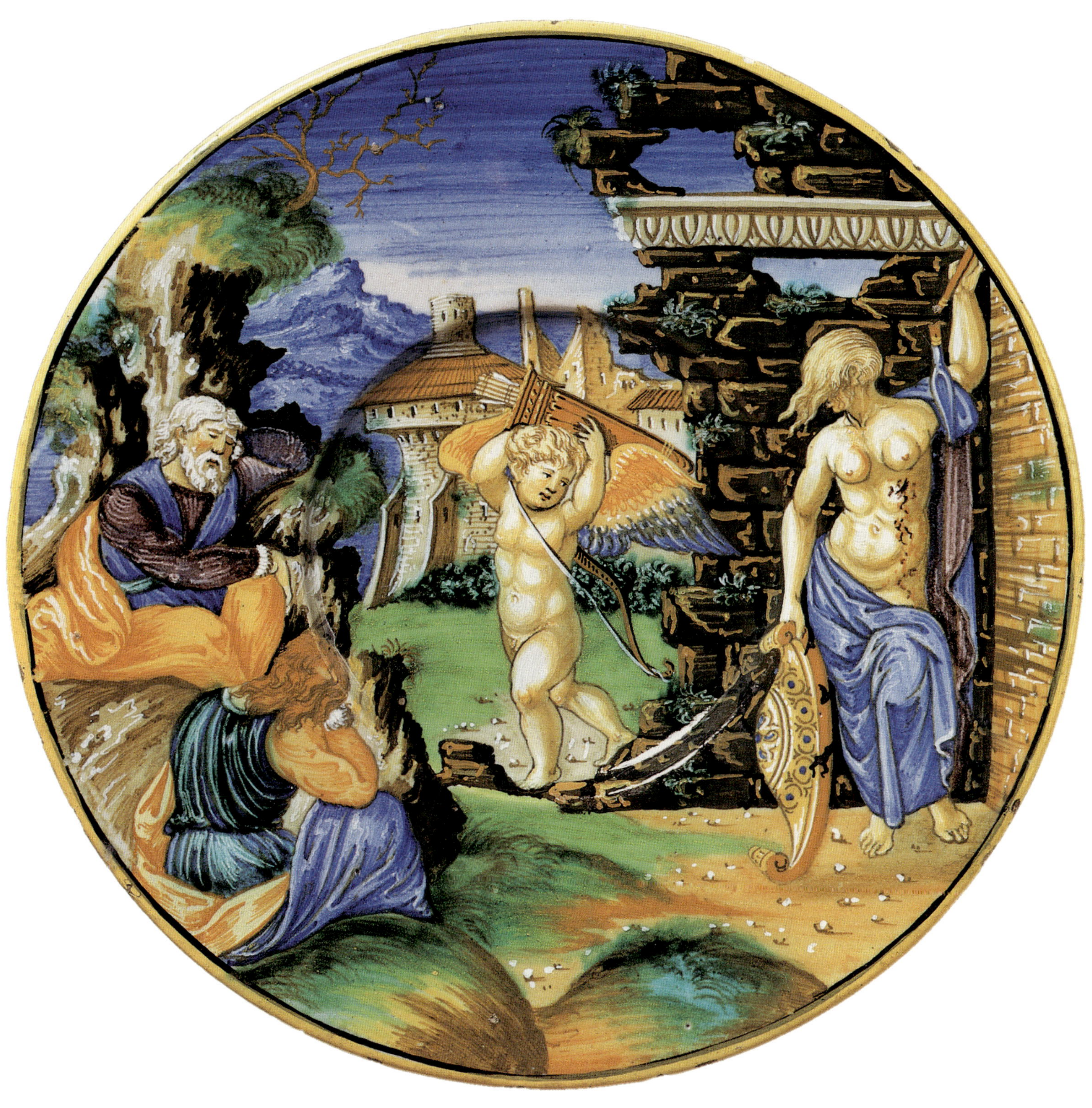

## 51. Plaque: *Sinon before Priam*

Attributed to Francesco Xanto Avelli, possibly assisted by
'Lu Ur', Urbino, *c.*1536

H: 30.3 cm; W: 27.7 cm
London, British Museum, PG&E 1906, 12-10, 1


PROVENANCE

Fountaine collection by 1835; given by
Sir Henry Howorth.

BIBLIOGRAPHY

Moore 1988, p. 441 (1835 inventory, no. 56);
Fountaine sale 1884, lot 367; Wilson 1987,
no. 215; Moore 1988; Lessmann 1991,
p. 27 and fig. 8; Lessmann 1990, p. 349
and fig. 68; Wilson 1993A; Wilson 1996,
especially no. 88; Thornton and Wilson,
2007, no. 159.

NOTES

1. *Ill. Bartsch* 27, p.119, 442 (332).
2. *Ill. Bartsch* 29, p. 301, 43-I (261).
3. *Ill. Bartsch* 26, p. 135, 104-I (89).
4. Holcroft 1988, p. 234.
5. Verdier 1967, p. 75; Lessmann 1991,
   p. 28 and p. 29, note 40; Caroselli 1993,
   pp. 26 and 76.
6. Lessmann 1991, pp. 25–31. See also
   Lessmann 1979, nos. 134–137 (Nicola and
   school); nos. 143–45 (Xanto, perhaps
   with assistants); Lessmann 1990;
   Lessmann 2004.
7. Wilson 1996, nos. 88–91. For the early
   dating see p. 203, no. 88.


Polychrome. Right, an enthroned king, named on the daïs to the throne: *.PRIAMO./ .T.R.*. Before him kneels a man with bound wrists, named on the wall behind as *SINON .G.*. To the left, shepherds. On a strip below is inscribed in black: *[Tra]ditor Sino[n] da Pastor molti vie[n] preso e'l falso alfi[n] co[n] parla….. I[n]ganna.* (the betrayer Sinon is captured by many shepherds, and in the end the treacherous man deceives by talking).
Reverse: unglazed.
Broken in five pieces, repaired with some re-touching; made up at the bottom-left corner, at the end of the inscription on the lower right corner and on a crack running from the top-right edge to the lower right and over a lion on the throne.

The legs and lower body of the seated King Priam seem to derive from Marcantonio Raimondi's *Seated Emperor*, after Raphael (fig. 18, p. 29),[1] the print on which the 1521 bowl bearing Nicola da Urbino's monogram is based (figs. 16, 17, p. 29); Sinon derives from *The Sacrifice of Iphigenia* by Beatrizet after Michelangelo or Bandinelli;[2] the shepherd leaning on his crook may derive from a figure just left of centre in the upper row of Marcantonio's *Martyrdom of St. Lawrence* after Baccio Bandinelli.[3]

The Greek, Sinon, is persuading the Trojan King Priam to have the wooden horse, in which Greek soldiers were concealed, pulled inside the walls of Troy, where the Greeks could emerge and capture the city. Xanto probably knew an Italian translation of Virgil's *Aeneid*;[4] the *Iliad* was little known in early sixteenth-century Italy.

Plaques like this are quite distinct from devotional plaques (see cat. 21). The secular plaques may have been mounted on furniture or, as has been suggested in connection with Limoges enamel plaques by the Aeneid Master, incorporated in room-decoration, as in Catherine de Medici's *Cabinet d'Émail*.[5] Xanto's historical tile-paintings come in cycles, one of which, with the history of Cyrus of Persia, is numbered from 1–39. The present tile would have initiated a comparable set narrating the Fall of Troy, of which only eight remain, possibly not all from the same set, since three are attributable to Nicola da Urbino and a follower.[6] None of the others, at Brunswick, St Petersburg or formerly in the Sprovieri collection, is dated, but they are so like the Persian series, five of which are dated 1536, as to make one doubt datings of *c.*1530 for the Troy series, based on the presence of the y/Φ flourish on the plaque in Brunswick. The ampersand and y/Φ mark occur on cat. 47, by Xanto's close associate, Giulio da Urbino, dated as late as 1534.[7]

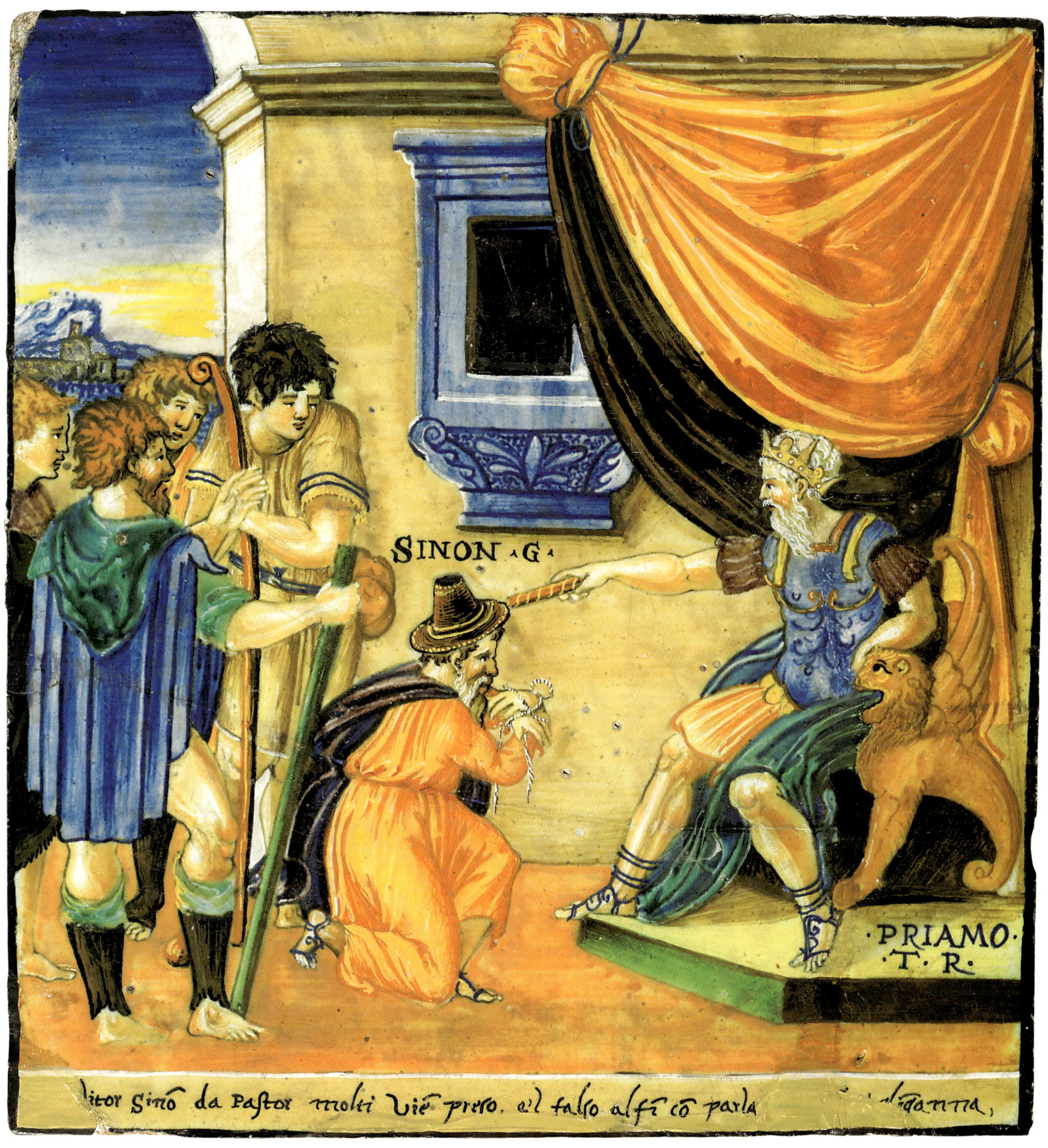


litor sinõ da pastor molti viẽ prero. e'l falso alfi cõ parla

52. Dish on low foot (*Coppa*): *A Head composed of Penises*

Attributed to Francesco Urbini, Gubbio, bearing his symbol
flanked by the initials *F. R.* and dated 1536

D: 23.2 cm
Oxford, Ashmolean Museum, WA 2003.136 (Purchased with the aid of the National Art Collections
Fund, the Resource/V&A Purchase Grant Fund, and numerous private donations, 2003)

PROVENANCE

Auctioned in Paris, February 1855;
Le Carpentier collection, Paris; Roger
Peyrefitte collection, Paris; Carlo di
Carlo collection, Florence.

BIBLIOGRAPHY

*Catalogue d'une Jolie Collection de Majoliques
Italiennes*, Paris, 12–15 February 1855,
lot 105; Darcel and Delange 1867-69, p. 43
(mark only is illustrated); Borenius 1928,
pp. 5–7; Mallet 1979, p. 273, no. 12; Mallet
2004, pp. 53–54 and figs. 20–21; Wilson
2005B (further bibliography on pp. 36–37,
note 3); Biscarini and Nardelli 2006.

NOTES

1. Wilson 2005B. As this catalogue was
   going to press an article placing the
   dish in the context of attitudes to the
   Jewish community in the Duchy of
   Urbino was published (Biscarini and
   Nardelli 2006).
2. Ballardini 1940, pls. xxvii a and b. This
   piece did not survive World War II.
3. Mallet 1979, pl. xcv a and b; Fiocco and
   Gherardi 1989, p. 430, figs. 137–138 and
   p. 447, pl. lii a and b.
4. Thornton and Wilson 2007, nos. 304
   and 306.
5. Barral 1987, no. 11. The date is vouched
   for by Francesco Urbini's Xantesque
   political allegory bearing the same
   initials and only slightly varied arms.
   Giacomotti 1974, no. 847.
6. Rackham 1940, nos. 778 and 779;
   Mallet 1979, pp. 283–84.

Polychrome. A profile head, composed of penises, with a green ribbon tying
a lock; dark blue ground with twisting fictive scroll inscribed backwards:
*.OGNI.HOMO.ME.GUARDA.COME.FOSSE.UNA.TESTA.DE.CAZI* (Everyone looks at
me as if I were a head of dicks).
Reverse: within the foot, in dark blue, the inscription: *1536/El breve de[n]tro voi
/legerite/Como giudei se i[n]tender/el vorite* (1536. If you want to understand the
inscription inside you will read it like the Jews) – ie. from right to left, as in
Hebrew script.
Below this is a mark that has been variously described as a trestle (*cavalletto,
trespolo*) or a pair of scales without the pans, here flanked by the initials F R.

This unique piece sends up a well-known genre of dish painted either with
a heroic male head or a beautiful female one. Timothy Wilson, in the fullest
study of the piece to date,[1] makes comparisons with works of art including
a portrait medal of Pietro Aretino and the fantastic heads painted by
Arcimboldo. The present dish is earlier than either. Its authorship is declared
by the *cavalletto* mark associated with Francesco Urbini's rather unskilful
*istoriati*, of which cat. 44 is an unmarked example. Such work was, however,
exceptional for Francesco Urbini who, on the evidence of a lustred *cavalletto*
mark,[2] was also employed at Gubbio adding lustre to ware, not improbably
including *istoriati* sent from Urbino by Xanto, with whose work of all periods
he was familiar. One of the two *istoriati* inscribed in blue by Francesco
Urbini as executed in 1534 at Gubbio[3] has, on the front of the bier on which
Coronis is dying, a design of foliate dolphins and masks that enables one
with reasonable confidence to identify his hand on decorative borders
attributable to Gubbio, including some 'S' service pieces of 1524[4] and the
border of cat. 10, whose central figure-subject is here attributed to Xanto.
An *istoriato* dish wholly by Francesco and dateable *c.* 1531[5] shows how
sophisticated a sense of flat pattern he had, a skill he took to Deruta in 1537.[6]
In 1536, on the eve of his departure for Deruta, he painted the phallic dish;
is it possible the initials *F.R.* stand for the man he would have known
as *Francesco Rovigiese* at Gubbio in 1524–25 and with whose later work he could
have remained familiar through enriching it with lustre? Is it also possible
he painted a caricature of his old colleague, enlivening it with one of
Xanto's saltier sayings?

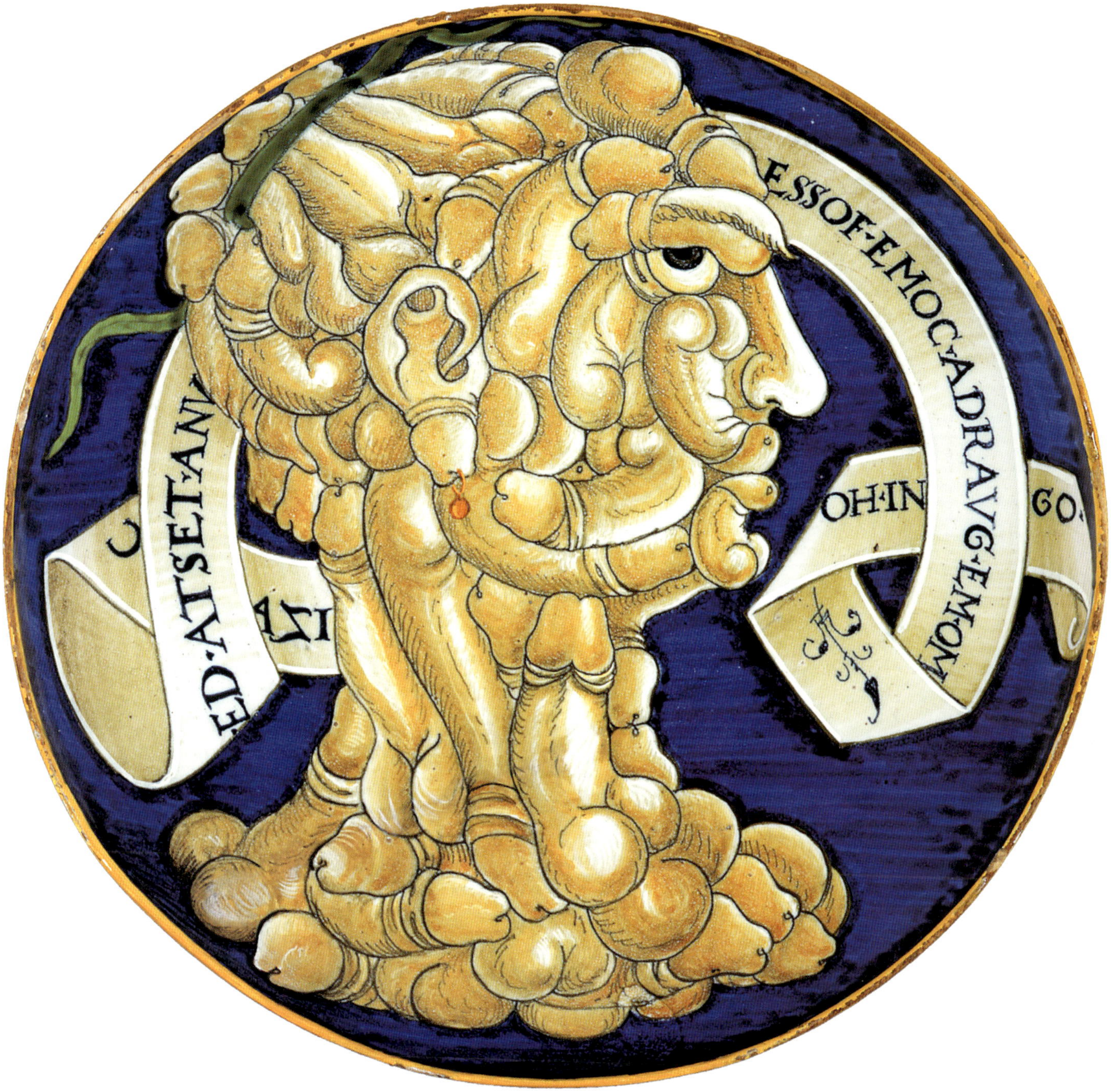

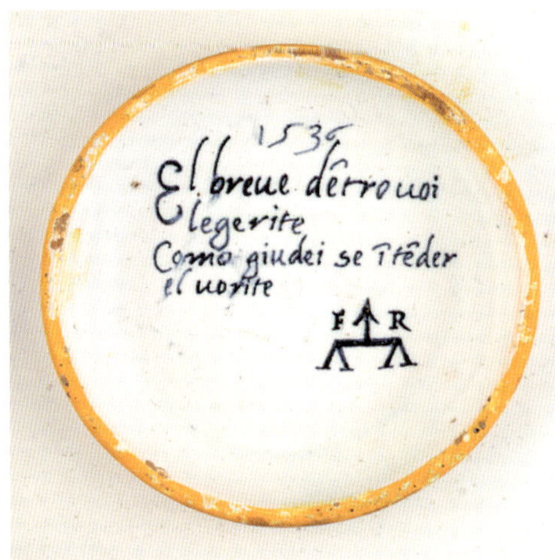

52 reverse (detail)

## 53. Plate: *The Vestal Virgin Tuccia carries Water in a Sieve to the Temple of Vesta*

By Francesco Xanto Avelli, Urbino, signed with initial and dated 1538

D: 25.9 cm
London, Wallace Collection, C93


PROVENANCE

Pasolini collection, Faenza; comte de Nieuwerkerke.

BIBLIOGRAPHY

Frati 1852, no. 61; Pasolini sale 1853, lot 72; Bethnal Green 1872-75, no. 1488; Demmin 1875, pl. cxli; Hausmann 1972, no. 196; Norman 1976, no. C93; Ivanova 2003, no. 50.

NOTES

1. *Ill. Bartsch* 28, p. 192, 53 (89).
2. *Ill. Bartsch* 26, p. 135, 104-I (89).
3. Rackham and Ballardini 1933, p. 398 and fig. 8.s.


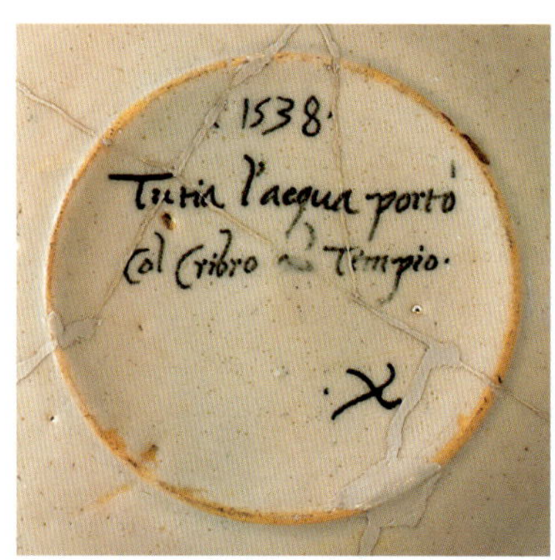

53 reverse (detail)

Polychrome. Left, Tuccia, a Vestal Virgin, designated by the initials *T.V.V.* at her feet, holds a sieve full of water and leads two other women towards a priest, an attendant and two other women who are grouped round a flaming altar beneath a canopy inscribed *.VEST. TEM.*.
Reverse: inscribed in black within the foot: *.1538./Tutia l'acqua portò/ Col Cribro al Tempio./ .X.* (1538, Tuccia carried the water in the sieve to the Temple. X.). Broken into seventeen pieces and reassembled.

Tuccia and the two women accompanying her, to the left, are taken (in reverse) from Gian Giacomo Caraglio's *The Muses and Pierides* after Rosso Fiorentino (fig. 43, p. 114);[1] the two women to the right are from the same print, but are not reversed; in the centre, the bearded priest by the altar and the young man behind him derive, in reverse, from figures towards the top right in Marcantonio Raimondi's *Martyrdom of St Lawrence* after Baccio Bandinelli.[2]

According to Pliny, *Natural History*, Book XXVIII, 12, Livy, IV, and Valerius Maximus, *Factorum Dictorumque Memorabilium*, IX, VIII. I. 5, the Vestal Virgin Tuccia was accused of unchastity, but proved her innocence by successfully carrying a sieve full of water from the Tiber to the Temple of Vesta.

As can be seen from *Appendix C*, Xanto painted this subject in 1535, twice in 1538 (of which cat. 53 is one), once in 1539 and once in 1540. He had, however, earlier depicted the Vestal Tuccia, showing three scenes of the story on a single *tondino* from the mid-1520s signed *F.R.*, formerly in the Berlin Schlossmuseum but lost during World War II.[3] That the closely similar piece in the Hermitage at St Petersburg, also dated 1538, is not the one formerly in the Pasolini collection is shown by the fact that Frati quotes the inscription *Vest. Tem,* absent on the Hermitage's example.

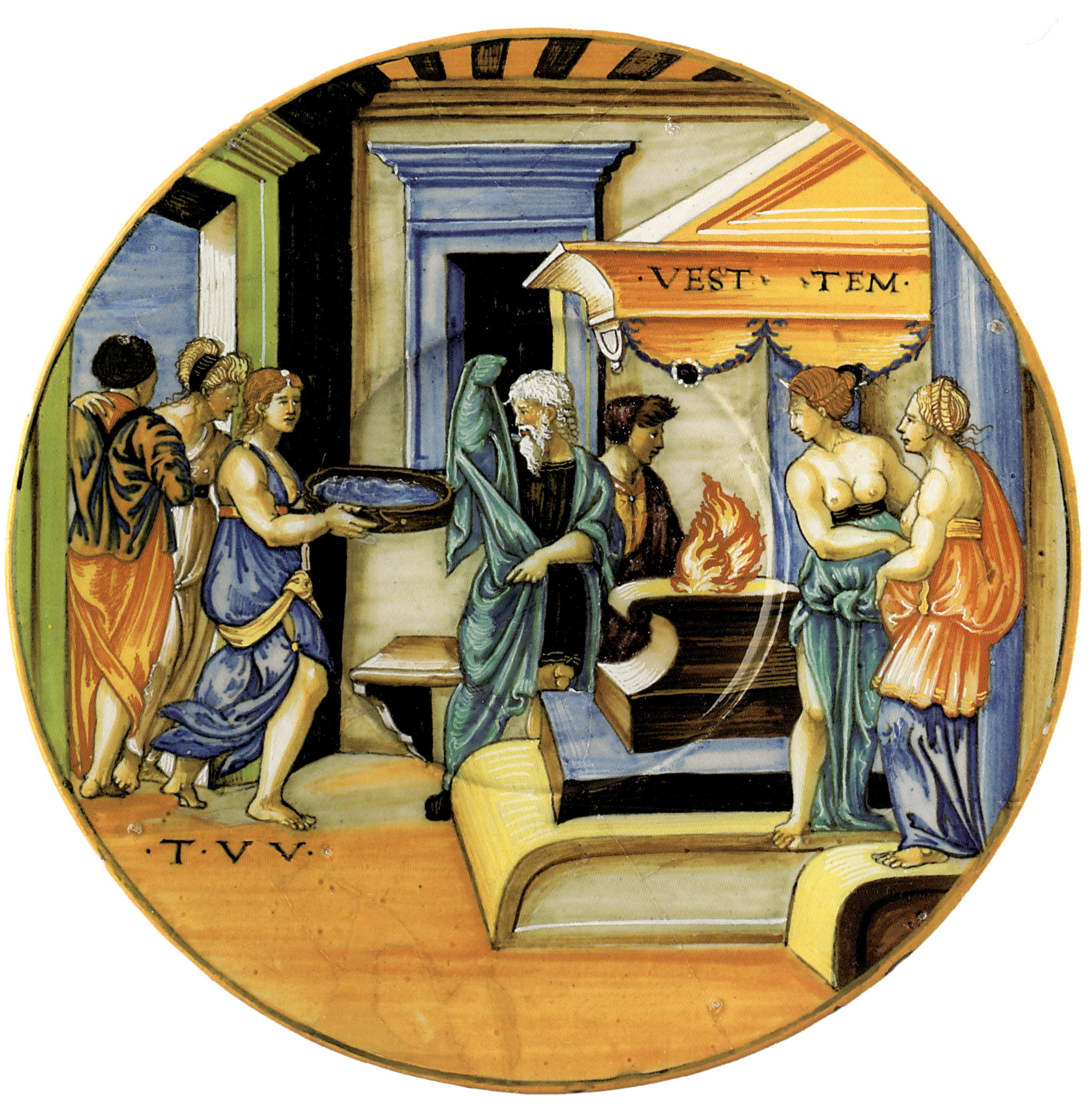

·VEST· ·TEM·
·T·V·V·

## 54.  Plate: *Metabus and Camilla*

Attributed to Francesco Xanto Avelli, possibly with slight collaboration
from Sforza di Marcantonio, Urbino, not signed but with lustred date, 1538;
lustre probably added at Gubbio

D: 27.3 cm
London, Ranger's House, English Heritage, Wernher Foundation, 219-179


PROVENANCE

Debruge-Duménil (bought in Italy);
Prince P. Soltykoff; M. Sellière.

BIBLIOGRAPHY

Labarte 1847, p. 679, no. 1145 (lustre
decoration implausibly read as a signature
F.X.); Debruge-Duménil sale 1849, lot
1145; Labarte 1875, III, p. 289 and pl. lxviii;
said to have been in the *Art Treasures and
Industrial Exhibition*, Wrexham, 1876; Wilson
1993B, pp. 212–13, figs. 5–6 and note 10;
Triolo 1996, p. 368–69, no. 13.2.

NOTES

1. *Ill. Bartsch* 27, p. 108, 420 (316).
2. *Ill. Bartsch* 26, p. 33, 21 (24).
3. *Ill. Bartsch* 26, p. 244, 247 (200).
4. Lessmann 1979, no. 148; Mallet 1978,
   p. 43, fig. 5.
5. Wilson 1993B, pp. 210–14, inv. no.
   1942.9.337 (C-62).


Polychrome and lustre. Left, Metabus prepares to hurl the infant Camilla
to safety over the river Amasenus on his spear; right foreground, the river
god pours water; middle-distance right, Diana and attendants stand in a
grotto ready to receive the child. In the centre, above the child, is a shield
of arms: *azure, six teasels (?) or, in chief, a label of Anjou*.
Reverse: three concentric antimony-yellow circles, those at the rim and foot
partly covered with red lustre; outside the foot two spiral leaf-scrolls and two
arrangements of concentric circles, all in red lustre; within the foot further
leafy scrolls and the date *1538* in red lustre.
Crack running from rim to foot ring; minor chips to rim.

The figure of Metabus is adapted from a spearman (used also for cat. 7, 25
and 34) in the *Battle Scene* print probably by Marco Dente, after Raphael or
Giulio Romano (fig. 32, p. 60).[1] The river god in the foreground, right, is
from Marco Dente's print of *The Massacre of the Innocents* after Baccio Bandinelli
(fig. 42, p. 108).[2] Camilla and Diana and her attendants derive from
Raimondi's *Parnassus* (fig. 44, p. 116).[3]

According to Virgil (*Aeneid* XI, 561) Metabus, King of the Volscians, was
fleeing from his enemies when, unable to swim the river Amasenus with
his baby daughter Camilla in his arms, he hurled her across attached to
his javelin, entrusting her to the goddess Diana. In *Appendix C* Elisa Sani lists
this subject no less than twelve times among Xanto's works between 1532
and 1542. It was also copied by followers in 1539 and 1543.[4]

The arms on this plate and on cat. 55 have not been identified; the charge
described as teasels has also been interpreted as oak-leaves, lobsters, torches
or pine-cones. Xanto seems to have collaborated on the service, probably
with Sforza di Marcantonio. Two other plates from it are recorded: *Hero and
Leander*, in the National Gallery of Art, Washington,[5] and *Joseph and Potiphar's
Wife* in the Victoria and Albert Museum (cat. 55). The Camilla and the
Leander plates (lustre apart) seem almost wholly by Xanto, though the
Leander plate is inscribed in handwriting that is not his. The lustre on all
three was probably added at Gubbio.

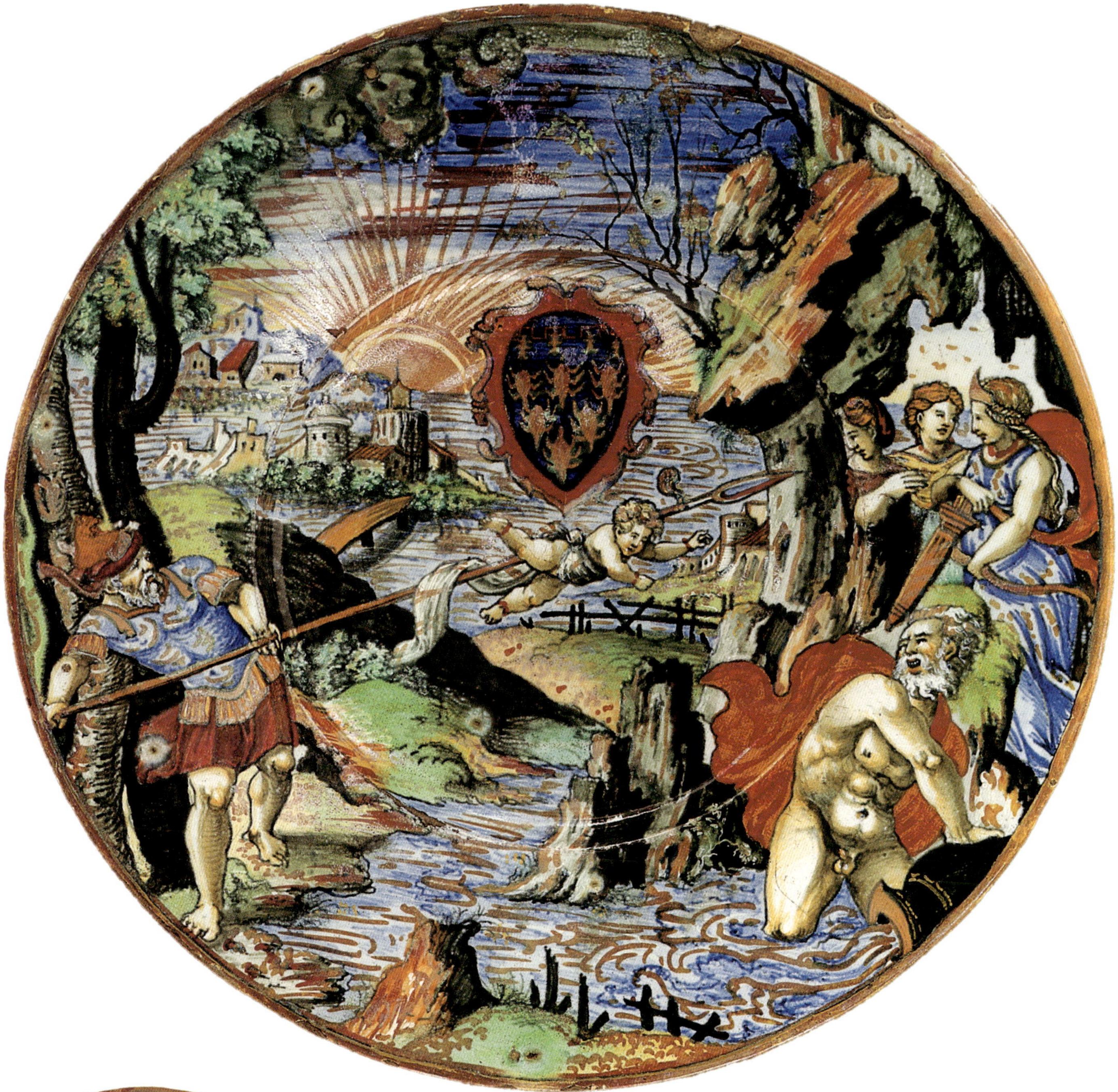

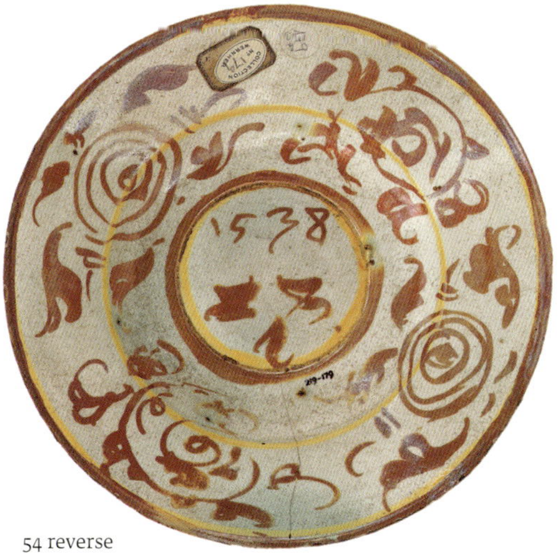

54 reverse

## 55.  Dish on low foot (*Coppa*): *Joseph and Potiphar's Wife*

Attributed to Sforza di Marcantonio, his presumed signature *S*
on the reverse; Urbino, the lustre probably added at Gubbio, *c.* 1538

D: 27.0 cm
London, Victoria and Albert Museum, C.481-1921

PROVENANCE
Bequeathed by David M. Currie.

BIBLIOGRAPHY
Rackham 1940, no. 729 (unillustrated);
Wilson 1993B, pp. 210–14, inv. no.
1942.9.337 (C-62); Fiocco and Gherardi
1996, pp. 147–48; Triolo 1996, p. 369, 13.3;
Triolo 2002, pp. 133–34, pl. xxxvi and
fig. 14.

NOTES
 1. *Ill. Bartsch* 26, p. 18, 9 (10).
 2. Rasmussen 1989, no. 87.
 3. Giacomotti 1974, 858.
 4. Conti 1971, no. 194.
 5. Lippmann 1895, pl. F.V.
 6. Wilson 1993B, pp. 210–14, figs. 7–8
    and note 11.
 7. Fiocco and Gherardi 1996, pp. 145–51.
 8. Norman 1976, no. C90. The lustred
    date on Wilson and Sani 2006, no. 36,
    might be 1535.
 9. Bonali and Gresta 1987, p. 37, note 54.
10. Bettini 1997, p. 79, fig. 52; *idem* in
    Dal Poggetto 2004, p. 428, XII.70.

Polychrome with lustre. The wife of Potiphar sits on the edge of a bed, clutching at the garment of Joseph, who flees to the right. Behind the bed stands a horned devil; above, right, Cupid descends holding flaming torches. Above, centre, is a shield of arms, as on cat. 54 but with the label somewhat differently treated.
Reverse: the border decorated in lustre with leafy spirals alternating with crossed lozenges. Within the foot are further 'c' shaped scrolls in lustre and, in blue: *fugie iosefe il di / sonesto efetto / S.* (Joseph flees from the shameful deed. S.).

Joseph and Potiphar's wife are closely modelled on Marcantonio Raimondi's print of the subject after Raphael,[1] in which the devil is less prominent, in a niche to the right, and probably meant for an Egyptian idol; Cupid does not appear in the print.

Like a lustred dish in the Lehman collection,[2] similar in composition and painted and inscribed by the same hand, cat. 55 reflects a much superior original by Xanto in the Louvre, inscribed in blue: *1538. Gioseppe fuggie il scelerato affetto / X.*[3] As in cat. 55, Cupid has been added in the sky, as he has also on a large dish with additional figures, dated 1537, in the Bargello.[4] This Cupid is seemingly adapted from the one in the woodcut of *The Planet Venus* published by Gabriele Giolito De' Ferrari (fig. 56, p. 160).[5] The intrusion of a pagan Cupid is hard to accept in the biblical story of the wife of Potiphar, captain of Pharaoh's guard, who accused Joseph when he had rejected her advances (Genesis 39).

A thinly drawn 'S' that appears on cat. 55, on the 'Teasel' service piece in Washington[6] and on a few other pieces, has been convincingly identified by Fiocco and Gherardi as a signature of the painter Sforza di Marcantonio del fu Marcantonio de Julianis di Castel Durante, who was presumably of Castel Durante origin.[7] On the evidence of a lustred dish in the Wallace Collection, it would seem that he was already in Urbino and close to Xanto as early as 1535.[8] By 17 May 1548 he is documented in Pesaro[9] where, with a few unexplained gaps, his work can be traced to as late as 1576, and where he made a will and died in 1580. He was evidently in Urbino working on the 'Teasel' service in 1538, but it is harder to determine where he executed a range of work dated from 1543 onwards. I am tempted to ascribe to Sforza a *coppa* in the Bettini collection with the *Adoration of the Shepherds*, inscribed in what looks like Sforza's hand *fatto in pessaro / 1543*. If this were accepted as his,[10] we could be sure he had moved to Pesaro soon after Xanto's work peters out. Such an early move to Pesaro might explain the lack of later lustred work attributable to Sforza.

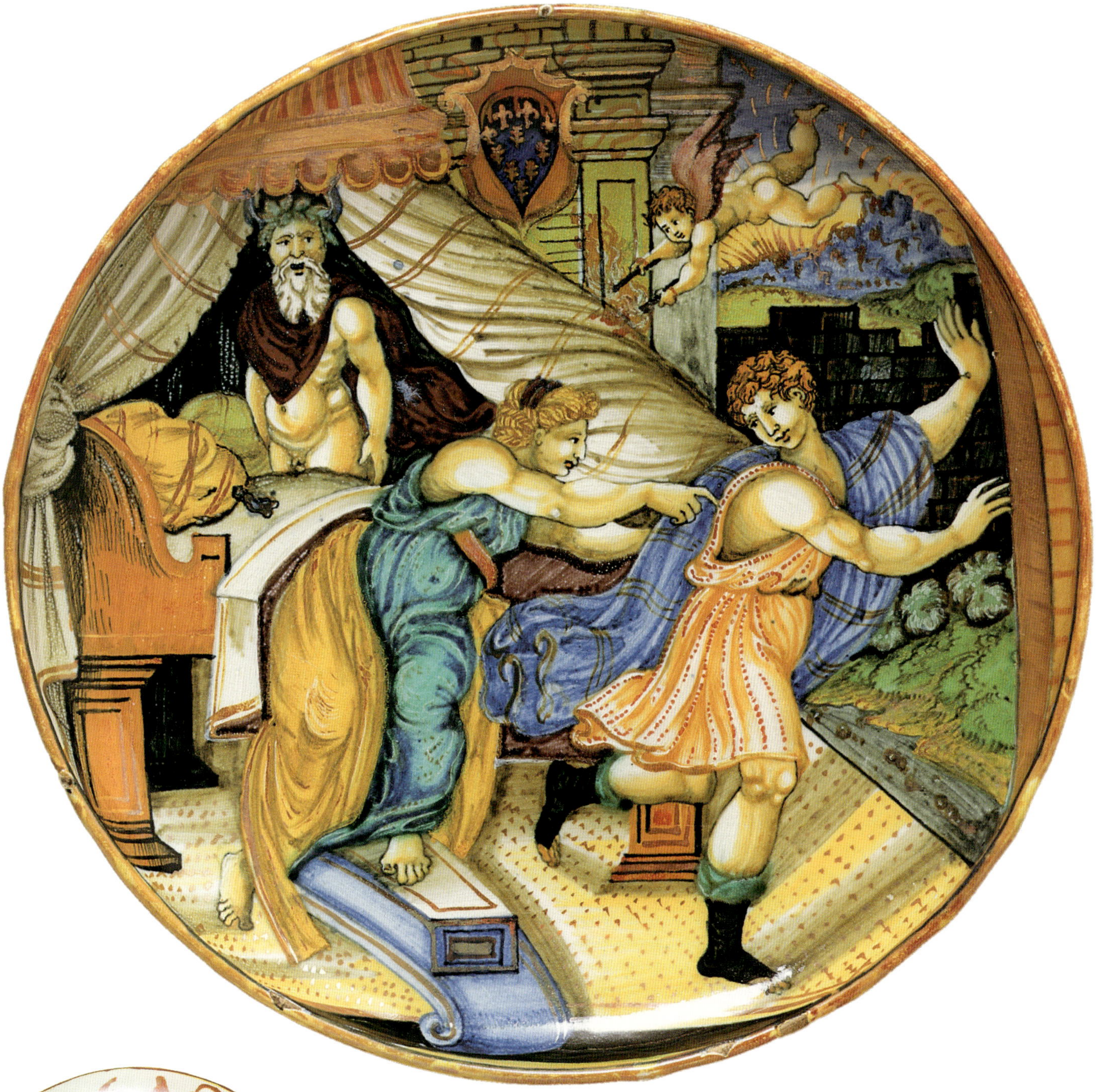

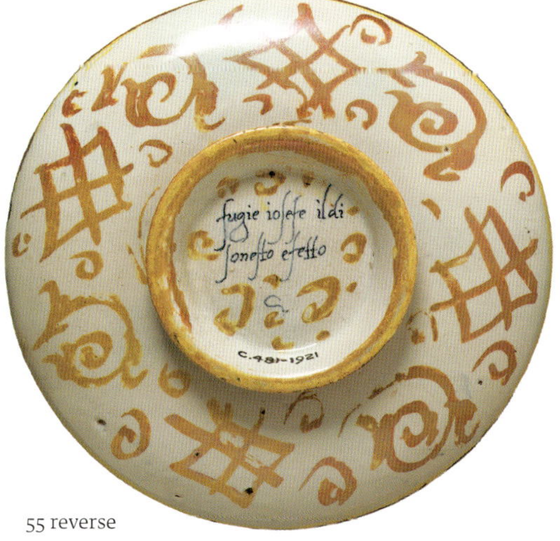


55 reverse

# 56. Plate: *The Children of the Planet Venus*

Attributed to Francesco Xanto Avelli, Urbino, unsigned but dated *1542*

D: 28.0 cm
London, Victoria and Albert Museum, C.2240-1910

PROVENANCE

Frédéric Spitzer; bequeathed in 1910 by
George Salting.

BIBLIOGRAPHY

Molinier 1892, p. 56, no. 131 (as Castel
Durante or Urbino); Rackham 1913, p. 195
(as by Orazio Fontana of Urbino);
Rackham 1940, no. 868 (as by 'The Painter
of the Myths in Modern Dress'); Wilson
and Sani 2006, p. 106 (as by Xanto).

NOTES

1. Lippmann 1895, pl. F.V.
2. Rackham 1940, pp. 243 and 289.
3. Wilson and Sani 2006, no. 40.
4. Kunstindustrimuseet, no. O.K. 12045.
5. Triolo 2000, no. 215.
6. Mancini Della Chiara 1979, no. 217;
   Giardini 1996, no. 12.
7. Ravanelli Guidotti 1985, no. 99.

Polychrome. In the centre, a group of musicians in costume of the period
play the harp, the lute and a wind-instrument. To the left, two young lovers
sit on the ground; to the right stand two further lovers. In the background
is a landscape with rocks, hills and buildings.
Reverse: inscribed in dark blue: *Omnia vincit/Amor./.1542.*

The figures are taken, in reverse and with the omission of a further couple,
from the terrestrial portion of the woodcut of *The Planet Venus*, published in
1533 by Gabriele Giolito De' Ferrari of Venice (fig. 56).[1]

Rackham assigned this plate to a group for which he devised the name
'The Painter of the Myths in Modern Dress',[2] but its style is typical of Xanto's
latest work, which is quite often unsigned and, if inscribed at all, often
displays a new style of calligraphy executed with a thicker brush than
formerly. Cat. 56 has recently been compared to another unsigned piece of
1542 with *Parnassus* and attributed to Xanto.[3] Amongst plates dated 1542
and signed *.x.* is one with *Apollo and the Muses on Parnassus*, in Oslo's Kunstindustrimuseet.[4] That Xanto was familiar with the *Planet Venus* woodcut is
shown by a *tagliere* in Milan which also uses the figures from it in reverse.[5]
The Cupid who accompanies Venus in the celestial part of the woodcut
seems to have been appropriated by Xanto for his *Joseph and Potiphar's Wife* in
the Bargello and thence passed into the repertory of his follower, Sforza di
Marcantonio (cat. 55) and probably into a more mature work of Sforza's,
his *Apollo and Daphne* of 1545 at Pesaro.[6]

    The Virgilian tag *Omnia vincit Amor* is understandable enough on a plate
depicting those under the astrological influence of Venus. Xanto had used
it on a signed *coppa* with the marriage of Alexander and Roxana, dated 1537,
which survives as a fragment at Bologna.[7] It also features on cat. 1 which,
with its date 1522, is the earliest piece for which Xanto's authorship can
confidently be claimed.

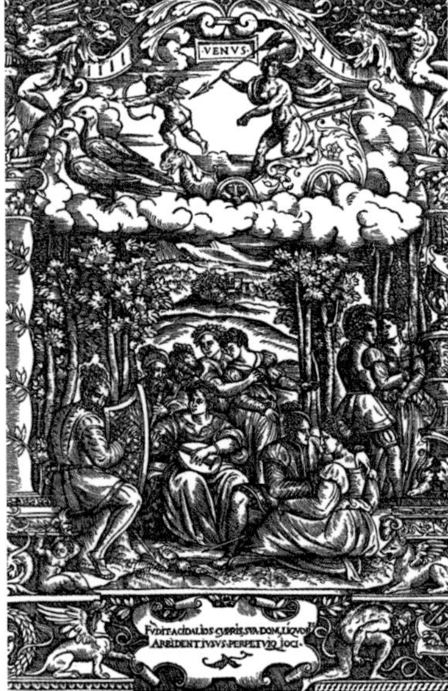

Fig. 56. *The Planet Venus*, 1533, woodcut
published by Gabriele Giolito De'Ferrari

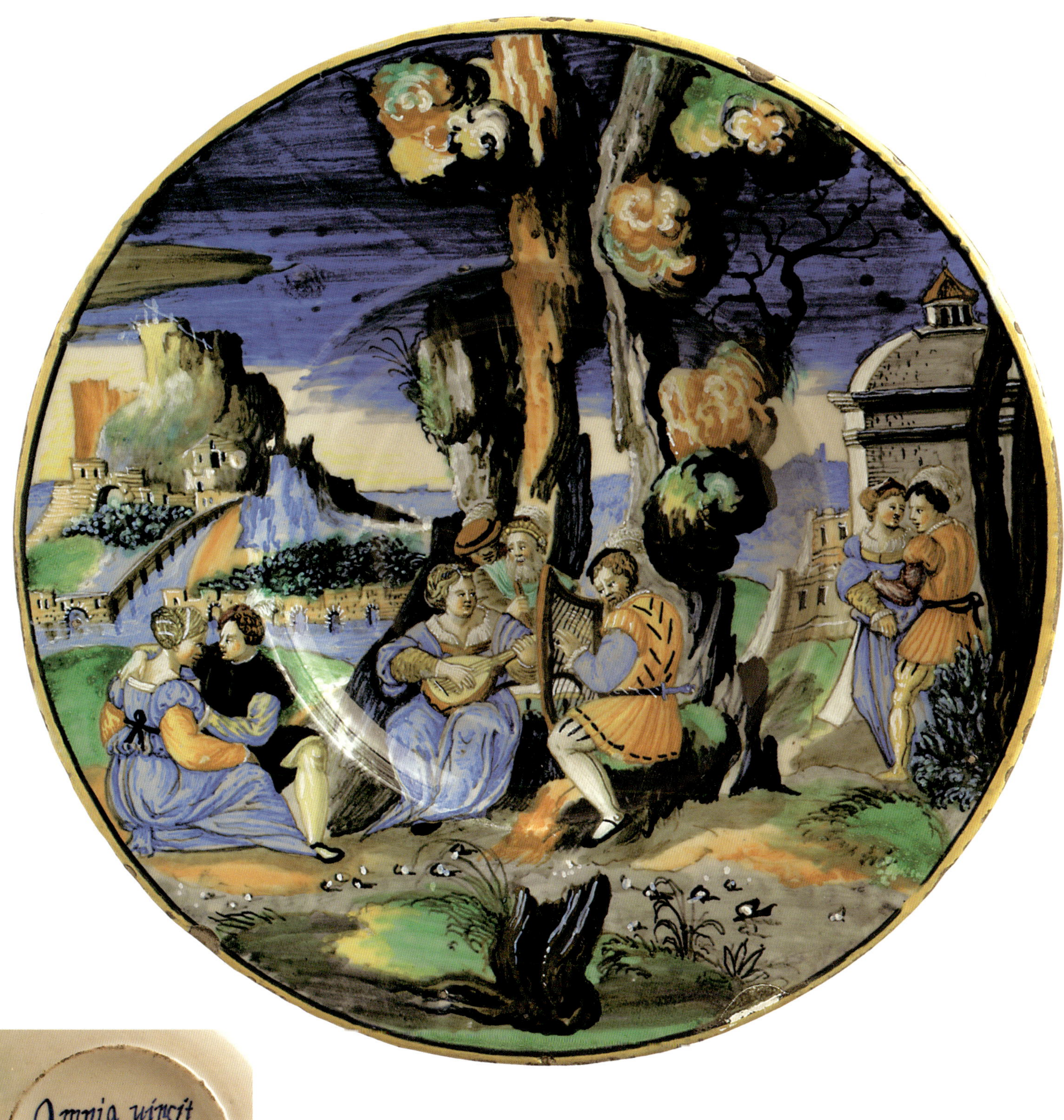

56 reverse (detail)

# Il *Ritratto*, a sonnet sequence by Francesco Xanto Avelli

GIOVANNA HENDEL

## I. THE MANUSCRIPT

Xanto's forty-four sonnets have come down to us in a single manuscript copy clearly made by a professional scribe and now kept in the Vatican Library.[1] It forms part of the *Fondo Urbinate*, the collection that formerly belonged to the Dukes of Urbino and passed to the Vatican in 1657, after the Urbino branch of the Della Rovere family became extinct. The manuscript is first recorded in the Castel Durante collection of Francesco Maria II (1549–1631), grandson of Francesco Maria I.[2] However, it might well have been in the possession of the Dukes of Urbino before Francesco Maria II's time. It could even be Xanto's presentation copy, given to Francesco Maria I before his death in 1538, because Francesco Maria II's library included some manuscripts that he had inherited, even though they are not listed in earlier inventories.[3]

This possibility is supported by the fact that the scribe's hand can be dated to approximately the first half of the sixteenth century.[4] Moreover, the level of sophistication of the script, with its decorated initial at the opening of the first sonnet and its ornamented letters, is appropriate for a presentation copy.

Furthermore, another indication that the manuscript dates from the Duke's lifetime came to light during close examination of the manuscript. In fact, I realised that one leaf (corresponding to Sonnets XXXIX, XL) had been added after completion of the rest of the text. The manuscript was originally made of seven quires of four leaves each. The first leaf of the first quire and the fourth leaf of the seventh quire were pasted onto the front and back boards respectively. The fourth leaf of the first quire, which probably corresponds to a blank leaf, judging by what would have been its position in the text, was cut. An extra leaf was then added after the third leaf of the sixth quire.[5] The hand on the additional leaf ($E(\chi^1)$) would appear to be identical to the hand responsible for the rest of the manuscript.[6] However, on this leaf the ink is richer, the script is slightly larger and the margins narrower than on other leaves. This suggests that the scribe of the additional leaf is also the scribe responsible for the rest of the manuscript, but that he wrote it at a later date than the other leaves. Perhaps he could not refer back to the original document in order to ensure that the size of the script and the width of the margins of the new leaf would correspond to it.

Now, it is highly improbable that the scribe added the new leaf to remedy an error, since he is most unlikely to have omitted two whole sonnets when transcribing Xanto's work. Moreover, Sonnets XXXIX and XLI do not even begin in the same way, thus ruling out the possibility that the scribe inadvertently copied out Sonnet XLI instead of Sonnet XXXIX, mistaking one for the other. Besides, the differences between the additional leaf and the rest of the manuscript, described above, appear to rule out the possibility that the leaf was added when the scribe could still refer directly to his manuscript simply to replace an original, damaged leaf bearing Sonnets XXXIX and XL.

A more probable explanation for the additional leaf, in line with the idea that the scribe's hand can be dated to the first half of the sixteenth century, is that it was inserted at Xanto's request. This would support the idea that the manuscript was written in the first half of the sixteenth century, since Xanto probably died in or shortly after 1542 (see Introduction, p. 14).

The addition of the extra leaf might also have interesting implications for some of the episodes referred to in the sonnets and for Xanto's relationship to his patron/s.

The transcription has been as faithful as possible to
the text as given in the manuscript. These are the only
changes that have been made made:
(i) 'u' is replaced with 'v' where appropriate.
(ii) Accents from all the 'i's have been removed. This is
because the 'i's in the manuscript are accentuated quite
ubiquitously, as if the scribe used accents, in the case
of 'i's, as dots. By contrast, the other vowels in the
manuscript are sometimes accentuated and sometimes
not. So no changes to accommodate the other vowels in
the manuscript have been made.
(iii) Commas at the ends of sonnets have been turned into
full-stops. This is the only change made to the punctuation.
However, the fact that in sixteenth century Italian there
were still not any standard rules of punctuation has
allowed me to translate, in some cases, as if there had
been a punctuation-mark where there was none or where
there was one otherwise placed than it would be in
modern Italian.
(iv) When there is an obvious scribal mistake, this is
reproduced it within square brackets, followed by the
equal sign and the correct reading. When the correct
reading requires the removal of letters, the equal sign is
followed by '/'. So, for example, the fact that the correct
reading of the text should have been 'ha' instead of 'hai'
is expressed as 'ha[i = /]'.



The aim has been to provide a translation which is as close
as possible to the original text. Thus the translation has
been as literal as possible. This has resulted in the English
text sounding awkward in places, but the non-Italian
reader can be assured that the original text also reads far
from well. Resisting the temptation to 'improve' on the
original, the translation attempts to recreate in English
the same impression as the original text makes
on an Italian reader.*

---

1. Vatican manuscript Urb. lat. 794, 20.6 × 14.1 cm, ink on paper,
   parchment binding. The sonnets are not numbered in the original
   manuscript, but they are numbered here, for convenience's sake,
   using Roman numerals as in the previous editions of the sonnets,
   Vitaletti (1918) and Cioci (1987).
2. See the concordances in Stornajolo 1902-1921, vol. III, p. xiv.
3. Compare with Stornajolo 1902-1921, vol. III, p. xiv*.
4. For examples of similar hands, see Casamassima 1966.
5. Thus the collational formula is: $\pi^3$ (of 4, i used as front pastedown,
   iv cancelled) A-D$^4$ E$^4$ (E$_3$ + $\chi^1$) F$^4$ (iv used as back pastedown) [$\$_1$ signed].
6. Moreover, the same ways of abbreviating the 'et's on E($\chi^1$) can be
   found in the rest of the manuscript but they do not just repeat
   the ones on the adjoining ff. E$_3$$^b$ & E$_4$$^a$. This suggests that the
   hand of E($\chi^1$) is not merely that of a scribe trying to imitate the
   adjoining pages.

---

* The translation has benefitted greatly from invaluable comments
  by John Mallet, to whom I am very grateful. I would also like to
  thank Andrea Gilbert, Suzanne Higgott, Jeremy Warren and, for
  advice on the manuscript, Mirjam Foot, Laura Nuvoloni and, in
  particular, Paolo Vian.

Il Ritratto dell'Ill.<sup>mo</sup>, & Inuit=
tissimo Principe' Francesco Maria
Feltrio dalla Rouer. iiij.
Duca d'Urbino
Per Francesco xanto da Rouigo.

*Il Ritratto dell'Illmo, et Invit.*
*tissimo Principe Francesco Maria*
*Feltrio dalla Rovere .iiii.*
*Duca d'Urbino*
*Per Francesco Xanto da Rovigo.*

The Portrait of the Most
Illustrious and Indomitable
Prince Francesco Maria Feltrio dalla
Rovere Fourth Duke of Urbino,[1]
by Francesco Xanto of Rovigo.

1. Here Francesco Maria is called 'Fourth Duke of Urbino', whereas in the dedication at the head of the first sonnet, he is called 'Third Duke of Urbino'. As Cioci (1987) points out, this is, probably, to be explained by the fact that in the first case but not in the second, Oddantonio da Montefeltro, half-brother of Federico da Montefeltro, has been counted as the first Duke of Urbino, thus making Francesco Maria fourth in the line of succession.



OPPOSITE:
Fig. 57. Dedication from Xanto's sonnet sequence *Il Ritratto*, sixteenth century, manuscript, Biblioteca Apostolica Vaticana (Vatican), Urb. lat. 794, f. 1r

I

All'Illustriss.o Francesco Maria Feltrio
dalla Rovere, III Duca d'Urbino.

*Duca viril' che d'honorato ammanto*
*Fra i monti Etrurij et l'onde d'Adria vai*
*Pomposo alzando al ciel' col valor' c'hai*
*Il chiaro nome tuo lodato tanto,*

*Non ti sdegnar' se fedelmente io canto*
*Que liberali effetti con che dai*
*Pace à virtute et di par nome fai*
*L'umbro Metauro gir col Phrigio Xanto*

*Ne maraviglia partorisca il crudo*
*Et rozzo stil, che sott'humil ricetto*
*Natura al mondo die povero et gnudo*

*Chel' tuo gentile et ben cortese affetto*
*E tal' delle virtú custode et scudo*
*Ch'ogn'anima et ogni cor ti fai soggietto*

---

I

*To the Most Distinguished Francesco Maria Feltrio*
*della Rovere Third Duke of Urbino.*

Oh manly duke,[1] who, between the Etruscan
mountains and the Adriatic's waves,[2] go, with a
mantle of glory, magnificently raising to heaven by
your valour your renowned name, so much lauded,

Do not be disdainful if I faithfully sing your liberal
deeds by which you give peace to virtue and you make
the Umbrian Metaurus run with the same glory as
the Phrygian Xanthus.[3]

And don't let this rough and unrefined style, which
nature bore to the world plain and bare under a
humble shelter, engender wonder;

Since your gentle and most kind affection is such a
guardian and shield to all virtues that you subjugate
every soul and heart.

---

[1] *Oh manly Duke.* Perhaps the fact that Guidobaldo I, Francesco Maria's uncle and predecessor, was impotent is behind Xanto's choice of this address.

[2] *between … waves.* The extent of the ancient district of Etruria varied considerably throughout the centuries, but the term 'Etruscan mountains' (the Appennino Centrale) is here used in a general way to define the western borders of the Duchy of Urbino, as the Adriatic sea is used to mark the eastern borders.

[3] *you … Xanthus.* The river Metaurus flows through the territory of the Duchy of Urbino, which at least partly overlapped with the region of Umbria, larger than today's Umbria and including Gubbio, with which Xanto's work is linked. The river Xanthus is called 'Phrygian' because it flows in Phrygia, formerly region of the classical Asia Minor and now part of Turkey. Probably the general idea, here, is that the Duke's deeds raise his duchy to the fame earned by Classical Antiquity. Then Xanto takes pride, of course, in associating himself, through his name, with the fame of Classical Antiquity. In addition, Cioci (1987, p. 93) sees here a reference to planned expeditions/crusades against the Turks in which the Duke was meant to take a part.

---

II

*Qual' se per farsi alla miglior stagione*
*Bella ghirlanda d'odorosi fiori*
*Avien che'n prato pien' di bei colori*
*Vergine arrivi con sue gratie buone.*

*Che piena al fin' di molta ammiratione*
*Per l'abbondanza bella ch'entro et fuori*
*La cinge e 'ngombra spesso tra gli odori*
*Manda l'opra sua vaga in oblivione.*

*Tal' io Signor, al cominciar' sospeso*
*Mi truovo nel giardin' di vostre lodi*
*Da miglior' voci già per fama inteso,*

*Ov'amor' et virtute in mille modi*
*Lusingandomi dicon' poi ch'asceso*
*Sei al costui valor cantando godi.*

---

II

Like a virgin who, with her good graces, in order
to make herself a beautiful garland of fragrant flowers
in the gentler season, comes to a meadow full of
beautiful colours

And who, full in the end of much admiration for the
beautiful plenty that inside and outside surrounds and
often encumbers her amongst the various perfumes,
becomes oblivious of her lovely work,

Such, my lord, I find myself, suspended in my
beginning, in the garden of your praises, which has
already been made famous by better voices than mine,

And where love and virtue, flattering me in a
thousand ways, tell me: 'Now that you have risen
to his greatness, rejoice in your singing'.

*Ornata di diversi et bei colori*
*L'alma pittura et mia fedel' nutrice*
*Sperando farmi tal' qual' far' le lice*
*Tutto m'infuse ne suoi sacri odori.*

*Et trassemi à mostrar' l'armi et gli amori*
*Del stuol' dannato et del splendor' felice*
*Si come del mio ben' vera radice*
*E luce et aura alli miei primi fiori.*

*Ma non ancho venuto à gli sei lustri*
*Er'io per tal sentier', ch'à un Rover' d'oro*
*Amor mi trasse et disse hor scrivi il vero.*

*Cosi tra due di par canto et coloro*
*L'antiche historie et gli honorati Illustri*
*Hoggi per lor virtú degni d'impero.*



Adorned with various and beautiful colours, divine Painting, my faithful nurse, hoping to make me such as she can make me, infused into my whole self her sacred scents.

And she brought me to tell the martial and amorous deeds of the doomed multitude and of the blessed bright ones,[1] as the true root of my good and as the light and breeze of my first bloom.

But I had not yet been for six *lustra* on such a path,[2] when Love drew me to a golden Oak[3] and told me: 'Now write the truth'.[4]

Thus between the two[5] I both sing and paint the ancient stories and the honoured illustrious men who today for their valour[6] deserve to reign.

1 *she…ones.* Here Xanto seems to refer to some early poetical endeavour of his, perhaps a poem on the afterlife following the example of the *Divine Comedy*.
2 *But…path.* That is to say: 'But, engaged in such pursuits, when I was not yet thirty…' A 'lustrum' denotes, in Latin, a period of five years.
3 *a golden Oak.* Clearly representing Francesco Maria Della Rovere: a golden 'rovere', or oak, featured in the coat of arms of the Della Rovere family.
4 *Now write the truth.* Here Xanto is probably contrasting the fictional character of his early poetical work with the historical and, allegedly, descriptive one of *Il Ritratto*.
5 *between the two.* That is, between poetry and painting.
6 *for their valour.* As John Mallet points out in the Introduction (p. 16), the term 'virtù' in the sixteenth century not only meant 'virtue' in our modern English sense, but was also understood to encompass a wide range of skills in statecraft and war. Here it is translated with 'valour', as a single word had to be chosen.



*Colei che gia sovra 'l paterno fiume*
*Divenne pianta celebre et gentile*
*Per cui del Gange et dell'estrema Tile*
*Godeo sovente il bel Roman' costume.*

*Porga alle luci mie suo chiaro lume*
*Et orni me d'un si leggiadro Aprile*
*Ch'io possi insiem col mio Signor virile*
*Levarmi al ciel con gloriose piume.*

*Ne mi sfido di cio per ch'io so ch'ella*
*Mirand'io l'alt'Urbin' mi disse allegra*
*Quinci si va, chi vuol andar' per fama,*

*Peró svegliati homai non esser pegra*
*Man', se del tuo Signor la nuova stella*
*Speri à Mart' agguagliar ch'altro non brama.*



She who once, by the paternal river, became a famous and noble plant[1] in which rejoiced the beautiful Roman costume[2] from the Ganges to the furthest Thule,[3]

Let her offer to my eyes her bright light and let her make me as graceful as April, so that, with my manly lord, I can rise to heaven on glorious wings.

And I do not despair of doing that, because I know that, while I was gazing high at Urbino, she told me cheerfully: 'Hence go those who want to pursue fame'.

So, rise, my hand, do not be sluggish, if you hope to make equal to Mars the new star of your lord, who longs for nothing else.

1 *She…* This is Daphne, daughter of the river god Peneus, who, pursued by Apollo, successfully implored her father to turn her into a laurel bush. Laurel was then chosen by Apollo as his sacred plant and thus became the emblem of poetry, used to crown the winners of poetical contests. So Xanto invokes Daphne as a personification of poetry.
2 *in which rejoiced the beautiful Roman costume.* Laurel was also used, in ancient Greece and Rome, to crown the winners of the Pythian games, held in honour of Apollo. It thus became a symbol of victory in general and it is as such that it is probably referred to here.
3 *from the Ganges to the furthest Thule.* That is, in all lands up to the furthest eastern and northern borders of the known world.

V

*Vaga bella diletta alma pittura*
*Che'n terra hoggi di sei l'aura seconda*
*Che spinge al secur' porto fuor del'onda*
*Le piu chiare memorie di natura,*

*Per l'alta luce tua che splende et dura*
*Ov'util' pace piu tra nostri abonda*
*Mentr'al contempio tua beltá gioconda*
*Gli desti spirti piu ci rape et fura,*

*Spira nel servo tuo quel dolce fiato*
*Che suol l'huomo levar' da terra et lieto*
*Porlo nel ciel di chiara fama ornato.*

*Tanto chel vaso lucido et repleto*
*Del vero essempio del signor mio grato*
*I mostri, astretto da immortal decreto.*

VI

*Gia sent'in me 'l calor del sacro nume*
*Potente et l'aura al vel del mio bel legno*
*Spirar con tal favor' ch'io scopro 'l segno*
*Di mia salute et del promesso lume,*

*Ond'hor l'inculto mio thema et costume*
*Seguendo et remiggiando il turbo Regno*
*Andrò solcando in sin ch'al gran disegno*
*Aggiunga l'armi et l'honorate piume,*

*Ne resterò quantunque inquietan' hora*
*L'humil mia cimba l'ond'empie et spumose*
*Di retrarla mai sempre verso 'l porto,*

*Acciò fortuna vegga à piu tard'hora*
*Chi piu tener' credea nel' golfo sorto*
*Quant'intrepido contra se' l'oppose'.*

---

V

Oh graceful, beautiful, beloved, divine Painting,
who today on earth are the favourable breeze that
drives to safe harbour, away from the waves, the
most illustrious memories taken from nature,

By means of your bright light that shines and lasts
where fruitful peace is most plentiful amongst our
friends, whilst, at the same time, your cheerful beauty
most enraptures and ravishes our awakened spirits,[1]

Infuse into your servant that sweet breath that always
raises man from earth and sets him happy in heaven,
adorned by bright fame,

So that I can gratefully show the shining and brim-full
vessel of the true example of my lord, bound to fame
by divine decree.[2]

VI

I already feel in me the ardour of the sacred powerful
*numen*[1] and I feel that its breeze blows in the sail of my
beautiful ship in such a favourable way that I already
see the goal of my good and of my promised light.

Hence, now pursuing my rough topic and style,
I shall row and plough through the dark Kingdom[2]
until to the great design I shall add the Duke's arms
and honoured plumes.[3]

Nor, in spite of the cruel and foamy waves that distress
my humble ship, shall I cease to continue to direct it
towards the harbour,

So that at last sees good fortune he who thought to
have the firmest grip in the gulf within reach on that
which fearlessly set itself against him.[4]

---

1 *Oh graceful … spirits.* Here it is not very clear
what Xanto wants to say. Along the lines
suggested by Cioci (1987, p. 101), the general
idea seems to be that Painting saves from
mortality ('spinge al secur porto fuor
del'onda') what is worthiest of being
remembered in the world ('le più chiare
memorie di natura'). The reference to nature
is probably to be understood in the context
of the aesthetic theory, common in Xanto's
time, of painting as a copy of nature. In the
second quatrain*, then, Xanto contrasts
the generosity of Painting, particularly in
a peaceful milieu like the Duchy of Urbino,
with the way she 'enraptures and ravishes'
her followers' inspired spirits.

2 *bound to fame by divine decree.* Here the words
'to fame' have been added to the translation,
because to translate literally as just 'bound
by divine decree' would lead one to ask:
'bound to what?'. Clearly Xanto has some
positive destiny in mind for his Duke, which
probably can be best captured by the general
idea of the Duke being bound to fame. Note,
however, that, as Cioci (1987, p. 101, note 14)
has pointed out, Xanto's own words to
express this are quite unfortunate, as they
can also suggest the idea of being negatively
bound by fate – in English one could also
translate 'doomed by divine decree'.

* Quatrain = A verse** of four lines.
** Verse = A group of lines that form a unit
in a poem.

1 *Numen.* Deity of unspecified gender. Here it is,
probably, Painting, continuing the address
to 'l'alma pittura' made in the previous
sonnet in similar nautical metaphors.

2 *The dark Kingdom.* Probably the sea, pursuing
the nautical metaphor begun in the first
quatrain. It is, however, unclear what
exactly this is meant to stand for within
the whole metaphor. Perhaps it just refers
in general to the labour of Xanto's work.

3 *Plumes.* This is a literal translation of 'piume',
perhaps taken in this context as a general
emblem of chivalry, as in crests, or even,
more specifically, as referring to the eagle
present in Francesco Maria's coat of arms.
Less literally, one could take 'piume' to
stand for wings, as in Sonnet IV.

4 *So that at last sees good fortune he who … against
him.* The sense of this passage (translated
as literally as possible) is obscure. Taking
Xanto, here, to be talking about the Duke,
the general idea seems to be that Xanto
wishes him 'good fortune' after a trouble-
some period following a time in Francesco
Maria's life when he thought to have a grip
on that which, on the contrary, turned
against him. Perhaps this refers to the
period when Francesco Maria thought to
have secured an alliance with Pope Leo X,
who, however, having at first confirmed
Francesco Maria in the possession of the
Duchy of Urbino, subsequently turned
against him (see Introduction, p. 17).

VII

*Voi selve ombrose d'Umbria et piagge apriche*
*Et voi Hetrurij monti che i lamenti*
*Hor d'Arno odite in dolorosi accenti*
*Delle perdute sue tante fatiche,*

*Pieghivi à noi per l'honorate spiche*
*De vostri campi amor s'udir contenti*
*Siete dei spirti di virtute ardenti*
*L'attioni et gratie delle gratie amiche.*

*Che ben ch'io sia di cio narrarvi indegno*
*Io chiamero 'l mio Duca albergo et sede*
*Di tutto quell che fa l'huom' del ciel degno*

*Quindi vedrete et lealtate et fede*
*Tal che direte sol mancargli il regno*
*Per por di pari al Macedone il piede.*

Oh you, shadowy woods of Umbria and shores open
to the sun, and you, Etruscan mountains,[1] that now
hear the Arno lament in sorrowful cries its many
and lost labours,[2]

Let love bend you towards us, for the honoured ears
of corn of your fields, if you are happy to hear the
deeds and graces, friends of the Graces, of those
spirits burning with ardour.

For, although I am not worthy of telling you this,
I shall call my Duke abode and seat of all that makes
man worthy of heaven.

Hence you will see such loyalty and faith that you
will say that he lacks only a kingdom to set his foot
in the same way as the Macedonian.[3]

1 *Oh you…mountains.* For geographical references to the Duchy of Urbino, see notes to Sonnet I.
2 *that…labours.* A couple of interpretations are possible concerning the episode in the history of Florence referred to in this verse. One possibility is that it refers to the wars between Francesco Maria and the Medici, who were trying to impose Lorenzo De Medici as Duke of Urbino. These wars (1516–22) were very costly for Florence and, in the end, from the Medici's point of view, fruitless, since Francesco Maria succeeded in securing possession of the Duchy in 1522 (hence the 'many and lost labours' of Florence). Alternatively, one could take these lines to refer to the surrender, in August 1530, of the short-lived (1527–30) republic of Florence to the Imperial army of Charles V, after a ten month siege.
3 *…the Macedonian.* Alexander the Great.

VIII

*La mesta donna il cui bel corpo irriga*
*Con le dolci acque sue l'Arno pregiato*
*Mostrava per essempio all'human stato*
*Del petto suo la sanguinosa riga,*

*Guidava 'l tempo che l'età gástiga*
*L'Augusto d'Austria, da fortuna amato,*
*Nel regno infido del crudel' pirato*
*Per dargli in armi lagrimosa briga,*

*Quando l'immenso et prosperevol' raggio*
*Ch'hoggi riscalda d'Umbri il sito ameno*
*Guardandol' sempre d'ogni strano oltraggio,*

*Quel fonte mi scoperse d'amor pieno*
*Ch'alfin' dovea del mio longo viaggio*
*La bocca rinfrescarmi e 'l fronte e 'l seno.*

The sad woman, whose beautiful body is washed
by the sweet waters of the precious Arno, showed
as an *exemplum*[1] to all men the bloody wound on
her breast,[2]

The Augustus of Austria,[3] cherished by fortune,
led the time that punishes our age, in the faithless
kingdom of the cruel pirate,[4] in order to give him
in arms tearful trouble,

When the vast and generous ray, which today
warms the delightful country of the Umbri,[5] always
protecting it from any foreign harm,

Uncovered that source full of love that eventually,
after my long journey, was to refresh my mouth,
my brow and my bosom.[6]

1 *exemplum.* Here the Italian 'essempio' has been translated with the Latin 'exemplum' because this is probably the best way to convey the idea, not quite captured by the English word 'example', of an event or fact by reference to which men can draw a lesson for the future from what happened in the past.
2 *The sad woman…* This is Florence, 'wounded' by the Imperial troops of Charles V, who in August 1530, after a ten month siege, took hold of the city and reinstated the Medici to power.
3 *The Augustus of Austria.* Charles V of Austria, crowned Holy Roman Emperor in 1530.
4 *cruel pirate.* As Triolo (1996, p. 106) has suggested, this may refer to the pirates' stronghold of Cherchell, to the west of Algiers, conquered by Charles V in 1530. The siege of La Goletta, near Tunis, in 1535, was suggested by Mallet (1984, p. 399), but he now believes that the date is too late to be compatible with the siege of Florence referred to in the first quatrain.
5 *The delightful country of the Umbri.* The Duchy of Urbino.
6 *Uncovered…bosom.* Here Xanto apparently refers to some important favour granted to him by the Duke. We do not know, however, exactly what this favour was. Similarly, we do not know whether the 'long journey' Xanto is talking about is meant to refer to an actual journey or to a metaphorical one. (For discussion of this, see Introduction, p. 26).

*Sopita musa mia destati homai*
*Et manda al ciel' con chiara fama il nome*
*Del mio signor, che ben' sai quanto et come*
*Le virtut'ama et chiar certezza n'hai,*

*Gia gran temp'e ch'i sfavillanti rai*
*Che fan diadema a sue fulgenti chiome*
*Et l'antico et preclaro alto cognome*
*Per fama ti son noti ovunque vai,*

*O fortunato il giorno che far lieve*
*Sentami 'l grave giogo et che l'ardente*
*Sol, mi riscald'il cor benigno et grato*

*Et con ingegno e arte piu potente*
*Lodando il Duca mio quanto si deve*
*Perpetuo 'l lassi et di su[o = a] gloria ornato.*

My slumbering Muse, now awake and send to heaven
with bright fame my lord's name, for you know well
how much he loves all virtues and you are thoroughly
certain of this.

For a long time you have known by renown,
wherever you go, of the shining rays which crown
his bright locks, and his ancient and illustrious
noble name.

Oh happy day when I might feel the heavy yoke become
light and that the burning sun may warm my good and
grateful heart,

And when with more powerful ability and art, praising
my Duke as much as is his due, I shall leave him
immortalized, adorned with his glory.



*Fra gli Emilij, e'l Truento, e 'l bel paese*
*Che l'Augusta città circonda et mura*
*Volse mostrar à noi l'alma natura*
*Quanto dell'opre sue fusse cortese,*

*Et per segno di cio chiaro et palese*
*Produsse 'l mio Signor' et diegli in cura*
*D'immensa cortesia quell'armatura*
*Con che n'ha[i = /] retti in mille chiar'imprese,*

*Per vera lode adunque in darno mira*
*Chi del mio Duca il bell'oprar non vede*
*Pien di dolcezza in usitata et mira,*

*Ne sà come virtute à suoi provede*
*Chi non sà con che part'egli à se' tira*
*Ogn'anima gentil' ricca di fede.*

In the land encircled by the Emilii and the Tronto and
by the beautiful country that surrounds the walls of
the August City,[1] divine Nature wanted to show us
how generous she was with her works,

And as a clear and apparent mark of that, she created
my lord and entrusted him with that armour of
great chivalry with which he led many in a thousand
famous deeds.

So in vain looks for true praise he who does not see
and admire the beautiful deeds of my Duke, full of
uncommon sweetness,

Nor does he know how virtue provides for her friends
he who does not know in which way he draws to him
every noble and faithful soul.[2]

1  *In the land … August City.* Once again, the
   Duchy of Urbino, marked by its borders: to
   the North the region more or less corresponding to today's Emilia Romagna, called after
   the Emilii, i.e. its inhabitants in ancient
   times; to the South the river Tronto; to the
   West the Papal States, 'surrounding and
   walling' Rome.
2  *every noble and faithful soul.* Here 'ricca di fede'
   has been translated with 'faithful'. Literally,
   however, it means 'rich of faith'. So Xanto's
   intended meaning is ambiguous. He could
   also mean that the Duke knows how to draw
   to him people who are 'rich in faith' in the
   sense of hopeful of rewards.

## XI

*Mentre del mio Signor negli alti essempi*
*Mi specchio, forza tal sento donarmi*
*Che' innerbo il debol' stil' tanto ch'armarmi*
*Oso al contrasto de' moderni scempi,*

*Ne temo di fortuna in furor' empi*
*Et men' di mort' horrenda gli urti et l'armi*
*Si che pieno di speme et d'amor trarmi*
*Sicuro ardisco à gli honorati tempi,*

*La 've col pletro eburno et vivo inchiostro*
*De bei cristalli al mormorio suave*
*Tra dolci fiati di piacevol' venti,*

*L'oprar senza alcun' par' temprato et grave*
*Del fedel' Duca mio ver Borea et Ostro*
*Cantando spargero con dolci accenti.*

While I look at myself in the mirror of my lord's great exemplary deeds, I feel that such strength is given to me that I make more robust my weak style, so much that I dare arm myself for the battle against the destructions of our times,[1]

Nor do I fear the attacks of Fortune in her fury, nor the arms and blows of horrible death, so that full of hope and love I dare draw myself to safety in the honoured temples,

There where with a plectrum* of ivory and with vivid ink, accompanied by the gentle murmur of beautiful crystal-clear waters, amongst the sweet breaths of gentle breezes,

I shall spread to Boreas and Auster,[2] singing in sweet accents, my faithful Duke's deeds, unrivalled in their good measure and thoughtfulness.

1 *I dare arm myself for the battle against the destructions of our times.* Clearly to be taken in a metaphorical sense. However, the precise meaning is unclear.
2 *to Boreas and Auster.* To the North (wind) and to the South (wind).

* Plectrum = A thin flat piece of tortoiseshell or another hard material used to pluck a stringed instrument.



## XII

*Ben provide 'l signor che l' tutto muove*
*Alla nostra quiete et nostra pace*
*Quando fra noi con amorosa face*
*Leonora aggiunse al bel' arbor di Giove,*

*Acció con gratie inusitate et nuove*
*Prole cotal' n'uscisse et sí vivace*
*Ch'ornasse 'l mondo et fesse altrui capace*
*Della virtú che l'alme sveglia et fove,*

*O Francesco Maria, O vivo raggio*
*Se'l ciel' ti elesse à tale esser consorte*
*Fu per esser' previsto al tuo buon frutto*

*Dico il tuo Guid'Ubaldo giusto et forte*
*Peró che tra le Muse et Marte instrutto*
*Detto sara nel mondo invitto et saggio.*

Our Lord, Prime Mover,[1] saw well to our peace and quiet when, amongst us, with loving light, he added Leonora to the beautiful tree of Jove,[2]

So as to engender a lively offspring, possessing uncommon and new charms, and such that he adorned the world and made others capable of that virtue that awakens and supports all souls.

Oh Francesco Maria, oh bright ray, if heaven chose you to be the husband of such a woman, it was to provide for your good fruit;

I mean, your Guid'Ubaldo,[3] just and strong, for, raised amongst the Muses and Mars, he will be called on earth invincible and wise.

1 *Prime Mover.* One of the attributes of God in Scholastic doctrines.
2 *he added Leonora to the beautiful tree of Jove.* Eleonora Gonzaga (1493–1550), daughter of Francesco II Gonzaga, fourth Marquess of Mantua, and Isabella d'Este, married Francesco Maria Della Rovere in 1509. The oak tree was sacred to Jove and features in the Della Rovere family's coat of arms ('rovere' means 'oak').
3 *your Guid'Ubaldo.* Guidobaldo (1514–1574) was the first son of Francesco Maria to survive infancy. He became Duke of Urbino as 'Guidobaldo II', succeeding his father in 1539.

*Non oro, o gemme over purpura et ostro*
*Ne riche spoglie et forbit'armi et scanni*
*De principi superbi et de' Tiranni*
*Ch'infettan' con lor opre il secul' nostro,*

*Giamai, Signor, potranno al nome vostro*
*Nom' alcuno agguagliar', però ch'i panni*
*D'avar' moderni immersi in stolti affanni*
*Assai men duran' chel ben speso inchiostro,*

*Ma ben quella virtù c'hor mal si stima*
*Fra l'imperita plebe inutil' tanto*
*Attinger sol potrà vostr'alta cima,*

*Vostr'alta cima alla qual dassi 'l vanto*
*Di vera integritade et c'hora in rima*
*Con giusta occasion' divolgo et canto.*



Not gold, nor gems, nor purple cloth, nor rich
spoils, nor the magnificent arms and thrones of the
proud princes and tyrants who infect our age with
their deeds,

Never, my lord, will they be able to make your name
equal to any other, for the miser's modern clothes
dipped in foolish labours last considerably less than
well spent ink.

But only that virtue, now despised as useless
by the ignorant mob, will be able to attain your
high peak,

Your high peak, to which the boast of genuine
integrity is due and which now, on just pretext,
I spread abroad and sing in rhyme.

XIV

*Con molta pace del sacrato alloro*
*Stavami un giorno assai vicino all'acque*
*In che Phetonte ruinando giacque*
*Con longa infamia d'ogni suo decoro,*

*Et dell'eccelsa et fertil' Rover d'oro*
*L'alt'et chiare virtú con ch'ella nacque*
*I volea gia cantare, quand'in se tacque*
*La lingua, ond'io mancai del bel lavoro,*

*Non senza gran cagion perdei la voce*
*Nel cominciar' dell'honorato canto*
*La' ve disio d'honor sol' m'havea spinto,*

*Peró che in grembo alla Thebana manto*
*Salvarsi vidi da un' leon' feroce*
*Di dolente cipresso il mio sol cinto.*



One day I was standing, in the great peace of the
sacred laurel, very close to the waters in which
Phaeton fell, crashing down with lasting disgrace
from all his pride,[1]

And I already wanted to sing the high and renowned
virtues with which the sublime and fruitful golden
Oak[2] was born, when my tongue was silenced, so that
I missed the beautiful work.

In the beginning of my honourable singing, when
only a desire for glory had pushed me, I did not lose
my voice without a serious reason,

For in the bosom of the Theban Manto[3] I saw escape
from a ferocious lion my sun,[4] crowned by sorrowful
cypress.

1 *One day…pride.* Phaeton, the son of Helios
the sun-god, convinced his father to let
him drive the chariot of the sun across
the sky, but, having lost control of it and
coming too close to the earth, was killed by
Zeus's thunderbolt in order to prevent the
destruction of the earth. His body fell into
the river Eridanus, today's Po. So here
Xanto is telling us that he first conceived
the project of writing about the Duke (see
second quatrain) when he was close to the
Po. His reference to the 'sacred laurel' seems
to suggest that at that time he was already
writing poetry.
2 *the sublime and fruitful golden Oak.* Once again,
the Oak stands for Francesco Maria Della
Rovere, as there is a golden oak in the
Della Rovere family's coat of arms.
3 *the Theban Manto.* Manto, daughter of the
diviner Tiresias, fled from Thebes to escape
the rule of Creon and founded Mantua in
the middle of the swampy lagoons of the
river Mincio.
4 *I saw escape from a ferocious lion my sun.* In 1516
Francesco Maria had to take refuge in
Mantua, at the court of his father-in-law
Francesco II Gonzaga, as Pope Leo X (the
'ferocious lion') had turned against him,
revoking his previous appointment to him
of the Duchy of Urbino and even going so
far as to excommunicate him. Xanto thus
dates to this year his first idea of writing
about Francesco Maria.

XV

*Signor che sempre come raggio in vetro*
*Penetri sí con l'intelletto chiaro*
*Ai naturai secreti che ben raro*
*Fia quel ch al corso tuo seguira dietro,*

*Lascia il cordoglio, et l doloroso metro*
*Al volgo feminil' ch'altro riparo*
*Non ha dal ciel che'l suo dolor' amaro*
*Acqueti et sfoghi in quest'antr'aspro et tetro,*

*Peró che'l saggio mai d[i = e]e contristarsi*
*Per alcun' morso di fortuna audace*
*Ne superbir s'al ciel ben ved' alzarsi,*

*Quest'e 'l dritto camin' chiaro et verace*
*Ove celebri al mondo vediam farsi*
*Dunque, tu che cio sai, donati pace.*

My lord, you who like a ray through glass with your
sharp intellect always get through to the secrets of
nature in such a way that it will be very rare indeed
to find someone who can keep up with you,

Leave grief and sorrowful verse to the female throng
which receives nothing else from heaven other than
this as a remedy to calm and relieve its bitter grief
in this harsh and dark den,

For the wise man should never grieve for any bold blow
of fortune, nor should he become haughty if he sees
himself risen to heaven.

This is the right path, clear and true, where we see
men become famous in the world. So, you who know
that, set your mind to rest.

XVI

*O quanto gaudio fu per gli alti monti*
*Tra fauni, all'hor che 'l mio gran Duca in sella*
*Duo mes'innanzi alla stagion' novella*
*Passó d'Emilia le fortezze e i ponti,*

*O che letitia per le rive et fonti*
*Mostró ciascuna nimpha vaga e bella*
*Quand'il mio Duca in questa part'e 'nquella*
*Apparse d'Umbria tra guerrier suoi pronti,*

*O ch'allegrezza et che triompho dico*
*Fece Marte nel ciel' veduto in guerra*
*Il vero suo figliuol' col ferr'in mano*

*Sgombrar 'l'imperial' cangiar' la terra*
*Et l'acque Arimnesi in sangue humano*
*Et 'l Metauro passar' contra 'l nemico.*

Oh what a joy the fauns in the high mountains
had, when, two months before the new season, my
great Duke passed in the saddle the fortresses and
bridges of Emilia.[1]

Oh what a delight was shown by every graceful
and beautiful nymph among the brooks and springs,
when my Duke appeared here and there[2] from
Umbria amongst his eager soldiers.

Oh what mirth and triumph, I say, was celebrated
by Mars in heaven, when he saw his true son at war,
armed with his sword,

Clear the Imperiale,[3] turn the land and waters of
Rimini into human blood[4] and cross the Metauro to
meet the enemy.[5]

1 *two months before the new season… Emilia.*
In January 1517 (two months before the
beginning of spring), Francesco Maria set
out on an expedition to regain his duchy.
This, together with the various episodes
of the campaign mentioned below, is the
subject of the present sonnet.
2 *here and there.* Francesco Maria waged his
war in many parts of the duchy.
3 *Clear the Imperiale.* This refers to the taking
of the Villa Imperiale, near Pesaro, on
6 May 1517.
4 *turn the land and waters of Rimini into human blood.*
This refers to the battle of the borgo San
Giuliano, on the outskirts of Rimini.
5 *cross the Metauro to meet the enemy.* Francesco
Maria pursued his successful campaign
south of the river Metauro.

## XVII

*Deh perche sí com'hor non vidío quanto*
*Splendea del mio signor la chiara fronte*
*All'hor che tolto fui dal sacro fonte*
*Prima cagion' d'andar' nel regno santo,*

*Lasso che 'ndarno non harei tra'l'pianto*
*D'amor' cantate l'aspr'ingiurie et l'onte*
*Sperando et ardendo, hor sol da me fian conte*
*L'alte sue cortesie, l'honor suo tanto,*

*Ma converrami essendo 'l camin' lungo*
*Et l'hora tarda, il corso affretar' molto*
*S'io vorró dirne à pien nell'età mia,*

*Ben che 'l vago disio ch'amando aggiungo*
*Al bel suggietto con allegro volto*
*Mi trarrà forse à quell' ch'accio m'invia.*

Ah, why did not I see then, as I do now, how much my
lord's bright brow shone, when I was taken away from
the sacred river, which was the first cause of my going
to the blessed kingdom?[1]

Alas, I would not have vainly sung in amorous lament
the bitter offences and injuries, hoping and being
fired with passion.[2] Now only shall I recount his high
virtues, his great honour.

But, since my road is long and it is late, I really must
hasten my course if, at my age,[3] I want to recount
that in full,

Although the sweet yearning that, in my love, I add to
the beautiful subject with cheerful face will, perhaps,
draw me to what leads me to that.[4]

1 *when I was taken away … to the blessed kingdom.*
This interpretation follows Cioci (1987, p. 135)
in understanding the 'sacro fonte' to refer to
the Po and the 'regno santo' to refer to the
Duchy of Urbino – hence 'fonte' has been
translated by 'river' and 'santo' by 'blessed'
and not 'sacred'. So, according to this interpretation, Xanto is regretting the fact that
he was not yet fully aware of the virtues of
the Duke at the time when, for some reason
not quite in accord with his will (he was
'tolto', 'taken away'), he left his native
country in the Po region to set out on the
journey that eventually led him to the Duchy
of Urbino.
2 *Alas … passion.* As pointed out by Cioci (1987,
p. 135), Xanto, like many of his contemporaries, was trying to follow Petrarch not only
in style but also, whenever at all possible, in
subject matter. Thus here he tells us of some
unrequited love that was, apparently, the
subject of previous poetical endeavours of his.
3 *at my age.* The chronology of Xanto's life is
the subject of much debate, partly based,
indeed, on his sonnets (see Introduction).
However, scholars agree that Xanto was at
least in his early thirties when he started
writing the sonnets and at the time people
in their thirties were not considered young
– the average life expectancy was forty.
4 *what leads me to that.* Here Xanto probably
means the Duke's virtues. So the general
gist of this verse is that Xanto hopes that
his yearning to recount the Duke's virtues
will help him to achieve his poetical project,
which was, in fact, inspired by the existence
of these virtues.



## XVIII

*Vidi levarsí il mio lucente sole*
*Per impartir' tra noi suo chiari lumi*
*Et via troncar gli venenosi dumi*
*Dal suo patrio terren che tant'ei cole,*

*Vidi al sonar' di sue sante parole*
*Atte à fermar' gli piu correnti fiumi,*
*Gli ornati et alti suoi regai costumi*
*Di rose tutti sparsi et di viole,*

*Lo vidi poi con piu felice corso*
*Saltar' il Rubicon l'Isauro e 'l Metro*
*Et del fero Griphon calcar' il dorso,*

*Et' l manto puoc'avanti oscuro et tetro*
*Per dolente cypresso in cotal' corso*
*Vidi rivolto in glorioso metro.*

I saw my shining sun rise to bestow on us
his bright light and to cut off the poisonous thorns
from his native land he so much reveres,[1]

I saw at the sound of his blessed words, capable to
stay the most impetuous rivers, his adorned and
noble royal costumes all covered with roses
and violets,

I then saw him, in a happier course, leap the Rubicon,
the Isauro and the Metauro[2] and bow the proud
Gryphon's back,[3]

And I saw his mantle, shortly before dark and dismal
in its sorrowful cypress, convert into glorious poetry
by his feat.

1 *I saw … reveres.* In this verse and in the rest
of the sonnet, Xanto celebrates the final,
definitive reconquest of the Duchy of
Urbino by Francesco Maria, achieved
within a few weeks of the death of Leo X
on 2 December 1521.
2 *I then saw him … leap the Rubicon, the Isauro and the
Metauro.* These three rivers mark Francesco
Maria's reconquest from North to South, as
the Rubicon formed the boundary between
Italy and the province of Cisalpine Gaul
(today's Northern Italy) in Roman times,
the Isauro (today's Foglia) is the river of
Pesaro and the Metauro flows through Castel
Durante (the modern Urbania) and close to
Urbino, before reaching the sea just south
of Pesaro, a little south-east of Fano.
3 *and bow the proud Gryphon's back.* This refers to
the taking of Perugia, whose charge is the
Gryphon, on 6 January 1522.

X I X

*Se'l ciel' tanto favore alla mia musa*
*Prestasse ch'io potessi quant'io bramo*
*Fornir la tela che tutt'hora io tramo*
*Con quell'amor' che rar'hoggi dí s'usa,*

*Forse Sequana Ilerda et Arethusa*
*Mirando nel signor' ch'honoro et amo*
*Vinte da invidia in atto mesto et gramo*
*Ira et doglia n'harian senz'altra scusa,*

*Ma quella instabil dea che mal' comparte*
*La fertil' terra con diversi assalti*
*Retrarmi tenta ogn'hor da tal'impresa*

*Non potrá gia l'iniqua far' che gli alti*
*Effetti del mio Duca in mille carte*
*Non lassi al mondo con memoria illesa.*

X X

*D'Italia l'alte et honorate sponde*
*Smembrate et rotte in mille pezzi et parte*
*Sotto'l furor del bellicoso Marte*
*Da Galli et Sparti et Cimbri in terra e in onde,*

*Tal che le guancie pria chiare et gioconde*
*Di cinereo color fatto sanz'arte*
*Eran venute et le proprie armi sparte*
*Giacean' tra spine ree fetid'e immonde,*

*Quando da Marco et dalla santa chiesa*
*Il saggio Duca mio fu eletto solo*
*A sovenir' Italia al maggior uopo,*

*Il qual tanti trophei di tal' impresa*
*Addusse, ch'hora Urbin' con lieto volo*
*Al ciel' s'inalza chiar' piu che piropo.*

X I X

If heaven bestowed on my Muse so much favour
that I could endow as much as I wish the cloth
that I am still weaving with that love that today is
rarely found,

Perhaps Sequana, Ilerda and Arethusa,[1] marvelling
at the lord I honour and love, would be overcome by
envy and, with a sad and wretched gesture, would
feel wrath and sorrow with no other excuse.

But that fickle goddess, who distributes unevenly
the fruitful lot, with various assaults, continues to
try and turn me away from this undertaking.

But the evil goddess will not be able to prevent me from
leaving to the world, for unsullied remembrance, the
great deeds of my Duke, written in a thousand pages.

X X

The noble and honoured lands of Italy were
dismembered, torn and ripped in a thousand pieces,
under the fury of the bellicose Mars, by the Gauls,
the Sparti and the Cimbri, on land and water,[1]

So that her cheeks previously bright and cheerful
had become of an ashen colour made without any art
and her arms lay scattered amongst cruel, foul and
loathsome thorns,

When my wise Duke was the one appointed by
Mark and by the Holy Church to aid Italy in her
major need,[2]

And from this feat he gathered so many trophies, that
now Urbino, brighter than pyrope,[3] rises to heaven in
a happy flight.[4]

1 *Sequana, Ilerda and Arethusa.* That is: the Seine; the Spanish city that today is called Lerida and that is remembered for the battle between Caesar and Pompey's generals Afranius and Petreius in 49 B.C.; the renowned spring in Syracuse, named after the nymph Arethusa. The only thing that these have in common and that seems to be the reason for Xanto's choice is their being famous and thus good candidates for feeling 'wrath and sorrow' at being overshadowed by the Duke's fame.

1 *The noble … water.* Given the reference in the lines below to Francesco Maria's role as commander in chief of the troops of the participants of the Holy League of Cognac, Xanto should probably be understood here to refer to the period leading up to the Sack of Rome in May 1527. We could then take his allusion to the Sparti to refer to the civil strife (e.g. amongst different parties in Florence) which was ripping Italy apart at this period. In fact, in classical mythology, the Sparti are the warriors who rose from the dragon's teeth sown by Cadmus and fought each other. The Gauls and the Cimbri (standing for Teutonic/Northern populations in general) could be understood to refer to the French and Hapsburg armies, which had made Italy their battlefield in the years preceding the Sack of Rome. Alternatively, taking Xanto to write of the period immediately preceding the Sack of Rome, the Gauls could stand for the army of Charles V, which was led by a Frenchman, Charles de Bourbon. The Cimbri would stand for the Landsknechts, the German mercenary foot-soldiers employed in Charles V's army.

2 *When … need.* Francesco Maria had been, since June 1523, Captain General of Venice. As leader of the largest contingent, he was thus commander in chief of the troops of the participants of the Holy League of Cognac who were opposing the advance of Charles V's army down the Italian peninsula in 1527. These included the papal troops, although the latter were under the direct command of Francesco Guicciardini.

3 *pyrope.* A precious stone, flaming red.
4 *And … flight.* Historically, Francesco Maria's role was far from being so glorious. He is, in fact, remembered for having failed to prevent Charles V's army from sacking Rome.

XXI

*Preso m'ha signor mio tua fama et fede*
*Tra si cortesi effetti che s'io tento*
*Da lor retrarmi un' minim' atto sento*
*Sottrarmi à tal' passion' c'ogn'altra eccede,*

*Che potrian' quelli ogni gran scettro et sede*
*Ornar' d'un' tant'honor' ch'[altro avento ogn'*
*= ogn'altro avento]*
*Quantunque fusse egual' fora contento*
*Esser chiamato del tuo nome herede,*

*Nulla poss'io levar' del peso caro*
*Perche natura, il ciel, gratia et virtute*
*Nascendo à servitu tal mi legaro,*

*Nella qual forse anchor' cotal' salute*
*Trovar potrei ch'al mio stil hoggi amaro*
*Sarian' dolcezze et gratie concedute.*

XXI

Your fame and faith have taken me, my lord, amongst
such gracious effects that if I try to withdraw only a
little, I feel that I am taking myself away from such
a passion, which exceeds all others.

For these effects could adorn every sceptre and
seat with such honour that any other event, even
if equal to them, would be happy to be called heir
to your name.

I cannot relieve myself of the dear burden, for nature,
heaven, grace and virtue bound me by birth to such
servitude,

In which, perhaps, I could still find such good that
sweetness and grace would be granted to my style,
now harsh.

XXII

*Eccelso Duca che guarnito d'armi*
*Sovra 'l spumante tuo corsier disioso*
*D'honor tenti arrivar tutt'animoso*
*La' ve teco col cor' esser' gia parmi,*

*Vattene invitto et fra gli santi marmi*
*O di Goffredo imitator famoso,*
*Col tuo severo oprar' chiaro et pietoso*
*Mostrarti sí che ne risuoni in carmi,*

*Ivi e d'entrare à fama occasion' vera*
*Che ben ti condurrà du' le virtudi*
*S'approvano con fe da man' à sera.*

*Fa, Signor mio che i Barbareschi scudi*
*Sentin' l'ardir' che 'n l'età tua primera*
*Notasti, inteso agli honorati studi.*

XXII

Excellent Duke, who, equipped with arms, on your
foaming steed, longing for glory, try to reach, all full
of courage, the place where, in my heart, I already feel
myself with you;[1]

Go, invincible and amongst the sacred marbles, oh
famous follower of Godfrey,[2] to make such a fine
showing, by your austere, renowned and pious deeds,
that it may resound in song.

Here is a true opportunity to reach fame that will lead
you where virtues are commended with faith from
morn to eve.

Oh my lord, make the Barbaresque shields[3] feel the
courage that you noted in your prime, when you were
bent upon honoured studies.[4]

1 *Excellent…you.* As is made clear by the
references to Godfrey of Bouillon and to the
'Barbaresque shields' in the verses below,
Xanto is here talking about some planned
military expedition against the infidel in
which the Duke was involved. Vitaletti
(1918, p. 13) suggests that this might be
the expedition planned in January 1538 by
Venice, the Pope and Charles V against the
Turks, in response to the attacks carried out
in the Aegean in 1537. (Vitaletti incorrectly
writes that this anti-Turk coalition was
formed in January 1537. For the correct dating
to January 1538, see Setton [1976, vol. 3,
p. 429].) Francesco Maria was chosen to be
the leader of this expedition, but before he
could set out he was struck by the illness
that led to his death on 20 October 1538.
However, the evidence we have is not
conclusive for Vitaletti's interpretation. As
Cioci (1987, pp. 56–59) points out, the 1538
plan against the Turks was not the only one
which was made during Francesco Maria's
lifetime and in which he was meant to take
an important part. In this sonnet Xanto
might refer to plans made in the early 1530s
rather than in the late 1530s.
2 *oh famous follower of Godfrey.* Godfrey of Bouillon
(*c.* 1060–1100), Duke of Lower Lorraine and
one of the leaders of the first Crusade.
3 *the Barbaresque shields.* This could mean
'shields of Barbary' and stand, in particular,
for the fleet of Khaireddin Barbarossa,
Beyler Bey of Algiers, who, in the 1530s,
carried out numerous attacks in the
Mediterranean. Alternatively, it could mean
'barbarian shields' and stand for the infidel
in general.
4 *the courage…studies.* Here Xanto seems to
urge the Duke to follow the heroic models
studied as part of his historical and literary
education.

### XXIII

*Magnanimo Signor', qualunque parte*
*Del mondo gia conobbe il Latin' regno*
*Non puo di largità toccare il segno*
*Se pria non ha di te contezza in parte,*

*Ne quel' si speri mai che sol si parte*
*Da luoco men d'unaltro ricco et degno*
*Di ritrovar pietà senza gran sdegno*
*Se pria 'l sentier ver te ben non comparte,*

*Che certo essempio sei hoggi dí in terra*
*Di vera cortesia, peró ch'osservi*
*D'Agrigentino Sylla il viver' chiaro.*

*Questo non solo il sa tua patria et terra*
*Ne tuoi congiunti et ne fidati servi*
*Ma quanto cigne il mar tra l alpi, e 'l faro.*

### XXIV

*Havendomi con fraude il dolce sonno*
*Vinto d'un' lauro alla soave ombrella*
*Nella stagion' che l'amorosa stella*
*Desta al danno comun' l'altero donno,*

*Signor', chiaro vid'io tra quei che ponno*
*Per virtute apparir' potenti in sella*
*Vostro aspetto regal' nel grembo à quella*
*Aligera immortal nemica al sonno,*

*Dalla qual' vidi all'honorata testa*
*Porvi di Lauro una viril' ghirlanda*
*Di gemme tutta oriental contesta,*

*Con aurei lacci cinta d'ogni banda*
*Ond'io cantai o lieta notte o festa*
*Dell'humilmente mia grata vivanda.*

### XXIII

Oh magnanimous lord, no part of the world
that once knew the rule of Rome can attain
true generosity unless it knows you at least
in part.

Nor can he who, alone, leaves a place less rich
and worthy than another[1] ever hope to find pity
without great scorn, unless he directs his way
towards you,

For today on earth you are a sure example of true
courtesy, as you follow the illustrious conduct of the
Agrigentine Sulla.[2]

This is known not only by your relatives and by your
faithful servants in your country and land, but also by
all that the sea girdles from the Alps to Cape Faro.[3]

### XXIV

Sweet sleep having tricked me while I was lying
in the fresh shade of a laurel at the time that
the star of love[1] awakes the proud master[2] to the
common harm,

I clearly saw, my lord, amongst those who can,
by their valour, look mighty in the saddle, your regal
aspect on the lap of that immortal winged one,
enemy to sleep.[3]

By whom I saw your honoured head crowned
by a manly garland of laurel, all entwined with
oriental gems

And tied on all sides by golden laces;
Hence I sang: 'Oh merry night, oh feast of my food
humbly and gratefully received!'

1. *he who, alone, leaves a place less rich and worthy than another.* That is, leaves a poor place to seek fortune in wealthier lands – probably an autobiographical reference.
2. *as you follow the illustrious conduct of the Agrigentine Sulla.* Lucius Cornelius Sulla (138–78 B.C.), renowned, amongst other things, for his liberality. It is not clear, however, why Xanto calls him 'Agrigentine'. Perhaps it is because, as suggested by Cioci (1987, p. 149), part of the civil wars between the followers of Sulla and those of Marius were fought in Sicily.
3. *all that the sea girdles from the Alps to Cape Faro.* That is, by everybody in Italy – Cape Faro in Sicily stands for the southernmost place in Italy.

1. *the star of love.* Venus, the morning star.
2. *the proud master.* Cupid.
3. *that immortal winged one, enemy to sleep.* Fame.

XXV

*Pace sempre dal ciel' sovra noi tanto*
*Discenda Signor mio che l'aurea etade*
*Ritorni al mondo e 'n quella pria bontade*
*Ch'anchora osserva de migliori il vanto,*

*Ne piu canggiar si vegga insegna o manto*
*Alla corrotta Italia, in sua beltade*
*Onde mendici nell'altrui contrade*
*Avien' ch'andiamo ad isfogar il pianto,*

*Acció che 'l favor tuo sí ricco et grande*
*Possi con maggior tuo gaudio e riposo*
*Usar' ver noi, nel dar preghi et ghirlande,*

*Peró che talhor l'aspro et bellicoso*
*Marte nel mondo cotal nebbia spande*
*Che 'l sol sovente par esserci ascoso.*

XXV

May peace,[1] oh my lord, always descend from heaven
on us, so that the golden age may come back in the
world and that we may revert to that first goodness
that still follows the virtue of the best,

And let us no longer see the corrupt Italy change
her flag and her coat, in her beauty, causing
us to go begging in foreign lands to give vent to
our tears,[2]

So that you may be able to bestow on us, who offer you
prayers and garlands, your favour, so rich and great,
for your greater happiness and peace,

For sometimes the harsh and bellicose Mars spreads
such a mist in the world that it looks as though the
sun is hidden from us.

1 *May peace… * If we wish to establish a correspondence between this sonnet and a specific time in the life of Francesco Maria, the best candidate is certainly the year 1530. In fact, one of the outcomes of the Congress of Bologna in March 1530 was the official investment of Francesco Maria with his duchy and titles, ending the year-long confrontation with the Pope and opening a period of security and peace for Francesco Maria, in so far as the territory of the Duchy of Urbino was concerned.

2 *And let us no longer see…tears.* Probably a reference to Francesco Maria's exile in Mantua (compare with Sonnet XIV).

XXVI

*A qualunque virtù suprema et alma*
*Fu mai la cima et l'honorata altezza*
*Sperai cantando o folle mia bassezza*
*Del mio Duca agguagliar' l'horrevol' palma,*

*Hor solo à rimembrar la voce e l'alma*
*Et la mano et lo stil colmo d'asprezza*
*Paventa et trema, perche tal bellezza*
*Tropp' all' ingegn' human' è greve salma,*

*Che debb'io dunque far' per spiegar' l'ale*
*In sí gran dubbio vers' u' trarmi ardisco?*
*O immenso mio disire o vil timore,*

*O crudo cielo al bel' lavor' ch'ordisco*
*Perche non doni à me tuo gran favore?*
*Poi chel mio Duca festi et tanto et tale.*

XXVI

To whatever supreme and immortal virtue,
whatever its summit or honoured height, I hoped,
oh miserable fool that I am, to equal the honoured
palm of my Duke,[1]

Now, at the mere memory of it, my voice, my soul,
my hand and my style, which is so rough, fear and
tremble, because such beauty is a burden too heavy
for the human intellect.

What shall I do, then, to spread my wings, in such
a great doubt, towards where I dare draw myself?
Oh immense desire! Oh coward fear!

Oh cruel heavens, why do not you bestow your great
favour on the beautiful work that I am preparing and on
me, since you celebrate so much my Duke for his worth?

1 *the honoured palm of my Duke.* Palm leaves were symbols of victory and glory. Here, however, there is also a more specific reference to Francesco Maria's device, conceived by Paolo Giovio in 1522 at the Duke's request. The device consists of a palm tree weighed down by a block of marble, together with the motto 'Inclinata Resurgit' ('Having been bent low, it springs upright again'). This was to signify Francesco Maria's resilience against adverse fortune, with particular reference to the years of struggle against Pope Leo X and to Francesco Maria eventually regaining his duchy in 1522. (For reproductions of Francesco Maria's device, see Cioci [1987, p. 159].)

*Ben puoi crudel' Fortuna in vari modi*
*Urtarmi et tormi et impedirmi ogn'ora*
*La forza e 'l bel sentier' che d'hora in hora*
*Mi scuopre 'l ciel' con gran promesse et lodi,*

*Ben puoi proterva con tu[o = e] tante frodi*
*Far' che 'l corpo mortal ogni dí mora*
*Et 'n tant'aspro penar con rea dimora*
*M'astringan' l'alma mill'infesti nodi,*

*Ma non però potrai gia farmi tale*
*Ch'io resti di cantar l aurata pianta*
*Se pria non lassi me del spirto privo,*

*Il qual' fra 'l choro eletto celestiale*
*Forse poi narrerá la gloria tanta*
*Qual merta quel di chi sol parlo et scrivo*

XXVII

Oh Fortune, you may well knock me in various ways, and you may well take away and continuously obstruct the strength and the beautiful path that gradually reveals to me heaven with great promises and praises,

You may well, arrogant one, by your many deceits, make it so that my mortal body dies every day and that in such a bitter suffering a thousand evil ties bind me with pitiless persistence.

But you won't be able to make me such that I cease to sing the golden plant[1] unless you first deprive me of my soul,

Which, amongst the elect celestial choir, will then, perhaps, tell of such great glory, as befits the one of whom I talk and write.

1 *the golden plant.* As already pointed out, a golden oak featured in the coat of arms of the Della Rovere family.



*Almo paese che fra 'l mare et Catri*
*Contempli 'l grato et liberal' valore*
*Di quel gran Duca c'hoggi in tuo favore*
*Adorna d'alto honor' tempi et theatri.*

*Quest'hora invola degli antichi patri*
*Quel pregio di bontà quel vero honore*
*Gia per tant'anni et mesi et giorni et hore*
*Celato à noi da i tempi oscuri et atri.*

*Quest'e quel vero ben quest'è quell sole*
*Che 'n te farà svegliar que' tanti ingegni*
*Che pel dormir d'altrui son' dati al sonno,*

*Et se non fallan gli mostrati segni*
*Et favorisca 'l ciel come far suole*
*Virtù, trarrom'anch'io sveglio à tal donno.*

XXVIII

Oh noble country, which, between the sea and mount Catria,[1] behold the welcome and generous virtue of that great Duke who, today, for your benefit, adorns your temples and theatres with noble honour.

This hour ravishes that prize of excellence and that true honour of our ancestors, which already for many years and months and hours was concealed to us by dark and gloomy times.

This is that true good, this is that sun that will awake in you the many talents which have been asleep because of the slumbering of others,

And if the manifested signs do not betray us and if heaven favours virtue, as it usually does, I too shall draw myself, awake, to such a lord.

1 *between the sea and mount Catria.* Marking, respectively, the eastern and western borders of the Duchy of Urbino.

## XXIX

*Non mai tra gli Umbri signor' mio Saonda*
*Cotanto per gran pioggia alzò la fronte*
*Delle cui forze spesso audaci et pronte*
*Il Chiaso e 'l Tebro e 'l gran Tyrreno abbonda,*

*Ne il mio natio paese immerge et inonda*
*L'Adice altero, tra le valli e 'l monte*
*Ch'innalza d'Este le fattezze conte*
*Con quanto d'Adria il sit'orna et circonda,*

*Quant'io tra sacri et spirital' delubri*
*M'innalzo et empio il vostro honor notando*
*Senza timor' alcun' d'aspri colubri,*

*M'innalzo et empio dico d'amor' quando*
*Odo sí come fama e à caspi e à rubri*
*Vostra inviolabil fe va celebrando.*

Never, my lord, did the Saonda, amongst the Umbrians, rise so high, due to heavy rain, whose force, often bold and swift, fills the Chiascio, the Tiber and the great Tyrrhenian Sea.[1]

Nor does the haughty Adige soak and flood my native country, between the valleys and the mountain that raises the famous features of Este with that which the site of Adria adorns and surrounds,[2]

As much as I rise and fill, amongst sacred and holy temples, beholding your glory, without any fear of bitter serpents,

I rise and fill, I say, with love when I hear how Fame goes celebrating your unbroken faith to the Caspi and the Rubri.[3]

1 *the Saonda…whose force, often bold and swift, fills the Chiascio, the Tiber and the great Tyrrhenian Sea.* The Saonda is a torrent that flows into the river Chiascio, which is, in turn, a tributary of the Tiber, whose mouth is in the Tyrrhenian Sea. The Saonda and the Chiascio flow through territory that once belonged to the Duchy of Urbino; the Tiber marked the western borders of the Duchy.

2 *between…surrounds.* The Po valley and the Mount Este are used to mark, respectively, the southern and northern borders of the region referred to here. The town of Adria (or Atria) is situated between the mouths of the Adige and the Po.

3 *when I hear how Fame goes celebrating your unbroken faith to the Caspi and the Rubri.* The Caspi stand for the inhabitants of the region around the Caspian Sea and the Rubri (from the Latin *ruber*, red) stand for the inhabitants of the region around the Red Sea. Here we can take this reference to the Caspi and the Rubri to be used only generally to say that the Duke's fame spreads as far as distant, exotic regions. Alternatively, as is suggested by Cioci (1987, p. 165), a more specific reference to a planned crusade to the East (compare with Sonnet XXII) may be intended.



## XXX

*Quantunque talhor sol tra inhabitati*
*Boschi di fere nidi et di serpenti*
*Vad'io non punto in me dal timor' spenti*
*Entrar puo di vilta gli estremi agguati,*

*Anzi co miei pensier' d'ardir' armati*
*Me n' vo sicur cantando o rami olenti*
*Dell'alta Rover' d'or sempre presenti*
*Sarete à fama et di vittorie ornati.*

*Parmi d'udir' sovente in mezzo 'l canto*
*Voce cotale o pien' d amor' et fede*
*A tempo anchor ti sei dal sonno tolto,*

*Raro suggietto tale accade o Xanto,*
*Et raro in darno anchor sparger si vede*
*Di virtu 'l seme in Giardin' raro et colto.*

Although sometimes I wander alone[1] in uninhabited woods, full of dens of wild beasts and of serpents, the worst snares of cowardice due to fear cannot conquer me.

On the contrary, my thoughts armed with courage, I stride, confidently singing: 'Oh fragrant branches of the tall golden Oak, you will always be where fame is and you will always be adorned by victories'.

I often seem to hear, in mid song, a voice saying: 'Oh you, full of love and faith, you rose in time from your slumber;

Rarely does such a subject present itself, oh Xanto, and also rarely can it be seen that the seed of virtue is spread to no avail in a rare and cultivated Garden'.

1 *Although sometimes I wander alone.* As pointed out in the Introduction (p. 26), Francesco Maria was rarely present in Urbino. This sonnet may refer, therefore, to times when the Duke is away and Xanto 'wanders alone', in the middle of all the snares of his rivals and/or enemies.

*Glorioso Duca poi che nel tuo petto*
*Le gratie son ridotte à trastullarsi*
*Et sento et odo ogn hor' di te lodarsi*
*Virtù con vero nome et vero effetto,*

*Assente anchor dal tuo leggiadro aspetto*
*Ti diei mia libertade ond'alsi et arsi*
*In sí soave fuoco e tal ch'armarsi*
*Mia lingua vidi d'arte et di soggietto,*

*Sol per far risentire al cieco mondo*
*L'util' odor' della bollente massa*
*Che tra l'incude et 'l gran martel s'affina.*

*Et quanto ami colei che anulla et cassa*
*Ogni error' di ricchezza et la reina*
*Che l'huom' richiama al viver suo secondo.*



Glorious Duke, since in your breast the Graces
can only take delight and every hour I sense and
hear praise of your worth in its true name and in
its true effect,

When I was still absent from the noble sight of you,
I surrendered my liberty to you,[1] whence I froze and
I blazed in such a gentle fire that I found my tongue
armed with skill and with a subject,

Only in order to make the blind world smell the useful
odour of the boiling metal that is refined between the
anvil and the great hammer,

And in order to make the world feel how you love her
who removes and cancels all fault derived from wealth[2]
and that queen who recalls a man to posthumous life.[3]

1 *When I was still absent from the noble sight of you, I surrendered my liberty to you.* This seems to suggest that Xanto was first inspired by the Duke's virtues and started writing about him when he was not yet settled in Urbino. Perhaps he is referring to the time alluded to in Sonnet XIV, when he first conceived the project of writing about the Duke but was then silenced, at the very beginning, by the shock of hearing of the Duke's disgrace. However, it is also possible that Xanto refers rather to a later time, when, still not yet in Urbino, he eventually embarked on the project that had such an abortive beginning.
2 *her who removes and cancels all fault derived from wealth.* This is probably Temperance.
3 *that queen who recalls a man to posthumous life.* Fame.



*Se mai fama nel mondo alta et sonora*
*Accese in gemtil' cor giusti disiri*
*Pe quai dal pianto spesso et da i sospiri*
*Levati siam al ciel' con piu san' ora,*

*Inclito Duca lo prov'io pur hora*
*Quanto mia stella à te par che mi tiri*
*Et se cio sol fa 'l specchio in ch'ogn' hor miri*
*Che farà tua presenza alma et decora ?*

*Et se non che legato qui son tanto*
*Colpa del mio destin' ch'à mio dispetto*
*Fa ch'io raffreni i bei pensieri alquanto,*

*Al tuo verendo et signoril cospetto*
*Gia venuto sarei con l'humil canto*
*Sol per tua buona fama à te soggietto.*



If ever Fame in the world high and sonorous inflamed
in a noble heart legitimate desires, by which, from
tears and sighs, we are often raised to heaven for a
healthier time,

Oh glorious Duke, I certainly experience it now, how
much my star appears to draw me to you, and if this is
already made so by the mirror in which you constantly
see yourself, what will be achieved by your noble and
decorous presence ?[1]

And if it were not for the fact that I am so much bound
here, my destiny being to blame, which against my will
causes me to restrain my beautiful thoughts considerably,

I would already have come with my humble song to
your venerable and noble presence, being subject to
you only by your good fame.

1 *if this is already made so by the mirror in which you constantly see yourself…* As pointed out for Sonnet XXX and in the Introduction, Francesco Maria was seldom in Urbino. This sonnet seems to refer to a time when he was away. The question is what Xanto means by the mirror in which the Duke constantly sees himself. Cioci (1987, p.171) suggests that this refers to a portrait of the Duke. This does not explain, however, why Xanto says that the Duke *constantly* ("ogn'or") sees himself in this portrait. Xanto could be referring, instead, to Eleonora Gonzaga, who has already been presented, in Sonnet XII, as the Duke's worthy spouse, mirror of his virtues, as we could say. She was certainly more consistently present in Urbino than the Duke. Alternatively, if this sonnet refers to one of the Duke's periods of absence when his son Guidobaldo was already old enough to be left in charge, the 'mirror' could refer to Guidobaldo, who is, indeed, referred to in the next sonnet.

XXXIII

*Non la presenza tua non tue parole*
*Constretto m'ha nelle tue giuste lodi,*
*Ma gli essempi che dai del ben che godi*
*M'hanno tirato à sí gradite scole,*

*Poi che tua gratia ch'ogni gratia cole*
*Con mille et piu lodate imprese et modi*
*M'accinge l'alma d'amorosi [m = n]odi*
*Fra chiare cortesie nel mondo sole.*

*Allegro gli honorati et chiari fregi*
*Del sangue tuo, Signor, et l'util parte*
*Degli acquistati et dispensati pregi,*

*Sotto l'alma Minerva, e 'l fero Marte*
*Fra spirti chiari, per costumi egregi,*
*Lassero noti in piu di mille charte.*

XXXIII

Not your presence, nor your words have compelled
me to laud you deservedly, but the examples you give
of the blessing you enjoy have drawn me to such an
agreeable practice,

For your graces, which are revered by all the Graces, by
a thousand and more praiseworthy feats and manners,
bind my soul in affectionate ties, amongst illustrious
virtues unique in the world.

I shall happily confer fame, in more than a thousand
pages, oh my lord, on the honoured and noble
ornaments of your blood,[1] on prizes you have won
and dispensed under divine Minerva and fierce
Mars, amongst famous spirits illustrious for their
behaviour.

1 *the honoured and noble ornaments of your blood.*
Francesco Maria's son Guidobaldo.

XXXIV

*Deh quando mai potro veder' l aspetto*
*Del mio gran Duca di tal laude degno*
*Qual si conviene à chi d'imperio, o regno*
*Per virtù merta il possidente effetto ?*

*Tosto ch'all'ampia selva et regal tetto*
*Le figlie di Pandion pel vecchio sdegno*
*Faran ritorno, et che 'l bel' sole al segno*
*Del Tauro, mostrer[anno = à] l'aurato petto,*

*Hor ch'io discerno il dur terrestre smalto*
*Di bianche nevi ricoperto, fiso*
*Starommi à contemplar' gli ornati inchiostri,*

*Ne stanco sarò mai di cantar' l'alto*
*Splendor' che l'Umbria alluma et 'l fido aviso*
*Di quanto oprar' debbiam ne i giorni nostri.*

XXXIV

Ah, when shall I ever be in the presence of my great
Duke, worthy of praise as it befits him who as a
result of his valour deserves to possess an empire or
a kingdom?

As soon as Pandion's daughters come back to the
vast forest and the regal roof to sing their old
indignation,[1] and the beautiful sun shows its
golden breast in the sign of Taurus,[2]

I, who now see the hard surface of the earth
covered with white snow, will gaze steadily at
the adorning ink,

Nor will I ever tire of singing the high splendour
that inflames Umbria and the true inspiration for
what we must do in our days.

1 *As soon as Pandion's daughters…* In classical
mythology, Procne and Philomela,
Pandion's daughters, were wronged by
Tereus, Procne's husband, who raped
Philomela. In revenge, Procne killed Itys,
the son she had by Tereus, and served
him as food to the unknowing Tereus.
Procne and Philomela escaped Tereus's
wrath by being turned into a swallow and
a nightingale respectively. The singing of
these birds is thus traditionally associated
with a lament, although they are also
associated, as here, with the coming of
spring.
2 *and the beautiful sun shows its golden breast in
the sign of Taurus.* That is, when the sun
enters the sign of Taurus, in the third
week of April.

### XXXV

*Pien' d'allegrezza inusitata et nuova*
*Che l'operato bene un'alma avviva,*
*Vengo a te signor' mio, dal qual deriva*
*Quel ben ch'al ben' oprar tanto mi giova,*

*Per farti noto con verace pruova*
*Quanto la donna al mondo alata et diva*
*Mi sculse al petto tua virtu visiva*
*Per trarmi à quel' che raro hoggi si truova.*

*Et tu quel raro sei et tale e tanto*
*Che ben m'affido ch'al tuo nome in terra*
*Non possa danno dar morte ne tempo.*

*Et s'humil troppo in cio sara 'l mio canto*
*Spero che splendera nel nuovo tempo*
*L'integra fede mia che in lui si serra.*

### XXXV

Full of uncommon and new happiness, since your
good deeds invigorate one's soul, I come to you,
my lord, from whom springs that good that is so
propitious to my good deeds,

To let you know by a true proof how much the
woman, winged and divine[1] for the world, carved in
my heart your virtue made visible to draw me to what
today is rarely found.

And you are this rare good and so much and such
that I trust that neither death nor time can blemish
your name on earth,

And if my song will be too humble for that, I hope
that my flawless loyalty which is contained in it will
shine in the future.

1  *the woman winged and divine*. Fame.

### XXXVI

*Lung'alla plebe tumida et ventosa*
*Trattomi e all'alta cima del bel colle*
*Venuto ov'hora al ciel' con fama estolle*
*Gli aurati rami suoi la quercia annosa*

*Vidi fortuna come fresca rosa,*
*Rider' sol dal mattin' fin' che ne tolle*
*Apollo il giorno et dopo infetta et molle*
*Lasciar' del mondo quasi ogni gran cosa,*

*Poi vidi nel bel luogo alzarsi al cielo*
*Col felice favor di virtute alma*
*Del mio gran Duca l'honorato nome,*

*Et l'aura sì soave al bianco velo*
*Spirar del legno suo, ch'al fin' le chiome*
*S'ornó di gloriosa et immortal palma.*

### XXXVI

Having taken myself away from the haughty and
conceited throng and having come to the high
summit[1] of the beautiful hill where now the ancient
oak lifts up with fame its golden boughs,

I saw Fortune, like a fresh rose, smile only from the
morning until Apollo took away the day from it and
then I saw it, corrupt and slack, abandon almost every
great thing in the world.[2]

Then I saw, in this beautiful place, the honoured
name of my great Duke rise to heaven by the happy
favour of great valour

And I saw a breeze blow so gently in the white sail
of his boat, that eventually he crowned his locks with
glorious and immortal palms.[3]

1  *the high summit*. Probably meaning Urbino.
2  *I saw Fortune…* Probably referring to the relatively short-lived fortune of the Medici in their Wars of Urbino against Francesco Maria. (Compare with Sonnet VII and Introduction, p. 17)
3  *And I saw a breeze…* That is to say, the Duke eventually won a glorious victory over his enemies. For the symbolic meaning of palms and their more specific meaning when associated with Francesco Maria, see Sonnet XXVI, note 1.

*L' honorat'uso da cui trar' solete*
*Quel immortal splendor ch'Italia honora*
*Con l'alta gratia sua piu m'innamora*
*Ch'ogn'altra vista, la disiata sete,*

*Quest'é 'l nodo Signor', con che m'havete*
*Avinto et tratt'à piu gioconda aurora*
*Ben per me lieto giorno et felic'hora,*
*Tra lustri raggi ove voi solo siete,*

*Solo dico Signor', perche' sei raro,*
*Et quel che' men la possession' che l'uso*
*Delle ricchezze, in terra apprezza et ama,*

*Peró sel bel disio nel petto chiuso*
*Tenessi i sarei certo ingrato ò avaro*
*Troppo à chi debbo et che l'honor' mio brama.*



Those honoured customs from which you take that
immortal splendour which does honour to Italy with
its high favour inflame my longing thirst more than
any other sight.

This is, my lord, the tie by which you bound me and
by which you drew me to a more cheerful dawn,
oh for me happy day and fortunate hour, amongst
the shining rays where you alone are.

Alone, I say, my lord, because you are a rare example
of one who values and cherishes on earth less the
possession than the use of his riches.

So, if I kept my beautiful desire locked in my heart,
I would certainly be ungrateful and too mean towards
him to whom I am indebted and who wishes me success.



*D'humil frondente et verde perizoma*
*S[uo =ov]ra 'l Metauro in Umbria, mentr'altera*
*Iva tra noi fiorita primavera*
*Cinto vidi un pastor di bianca chioma,*

*Ch'à sciolta voce ver l'infetta Roma*
*Animandol[a = o] 'l bene o pieta vera,*
*Le diceva esclamando et mane et sera*
*Con quell amor che raro hoggi si noma,*

*Donna caduta per furor' insano*
*D'avara ambítion', se vuoi rihaverti*
*Et fuggir' l'otio periglioso et strano*

*Convoca al scampo tuo gli spirti esperti*
*Honor del sangue illustre Ferretrano,*
*Se non gia son' per te gli abissi aperti.*



When Spring in her bloom was proudly going
amongst us,[1] I saw by the Metaurus, in Umbria,
a white-haired shepherd[2] clothed of a simple leafy
and green loincloth,

Who in a ready tongue inspired by the good or by true
piety was addressing corrupt Rome and was telling her,
inveighing from morn to eve, pushed by that love that
today can rarely be found:

'Oh woman fallen because of your insane frenzy of
avaricious ambition, if you want to recover and to
escape your dangerous and outrageous sloth,[3]

Call to your rescue those expert spirits who are the
honour of the illustrious blood of Feretrius,[4] otherwise
the abysmal depths of Hell are already gaping for you'.

1  *When … us.* This probably refers to the spring
of 1536, marking the conclusion of the
Camerino dispute between Francesco Maria
and the Pope – see Introduction, p. 23.

2  *a white-haired shepherd.* Cioci (1987, p. 183) takes
this white-haired shepherd to be Francesco
Maria. However, perhaps Xanto meant
rather to identify himself with the shepherd,
in line with the classical tradition of the
shepherd-poet. In this guise he would be
defending his Duke, "pushed by that love
that today can rarely be found", as he tells us
below, using the same words as are used in
Sonnet XIX. Also, the exhortation below to
Rome to be rescued by the Della Rovere
family, makes more sense if spoken by Xanto
instead of by the Duke, referring to himself.
Moreover, the guise of a shepherd appears
to be too humble for Francesco Maria.

3  *if … sloth.* As suggested by Cioci (1987, p. 183),
the reproach of laziness is probably to be
understood in relation to the need, in those
years, to mobilize all Christian powers
against the Turks. In fact, the intervention
of Venice and Charles V on behalf of
Francesco Maria in the Camerino dispute
was motivated by their desire that the Pope
and Francesco Maria come to an agreement,
so that the latter could be employed in the
fight against the infidel.

4  *Call … Feretrius.* 'Feretrius' (meaning 'who
carries away [the spoils of war]') was one of
the titles of Jove. The Montefeltro family's
territory around San Leo was called 'Mons
Feretri' because of a temple sacred to Jove
Feretrius in San Leo. It is possible that this is
the origin of the name 'Montefeltro'. The
"illustrious blood of Feretrus" would, thus,
be the descendants of the Montefeltro
family, most notably Francesco Maria.
However, there is also an association with
the Della Rovere family, whose arms feature
the oak, the sacred tree of Jove.

**XXXIX**

*Se risplendenti piu che fiamma et oro*
*Sisto et Giulio regnaro in l'alta sede*
*Quella innalzando con speranza et fede*
*Di poi gustar' nel ciel' l'etterno choro,*

*Via piu che fiamma, o 'l sol' sceso del Toro*
*L'alto et chiaro mio Duca hoggi si vede*
*Raggiare, et fatto di duo padri herede*
*La quercia innalza al par del sacro alloro,*

*Et di quest'un' ch'io dico hoggi si raro*
*Vedrem' ch'Apoll' mi detta, uscir fra noi*
*Giulio minor di Guid'Ubaldo frate,*

*Piu che piropo chiaro, et údrem poi*
*Di Lisabetta et Giulia l'honestate*
*Volar con fama eterna oltr'Ethna et Varo.*

**XXXIX[1]**

If, shining more than fire and gold, Sixtus and Julius[2] reigned in the high see, raising it with hope and faith, and then enjoyed in heaven the eternal choir,

Much more than fire, or than the sun in the constellation of the Taurus,[3] my noble and illustrious Duke is seen to shine and, heir of two fathers,[4] he raises the oak as well as the sacred laurel.[5]

And, as Apollo tells me, we shall see that from this man, whom today I call so rare, will spring amongst us Julius Minor,[6] brother of Guidubaldo,[7]

Shining more than pyrope,[8] and we shall then hear the virtue of Lisabetta and Giulia[9] fly with eternal fame beyond the Etna and the Varo.[10]

1 This is the sonnet on the recto of the added leaf (see the introductory Notes to the Manuscript).

2 *Sixtus and Julius.* Sixtus IV, i.e. Francesco Della Rovere (1414–1484), who was pope from 1471; Julius II, i.e. Giuliano Della Rovere (1443–1513), pope from 1503.

3 *the sun in the constellation of Taurus.* That is, the sun in April and May, when it is particularly bright.

4 *heir of two fathers.* The renowned Sixtus and Julius mentioned in the first quatrain.

5 *he raises the oak as well as the sacred laurel.* That is, he brings fame to the Della Rovere family as well as being an excellent patron of poets.

6 *Julius Minor.* Giulio Feltrio Della Rovere (1533–1578), second son of Francesco Maria. The epithet 'Minor' is used in anticipation of a fame which will place him next to his grand-uncle Julius II.

7 *Guidubaldo.* Guidobaldo Della Rovere (1514–1574), first son of Francesco Maria and heir to the Duchy of Urbino.

8 *pyrope.* Precious stone, flaming red.

9 *Lisabetta and Giulia.* Elisabetta Della Rovere (1529–1561) and Giulia Della Rovere (1527–1563), third and second daughters respectively of Francesco Maria.

10 *beyond the Etna and the Varo.* Marking the southern and northern extremities of Italy. The river Varo flows near Nice.

**XL**

*Non molto andrà che le superbe spoglie*
*Et gli helmi e i scudi fessi e i sparsi usberghi*
*Levati dagli petti et dagli terghi*
*De i spirti colmi d'orgogliose voglie,*

*Saranno al tempio ov'alt'honor s'accoglie*
*Fisse, sgombrando i Barbareschi alberghi*
*Et spenti et tronchi mille strani gerghi*
*Vedrem fugir' dal mondo et brighe et doglie,*

*Poi la robusta pianta et i rami d'oro*
*Al manco lato del Metauro antico*
*Vedrem sola posar' cinta d'alloro,*

*O ch'allegrezza in ciel' n'haurà Fedrico*
*Veggiend'unir' con grid'alt'e sonoro*
*Si bella pianta, al suo bell' colle aprico.*

**XL[1]**

It will not be long before the proud spoils, the helmets, the broken shields and the scattered armour taken from the breasts and the backs of those spirits full of haughty appetites

Will be hung in that temple, home to high Fame, clearing the Barbaresque abodes, and we shall see a thousand strange tongues, extinguished and cut, flee from the world, troubles and pains.[2]

Then we shall see the robust tree and the golden boughs[3] rest alone, crowned with laurel, to the left of the ancient Metaurus.[4]

Oh how happy will Fedrico[5] be in heaven, seeing that, with a loud and resounding cry, such a beautiful tree is joined to his beautiful bright hill.

1 This is the sonnet on the verso of the added leaf (see the introductory Notes to the Manuscript).

2 *It will not be long before…* In this sonnet, Xanto is, once again, talking about some military expedition against the infidel in which the Duke was involved. As in Sonnet XXII, this could be the expedition planned in January 1538, which Francesco Maria was meant to lead (see note 1 to Sonnet XXII). However, Xanto might refer rather to another of the variously planned expeditions against the Turks of the 1530s. As in Sonnet XXII, the term 'Barbaresque' could mean 'of Barbary' and could be taken to refer specifically to the army of Khaireddin Barbarossa, Beyler Bey of Algiers, or it could mean 'barbarian' and could be taken to refer to the infidel in general (see Sonnet XXII, note 3).

3 *the robust tree and the golden boughs.* The oak tree, which featured, in gold, in the arms of the Della Rovere.

4 *to the left of the ancient Metaurus.* Urbino is located to the left of the river Metaurus.

5 *Fedrico.* Federico Da Montefeltro (1422–1482), first Duke of Urbino. The 'tree' of the Della Rovere was 'joined' to Urbino by the marriage of Federico's daughter Giovanna to Giovanni Della Rovere and by their son Francesco Maria becoming Duke of Urbino on the death of his childless uncle Guidobaldo I Da Montefeltro, son of Federico.

*O, cultor di giustitia, o fido amico*
*Di quelle alte virtu che fra gli dei*
*Prezzando i buoni et castigando i rei*
*Albergo ti daran, me ch'io non dico,*

*Il nome tuo, terror d'ogni nemico,*
*Il fedel stato in cui si forte sei,*
*Et le bandiere vinte et gli trophei*
*Fanno che agguagli ogni famoso antico,*

*De tuoi giusti consigli il chiaro lume*
*Cotal lampeggia, ch'ogni ver' guerriero*
*Non meno istima te, che 'l martial' nume,*

*Quindi nascie signor, ch'io t'amo e spero*
*Passar con teco insieme il sacro fiume*
*De miei cognome, per dio vivo et vero.*



Oh lover of justice, oh faithful friend of those high virtues which, before I can even say that, will give you abode amongst the gods, who value the good and punish the evil,

Your name, terror to all your enemies, your faithful state, in which you are so strong, and the banners and the trophies won make you the equal to any famous ancient hero.

The bright light of your good judgement shines so that every true warrior respects you no less than the martial god,[1]

Hence it comes about, my lord, that I love you and I hope to cross together with you the sacred river that bears the surname of my family, for the living and true God.[2]

1 *the martial god.* Mars, god of war.
2 *I hope…God.* Here Xanto expresses the hope of accompanying the Duke in his expedition against the Turks, probably the one Francesco Maria was meant to lead in 1538, the year of his death. The Turks are referred to via a pun with the name 'Xanto': the river Xanthus flows in Phrygia, quite close to Constantinople, capital of the Ottoman Empire.



*Il ricco Tago il geminato Beti,*
*L'Hiber famoso, la risurgent' Ana,*
*L'antico Atlante quasi in forma humana*
*Tra i fianchi ombrosi suoi d odor repleti,*

*Gl'Itali poggi, i campi ameni et lieti,*
*L'onde che 'n doran' la regione Hircana,*
*Pattol, Cori[n]to, Olimpo, e 'l Boreal' Tana*
*Tendente à molti, per divin decreti,*

*L'ampia Heritymia et gli sestiani altari*
*Al gran Cesare Augusto dedicati*
*Et 'l scoglio di Cepion', freddo sepulcro,*

*Questi tutti sarian pe i gesti rari*
*Del mio Duca viril con modo pulchro*
*A farne 'l paragon', men celebrati.*



The rich Tago, the twinned Baetis, the famous Hiber,[1] Ana,[2] that rises again, the ancient Atlas, of almost human form betwixt his shady flanks replete with scent,[3]

The Italian hillocks, the pleasant and happy meadows, the waves that touch Hircania with gold,[4] Pattol,[5] Corinth, Olympus and the boreal Tana,[6] that reaches out to many, by divine decree,

The vast Heritymia and the altars of Sestos,[7] dedicated to the great Caesar Augustus, and the rock of Caepio, cold sepulchre,[8]

All of these would be less extolled, if we drew a beautiful comparison with the uncommon feats of my manly Duke.

1 *The rich Tago, the twinned Baetis, the famous Hiber.* All rivers in Spain. The Baetis (today's Guadalquivir) is called 'twinned' because in the swampy region of Las Marnias it splits into two subsidiary channels.
2 *Ana.* City by the river Euphrates.
3 *the ancient Atlas, of almost human form…* The Atlas mountains, in Mauritania, are said to be 'of almost human form' because they are named after the Titan Atlas who, having unsuccessfully waged war against the Olympian gods, was punished by being turned into the chain of mountains thought to hold up the heavens.
4 *the waves that touch Hircania with gold.* That is, the Caspian Sea, north of the ancient Persian region of Hircania.
5 *Pattol.* Or Pattolo, a river in Lydia.
6 *the boreal Tana.* Today's Don, in Western Russia.
7 *Sestos.* Town of the Thracian Chersonese, the modern Gallipoli peninsula in European Turkey.
8 *the rock of Caepio, cold sepulchre.* Possibly meaning Smyrna, in Asia Minor, where Quintus Servilius Caepio died in exile.

XLIII

*Se d'ove il Gange in mar' pon l'alte corna*
*Al Sardo, al Pireneo à Calpe et à Gade*
*Et al Tile e in Ponto e 'n l'oriental contrade*
*Dell alta Rover' d'oro il nome adorna,*

*Et se qualunque hoggi 'n virtù soggiorna*
*Dal sen d'Adria, al Tyrhen, fra nostre strade*
*Per colpa di fortuna ò piega ò cade*
*Per l'alta Rover' d'oro in pie ritorna,*

*Et s'ancho il popol' dell'altero colle*
*Che'n fronte all'Austro il freddo Catri mira*
*All'alta Rover' d'oro è fedel tanto,*

*Non prenda ammiration ne caschi in ira*
*Alcun di quei che la ricchezza estolle*
*Se l'alta Rover' d'oro honoro et canto.*

XLIII

If the name of the noble golden Oak adorns the
region where the Ganges pours into the sea his lofty
horns,[1] Sardinia, the Pyrenees, Calpe,[2] Cadiz, Thule,
the Pontus and the eastern countries,[3]

And if any virtuous man, from Adria's bosom to the
Tyrrhenian sea, in our streets is bent by Fortune or
falls because of her fault and then regains his feet
thanks to the noble golden Oak,

And, also, if the people of the lofty hill that on its
southern side looks towards cold Mount Catria,[4]
is so faithful to the noble golden Oak,

Any of those who extol wealth be not surprised
nor angry if I honour and sing the noble
golden Oak.

1 *the Ganges pours into the sea his lofty horns.* Here
the 'corna', or 'horns', are, possibly, to be
understood by reference to the classical
representations of river gods as horned men
with bodies of serpentine fish below the
chest. Alternatively, Xanto may simply be
referring to the bifurcating distributaries
of the Ganges.
2 *Calpe.* One of the Pillars of Hercules,
today's Gibraltar.
3 *If the name…* There doesn't seem to be any
reason for the choice of all these different
places in the world as opposed to others
except that they provide a good range for the
claim that the name of the Duke is extolled
all over the world, from East to West, from
North to South.
4 *the people… Catria.* These are the inhabitants
of Urbino. In the original text, the idea of
the southern side of Urbino is conveyed by
reference to the South wind Auster.

XLIV

*Questi, che qui tra noi, dal ciel' discese*
*Per gratia, sotto humano et mortal' velo*
*Con sue tante virtuti al caldo et al gielo*
*Farassi chiaro in mille chiare imprese,*

*Le sacre menti et l'alte penne accese*
*Di divino furore et divin' zelo*
*Pria che l'incerta età gli cangi il pelo*
*Lassera stanche in dir quant'egli ascese,*

*Che quanto il rozzo et mio mal culto stile*
*Ha di lui dett' é una favilla appresso*
*Quel che merta 'l suo lume immenso et alto.*

*Ma sol cio fei, per dimostrar' l'impresso*
*Mio cor dell'amor' suo raro et gentile,*
*Non che strana ambition mi fesse assalto.*

*Finis, ad laudem*
*Omnipotentis Dei*

XLIV

This creature, who by divine grace descended
amongst us from heaven, under a human and mortal
veil, will by his many virtues make himself famed,
in heat or frost, through a thousand glorious feats.

He will leave sacred minds and great pens, alight
with divine inspiration and zeal, worn out by telling
how high he rose, long before faltering age shall
change the colour of his hair.

What my rough and uncultivated style has said of
him is a spark compared to what his immense and
high light deserves,

But I did that only to show my heart impressed by his
rare and noble love, and not because I had been seized
by some strange ambition.

The end, to the glory
Of God Almighty

Questi, che qui tra noi dal ciel discese

Per gratia, sotto humano & mortal velo

Con sue tutte virtuti al caldo & al gielo

Farassi chiaro in mille chiar imprese,

Le sacre meti & l'alte pene accese

Di divino furor & divin zelo

Pria che l'incerta età gli cangi il pelo

Lassera stanche in dir qua tu egli ascese,

Chi ciato di rozzo & mio mal culto stile

Ha di lui dett'e una favilla appresso

Quel che merta il suo lume imenso & alto,

La sol ciò fei, per dimostrar l'impresso

Mio cor dell'amor suo raro & gentile

No che strana ambitio mi fosse assalto.

# Petrarch's Sonnets x and xxxiii

### x

*Glorïosa Colonna, in cui s'appoggia*
*Nostra speranza e 'l gran nome latino,*
*Ch'ancor non torse dal vero cammino*
*L'ira di Giove per ventosa pioggia,*

*Qui non palazzi, non theatro o loggia,*
*Ma 'n lor vece un abete, un faggio, un pino,*
*Tra l'erba verde e 'l bel monte vicino,*
*Onde si scende poetando et poggia,*

*Levan di terra al ciel nostr'intellecto;*
*E 'l rosigniuol che dolcemente all'ombra*
*Tutte le notti si lamenta et piagne,*

*D'amorosi pensieri il cor ne 'ngombra.*
*Ma tanto ben sol tronchi, et fai imperfecto,*
*Tu che da noi, Signor mio, ti scompagne.*

### xxxiii

*Già fiammeggiava l'amorosa stella*
*Per l'orïente, et l'altra, che Giunone*
*Suol far gelosa, nel septentrïone*
*Rotava i raggi suoi lucente et bella;*

*Levata era a filar la vecchiarella,*
*Discinta et scalza, et desto avea 'l carbone,*
*Et gli amanti pungea quella stagione*
*Che per usanza a lagrimar gli appella;*

*Quando mia speme, già condutta al verde,*
*Giunse nel cor, non per l'usata via,*
*Che 'l sonno tenea chiusa, e 'l dolor molle;*

*Quanto cangiata, oimè, da quel di pria !*
*Et parea dir : « Perché tuo valor perde ?*
*Veder quest'occhi anchor non ti si tolle ».*

### x

Oh glorious Colonna, that supports our hope
and the great Latin renown and that Jupiter's
wrath by its gusts of rain has still not driven from
the right path,

Here no palaces, no stage nor loggia, but in their
stead, a fir, a beech, a pine, between a green meadow
and the beautiful mountain nearby, where one goes
downhill and up composing poems,

These raise our intellect from earth to heaven. And
the nightingale, that sweetly in the dark every night
laments and complains,

Crowds one's heart with thoughts of love. It is only you,
my lord, who, being parted from us, curtail and make
incomplete so much joy.

### xxxiii

The star of love was already shining in the East
and the other bright and beautiful one, who
makes Juno jealous, was turning her rays in
the West,

Meanwhile, half-dressed and barefoot the old
woman had risen to spin and had stirred the embers
and it was that time of the day that spurs and calls
lovers to their accustomed lament,

When my love and hope, already close to her last breath
and, alas, how different from what she used to be,
reached my heart, but not through the accustomed way,

Which was kept closed by sleep and moist with sorrow,
and looked as though she was saying: « Why do you lose
heart? You are not yet deprived of the sight of these eyes ».

# List of works by or attributable to Francesco Xanto Avelli

ELISA PAOLA SANI

This list makes no claim to completeness, though it is hoped that it may lead to identification of further pieces. An attempt has been made to select only the fullest, most recent or most easily accessible bibliographical references.[1]

The following abbreviations are used for the most recent public locations (excluding auction houses) which are listed at least three times:

| | | | |
|---|---|---|---|
| AM | Ashmolean Museum, Oxford | MCMB | Museo Civico Medievale, Bologna |
| BM | British Museum, London | MCP | Musei Civici, Padua |
| BVBM | Boymans Van Beuningen Museum, Rotterdam | MIC | Museo Internazionale delle Ceramiche, Faenza |
| CGA | Corcoran Gallery of Art, Washington | MMA | Metropolitan Museum of Art, New York |
| DMAD | Danish Museum of Art and Design, Copenhagen | MNCS | Musée National de la Céramique de Sèvres, Paris |
| FM | Fitzwilliam Museum, Cambridge | MPP | Musée du Petit Palais, Paris |
| GCC(M) | Glasgow City Council (Museums) | MSA | Museo Statale d'Arte Medievale e Moderna, Arezzo |
| GM | Gardiner Museum, Toronto | NGA | National Gallery of Art, Washington |
| HAU-M | Herzog Anton Ulrich-Museum, Brunswick | NGV | National Gallery of Victoria, Australia |
| HSM | Hermitage State Museum, St Petersburg | PL | Polesden Lacey, Surrey, The National Trust |
| KB | Kunstgewerbemuseum, Berlin | SB | Schlossmuseum, Berlin |
| LACMA | Los Angeles County Museum of Art, Los Angeles | SF-P-M | Stiftung Fürst-Pückler-Museum, Park und Schloß Branitz |
| ML | Musée du Louvre, Paris | | |
| MAACS | Museo d'Arti Applicate, Castello Sforzesco, Milan | VAM | Victoria and Albert Museum, London |
| MADL | Musée des Arts Décoratifs, Lyon | WAM | Walters Art Museum, Baltimore |
| MC | Museo Correr, Venice | WC | Wallace Collection, London |

There is an alphabetical index to the locations cited in this List on pp.202-03.

1. I am indebted to many museum curators, collectors and dealers for providing information on published and unpublished works by or attributable to Xanto. I would particularly like to thank Dora Thornton and Timothy Wilson for generously making available the entries on Xanto from their forthcoming catalogue of Italian ceramics in the British Museum (Thornton and Wilson 2007). I must acknowledge here the use of all recent literature on Xanto in compiling this list; in particular Triolo 1996, for Xanto table services, and Lessmann 2004, for Xanto panels. I am extremely grateful to Suzanne Higgott for careful reading and editing, to Jeremy Warren for suggestions and to Timothy Wilson for help and advice. The present work started upon John Mallet's suggestion and it is based on his records and studies on Xanto; I wish to thank him dearly for precious advice and constant inspiration.

### Early, unsigned pieces attributed to 'F.R.'/Xanto

1.  1522. Bowl with broad border (*Tondino*): *Hercules and Omphale*. D: 30.0 cm. VAM, 2572-1856. Rackham 1940, no. 793, pl. 125. This cat. 1.
    On front, on a tablet: *.OMNIA. / VINCIT. / AMOR. 1522.*
2.  *c.* 1522. Fragment from centre of a dish: *Samson rending the Lion*. D: 23.5 cm. VAM, 658-1884. Rackham 1940, no. 794, pl. 125. This cat. 2.

### Lustred pieces arguably by 'F.R.'/Xanto working at Gubbio in Maestro Giorgio Andreoli's workshop, 1524–25

3.  1524. Bowl with broad border (*Tondino*): *A River God in a Landscape*. Lustred. D: 24.0 cm. BM, P&E 1851, 12-1, 7. Wilson 1987, no. 163; Thornton and Wilson 2007, no. 298. This cat. 4.
    REVERSE: in red lustre, floral scrolls and *1524/M°.G°.*
4.  1524. Bowl with broad border (*Tondino*): *The Judgement of Paris with Mercury*. Lustred. D: 26.5 cm. BM, P&E 1851, 12–1, 8. Wilson 1987, no. 68; Thornton and Wilson 2007, no. 299. This cat. 5.
    REVERSE: in lustre, *1524/M°. G°.*
5.  1525, 6 April. Large dish without foot ring: *Women Bathing*. Lustred. D: 44.6 cm. WC, C66. Norman 1976, no. C66. The centre here attributed in whole or in part to Francesco Xanto Avelli. This cat. 10.
    REVERSE: in lustre, *Mastro Giorgio/da ugubio Adj 6/daprile/1525*
6.  1525. Flat plate: *The Three Graces*. Lustred. D: 30.5 cm. VAM, 175-1885. Rackham 1940, no. 673, pl. 106. This cat. 9.
    REVERSE: in lustre, *1525/M°. G°.*
7.  1525. Plate: *The Prodigal Son amid the Swine*. Lustred. D: 28.3 cm. MMA, Robert Lehman Collection, 1975. I. 1105. Rasmussen 1989, no. 119.
    REVERSE: in lustre, *1525/M° G°* and scrolls.
8.  1525. Flat plate: *Three Soldiers Fighting*. Lustred. D: 30.3 cm. NGA, Widener Collection, 1942.9.334. Wilson 1993B, pp. 180–83.
    Here figs. 20–21.
    REVERSE: in lustre, *1525/M° G°* and scrolls.
9.  1525. Bowl with broad border (*Tondino*): *Juno in her Chariot*. Lustred. D: 27.9 cm. MMA, 41.100.279. Wilson 2002B, no. 20.
    REVERSE: in lustre, *1525/M°. G°.*
10. 1525. Bowl with broad border (*Tondino*): *Juno in her Chariot*. Lustred. D: 27.9 cm. MMA, 41.100.280. Wilson 2002B, no. 21.
    REVERSE: in lustre, *1525/M°. G°.*
11. 1525. Large dish without foot ring: *An Allegory of Envy*. Lustred. D: 40.5 cm. VAM, C. 2200-1910. Rackham 1940, no. 674, pl. 106. This cat. 11.
    REVERSE: in lustre, an ewer and *1525/M°. G°.*
12. Dish on a low foot (*Coppa*): *An Allegory of Envy*. Lustred. D: 20.0 cm. VAM, 8939-1863. Rackham 1940, no. 675, pl. 106.
    REVERSE: in lustre, *M°G°* and sprays.
13. Bowl with broad border (*Tondino*): *Dance of Cupids*. Lustred. D: 27.8 cm. New York, The Pierpont Morgan Library. Wilson 2002B, fig. 1.
    REVERSE: in lustre, *1525*



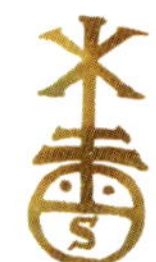

14. 1524. Bowl with broad border (*Tondino*): A putto approaching an altar on which is an owner's mark incorporating a double cross and an *S*, grotesques and shields. D: 20.8 cm. The putto here attributed to Xanto Avelli. BM, P&E 1851, 12–1, 13. Wilson 1987, no. 164; Thornton and Wilson 2007, no. 305. This cat. 6.
    REVERSE: in lustre, *1524/M°. G°*
15. *c.* 1524. Bowl with broad border (*Tondino*): A putto holding an owner's mark incorporating a double cross and an *S*, grotesques and shields. D: 20.7 cm. The putto here attributed to Xanto Avelli. BM, P&E 1851, 12–1, 15. Wilson 2002B, pl. xix; Thornton and Wilson 2007, no. 306.
16. 1525. Plate: *The Reconciliation of Cupid and Minerva*. Lustred. D: 26.0 cm. NGA, Widener Collection, 1942.9.333. Wilson 1993B, pp. 177–79.
    REVERSE: in lustre, *1525/M° G°* and an owner's mark incorporating a double cross and an *S*.
17. 1525. Bowl with broad border (*Tondino*): *Battling Figures and Cupid*. D: 26.3 cm. BM, P&E 1851, 12–1, 10. Wilson 1987, no. 167; Thornton and Wilson 2007, no. 301. This cat. 7.
    REVERSE: in lustre, *M°.G°./1525* and an owner's mark incorporating a double cross and an *S*.
18. 1525. Bowl with broad border (*Tondino*): *A Horseman with a Standard*. D: 24.5 cm. BM, P&E 1851, 12–1, 12. Wilson 2002B, pl. xxii; Thornton and Wilson 2007, no. 302. This cat. 8.
    REVERSE: in lustre, *1525/.M°.G°.* and an owner's mark incorporating a double cross and an *S*.
19. 1525. Bowl with broad border (*Tondino*): *Three Men in Academic Dress Debating*. D: 26.1 cm. BM, P&E 1851, 12–1, 9. Wilson 2002B, pl. xx, fig. 9; Thornton and Wilson 2007, no. 300.
    REVERSE: in lustre, scrolls, *1525/.M° G°.* and an owner's mark incorporating a double cross and an *S*.

### Pieces signed F.R. and related pieces

20. *c.* 1522–25. Large dish: *The Israelites gathering Manna*. D: 41.0 cm. VAM, 7680-1861. Rackham 1940, no. 796, pl. 126. This cat. 3.
    On front: *F.R.* (blurred) in foreground.
21. *c.* 1522–25. Dish on low foot (*Coppa*): *St Jerome in the Wilderness*. D: 26.0 cm. Sotheby's, London, 10–11 May 1962, lot 34 (ill.).
    On front, in the rockwork on the right: *F.R.*, in white.
22. *c.* 1525–26. Plate with broad border (*Tondino*): *Dido entertaining Aeneas*. D: 25.5 cm. VAM, C.2117-1910. Rackham 1940, no. 795, pl. 126. This cat. 14.
    On front: *F.R.* in foreground.
23. *c.* 1525–26. Fragment of plate: *Horsemen and Hunter with dead Hare on Stick*. D: 27.7 cm. KB, 98,160. Hausmann 1972, no. 129 (attributed to Faenza).
24. *c.* 1525–26. Plate with broad border (*Tondino*): *Narcissus at the Fountain of Love*. D: 27.6 cm. WC, C47. Norman 1976, no. C47. This cat. 12.
25. *c.* 1525–27. Dish on a low foot (*Coppa*): *Solomon building the Temple*. D: 27.8 cm. BM, P&E 1855, 12–1,102. Wilson 1987, no. 69; Thornton and Wilson 2007, no. 154. This cat. 13.
    On front, in blue black on the upturned rim at 4 o' clock: *F.R.*
26. *c.* 1525–27. Bowl with broad border (*Tondino*): *Aeneas receiving Dido* and in the centre, *The Suicide of Dido*. D: 25.3 cm. NGV, Felton Bequest, D4/1976. Mallet 1976, fig. 1.
    Front: on a tablet in the foreground, *AENEAM RECIPI/T PULCRA. CAR/TAGINE/DIDO* and *.F.R.*
27. *c.* 1525–27. Plate: *The Vestal Tuccia carrying Water in a Sieve to the Temple of Vesta*. D: 22.0 cm. Formerly SB, K1790, presumed destroyed in World War II. Rackham and Ballardini 1933, fig. 8.
    On front, at foot of masonry: *F.R.*
28. *c.* 1525–27. Plate: *The Fall of Icarus*. D: 25.5 cm. GM, G83.1.0333.
29. *c.* 1525–27. Plate: *The Metamorphosis of Callisto* with arms of the Bonzi family of Florence. D: 27.5 cm. VAM, C.19-1922. Rackham 1940, no. 548. This cat. 17.

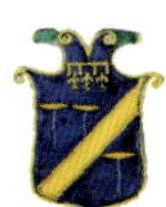

30. *c.* 1525–28. Plaque: *Christ Carrying the Cross (Spasimo di Sicilia)*. H: 51.0 cm; W: 33.5 cm. VAM, 4351-1857. Rackham 1940, no. 799, pl. 126 (disputable attribution. Possibly by another painter signing *F.R.* working in Forlì). This cat. 15.
    On front: *F.R.* on plaquette in foreground.
31. *c.* 1525–28. Dish on low foot (*Coppa*): *Apollo and Marsyas*. Formerly SB, presumed destroyed in World War II. Rackham and Ballardini 1933, fig. 9.
32. *c.* 1527–28. Dish on low foot (*Coppa*): *Dance of Cupids*. D: 26.9 cm. WC, C46. Norman 1976, no. C46. This cat. 19.
33. *c.* 1527–28. Dish on low foot (*Coppa*): *The Death of Lucretia*. D: 27.5 cm. VAM, C.2228-1910. Rackham 1940, no. 797, pl. 126.
34. *c.* 1527–28. Dish on low foot (*Coppa*): *The Death of Cleopatra*. D: 27.0 cm. VAM, C.2238-1910. Rackham 1940, no. 798, pl. 126.
35. *c.* 1527–28. Dish on low foot (*Coppa*): *The Conversion of Saul*. D: 26.6 cm. NGA, Widener Collection, 1942.9.349 (C-74). Wilson 1993B, pp. 202–04.

### Pieces signed F.L.R of *c.* 1529

36. 1529. Dish on low foot (*Coppa*): *Jupiter and Semele*. D: 25.8 cm. Budapest, Iparművészeti Muzeum. Mallet 2004, p. 38, pl. 2.
    REVERSE: in blue, *De giove & Semele/.f.L.R* and in lustre, *1529. M°. Giorgio/ da Ugubio*
37. *c.* 1528–30. Large dish on low foot (*Coppa*): *Roman Lion-Hunt*. D: 38.0 cm. BM, P&E 1970, 12–11, 1. Wilson 1987, no. 70; Thornton and Wilson 2007, no. 155. This cat. 16.
    REVERSE: *Que stabant uix hosptibus/ spectanda sepulchra:/quellibet arbitrio iam uidet/.illa suo./.f.L.R*
38. *c.* 1529. Fragment of a dish: *Venus and Cupid*. D: 16.5 cm. Florence, Museo Nazionale del Bargello, 1970–2021. Conti 1971, no. 41.
    REVERSE: *Nosce te ipsum. F.L.R.*

### The so-called 'Y/Φ series' (1527–30)
DATED WORKS

39. 1528. Dish on low foot (*Coppa*): *Hercules and Deianira (Omphale?)*. Lustred. D: 27.2 cm. MSA, 14582. Fuchs 1993, no. 144. This cat. 20.
    REVERSE: in lustre, *1528, M° Giorgio/ da ugubio*, red and yellow lustre scrolls; in antimony yellow, *De Hercule et Deianira* followed by the y/Φ flourish.
40. 1528. Dish: *Leda and the Swan*. Lustred. D: 27.0 cm. MPP, Dutuit 1092. Join-Dieterle 1984, no. 70.
    REVERSE: in blue, *Giove/Cygno* followed by the y/Φ flourish and in yellow lustre, *1528 M° Giorgio da Ugubio*

41. 1528. Plate: *A Love Scene (Venus and Jupiter)* and *Venus and Cupid*. Lustred. D: 29.7 cm.
DMAD, 57/1951.
Houkjaer 2005, no. 154.
REVERSE: in lustre, *1528/M° Giorgio/Ugubio* and scrolls; in blue, *A latto venere e/ Giove samano/fabula* followed by the y/Φ flourish.

42. 1528. Plate (*Tagliere*): *The Fable of Picus*. Lustred. D: 27.5 cm. Gubbio, Palazzo dei Consoli. Fiocco and Gherardi 1998, no. 13.
REVERSE: in lustre, *1528/M° Giorgio/da Ugubio* followed by the y/Φ flourish and scrolls; in blue, *De Pico et Cane[n]te/* followed by the y/Φ flourish.

43. 1528. Plate: *Ino and Athamas*. Lustred. D: 27.1 cm. Vienna, Österreichisches Museum für Angewandte Kunst, KHM4/3147. Ballardini 1933, 218, 203, 340 R.
REVERSE: in lustre, *1528//M° Giorgio/da Ugubio*; in blue, *ino et athama[n]te* followed by the y/Φ flourish.

44. 1528. Plate: Allegorical scene with an old man with a vase walking in a river with dolphins. Lustred. D: 27.5 cm. Formerly Sir Stephen Courtauld collection; Sotheby's, London, 18 March 1975, lot 26; Carbonara collection, Fiorano Modenese. Fiocco and Gherardi 1998, no. 14.
REVERSE: in lustre, *1528 M° Giorgio da Ugubio* followed by a flourish.

45. 1528. Plaque: *St Sebastian and St Roch*. H: 15.5 cm; W: 13.0 cm. VAM, C.2253-1910. Rackham 1940, no. 628, pl. 99. This cat. 21.
REVERSE: plain except for the date *1528* in black.

46. 1529. Bowl with broad border (*Coppa*): *Isaac and Esau*. Lustred. D: 32.0 cm. MIC, Fanfani Bequest, 24938. Ravanelli Guidotti 1990, no. 123.
REVERSE: in lustre, *1529/M°G°/da Ugubio* and scrolls.


UNDATED WORKS *c.* 1527–30

47. Dish on low foot (*Coppa*): *Hercules and Omphale?*. D: 27.1 cm. WAM, 48.1344. Prentice Von Erdberg and Ross 1952, no. 48. This cat. fig. 19.
REVERSE: *Hercule et/Deianira* followed by the y/Φ flourish.

48. Plate: *Hercules and Lichas*. MIC, 17398. Ravanelli Guidotti 1996, pl. 26a.
REVERSE: *Hercule il suo Lica/ in mare an[n]eta/ fabula* followed by the y/Φ flourish.

49. Bowl with broad border (*Tondino*): *Hippolytus escaping from the Wrath of Theseus*. D: 27.1 cm. WC, C86. Norman 1976, no. C86. This cat. 24.
REVERSE: *phedra da amore et/da luxuria oppresa/sporcitia* followed by the y/Φ flourish.

50. Bowl with broad border (*Tondino*): *A Political Allegory*. D: 27.0 cm. FM, C.14-1953. Poole 1995, no. 385. This cat. 30.
REVERSE: *Fuggi Spagna: Marcho/ et francia./nota* followed by the y/Φ flourish.

51. Bowl with broad border (*Tondino*): *Pyramus and Thisbe*. D: 26.0 cm. FM, C.15-1953. Poole 1995, no. 386.
REVERSE: *Vedi Piramo & Tisbe/i[n] sieme all ombra./Historia* followed by the y/Φ flourish.

52. Bowl with broad border (*Tondino*): *Scylla, Cupid and Four Nymphs Bathing*. D: 26.2 cm. FM, C.83-1961. Poole 1995, no. 387.
REVERSE: *Di C...:de et Scilla/il parlame[n]to./fabula* followed by the y/Φ flourish.

53. Plate: *Allegory of the Sufferings of Italy*. D: 26.7 cm. MCP, 154. Munarini and Banzato 1993, no. 294.
REVERSE: *Nota gli affanni/tuoi misera Italia./ pe[n]sa* followed by the y/Φ flourish.

54. Bowl with broad border (*Tondino*): Allegory with a female figure, perhaps Diana, a dog and two soldiers. D: 26.5 cm. MCP, 153. Munarini and Banzato 1993, no. 295.
REVERSE: *Mirate il tempo bell'/ch'anoi ritorna./ nota* followed by the y/Φ flourish.

55. Large plate: *Ino and Athamas*. D: 44.5 cm. MIC, 7612. Zauli Naldi 1956, p. 123, pl. lxv.
REVERSE: *De Atama[n]te et Ino i[n]furiati/fabula* followed by the y/ Φ flourish.

56. Plate: *Narcissus and Echo*. Turin, Museo Civico. Mallé 1974, no. 34.
REVERSE: *Di Ecco i[n] saxo p[er] il crudo ama[n]te./fabula* followed by the y/Φ flourish.

57. Bowl with broad border (*Tondino*): *Two Cupids and a Dog*. D: 21.0 cm. Formerly Paul Gillet collection. Gillet Collection 1943, no. 117. Exhibited at the Biennale des Antiquaires, Paris, September 2006. 'Collection Paul Gillet', Lefebvre & Fils, p. 51.

58. Plate: *Hero and Leander*. Vienna, Kunsthistorisches Museum, Gemäldegalerie, H.E. 2733.
REVERSE: *Leandro i[n] mare; & Hero/alla finestra./historia* followed by the y/Φ flourish.

59. Bowl with broad border (*Tondino*): *Perseus with the Head of Medusa*. D: 27.0 cm. With Cyril Humphris in 1965.

60. Large Plate: *The Massacre of the Innocents*. D: 48.9 cm. CGA, William A. Clark Collection, 26.350. Watson 1986, no. 49.
REVERSE: *P[er] Cristo morse l innocenti i[n] infantia./* followed by the y/Φ flourish.

61. Bowl with broad border (*Tondino*): *Aeneas invoking the Aid of Aeolus, God of the Winds*. D: 27.5 cm. Formerly Berney collection; Sotheby's, London, 11 March 1980, lot 17.
REVERSE: in blue, *Gli feri venti ad Eulo ubidienti/fabula* followed by the y/Φ flourish.

62. Bowl with broad border (*Tondino*): an allegorical scene with a woman and a putto. D: 19.8 cm. CGA, William A. Clark Collection, 26.331.Watson 1986, no. 50.
REVERSE: *mech, moch./leggi* followed by the y/Φ flourish.

63. Plate: *Allegory of the Sack of Rome*. D: 29.3 cm. Private collection, Berlin. Hausmann 2002, no. 66.
REVERSE: *Roma prostrata fra/ lascivi et scalci. Nota* followed by the y/Φ flourish.

64. Bowl with broad border (*Tondino*): *Phrixus escaping on the Ram and sacrificing it to Mars at Colchis*. D: 26.9 cm. AM, Barlow loan, LI180.3. Mallet 2004, no. 18. This cat. 23.
REVERSE: in blue, *Come phrixo/ Sacrificho il mo[n]tone/ a marte/* followed by the y/Φ flourish.

65. Dish on low foot (*Coppa*): *The Judgement of Paris*. D: 27.3 cm. Formerly Sprovieri collection, Italy. Wilson 1996, no. 19.
REVERSE: *Sententia de Paris/* followed by the y/Φ flourish.

66. Fragments of a plate: *The Death of Laocoon and his Two Sons*. D: 27.7 cm. HAU-M, 963. Lessmann 1979, no. 140.
REVERSE: in blue, the incomplete inscription *Da e serpi lao.../ e, i figli mor[t]./ histo...* followed by the y/Φ flourish.

67. Plate: *The Death of Laocoon and his Two Sons*. D: 35.0 cm. Formerly HAU-M, 752. Lessmann 1979, Appendix I, no. V.
REVERSE: *Eccoti pi[n]to il fer' Laocoonte/ vibrar il hasta nel caval Troiano et due Serpenti, ognu[n] feroce et strano/ Tutto vorarlo co[n] lor voglie pro[n]te historia*

68. Dish on low foot (*Coppa*): *The Emperor Charles V in all'antica Armour with an Angel*. D: 27.6 cm. MADL, Damiron no. 1897. Fiocco et al. 2001, no. 151.
REVERSE: in dark blue, *Cerco la monarchia/per punir' molti./immaginationi* followed by the y/Φ flourish.

69. Plate: *The Last Combat of Cygnus, Son of Neptune*. D: 26.6 cm. MADL, Damiron no. 2022. Fiocco et al. 2001, no. 152.
REVERSE: *De Cygno i[n] cigno da Nep/tu[n] co[n]verso./ fabula* followed by the y/Φ flourish.

70. Bowl with broad border (*Tondino*): *Alpheus and Arethusa*. D: 25.7 cm. HAU-M, 255. Lessmann 1979, no. 142.
REVERSE: in blue, *Il sviscerato amor' del'/ fiume Al/pheo. / fabula* followed by the y/Φ flourish.

71. Dish on low foot (*Coppa*): *Aeneas, Anchises and Ascanius fleeing Troy*. D: 27.0 cm. HAU-M, 800. Lessmann 1979, no. 141.
REVERSE: in blue, *trass' il padre d'il fuoco/il pio Enea./ historia* followed by the y/Φ flourish.

72. Plate: *St Jerome and the Beato Colombini at Prayer*. D: 26.0 cm. GCC(M), 1893.93.b. Mallet 1988, p. 90, fig. 1. This cat. 31.

73. Plate: An allegory, an old man with a crescent with two putti carrying windmills. D: 20.0 cm. GCC(M), 1896.76.b. Mallet 1988, p. 92, figs. 2 and 2R. This cat. 27.
REVERSE: *Tich, Tach./ nota* followed by the y/Φ flourish.

74. Plate (*Tagliere*): *Hercules and the Hydra*. D: 29.0 cm. Formerly HAU-M, 1050. Lessmann 1979, Appendix I, no. IV.
REVERSE: *Hercule forte l'idra ucide a forza./ fabula*

75. Plate: *Danae and Perseus put out to Sea*. D: 41.3 cm. BM, P&E 1855, 12–1, 113. Wilson 1987, no. 71; Thornton and Wilson 2007, no. 156.
REVERSE: *De Danae/e/Perseo il fer' destino./o/fabula/o/historia* followed by the y/Φ flourish.

76. Plate: *Cupid escaping from Psyche*. D: 25.8 cm. BM, P&E 1855, 3–13, 13. Thornton and Wilson 2007, no. 158.
REVERSE: in blue, *Psiche segue Cupido/ et lui la fuggie./fabula* followed by the y/Φ flourish.

77. Bowl with broad border (*Tondino*): *The Story of Portia*. D: 26.5 cm. Sotheby's, London, 14 April 1981, lot 28.
REVERSE: *vedi Portia ch'il ferro al/ fuoco affina/, historia* followed by the y/Φ flourish.

78. Dish on low foot (*Coppa*): *Venus under attack from a Man with a Dagger while Two winged Putti walk away*. D: 25.9 cm. BM, P&E 1855, 12–1, 95. Wilson 1987, no. 72; Thornton and Wilson 2007, no. 157.
REVERSE: *"Vener' stratiata et il figliolo i[n] fuga. nota* followed by the y/Φ flourish.

79. Large plate: *The Death of Laocoon and his Two Sons*. D: 47.7 cm. HSM, Φ 373. Ivanova 2003, no. 42.
REVERSE: in black, *Co[n]templa exa[n]gue il fier' Laocoonte./historia* followed by the y/Φ flourish.

80. *c.* 1528–30. Plate with broad border (*Tondino*): *Vulcan forging an Arrow, watched by Venus and Cupid*. D: 25.5 cm. WAM, 48.1492. Prentice Von Erdberg and Ross 1952, no. 49.
REVERSE: in blue, *Vulcano* followed by the y/Φ flourish.

81. Large plate: *Aeneas, Anchises and Ascanius fleeing Troy*. D: 49.5 cm. Formerly Fountaine collection, now MMA, 27.97.27. Fountaine sale 1884, no. 209.
REVERSE: *Arde Troi' et Enea via'l padre porta./Historia* followed by the y/Φ flourish.

82. Bowl with broad border (*Tondino*): *Vulcan, Venus and Cupid*. D: 26.0 cm. MMA, 04.9.19.
REVERSE: *Vulcano alla fuci/na a botte batte./fabula* followed by the y/Φ flourish.

83. *c.* 1530. Plate (*Tondino*): *Leuchotoe being buried Alive*. Lustred. D: 27.3 cm. HSM, Φ 850. Ivanova 2003, no. 46.
REVERSE: *La vergine vestal/ Sottrata viva/ historia.* followed by the y/Φ flourish.

84. Plate: *Allegory of the Sack of Rome*. D: 26.3 cm. Formerly Sackler collection, present whereabouts unknown. Mallet 1988, nos. 13, 13R.
REVERSE: *Di Cleme[n]te al conspetto/ Roma la[n]gue./ nota* followed by the y/Φ flourish.

85. Dish on low foot (*Coppa*): *Ino and Athamas*. D: 26.5 cm. Private collection. Leonardi 1996, no. 31.
REVERSE: *Di Ino* (partly erased) *...Atama[n]te i[n]furi/ati./fa...la* followed by the y/Φ flourish.

86. Plate: *Allegory of the Triumph of Germany*. D: 26.6 cm. WC, C87. Norman 1976, no. C87. This cat. 29.

87. Plate: *Men fighting in a Classical Building*. D: 26.7 cm. HAU-M, 783. Lessmann 1979, no. 147.

88. Plate: *Vulcan, Cupid and Venus*. D: 30.3 cm. NGV, Felton Bequest, 3862.3. Mallet 1976, fig. 5.

89. Plate: *Men Fighting*. D: 27.0 cm. MB-AD, 1063. Barral 1987, no. 12.

90. Dish on low foot (*Coppa*): *Charity*. D: 26.3 cm. PL, POL/C/17. Mallet 1971A, no. 1. This cat. 22.

91. *c.* 1530. Plaque: *The Virgin and Child in the Sky surrounded by Angels playing Music*. Lustred. H: 20.5 cm; W: 26.0 cm. Fondazione Cassa di Risparmio di Perugia collection. Gardelli 1987, no. 29; Wilson and Sani 2007.

with arms *vert two pallets or, on a chief
of the second an eagle displayed sable, impaling or
an eagle displayed gules, c.1528–30*

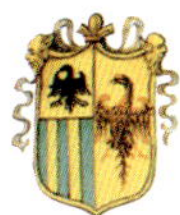

92. Plate: *Hercules and the Nemean Lion with St Veronica*.
D: 27.7 cm. Modena, Galleria Estense, 1993.
F. Liverani 1979, no. 8.
REVERSE: *Hercole che la pelle al leo[n] toglie/p[er] fare agli
humer'sui sup[er]be spoglie/sola vir:[tus]*
93. Plate: *Scylla and Galatea*. D: 26.0 cm. VAM, 2233-1910.
Rackham 1940, no. 635, pl. 100.
REVERSE: *Exorta Galathea silla ad amare fabula* followed
by the y/Φ flourish.
94. Dish on low foot (*Coppa*): *Aeneas, Anchises and Ascanius
fleeing Troy*. D: 26.0 cm. Cologne, Museum für
Angewandte Kunst, E1602. Klesse 1966, no. 309.
REVERSE: *Quest'e colui ch'a troia il/padre Anchise/Trasse d'il
fuoco, et dopo lo[n]go/ errore [errare]/Sotto la ripa Antantra
a/posar'mise./historia* followed by the y/Φ flourish.



with arms *azure an eagle displayed argent,
c.1528–30*

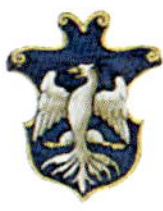

95. Plate: *Leda and the Swan*. D: 26.5 cm. Sotheby's, London,
11 March 1980, lot 18. Chompret 1949,
p. 190, fig. 970.
REVERSE: *Di Giove/i[n] Cigno per/ Amor cangiato/ fabula*
followed by the y/Φ flourish.
96. Plate: *The musical Contest of Apollo and Pan*. D: 29.8 cm.
LACMA. William Randolph Hearst Collection, 50.9.15.
Mallet 1988, p. 70, fig. 5.
REVERSE: *De Apollo & Pa[n] gli musicali/ acce[n]ti./fabula*
followed by the y/Φ flourish.
97. Plate: *Hercules and Cacus*. D: 30.0 cm. ML, OA 1513.
Giacomotti 1974, no. 872.
REVERSE: *Hercule Cacco co[n] gra[n] fretta uccide/ Sola vir:*

An additional piece from the set is attributed to
'The Milan Marsyas Painter'.



*azure, three crescents, addorsed, argent, c.1529–30*,
no. 98, of 1530, being the only dated piece

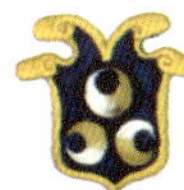

98. Plate: *Venus appears to Aeneas and Achates*. D: 25.8 cm.
MMA, Robert Lehman Collection, 1975.1.1136.
Rasmussen 1989, no. 76.
REVERSE: *Troianos q uagos/libicas expellit i[n]/oras./1530*
followed by the y/Φ flourish.
99. Plate: *The Burial of Leucothoe* (or *Rhea Silvia and King
Amulius*). D: 25.0 cm. Formerly Cottreau collection.
Cottreau sale, Paris, 28–29 April 1910, lot 8.

100. Plate: *Apollo and Daphne*. D: 26.0 cm. GCC(M),
1893.93.a. Mallet 1988, fig. 3, p. 92. This cat. 25.
REVERSE: *Apollo che sua Daph[ne]/segue et. ama./fabula et
hist:*
101. Plate: *Narcissus and Echo*. D: 26.8 cm. Chicago Art
Institute, 1937.848. Formerly Spitzer collection.
Molinier 1892, no. 49.
REVERSE: *P[er] Narcis'Ecco trasforma/ta i[n] saxo./ fabula*
followed by the y/Φ flourish.
102. Plate: *Diana and Actaeon*. D: 28.9 cm. AM, on loan from
a private collection. Rackham 1957, p. 109, pl. 54;
Wilson 1996, p. 188, no. 2.
REVERSE: *Dov'alsuo ama[n]te si/ Diana piacque./fabula*
followed by the y/Φ flourish.
103. Plate: *Ino and Athamas*. D: 26.5 cm. Present whereabouts unknown. Triolo 1996, no. 3A.6, fig. 13.
REVERSE: *De ino et Athama[n]te i[n]furiati. Fabula.*
104. Plate: *Leda and the Swan*. D: 26.0 cm. GM, G83.1.387.
Sotheby's, London, 14 April 1981, lot 29.
REVERSE: *Giove fece di Leda il ve[n]/tre pregno.: fabula*
followed by the y/Φ flourish.
105. Plate: *Phrixus and Helle*. D: 29.5 cm. Deaccessioned by
the Kunstgewerbemuseum, Cologne, 1931. Present
whereabouts unknown. Triolo 1996, no. 3A.8, fig. 15.
REVERSE: *De Elle Phrixo o del mo[n]ton d'l'oro fabula*
followed by the y/Φ flourish.
106. Plate: *Dedalus and Icarus*. D: 26.0 cm. Sotheby's,
London, 3 November 1970, lot 49.
REVERSE: *Dedalo ch'al gra[n] volo il figliuol perde. fabula*
107. Plate: *Cupid, Psyche and a River God*. D: 26.2 cm. PL,
POl/C/25. Mallet 1971A, pl. ii and 13.
REVERSE: *Sdegnato il bel Cupido co[n] sua Psiche./ fabula*
followed by the y/Φ flourish.
108. Bowl with broad border (*Tondino*): *Allegory of the Sack of
Rome*. D: 27.0 cm. PL, POl/C/18. Mallet 1971A, no. 4.
This cat. 28.
REVERSE: *Tybri avaritia co[n] las/civia aggiunti./nota*
followed by the y/Φ flourish.
109. Plate: *Allegory of the Sack of Rome*. D: 30.0 cm. Formerly
MIC, 9764, 1. Destroyed in World War II. Triolo 2001,
fig. 4a–b.
REVERSE: *Cleme[n]te i[n] Castell'chiu/ so & Roma la[n]gue./
nota* followed by the y/Φ flourish.
110. Plate (*Tagliere*): *Allegory of the Sack of Rome*. D: 27.0 cm.
Formerly Bohnewand collection. Vossilla 2002,
pp. 109–16.
REVERSE: *Dal fortunato Carlo Roma afflitta*
111. Bowl with broad border (*Tondino*): *A River God with
Cupid*. D: 19.7 cm. Formerly Arthur Sackler collection,
82.8.6. Christie's, New York, 13 January 1993, lot 24.
112. Bowl with broad border (Tondino): *A Man in a winged
Helmet chasing Cupid*. D: 19.3 cm. Formerly Sprovieri
collection. Wilson 1996, no. 84.
113. Plate: *Amphiaraus and Eriphile*. D: 26.0 cm. Formerly
Alexander Barker collection. Triolo 1996, no. 3A.15,
fig. 22.
114. Dish on low foot (*Coppa*): *Orpheus descending into Hades*.
D: 26. 7 cm. Achille Seillière sale, Paris, 5–10 May
1890, lot. 55.
REVERSE: *Orpheo sceso/nel' i[n]ferno/?*followed by the
y/Φ flourish.

Other pieces from the set, with the crescents
differently arranged, are attributed to 'The Milan
Marsyas Painter'.


## Signed pieces by Xanto, Urbino, 1530–42

115. *c*. 1527–30. Bowl with broad border (*Tondino*): *Dedalus
flying above with his Son falling behind him, a River God in the
Foreground*. Lustred. D: 26.7 cm. GM, G.83.1.0362.
REVERSE: *fran: Avello R: pi[nse]:/Dedalo; còl figliol i [n]Aere/
à volo./fabula* followed by the y/Φ flourish and lustre
scrolls.

116. *c*. 1530–32. Dish: *Apollo and the Muses on Mount Parnassus*.
D: 27.1 cm. KB, 32.48. Hausmann 1972, no. 193.
REVERSE: *fra[n]: xa[n]to, Avelli, R: pi[n]:/ Il radiante Apollo,
& l'alme Mu/se./ Sola virt:* followed by the y/Φ flourish.
117. *c*. 1530–32. Bowl with broad border (*Tondino*): *Jason
discovering that Medea has killed her Children*. D: 26.8 cm.
Formerly Hannaford collection, Sotheby's, Florence,
12 October 1969, lot 92.
REVERSE: *f.X.A.R./ del....udel Medea/ l'op...crudele/...ria*
followed by the y/Φ flourish.


### 1530

118. Pilgrim Flask: *Mercury conducting Psyche to Olympus* and
an unidentified scene of a man tossing a wineskin.
H: 36.5 cm. WAM, 48.1373. Prentice Von Erdberg and
Ross 1952, no. 51.
Inscribed in a cartouche on one side, *.F.A.R.* and on
the other side the date *M.D.XXX*
119. Bowl with broad border (*Tondino*): *Allegory of the New
Year*. D: 21.9 cm. MAACS, 232. Triolo 2000, no. 207.
REVERSE: *f.x.a.r./ i[n] Urbino./.1530.* on the front, on a
chariot, *M.D.XXXI*, maybe referring to the new year.


### 1531

120. Bowl with broad border (*Tondino*): *Mars and Venus*.
D: 25.4 cm. London, Ranger's House, English
Heritage, Wernher Foundation, 218–127. Wilson
2002C, fig. 9. This cat. 34.
REVERSE: *1531.Stan[n]osi i[n] pace Vene.../bella &
Marte./Spere./fra: Xa[n]to Ave: Ro/vigiese pi[nse]: i[n] Urbino*
121. Dish on low foot (*Coppa*): *St Jerome*. D: 27.5 cm. ML,
MR 2216. Giacomotti 1974, no. 848.
REVERSE: *1531/Specchio di penite[n]za honor d'il
clero/historia./Fra[n]cesco Xanto A. Rovigiese pi[nse] i[n]
Urbino.*
122. Plate (*Tagliere*): *St Jerome*. Lustred. D: 30.2 cm. HSM,
Φ 370. Kube 1976, no. 73.
REVERSE: in lustre, 1531 and scrolls; in blue, *Francesco
Xa[n]to Avelli rov:/ pi[n]/Specchio di penite[n]tia, hono/r dil
clero./historia* followed by the y/Φ flourish.
123. Bowl with broad border (*Tondino*): *Amphiaraus and
Eriphyle*. Lustred. D: 26.6. HSM, Φ 3078. Ivanova 2003,
no. 39.
REVERSE: with lustre scrolls that cover the signa-
ture, *1531./l'avara & rea moglier/ di Amphirao./ .historia./ Fra:
Xanto. Avl:/Rovigo in Urbino pin.*
124. Plate: *Amphiaraus and Eriphyle*. Lustred. D: 29.0 cm.
Brussels, Musées Royaux d'Art et d'Histoire, 2681.
Dumortier 2002, pl. lxvi, fig. 10.
REVERSE: *1531./L'Avara & rea mo/glier di
Amphiarao./.historia./ fra[n]: Xanto, Avelli/ Rovigiese, i[n]
Urbino/ pi[n]:* and lustred scrolls covering the
signature.
125. Plate: *Amphiaraus and Eriphyle*. Lustred. D: 29.3 cm.
Philadelphia Museum of Art. The Howard I. and
Janet H. Stein Collection. Watson 2001, no. 50.
REVERSE: *.1531./L'avara & rea moglier/di Amphiarao./
.historia./fra[n]cesco Xanto, Avelli/da Rovigo, i[n]
Urbino/pi[n]se.* and lustred scrolls covering the
signature.
126. Plate: *The Death of Cleopatra*. Lustred. D: 27.2 cm.
HSM, Φ 369. Ballardini 1938A, 22, 19.
REVERSE: in lustre, the date *1531*; in blue, *Fra[n]cesco
Xa[n]to Avelli/Rovigiese pi[n]se i[n] Urbino/Viss'Anton vivo, et
morì morto lui./Historia* followed by the y/Φ flourish and
lustred scrolls covering the signature.
127. Dish on low foot (*Coppa*): *Bacchus, Cupid and a Woman*.
D: 27.6 cm. KB, K 1771. Hausmann 1972, no. 194.
REVERSE: *.1531./Il vinole[n]te Bacco, & Sua malitia./ favola/
fra[n]: xa[n]to Ave:/ Rovigiese i[n] Urbi/ no.*

128. Bowl with broad border (*Tondino*): *The Legend of Romulus and Remus*. Lustred. D: 27.0 cm. Formerly Sprovieri collection, now private collection, Italy. Wilson 1996, no. 85.
    REVERSE: in blue, *.1531./Gli primi fo[n]dator' del'/alma Roma/historia./fra[n]: Xa[n]to Avello/Rovigiese i[n] Urbino/pi[n]se.* and lustred scrolls covering the signature.

129. Dish on low foot (*Coppa*): *The Judgement of Paris*, with arms of Eliseo Piani, *vert, a fess or, a chief party per pale gules* (shown as orange) *and argent two rosettes counterchanged* flanked by *Eli* and *PYA*. D: 26.0 cm. FM, C.86-1961. Poole 1995, no. 388. This cat. 33.
    REVERSE: *1531/Per cui Troia superba fu/combusta./Favola/Fra[n]cesco Xanto Avelli, da Rovigo, i[n] Urbino/Pi[n]se.*

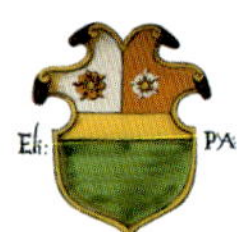

130. *c.* 1531. Cover (*Tagliere*) from an accouchement set: inside, *The Holy Family*.
    REVERSE: two putti holding the coat of arms of Eliseo Piani. D: 19.2 cm. FM, MAR.C.60-1912. Poole 2003, pl. Ia, b, as probably by Xanto.

131. Dish on low foot (*Coppa*): *The Musical Contest between Apollo and Pan*. D: 26.7 cm. FM, C.88-1961. Poole 1995, no. 390.
    REVERSE: *.1531./De Apollo & Pa[n] gli musi/cali acce[n]ti./.favola./fra[n] Xanto, Av: Ro/vigiese i[n] Urbino/pi[n]:*

132. Bowl with broad border (*Tondino*): *The Musical Contest between Apollo and Pan with Cupid*. D: 21.0 cm. Formerly Adda collection, now private collection, Italy. Gardelli 1987, no. 24.
    REVERSE: *f.X.A./i[n] Urbino./1531*

133. Plate: Unidentified subject with an old man with a bunch of flowers and a woman playing a lyre; above, Cupid flies with a wreath of flowers. D: 20.0 cm. VAM, 1865-1855. Rackham 1940, no. 630, pl. 99.
    REVERSE: in blue, *1531./F.X.A.R. i[n] Urbino*

134. Plate: *Pyramus and Thisbe*. D: 25.5 cm. VAM, 1780-1855. Rackham 1940, no. 631, pl. 99.
    REVERSE: *1531./Vidi piramo e Tisbe Isieme à l'ombra./historia.] Xanto av: Ro: i[n] Urbino pi[n]se]*

135. Bowl with broad border (*Tondino*): *Allegory of Good and Bad Fame*. D: 21.9 cm. MAACS, 231. Triolo 2000, no. 208.
    REVERSE: in blue, *f.X.A.R./i[n] Urbino/.1531.*

136. Bowl with broad border (*Tondino*): *Conversation with flying Putto with little Shield*. Lustred. Formerly Pietro Fassini collection. Ballardini 1953, figs. 2–3.
    REVERSE: *F.X.A.R. i[n] Urbino/1531*

137. Bowl with broad border (*Tondino*): *Allegory of Fame*. D: 25.5. Formerly Boulton collection, Sotheby's, London, 7 December 1965, lot 60. Ballardini 1938A, 17, 12.
    REVERSE: *.1531./Prostrato il vitio a'pie/ di Fama giace./Nota./fra[n]: Xanto.A.Ro/vigiese i[n] Urbino/p[i]:*

138. Large plate: *The Flooding of the Tiber*. D: 45.0 cm. MAACS, 125. Triolo 2000, no. 209.
    REVERSE: in blue, *.MDXXXI./Versando il Regal Tibro turbid'acque/ Nel trenta, e'l mar spi[n]gendo l'onde à terra,/ Roma sott'esse be[n] tre giorni giacque./ .historia./ fra[n]cesco Xanto Avelli da/ Rovigo pi[n]se i[n] Urbino*

139. Large plate: *Ruggiero on the Hippogriff*. D: 45.0 cm. LACMA, 49.26.3. Wilson 1990, no. 15.
    REVERSE: *.M.D.XXXI. sopra l'Hyppogripho/progenitor di sangue Este[n]se qual'è/ & sempre fù, d'ogni reo vitio schifo./ Nota./ Fra[n]: Xanto, Av: da/ Rovigo i[n] Urbino pi[n]se.*

140. Plate: *Leuchotoe being buried Alive*. Lustred. D: 28.0 cm. Sotheby's, London, 17 March 1982, lot. 40; private collection, Rome. Fiocco and Gherardi 1998, no. 16.

---

REVERSE: in black, *1531./La Vergine vestal/Sottratta viva./.historia./Fra: xa[n]nto, Ave:/Rovigiese, i[n] urb/ino pi:* and lustred scrolls covering the signature.

141. Plate: An allegory, a man with books and scrolls at his feet bowing before a woman to the right, Cupid in front of her holding out a wreath towards him, Mercury to the left. Lustred. Formerly Cook collection. Rackham 1904, no. 118. Exhibited by Galleria Bellini, Florence, at *Il Mostra –Mercato della ceramica d'antiquariato*, Faenza, 28 June–15 July 1962, pl. 2 in catalogue.
    REVERSE: *1531/Premiasi alfi[n] ciascu[n]/ seco[n]do il merto. Nota/fra[n]: Xanto da Rovigo i[n] Urbino pi[nse].* within lustre scrolls.

142. Plate: *Alpheus and Arethusa*. Lustred. D: 30.0 cm. Philadelphia Museum of Art, The Howard I. and Janet H. Stein Collection, 1943-1-3. Watson 2001, no. 17.
    REVERSE: in lustre, the date, *1531* and scrolls; in blue, *fra:[n] Xa[n]to, Avelli, R: pi:[nse]/Alpheo ama[n]te, & Arethusa i[n]/fuga./fabula* followed by the y/Φ flourish.

143. Pilgrim Flask: perhaps *The Dance of Numis* and *The Death of Psyche*. MC, 236. Petruzzellis-Scherer 1988, nos. 3–4. Around the neck of the flask, one cartouche with the initials: *F.X.A.R.*; another with the date: *M.D.XXXI*

144. *c.* 1531. Bowl with broad border (*Tondino*): *Aristaeus, Eurydice killed by a Snake and Orpheus*. D: 27.2 cm. MAACS, 138. Triolo 2000, no. 210.
    REVERSE: in blue, *fra[n]cesco Xa[n]to Ave:/ Rovigiese pi[n]se i[n] Urbino/ Euridice fuggir' vidi Aris/ teo./ fabu. Hist.*

145. *c.* 1531. Bowl with broad border (*Tondino*): *Daedalus and Talus*. D: 27.5 cm. MAACS, 217. Triolo 2000, no. 211.
    REVERSE: *fra[n]cesco Xa[n]to Avelli pi[nse]:/ i[n] Urbino./ Opra l'invidia i[n] Dedal' Xtu/ oso/ historia y/Φ flourish.*

146. *c.* 1531. Bowl with broad border (*Tondino*): *Allegory of the Four subdued Cities*. D: 27.5 cm. MAACS, 226. Triolo 2000, no. 212.
    REVERSE: in blue, *.fra[n]: Xa[n]: Avel:/ Rov: pi[nse]: i[n] urbi:/ Partenope, Fiore[n]za, Genua/ & Roma./ nota y/Φ* flourish.

147. *c.* 1531. Plate: *Allegory of the lost Fame of Rome*. D: 27.5 cm. MAACS, 142. Triolo 2000, no. 213.
    REVERSE: in blue, *Fra[n]cesco Xa[n]to Avelli da/ Rovigo pi[n]se./ Quella che gia' di Roma fò/ reina. Nota y/Φ* flourish.

---

THE 'HERCULES' SERVICE WITH ARMS *or, Hercules rending the Nemean Lion*, 1531–32

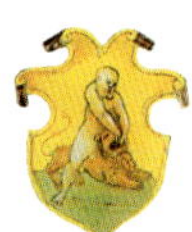

148. Plate: *Aeneas carrying Anchises from Troy, accompanied by Ascanius*. D: 25.9 cm. BM, P&E 1855, 12-I, 45. Wilson 1987, no. 73; Thornton and Wilson 2007, no. 160.
    REVERSE: *.1531./ Quest'è colui che pia[n]se sotto Antandro./ historia./ Fra[n]cesco/ Xanto, Avelli da/ Rovigo I[n] Urbino pi[n]se.*

149. Plate: *Pyramus and Thisbe*. D: 25.5 cm. VAM, 1780-1855. Rackham 1940, no. 631, pl. 99.
    REVERSE: *1531 Vidi piramo & Thisbe i[n]sieme à l'ombra. historia. fra[ncesco]:Xanto Av: Ro: i[n] Urbino pi[n]se:*

150. Plate: *Hercules and Cacus*. D: 26.0 cm. MIC, 11530. Ravanelli Guidotti 1990, no. 124b.
    REVERSE: *1531./Hercol che cacco ro/ batori ucide./viritù./fra Xanto Avelli/ da Rovi[go] i[n] Urbi[no] pi[nse].*

151. Plate: *Scylla and Charybdis*. D: 26.6 cm. Newcastle-on-Tyne, Hatton Gallery, University of Newcastle. Triolo 1996, no. 5.5, figs 38, 38a.
    REVERSE: *.1531./ Di Silla & di Carib/ di parlamenti./ .favola./ fra[ncesco]: Xa[n]to .A. Ro./ vigiese i[n] Urbino/ pi[nx]i[t].*

---

152. Bowl with broad border (*Tondino*): *Old man, young Woman and Cupid*. D: 20.0 cm. VAM, 1685-1855. Rachkam 1940, no. 630, pl. 99.
    REVERSE: *1531. F.X.A.R. i[n] Urbino.*

## 1532 (from above service)

153. Plate: *Amphiaraus and Eriphyle*. D: 25.9 cm. CGA, Clark Collection, 26.354. Watson 1986, no. 51.
    REVERSE: *1532/ Quell'avara moglie/ di Amphiarao / Nel VIIII L de Ovidio Meth:/ fra : Xanto A Rovi/giese, I Urbino/ pi :*

154. Plate: *Death of Calanus*. D: 27.0 cm. BM, P&E 1913, 12–20, 120, Barwell Bequest. Wilson 1987, no. 216; Thornton and Wilson 2007, no. 163.
    REVERSE: *.1532. Calano i[n] fuoco ad Ales/sandro disse: Nel cap: VI. D[e]I. L. I. di Vale/rio Mass:/ .fra[ncesco] Xanto .A./ da Rovigo, i[n]/Urbino pi[nse]:*
    On front: IO TI VEDRÓ DI CORTO

155. Plate: *The Death of Cleopatra*. D: 26.7 cm. MADL, Damiron no. 1901. Fiocco et al. 2001, no. 153.
    REVERSE: *1532./ Morto ch'Antonio/ fù morir vogl'io./ Nel XL. L. D[e] Trogo/ pompeio./ .fra[n]: Xa[n]to .A. da/ Rovigo. I[n] Urbino.*

## *c.* 1532 (from above service)

156. Plate (*Tondino*): *Two Goddesses and Mercury*. D: 20.0 cm. MIC, Fanfani Bequest, 24920. Ravanelli Guidotti 1990, cat. 124.

157. Bowl with broad border (*Tondino*): *Three Figures and Cupid*. Formerly Buckley collection, present whereabouts unknown. Triolo 1996, no. 5.10, fig. 43.

## 1532

158. Bowl with broad border (*Tondino*): *Hero and Leander*. Lustred. D: 25.5 cm. ML, MR 2219. Giacomotti 1974, no. 862.
    REVERSE: *1532.Lea[n]dro i[n] mare, & Hero a' la finestra./.Nel II. cap: d[e] amore dil .I. tri/u[m]pho d[e].M.F.P. com[m]entato./f. Xanto.A. da Rovigo, i[n] Ur/bino*

159. Plate: *Mars, Venus and Cupid*. Lustred. D: 26.2 cm. BM, P&E 1855, 3–13, 12. Wilson 1987, no. 75; Thornton and Wilson 2007, no. 164. This cat. 35.
    REVERSE: in blue, *.1532./ Marte tornato i[n] Ciel,/Vener[e] contempla./ Nel XXV canto dil Rovere/ vittorioso, di F.X.A.R. pittor./.fra[ncesco]:/ Xanto .A. da Rovigo,/ i[n] Urbino pi[nxit]* and lustred floral sprays.

160. Bowl with broad border (*Tondino*): *Saturn, Mercury and Jupiter*. Lustred. D: 25.8 cm. KB, K 1769. Hausmann 1972, no. 195.
    REVERSE: *.1532./ Qual nube al fur gli antiqui Iddei./ Nel [se?]/ fra[n]: Xanto. A. Da Rovigo, i[n] Urbino.* and lustred scrolls covering the signature.

161. Bowl with broad border (*Tondino*): *Bacchantes transformed into Trees*. Lustred. D: 26.5 cm. VAM, C.2204-1910. Rackham 1940, no. 723, pl. 114.
    REVERSE: in dark blue, *1532/ In Arbori co[n]verse le Baccanti./ Nel. XI L. d'ovidio Meth: Fr: X.A.R. i[n] Urbino* and rough leafy scrolls in lustre.

162. Plate: *Astolfo attacking the Harpies*. Lustred. D: 26.0 cm. VAM, C.2201-1910. Rackham 1940, no. 724, pl. 114.
    REVERSE: in dark blue, *1532/ Astolpho che l'Harpie persegue E scaccia./ Nel. XXX. Canto dil Furioso d. M.L. Ariosto. fra: Xanto. A. da Rovigo, i[n] Urbino pt:* and lustre scrolls.

163. Plate: *The Transformation of the Nymphs into the Echinades Islands*. Lustred. D: 25.9 cm. Formerly Pringsheim collection, now MMA, Robert Lehman Collection, 1975.I.II30. Rasmussen 1989, no. 81.
    REVERSE: *.1532./Echinade già Nimphe, hor/ Scogli i[n] mare./ Nel.IX.L.d[e]. Ovidi meth:/ fra[n]:xa[n]to.A.da/ Rovigo, i[n] urbi/ no.* and lustred scrolls covering the signature.

164. Dish on low foot (*Coppa*): *The Death of Laocoon and his two Sons*. Lustred. D: 26.0 cm. MMA, 1975.I.II29. Rasmussen 1989, no. 82.
REVERSE: *.1532./Da Serpi Laocoonte,e,i figli/uccisi, /Nel.II.de la Eneida d[e] Vigilio.M./.fra[n]: xanto.A./da Rovigo, i[n]/Urbino* and lustred scrolls covering the signature.

165. Bowl: *Aeneas and Anchises escaping from Troy*. Lustred. D: 26.5 cm. Formerly Caruso collection, Sotheby's, London, 20 March 1973, lot 37. Ballardini 1938A, 69, 66.
REVERSE: in blue, *1532/Enea col padre Anchise el figlio Ascanio/ Nel II/Li: d[e] L'Eneida d[i] /V/M/Fra[n] Xanto A da Rovigo i[n] Urbino*; in lustre, N and scrolls.

166. Bowl with broad border (*Tondino*): *The Story of Procne and Philomela*. D: 26.5 cm. Formerly Berney collection, Sotheby's, London, 14 April 1981, lot 27.
REVERSE: *1532/Di Progne & Philomela, & di Thereo/ Nel VI. Libro de Ovidio M:/.fra: Xanto A./Rovigiese, i[n]/Urbino*

167. Plate: *Hermaphroditus with the Nymph Salmacis*. St Louis Art Museum, 120:50. Detroit 1958, no. 108.
REVERSE: *.1532./Nel fo[r]te di Salma:/ce Hermafrodito./Nel IIII.L. d[e] ovidio Meth:/.fra[n]: Xanto .A. da Rovigo, i[n] Urbino.*

168. Plate: *Camilla's Rescue*. D: 26.5 cm. Formerly Adda collection, now private collection. Rackham 1959, no. 420, pl. 191a.
REVERSE: *.1532./Methabo oltr'Amasse/lancio' Camilla./Nel XI.Libro de l'Eneide../..fra:[n] Xanto./da Rovigo, i[n]/Urbino.*

169. Plate (*Tagliere*): *The Legend of Picus*. Lustred. D: 27.0 cm. Semenzato, Venice, 31 January 1993, lot 201. *CeramicAntica*, iii, 3, March 1993, p. 64.
REVERSE: *. 1532. Dil Sol' la figlia, &/Pico il porco trancia./Nel XIIII.Libro di' Ovidio Meth:/f.Xanto.A./Rovigiese, i[n] Urbino.*

170. Bowl with broad border (*Tondino*): *St Christopher*. D: 20.0 cm. Formerly Adda collection. Rackham 1959, no. 421, plate 192a.
REVERSE: *1532/i[n]Urbino.f.X.A.R.*

171. Bowl with broad border (*Tondino*): *The Descent of Orpheus into Hades*. Lustred. D: 26.5 cm. WC, C88. Norman 1976, no. C88. This cat. 38.
REVERSE: *.1532./Alla Caro[n]thea Cimba arri/va Orpheo/Nel..X.L. d[e] Ovidio Meth:/ .fra[n]: Xa[n]to. A/da Rovigo, i[n]/Urbino.* and scrolls covering the signature.



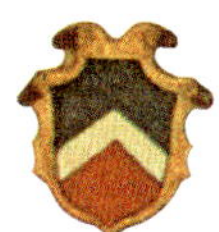

172. Large Plate: *The Abduction of Helen*. D: 48.0 cm. Private collection, Italy. Ballardini 1938A, 41, colour plate v.
REVERSE: *M.D.XXXII./Quest'è il pastor che mal mirò il bel volto/d'Helena greca,/e quel fumoso rupto/pcl qual fu 'l mondo sotto sopra volto./Nel. IX. Libro de Ovidio Methamor:/ Fra[n]: Xanto, Avelli da Rovigo, i[n] Urbino.*

173. c. 1532. Bowl with broad border (*Tondino*): *Aurora and Cephalus*. D: 20.0 cm. Pesaro, Museo Civico, C.A.S. 155. Giardini 1996, no. 113. This cat. figs. 22–23.
REVERSE: inscribed in a hand that is not Xanto's and is probably that of Nicola da Urbino, *de aurora e ciefallo* and perhaps an *M*

Other pieces of the set attributed to other painters.



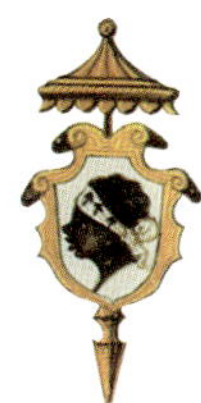

1532 (from above service)

174. Large plate: *The Hunt of Aeneas and his Companions*. D: 49.0 cm. Formerly Pringsheim and Strauss collections; private collection. Falke 1994, II, no. 261.
REVERSE: *M.D.XXXII./ In libia giunto Enea co[n] sette Navi/ co[n] li compagni tiro/ dal bosco al Lito/ Sette gra[ndi] cervi po[n]derosi & gravi./Nel. I. Libro della Eneida Xgiliana./ .F. Xa[n]to.A.R/ i[n] Urbino.*

175. Large plate: *The Decadence of Rome*. D: 38.0 cm. ML, 7588. Giacomotti 1974, no. 849.
REVERSE: *.M.D. XXXII./ Fiamma dal Ciel su le tue treccie piova/ malvagia, che dal fiume, & da le ghia[n]de/pe[r] laltrui impoverir se ricca & gra[n]de/ poi che di male oprar ta[n]to ti giova/ Nel C.XVI. Sonetto d[e] M.F. Petrarca./ .fra[n]: Xanto .A. da Rovigo. i[n]/Urbino.*

176. c. 1532. Large plate: *The Death of the Woman of Sestos*. D: 40.6 cm. MMA, The Friedsam Collection 1931, 32.100.378. Rasmussen 1989, Appendix I, no. 80.6.
REVERSE: *.M.D.XXXII/ A l'uso antico u[n] xgi[ne] corpo ard/e[n]do/ un'Aquila da quell nutrito, anch'ella//volse partecipar dil fuoco horre[n]do./ Nel .X. Libro d[e] Caio Plinio seco[n]do, al/Cap.: V./fra[n]: Xanto .A./ da Rovigo, i[n] Urbino.*

177. Plate: *Aeneas contemplates the Trojan Battles*. D: 27.3 cm. Knightshayes Court, Devon, The National Trust. Rasmussen 1989, Appendix I, no. 80.30.
REVERSE: *.1532./ Le battaglie Troiane Enea co[n]templa/nel .1. libro de l'Eneida. V./ F. Xanto A./ da Rovigo, i[n]/ Urbino.*

178. Triangular Salt Cellar: on the top three pairs of winged *putti* joined at the legs, holding a coat of arms. W: 15.7 cm. BM, P&E 1855, 12–1, 110. Wilson 1987, no. 74; Thornton and Wilson 2007, no 162. This cat. 37.
In the depression for the salt: *Fran: Xanto. A. Rovi*, on the sides in cartouches: *1532*.

179. Plate: *The Departure of Aeneas and Ascanius with the Celestial Flame*. D: 27.2 cm. Private collection, Italy. Rasmussen 1989, Appendix I, no. 80.23.
REVERSE: *1532/ Sovra Ascanio larde una/ Celeste fiamma./ Nel. II. Libro della Eneida .V./ fra[n]: Xanto A./ da Rovigo. i[n]/ Urbino.*

180. Plate: *Aeneas at the Tomb of Polydorus*. Lustred. D: 29.5 cm. MMA, Robert Lehman Collection, 1975.1.1131. Rasmussen 1989, no. 80.
REVERSE: within lustre scrolls that partly cover the signature, *.1532./ Enea, d[e] Polidor giunto/ al sepulcro. Nel .III. libro d[e] l'Eneida. V./ .fra[n]: Xanto .A./ da Rovigo, i[n]/ Urbino.*

181. Plate: *The Death of Palinurus*. D: 28.0 cm. LACMA, William Randolph Hearst Collection, 50.9.28. Rasmussen 1989, Appendix I, no. 80.24.
REVERSE: *.1532./ Palinuro nochier tra l'on/ de affoga./ nel. V. Libro de l'Eneida. V./. fra[n]; Xanto .A./ da Rovigo, i[n]/ Urbino*

182. Plate: *Camilla's Rescue*. D: 26.0 cm. Formerly Beit collection. Rasmussen 1989, Appendix I, no. 80.16.
REVERSE: *1532/ Al fiume d'Amassen'/Camilla, e'l padre./ nel .XI. lib: d[e] l'Eneida Virg:/ Fra[n]: Xanto/ A: da Rovigo i[n]/ Urbino.*

183. Plate: *Astolfo in the Land of Women*. D: 26.0 cm. BM, P&E 1913,12–20, 121. Wilson 1990, no. 20; Thornton and Wilson 2007, no. 161. This cat. 36.

184. Plate: *Orlando Finds Ruggiero's Charger Frontino, his Armour and Sword*. D: 26.5 cm. FM, C. 10-1953. Poole 1995, no. 392.
REVERSE: *.1532./ nel agitato Legno trova/ Orlando di Ruggier' l'armi/ Nel XXXVII. ca[n]to del furioso d[e]: M.L.Ariosto/ fra[n] Xa[n]to .A./ da Rovigo, i[n] Urbino.*

185. Plate: *Hero and Leander*. D: 26.3 cm. LACMA, William Randolph Hearst Collection, 50.9.14. Rasmussen 1989, Appendix I, no. 80.25.
REVERSE: *1532/ Lea[n]dro i[n] mare, & Hero alla finestra./ Nel. Libro d[e]:....../ f. Xa[n]to .A. da/ Rovigo, i[n]/ Urbino.*

186. Plate: *Apollo, Daphne and Cupid*. D: 26.6 cm. MMA, Robert Lehman Collection, 1975.1.1137. Rasmussen, 1989, no. 79.
REVERSE: *.1532./ Apoll, Daphne, e, Cupi/do e, l'arco, e Strali./ Nel .I. Li, de Ovidio Meth:/ .f.X.A. da/ Rovigo, i[n] Urbino.*

187. Plate: *Transformation of Cygnus and Phaeton's Sisters*. D: 26.9 cm. MMA, Robert Lehman Collection, 1975.1.1135. Rasmussen 1989, no. 78.
REVERSE: *.1532./ in Cigno e, i[n] olmi/ de Clymene i figli./ Nel II. L. d[e] Ovidio Met:/.fra[n]: Xa[n]to .A./ da Rovigo, i[n]/ Urbino.*

188. Plate: *Pyramus and Thisbe*. D: 28.7 cm. Boston, Museum of Fine Arts, Otis Norcross Fund, 1975.809. Triolo 1991, fig. 4, p. 45.
REVERSE: *1532/ Vedi Piramo e, Tisbe i[n] sieme à l'ombra/ Nel V: Libro d[e] Ovidio Meth./ f.X.A.R./ i[n]/ Urbino.*

189. Plate: *Perseus, Medusa and Pegasus*. Private collection. Rasmussen 1989, Appendix I, no. 80.18.
REVERSE: *1532/ Perseo. Medusa. e'l bel caval/ Pegaso/ Nel IIII. Libro d[e] Ovidio Meth:/ fra[n]: Xanto/ da Rovigo, i[n]/ Urbino.*

190. Plate: *Neptune raping the Nymph Basalis*. D: 26.3 cm. NGA, 1942.9.345 (C-70). Wilson 1993B, pp. 205–09.
REVERSE: *.1532/ Rape i[n] castro[n] Nettu[no]/ Basali nimpha/ Nel VI. Li: de Ovidio Met:/ fra[n]: Xanto A. / da Rovigo, i[n]/ Urbino.*

191. Plate: *Hercules and Cacus*. D: 25.7 cm. Formerly Pringsheim collection. Rasmussen 1989, Appendix I, no. 80.15.
REVERSE: *1532./ D'Hercule e Cacco e l'Aventino monte. / Nel VIIII. Libro de Ovidio Met: fra[n]: Xanto: A. Da Rovigo, i[n] Urbino.*

192. Plate: *Hercules and Lichas*. D: 29.1 cm. MMA, Rogers Fund 1904 (04.9.7). Rasmussen 1989, Appendix I, no. 80.7.
REVERSE: *1532/ Da hercol'Licha/ i[n] mar scagliat[o] à furia/ Nel VIIII. Libro d[e] Ovidio Met:/ fra[n] Xa[n]to A./ da Rovigo, i[n]/ Urbino.*

193. Plate: *Tydeus and Polynices*. D: 28.0 cm. GM, G83.1.0384. Rasmussen 1989, Appendix I, no. 80.26.
REVERSE: *.1532./ Thideo & Polynice i[n] sieme à fro[n]te./ VIIII. Libro de Ovidio Met./f.X.A./ Rovigiese i[n]/ Urbino.*

194. Plate: *The Vision of Alchmeon and the Matricide*. D: 25.7 cm. Private collection, Italy. Gardelli 1987, no. 26.
REVERSE: *.1532./ La moglie d'Amphia/ rao dal figlio uccisa/ Nel VIIII. Libro d[e] Ovidio M./ fra[n]: Xanto A./ da Rovigo, i[n] Urbino.*

195. Plate: *The Bacchantes turned into Oak Trees*. D: 26.0 cm. Formerly Harris collection, now PL, Pol/C/26. Mallet 1971A, figs. 7, 14.
REVERSE: *1532. Le Baccanti co[n]verse i[n]/ verdi frasche/ Nel XI libro d[e] Ovidio Meth: fra[n]: Xanto A./ da Rovigo, i[n]/ Urbino.*

196. Plate: *Aesacus and Hesperia*. D: 26.3 cm. Sotheby's, London, 18 October 1988, lot 256.
REVERSE: *1532./ Esaco i[n] smergo, & la/ sua Nimpha morta./ Nel XI. libro d[e] Ovidio meth:/ fra[n]: Xanto/ A. Da Rovigo/ i[n] Urbin/o.*

197. Plate: *King Anius' Daughters turned into Doves*. D: 26.4 cm. MMA, Robert Lehman Collection, no. 1975.1.1134. Rasmussen 1989, no. 77.
REVERSE: *.1532./ Dil Re Anio le figlie/ i[n] più Colombe/ Nel. XIII. L: d[e] Ovidio Met:/ fra: Xanto A./ da Rovigo, i[n] Urbino.*

198. Plate: *Scylla and Galatea*. D: 26.5 cm. Formerly
Pringsheim collection. Falke 1994, II, no. 263.
REVERSE: *.1532./A' Scylla parla Galath/ ea d'amore./
Nel XIII. Lib: d[e] Ovidio M./fra[n] Xa[n]to A./ da Rovigo,
i[n] Urbino*

199. Plate: *Ulysses and Circe*. D: 26.0 cm. FM, C.11-1953.
Poole 1995, no. 391.
REVERSE: *1532/ Ulisse chiede à Circe/ i suoi compagni/ Nel
XIIII Li d[e] Ovidio met:/fra[n]: Xanto A. Da Rovi[go], i[n]/
Urbin[o]*

200. Plate: *The Death of Calanus*. D: 25.5 cm. HSM, Φ 1709.
Ivanova 2003, no. 41.
REVERSE: *1532/ Calano ad Alessandro disse/ arde[n]do./
Nel I. Libro d[e] Valerio Massimo/ al Cap: VI/ fra[n]: Xanto A./
da Rovigo, i[n] Urbino.*

201. Plate: *Alexander the Great's Act of Piety*. D: 26.0 cm.
Pesaro, Altomani collection. Rasmussen 1989,
Appendix I, no. 80.19.
REVERSE: *1532. /Dil magno Re Alessandro/ un' pietoso atto.
Nel V. Libro de Valerio Mass./ al Cap: 1/ fra[n]: Xanto A/ da
Rovigo, i[n] Urbino.*

202. Plate: *The Sinking of the Fleet of Seleucus II*. D: 25.7 cm.
CGA, 26.361. Watson 1986, no. 52.
REVERSE: *1532/ La Classe di Seleuco i[n]/ mar' sommersa./
Nel XXVII. Libro d[e] Iustino Histo: / fra[n]: Xanto A. da Rovigo,
in Urbino.*

203. Bowl with broad border (*Tondino*): *A Man, the Muse of
Music and Cupid*. D: 19.0 cm. MIC, Fanfani Bequest.
Ravanelli Guidotti 1990, no. 125.
REVERSE: in blue, *1532/ f.X. A.R./ i[n] Urbino.*

204. Bowl with broad border (*Tondino*): *Soldier, Man and
Cupid*. D: 19.0 cm. Göteborg, Röhsska
Konstslöjdmuseet, RKM 65-47. Rasmussen 1989,
Appendix I, no. 80.21.
REVERSE: *1532/ f. X.A.R./ i.[n] Urbino*

205. Dish on low foot (*Coppa*): *Musical Contest with Cupid*.
D: 19.5 cm. Formerly Pringsheim and Adda
collections. Rackham 1959, no. 422.
REVERSE: *1532, f.X.A.R. i[n] Urbino*

206. Bowl with broad border (*Tondino*): *Two Figures in the
Clouds, with Cupid*. D: 19.2 cm. Cleveland, The
Cleveland Museum of Art, 42.625. Rasmussen 1989,
Appendix I, no. 80.31.
REVERSE: *1532/ F.X.A.R./ i[n] Urbino.*

207. Bowl with broad border (*Tondino*): *Two Figures in the
Clouds, with Cupid*. D: 19.1 cm. Cleveland, The
Cleveland Museum of Art, 42.626. Rasmussen 1989,
Appendix I, no. 80.32.
REVERSE: *1532/ F.X.A.R./ i[n] Urbino.*

208. Bowl with broad border (*Tondino*): *Two Figures and Cupid*.
D: 19.1 cm. Formerly Fountaine and Pringsheim
collections, present whereabouts unknown.
Rasmussen 1989, Appendix 1, no. 80.31.
REVERSE: *1532, f.X.A.R. i[n] Urbino.*


### 1533 (from above service)

209. Plate: *Juno changes Antigone into a Stork*. D: 25.9 cm.
MSA, 14586. Fuchs 1993, no. 145.
REVERSE: *1533/ Co[n]verte Giuno Antigo/ ne i[n] Cicogna/
Nel.VI. libro de Ovidio met:/fra[n]: Xanto A./ Rovig: i[n]/ Urbino.*

210. Plate: *Cynyras' Daughters turned into Temple Steps*.
D: 29.0 cm. Formerly Lindsay Fleming collection.
Rasmussen 1989, Appendix I, no. 80.27.
REVERSE: *1533. I[n] gradi d[e] Cynara/ le figliole/ Nel VI. libro
d[e] Ovidio Met./ fra[n]: Xa[n]to A./ Rovig: i[n]/ Urbino.*


### 1533

211. Plate (*Tagliere*): *The Death of Aesacus*. Lustred.
D: 27.0 cm. ML, MR 2218. Giacomotti 1974, no. 864.
REVERSE: elaborate lustre pattern and in blue,
*1533/Esaco vol morir'/morta sua donna/ Nel XI. Lib[ro] d[e]
Ovidio .M./.f.X..A.R./i[n] Urbino*

212. Dish on low foot (*Coppa*): *Ulysses and Circe*. D: 25.5 cm.
ML, 1509. Giacomotti 1974, no. 863.
REVERSE: *1533./Ulisse, chiede à Circe/ i sua compagni/.
Nel XIIII. Libro d[e] Ovidio .M./.fra[n]: Xanto .A./ Rovigiese
i[n]/Urbino*

213. Bowl with broad border (*Tondino*): *Romulus and Remus
suckled by the She-Wolf*. D: 26.5 cm. BM, P&E 1854, 2–13,
1. Wilson 1987, no. 76; Thornton and Wilson 2007,
no. 165. This cat. 43.
REVERSE: in lustre, foliate scrolls, an N in gold
lustre and, in blue, *1533./De Marte I figli/ alla pietosa
Lupa./Nel.XLIII. Lib: de Trogo po[m]peio./.fra[n].Xanto/.A.
da Rovigo/ i[n] Urbino*

214. Plate: *Polemon entering the School of Xenocrates*. Lustred.
D: 26.4 cm. WAM, 48.1362. Prentice Von Erdberg and
Ross 1952, no. 53.
Front, on a book: *Scola/ di/ Xeno/ crate/ phi:*.
REVERSE: floral scrolls in red and gold lustre that
cover the signature: *.1533/ Palemo[n] sciocco, al gra[n]/
Studio converso/ Nel VI libro d[e] Valerio Mass:/ al cap: ix./
fra[n] Xanto A./ da Rovigo, i[n]/ Urbino*

215. Broad-rimmed bowl (*Tondino*): *Amphiaraus and Eriphyle*.
D: 25.7 cm. BM, P&E 1855, 12–1, 53. Wilson 1987,
no. 77; Thornton and Wilson 2007, no. 166.
REVERSE: *.1533. L'avara, e, rea moglier di Amphiarao. Nel
.libro d Ovidio..F. Xa[n]to. A. Rovig: i[n] Urbino.*

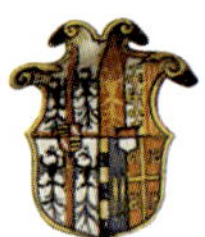

216. Large plate: *The Marriage of Ninus and Semiramis*,
with arms of Gonzaga-Paleologo of Montferrat.
D: 46.2 cm. VAM, 1748-1855. Rackham 1940, no. 632.
This cat. 40.
REVERSE: *M.D.XXXIII/ Hor vedi la magnanima Reina/
ch'una treccia rivolta, e, l'altra sparsa/ Corse alla, Babilonica
ruina./ nel I libro di Trogo Pompeio/ Fra[n]: Xa[n]to A./ da
Rovigo, i[n] Urbino.*

217. Dish on low foot (*Coppa*): *The Birth of Venus*. Lustred.
D: 30 cm. LACMA. William Randolph Hearst
Collection, 50.9.17.
REVERSE: *.1533./Dil terzo Cielo l'amo/rosa stella./.Nel. &
y/Φ ./Fra[n]: Xanto .A./da Rovigo, i[n]/Urbino.*

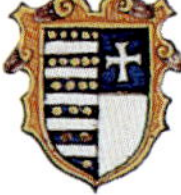

218. Large dish: *The Triumph of Neptune and Venus*, with arms
of Michiel-Gritti. D: 48.0 cm. WC, C89. Norman
1976, no. C89. This cat. 39.
REVERSE: four little leaves around the inscription,
*M.D.XXXIII/Triumpha qui Nettu[n] nelle salse onde,/ Su le
qual gode l'amorosa stella/ Ignuda frà suoi figli, e, vaga e, bella/
Vien Coronata de fioretti, e, fronde./ Fra[n]: Xanto A. da Rovigo
i[n]/ Urbino.*

219. Large plate: *The Battle of Roncevaux*. D: 43.4 cm. CGA,
26.356. Watson 1986, no. 53.
Front: on a banner *M./.Y./.X./.H./.Q.*, on a shield
*M D X/ XX/II/I*.
REVERSE: *M D XXXIII/ Arme, Co[?]tasti, guerre & gra battaglie / Dio no si truova i[n] terra altro che Marte / Co[?]i[?]gi,
saccomani, ombre, e bagaglie / Nel []so libro del Vescovo Turpino
/ o credi o no & y/Φ flourish/f X A/ Rovigiese i[n] / Urbino*

220. Broad-rimmed bowl (*Tondino*): *The Destruction of Seleucus
II's Fleet*. Lustred. D: 25.6 cm. MADL, Damiron
no. 1904. Fiocco et al. 2001, no. 154.
REVERSE: in dark blue, *.1533./ Seleuco sol della sua /
Classe selvo. / Nel.XXVII. Lite de Justino His : / .ff : Xanto. A. /
da Rovigo, i[n] [urbi]no*; in lustre, scrolls that cover
signature and F.P.

221. Plate: *The Destruction of Seleucus II's Fleet*. D: 28.6 cm.
FM, C.87-1961. Poole 1995, no. 393.
REVERSE: *.1533./Della sua Classe sol/Seleuco scampa. /
Nel .XXVII. Libro d[e] Iustino/Histo:/.f.X.A.R./i[n] Urbino*

222. Dish on low foot (*Coppa*): *The Crushing of Tarpeia by the
Sabines*. D: 29.5 cm. MSA, 14585. Fuchs 1993, no. 146.
REVERSE: *1533/Tarpea raccoglie del/ suo seme il frutto./nella
Deca de .T. Livio./ Fsco Xa[n]to/ da Rovigo/ Urbino*

223. Plate: *Deucalion and Pyrrha*. Lustred. D: 25.2 cm. MADL,
Damiron no. 1902. Fiocco et al. 2001, no. 155.
REVERSE: in blue, *.1533. / Pyrrha col sposo suo riempir/no il
mondo. / Nel. I. libro de Ovidio Meth:/ .fra[n] : Xanto. A. / da
Rovigo, i[n] Urbino*

224. Plate: *Actaeon changed into a Stag*. D: 26.0 cm. VAM,
1700–1855. Rackham 1940, no. 633, pl. 100.
REVERSE: in blue, *1533./ il misero Atho[n] converso i[n] cervo
Nel III. Libro de Ovidio. Me: /Fra[n]: Xa[n]to. A. da Rovigo, i[n]
Urbino*

225. Bowl with broad border (*Tondino*): *Actaeon changed into
a Stag*. Lustred. D: 26.0 cm. VAM, C.2206-1910.
Rackham 1940, no. 725, pl. 114. This cat. 45.
REVERSE: within lustre scrolls, *1533/Il misero Atteo[n]
co[n]verso i[n] cervo Nel. III: L. de Ovidio. M. fra[ncesco]: Xanto
A. da Rovigo i[n] Urbino*

226. Dish on low foot (*Coppa*): *Cephalus and Procris*. Lustred.
D: 28.6 cm. Formerly Fountaine collection, now
MMA, 27.97.41. Ballardini 1938A, 96, 90, 283R.
REVERSE: an E reversed and: *.1533. /inaveduto cephal/
procri uccide./Nel.VII. libro d[e] Ovidio Met/.fra[n]. Xanto. A./
Rovigiese. i[n]/ urbino*

227. Plate (*Tagliere*): *Camilla's Rescue*. D: 26.0 cm. ML, N 75.
Giacomotti 1974, no. 850.
REVERSE: in blue, *1533/il fortunato sca[m]po de Camilla nel
XI libro del Eneida V/Fra: Xa[n]to. A. da Rovigo. i[n] Urbino.*

228. Plate: *Narcissus*. Lustred. D: 26.0 cm. Formerly SB,
K1770, presumed destroyed during World War II.
Ballardini 1938A, 95, 89, 276R.
REVERSE: *.1533/ il vano amante di/ sua propia imago./
Nel III. Libro d[e] Ovidio met:/ fra[n]: Xa[n]to .A./ Rovigiese./
i[n] Urbino*

229. Dish on low foot (*Coppa*): *Mutius Scaevola burning his
Hand in the Presence of Lars Porsenna*. Lustred. D: 29.2 cm.
FM, C.12-1953. Poole 1995, no. 394.
REVERSE: *.1533./ Mucio che la sua des/tra erra[n]te cuoce./
Nella. Deca d[e] Tito livio/ Fra[n]: Xa[n]to .A./ da Rovigo/
i[n] Urbino and lustre scrolls.*

230. Dish on low foot (*Coppa*): *The Killing of the Ass*.
D: 26.5 cm. Hamburg, Museum für Kunst und
Gewerbe, 1907.138, 1907. Rasmussen 1984, no. 123.
REVERSE: *.1533./ La pelle serbarem' per/ far le scarpe./
Nel cy/?/ .F.X.A.R. i[n] Urbino*

231. Plate (*Tagliere*): *The Bacchantes turned into Oak Trees*.
D: 25.5 cm. MNCS, 4403. Giacomotti 1974, no. 851.
REVERSE: in blue, *.1533./Converse i[n] arboscelli/le
baccanti./Nel. . libro de Ovidio Met:/fra[n]: Xa[n]to .A./
Rovig: i[n]/ Urbino.*


### 1534

232. Plate (*Tagliere*): *The River God Alpheus and the Nymph
Arethusa*. Lustred. D: 25.7 cm. MMA, 1975.I.Io90.
Rasmussen 1989, no. 83.
REVERSE: within lustre scrolls, *.1534./ De Alpheo, e,
d'Arethusa/ il vano amore./.F.X.*

233. Bowl with broad border (*Tondino*): *Dionysus the Tyrant
(The Sword of Damocles)*. D: 25.5 cm. Sotheby's, London,
16 March 1976, lot 25. Private collection, Italy.
Gardelli 1987, no. 27.
REVERSE: *1534 Del tirannico fato di Dioniso Syragu/sano,
essempio. / F.X.*

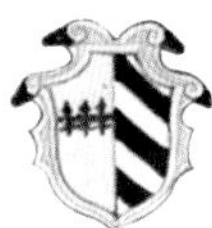

234. Dish on low foot: *Mutius Scaevola burning his Hand in the Presence of Lars Porsenna*, with unidentified arms, *or, three fleur-de-lys azure in fesse impaling bendy argent and sable*. D: 26.6 cm. NGV, Felton Bequest, 4673.3. Mallet 1976, p. 15, fig. 6.
    REVERSE: *.1534./ Mutio che la sua destra/ erra[n]te cuoce/ Fra[n]: Xa[n]to/ da Rovigo, i[n] Urbino.*
235. Plate: *Camilla's Rescue*. Lustred. D: 26.0 cm. 1534. Scott-Taggart 1972, p. 49; Sotheby's, London, 16 March 1976, lot 26. Now GM, G83.1.0363.
    REVERSE: *1534/Metabo oltre Amasse/lancio Camilla/Nel .XI libro de L'Eneida.x./Fra.Xa./a/Rovigiese i[n] Urbino*
236. Bowl with broad border (*Tondino*): *Camilla's Rescue*. D: 26.5 cm. MC, 214. Petruzzellis-Scherer 1988, no. 6.
    REVERSE: *.1534./il fortunato sca[m]po/ de Camilla./. F.X./i[n] Urb:*
237. Bowl with broad border (*Tondino*): *Camilla's Rescue*. D: 25.5 cm. MC, 243. Petruzzellis-Scherer 1988, no. 7.
    REVERSE: *1534./Methabo oltr'Amas/sen lancio' Camilla/ F.X./i[n]/Urb.*
238. Bowl with broad border (*Tondino*): *The Story of Procne and Philomela*. D: 25.5 cm. MC, 239. Petruzzellis-Scherer 1988, no. 5.
    REVERSE: *.1534./ De l'onta di The:/reo l'iniquo i[n]ditio./ .F.X.A.R./ i[n] Urbino*
239. Bowl with broad border (*Tondino*): *The Transformation of the Nymphs into the Echinades Islands*. D: 26.5 cm. MC, 246. Petruzzellis-Scherer 1988, no. 8.
    REVERSE: *.1534./L'Echinade i[n] Scogliet/ti fur converse/ /F.X./i[n] urb:*
240. Bowl with broad border (*Tondino*): *The Transformation of the Nymphs into the Echinades Islands*. D: 25.5 cm. MC, 245. Petruzzellis-Scherer 1988, no. 9.
    REVERSE: *1534/l'Echinade co[n]ve/rse in duri schogli./.F.X.*
241. Bowl with broad border (*Tondino*): *Aesacus and Hesperia*. D: 25.5 cm. MC, 242. Petruzzellis-Scherer 1988, no. 10.
    REVERSE: *1534./Cadendo Esaco si co[n]verse i[n] smergo./. F.X./i[n]/Urbino*
242. Bowl with broad border (*Tondino*): *Aesacus and Hesperia*. D: 25.5 cm. MC, 241. Petruzzellis-Scherer 1988, no. 11.
    REVERSE: *1534/Da l'alto sasso i[n]/ mar si getta Esaco/ F.X./ i[n] Urbino*
243. Bowl with broad border (*Tondino*): *The Wedding of Alexander and Roxana*. D: 25.5 cm. MC, 238. Petruzzellis-Scherer 1988, no. 13.
    REVERSE: *.1534./ Ecco la babilonica reina./F.X.A.R.*
244. Bowl with broad border (*Tondino*): *Leuchothoe being buried Alive*. D: 25.5 cm. MC, 240. Petruzzellis-Scherer 1988, no. 12.
    REVERSE: *.1534./Sottrata Leucotoe/dal padre viva./. F.X.A.R/i[n] Urbino.*
245. Bowl with broad border (*Tondino*): *Aeneas and Anchises in the Elysian Fields*. Lustred. D: 25.5 cm. MC, 247. Petruzzellis Scherer 1988, no. 14 (dating this piece 1535).
    REVERSE: *.1534.* (or possibly 1535) */pie[n] di letitia An/chise al figliol cor/re./.F.X./.R.*
246. Plate: *Charles V punishing Rome*. Lustred. D: 26.5 cm. HSM, Φ 3040. Kube 1976, no. 76; Ivanova 2003, no. 37.
    REVERSE: lustre scrolls and the letter N in lustre; in blue, *1534/Roma lasciva dal buo[n]/ Carlo quinto partita à/ mezzo./ fra[n].Xanto.A./ da Rovigo, i[n]./Urbino*
247. Plate: *The Death of Cleopatra*. D: 26.3 cm. HSM, Φ 3044. Ivanova 2003, no. 50.
    REVERSE: in blue, *1534/morto ch'Antonio fu ,/ morir vols'io/.F.X.A./.R./i[n] Urbino.*
248. Plate: *The Battle of Pavia*. D: 28.3 cm. BM, P&E 1855, 3–13, 11. Thornton and Wilson 2007, no. 167. This cat. 46.

REVERSE: in blue, *.1534./ Cadette il re Cristian[n]/sotto Pavia./.F.X.*
249. Large plate: *The Abduction of Helen*. D: 46.1 cm. Malibu, The J. Paul Getty Museum, 84.DE.118. Hess 2002, no. 29.
    REVERSE: *.M.D.XXXIII./Quest'é'l pastor che mal mirò'l bel/ volto/D'Helena Greca, e, quel famoso rapto/.Pel qual fu'l mondo sotto sopra volto./ .Fra[n]: Xa[n]to. A/ da Rovigo, i[n]/ Urbino.*
250. Large plate: *The Wedding of Alexander and Roxana*. Lustred. D: 47.5 cm. MMA, 18.129.2. Ballardini 1938A, 135, 129, 307R.
    REVERSE: written in blue in an elaborate lustred polygonal frame, *.M.D.XXXIIII./Hor vedi la magnanima Reina/ ch'una trama rivolta ,e, l'altra sparsa/ corse alla Babylonica ruina./.fra[n]: Xanto. A. da Rovigo .F./ Urbino.*
251. Plate (*Tagliere*): *Venus and Mars*. D: 26.5 cm. Formerly HAU-M, 644, presumed destroyed in World War II. Lessmann 1979, Appendix 1, no. vi.
    REVERSE: *.1534./ Gia fiammegiava l'a/morosa stella p[er] l'Oriente./.F.X.A.R /i[n]/Urbino*
252. Bowl with broad border (*Tondino*): Allegory: a soldier with a shield, a man walking away, an old man and a putto hiding his face in his hands. D: 25.8 cm. FM, C.82-1961. Poole 1995, no. 395.
    REVERSE: *.1534./Gia fiam[m]egiava l'/amorosa stella./.F.X.A.R./i[n]/Urbino*
253. Large plate: *Actaeon changed into a Stag*. D: 45.0 cm. Christie's, New York, 3 December 1973 and 3 October 1983. Ballardini 1938A, 151, 147.
    REVERSE: *.1534./Il misero Atheon converso/in Cervuo,/.F.X.*
254. Plate (*Tagliere*): *The Crushing of Tarpeia by the Sabines*. D: 26.0 cm. With Cyril Humphris in 1962; Peel & Humphris catalogue, 1962.
    REVERSE: signature and date 1534.
255. Plate: *Deucalion and Pyrrha*. D: 26.0 cm. Vienna, Österreichisches Museum für Kunst und Industrie (MAK), Ke 03598. Ballardini 1938A, 150, 145, 318R.
    REVERSE: *.1534./Deucalione ,e, Pirrha ,e,/ lor' buone opre./.F.X.*

## 1535

256. Dish on low foot (*Coppa*): *The Dream of Alcyone*. Lustred. D: 26.5 cm. ML, OA 2230. Giacomotti 1974, no. 865.
    REVERSE: *1535/D'Alcyone la visio[n] treme[n]da/ e vera/Fra[n]: X./R/*
257. Large plate: *Aeneas and Anchises in the Elysian Fields*. D: 41.8 cm. Formerly Leipzig, Kunstgewerbe-museum, 99.204, presumed destroyed in 1945. Ballardini 1938A, 193, 186, 348R.
    REVERSE: *.M.D.XXXV./Mostra suoi desce[n]denti Anchise al figlio/ ne i campi Elisi./ .F.X.*
258. Large plate in fragmentary state: *Aeneas and Anchises in the Elysian Fields*. D: 45.0 cm. ML, R 200. Giacomotti 1974, no. 853.
    REVERSE: *MDXXXV/Mostra suoi descendenti Anchise al figlio...Campi Elisi/F.X.*
259. Dish: *Cupid in the Guise of Ascanius conducted to Dido by Achates*. Lustred. D: 28.0 cm. VAM, C,479-1921. Rackham 1940, no. 726, pl. 115.
    REVERSE: in blue, within lustre scrolls, *1535/ Mena Achate i[n] Cartago Aschanio à Dido./F.X.R.*
260. Plate: *The Death of Palinurus*. Lustred. D: 28.0 cm. VAM, 272-1871. Rackham 1940, no. 727, pl. 115.
    REVERSE: in dark blue within lustre scrolls, *1535./ Rovina Palinur' dil mar nel fondo./Fra[n]: X.R.*
261. Bowl with broad border (*Tondino*): *The Death of Palinurus*. Lustred. D: 29.7 cm. Cincinnati, Taft Museum. McNab 1995, p. 531.
    REVERSE: lustre scrolls and, *1535/Rovina Palinur'nelle Sals'onde-F.Xa[n]to. R.*
262. Bowl with broad border (*Tondino*): *Hero and Leander*. Lustred. D: 25.5 cm. VAM, C.756-1925. Rackham 1940, no. 728, pl. 115.

REVERSE: in greenish black among lustred scrolls and an N in lustre, *1535/ Lea[n]dro i[n] mare e Ero alla finestra F.X.*
263. Dish on low foot (*Coppa*): *Glaucus and Scylla*. Lustred. D: 25.4 cm. WC, C91. Norman 1976, no. C91. This cat. 49.
    REVERSE: lustre scrolls and in black, *.1535./Scilla i[n] reo fo[n]te la[n]gue/e, Glauco i[n] pesce./Fra[n]: X/.R*
264. Plate (*Tagliere*): *Pyramus and Thisbe*. D: 26.5 cm. MCMB, 977. Ravanelli Guidotti 1985, no. 96.
    REVERSE: *.1535./Vedi piramo, e, Tisbe/ i[n]sieme à l'ombra./Fra[n]: X./.R.*
265. Large plate: *The Abduction of Helen*. D: 44.0 cm. Formerly SB, 1767, presumed destroyed during World War II. Ballardini 1938A, 191, 183, 349R.
    REVERSE: *.M.D.X.X.X.V/ Ecco 'l Pastor che mal mirò 'l bel volto/D'Helena greca/ ond'uscir gra[n] tempeste / E, funne il mo[n]do sotto sopra volto./.F.X.*
266. Large plate: *The Abduction of Helen*. D: 47.0 cm. Formerly Pringsheim collection. Falke 1994, II, no. 267.
    REVERSE: *.M.D.XXXV./Helena vedi per cui ta[n]to reo/ tempo si volse/ .F.X.*
267. Plate (*Tagliere*): *The Vestal Tuccia carrying Water in a Sieve to the Temple of Vesta*. Lustred. D: 27.5 cm. Private collection, Berlin. Hausmann 2002, no. 67.
    REVERSE: within gold lustre scrolls, *.1535./Tutia l'acqua portò/ col cribro al Tempio./.F.Xa[n]:/.R.*
268. Dish: *The Story of Portia*. D: 24.5 cm. Phillips, London, 17 September 1997, lot 46 (perhaps in collaboration with 'Lu Ur').
    REVERSE: *.1535./Vidi Portia del ferro al fumo affina./.F.X..R.*
269. Bowl with broad border (*Tondino*): *The Martyrdom of Saint Catherine*. D: 25.8 cm. Ecouen, Musée de la Renaissance, 2344. Giacomotti 1974, no. 852.
    REVERSE: *1535/La vergi[n] Catherina/ al gra[n] martirio./.F.X.*
270. Plate: *Narcissus and Echo*. D: 30.0 cm. BVBM, B19 (NK 2954), on loan from Institute Collection Netherlands, The Hague. Boymans Van Beuningen Museum 1994, p. 210.
    REVERSE: *1535.Echo cham[b]iado in duro sasso fosti F.X.*
271. Plate: *The Dream of Astyages*. Lustred. D: 26.0 cm. Formerly Parpart collection. New York, 10–12 April 1930, lot 610 (The Estate of Mrs. Havemeyer, part II, illustrated).
    REVERSE: *1535./Dil vecchio Astiage Re l'alta/visione/F.X.R.*
272. Fragment of a plate: *The Dream of Astyages*. Lustred. D: *c.* 27 cm. Excavated in the courtyard of the Palazzo della Cancelleria in Rome. Palmer 1991.
    REVERSE: signed and dated 1535.
273. *c.* 1535. Fragment of plate: *The Death of Palinurus*. Lustred. D: *c.* 27 cm. Excavated in the courtyard of the Palazzo della Cancelleria in Rome. Triolo 1996, pp. 136–37 and p. 151, note 3.
    REVERSE: signed, rest of inscription missing
274. *c.* 1535. Salt: *Flying Cupids*. H. 5.7 cm. KB, K 2115. Hausmann 1972, no. 198.
    On the depression for the salt: F.X.
275. *c.* 1535. Plaque: *The Flight of Aeneas and the Death of Creusa*. H. 30.2 cm; w. 27.6 cm. HAU-M, 1046. Lessmann 1979, no. 143 (unsigned).
    On front: on bottom right, *Questo è colui/ che pianse sotto / Antandro/ La morte di Cre/ usa. e* followed by the y/Φ flourish.
276. *c.* 1535. Fragment of a plate (*Tondino*): *The Burial of Leucothoe*. MIC, Paolo Mereghi Bequest. Ravanelli Guidotti 1994B.

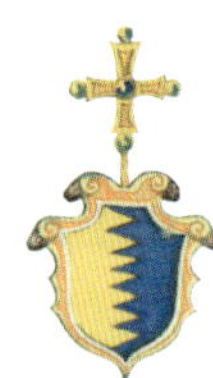

277. Bowl with broad border (*Tondino*): *Allegory of Prudence*. Lustred. D: 18.7 cm. AM, Fortnum collection, WA 1899. CDEF.C446. Wilson 1995, pp. 50–51, figs. 8a–8b.
REVERSE: *.1535./Quel' é prude[n]te [p]e c'hor [h]a piu for/[z]a/F.X.*
278. Bowl with broad border (*Tondino*): *Allegory of Disaster*. D: 18.5 cm. BM, P&E 1878, 12–30, 403. Wilson 1987, no. 200; Thornton and Wilson 2007, no. 168.
REVERSE: *.1535.Qua[n]to rovina al fi[n] chi troppo sforzasi .X.*
279. Plate: *Jupiter and Dionysus, Tyrant of Syracuse*. Lustred. D: 28.0 cm. Turin, private collection. Wilson 1996, p. 200, fig. c.
REVERSE: N in lustre and in blue, *1535/F.X.R*
280. Plate: *Theseus entering the Labyrinth*. D: 25.1 cm. Formerly Sprovieri collection. Wilson 1996, no. 87.
REVERSE: inscribed in blue, *1535/Theseo nel Laberi[n]to animoso e[n]tra/ .F.X.*
281. Plate: *The Vision of Alcyone*. D: 25.4 cm. MMA, 52.192.3. Triolo 2002, fig. 6.
REVERSE: *1535/D'Alcyone la visio[n] tre/ me[n]da, e, vera/F.X.*
282. Bowl with broad border (*Tondino*): *Polyphemus, Acis and Galatea*. Lustred. D: 25.3 cm. HSM, Φ 826. Ivanova 2003, no. 44.
REVERSE: *1535. Muore Aci e in fiume Galatea si cangia F.X.*
283. Plate: *Judith and Holofernes*. Lustred. D: 25.0 cm. Formerly SB, Lg 272. Destroyed in World War II. Wilson 1996, p. 200, fig. f.
REVERSE: *1535./Iudit Hebrea la saggia ,e,/ casta. E, forte./F.X.*
284. Plate: *Aeneas, Anchises, Creusa and Ascanius with the miraculous Flame*. Lustred. D: 27.5 cm. VAM, C.29-1943. Wilson 1996, no. 1, p. 200, fig. b.
REVERSE: *.1535./Anchise, Enea Creusa/ e Ascanio figlio./F.X.*

## 1536

285. Plaque: *The Dream of Astyages*. H: 30.0 cm; w: 27.5 cm. Formerly HAU-M. Lessmann 2004, no. 1.
On the front: ASTIAGE RE and ASIA. On a tablet on top right corner; *De Astyage Re' di Media il / sogno grave. De iustino/ historico nel libro primo/ 1536 .no 1*. Bottom left, F.X.
286. *c.* 1536. Plaque: *The Birth and Exposure of Cyrus*. H: 30.0 cm; w: 27.5 cm. Formerly HAU-M, lost during World War II and later found in a fragmentary state at KB. Lessmann 2004, no. 2.
On the front: ASTIA/GE and ARPAG;
in a roundel: *Astiage Re die/de il parto della figliuola ad Arpago/ suo secretario che /l'uccidesse/ no. 2*.
At the base of a plinth:
F.X.R.
287. *c.* 1536. Plaque: *The Infant Cyrus found by a Shepherd*. H: 30.0 cm; w: 27.8 cm. ML, OA 9028. Giacomotti 1974, no. 854, Lessmann 2004, no. 3.
On the pavement of the stable: *Mosso il pasto/re dil Re Astia/ge a pieta racco/lse il gettato/parto e quello element...come padre. n. 3*. At the base of the fireplace: F.X.R.
288. *c.* 1536. Plaque: *The Wife of the Shepherd abandons her own Child and adopts the little Cyrus* (?). H: 31.75; w: 28.6 cm. Formerly Fountaine collection. Lessmann 2004, no. 4. Signature, date and number unknown, possibly no. 4 of series.

289. Plaque: *Cyrus proclaimed King by the Children of the Village*. H: 30.0 cm; w: 30 cm. ML, OA 9029. Giacomotti 1974, no. 855.
On panel at base: *Fan[n]o e familli[i fanciulli]/ Re Ciro gioca[n]do ond'hebbe Il Reger'suo pote[n]te augurio come Troge'l descrive e dove e qua[n]do* On a pedestal: *1536/i[n] Urbino/no. 5*. On a plinth: F.X.R.
290. *c.* 1536. Plaque: *Cyrus recognized by Astyages as his Grandson*. H: 30.2 cm; w: 27.6 cm. HAU-M, 1049. Lessmann 2004, no. 6.
On the front, at the bottom: *Ciro accusato, e, Fa[n]ciullo Anchora Dil suo superbo oprar, na[n]t'[dinanzi] al Ré Astiage Ond' ei rispose altier, qual vedete hora. no. 6*. On the base of the throne: F.X.R.
291. *c.* 1536. Plaque: *The Feast of Cyrus at Persepolis*. H: 31.7 cm; w: 28.6 cm. Formerly Fountaine collection. Lessmann 2004, no. 7. Date and number unknown.
On the lower edge: F.X.R.
292. Plaque: *Cyrus at the Conquest of Babylon*. H: 27.6 cm; w: 30.2 cm. HAU-M, 1050. Lessmann 2004, no. 8 (unsigned).
On the front, on a tablet: *Ciro espugna[n]do Babilonia punto / Creso gran Ré di Lydia lasciò ch'era / Per soccorrere tal terra armata giunto. / Nel .I. libro de Iustino historico . no. 13*.
On a shield the date: *1536*
293. *c.* 1536. Plaque: *The Capture of the King of the Lydians, Croesus*. H: 30.6; w: 27.6 cm. SF-P-M, VII 1894 Kc. Lessmann 2004, no. 9.
On the bottom, on a strip: *Eccoti preso d'ogni sperme ignudo il [Ré] di Lidia, manifesto ese[m]pio, Che puoco v... contra Fortuna...and nº 14*. Signed in red in foreground, on the left: *Fra[n]cesco/ Xanto/ da/ Rovigo/* and on the right: *i[n] urbino*
294. *c.* 1536. Plaque: *The Looting of the Horses and Arms of the Lydians by Cyrus' Army*. H: 30.5 cm; w: 27.6 cm. SF-P-M, VII 1894 Kd. Lessmann 2004, no. 10 (unsigned).
On the front, to the right: *Cirro Lydia spoglió/ d'armi, e, cavalli./ n° 15. Quelle: Justinus I, 7, 11*.
295. *c.* 1536. Plaque: *The Death of Cambyses, the Murder of Smerdis and the Coronation of Horopastes as the King of Persia*. H: 30.5 cm; w: 27.6 cm. Formerly Sprovieri collection. Wilson 1996, no. 89; Lessmann 2004, no. 11 (unsigned, possibly with assistance from 'Lu Ur').
On the bottom, on a strip: *Di Gambise, e, Horopaste i brutti essempii Successi i[n] Persia, e, da Iusti[n] narrati. no. 19*
296. *c.* 1536. Plaque: *Darius and the Conspirators swearing to kill Horopastes, the False King of Persia*. H: 30.0 cm; w: 28.2 cm. Warsaw, Narodowe Museum. Lessmann 2004, no. 12.
On the front: *.DARIO., .ORTANO. F.X.*
297. Plaque: *The Assassination of Horospastes*. H: 30.5 cm; w: 27.6 cm. SF-P-M, VII 1894 Ke. Lessmann 2004, no. 13.
On the front, on a strip: *Gli sette congiurati di Persia uc[ci] dono Horopaste loro fittitio Ré. 1536. i[n] Urbino. F.X.R. no. 22*
298. Plaque: *The Marriage of Darius the Great with the Daughter of Cyrus*. H: 30.4 cm; w: 27.7 cm. Private collection, Italy. Lessmann 2004, no. 22.
On the front, on a scroll: *Eletto che fu Ré, p[er] gra[n] fortuna, Di Persia il primo Dario. Toll' p. Donna Di Ciro la figliola, tuer sol/ n. 25* and above: *DARIO R.P.* On the side: F.X.R.
299. *c.* 1536. Plaque: *Gobrius and Darius*. H: 30.4 cm; w: 27.2 cm. Formerly Sprovieri collection. Wilson 1996, no. 90 (perhaps with assistance from 'Lu Ur').
On a plinth, the inscription: *Rivela Go/brio sua i[n]te[n]/tione à Da/rio. Iust: hist:/ i[n] lib:.I. d[e/] bellis extern/is* On a plinth on the right: *.n. 26*. On a step at the left edge, the signature: *.F.X.R.*
300. *c.* 1536. Plaque: *Gobrius fleeing from Darius*. H: 30.3 cm; w: 27.6 cm. SF-P-M, VII 1894 Kb. Lessmann 2004, no. 15.
On front: *DARIO RE* and *GOBRIO*. *nº 28*. Signed on the right handside corner: F.X.R.
301. Plaque: *Themistocles and the Ionians*. H: 30.3 cm; w: 27.6 cm. SF-P-M, VII 1894 Kh. Lessmann 2004, no. 18.

On a block in the foreground: *O Ionii ch[e]/ material vi/ muove che,/l Iustino historico ne/l libro seco[n]do d[ei] bellis / externis* On a step in the foreground: *1536/F.X.*
302. Plaque: *Xerxes and his Soldiers defiling the Temple of Apollo at Delphi*. H: 30.0 cm; w: 27.5 cm. Warsaw, Narodowe Museum. Lessmann 2004, no. 19.
On a tablet at the front: *Xerse mando/ à Delpho à gua/stare il tempio/ d'Apollo.no 34./.1536 /F.X.R./ TEMPLU[M] APOLONIS*
303. *c.* 1536. Plaque: *Themistocles against Maradonius*. H: 30.4 cm; w: 28 cm. SF-P-M, VII 1894 Kg. Lessmann 2004, no. 20.
Signed on *a shield*: F.X./R. In the foreground: *Mardonio fu i[n] Boetia, e, rotto, e, vinto. nº 39/ i[n] Urbino*
304. *c.* 1536. Plaque: *The Escape of Xerxes*. H: 30.4 cm; w: 27.6 cm. SF-P-M, VII 1894 Kf. Lessmann 2004, no. 21 (unsigned).
On a strip of wood: *Fuggie Xerse pauroso i[n] picciol legno. Iust: hist: libr: II de bellis externis*
305. *c.* 1536–38. Plaque: *The Combat between Achilles and Hector*. H: 27.6; w: 30.2 cm. HSM, Φ 858. Ivanova 2003, no. 48 (unsigned).
On front: *HECTOR* and *PA[N]TASILEA* and at the bottom *Passa[n]do Hechtorre il bel fiume di XA[N]TO Fu dal superbo Achill' per forza ucciso &..* followed by the y/Φ flourish.
306. *c.* 1536. Plaque: *Sinon before Priam*. H: 30.3 cm; w: 27.7 cm. BM, P&E 1906, 12–10, 1. Wilson 1987, no. 215; Thornton and Wilson 2007, no. 159. This cat. 51 (unsigned).
On a brown strip at the base in brown-black: *[Trad]itor Sino[n] da Pastor molti Uie[n] preso. E'l falso alfi co[n] parla...[in]ganna*
307. Plate (*Tagliere*): *The Dream of Astyages*. D: 26.5 cm. MCMB, 979. Ravanelli Guidotti 1985, no. 97.
Front: *Cirus*, and *ASTA/GES/.M.R.*
REVERSE: in blue, *.1536./D'Astiage Rè di Me/dia il sogno grave./Fra[n]:X./.R.*
308. Bowl with broad border (*Tondino*): *Aesacus and Hesperia*. D: 26.3 cm. MCMB, 978. Ravanelli Guidotti 1985, no. 98.
REVERSE: *.1536/A' volo[n]taria morte/Esaco corre./F.X./Ro:*
309. Bowl with broad border (*Tondino*): *Pyramus and Thisbe*. D: 26.1 cm. CGA, 26.360. Watson 1986, no. 54.
REVERSE: *1536 /Vedi piramo, e, Tisbe/i[n]sieme a l'ombra /F X / Rovi:*
310. Plate: *Dionysus the Tyrant (The Sword of Damocles)*. Lustred. D: 24.4 cm. MADL, Damiron no. 1900. Fiocco et al. 2001, no. 156.
REVERSE: in dark blue, *1536./L'inquieta vita dil /Tira[nno] Dionigi. / .F.Xa[nto] : /.R.*
311. Plate: *Allegory of the Discords of Italy*. D: 26.0 cm. VAM, 1698-1855. Rackham 1940, no. 636, pl. 100. This cat. 50.
REVERSE: in black, *1536/ Di tua discordia Italia il premio hor hai./F: co./X /Rov:*
312. Dish on low foot (*Coppa*): *The States governed by Saturn*. Lustred. D: 25.9 cm. Cincinnati, Taft Museum. McNab 1995, pp. 533–34.
REVERSE: *.1536./Sotto la fredda stella di/ Saturno. /FX. /.RO:*
313. Plate: *Hercules and Cerberus*. Brescia, Museo Civico. Ravanelli Guidotti 1988, figs. 5a–b.
REVERSE: *.1536./Contra'l trifauce Ca[n] Hercol/ possente./.F.X./.R.*
314. Plate: *Isaac and Esau*. D: 36.5 cm. Paris, private collection. Conti 1992, p. 53.
REVERSE: signed and dated 1536.
315. 1536. Plate: *Demeratus, King of Sparta warning his Subjects of the Hostile Plans of Xerxes* (possibly with 'Lu Ur'). D: 34.0 cm. Formerly Adda collection. Rackham 1959, no. 423, pl. 190a.
REVERSE: *1536 Demato avisa suoi Spartani chome controlar/ sarma il foribondo Xerse p[er] torli larmi elstato elchiaro nome*
316. Plate: *An old man wounded on the floor, a standing warrior with a sword, Fame and Cupid*. Lustred. D: 26.0 cm. Castellani sale, Rome, 31 March 1884, lot 35.

REVERSE: *1536./Tal atto imita chi vuol pregio in armi* and 'le sigle de l'artiste'.

317. Dish on low foot (*Coppa*): *The Entombment*. Lustred. D: 27.3 cm. Formerly Lord Amherst of Hackney. Christie's, London, 11 December 1908, lot 6. Now MMA, 27.97.30.
REVERSE: */Ite superbi e miseri Christia/ni/ Consumando l'un l'altro, e, non/ vi caglia/ che'l sepulcro di Cristo/ è in man dei Cani/ F.X./ Rovi:/1536*

### 1537

318. Large plate: *The Abduction of Helen*. D: 46.0 cm. Formerly Octavius Coope collection, Christie's, London, 3 May 1910, lot 38.
On front on a tablet: *RAPTUS HELENAE*
REVERSE: *1537.Quest' e 'l Pastor che mal miro 'l bell' volto/d'Helena greca, e, quel famoso ratto Pel qual fu 'l mo[n]do sotto sopra volto/Fra[n] X.R.*

319. Large plate: *The Abduction of Helen*. D: 44.0 cm. ML, OA 1847. Giacomotti 1974, no. 856.
REVERSE: *M.D. XXXVII./Quest' e 'l Pastor che mal miro'l bell'volto/D'Helena Greca, e quel famoso rapto/Pel qual f[u] el mo[n]do sotto sopra volto/fra[n]: Xanto/Rovigiese*

320. Plate: *Grifone fighting with the People of Damascus*. D: 27.5 cm. Formerly Castellani and Pringsheim collections. Falke 1994, III, no. 394 (363).
REVERSE: *1537/Solo Griphon[n] co[n]tra Damasco tutto/F.X.R.*

321. Bowl with broad border (*Tondino*): *Aeneas and Anchises in the Elysian Fields*. D: 25.8 cm. HAU-M, 968. Lessmann 1979, no. 146.
REVERSE: in dark blue, *.1537. / Nei ca[m]pi Elisi il pio Troiano, e'l padre./ F.X./R.*

322. Plaque: *The Adoration of the Shepherds*. H: 34.0 cm; W: 29.0 cm. Pesaro, Museo delle Ceramiche. Giardini 1996, no. xxvii, pl. 214.
On a plinth column the date *.M./D./XXX/V/II*, on the base of the column: *.F.X.R.*

323. Large plate: *The Retreat of Xerxes*. D: 40.5 cm. AM, WA 1888.CDEF.C448. Wilson 2003A, no. 16.
On the boat: *.XERSES.PERSA [RUM].REX.*
REVERSE: *.1537./Fuggie Xerse pauroso i[n] picciol Legno/ Solcando il mar d'Abido tremebo[n]do/No[n] gli reusce[n]do i[n] armi il suo disegno/ .F.X./.R.*

324. Plate (*Tagliere*): *The Retreat of Xerxes*. D: 25.5 cm. Formerly Pringsheim collection. Sotheby's, London, 21 November 1977, lot 18. Falke 1994, III, no. 395 (365).
REVERSE: *.1537./Fuggie 'l superbo Ré/ le greche astutie./.F.X./R.*

325. Plate: *Hero and Leander*. D: 26.3 cm. Modena, Galleria Estense. F. Liverani 1979, no. 9.
REVERSE: *.1537./Lea[n]dro i[n] mare et Hero / alla finestra./.F.X./.R.*

326. Plate: *Samson and the Philistines*. D: 25.5 cm. HSM, Φ 3041. Ivanova 2003, no. 47.
REVERSE: in blue, *1537, / Sa[n]son che lalto Tem/pio à terra tira / F.X./R.*

327. Dish on low foot (*Coppa*): *The Virgin and Child in the Clouds*. D: 26.5 cm. MAACS, 225. Triolo 2000, no. 214.
REVERSE: in blue, *.1537./Ave Regina Angelo/ .F.X./ .R.*

328. Bowl with broad border (*Tondino*): *Hypermnestra watching Lynceus Threaten her Father Danaus*. D: 25.5 cm. WAM, 481324. Prentice Von Erdberg and Ross 1952, no. 52.
On front, under the figures: *Lino, Danao* on a tablet supported by Cupid: *Omnia Vincit/ Amor*
REVERSE: in black, *.1537./Tratta Hipermestra fu/dal Carcer tettro./ F.X.R.*

329. Centre of a bowl: *The Wedding of Alexander and Roxana*. H: 22.0 cm; W: 18.9 cm. MCMB, 976. Ravanelli Guidotti 1985, no. 99.
REVERSE: *.MDXXXVII./OMNIA VINCIT/AMOR./.F.X.R.*

330. Plate (*Tagliere*): *Leda and the Swan*. D: 27.5 cm. MCMB, 280. Ravanelli Guidotti 1985, no. 100.

331. Plate (*Tagliere*): *Alcyone and Ceyx*. MC, 105. Petruzzellis-Scherer 1988, no. 15.
REVERSE: *.1537./D' Halcione e, Ceyce i[n] riva'l mare./.F.X./.R.*

332. Plate: (*Tagliere*): *Alcyone and Ceyx*. MC. Petruzzellis-Scherer 1988, no. 16.
REVERSE: *.1537./D' Halcione, e, Ceice i[n] riva'l mare./.F.X./.R.*

333. Large plate: *Leonidas conquering the Persians*. D: 46.0 cm. Formerly HAU-M, 1050. Lessmann 1979, Appendix I, no. ix.
REVERSE: *.1537./Leonida ch'a suoi lieto propose / un' duro pra[n]dio, e, una terribil cena/ E i[n] puoca piazza fe mirabil cose / F.X./R.*

334. Plate (*Tagliere*): *Cephalus and Procris*. D: 26.0 cm. Private collection, Italy.
REVERSE: *.1537./L'i[n]avvertito Cephal/Procri uccide./.F.X./.R.*

335. Plate (*Tagliere*): *Candaules showing his Wife to Gyges*. D: 26.0 cm. Formerly Pringsheim collection. Falke 1994, II, no. 268.
REVERSE: *.1537./Mostra Candauli Ré sua/Donna à Gigio./.F.X./.R.*

336. Large plate: *Joseph and Potiphar's Wife*. D: 45.0 cm. Florence, Museo Nazionale del Bargello, Carrand Bequest, 22.10.1888. Conti 1971, no. 194.
REVERSE: *M.D.XXXVII.Quel Savio che ha le voglie sue modeste/ No[n] s'intraugli i[n] quei lacci che fanno/ Parer le vite altrui spesso moleste/ Fra[n] Xa[n]to da Rovigo*

337. Plate: *Apollo and the Muses on Mount Parnassus*. D: 26.0 cm. Formerly Pasolini dall'Onda collection. Adams sale, Bonhams, London, 22 May 1996, lot 136.
REVERSE: *1537. Il bio[n]do Apollo e le/Sacrate muse/F.X./.R.*

338. Bowl with broad border (*Tondino*): *Aesacus and Hesperia*. D: 26.0 cm. Detroit Institute of Arts, 57.36.
REVERSE: (small areas of the inscription are missing) *1537. /Dal sasso i[n] le sals'/ o[n]de Esaco gittasi./ F.X./R.*

339. Plate: *A Fishing Scene*. D: 27.0 cm. Formerly Woodward collection. Borenius 1928, no. 41.
REVERSE: *.1537./Tutti siamo pes/catori./.F.X./.R.*

340. Plate: *Hercules and Cerberus*. D: 28.0 cm. Formerly Woodward collection. Borenius 1928, no. 40.
REVERSE: *.1537./co[n]tra 'l trifauce ca[n]/Hercole ardito/F.X./R.*

### 1538

341. Plate: *Apollo and Daphne*. Lustred. D: 25.7 cm. BVBM, T 8. Boymans Van Beuningen Museum 1994, p. 209.
REVERSE: lustre scrolls and, in blue, *.1538. Fuggie dal bio[n]do Apollo/Daphne ge[n]tile..X.*

342. Plate: *Hector and Achilles*. D: 26.0 cm. Formerly Pringsheim collection. Falke 1994, II, no. 269. Here fig. 14.
REVERSE: *1538./Entr'al fiume Troia[n] Hettor' oppresso/.X.*

343. Large plate: *Horatius Cocles holding the Bridge against the Etruscans*. D: 46.0 cm. FM, Ç, 55-1927. Poole 1995, no. 396.
REVERSE: *.M.D.X.X.X.VIII./Vedi su'l ponte i[n]trepido, e, feroce/ Oratio sol co[n]tra Thoscana tutta/ Che ne ferro, e, ne fuoco a vertù nuoce.*

344. Dish on low foot (*Coppa*): *Florence bewailing her Children*. Lustred. D: 27.8 cm. MPP, Dutuit 1098. Join-Dieterle 1984, no. 71.
REVERSE: *1538/ Fiore[n]za mesta i morti figli/ piagne./ .X.*

345. Dish on low foot (*Coppa*): *Tarquin and Lucretia*. Lustred. D: 27.5 cm. Paris, MPP, Dutuit 1099. Join-Dieterle 1984, no. 72.
REVERSE: in blue, *.1538./Lucretia da ma destra/ tra la prima/.X.*

346. Bowl with broad border (*Tondino*): *The Death of Cleopatra*. Lustred. D: 26.1 cm. Hamburg, Museum für Kunst und Gewerbe, 1900.160. Rasmussen 1984, no. 124.
REVERSE: *.1538./vissi A[n]ton' vivo, e ,/ mori morto lui/ .X.*

347. Plate: *The Vestal Tuccia carrying Water in a Sieve to the Temple of Vesta*. D: 26.0 cm. HSM, Φ 3043. Ivanova 2003, no. 51.
On the front, under the figure of Tuccia: *.T.T.V*
REVERSE: *.1538./Tucia l'acqua portò/ col cribro al Tempio./ .X.*

348. Plate: *The Vestal Tuccia carrying Water in a Sieve to the Temple of Vesta*. D: 25.9 cm. WC, C93. Norman 1976, no. C93. This cat. 53.
On the front on a canopy: *.VEST.TEM*, under the Vestal: *T.U.V.*
REVERSE: in black, *.1538/ Tucia l'acqua portò/ Col Cribro al Tempio./.X.*

349. Bowl with broad border (*Tondino*): *Leda and the Swan*. D: 25.8 cm. Formerly Sprovieri collection, now private collection. Wilson 1996, no. 92.
REVERSE: *.1538./ Di Leda bella il gene/roso parto./ .X.*

350. Plate: *The Dream of Constantine*. D: 26.0 cm. Formerly Pringsheim collection. Falke 1994, III, no. 398 (368).
REVERSE: *.1538./Del nobil Costati[n] l'alta visione/.X.*

351. Dish on low foot (*Coppa*): *Joseph and Potiphar's Wife*. D: 29.5 cm. ML, OA 1815. Giacomotti 1974, no. 858.
REVERSE: *1538./Gioseppe fuggie il scelerato affetto/.X.*

352. Plate: *Noli Me Tangere* (Christ, Mary Magdalene and Three Angels seated on the Sepulchre). Lustred. D: 26.0 cm. Formerly G.H. Morland collection. Robinson 1863, no. 5,256.
REVERSE: *.1538./Noli me tangere/Xpo a Maria disse. X.*

353. Dish on low foot (*Coppa*): *The Nativity*. Lustred. 26.7 cm. MMA, 27.97.36.
REVERSE: *.1538. l'util Natal d'il Re/de[n]tor del mo[n]do./. X.*



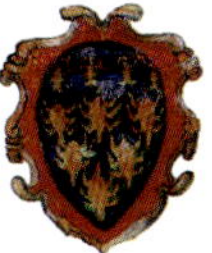

354. Plate: *Camilla's Rescue*. Lustred. D: 27.0 cm. London, Ranger's House, English Heritage, Wernher Foundation, 219-179. Wilson 1993B, pp. 212–13, figs. 5–6. This cat. 54.
REVERSE: in lustre, *1538*.

355. Plate: *Hero and Leander*. D: 26.7 cm. NGA, Washington, 1942.9.337 (C-62). Wilson 1993B, pp. 210–214 (signed S in blue and attributable to Xanto probably collaborating with Sforza di Marcantonio).
REVERSE: *Leandro in mare/etera ale finestra* and *1538*

Another piece in the set (this cat. 55) is attributed to Xanto's collaborator Sforza di Marcantonio.

SERVICE WITH UNIDENTIFIED COAT OF ARMS *helmet, crest, a lion passant guardant azure and mantling, set against an oval medallion divided or and azure; the shield is blazoned: quarterly, 1 and 4, gules three bars argent, 2 and 3, argent on a point enty two lions affrontant gules, 1538*

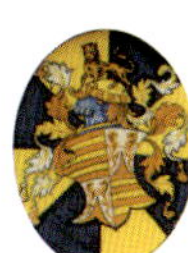

356. Plate: *Pyramus and Thisbe*. D: 25.5 cm. MNCS, 21047. Giacomotti 1974, no. 857.
REVERSE: *1538 vedi piramo e tisbe...sieme allo[m]bra X*

357. Bowl with broad border (*Tondino*): *Narcissus*.
D: 26.2 cm. DMAD, 701/1962.
Houkjaer 2005, no. 153.
REVERSE: *1538/ Il vano ama[n]te di sua propria imago./.X.*

358. Bowl with broad border (*Tondino*): *Picus and Circe*.
D: 25.3 cm. DMAD, A38/1922.
Houkjaer 2005, no. 152.
REVERSE: *.1538./Picco l' u[n] gia de no/stri Regi, e, Circe./.X.*

359. Plate: *The Philistines burning Samson's Father-in-law's House*.
D: 25.5 cm. Formerly Adda collection. Rackham 1959,
p. 424, pl. 192B.
REVERSE: *1538 Il suocer di Sanso[n] arso i[n] suo demo X*

360. Plate: *Samson battling the Philistines*. D: 26.0 cm.
Formerly Adda collection. Rackham 1959, p. 425,
pl. 193A.
REVERSE: *1538 Sanso[n] co[n] la massella uccide, e, fuga X*

361. Plate: *The Death of Samson*. D: 25.5 cm. Formerly Adda
collection. Rackham 1959, p. 425, pl. 193B.
REVERSE: *1538 Mora saso[n] co[n] tutti I suoi nemici X*

362. *c. 1538*. Pligrim Flask. *The Feast of Pirithous and
Hippodamia*. H: 35.5 cm. Private collection. Mallet
2002, figs. 8–10. Unsigned and undated.


## 1539

363. Plate: *The Killing of Virginia by her Father Virginius*. Lustred.
D: 27.4 cm. St Louis, City Art Museum, 10: 1953.
Triolo 1993, pp. 214–15.
REVERSE: *.1539./Quel ch'à sua figlia/,e, à Roma ca[n]ggio
stato/.X.*

364. Dish on low foot (*Coppa*): *The Transfiguration*. Lustred.
D: 27.2 cm. MADL, Damiron no. 1903. Fiocco et al.
2001, no. 157.
REVERSE: in dark blue, *.1539./Trasfiguross' il Salva/tor
del mo[n]do./.X.*

365. Dish on low foot (*Coppa*): *Alcyone and Ceyx*. Lustred.
D: 26.0 cm. VAM, C.480-1921. Rackham 1940,
no. 730, pl. 115.
REVERSE: in black, within lustre scrolls, *1539./
Alcyone, e, Ceyce i[n] riva `l mare. X.*

366. Bowl with broad border (*Tondino*): *Pyramus and Thisbe*.
D: 25.3 cm. KB, K 1772. Hausmann 1972, no. 197.
REVERSE: *.1539./ Vedi piramo, e, Tisbe i[n]sieme allombra.
/.X.*

367. Dish: Allegorical subject with a man wearing a
turban and four women; above, a scroll with *Omnia
p pecuniam facta sunt*. D: 26.0 cm. VAM, 1698-1855.
Rackham 1940, no. 637, pl. 100.
REVERSE: *MDXXXVIIII./Cossi va'l mo[n]do, e, l'esperienza é
fatta/.X.*

368. Bowl with broad border (*Tondino*): *Camilla's Rescue*.
D: 31.0 cm. Formerly Castellani collection.
Sotheby's, London, 16 July 1991, lot 17.
REVERSE: *1539/Methabo olter'Am/ase la[n]cio' Camil/la/.X.*

369. Plate (*Tagliere*): *Camilla's Rescue*. Lustred. D: 29.7 cm.
MMA, 1975.1.II33. Rasmussen 1989, no. 84.
REVERSE: within lustre scrolls, *.1539./Methabo oltr'a-
mase/la[n]ciò Cammilla/.X.*

370. Plate: *The Vestal Tuccia carrying Water in a Sieve to the Temple
of Vesta*. D: 30.5 cm. Sotheby's, London, 18 March
1975, lot 24.
REVERSE: *1539/Tucia l'acqua porto/ col cribro al tem/pio./.X.*

371. Fragmentary dish on low foot (*Coppa*): *The Faliscan
Sons*. D: 26.6 cm. MCP, H 11287. Munarini and
Banzato 1993, no. 296.
REVERSE: *.1539./Re[n]de Camillo alli Falischi/i figli./.X.*

372. Plate (*Tagliere*): *Hero and Leander*. D: 29.0 cm. Sotheby's,
London, 5 July 1957, lot 58.
REVERSE: *1549 (sic 1539)/Leandro i[n] mare, et Hero alla
finestra.
X.*

373. Plate: *Dionysus the Tyrant (The Sword of Damocles)*. Lustred.
D: 27.5 cm.
BVBM, T9. Boymans Van Beuningen Museum 1994, p. 207.
REVERSE: lustre scrolls, and in blue, *1539. l'inquieta vita
del/tira[n] Dionisi./.X.*


## 1540

374. Plate: *Apollo and the Muses on Mount Parnassus*. Formerly
Parpart collection. Lepke, Berlin, 18–22 March 1912,
lot 172.
REVERSE: *1540/X.*

375. Large Plate: *The Abduction of Helen*. Lustred.
D: 42.0 cm. ML OA 1839. Giacomotti 1974, no. 866.
REVERSE: in lustre, scrolls and N; in blue,
*M.D.X.L./Quel famoso rapto, pel qual fu [i]l mo[n]do sotto
sopra volto/.X.*

376. Bowl with broad border (*Tondino*): *The Vision of
Constantine*. D: 26.0 cm. Weimar, Kunstsammlungen
zu Weimar, A 2153. Reissinger 2000, no. 11.
REVERSE: *.1540/Del nobil consta[n]ti[no]/ l'alta. Visione./.X.*

377. Plate: *The Prophetic Dream of the Woman of Himera*.
D: 25.5. cm. VAM, 1696-1855. Rackham 1940,
no. 638, pl. 100.
On the front, above an angel: *Hic ille Dionysius Sicilie
Tirannus*
REVERSE: *1540. L'alta visio[n] d'Imera i[n] Siragusa./ .X.*

378. Plate: *The Prophetic Dream of the Woman of Himera*.
D: 26.0 cm. Formerly Pringsheim collection. Falke
1994, III, no. 399.
On the front, above an angel: *Hic ille Dionysius Sicilie
Tirannus*
REVERSE: *1540. L'alta visio[n] d'Imera i[n] Siragusa./.X.*

379. Plate: *Dionysus the Tyrant (The Sword of Damocles)*.
D: 30.0 cm. Prague, Umeleckoprumyslové Museum,
11.571. Vydrová 1973, no. 50.
REVERSE: *.1540./L'inquieta vita dil/ tyra[n] dionysio./.X.*

380. Plate: *The Burial of Leucothoe*. D: 27.5 cm. VAM, 1695-
1855. Rackham 1940, no. 639, pl. 101.
REVERSE: in black, *1540 Sottrata leocothoe dal padre viva. X.*

381. Bowl with broad border (*Tondino*): *The Death of
Cleopatra*. D: 25.9 cm. Stuttgart, Württembergisches
Landesmuseum, B 139/92. Hesse 2004, p. 103,
fig. 16–17.
On the front: *M.D.X.L and C.R.E*
REVERSE: in black, *.1540./vissi Anto[nio] vivo, e, mori
morto/ lui./.X.*

382. Bowl with broad border (*Tondino*): *The Fall of Icarus*.
D: 25.0 cm. Stockholm, Nationalmuseum, CXV 691.
Dahlbäck Lutteman 1981, no. 1.
REVERSE: in green, *1540/Quello ch'all'od'/Icarie deve il
no/me./X.*

383. Plate (*Tagliere*): *The Death of Aeschylus*. D: 28.5 cm.
Private collection, Berlin. Hausmann 2002, no. 68.
REVERSE: *1540/ Quel che fu vi[nto]/ dal suo fier destino/.X.*

384. Dish on low foot (*Coppa*): *The Death of Aeschylus*.
D: 27.0 cm. ML, OA 1510. Giacomotti 1974, no. 859.
REVERSE: *1540/Suo destino ha ciascu[n] dal di chel nasce/.X.*

385. Bowl on low foot (*Coppa*): *Polyphemus, Acis and Galatea*.
D: 27.0 cm. Formerly Cook collection, Sotheby's,
London, 7 December 1965. Rackham 1904, no. 65.
REVERSE: *1540.* (rather smudged, above, a line) */vedi
Aci,e, Galatea/ch'n grembo gl'* (smudged) *era./.X.*

386. Plate (*Tondino*): *The Death of Cleopatra*. D: 27.0 cm.
Columbus Gallery of Fine Arts, 31.31. Cole 1977,
no. 16.
REVERSE: *1540/ viss Anton[io] vivo e mori morto lui. /.X.*

387. Plate: *The Vestal Tuccia carrying Water in a Sieve to the Temple
of Vesta*. D: 27.2 cm. Murray Sale, Sotheby's, Florence,
November 1929, lot 114, pl. xxiii.
REVERSE: *.1540./Tutia l'acqua porto'/col cribo al Tempio./X.*

388. Dish on low foot (*Coppa*): *Plautius and Orestilla*.
D: 27.2 cm. MNCS, 21046. Giacomotti 1974, no. 860.
REVERSE: *1540 L' uno Plautio si é l'a[l]tr [a] Orestilla/.X.*

389. Dish on low foot (*Coppa*): *Descent from the Cross*.
D: 27.2 cm. Stoke-on-Trent, Potteries Museum and
Art Gallery. Brody 2001, no. 70, p. 55, fig. 8.
REVERSE: *.MD. XL./De l'alto legno giù Xpo vie tolto/ .X.*


## 1541

390. Plate: *The Dream of Astyages*. D: 28.0 cm. Testart
collection, Testart sale, Paris, 24–25 June 1924, lot 23.
REVERSE: inscription, date and signature.

391. Plate: *The Story of Portia*. D: 27.5 cm. VAM, 1790-1855.
Rackham 1940, no. 640, pl. 101.
REVERSE: *1541./Vedi Portia chel ferro al pie percuote./.X.*

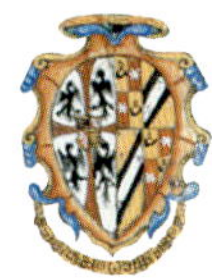

392. Large plate: *The Storming of Goletta*, with coat of arms
of Ferrante Gonzaga-Guastalla. D: 45.6 cm. Formerly
Marryat collection, now France, private collection.
Mallet 1984, p. 399, pls. cix and cx. Here figs. 26, 27.
Front: *M.D.XXXXI./ Da Carlo d'Austria Imperator potente/
L'alta Goletta inespugnabil tanto/ Astretta, e presa
con furor repena./ In Urbino nella/ botteg di Francesco/ de
Silvano/.*

393. Dish on low foot (*Coppa*): *Noli me Tangere*. D: 28.9 cm.
MPP, Dutuit 1070. Join-Dieterle 1984, no. 73.
REVERSE: *.1541.Noli me tanger, Xpo, à maria disse./.X.*

394. Dish on low foot (*Coppa*): *Turnus attacking the 'New Troy'*.
D: 27.8 cm. MADL, Damiron no. 1896. Fiocco et al.
2001, no. 158.
REVERSE: *.1541./Turno d'intorno/ alla novella Troia./ .X.*

395. Dish on low foot (*Coppa*): *The Martydom of St Ursula*.
D: 27.0 cm. Christie's, London, 11 October 1993,
lot 128.
REVERSE: *.1541./Orsola in mar /tiriggiata muore./.X.*
On front, written on the boat, in white: *Orsola*

396. Plate: *Camilla's Rescue*. D: 28.0 cm. MNCS, 21048.
Giacomotti 1974, no. 861.
REVERSE: *1541/ Metabo oltr' ama sen lancio Camilla/.X.*

397. *c. 1540–42*. Dish on low foot (*Coppa*): *Ulysses arriving
Home at Troy*. D: 26.7 cm. Hotel Drouot, Picard, 11 June
1997, lot 58 (formerly Gustave and Robert de
Rothschild).
REVERSE: *l'astuto Ulis/se, e, la sua/fera amante,/.X.*


## 1542

398. Plate: *Vulcan forging Cupid's Arrows*. D: 26.5 cm. HSM,
Φ 1896. Ivanova 2003, no. 49.
REVERSE: *1542. Per Cupido/ Vulca[no] tempra li stra/li .X.*

399. Plate: *Aeneas and Anchises escaping from Troy*. Formerly SB,
K1768, destroyed in World War II. Wilson 1996, fig. b,
p. 219.
REVERSE: *.1542./ Quest'é colui ch'à Troia/ il padre Anchise/
Traße del fuoco./ .X.*

400. Plate: *Hero and Leander*. Formerly Barker collection,
exhibited at the 1862 South Kensington Museum
Exhibition (listed in *Supplemental List of Loans to the Art
collections*, 1864, p. 35). Fortnum 1896, mark no. 206.
REVERSE: *1542/ Lea[n]dro i[n] mare &/Ero alla finestra/.X.*

401. Plate: *The Death of Cleopatra*. D: 26.4 cm. Boston,
Museum of Fine Arts, 95.371.
REVERSE: *.1542./Di Marcantonio , e ,/ Cleopatra il fine./.X.*

402. Plate: *Apollo and the Muses on Mount Parnassus*.
D: 29.4 cm. Formerly Sellière collection; Oslo,
Kunstindustrimuseet, O. K. 12045. Seillère sale,
Paris, Galerie Georges Petit, 5–10 May 1890, lot 82.
REVERSE: *.1542./Lalto Parnaso, e, le/Sacrate muse./.X.*

**Unsigned pieces attributable to
Xanto from *c.* 1530–42**

403. 1530. Broth-bowl (*Scodella*) and Cover (*Tagliere*) from
an accouchement set: inside the bowl, an accouche-
ment scene; outside, putti; on the cover, *The Holy
Family* (D: 20.0 cm). MC, Venice, 236. Petruzzellis-
Scherer 1988, Nos. 1, 2.
On the foot of the bowl: *MDXXX*

404. *c.* 1531. Broth-bowl (*Scodella*) from an accouchement
set: inside, an accouchement scene; outside, *The
Abduction of Europa*. D: 17.0 cm. Formerly Pringsheim
collection. Falke 1994, II, no, 259 a–b.

405. *c.* 1530–31. Broth-bowl (*Scodella*) from an accouchement set: inside, a birth-scene, *The Birth of Achilles* (?).
Outside, Cupids in pairs with scrolls, supporting
baskets and grotesques. D: 16.5 cm. VAM, C.2241-
1910. Rackham 1940, no. 629, pl. 99. This cat. 32.
On the outside, two labels, one with *M.X.A.R.* and
the other one *.M.A.XX*

406. *c.* 1530–35. Three-lobed dish: inside, a figure of
Fortune. Outside, interlaced oak-branches in relief
and a row of oak-leaves in *bianco sopra bianco*. H: 7.0
cm. VAM, 4692-1858. Rackham 1940, no. 599.

407. 1532. Bowl with broad border (*Tondino*): *Cupid and Two
Women*. Lustred. D: 22.0 cm. Formerly Sprovieri
collection. Wilson 1996, no. 86.
Reverse in lustre: *1532/M°G°*.

408. 1533. Plate: *Picus and Circe*. D: 27.0 cm. Formerly
Pringsheim collection. Falke 1994, II, no. 265.
REVERSE: *1533/De Pico & can[n]ete* y/Φ flourish/*M
Giorgio/ da Ugubio* and a flourish

409. *c.* 1535. Large plate: *The Death of Laocoon and his Two Sons*.
D: 45.0 cm. GM, G83.1.0390. Wilson 1993B, p. 217.

410. 1536. Plaque: *The Adoration of the Shepherds*. H .29.0 cm;
w: 29.0 cm. Formerly S. Addington collection.
Robinson 1863, no. 5, 248.
On a pedestal, the date *1536*, on the bottom, on a
strip: *Vergine sacra gloriosa, e, eterna, che gia portasti, nel tuo
ventre sa[n]to quel che la terra e 'l ciel governa.*

411. *c.* 1538–40. Dish on low foot (*Coppa*): *The Vestal Tuccia
carrying Water in a Sieve to the Temple of Vesta*. D: 26.6 cm.
KB, K 1844. Hausmann 1972, no. 196.
REVERSE: *Tucia lagua porta col chribro al tempio*

412. *c.* 1539. Saucer-dish: *Vulcan forging an Arrow, watched by
Venus and Three Cupids*. D: 17.1 cm. BM, P&E 1878, 12–30,
373. Wilson 1987, no. 78; Thornton and Wilson 2007,
no. 169.
REVERSE: in a cloudy sky, Saturn and his children
in a chariot drawn by dragons, Apollo in a chariot
drawn by horses, and *.M.D.XXXVIIII*

413. 1539. Plate: *The Death of the Laocoon and his Two Sons*.
Lustred. D: 27.0 cm. NGA, Widener Collection,
no. 1942.9.338. Wilson 1993B, pp. 215–17.
REVERSE: *1539/da duo gra[n] serpe/Laocaonte ucciso* and
lustre scrolls

414. 1539. Fragment of dish: *Cupid in a Landscape*. Lustred.
D: 12.0 cm. Dated 1539. Christie's, London,
11 December, 1908, lot 10.

415. *c.* 1540. Plate: Mythological subject, perhaps Perseus
beheading the Medusa and other figures, possibly
Phineus and his followers. D: 26.0 cm. Sotheby's,
London, 29 June 1964, lot 22.
REVERSE: uninscribed

416. 1542. Dish on low foot (*Coppa*): *Apollo and the Muses on
Parnassus*. D: 27.5 cm. Fondazione Cassa di Risparmio
di Perugia collection. Wilson and Sani 2006, no. 34.
REVERSE: in dark blue, *.1542./Il Sacro Apollo, e', le/
Sorelle nove*

417. 1542. Plate: *Camilla's Rescue*. D: 26.6 cm. MCP, 178.
Munarini and Banzato 1993, no. 297.
REVERSE: *.1542./Metabo oltre Ama/se lancio' Camilla.*

418. 1542. Plate: *The Dream of Astyages*. D: 27.5 cm. BM, P&E
1878, 12–30, 439. Wilson 1987, no. 79; Thornton and
Wilson 2007, no. 170.
REVERSE: *.1542. D'Astiage Rè di Media il sogno grave*

419. 1542. Fragmentary bowl: *The Adoration of the Magi,*
Phillips, London, 11 September 1991, lot 205.
REVERSE: *.1542./Gia fiammeggiava/l'honorata stella.*

420. 1542. Dish on low foot (*Coppa*): *Children of Venus*.
D: 28.0 cm. VAM C.2240-1910. Rackham 1940,
no. 868. This cat. 56.
REVERSE: *Omnia vincit /Amor./.1542.*

---

# Addendum

115a. *c.* 1530. Bowl with broad border (*Tondino*): *The Contest
of Minerva and Neptune*. D: 26.5 cm. Vercelli, Museo
Leone. Casati Migliorini 2001, p. 30.
REVERSE: *Faula* followed by the y/Φ flourish / *Di la
dotta Minerva / di Nettuno / Fra[n]cesco Xa[n]to A:R:/
pi[nxit] i[n] Urbino.*

# Index to locations cited in Appendix C

# Bibliography


ALBARELLI 1986
Giuseppe M. Albarelli, *Ceramisti Pesaresi nei Documenti Notarili dell'Archivio di Stato di Pesaro, Sec. XV–XVII*, Bologna, 1986

ALVERÀ BORTOLOTTO 1988
Angelica Alverà Bortolotto, *Maiolica a Venezia nel Rinascimento*, Bergamo, 1988

AUSENDA 2000
Raffaella Ausenda (ed.), *Musei e Gallerie di Milano. Museo d'Arti Applicate. Le ceramiche. Tomo Primo*, Milan, 2000

BALLARDINI 1933
Gaetano Ballardini, *Corpus della maiolica italiana*, 1, Rome, 1933

BALLARDINI 1938A
Gaetano Ballardini, *Corpus della maiolica italiana*, 2, Rome, 1938

BALLARDINI 1938B
Gaetano Ballardini, 'Il Trentennio', *Faenza*, xxvi, 1938, 6, pp. 123–27

BALLARDINI 1940
Gaetano Ballardini, 'Nuovi acquisti al museo', *Faenza*, xxviii, 1940, 5–6, pp. 104–11

BALLARDINI 1953
Gaetano Ballardini, 'Per una collezione di maiolica', *Faenza*, xxxix, 1953, 2, pp. 27–29 (P. Fassini collection)

BALLARDINI NAPOLITANI 1940
Doda Ballardini Napolitani, 'Ispirazione e fonti litterarie nell'opera di Francesco Xanto Avelli, pittore su maiolica in Urbino', *La Rinascita*, 3, 1940, pp. 905–22

BALZANI AND REGNI 2002
Serena Balzani and Marina Regni, 'La bottega di Ottaviano Dolci e di Giovanni Maria Perusini soci in arte picture', in Bojani 2002A, pp. 49–53

BALZANI AND REGNI 2004
Serena Balzani and Marina Regni, *Vasai e pittori a Casteldurante nei primi due decenni del secolo XVI, nuovi apporti documentari*, Urbino, Accademia Raffaello, 2004

BARRAL 1987
Claudie Barral, *Catalogue Raisonné du Musée des Beaux-Arts de Dijon*, Dijon, 1987

BARTRUM 2002
Giulia Bartrum, *Albrecht Dürer and his Legacy*, exh. cat., British Museum, London, 2002

BATTINI 1974
Giorgio Battini, *L'Amico della Ceramica*, Florence, 1974

BERARDI 1984
Paride Berardi, *L'Antica Maiolica di Pesaro*, Florence, 1984

BETTINI 1997
Alessandro Bettini, 'La ceramica a Fano tra XIV e XVII secolo', in Bojani 1997, pp. 137–45

BETHNAL GREEN 1872–75
C. C. Black, *Catalogue of the Collection of Paintings, Porcelains, Bronzes, Decorative Furniture and other Works of Art, lent for exhibition in the Bethnal Green Branch of the South Kensington Museum, by Sir Richard Wallace, Bart., M.P., June 1872*, London, 1872. The eighth edition, published in 1874, includes more objects.

BIGANTI 2002A
Tiziana Biganti, 'Sulle Tracce di Maestro Giorgio. L'Affermazione di un Lombardo nella Città di Gubbio', in Bojani 2002B, pp. 49–60

BIGANTI 2002B
Tiziana Biganti (ed.), *Maestro Giorgio nei Documenti Eugubini (Regesti 1488–1575)*, Florence, 2002

BISCARINI 2002
Patrizia E.P. Biscarini, 'Splendore e Decadenza di Una Città: Gubbio tra la Fine del Quattrocento e la Prima Metà del Cinquecento, Alcune Note di Storia', in Bojani 2002B, pp. 31–48

BISCARINI AND NARDELLI 2006
Patrizia E. P. Biscarini and Giuseppe M. Nardelli, 'Alcune Riflessioni sulla Coppa Erotica dell'Ashmolean Museum di Oxford', *CeramicAntica*, xvi, 10, November 2006, pp. 48–50

BOBER AND RUBINSTEIN 1986
Phyllis Pray Bober and Ruth Rubinstein, *Renaissance Artists and Antique Sculpture*, London, 1986

BOHN 1876
Henry Bohn, *A Guide to the Knowledge of Pottery, Porcelain and Other Objects of Vertu* (Reprint of the sale catalogue of the Ralph Bernal collection, Christie's, London, 23 March, 1855), London, 1876 edition

BOJANI 1997
Gian Carlo Bojani (ed.), *Fatti di ceramica nelle Marche dal Trecento al Novecento*, Macerata (Fondazione Cassa di Risparmio della Provincia di Macerata), 1997

BOJANI 1998
Gian Carlo Bojani (ed.), *Mastro Giorgio da Gubbio: una carriera sfolgorante*, exh. cat., Gubbio, 1998

BOJANI 2001
Gian Carlo Bojani (ed.), *La maiolica italiana del Cinquecento. Capolavori della Collezione Strozzi Sacrati. Atti del convegno di studi, Museo Internazionale delle Ceramiche Faenza, 25, 26, 27 settembre 1998*, Florence/Faenza, 2001

BOJANI 2002A
Gian Carlo Bojani (ed.), *I Della Rovere nell'Italia delle corti, Atti del convegno di Urbania 1999*, IV, *Arte della maiolica*, Urbino/Urbania, 2002

BOJANI 2002B
Gian Carlo Bojani (ed.), *La maiolica italiana del Cinquecento. Il lustro eugubino e l'istoriato del ducato di Urbino, Atti del convegno di studi, Gubbio, 21, 22, 23 settembre 1998*, Florence, 2002

BONALI AND GRESTA 1987
Piero Bonali and Riccardo Gresta, *Girolamo e Giacomo Lanfranco dalle Gabicce, Maiolicari a Pesaro nel Secolo XVI*, Rimini, 1987

BORENIUS 1928
Tancred Borenius, *Catalogue of a Collection of Pottery belonging to W.H. Woodward*, London, 1928

BORENIUS 1930
Tancred Borenius, *Catalogue of a Collection of Italian Maiolica belonging to Henry Harris*, London, 1930

BOYMANS VAN BEUNINGEN MUSEUM 1994
*Kunstnijverheid Middeleeuwen en Renaissance, Decorative Art Middle Ages and Renaissance* (texts by H. Vreeken), Boymans van Beuningen Museum, Rotterdam, 1994

BRAGHIROLLI 1878
Willelmo Braghirolli, *Lettere Inedite di Artisti del Secolo XV Cavate dall'Archivio Gonzaga*, Mantua, 1878

BRESSAN 1857
Bartolomeo Bressan (ed.), *Lettere Storiche di Luigi Da Porto Vicentino, dall'anno 1509–1528*, Florence, 1857

BRODY 2001
Michael Brody, 'Italian Renaissance pottery at Stoke-on-Trent', *Apollo*, clxxx, January 2001, pp. 9–17

BURLINGTON FINE ARTS CLUB 1887
*Burlington Fine Arts Club. Catalogue of Specimens of Hispano-Moresque and Majolica Pottery Exhibited in 1887*, London, 1887

CAROSELLI 1993
Susan L. Caroselli, *The Painted Enamels of Limoges, A Catalogue of the Collection of the Los Angeles County Museum of Art*, Los Angeles, 1993

CASAMASSIMA 1966
E. Casamassima, *Trattati di scrittura del Cinquecento italiano*, Milan, 1966

CASATI MIGLIORINI 2001
Paola Casati Migliorini, 'La collezione di maioliche e porcellane del Museo Leone di Vercelli', *CeramicAntica*, xi, 11, December 2001, pp. 30–44

CHAPMAN 2006
Hugo Chapman, *Michelangelo Drawings: Closer to the Master*, exh. cat., London, British Museum, 2006

CHASTEL 1983
André Chastel, *The Sack of Rome, 1527*, Princeton, 1983

CHOMPRET 1949
Joseph Chompret, *Répertoire de la majolique italienne*, 2 vols, Paris; reprinted, Milan, 1986

CIOCI 1979
Francesco Cioci, 'La proposta per una ristampa: due sonetti inediti di Francesco Xanto Avelli', *Faenza*, lxv, 1979, 6, pp. 297–301

CIOCI 1987
Francesco Cioci, *Xanto e il Duca di Urbino*, Milan, 1987

CIOCI 1988
Francesco Cioci, 'Francesco Xanto da Rovigo: Poeta, Maiolicaro e Politico', in Rovigo 1988, pp. 53–60

CIOCI 1991A
Francesco Cioci, 'La Bibliografia di Xanto dal 1980 ad Oggi: il Perchè di Una Rinuncia' in Wilson 1991, pp. 32–35

CIOCI 1991B
Francesco Cioci, 'Xanto e il Duca di Urbino, l'iconografia o del Soggetto Nascosto nella Maiolica Cinquecentesca: Mech, Moch. Leggi Y', *Faenza*, lxxvii, 1991, 1–2, pp. 5–11

CIOCI 1993
Francesco Cioci, 'Xanto a Gubbio nel 1528–29', *CeramicAntica*, iii, 11, December, 1993, pp. 28–45

CIOCI 1995
Francesco Cioci, 'Xanto a Rimini', *Faenza*, lxxxi, 1995, 1–6, pp. 241–49

CIOCI 1997A
Francesco Cioci, 'Fatti urbinati del Rinascimento: Nicola da Urbino e Xanto da Rovigo', in Bojani 1997, pp. 195–205

CIOCI 1997B
Francesco Cioci, 'Xanto e il Duca di Urbino. Il servizio Pucci e il suo titolare. Un omaggio all'Impero', *Faenza*, lxxxiii, 1997, 4–6, pp. 205–30

CIOCI 2002A
Francesco Cioci, 'Nicola da Urbino e Francesco Maria I Della Rovere', in Bojani 2002A, pp. 67–88

CIOCI 2002B
Francesco Cioci, 'Il Servizio Pucci di Xanto: I Soggetti dall'Eneide e il Contributo di Mastro Giorgio', in Bojani 2002A, pp. 69–84

CIOCI 2002C
Francesco Cioci, "in Urbino nell'Anno 1534", *Faenza*, lxxxviii, 2002, 1–6, pp. 110–21

CIOCI 2003
Francesco Cioci, "In Urbino, nell'anno 1538. Fiore[n]za mesta i morti figli piagne", *CeramicAntica*, viii, 5, May 2003, pp. 24–31

CIOCI 2004
Francesco Cioci, 'Francesco Maria I Della Rovere e Francesco Xanto Avelli da Rovigo: le Maioliche Politiche', in Dal Poggetto 2004, pp. 217–220 and pp. 405–11

CIOCI 2006
Francesco Cioci, 'Xanto e il Duca di Urbino. Antonio Pucci...: "ma chi diavolo era costui?" ', *Faenza*, xcii, 2006, 1–3, pp. 47–59

CLERI *et al.*, 2002
Bonita Cleri, *I Della Rovere nell'Italia delle corti, Atti del convegno di Urbania 1999*, 4 vols, *Storia del Ducato*, Urbino/Urbania, 2002

CLOUGH 2002
Cecil H. Clough, 'La Successione dei Della Rovere nel Ducato di Urbino', in Cleri *et al.* 2002, I, pp. 35–62

CLOUGH 2005
Cecil H. Clough, 'Clement VII and Francesco Maria Della Rovere', in Gouwens and Reiss 2005, pp. 75–108

COLE 1977
Bruce Cole, *Italian Maiolica from Midwestern Collections*, exh. cat., Indiana University Art Museum, 1977

COLLINS 1987
Patricia Collins, 'Prints and the Development of Istoriato Painting on Italian Renaissance Maiolica Painting', *Print Quarterly*, iv, 3, 1987, pp. 223–35

CONTI 1971
Giovanni Conti, *Museo Nazionale di Firenze, Palazzo del Bargello, Catalogo delle Maioliche*, Florence, 1971

CONTI 1980
Giovanni Conti, *L'arte della maiolica in Italia*, 2nd ed., Busto Arsizio, 1980

CONTI 1992
Giovanni Conti, *Nobilissime ignobiltà della maiolica istoriata*, Faenza, 1992

CURNOW 1992
Celia Curnow, *Italian Maiolica in the National Museums of Scotland*, (National Museums of Scotland Information Series, no. 5), Edinburgh, 1992

DAHLBÄCK LUTTEMAN 1981
Helena Dahlbäck Lutteman, *Majolika från Urbino och andra orter i Italien i Nationalmuseum Stockholm*, Stockholm, 1981

DAL POGGETTO AND DAL POGGETTO 1983
Maria Ciardi Dupré Dal Poggetto and Paolo Dal Poggetto (eds.), *Urbino e le Marche prima e dopo Raffaello*, exh. cat., Florence, 1983

DAL POGGETTO 2003
Paolo Dal Poggetto, *La Galleria Nazionale delle Marche e le Altre Collezioni del Palazzo Ducale di Urbino*, Urbino, 2003

DAL POGGETTO 2004
Paolo Dal Poggetto (ed.), *I Della Rovere. Piero Della Francesca, Raffaello, Tiziano*, exh. cat., Senigallia, Urbino, Pesaro, and Urbania, Milan, 2004

DARCEL AND DELANGE 1867–69
A. Darcel and H. Delange, *Recueil de Faïences Italiennes*, Paris, 1867–69

DELANGE 1853
Henri Delange, 'Appendice' in Passeri 1853, pp. 97–119. Translated into Italian in Vanzolini 1879, i, pp. 249–81

DELUCCA 1998
Oreste Delucca, 'Ceramisti e Vetrai a Rimini in Età malatestiana', in *Rassegna di Fonti Archivistiche*, Rimini, 1998, pp. 267–68

DEMMIN 1875
A. Demmin, *Histoire de la Céramique*, 2 vols, Paris, 1875

DETROIT 1958
*Decorative Arts of the Italian Renaissance 1400–1600*, exh. cat., The Detroit Institute of Art, 1958

DENNISTOUN 1909
James Dennistoun, *Memoirs of the Dukes of Urbino*, 1851, 3 vols, 2nd ed., London and New York, 1909

DUBRUJEAUD 1911
A. Dubrujeaud, *Faïences Italiennes de la Collection Al. Imbert*, Paris, 1911

DUMORTIER 2002
Claire Dumortier, 'Majoliques lustrées des Musées royaux d'Art et d'Histoire', in Bojani 2002B, pp. 171–76

EICHE 1986
Sabine Eiche, 'La Corte di Pesaro' in M. R. Valazzi, *La Corte di Pesaro*, Modena, 1986

EICHE 2001
S. Eiche, 'I Della Rovere Mecenati dell' Architettura' in S. Mariotti (ed.), *Pesaro nell'Età dei Della Rovere*, 2 vols., Venice, II, 2001, pp. 231–66

FAIETTI AND OBERHUBER 1988
Marzia Faietti and Konrad Oberhuber (eds.), *Bologna e l'Umanesimo 1490–1510*, Bologna, 1988

FALKE 1934
Otto von Falke, 'Der Majolikamaler Giorgio Andreoli von Gubbio', *Pantheon*, xiv, 1934, pp. 328–33

FALKE 1994
Otto von, Falke, *Le maioliche italiane della collezione Pringsheim / Die Majolikasammlung Alfred Pringsheim / Italian Maiolica of the Pringsheim Collection*, 3 vols. Amplified reprint of Falke 1914–23 with essays by Carmen Ravanelli Guidotti, Tjark Hausmann, and Timothy Wilson, Ferrara, 1994

FERRIANI 1983
Daniela Ferriani, after Ferriani, 'Primi Influssi di Rafaello nelle Marche (Seconda Decade del Cinquecento), XLII. Timoteo Viti', in Dal Poggetto and Dal Poggetto 1983, pp. 315–21

FILIPPINI 1942
Francesco Filippini, 'Nuovi documenti intorno a Mastro Giorgio e alla sua bottega (1516–1517)', *Faenza*, xxx, 1942, 5–6, pp. 76–78

FIOCCO AND GHERARDI 1988
Carola Fiocco and Gabriella Gherardi, *Ceramiche Umbre dal Medioevo allo Storicismo*, Catalogo generale del Museo Internazionale delle Ceramiche in Faenza, vol 5, parte prima, Faenza, 1988

FIOCCO AND GHERARDI 1989
Carola Fiocco and Gabriella Gherardi, *Ceramiche Umbre dal Medioevo allo Storicismo*, Catalogo generale del Museo Internazionale delle Ceramiche in Faenza, vol 5, parte seconda, Faenza, 1989

FIOCCO AND GHERARDI 1995
Carola Fiocco and Gabriella Gherardi, *Museo Comunale di Gubbio, Ceramiche*, Perugia, 1995

FIOCCO AND GHERARDI 1996
Carola Fiocco and Gabriella Gherardi, 'Il Pittore "S" e la Coppa di Tiberio', *Faenza*, lxxxii, 1996, 4–6, pp. 145–51

FIOCCO AND GHERARDI 1998
Carola Fiocco and Gabriella Gherardi, 'Maestro Giorgio, il Lustro di Gubbio e l'Istoriato del Ducato di Urbino', in Bojani 1998, pp. 15–90

FIOCCO AND GHERARDI 2002A
Carola Fiocco and Gabriella Gherardi, 'Tesori nascosti: la collezione di maiolica italiana del Musée de la Tour du Moulin à Marcigny', *Faenza*, lxxxviii, 2002, 1–6, pp. 73–109

FIOCCO AND GHERARDI 2002B
Carola Fiocco and Gabriella Gherardi, 'Maestro Giorgio, Il lustro a Gubbio, e l'istoriato del ducato di Urbino', in Bojani 2002B, pp. 61–68

FIOCCO AND GHERARDI 2004
Carola Fiocco and Gabriella Gherardi, "Ceramica forlivese della prima metà del '500: 'Petrus'", *Keramos*, 186, 2004, pp. 9–36

FIOCCO *et al.* 2001
Carola Fiocco, Gabriella Gherardi and Liliane Sfeir-Fakhri, *Majoliques italiennes du Musée des Arts Décoratifs de Lyon. Collection Gillet*, Dijon, 2001

FORTNUM 1873
C. Drury E. Fortnum, *A Descriptive Catalogue of the Maiolica, Hispano-Moresco, Persian, Damascus, and Rhodian Wares, in the South Kensington Museum*, London, 1873

FORTNUM 1896
C. Drury E. Fortnum, *Maiolica*, Oxford, 1896

FRATI 1852
Luigi Frati, *Del Museo Pasolini in Faenza Descrizione*, Bologna, 1852

FUCHS 1993
Charles Dominique Fuchs, *Maioliche istoriate rinascimentali del Museo Statale d'Arte Medioevale e Moderna di Arezzo*, Arezzo, 1993

GARDELLI 1987
Giuliana Gardelli, *Maioliche Rinascimentali dallo Stato di Urbino da Collezioni Private*, Urbino, 1987

GARDELLI 1999
Giuliana Gardelli, *Italika, Maiolica Italiana del Rinascimento, Saggi e Studi*, Faenza, 1999

GIACOMOTTI 1974
Jeanne Giacomotti, *Catalogue des Majoliques des Musées Nationaux*, Paris, 1974

GIARDINI 1996
Claudio Giardini, *Pesaro. Museo delle Ceramiche*, Musei d'Italia – Meraviglie d'Italia, no. 33, Bologna/Milan/Rome, 1996

GILLET COLLECTION 1943
*Collection de faïences d'un amateur. 169 pièces de la collection de faïences Paul Gillet* (by Charles Damiron), Lyon, 1943

GLASER 2004
Silvia Glaser (ed.), *Italienische Fayencen der Renaissance. Ihre Spuren in internationalen Museumssammlungen*, Wissenschaftliche Beibände zum Anzeiger des germanischen Nationalmuseums, Band 22, Nuremberg, 2004

GOLDTHWAITE 1989/97
Richard A. Goldthwaite, 'The economic and social world of Italian renaissance maiolica', *Renaissance Quarterly*, 42, pp. 1–32 (translated into Italian in *Faenza*, lxxxiii, 1997, 4–6, pp. 176–204)

GOUWENS AND REISS 2005
Kenneth Gouwens and Sheryl E. Reiss (eds.), *The Pontificate of Clement VII, History, Politics, Culture*, Aldershot (England) and Burlington (USA), 2005

GRESTA 2002
Riccardo Gresta, 'Giulio da Urbino e Xanto Avelli: una collaborazione difficile?', in Bojani 2002B, pp. 145–56

F. GUICCIARDINI 1561
Francesco Guicciardini, *Storia d'Italia*, first published Florence, 1561

L. GUICCIARDINI 1993
Luigi Guicciardini, *The Sack of Rome*, translated and edited by James H. McGregor, New York, 1993

HAUSMANN 1972
Tjark Hausmann, *Majolika. Spanische und italienische Keramik vom 14. bis zum 18. Jahrhundert*, Kataloge des Kunstgewerbemuseums Berlin, VI, Berlin, 1972

HAUSMANN 1974
Tjark Hausmann, 'Maioliche italiane dello "Schlossmuseum" di Berlino perdute nella seconda guerra mondiale', *Faenza*, lx, 1974, 1–3, pp. 24–40

HAUSMANN 2002
Tjark Hausmann, *Fioritura, Blütezeit der Majolika, eine Berliner Sammlung*, Berlin, 2002

HESS 2002
Catherine Hess, *Italian Ceramics. Catalogue of the J. Paul Getty Museum Collection*, Los Angeles, 2002 [Revised edition of Hess 1988]

HESSE 2004
Sabine Hesse, *Die Majolikasammlung des Württembergischen Landesmuseums in Stuttgart*, in Glaser 2004, pp. 97–110

HIGGOTT 2003
Suzanne Higgott, 'Sir Richard Wallace's maiolica. Sources and display', *Journal of the History of Collections*, 15, 1, 2003, pp. 59–82

HIGGOTT 2004
Suzanne Higgott, 'New Light on Maiolica in the Wallace Collection', in Glaser 2004, pp. 55–78

HOLCROFT 1988
Alison Holcroft, 'Francesco Xanto Avelli and Petrarch', *Journal of the Warburg and Courtauld Institutes*, li, 1988, pp. 225–34

HOLLINGSWORTH 2004
Mary Hollingsworth, *The Cardinal's Hat*, London, 2004

HOUKJAER 2005
Ulla Houkjaer, *Tin-glazed Earthenware, 1300–1750, Spain, Italy, France*, Copenhagen, 2005

*Ill. Bartsch*
Walter L. Strauss (general ed.), *The Illustrated Bartsch*, New York, 1978–

*Ill. Bartsch* 10 (Commentary)
Walter L. Strauss (ed.), 10 (Commentary), *Sixteenth Century German Artists, Albrecht Dürer*, New York, 1981

*Ill. Bartsch* 16
Robert A. Koch (ed.), *Early German Masters Jacob Bink, Georg Pencz, Heinrich Aldegrever*, New York, 1980

*Ill. Bartsch* 25
Mark Zucker (ed.), *Early Italian Masters*, New York, 1980

*Ill. Bartsch* 25 (Commentary)
Mark J. Zucker, 25 (Commentary), *Early Italian Masters*, New York, 1984

*Ill. Bartsch* 26
Konrad Oberhuber (ed.), 26, *The Works of Marcantonio Raimondi and of his School*, New York, 1978

*Ill. Bartsch* 27
Konrad Oberhuber (ed.), 27, *The Works of Marcantonio Raimondi and of his School*, New York, 1978

*Ill. Bartsch* 28
Suzanne Boorsch and John Spike (eds.), 28, *Italian Masters of the Sixteenth Century*, New York, 1985

*Ill. Bartsch* 29
Suzanne Boorsch (ed.), *Italian Masters of the Sixteenth Century*, New York, 1982

IVANOVA 2003
Elena Ivanova, *Il Secolo d'Oro della Maiolica*, Milan, 2003

JESTAZ 1972
Bertrand Jestaz, 'Les modèles de la majolique historiée, bilan d'une enquête', *Gazette des Beaux-Arts*, 79, part 1, 1972, pp. 215–40

JOIN-DIETERLE 1984
Catherine Join-Dieterle, *Musée du Petit Palais, Catalogue de Céramiques*, vol. I, Paris, 1984

KLESSE 1966
Brigitte Klesse, *Majolika*, Kataloge des Kustgewerbemuseums Köln, Bd. II, Cologne, 1966

KUBE 1976
A.N. Kube, *Italian Majolica, State Hermitage Collection*, Moscow, 1976

LABARTE 1847
Jules Labarte, *Description des Objets d'Art qui Composent la Collection Debruge-Duménil*, Paris, 1847

LABARTE 1875
Jules Labarte, *Histoire des Arts Industriels au Moyen Age et à l'Époque de la Renaissance*, 3 vols, 2nd edition, Paris, 1875

LANDAU AND PARSHALL 1994
David Landau and Peter Parshall, *The Renaissance Print 1470–1550*, New Haven and London, 1994

LAW 2002
John E. Law, 'Relazioni Dinastiche tra i Della Rovere e i Varano', in Cleri *et al.*, 2002, pp. 21–34

LAWNER 1988
Lynne Lawner, *I Modi, the Sixteen Pleasures, an Erotic Album of the Sixteenth Century*, London, 1988

LEONARDI 1996
Corrado Leonardi, *Maiolica metaurense rinascimentale, barocca, neoclassica*, exh. cat., Palazzo Ducale, Urbino, 1996

LEONI 1605
Giovan Battista Leoni, *Vita di Francesco Maria di Montefeltro, IIII Duca d'Urbino*, Venice, 1605, cited by Bonita Cleri in John T. Spike (ed.), *Il Corteo Trionfale di Carlo V, Un Capitolo del Rinascimento in un'Acquaforte delle Collezioni Roveresche*, Urbania, 1999, pp.11–13

LESSMANN 1979
Johanna Lessmann, *Herzog Anton Ulrich-Museum, Braunschweig, Italienische Majolika*, Brunswick, 1979

LESSMANN 1990
Johanna Lessmann, 'Xanto's Panels', *Burlington Magazine*, cxxxii, May 1990, pp. 346–50

LESSMANN 1991
Johanna Lessmann, 'Istoriato Painting on Panels in the Workshop of Nicola da Urbino' in Wilson 1991

LESSMANN 2004
Johanna Lessmann, 'Bildfliesen von Francesco Xanto Avelli zur Geschichte Persiens', *Keramos*, 186, October, 2004, pp. 61–85

LIPPMANN 1895
F. Lippmann, *The Seven Planets*, Berlin, 1895

F. LIVERANI 1979
Francesco Liverani, *Le maioliche della Galleria Estense di Modena*, Faenza, 1979

F. LIVERANI 1991
Francesco Liverani, 'Sei Maioliche del Rinascimento Italiano: Preliminari allo Studio delle Iscrizioni nell'Istoriato Ceramico', in Wilson 1991, pp. 46–50

G. LIVERANI 1938
Giuseppe Liverani, 'Le 'Credenze' maiolicate d'Isabella d'Este Gonzaga e di Federico II Duca di Mantova', *Rassegna dell'istruzione artistica*, 9, 1938, pp. 330–46

G. LIVERANI 1955
Giuseppe Liverani, 'Un piatto di Nicola Pellipario al Museo', *Faenza* xli, 1955, 1–2, pp. 12–13

G. LIVERANI 1968
Giuseppe Liverani, 'La Fortuna di Raffaello nella Maiolica' in Mario Salmi (ed.), *Raffaello: L'opera, le Fonti, la Fortuna*, Novara, 1968, pp. 691–708; partly reprinted in *Faenza*, liv, 1968, 4–5, pp. 59–77

McCLUNG HALLMAN 2005
Barbara McClung Hallman, 'The "Disastrous" Pontificate of Clement VII: Disastrous for Giulio de'Medici?', in Gouwens and Reiss 2005, pp. 29–40

McNAB 1995
Jessie McNab, 'Sixteenth-Century Italian Maiolica' in Edward J. Sullivan (ed.), *The Taft Museum. Its History and Collections*, II, *European Decorative Arts*, New York, 1995, pp. 517–41

MALLÉ 1974
Luigi Mallé, *Maioliche italiane dalle origini al settecento*, Milan, 1974

MALLET 1971A
J. V. G. Mallet, 'Maiolica at Polesden Lacey III: A New look at the Xanto Problem', *Apollo*, lxxxiii, March 1971, pp. 170–83

MALLET 1971B
J. V. G. Mallet, in National Trust, *Polesden Lacey, Surrey*, 1971

MALLET 1974
J.V.G. Mallet, 'Alcune maioliche faentine in raccolte inglesi', *Faenza*, 1974, 1–3, pp. 3–23

MALLET 1976
J.V.G. Mallet, 'A Maiolica Plate Signed "F.R."', *Art Bulletin of Victoria*, Melbourne, 1976, pp. 4–19

MALLET 1978
J.V.G. Mallet, 'Pottery and Porcelain at Erddig', *Apollo*, cviii, July 1978, pp. 40–45

MALLET 1979
J.V.G. Mallet, 'Francesco Urbini in Gubbio and Deruta', *Faenza*, lxv, 1979, 6, pp. 279–96

MALLET 1981
J.V.G. Mallet, in David Chambers and Jane Martineau (eds.), *Splendours of the Gonzaga*, exh. cat., London, 1981, pp. 39–43, 175–78, 198–202

MALLET 1984
J.V.G. Mallet, 'La Biografia di Francesco Xanto Avelli alla Luce dei Suoi Sonetti', *Faenza*, lxx, 1984, 5–6, pp. 398–402

MALLET 1987
J.V.G. Mallet, Review of Wilson 1987, *Burlington Magazine*, cxxix, May 1987, pp. 331–32

MALLET 1988
J. V. G. Mallet, 'Xanto: i Suoi Compagni e Seguaci', in Rovigo 1988, pp. 67–108

MALLET 1992
J.V.G. Mallet, 'Amicus Amico Dilecto: Gaetano Ballardini e Bernard Rackham', *Faenza*, lxxviii, 1992, 3–4, pp. 134–56

MALLET 1994
J.V.G. Mallet, 'Michelangelo on maiolica: An *istoriato* dish at Waddesdon', *Apollo*, cxix, April 1994, pp. 50–55

MALLET AND DREIER 1998
J. V. G. Mallet and Franz Adrian Dreier, *The Hockemeyer Collection. Maiolica and Glass*, Bremen, 1998

MALLET 2002
J.V.G. Mallet, 'Considerazioni su Nicola da Urbino e le fonti delle sue composizioni su maiolica', in Bojani 2002B, pp. 89–99

MALLET 2004
J.V.G. Mallet, 'Xanto and Gubbio: New Thoughts and Queries', *Keramos*, 186, October 2004, pp. 37–60

MANARA 2002
Sandra Manara, 'Ancora le "Tre lune crescenti"', *Faenza*, lxxxviii, 2002, 1–6, pp. 217–24

MANCINI DELLA CHIARA 1979
Maria Mancini Della Chiara, *Maioliche del Museo Civico di Pesaro, Catalogo*, Pesaro, 1979

MASSING 1990
Jean Michel Massing, *Du Texte à l'Image. La Calomnie d'Apelle et son Iconographie*, Strasbourg, 1990

MASSING 1991
Jean Michel Massing, 'Nicola da Urbino and Signorelli's lost Calumny of Apelles', in Wilson 1991, pp. 150–56

MAZZOLA 1993
Maria Giuseppina Mazzola, *La Collezione della Marchesa di Torrearsa*, Palermo, 1993

MAZZUCATO 2004
Otto Mazzucato, 'Alcune Osservazioni Sui Ricettari' *Faenza*, xc, 2004, 1–6, pp. 208–09

MOLINIER 1892
Emile Molinier, 'Les faïences italiennes, hispano-moresques et orientales', in *La Collection Spitzer: antiquité, moyen-âge, renaissance*, Paris, 1890–92, 4 vols, 1892

MONTAGU 1968
Jennifer Montagu, "'Hercules and Iole' and some other bronzes by Foggini", *Apollo*, lxxxvii, March 1968, pp. 170–75

MOORE 1988
Andrew Moore, 'The Fountaine Collection of maiolica', *Burlington Magazine*, cxxx, June, pp. 435–47

MUNARINI 1990
Michelangelo Munarini, *Maioliche Istoriate delle Raccolte dei Musei Veneti*, Este, 1990

MUNARINI AND BANZATO 1993
Michelangelo Munarini and Davide Banzato, *Ceramiche Rinascimentali dei Musei Civici di Padova*, Milan, 1993

MUSÉE RETROSPECTIF 1865
*Catalogue des Objets d'Art et de Curiosité exposés au Musée Rétrospectif ouvert au Palais de l'Industrie en 1865*, Paris, 1865

NEGRONI 1985
Franco Negroni, 'Nicolò Pellipario: Ceramista Fantasma', *Notizie da Palazzo Albani*, xiv, 1985, 1, pp. 13–20

NORMAN 1965
A.V.B. Norman, 'Sources for the design on a Majolica Dish', *Apollo*, lxxi, June 1965, pp. 460–63

NORMAN 1969
A.V.B Norman, 'A note on the so-called Casa Pirota mark', *Burlington Magazine*, cxi, July 1969, pp. 447–48

NORMAN 1976
A.V.B. Norman, *Wallace Collection Catalogue of Ceramics 1, Pottery, Maiolica, Faience, Stoneware*, London, 1976

OLDING 1982
Simon Olding, *Italian Maiolica, Glasgow Museums and Art Galleries*, 1982

**PAATZ AND VALENTINER PAATZ 1952**
Walter Paatz and Elizabeth Valentiner Paatz, *Die Kirchen Von Florenz, Ein Kunstgeschichtliches Handbuch*, 10 vols, Frankfurt am Main, 1952

**PACIARONI 2002**
Raoul Paciaroni, 'Una raccolta di maioliche a Sanseverino dispersa agli inizi del XVIII secolo', *Faenza*, lxxxviii, 2002, 1–6, pp. 173–78

**PALMER 1991**
R. Palmer, 'A Palace Built, a Church Destroyed', *Apollo*, cxxxiv, September 1991, pp. 176–82

**PALVARINI GOBIO CASALI 1987**
Mariarosa Palvarini Gobio Casali, *La Ceramica a Mantova*, Ferrara, 1987

**PASSERI 1857**
Giambattista Passeri, *Storia delle Pitture in Majolica*, in Vanzolini 1879, I, pp. 1–101 (first ed. of Passeri, 1758)

**PETRARCA**
Francesco Petrarca (Petrarch), *Rime*

**PETRUZZELLIS-SCHERER 1988**
Jacqueline Petruzzellis-Scherer, 'Fonti iconografiche delle opere di Francesco Xanto Avelli al Museo Correr di Venezia', in Rovigo 1988, pp. 121–51

**PFUNGST 1890**
*A Descriptive Catalogue of a small collection of Italian Maiolica in the possession of Henry Pfungst, 22 Endsleigh Gardens*, London, 1890

**PICCOLPASSO 1980**
Ronald Lightbown and Alan Caiger-Smith (eds.), Cipriano Piccolpasso, *The Three Books of the Potter's Art*, London, 1980

**POOLE 1995**
Julia Poole, *Italian Maiolica and Incised Slipware in the Fitzwilliam Museum, Cambridge*, Cambridge, 1995

**POOLE 2003**
Julia Poole, 'The Identification of Maiolica from Sanseverino', *Faenza*, lxxxix, 2003, 1–6, pp. 93–100

**PRENTICE VON ERDBERG AND ROSS 1952**
Joan Prentice Von Erdberg and Marvin C. Ross, *Catalogue of the Italian Maiolica in the Walters Art Gallery*, Baltimore, 1952

**PRICE ZIMMERMANN 2005**
T. C. Price Zimmermann, 'Guicciardini, Giovio and the Character of Clement VII', in Gouwens and Reiss 2005, pp. 19–27

**PUNGILEONE 1879**
L. Pungileone, 'Notizie delle Pitture in Majolica Fatte in Urbino', in Vanzolini 1879, I, pp. 103–12

**RACKHAM 1904**
Bernard Rackham, 'Italian Maiolica and other Pottery', in *Catalogue of the Art Collection, vol. I, 8 Cadogan Square, SW (Cook Collection)*, London, 1904

**RACKHAM 1913**
Bernard Rackham, 'The Sources of Design in Italian Maiolica', *Burlington Magazine*, xxiii, July 1913, pp. 193–203

**RACKHAM 1922**
Bernard Rackham, 'A New Work by Nicola Pellipario at South Kensington', *Burlington Magazine*, xli, July 1922, pp. 21–27; September 1922, pp. 127–33

**RACKHAM AND BALLARDINI 1933**
Bernard Rackham and Gaetano Ballardini, 'Il Pittore di Maiolica "F.R."', *Bollettino d'Arte*, xi, 1933, pp. 393–407

**RACKHAM 1933**
Bernard Rackham, *Victoria and Albert Museum: Guide to Italian Maiolica*, London, 1933

**RACKHAM 1934**
Bernard Rackham, 'The De Pass Pottery in the Fitzwilliam Museum', *Connoisseur*, 93, April 1934, pp. 245–48

**RACKHAM 1940**
Bernard Rackham, *Victoria and Albert Museum: Catalogue of Italian Maiolica*, London, 2 vols, 1940 (re-issued with emendations and additional bibliography by J.V.G. Mallet, 1977)

**RACKHAM 1957**
Bernard Rackham, 'Xanto and "F.R.": An insoluble problem?', *Faenza*, xliii, 1957, 5, pp. 99–111

**RACKHAM 1959**
Bernard Rackham, *Islamic Pottery and Italian Maiolica. Illustrated Catalogue of a Private Collection*, London, 1959

**RASMUSSEN 1980**
Jörg Rasmussen, 'Die Majoliken "In Arimino"', *Jahrbuch der Hamburger Kunstsammlungen*, vol. 25, 1980, pp. 81–96

**RASMUSSEN 1984**
Jörg Rasmussen, *Museum für Kunst und Gewerbe, Hamburg, Italienische Majolika*, Hamburg, 1984

**RASMUSSEN 1989**
Jörg Rasmussen, *The Robert Lehman Collection: 10: Italian Majolica*, Princeton and New York, 1989

**RAVANELLI GUIDOTTI 1985**
Carmen Ravanelli Guidotti, *Ceramiche occidentali del Museo Civico Medievale di Bologna*, Bologna, 1985

**RAVANELLI GUIDOTTI 1988**
Carmen Ravanelli Guidotti, 'Le ceramiche delle collezioni rinascimentali', in Clara Stella (ed.), *Ceramiche nelle civiche collezioni bresciane*, Bologna, 1988, pp. 98–146

**RAVANELLI GUIDOTTI 1990**
Carmen Ravanelli Guidotti, *Museo Internazionale delle Ceramiche in Faenza. La Donazione Angiolo Fanfani. Ceramiche dal Medioevo al XX secolo*, Faenza, 1990

**RAVANELLI GUIDOTTI 1994A**
Carmen Ravanelli Guidotti, 'L'Ariosto "Istoriato" sulla Maiolica Italiana del Cinquecento', in Jadranka Bentini (ed.), *Signore Cortese e Umanesimo, Viaggio Intorno a Ludovico Ariosto*, Reggio Emilia, pp. 61–77

**RAVANELLI GUIDOTTI 1994B**
Carmen Ravanelli Guidotti, 'Un inatteso recupero nei fondi prebellici del Museo: un frammento di Xanto donato da Paolo Mereghi', *Faenza*, lxxx, 1994, 1–2, pp. 20–24

**RAVANELLI GUIDOTTI 1996**
Carmen Ravanelli Guidotti, 'Le Metamorfosi "vulgari" d'Ovidio sulla maiolica italiana', in Hermann Walter and Hans-Jürgen Horn (eds.), *Die Rezeption der Metamorphosen des Ovid in der Neuzeit: der antike Mythos in Text und Bild*, Proceedings of the International Symosium, Bad Homburg 1991, Berlin, 1996, pp. 85–97

**REISSINGER 2000**
Elisabeth Reissinger, *Kunstsammlungen zu Weimar: Kunst und Kunsthandwerk II: Italienische Majolika*, Berlin, 2000

**REYNOLDS 2005**
Anne Reynolds, 'The Papal Court in Exile: Clement VII in Orvieto, 1527–28', in Gouwens and Reiss 2005, pp. 143–61

**RICHA AND ZOCCHI 1754**
Giuseppe Richa and Giuseppe Zocchi, *Notizie Istoriche Delle Chiese Fiorentine, Divise Ne' Suoi Quartieri*, 10 vols, Florence, 1754

**ROBERTSON 1992**
Clare Robertson, *Il Gran Cardinale, Alessandro Farnese, Patron of the Arts*, New Haven and London, 1992

**ROBINSON 1856**
J. C. Robinson, *Catalogue of the Soulages Collection*, London, 1856

**ROBINSON 1863**
J. C. Robinson, 'Majolica wares', in J. C. Robinson (ed.), *Catalogue of the special exhibition of works of art of the mediaeval, renaissance, and more recent periods, on loan at the South Kensington Museum, June 1862*, London, 1863 edition, pp. 399–444.

**ROVIGO 1988**
G.B. Siviero (ed.), *Francesco Xanto Avelli da Rovigo. Atti del Convegno Internazionale di Studi 1980*, Accademia dei Concordi, Rovigo, 3–4 May 1980, 1988

**ROYER 2003**
Raymonde Royer, 'La Collection Pasolini. Sa dispersion en France', *Faenza*, lxxxix, 2003, 1–6, pp. 121–33

**SANTI 1893**
Giovanni Santi, *Cronaca Rimata*, Stuttgart, 1893

**SCATASSA 1904**
Ercole Scatassa, 'Artisti che lavorarano in Urbino nei secoli XVI e XVII', *Rassegna bibliografica dell' arte italiana*, 7, 1904, pp. 196–202

**SCARPELLINI 1984**
Pietro Scarpellini, *Perugino*, Milan, 1984

**SCOTT-TAGGART 1972**
John Scott-Taggart, *Italian Maiolica*, London, 1972

**SECCARONI 2004**
Claudio Seccaroni, 'Ricettari Quattrocenteschi per Coperte, Colori e Lustri', *Faenza*, xc, 2004, 1–6, pp. 196–207

**SETTON 1976**
K. M. Setton, 'The Papacy and the Levant (1204–1571)', 4 vols, Philadelphia: American Philosophical Society, 1976

**SOLON 1907**
Marc Louis Solon, *A History and Description of Italian Maiolica*, London, 1907

**SPALLANZANI 1994**
Marco Spallanzani, *Ceramiche alla Corte dei Medici*, Modena, 1994

**SPALLANZANI 1999**
Marco Spallanzani, 'Maioliche con stemma Pucci e cappello cardinalizio', *Faenza*, lxxxv, 1999, 1–3, pp. 71–83

**SPALLANZANI 2006**
Marco Spallanzani, *Maioliche Ispano-Moresche a Firenze nel Rinascimento*, Florence, 2006

**SPIKE 1999**
John T. Spike (ed.), *Il Corteo Triomfale di Carlo V*, Urbania, 1999

**STORNAJOLO 1902–1921**
C. Stornajolo, *Codices Urbinates Latini*, 3 vols, Rome: Typis Vaticanis, 1902–1921

**SYSON AND THORNTON 2001**
Luke Syson and Dora Thornton, *Objects of Virtue. Art in Renaissance Italy*, London, 2001

**TAIT 1976**
Hugh Tait, 'The Roman Lion-Hunt Dish, an Early Work by Xanto?', *British Museum Society Bulletin*, 21, March, 1976, pp. 3–6

**TALVACCHIA 1994**
Bette Talvacchia, 'Professional Advancement and the Use of Erotic in the Art of Francesco Xanto', *The Sixteenth Century Journal*, xxv, 1, Spring 1994, pp. 121–53

**TENNENT 1982**
Norman H. Tennent, 'Polymer for Art's Sake', *Shell World*, vol. 7, no. 6, September–October, 1982

**TERVARENT 1951**
Guy de Tervarent, 'Enquête sur le Sujet des Majoliques', *Kunstmuseets Årsskrift 1950*, Copenhagen, 1951, pp. 25–27

**THORNTON 1999**
Dora Thornton, 'An Allegory of the Sack of Rome by Giulio da Urbino', *Apollo*, cxlx, June 1999, pp. 11–18

**THORNTON 2003**
Dora Thornton, 'A *bella donna* from the Pasolini collection in the British Museum', *Faenza*, lxxxix, 2003, 1–6, pp. 134–49

**THORNTON AND WILSON 2007**
Dora Thornton and Timothy Wilson, *Italian Renaissance Ceramics: A catalogue of the British Museum collection*, London (forthcoming, late 2007)

**TRANIELLO 1988**
Leobaldo Traniello, 'Rovigo, Patria di Francesco Xanto Avelli' in Rovigo 1988, pp. 21–27

**TRINITY FINE ART 1994**
Trinity Fine Art Ltd., *An Exhibition of Old Master Drawings and European Works of Art*, New York, 5–17 May 1994

**TRIOLO 1988**
Julia Triolo, 'Francesco Xanto Avelli's Pucci Service (1532–1533): a catalogue', *Faenza*, lxxiv, 1988, 4–6, pp. 37–44; 228–84

**TRIOLO 1991**
Julia Triolo, '*L'Urbs e l'Imperatore*: a proposal for the interpretation of the Pucci service by Xanto Avelli', in Wilson 1991, pp. 36–45

**TRIOLO 1992**
Julia Triolo, 'New notes and corrections to 'The Pucci service: a catalogue'', *Faenza*, lxxviii, 1992, 1–2, pp. 87–89

**TRIOLO 1993**
Julia Triolo, 'Un piatto poco conosciuto di Francesco Xanto Avelli. 'L'uccisione di Virginia' (1539)', in *Metodologia della ricerca:*

*orientamenti attuali. Congresso internazionale in onore di Eugenio Battisti*, parte prima, *Arte lombarda*, nos. 2–4, 1993, pp. 108–13

TRIOLO 1995
Julia Triolo, 'Francesco Xanto Avelli in a document of 1542', *Faenza*, lxxxi, 1995, 3–4, pp. 214–15

TRIOLO 1996
Julia Triolo, *The Armorial Maiolica of Francesco Xanto Avelli*, Ph. D. thesis, UMI Dissertation Services, Pennsylvania State University, Ann Arbor, 1996

TRIOLO 2000
in Ausenda 2000, pp. 197–210

TRIOLO 2001
Julia Triolo, 'The astrologer plate', in Bojani 2001, pp. 52–63

TRIOLO 2002
Julia Triolo, 'The presence and absence of lustre on the armorial maiolica of Francesco Xanto Avelli', in Bojani 2002B, pp. 125–36

UGOLINI 1859
Filippo Ugolini, *Storia dei Conti e Duchi di Urbino*, 2 vols, Florence, 1859

VALAZZI 2004
Maria Rosaria Valazzi, 'Pesaro: i Duchi, la Città, il Palazzo', in Dal Poggetto 2004, pp. 164–69

VAN DE PUT AND RACKHAM 1916
Albert Van de Put and Bernard Rackham, *Catalogue of the Collection of Pottery and Porcelain in the Possession of Mr. Otto Beit*, London, 1916

VANZOLINI 1879
Giuliano Vanzolini (ed.), *Istorie delle fabbriche di majoliche metaurensi*, 2 vols, Pesaro, 1879 (reprinted Bologna, 1975)

VARCHI, ED. ARBIB
Lelio Arbib (ed.), Benedetto Varchi, *Storia Fiorentina*, 3 vols, 1843–44

VASARI, ED. MILANESI
Gaetano Milanesi (ed.), Giorgio Vasari, *le Vite*, Florence, 1878–1885

VENTURI 1914
Lionello Venturi, 'Poesie del Ceramista Francesco Xanto Avelli', *Studi sul Palazzo Ducale di Urbino*, 1914

VERDIER 1967
Philippe Verdier, *Catalogue of the Painted Enamels of the Renaissance*, The Walters Art Gallery, Baltimore, 1967

VITALETTI 1912
Guido Vitaletti, *Francesco Xanto Avelli*, Urbino, 1912

VITALETTI 1918
Guido Vitaletti, 'Le rime di Francesco Xanto Avelli', *Faenza*, vi, 1918, 1, pp. 11–15; 2, pp. 41–44

VOSSILLA 2002
Francesco Vossilla, 'Xanto Avelli, Francesco Maria Della Rovere e la Firenze di Bandinelli', in Bojani 2002A, pp. 101–16

VYDROVÁ 1973
Jirina Vydrová, *Italská Majoliká, Umeleckoprůmyslove Muzeum v Praze*, Prague, 1973

WALLEN 1968
Burr Wallen, 'A Majolica Panel in the Widener Collection', *National Gallery of Art, Report and Studies in the History of Art*, Washington, 1968, pp. 94–105

WARNKE 1993
Martin Warnke, *The Court Artist, On the Ancestry of the Modern Artist*, transl. David McLintock, Cambridge, 1993

WARING 1858
John Burley Waring (ed.), *Art Treasures of the United Kingdom from the Art Treasures Exhibition, Manchester*, London, 1858

WATSON 1986
Wendy Watson, *Italian Renaissance Maiolica from the William A. Clark Collection*, exh. cat., Corcoran Gallery of Art, Washington D.C., and Mount Holyoke College Art Museum, 1986

WATSON 2001
Wendy Watson, *Italian Renaissance Ceramics. The Howard I. and Janet H. Stein Collection and the Philadelphia Museum of Art*, exh. cat., Philadelphia, 2001

WILSON 1987
Timothy Wilson, *Ceramic Art of the Italian Renaissance*, exh. cat., British Museum, London, 1987

WILSON 1990
Timothy Wilson, 'Xanto and Ariosto', *Burlington Magazine*, cxxxii, May 1990, 132, pp. 321–27

WILSON 1991
Timothy Wilson (ed.), *Italian Renaissance Pottery. Papers written in association with a colloquium at the British Museum*, London, 1991

WILSON 1993A
Timothy Wilson, 'Il Pittore di Maioliche "LU UR", Compagno e Seguace di Francesco Xanto Avelli', *Fimantiquari, Arte Viva*, ii, 2, 1993, pp. 19–31

WILSON 1993B
Timothy Wilson, 'Renaissance Ceramics', in *Systematic Catalogue of the National Gallery of Art: Western Decorative Arts, Part I*, Washington and Cambridge, 1993, pp. 119–263

WILSON 1995
Timothy Wilson, 'La collezione Fortnum all' Ashmolean Museum di Oxford', *CeramicAntica*, v, 8, 1995, pp. 38–53

WILSON 1996
Timothy Wilson, *Italian Maiolica of the Renaissance*, Milan, 1996

WILSON 2000
in Ausenda 2000, pp. 182–97, pp. 213–16

WILSON 2002A
Timothy Wilson, 'La Maiolica a Castel Durante e ad Urbino fra il 1535 e il 1565: Alcuni Corredi Stemmati', in Bojani 2002A, pp. 125–50

WILSON 2002B
Timothy Wilson, 'Il Servizio Siglato "S", Eseguito nella Bottega di Maestro Giorgio negli Anni 1524–25', in Bojani 2002B, pp. 113–24

WILSON 2002C
Timothy Wilson, 'Italian maiolica in the Wernher Collection', *Apollo*, clv, 483, May 2002, pp. 35–39

WILSON 2003A
Timothy Wilson, *Maiolica. Italian Renaissance Ceramics in the Ashmolean Museum*, Oxford, 2003

WILSON 2003B
Timothy Wilson, ' "*Poca differenza…*" Some warnings against over-confident attributions of Renaissance maiolica from the Duchy of Urbino', *Faenza*, lxxxix, 2003, 1–6, pp. 150–75

WILSON 2003C
Timothy Wilson (ed.), *The Battle of Pavia*, Ashmolean Museum, Oxford, 2003

WILSON 2004A
Timothy Wilson, 'Committenza Roveresca e Committenza delle Botteghe Maiolicarie del Ducato di Urbino nell'Epoca Roveresca', in Dal Poggetto 2004, pp. 203–09

WILSON 2004B
Timothy Wilson, 'The Maiolica-Painter Francesco Durantino: Mobility and Collaboration in Urbino "Istoriato"', in Glaser 2004, pp. 111–45

WILSON 2004–2005
Timothy Wilson, '*Figulus et Pictor*: Alcune Osservazioni su Pittori 'Veri' e Pittori di Maiolica dal Quattrocento al Settecento', in *Centro Ligure per la Storia della Ceramica. Atti del Convegno XXXVII–XXXVIII*, Albisola, 2004–2005, pp. 155–63

WILSON 2005A
Timothy Wilson, 'Some *incunabula* of *istoriato*-painting from Pesaro', *Faenza*, xci, 2005, 1–6, pp. 8–24

WILSON 2005B
Timothy Wilson, 'Un Intricamento tra Leonardo ed Arcimboldo', *CeramicAntica*, xv, 2, February 2005, pp. 10–44

WILSON AND SANI 2006
Timothy Wilson and Elisa Paola Sani, *Le maioliche rinascimentali nelle collezioni della Fondazione Cassa di Risparmio di Perugia*, Perugia, 2006

WILSON AND SANI 2007
Timothy Wilson and Elisa Paola Sani (eds.), *Le Maioliche rinascimentali nelle collezioni della Fondazione Cassa di Risparmio di Perugia*, vol.II, Perugia (forthcoming 2007)

ZAULI NALDI 1956
Luigi Zauli Naldi, 'Recenti acquisti del Museo', *Faenza*, lxii, 1956, 6, pp. 123–26

*Sale catalogue bibliography*

Bernal sale 1855
*Catalogue of the Celebrated Collection of Works of Art… of that Distinguished Collector, Ralph Bernal*, Christie's, London, 5 March–30 April 1855

Castellani sale 1866
*Catalogue d'objets d'art antiques du Moyen-âge et de la Renaissance…composant la collection de M. Castellani*, Paris (Drouot: Pillet), 4–7 April 1866

Castellani sale 1871
*Catalogue of One Hundred and Fifty Choice Specimens of Majolica, Collected by that distinguished Connoisseur Signor Castellani of Rome and Naples*, Christie's, London, 12 May 1871

Debruge-Duménil sale 1849
*Catalogue des objets d'art qui composent la collection Debruge-Duménil*, Paris (Hôtel des ventes mobilières, rue des Jeuneurs: Bonnefons de Lavialle and Roussel), 23 January–12 March 1849

D'Yvon sale 1892
*Catalogue des Objets d'Art … de Mme d'Yvon*, Paris (Galerie Georges Petit), 30 May–4 June 1892

Fountaine sale 1884
*Catalogue of the Celebrated Fountaine Collection of Majolica, Henri II. Ware, Palissy ware, Nevers ware, Limoges enamels … Removed from Narford Hall, Norfolk*, Christie's, London, 16–19 June 1884

Pasolini sale 1853
*Catalogue d'une belle collection de Majoliques Italiennes des diverses fabriques des XVe, XVIe & XVIIe siècles*, Paris (Rue des Jeuneurs 42, Ridel and Roussel), 13–15 December 1853 [this sale was anonymous; the collection belonged to Roussel and consisted mainly of pieces from the Pasolini collection]

Pourtalès-Gorgier sale 1865
*Catalogue des Objets d'Art et de haute curiosité … de feu M. le Comte de Pourtalès-Gorgier*: Paris, 6 February–25 March 1865

Prince Napoleon sale 1872
*Catalogue of Works of Art from the Collections of his Imperial Highness the Prince Napoleon*, Christie's, London, 9–11 May 1872

Spitzer sale 1893
*Catalogue des objets d'art et de haute curiosité, antiques du moyen-âge & de la renaissance composant l'importante et précieuse collection Spitzer*, Paris (Chevallier), 17 April–16 June 1893

# Index (excluding Appendix C)

Maiolica by or attributed to Francesco Xanto Avelli is indexed by subject.
Works by or attributed to other maiolica painters are indexed under the
name of the painter.
Figures in *italics* refer to illustrations.

213

# Photographic Credits

AREZZO
Museo d'Arte Medievale e Moderna di Arezzo, cat. 20, 20 reverse.

BALTIMORE
The Walters Art Museum, Baltimore, fig. 19.

CAMBRIDGE
Fitzwilliam Museum, Cambridge, cat. 26, 30, 30 reverse, 33, 33 reverse.

EMILIA-GUASTALLA
Reproduced by kind permission of the Ufficio Diocesano per I Beni Culturali Ecclesiastici di Reggio Emilia-Guastalla, figs 3, 4.

FLORENCE
Galleria degli Uffizi, Florence, figs 6, 7.

GLASGOW
Glasgow City Council (Museums), cat. 25, 25 reverse, 27, 27 reverse, 31, 31 reverse.

LONDON
Permission The British Library (144.g.3.(1), page 37), fig. 10. © Copyright The Trustees of The British Museum, figs 9, 18, 29, 30, 34; cat. 4, 4 reverse, 5, 5 reverse, 6, 6 reverse, 7, 7 reverse, 8, 8 reverse, 13, 16, 16 reverse, 35, 35 reverse, 36, 36 reverse, 37, 42, 42 reverse, 43, 43 reverse, 46, 46 reverse, 47, 47 reverse, 51. Christie's, © Christie's Images Ltd. (1969), fig. 14. © Christie's Images Ltd. (1992), cat. 23, 23 reverse. Anonymous owner when published in Lynne Lawner, *I Modi, the Sixteen Pleasures, an Erotic Album of the Sixteenth Century*, 1988, Peter Owen Ltd, London, figs 45, 48, 52, 53. National Trust, © NTPL/Andrew Smart (A. C. Cooper Ltd), cat. 22, cat. 28, 28 reverse. V&A Images/Victoria and Albert Museum, figs 1, 2, 49, 50; cat. 1, 2, 3, 9, 9 reverse, 11, 11 reverse, 14, 15, 17, 18, 21, 21 reverse, 32, 32 details, 40, 40 reverse, 44, 44 reverse, 45, 45 reverse, 50, 50 reverse, 55, 55 reverse, 56, 56 reverse. © The Trustees of the Wallace Collection, London, fig. 51; cat. 10, 10 reverse, 12, 19, 24, 24 reverse, 29, 38, 38 reverse, 39, 39 reverse, 41, 41 reverse, 48, 48 reverse, 49, 49 reverse, 53, 53 reverse. Photo: Warburg Institute, figs. 31, 32, 33, 35, 36, 38, 39, 41, 42, 43, 44, 46, 47, 55, 56. Stefania Massari, *Giulio Romano pinxit et delineavit*, Rome, 1993, no. 40, illus. p. 47; fig. 28. © The Wernher Foundation, English Heritage Photographic Library, cat. 34, 34 reverse, 54, 54 reverse.

NAPLES
By kind permission of the Fototeca della Soprintendenza Speciale per il Polo Museale Napoletano, fig. 13.

OXFORD
Ashmolean Museum, figs 15, 52, 52 reverse.

PARIS
Capucine de Chabaneix, figs 26, 27.

PERUGIA
© Centro SMAArt, Universita' di Perugia, fig. 40.

PESARO
Servizio Musei del Comune di Pesaro, figs 22, 23, 24.

ROME
Schlecther, neg. 1 1986.0001, Deutsches Archäologisches Institut, Rome, fig. 37.

ST PETERSBURG
© The State Hermitage Museum, St Petersburg, figs 11, 16, 17.

URBINO
Su concessione del Ministero per i Beni e le Attività Culturali, fig. 12.

VATICAN
© Biblioteca Apostolica Vaticana (Vatican), figs 5, 57, 58 and back cover.

VIENNA
Akademie der bildenden Künste Wien, Kupferstichkabinett, fig. 54. KHM, Vienna, figs 8, 25.

WASHINGTON
© 2006 Board of Trustees, National Gallery of Art, Washington, figs 20, 21.